ESSENTIALS OF
SERVICES MARKETING

ESSENTIALS OF SERVICES MARKETING

K. Douglas Hoffman
University of North Carolina at Wilmington

John E. G. Bateson
Gemini Consulting

ⓓ
THE DRYDEN PRESS
Harcourt Brace College Publishers
Fort Worth Philadelphia San Diego New York Orlando Austin San Antonio
Toronto Montreal London Sydney Tokyo

87266

Publisher	George Provol
Acquisitions Editor	Bill Schoof
Product Manager	Lisé Johnson
Developmental Editor	Dona Hightower
Project Editor	Michele Tomiak
Art Director	Bill Brammer
Production Manager	Melinda Esco
Cover Image	Phil Cheung

ISBN: 0-03-015217-8

Address for orders: The Dryden Press, 6277 Sea Harbor Drive, Orlando, FL 32887-6777, 1-800-782-4479

Address for editorial correspondence: The Dryden Press, 301 Commerce Street, Suite 3700, Fort Worth, TX 76102

Website address:
http://www.hbcollege.com

THE DRYDEN PRESS, DRYDEN, and the DP logo are registered trademarks of Harcourt Brace & Company.

Printed in the United States of America

7 8 9 0 1 2 3 4 5 6 067 9 8 7 6 5 4 3 2 1

The Dryden Press
Harcourt Brace College Publishers

The Dryden Press Series in Marketing

Lindgren and Shimp
Marketing: An Interactive Learning System

Krugman, Reid, Dunn, and Barban
Advertising: Its Role in Modern Marketing
Eighth Edition

Oberhaus, Ratliffe, and Stauble
Professional Selling: A Relationship Process
Second Edition

Parente, Vanden Bergh, Barban, and Marra
Advertising Campaign Strategy: A Guide to Marketing Communication Plans

Rachman
Marketing Today
Third Edition

Rosenbloom
Marketing Channels: A Management View
Fifth Edition

Schaffer
Applying Marketing Principles Software

Schellinck and Maddox
Marketing Research: A Computer-Assisted Approach

Schnaars
MICROSIM
Marketing simulation available for IBM PC and Apple

Schuster and Copeland
Global Business: Planning for Sales and Negotiations

Shimp
Advertising, Promotion, and Supplemental Aspects of Integrated Marketing Communications
Fourth Edition

Talarzyk
Cases and Exercises in Marketing

Terpstra and Sarathy
International Marketing
Seventh Edition

Weitz and Wensley
Readings in Strategic Marketing Analysis, Planning, and Implementation

Zikmund
Exploring Marketing Research
Sixth Edition

Harcourt Brace College Outline Series

Peterson
Principles of Marketing

Preface

The primary objective of *Essentials of Services Marketing* is to provide instructional materials that not only introduce the student to the field of services marketing but also acquaint the student with specific customer service issues. Despite the phenomenal growth in service industries, business schools have only recently begun to react to this dramatic change in the business environment. Current marketing curricula and textbooks continue to emphasize traditional marketing strategies by focusing on tangible goods and offensive marketing strategies (i.e., recruiting new customers). Meanwhile, the business world now demands, in addition to these traditional skills, increasing employee competence in customer satisfaction, service quality, and customer service, skills that are essential in sustaining the existing customer base.

Essentials of Services Marketing consists of 15 chapters, making it much shorter than traditional services marketing texts, which generally contain 20 to 25 chapters. This book is written in an "essentials" format for two reasons. First, because of the lack of a "true" undergraduate services marketing textbook for a number of years, many services marketing instructors have been using their own materials such as articles, cases, and videos. The "essentials" textbook provides these instructors with the means of covering the basic concepts and at the same time provides the flexibility for instructors to insert their own materials as they see fit. Second, because services marketing is relatively young as an academic field, a framework from which to study services marketing that is acceptable to all instructors has yet to emerge. Hence, the "essentials" textbook provides an initial framework that may be easily modified, based on instructor and student suggestions, in future editions of the book.

STRUCTURE OF THE BOOK

Essentials of Services Marketing is divided into four main parts. The first part, **"An Overview of Services Marketing,"** concentrates on defining services marketing and providing the basic concepts that differentiate the marketing of services from the marketing of tangibles. The purpose of this part is to lay the foundation for the remainder of the book.

Chapter One provides the basic definitions of goods and services and discusses the importance of the service sector with regard to the world economy as well as the importance of adopting a market-focused management approach. Chapter Two focuses more deeply on the fundamental differences between goods and services and their corresponding managerial implications. Chapter Three provides an overview of the service sector and investigates the unique differences of various service industries. The classification schemes presented in Chapter Three highlight the similarities and differences of the various industries and provide the frameworks from which to study their managerial implications. Chapter Four focuses on consumer purchase decision issues as they relate to the services field. Consumers often approach service purchases differently from the way they approach the purchase of goods. The first part of the book concludes with Chapter Five, which takes an in-depth look at ethics in the service sector. Because of the differences between goods and services, unique opportunities arise that may encourage ethical misconduct.

The second part of the book, **"Service Strategy: Managing the Service Experience,"** is dedicated to topics that concern the management of the service encounter. Due to the consumer's involvement in the production of services, many new challenges are presented that do not frequently occur within the manufacturing sector. The primary topics of this part are strategic issues related to the marketing mix as well as the servuction model components discussed in Chapter One.

Chapter Six provides an overview of service operations, pinpointing the areas where special managerial attention is needed in the construction of the service process. Chapters Seven and Eight focus on pricing and communication issues as they relate specifically to service firms. Chapter Nine examines the development and management of the service firm's physical environment. Part 2 of the book concludes with Chapter Ten, which is devoted to topics regarding the hiring, training, and empowering of service personnel as well as the management of customers.

The third part of the book, **"Assessing and Improving Service Delivery,"** focuses on customer satisfaction and service quality issues. Methods for tracking service failures and employee recovery efforts as well as customer retention strategies are also presented. We believe that you will find this part particularly intriguing.

Chapter Eleven presents an overview of the importance and benefits of customer satisfaction and the special factors to consider regarding measurement issues. Chapter Twelve builds from the materials presented in Chapter Eleven and discusses conceptual and measurement issues pertaining to service quality and service quality information systems. Chapter Thirteen presents methods for tracking service failures and employee service recovery efforts. Chapter Fourteen focuses on the often forgotten benefits of customer retention and discusses strategies that maximize a firm's customer retention efforts. Chapter Fifteen concludes this part of the textbook with "Putting the Pieces Together: Creating the Seamless Service Firm." Chapter Fifteen is dedicated to pulling the ideas in the book together in a manner that demonstrates the delivery of flawless customer service.

Part 4 of the book, **"Cases,"** consists of nine cases that illustrate the topics discussed throughout the book. The cases are organized to correspond with the first three parts of the book and can be used at the instructor's discretion to give students "real-world" practice in using the concepts presented in the textbook.

INSTRUCTORS' RESOURCES

The *Instructor's Manual with Test Bank and Transparency Masters*, written by the authors, includes instructors' materials collected by the authors from professors all over the world. In addition, all test questions are available as computerized test banks on 3.5-inch disks in DOS, Windows, and Macintosh versions.

The Dryden Press may provide complimentary instructional aids and supplements or supplement packages to those adopters qualified under our adoption policy. Please contact your sales representative for more information. If as an adopter or potential user you receive supplements you do not need, please return them to your sales representative or send them to:

- ▲ Attn: Returns Department
- ▲ Troy Warehouse
- ▲ 465 South Lincoln Drive
- ▲ Troy, MO 63379

ACKNOWLEDGMENTS

Many thanks are owed to family, friends, colleagues, and the folks at The Dryden Press for their assistance, patience, and encouragement. This first edition has benefited greatly from the quality of reviewers' comments. We are very appreciative of the insightful comments of the following colleagues:

Kenneth D. Bahn, James Madison University
Julie Baker, University of Texas at Arlington
Ronald E. Goldsmith, Florida State University
Scott Kelley, University of Kentucky
Rhonda Walker Mack, College of Charleston
Gene W. Murdock, University of Wyoming
Susan Stites-Doe, SUNY-Brockport
Louis Turley, Western Kentucky University

Special thanks also go to the staff at The Dryden Press. A number of people have played a major role in the creation and production of this text, including Lyn Maize, former executive editor; Lisé Johnson, senior product manager; Butch Porter; Leigh Deal; Paul Stewart, product manager; Jim Lizotte, former acquisitions editor; Bill Schoof, acquisitions editor; Bill Brammer, art director; and Melinda Esco, production manager. Finally, we are particularly grateful for the efforts of Dona Hightower, developmental editor, and Michele Tomiak, project

▶▶▶▶ ◀◀◀◀

editor, who took ownership of the project and ultimately put the book together. Thank you, Dona and Michele!

In closing, we hope that you enjoy the book and your services marketing class. It will likely be one of the most practical courses you will take during your college career. Education is itself a service experience. As a participant in this service experience, you are expected to participate in class discussions. Take advantage of the opportunities provided you during this course, and become an integral component of the education production process. Regardless of your major area of study, the services marketing course has much to offer.

We would sincerely appreciate any comments or suggestions you would care to share with us. We believe that this text will heighten your sensitivity to services, and because of that belief, we leave you with this promise: We guarantee that after completing this book and your services marketing course, you will never look at a service experience in the same way again. This new view will become frustrating for most of you, as you will encounter many experiences that are less than satisfactory. Learn from these negative experiences, relish the positive encounters, and use this information to make a difference when it is your turn to set the standards for others to follow. As apostles of services marketing, we could ask for no greater reward.

Doug Hoffman
Associate Professor of Marketing
Department of Management and Marketing
The University of North Carolina at Wilmington
Wilmington, NC 28403
(910) 962-3072 (office)
(910) 962-3815 (fax)
hoffmank@uncwil.edu (E-mail)

John Bateson
Gemini Consulting
Four Milbank Street
London, England 3JA
United Kingdom

About the Authors

K. Douglas Hoffman is Associate Professor of Marketing at the Cameron School of Business Administration, The University of North Carolina at Wilmington. He received the 1992 Chancellor's Award for Teaching Excellence and is a former recipient of the Cameron Research Fellowship. As a recipient of a Faculty Reassignment Award, Dr. Hoffman spent the 1994 fall semester assisting John Bateson in the revision of the third edition of *Managing Services Marketing: Text and Readings* (Dryden) and began the framework for *Essentials of Services Marketing*.

Dr. Hoffman holds an undergraduate marketing degree from Ohio State University and a master's degree from the University of Kentucky. He received his Ph.D. from the University of Kentucky and started the first services marketing classes at Mississippi State University and The University of North Carolina at Wilmington.

Dr. Hoffman's research and consulting interests are primarily in the areas of customer service/satisfaction and services marketing education. His work has appeared in the *Journal of Retailing, Journal of Personal Selling and Sales Management, Journal of Business Ethics, Journal of Services Marketing, Journal of Professional Services Marketing, Journal of Marketing Education*, and *Marketing Education Review*. Doug is a past Education Coordinator for the Services Marketing Special Interest Group of the American Marketing Association.

John E. G. Bateson is a senior vice-president with Gemini Consulting. He was Associate Professor of Marketing at the London Business School, England, and a visiting associate professor at the Stanford Business School. Prior to teaching, he was a brand manager with Lever Brothers and marketing manager with Philips.

Dr. Bateson holds an undergraduate degree from Imperial College, London, a master's degree from London Business School, and a Ph.D. in marketing from the Harvard Business School. He has published extensively in the services marketing literature, including the *Journal of Marketing Research, Journal of Retailing, Marketing Science*, and *Journal of Consumer Research*. He is also the author of *Managing Services Marketing: Text and Readings* (Dryden) and *Marketing Public Transit: A Strategic Approach* (Praeger).

Dr. Bateson was actively involved with the formation of the services division of the American Marketing Association. He served on the Services Council for four years and has chaired sessions of the AMA Services Marketing Conference. He also serves on the steering committee of the Marketing Science Institute. Dr. Bateson consults extensively in the services sector.

Contents in Brief

CONTENTS

AN OVERVIEW OF SERVICES MARKETING

*This textbook is divided into three main parts. This first part, **An Overview of Services Marketing,** concentrates on defining services marketing and providing the basic concepts that differentiate the marketing of services from the marketing of tangible goods. The chapters in this part lay the foundation for the topics discussed in the remainder of the book.*

1

An Introduction To Services

"*To put it bluntly, the continued prosperity of Americans depends on management's success in changing its approach to services.*"

Michael E. Raynor, "After Materialismo . . . ," *Across the Board* (July–August 1992), p. 41

CHAPTER OBJECTIVES

This chapter introduces you to the field of services marketing. It establishes the importance of the service sector in the world economy and the need for services marketing education.
After reading this chapter, you should be able to

- Discuss the basic differences between goods and services.

- *Discuss the factors that influence the customer's service experience.*

- Discuss why the study of services marketing is important.

- *Discuss the fundamental differences between the industrial model and the new market-focused management model.*

- Describe the outcomes associated with a market-focused management approach as portrayed by the service-profit chain.

For Innovative Service, Run for the Border

While the vast majority of other food franchises have remained in the traditional management mode by focusing on more advertising, more promotions, more new products, and more new locations, Taco Bell has been focusing on the customer. Taco Bell believes that the company should be organized to support what the customer truly values . . . the food and the service delivery system.

Unlike other food franchises, Taco Bell has shifted its operation from manufacturing to assembly. Backroom tasks such as cleaning heads of lettuce, slicing tomatoes, shredding cheese, and making taco shells has been outsourced to other operations. As a result, labor's primary focus is now on serving customers as opposed to preparing food. In contrast, much of the remainder of the industry is expanding its on-site food manufacturing operations by offering products such as freshly baked biscuits and pizzas. Firms pursuing this strategy have complicated their operations and have placed their emphasis on production as opposed to service delivery.

Other changes within Taco Bell's operations have included a total revamping of the firm's managerial hierarchy. This change has translated into managers who coach and counsel rather than direct and control. In addition, a renewed emphasis on selecting and training public contact personnel has also occurred. An investment in advanced technology has also helped move Taco Bell and its employees to the forefront. Unlike other companies that utilize technology to monitor, control, and sometimes replace their employees, Taco Bell provides technology to employees as a resource to assist them in their duties.

Taco Bell has also recognized the importance of employee morale and loyalty to customer perceptions of service quality. To enhance employee morale, Taco Bell offers front-line employees higher-than-average wages compared with those throughout the rest of the industry. Moreover, because of a generous bonus system, managers are able to make 225 percent more than their competitive counterparts. Such actions have not only improved employee morale but have also resulted in lower employee turnover rates and an improved caliber of recruits.

Taco Bell's training efforts are also unique. Managers are encouraged to spend half their time on developing employees in areas such as communication, empowerment, and performance management. As a result, the majority of Taco Bell employees now feel they have more freedom, more authority to make decisions, and more responsibility for their own actions.

Overall, the consequences of Taco Bell's restructuring efforts to improve its service delivery systems have been overwhelmingly positive. In times of stagnant market growth for the rest of the industry, sales growth at company-owned Taco Bells has exceeded 60 percent, and profits have increased by more than 25 percent per year. In comparison, McDonald's U.S. franchises have increased their profitability during this same period at a rate of 6 percent. What makes the 25 percent increase in profits even more amazing is that Taco Bell has decreased the price on most menu items by 25 percent! Strategies such as these have led to value-oriented perceptions of Taco Bell that surpass competitive offerings.

Source: Leonard A. Schlesinger and James L. Heskett, "The Service-Driven Service Company," *Harvard Business Review* (September–October 1991), pp. 71–81. Reprinted by permission of *Harvard Business Review*. Copyright © 1991 by the President and Fellows of Harvard College.

INTRODUCTION

Services permeate every aspect of our lives. In fact, most of us enter life via one service encounter and spend the rest of our lives experiencing a multitude of other service encounters. Services are everywhere we turn, whether it be a visit to the doctor, a church service, a trip to our favorite restaurant, or a day at school. Services are so pervasive that only when they start to fail do we realize how dependent upon them we have become.

Given the pervasiveness of services, it is difficult to understand why only recently services marketing education has become an important component of a student's total learning experience at most colleges and universities. This fact is particularly disturbing when you consider that since 1900, the United States and Great Britain have had more jobs in the service sector than in manufacturing.[1] In the beginning, the work toward accumulating services marketing knowledge was slow. In fact, not until 1970 was services marketing even considered an academic field.[2] It then took 12 more years before the first national conference on service marketing was held in the United States in 1982.

Equally as surprising has been business educators' superficial treatment of the topic of customer service. Despite the importance marketing places on "the customer," it is amazing how little most business classes deal with issues directly related to customer service. Unfortunately, the current educational approach to customer service is to treat it as a "common sense" issue. Maxims such as, "The customer is always right," and "Treat your customers like you want to be treated yourself," are frequently the only guidance provided regarding direct interactions with customers. Although helpful, the common sense approach fails to develop within the student a true understanding of the complex relationships that exist among employees, the organization, and the customer when service is at issue.

WHAT IS A SERVICE?

The distinction between goods and services is not always perfectly clear. In fact, providing an example of a pure good or a pure service is very difficult. A pure good would imply that the benefits received by the consumer contained no elements supplied by service. Similarly, a pure service would contain no goods elements.

In reality, many services contain at least some goods elements, such as the hamburger at McDonald's or the bank statement from the local bank. Also, most goods at least offer a delivery service. For example, simple table salt is delivered to the grocery store. In fact, the company producing the salt may find it is

A service encounter deals not only in intangibles but can also include physical goods. This McDonald's employee is serving a customer who will take away more than a burger, fries, and a drink—an impression of McDonald's as a whole.

© Elena Rouraid/PhotoEdit.

able to differentiate its product by providing unique and/or exceptional service related to its delivery system. Firms that manufacture goods are increasingly using services of all kinds to differentiate their goods from those of competitors, such as free delivery, special credit arrangements, and "800" numbers that customers can call for free advice. In this era of relative product parity, service is becoming the driving force in establishing competitive advantage.

The distinction between goods and services is further obscured by firms that conduct business on both sides of the fence. For example, General Motors, the "goods" manufacturing giant, generates 20 percent of its revenue from its financial and insurance businesses, and the car maker's biggest supplier is Blue Cross-Blue Shield, not a parts supplier as you may have thought.[3]

Despite the confusion, the following definitions should provide a sound starting point in developing an understanding of the differences between goods and services. In general, **goods** can be defined as objects, devices, or things, whereas **services** can be defined as deeds, efforts, or performances.[4] Moreover, note that the term **product** refers to both goods and services and is used in such a manner throughout the remainder of this text. The primary difference between goods and services is the property of tangibility. Due to the difference in tangibility, a host of services marketing problems evolve that are not always adequately solved by traditional goods-related marketing solutions. These differences are discussed in detail in Chapter 2.

goods
Objects, devices, or things.

services
Deeds, efforts, or performances.

product
Either a good or a service.

scale of market entities
The scale that displays a range
of products along a continuum
based on their tangibility.

marketing myopia
Condition of firms that define
their businesses too narrowly.

tangible dominant
Goods that possess physical
properties that can be felt,
tasted, and seen prior to the
consumer's purchase decision.

intangible dominant
Services that lack the physical
properties that can be sensed
by consumers prior to the
purchase decision.

benefit concept
The encapsulation of the
benefits of a product in the
consumer's mind.

The Scale of Market Entities

The **scale of market entities** presented in Figure 1.1 displays a range of products based on their tangibility. Pure goods are tangible dominant, while pure services are intangible dominant. Businesses such as fast food, which contain both a goods and service component, fall in the middle of the continuum. Firms that manufacture goods and ignore, or at least forget about, the service (intangible) element of their offering are overlooking a vital component of their businesses.

By defining their businesses too narrowly, these firms have developed classic cases of **marketing myopia.** For example, the typical family pizza parlor may myopically view itself as being in the pizza business. However, a broader view of the business recognizes that it is providing the consumer with a reasonably priced food product in a convenient format. Recently, companies such as Little Caesar's Pizza have seen the light and have changed their businesses from strictly carry-out operations to include free home delivery services. The lesson to be learned is that no matter how good your product, you are only as good as your service delivery system.

According to the scale of market entities, goods are **tangible dominant.** As such, goods possess physical properties that can be felt, tasted, and seen prior to the consumer's purchase decision. For example, when purchasing a car, the consumer can kick the tires, look at the engine, listen to the stereo, smell that "new-car smell," and take the car for a test drive before making the actual purchase. The same cannot be said for the purchase of services—services are **intangible dominant.**

In contrast to goods, services lack the physical properties that can be sensed by consumers prior to purchase. As a result, a number of marketing challenges immediately become evident. For example, how would you (1) advertise a service that no one could see; (2) price a service that has no cost of goods sold; (3) inventory a service that could not be stored; and (4) mass-merchandise a service that needs to be performed by an individual? Due to the dominance of intangibility, service knowledge is acquired differently than is goods knowledge. For example, a consumer cannot sample a haircut, a surgical procedure, or a consultant's advice prior to purchase. Service knowledge is gained through the experience of receiving the actual service.

The Service Experience

When a consumer purchases a service, he or she purchases an experience. All products, be they goods or services, deliver a bundle of benefits to the consumer.[5] The **benefit concept** is the encapsulation of these benefits in the consumer's mind. For a good such as Tide, for example, the benefit concept might simply be cleaning. However, it might also include attributes built into the product that go beyond the mere powder or liquid, such as cleanliness, whiteness, and/or motherhood. The determination of what the bundle of benefits comprises—the benefit

SCALE OF MARKET ENTITIES

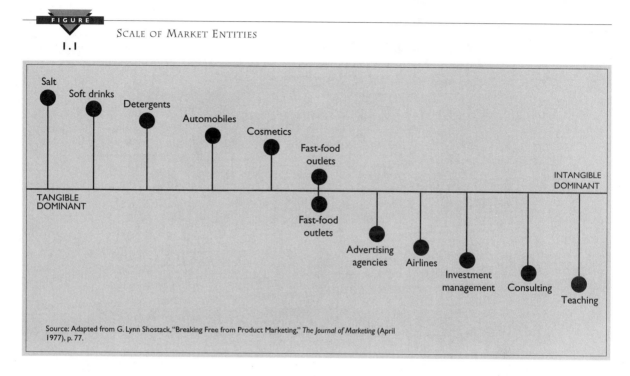

Source: Adapted from G. Lynn Shostack, "Breaking Free from Product Marketing," *The Journal of Marketing* (April 1977), p. 77.

concept purchased by consumers—is the heart of marketing, and it transcends goods and services.

In contrast to goods, services deliver a bundle of benefits through the experience that is created for the consumer. For example, most consumers of Tide will never see the inside of the manufacturing plant where Tide is produced; they will most likely never interact with the factory workers who produce the detergent or with the management staff that directs the workers; and they will also generally not use Tide in the company of other consumers. In contrast, restaurant customers are physically present in the "factory" where the food is produced; these customers *do* interact with the workers who prepare and serve the food as well as with the management staff that runs the restaurant. Moreover, restaurant customers consume the service in the presence of other customers, and they may all influence one another's service experience.

FRAMING THE SERVICE EXPERIENCE: THE SERVUCTION MODEL

One particularly simple but powerful model that illustrates factors that influence the service experience is the **servuction model** depicted in Figure 1.2. The

servuction model

A model used to illustrate the factors that influence the service experience, including those that are visible to the consumer and those that are not.

AN INTRODUCTION
TO SERVICES

FIGURE

1.2

THE SERVUCTION MODEL

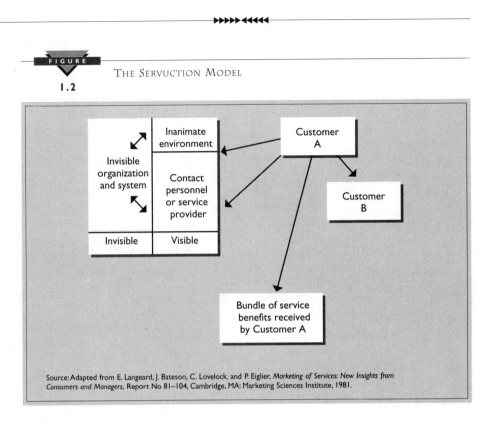

Source: Adapted from E. Langeard, J. Bateson, C. Lovelock, and P. Eiglier, *Marketing of Services: New Insights from Consumers and Managers*, Report No 81–104, Cambridge, MA: Marketing Sciences Institute, 1981.

servuction model is constructed of two parts: that which is visible to the consumer and that which is not. The visible part of the servuction model consists of three parts: the inanimate environment, the contact personnel/service providers, and other customers (denoted as Customer B in Figure 1.2). The invisible component of the model consists of the invisible organization and systems.

THE INANIMATE ENVIRONMENT

inanimate environment
All the nonliving features that are present during the service encounter.

The **inanimate environment** consists of all the nonliving features that are present during the service encounter. Because services are intangible, they cannot be objectively evaluated as can goods. Hence, in the absence of a tangible product, consumers look for tangible cues that surround the service on which to base their service performance evaluations. For example, you might partially assess the competence of your professor by observing the contents of his or her office. The inanimate environment is full of tangible clues such as furniture, flooring, lighting, music, odors, wall hangings, countertops, and a host of other inanimate objects that vary according to the service being provided. Due to the importance of the inanimate environment in consumer perceptions of service performance, Chapter Eight is devoted to the management of the inanimate environment.

FRAMING THE SERVICE EXPERIENCE:
THE SERVUCTION MODEL

Contact personnel are extremely important in service interactions, even if they interact only briefly with the customer, just as this supermarket employee is assisting the customer in her choice of produce.

© 1995 PhotoDisc, Inc. Image no. 21058.

CONTACT PERSONNEL/SERVICE PROVIDERS

Contact personnel are employees other than the primary service provider who briefly interact with the customer. Typical examples of contact personnel are parking attendants, receptionists, and hosts and hostesses. **Service providers** are the primary providers of the core service, such as a waiter or waitress, dentist, physician, or college instructor.

Unlike the consumption of goods, the consumption of services often takes place where the service is produced (inside the service factory) or where the service is provided at the consumer's residence or workplace. Regardless of the service delivery location, interactions between consumers and contact personnel/service providers are commonplace. As a result, the impact of contact personnel and service providers upon the service experience can be dramatic. Due to their importance within the service encounter, Chapter Nine is devoted to hiring, training, and empowering service personnel.

OTHER CUSTOMERS

To complete the visible portion of the servuction model, we need to introduce customers: A and B. **Customer A** is the recipient of the bundle of benefits that is created through the service experience. **Customer B** refers to all other customers who are part of Customer A's experience. As is the case with the other

contact personnel
Employees other than the primary service provider who briefly interact with the customer.

service providers
The primary providers of a core service, such as a waiter or waitress, dentist, physician, or college instructor.

Customer A
The recipient of the bundle of benefits that is created through the service experience.

Customer B
Other customers who are part of Customer A's experience.

visible components of the servuction model, other customers certainly affect the service experience.

For example, while eating at a fast-food restaurant, a customer was startled when his wife clutched her chest and exclaimed, "Don't look, don't look!" Believing that his wife was experiencing some sort of cardiac difficulty, the customer hastily inquired about the reason for the horrific expression now apparent on his wife's face. Still clutching her chest, she explained, "Somebody is getting sick over there. . . ." Upon hearing this unappetizing news, the husband's eyes fixated upon his wife's eyes as they both froze for an instant, deciding on their next course of action.

In this case, Customer B had indeed made a significant impact on all the restaurant's customers. This particular Customer B's actions cleared the entire restaurant in under 60 seconds. Particularly frustrating for the restaurant, it could not have foreseen the "upcoming event" and minimized its consequences. Even though the restaurant had no control over Customer B's actions, the event profoundly influenced the husband's and wife's future purchase intentions. The couple was unable to eat in any of the restaurant's franchises for more than a year and a half.

Customer B's influence on Customer A's experience can be active or passive. Unruly customers in a restaurant or movie theater are likely to affect other customers' experiences. Children who cry at church or run through department stores are also likely to affect others. More passive examples would include customers who show up late for appointments, making each subsequent appointment late; an individual who has "big hair" who sits directly in front of someone at a movie theater; and being part of a crowd, which as a collective group increases the waiting time for the service being sought.

INVISIBLE ORGANIZATION AND SYSTEMS

Thus far, the servuction model suggests that the benefits derived by Customer A are influenced by (1) the interaction with the inanimate environment, (2) contact personnel and/or service providers, and (3) other customers. The benefits are therefore derived from an interactive process that takes place throughout the service experience. Of course, the visible components of service firms cannot exist in isolation, and indeed, they have to be supported by invisible components.

invisible organization and systems
That part of a firm that reflects the rules, regulations, and processes upon which the organization is based.

The **invisible organization and systems** reflect the rules, regulations, and processes upon which the organization is based. As a result, although they are invisible to the customer, they have a very profound effect on the consumer's service experience. The invisible organization and systems determine factors such as information forms to be completed by customers, the number of employees working in the firm at any given time, and the policies of the organization regarding anything from the substitution of menu items to whether the firm accepts AARP cards for senior citizens' discounts.

The servuction system is what creates the experience for the consumer, and it is the experience that creates the bundle of benefits for the consumer. Perhaps the most profound implication of the model is that it demonstrates that consumers are an integral part of the service process. Their participation may be active or passive, but they are always involved in the service delivery process. This has a significant effect on the nature of the services marketing task.

WHY STUDY SERVICES?

Because of substantial changes in the business environment, a tremendous demand has developed for services marketing knowledge. Practitioners in the services field learned very quickly that traditional marketing strategies and managerial models did not always apply to their unique service industries. More specifically, the demand for services marketing knowledge has been fueled by (1) the tremendous growth in service-sector employment, (2) increasing service-sector contributions to the world economy, (3) the deregulation of many service industries, and (4) a revolutionary change of perspective in how service firms should organize their companies.

SERVICE SECTOR EMPLOYMENT

Throughout the world, the shifting of economies from agricultural to industrial to services is evident.[6] As indicated in the introduction, by 1900, both Britain and the United States had more jobs in the service sector than in the manufacturing sector. Today, manufacturing employs only one out of every six persons in the United States, one out of every five in Great Britain, and one out of three in Germany and Japan.

From 1970 to 1993, the U.S. labor force employed by manufacturing fell from 27 percent to 16 percent. Great Britain's labor force experienced a similar move away from manufacturing at a rate of 37 percent to 20 percent. In contrast, labor employed in the service sector has risen to 57 percent in Germany, 62 percent in Japan, 73 percent in Great Britain, and 78 percent in the United States. From 1970 to 1993, employment in the service sector rose from 66 percent to 78 percent in the United States and, astoundingly, from 50 percent to 73 percent in Great Britain (see Figure 1.3).

The increase in service employment is directly related to new service jobs. Between 1980 and 1990, 80 percent of all new jobs were developed in service industries.[7] Estimates suggest that 90 percent of all new jobs between 1990 and the year 2000 will also be service related. Experts project that by the year 2005, only 12 percent of U.S. workers will have manufacturing jobs, and this number is expected to decrease to 10 percent by the year 2020.[8]

ECONOMIC IMPACT

Service and service-related industries clearly dominate the U.S economy and will continue to do so in the foreseeable future. Similarly situated, the economies of

AN INTRODUCTION
TO SERVICES

FIGURE

1.3

WORLDWIDE CHANGES IN EMPLOYMENT

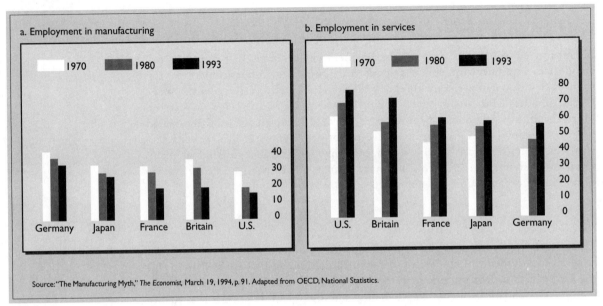

Source: "The Manufacturing Myth," *The Economist*, March 19, 1994, p. 91. Adapted from OECD, National Statistics.

other nations once known for their industrial might are also becoming predominantly service economies (see Figure 1.4). Countries such as Great Britain, Canada, France, Italy, Japan, and Germany have service economies that make up more than 50 percent of their gross domestic products (GDP).[9]

According to the U.S. Labor Statistics Bureau, the private service sector has increased its contribution to the GDP by more than 300 percent over the past 30 years. As a result, the private service sector now accounts for more than 70 percent of the GDP. In contrast, since 1970, GDP attributed to the manufacturing of goods has fallen from 26 percent to 19 percent. This means that for the first time in U.S. history, the majority of industries in our economy do not produce, they perform.

THE IMPACT OF DEREGULATION

The growth of the service sector is not the only reason that the demand for services marketing knowledge has increased. Over the past 15 years, an increasing interest in the marketing problems of service organizations has paralleled the emergence of competition in many parts of the service sector. The late emergence of services marketing as an academic field could then rightly be explained by the lack of a need for it in times when demand exceeded supply and competitive pressures were few. Deregulation has changed all that!

FIGURE

1.4

SERVICE SECTOR CONTRIBUTIONS TO GROSS DOMESTIC
PRODUCT BY COUNTRY (AS % OF GDP)

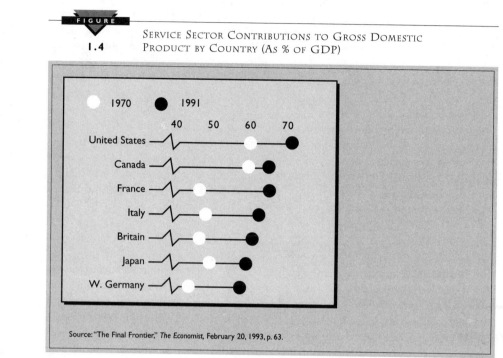

Source: "The Final Frontier," *The Economist*, February 20, 1993, p. 63.

During the 1980s, deregulation forced many traditional service industries such as airlines, financial services, telecommunications, and trucking into the competitive arena for the first time. These industries were forced to be competitive not only with existing firms within their industry, but also with new firms that were permitted to enter the industry due to deregulation. The new firms were leaner, more focused, and extremely competitive.

As competitive pressures increased within the deregulated industries, the need for services marketing knowledge became apparent. In addition to facing new competitors, the deregulated industries found themselves with excess supply and engaged in price wars with the competition. The consequences of deregulation upon the unprepared companies were devastating.[10] From 1980 to 1992, the U.S. airline industry declined from 36 operators to 11. The number of trucking companies that failed during the 1980s was more than the previous 45 years combined, and the number of commercial banks declined by 14 percent.

It became apparent that competing on pricing alone was leading to devastating results. Services marketing knowledge was needed in nonprice strategy areas such as customer service, customer retention, service differentiation, service quality, image enhancement, and the transformation of public contact employees into marketing-oriented personnel. Service industries such as the health-care industry, which in its recent past considered marketing a "dirty word" and beneath the dignity of its personnel, now embrace marketing techniques as a means for their firms' survival. However, even in the health-care field, the transformation remains incomplete. If you ask a room full of health-care workers to identify their primary customer, the majority of the room will still to this day answer "the physician," or perhaps more disturbing, "the insurance companies."

The Services Revolution: A Change in Perspective

Without a doubt, the United States is experiencing the most substantial period of change in its economic history since the industrial revolution. Accompanying this change has been a shift in the philosophy of how service firms should organize their businesses. Under the current industrial model of management, it is feared, services will not be able to create the wealth needed to maintain the United States standard of living.[11]

The Industrial Management Model

industrial management model

An approach to organizing a firm that focuses on revenues and operating costs and ignores the role personnel play in generating customer satisfaction and sustainable profits.

The **industrial management model** has its roots in the manufacturing sector and is still employed today by many service organizations. Organizations that follow this approach believe that (1) location strategies, sales promotions, and advertising drive sales revenue; and that (2) labor and other operating costs should be kept as low as possible. In sum, the industrial model focuses on revenues and operating costs and ignores (or at least forgets) the role personnel play in generating customer satisfaction and sustainable profits.

Followers of the industrial model believe that good employees are difficult to find nowadays. The industrial model supports the view that "all things being equal, it is better to rely on technology, machines, and systems than on human beings."[12] Followers of this approach believe that most employees are indifferent, unskilled, and incapable of fulfilling any duties beyond performing simple tasks. Consequently, jobs under the industrial model are specifically narrowly defined to leave little room for employees to exercise judgment. Moreover, employees are held to low job performance expectations, their wages are kept as low as possible, and few opportunities for advancement are available.

As opposed to valuing front-line employees, the industrial model places a higher value on upper and middle managers while viewing the people who deliver service to the customer as the "bottom of the barrel." The industrial approach assumes that only managers can solve problems; consequently, resolving customer problems quickly becomes almost impossible as additional steps are built into the service delivery process.

The industrial model guarantees a cycle of failure as service failures are designed directly into the system.[13] Due to its lack of support for front-line personnel, the industrial approach, albeit unintentionally, actually encourages front-line employees to be indifferent to customer problems. In essence, the system prohibits the front-line employee from taking any action even if the employee wants to assist in correcting the problem. Customer reactions to this type of treatment are not surprising. Two-thirds of customers who now defect from their former suppliers do so not because of the product, but because of the indifference and unhelpfulness of the person providing the service.

To further reduce operating costs, many firms that embrace the industrial model have replaced their full-time personnel with less experienced and less committed part-time personnel. These individuals are paid less than full-time personnel and receive few, if any, company benefits. In some instances, companies routinely release workers before mandatory raises and other benefits begin, in an attempt to keep operating costs down. Managerial practices such as this have created a new class of migrant worker in the United States—16 million people now travel from one short-term job to another.

The consequences associated with the industrial model in regard to service organizations have been self-destructive. The industrial model has produced dead-end front-line jobs, poor pay, superficial training, no opportunity for advancement, and little, if any, access to company benefits. Moreover, the industrial approach has led to customer dissatisfaction, flat or declining sales revenues, high employee turnover, and little or no growth in overall service productivity. In sum, many believe that the industrial approach is bad for customers, employees, shareholders, and the country.

THE MARKET-FOCUSED MANAGEMENT MODEL

In contrast to the industrial management model, proponents of the new **market-focused management model** believe that the purpose of the firm is to serve the customer.[14] Consequently, logic suggests that the firm should be organized in a manner that supports the people who serve the customer. By following this approach, service delivery becomes the focus of the system and the overall differential advantage in terms of competitive strategy.

The framework that supports this change in philosophy is based on the **services triangle** presented in Figure 1.5.[15] The services triangle depicts six key relationships. First, the firm's service strategy must be communicated to its customers. If superior service is the focus of the organization and the key point of differentiation on which it distinguishes itself from competitors, the customer needs to be made aware of the firm's commitment to excellence. Second, the service strategy also needs to be communicated to the firm's employees. Good service starts at the top, and management must lead by example. If top management is not committed to the process, front-line employees who interact with the firm's customers will be ineffective at best.

The third relationship depicted within the triangle focuses on the consistency of the service strategy and the systems that are developed to run the day-to-day operations. The systems like those discussed as components of the servuction model should flow logically from the service strategy and enhance the service encounter for employees and customers alike. The fourth relationship involves

market-focused management model
A new organizational model that focuses on the components of the firm that facilitate the firm's service delivery system.

services triangle
The framework that supports the market-focused management model by depicting the relationships among the systems, the service strategy, and the people, with the customer in the center of the triangle, interacting with each group.

AN INTRODUCTION
TO SERVICES

FIGURE

1.5

THE SERVICE TRIANGLE

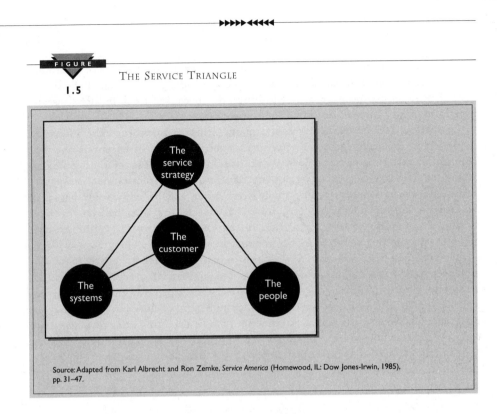

Source: Adapted from Karl Albrecht and Ron Zemke, *Service America* (Homewood, IL: Dow Jones-Irwin, 1985), pp. 31–47.

the impact of organizational systems upon customers. Interactions with the firm's systems should facilitate the customer's service experience. Too often, systems are designed for the sole purpose of keeping a small minority of customers from taking advantage of the company. Meanwhile, the majority of honest customers are forced to suffer through systems and policies that treat them as suspects instead of valued assets.

The fifth relationship within the services triangle pinpoints the importance of organizational systems and employee efforts. Organizational systems and policies should not be obstacles in the way of employees wishing to provide good service. For example, a frustrated Sam's Club employee informed a customer that policy dictated that he was not permitted to help customers load merchandise into their vehicles. His frustration stemmed from the firing of an employee who, a week earlier, turned down a woman's request for assistance. It later became apparent that the employee was fired not so much for his refusal, but due to the content of his response: "Hey, lady, this ain't Food Lion!" Finally, the last relationship is perhaps the most important of them all—the customer/service provider interaction. These interactions represent **critical incidents** or **"moments of truth."** The quality of this interaction is often the driving force in customer satisfaction evaluations.

critical incidents ("moments of truth")
The customer/service provider interaction that is often the key in customer satisfaction evaluations.

The market-focused management model, supported by the services triangle, is based on the belief that employees, in general, want to do good work. Hence, proponents of this model are more optimistic regarding their faith in human nature. As such, the market-focused management approach encourages investing in people as much as it does investing in machines. Consequently, as was the case for Taco Bell in the opening vignette, the primary purpose of technology should be to assist front-line personnel, not to replace them or monitor and control their activities. According to the market-focused management model, data once collected and controlled by middle managers should now be readily available to front-line personnel.

In further contrast to the industrial model, the market-focused management model recognizes that employee turnover and customer satisfaction are clearly related. Consequently, the market-focused management model emphasizes the recruitment and training of front-line personnel and ties pay to performance at every level throughout the organization. The benefits of superior training and compensation programs are clear. For example, the turnover rate for employees not participating in training programs at Ryder Truck Rental is 41 percent. In comparison, employees who did participate in training turned over at the rate of 19 percent.[16] Better-trained and better-paid employees provide better service, need less supervision, and are more likely to stay on the job. In turn, their customers are more satisfied, return to make purchases more often, and purchase more when they do return.

Past studies have also indicated that the correlation between customer satisfaction and employee turnover is also affected by the proportion of full-time to part-time employees.[17] As you might expect, the higher the proportion of full-time to part-time employees, the more satisfied the customers. Full-time employees tend to be more knowledgeable, more available, and more motivated to satisfy customers.

In contrast to the industrial management model philosophy, proponents of the market-focused management model refuse to sacrifice competent and motivated full-time personnel in the name of lower operating costs. The benefits of maintaining a highly motivated full-time staff are clear. As evidence, companies that pay their employees more than competitors pay often find that as a percent of sales, their labor costs are actually lower than industry averages.

One final difference between the industrial management model and the market-focused management model is that the latter attempts to utilize innovative data to examine the firm's performance by looking beyond generally accepted accounting principles. Traditional accounting principles reflect the sales orientation of the old industrial management model. New accounting measures that reflect the focus on customer orientation need to be developed and refined. The new measures of interest include the following: the value of customer retention over constantly seeking new customers, the costs of employee turnover, the value of employee training, and the monetary benefits associated with service recovery.

service-profit chain

The framework that illustrates the benefits of the market-focused management model and reveals that employee satisfaction and customer satisfaction are directly related.

PULLING IT ALL TOGETHER

The benefits of the market-focused management model are illustrated in the **service-profit chain** illustrated in Figure 1.6.[18] The links in the chain reveal that employee satisfaction and customer satisfaction are directly related. Employee satisfaction is derived from a workplace and job design that facilitate internal service quality. Hiring, training, and rewarding effective personnel are also major contributors to internal service quality.

Satisfied employees remain with a firm and improve their individual productivity. Hence, employee satisfaction is linked with increases in a firm's overall productivity and decreases in recruitment and training costs. Moreover, the increase in productivity coupled with a sincere desire to assist customers results in external service value. Employee attitudes and beliefs about the organization are often reflected in their behaviors. Given the customer's involvement in the production process, these behaviors are visible to the customer and ultimately influence the customer's satisfaction.

Customer satisfaction is directly related to customer loyalty, which is demonstrated through repeat purchases and positive word-of-mouth referrals to other customers. The net effects of customer retention are increased revenues and profitability for the firm.

Simultaneously, employees are also rewarded for their efforts. The outcomes associated with employee satisfaction—external service values, customer satisfaction, customer loyalty, revenue growth, and increased profitability—reinforce the company's commitment to continually improving internal service quality. As the recipients of internal quality improvements and positive customer responses, employees directly experience the fruits of their efforts. Employee satisfaction is subsequently reinforced, and the integrity of the service-profit chain is maintained.

The service-profit chain provides the logic behind the change in perspective that has led to the market-focused management model. The major lessons to be learned from the chain are twofold. First, a firm must satisfy its employees in order for customer satisfaction to become a consistent reality. Second, the chain proclaims the simple fact that service and quality pay!

SUMMARY

Services permeate every aspect of our lives; consequently, the need for services marketing knowledge is greater today than ever before. The distinction between goods and services is often unclear. In general, goods are defined as objects, devices, or things, whereas services are defined as deeds, efforts, or performances. Very few products can be classified as pure services or pure products. The scale of market entities presented in Figure 1.1 illustrates how various goods and services fall along a continuum based upon their tangibility.

FIGURE
1.6   THE SERVICE-PROFIT CHAIN

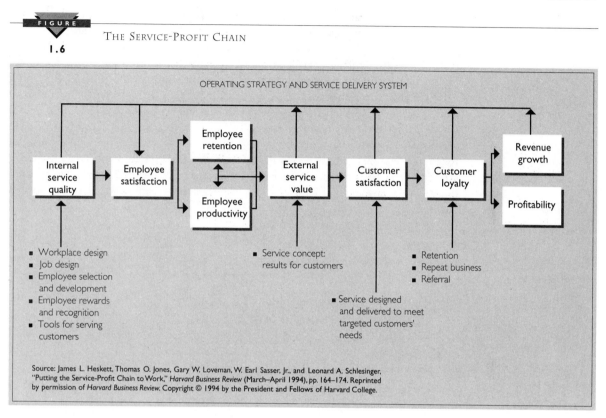

Source: James L. Heskett, Thomas O. Jones, Gary W. Loveman, W. Earl Sasser, Jr., and Leonard A. Schlesinger, "Putting the Service-Profit Chain to Work," *Harvard Business Review* (March–April 1994), pp. 164–174. Reprinted by permission of *Harvard Business Review*. Copyright © 1994 by the President and Fellows of Harvard College.

When a consumer purchases a service, he or she purchases an experience. The four components of the servuction system create the experience for the consumer—the inanimate environment, service providers/contact personnel, other customers, and the invisible organization and systems. In turn, the service experience that is created delivers a bundle of benefits to the consumer. In contrast to the production of goods, the servuction model demonstrates that service consumers are an integral part of the service production process.

Recent developments have fueled the demand for services marketing knowledge. First, tremendous growth has occurred in service-sector employment and in the service sector's contribution to many countries' gross domestic product. For example, experts suggest that by the year 2020, 90 percent of the United States labor force will be employed in service or service-related industries. The demand for services marketing knowledge has also increased due to the deregulation of many service industries. Many of these industries are facing situations in which supply exceeds demand, combined with fierce competitive pressures for the first time.

The demand for services marketing knowledge has also been fueled by a change in perspective in how service firms should manage their companies. Organizations that follow the traditional industrial model believe that (1) location strategies, sales promotions, and advertising drives sales revenue; and (2) labor and other operating costs should be kept as low as possible. The industrial model focuses on revenues and operating costs and ignores, or at least forgets, the role personnel play in generating customer satisfaction and sustainable profits.

In contrast, proponents of the new market-focused management model believe that the purpose of the firm is to serve the customer. Consequently, logic suggests that the firm should organize itself in a manner that supports the people who serve the customer. By following this approach, service delivery becomes the focus of the system and the overall differential advantage in terms of competitive strategy. The basic concepts and outcomes associated with the market-focused management approach are illustrated in the services triangle and the service-profit chain depicted in Figures 1.5 and 1.6.

KEY TERMS

goods	contact personnel
services	service providers
product	Customer A
scale of market entities	Customer B
marketing myopia	invisible organization and systems
tangible dominant	industrial management model
intangible dominant	market-focused management model
benefit concept	services triangle
servuction model	critical incidents
inanimate environment	Service-Profit Chain

DISCUSSION QUESTIONS

1. Discuss the current progress of services marketing education.

2. Why is it difficult to distinguish between many goods and services?

3. Define the following terms: goods, services, products.

4. Discuss the relevance of the scale of market entities to marketing myopia.

5. Discuss the consequences of the industrial management model.

6. What benefits are associated with better-paid and better-trained personnel?

7. Discuss the relevance of the services triangle to the market-focused management model.

8. Describe the major links in the service-profit chain as they relate to Taco Bell.

▶▶▶▶ ◀◀◀◀

NOTES

1. "The Final Frontier," *The Economist*, February 20th, 1993, p. 63.

2. Leonard L. Berry and A. Parasuraman, "Building a New Academic Field—The Case of Services Marketing," *Journal of Retailing* 69, (Spring 1993), pp. 1, 13.

3. "The Final Frontier," p. 63.

4. Leonard L. Berry, "Services Marketing Is Different," *Business Magazine* (May–June 1980), pp. 24–29.

5. This section adapted from John E. G. Bateson, *Managing Services Marketing*, 2nd ed. (Fort Worth, TX: The Dryden Press, 1992), pp. 8–11.

6. "The Manufacturing Myth," *The Economist*, March 19th, 1994, p. 91.

7. Stephen Keopp, "Pul-eeze! Will Somebody Help Me?," *Time*, February 2, 1987, pp. 28–34.

8. "The Manufacturing Myth," p. 91.

9. "The Final Frontier," p. 63.

10. Berry and Parasuraman, "Building a New Academic Field," pp. 17–18.

11. Leonard A. Schlesinger and James L. Heskett, "The Service-Driven Service Company," *Harvard Business Review* (September–October 1991), pp. 71–75.

12. Schlesinger and Heskett, "The Service-Driven Service Company," p. 74.

13. Schlesinger and Heskett, "The Service-Driven Service Company," p. 71.

14. Schlesinger and Heskett, "The Service-Driven Service Company," p. 77.

15. Karl Albrecht and Ron Zemke, *Service America* (Homewood, IL: Dow Jones-Irwin, 1985), pp. 31–47.

16. Schlesinger and Heskett, "The Service-Driven Service Company," p. 76.

17. Ibid.

18. James L. Heskett, Thomas O. Jones, Gary W. Loveman, W. Earl Sasser, Jr., and Leonard A. Schlesinger, "Putting the Service-Profit Chain to Work," *Harvard Business Review* (March–April 1994), pp. 164–174.

FUNDAMENTAL DIFFERENCES BETWEEN GOODS AND SERVICES

"It is wrong to imply that services are just like goods 'except' for intangibility. By such logic, apples are just like oranges, except for their 'appleness.'"

G. Lynn Shostack, "Breaking Free from Product Marketing," *Journal of Marketing* (April 1977)

CHAPTER OBJECTIVES

This chapter discusses the basic differences between goods and services, the marketing problems that arise due to these differences, and possible solutions to the problems created by these differences. After reading this chapter, you should be able to

- ► Define the characteristics of intangibility, inseparability, heterogeneity, and perishability.
- ► *Discuss the marketing problems associated with intangibility and their possible solutions.*
- ► Discuss the marketing problems associated with inseparability and their possible solutions.
- ► *Discuss the marketing problems associated with heterogeneity and their possible solutions.*
- ► Discuss the marketing problems associated with perishability and their possible solutions.
- ► *Discuss the impact of intangibility, inseparability, heterogeneity, and perishability on marketing's relationship to other functions within the service organization.*

THE AMERICAN AUTOMOBILE ASSOCIATION

The American Automobile Association (AAA) can claim to be one of the largest service organizations in the world, with more than 30 million members in the United States and Canada. Though its members still refer to it as "the auto club," the AAA prefers to describe itself as a travel service organization.

As a nonprofit firm, the AAA exists solely to provide service to its members. The spectrum of services provided is considerable, ranging from roadside emergency service to travel advice, auto insurance, road safety schemes, and even driving lessons and driver education courses. The AAA itself is actually an umbrella group of some 159 regional organizations, all of which have considerable leeway in the their ability to configure services to meet local demand.

The regional organizations first must operate global AAA services, such as breakdown assistance and insurance (the AAA regularly inspects member organizations to ensure that these services are provided according to standard), and then provide local programs to meet other traveler requirements. Travel advice, for example, is provided by more than a thousand regional offices across North America. However, while these services account for a great deal of the AAA's business with its customers, the core service and the principle reason that people join and remain members of the AAA is roadside emergency service.

When planning roadside emergency service, regional organizations have a number of factors to coordinate. Local population, geography, climate, and traffic patterns all play a part in the incidence of demand. However, demand is never predictable, as no one, not even the customer, knows exactly when the customer's car is going to break down.

When a breakdown does occur, the customer may not be aware of the cause or be able to move the vehicle to a place of the AAA's choice. In addition, the customer may be under considerable stress, particularly if the weather is bad or the hour is late. Consequently, the service will be perceived from the customer's viewpoint not only on the basis of whether the car was repaired, but on how long it took the service to arrive and on the helpfulness and courtesy of the service personnel, both on the telephone and with the recovery vehicle.

The challenge to AAA organizations is, then, to configure a service capable of meeting the demands of individual members, regardless of all other variables. The exact nature of these variables can never be known until the actual moment of the service.

Source: Adapted from John E. G. Bateson, *Managing Services Marketing*, 3rd ed. (Fort Worth, TX: The Dryden Press, 1995), p. 12.

INTRODUCTION

One of the reasons the field of services marketing was slow to grow within the academic community was that many marketing educators felt the marketing of services was not significantly different from the marketing of goods. Markets still needed to be segmented, target markets still needed to be sought, and marketing mixes that catered to the needs of the firm's intended target market still needed to be developed. However, since those early days, a great deal has been written regarding specific differences between goods and services and their corresponding marketing implications. The majority of these differences are primarily attributed to four unique characteristics—intangibility, inseparability, heterogeneity, and perishability.[1]

Services are said to be intangible because they are performances rather than objects, and they cannot be touched or seen in the same manner as goods. Rather, they are experienced, and consumers' judgments about them tend to be more subjective than objective. Inseparability of production and consumption refers to the fact that whereas goods are first produced, then sold, and then consumed, services are sold first and then produced and consumed simultaneously. For example, an airline passenger first purchases a ticket and then flies, consuming the in-flight service as it is produced.

Heterogeneity refers to the potential for service performance to vary from one service transaction to the next. This lack of consistency cannot be eliminated as it frequently can be with goods. Finally, perishability means that services cannot be saved; unused capacity in services cannot be reserved, and services themselves cannot be inventoried.[2]

The sections that follow focus on each of these four unique characteristics that service industries share and that differentiate their marketing from the marketing of goods. Because services fall in many places along the continuum that ranges from tangible dominant to intangible dominant as described by the scale of market entities in Chapter 1, the magnitude and subsequent impact that each of these four characteristics has upon the marketing of individual services will vary.

INTANGIBILITY

intangibility
A distinguishing characteristic of services that makes them unable to be touched or sensed in the same manner as physical goods.

Of the four unique characteristics that distinguish goods from services, **intangibility** is the primary source from which the other three characteristics emerge. As discussed in Chapter 1, services are performances, deeds, and efforts. As a result, services cannot be seen, felt, tasted, or touched in the same manner as tangible goods can be sensed.

For example, compare the differences between purchasing a movie ticket and purchasing a pair of shoes. The shoes are tangible goods, so the shoes can be objectively evaluated before the actual purchase. You can pick up the shoes, feel the quality of materials from which they are constructed, view their specific style and color, and actually put them on your feet and sample the fit. After the purchase, you can take the shoes home, and you now have ownership and the physical possession of a tangible object.

In comparison, the purchase of a movie ticket buys you an experience. Since the "movie experience" is intangible, services are subjectively evaluated. For example, consumers of services must rely on the judgments of others who have previously experienced the service for prepurchase information. Because the information provided by others is based on their own sets of expectations and perceptions, opinions will differ regarding the value of the experience. After the movie is over, the customer returns home with a memory of the experience and obtains the physical ownership of only a ticket stub.

Due to the intangibility of services, a number of marketing challenges arise that are not normally faced when marketing tangible goods. More specifically, these challenges include the lack of service inventories, the lack of patent protection, the difficulties involved in displaying and communicating the attributes of the service to its intended target market, and the special challenges involved in the pricing of services. The following sections address many of these challenges and offer possible solutions to minimize the effects.

MARKETING PROBLEMS CAUSED BY INTANGIBILITY

Lack of Ability to Be Stored Because of their intangibility, services cannot be inventoried. As a result, supplies of services cannot be stored as buffers against periods of high demand. For example, physicians cannot produce and store physical exams to be used at a later date; movie seats that are not sold for the afternoon matinee cannot be added to the theater for the evening show; and the AAA cannot inventory roadside service to be distributed during peak periods. Consequently, customers are commonly forced to wait for desired services, and service providers are limited in how much they can sell by how much they can produce. The bottom line is that the inability to maintain an inventory translates into constant supply and demand problems. In fact, the lack of service inventories presents so many challenges to marketers that it has earned its own name—perishability. Specific problems associated with perishability and the strategies associated with minimizing its effects are discussed in much greater detail later in the chapter.

Lack of Protection by Patents Due to the property of intangibility, services are not patentable. What is there to patent? Human labor and effort are not protected. Firms sometimes advertise that their processes are patented. However, the reality is that the tangible machinery involved in the process is protected, not the process itself. One challenge faced by the lack of patent protection is that new or existing services may be easily copied. Consequently, it is difficult to maintain a firm's differential service advantage over attentive competitors for long periods.

Difficulty of Displaying or Communicating Services The promotion of services presents yet another set of special challenges to the service marketer and is discussed in greater detail in Chapter Seven. The root of the challenge is this: How do you get customers to take notice of your product when they cannot see it? As an example, consider the insurance industry. Insurance is a complicated product for many people. As customers, we cannot see it, we are unable to sample it prior to purchase, many of us do not understand it, it seems to cost an awful lot of money, and the benefits of its purchase are not realized until some future point in time, if at all. In fact, if we do not use it, we are supposed to consider ourselves lucky. Why should spending thousands of dollars a year on something we never use make us feel lucky? To say the least, due to intangibility, the task of explaining your product's merits to consumers is highly challenging.

Difficulty of Pricing Services Typically, products' prices are often based on cost-plus pricing. This means that the producing firm figures the cost of producing the product and adds a markup to that figure. The challenge involved in the pricing of services is that there is no cost of goods sold! The primary cost of producing a service is labor.

As an example, let's say you are really strong in the field of mathematics, and you have been approached by another, less fortunate student who is struggling with his math assignments. Taking notice of your expertise in the field, this person wants to hire you as a tutor. What would you charge per hour? What costs are involved?

Based on feedback from other services marketing classes faced with this example, students usually begin giggling and indicate that they would engage in price gouging and charge the student $100.00 per hour. After the laughter subsides, past students quickly realize that it is very difficult to place a value on their time. Specific considerations usually emerge, such as how much money the tutor could make doing something else and the opportunity costs associated with not being able to lie around the apartment and enjoy free time. Typically, the general consensus is that the tutor should charge something comparable with the charges of all the other tutors. The problem with this response is that it still does not answer the original question, that is, how was this competitive-based price originally calculated?

POSSIBLE SOLUTIONS TO INTANGIBILITY PROBLEMS

The Use of Tangible Clues Given the absence of tangible properties, services are evaluated differently from goods. In many instances, consumers look at the **physical evidence** or tangible clues that surround the service to assist them in making service evaluations. **Tangible clues** may include such evidence as the quality of

physical evidence/ tangible clues
The physical characteristics that surround a service to assist consumers in making service evaluations, such as the quality of furnishings, the appearance of personnel, or the quality of paper stock used to produce the firm's brochure.

The benefits of intangible services such as insurance are difficult to assess until you need them. For example, this driver who has been in an auto accident must now contact her insurance agency for help in dealing with the very tangible damage to her car.

© 1995 PhotoDisc, Inc. Image no. 7173.

furniture in a lawyer's office, the appearance of the personnel in a bank, and the quality of paper used for an insurance policy.

Tangible clues are also often used in services advertising. As previously discussed, because of intangibility, firms often find it difficult to effectively communicate their service offerings to consumers. Returning to the insurance example, the major challenge of an insurance firm is to communicate to consumers in a 30-second television commercial what the specific firm has to offer and how the firm is different from every other insurance firm. One strategy embraced by many service firms is to use some form of tangible clues in advertising. Prudential uses "the rock" and promises "rock-solid protection." Allstate shows us "helping hands" and promises that "you're in good hands with Allstate." The list goes on and on . . . Merrill Lynch has "the bull," Nationwide promotes "blanket-wide protection," Kemper has "the cavalry," Travelers utilizes "the umbrella," and Transamerica promotes the shape of its office building as "the power of the pyramid." The lesson that all these companies have learned over time is that the services they sell are abstract to the consumer and, therefore, difficult for the average consumer to understand. The answer to this challenge was to provide tangible clues that were easily understood by the public and directly related to the bundle of benefits the services provided.

The Use of Personal Sources of Information Because consumers of services lack any objective means of evaluating services, they often rely on the subjective evaluations

nonpersonal sources
Sources such as mass
advertising that consumers use
to gather information about a
service.

personal sources
Sources such as friends, family,
and other opinion leaders that
consumers use to gather
information about a service.

organizational image
The perception an organization
presents to the public, and, if
well-known and respected,
lowers the perceived risk of
potential customers making
service provider choices.

inseparability
A distinguishing characteristic of
services that reflects the
interconnection among the
service provider, the customer
involved in receiving the service,
and other customers sharing
the service experience.

relayed by friends, family, and a variety of other opinion leaders. For example, when moving to a new town and seeking a family physician, consumers will often ask co-workers and neighbors for referrals. Hence, in purchasing services, personal sources of information become more important to consumers than **nonpersonal sources** such as the mass media.

Personal sources of information are a source of word-of-mouth advertising. One strategy often used to stimulate word-of-mouth advertising is to offer incentives to existing customers to tell their friends about a firm's offerings. Apartment complexes often use the incentive of a free month's rent to encourage tenants to have their friends rent vacant units. Service firms sometimes simulate personal communication while using the mass media. Mass advertising that features customer testimonials simulates word-of-mouth advertising and can be very effective. Examples include hospital advertisements featuring former recipients of major surgery who are now living normal and happy lives and insurance companies that feature victims of hurricanes, fires, and earthquakes who were satisfied with their insurance protection when they needed it most.

Creation of a Strong Organizational Image   Another strategy utilized to minimize the effects of intangibility is to create a strong **organizational image.** As will be discussed in much greater detail in the chapter about consumer behavior, intangibility and the lack of objective sources of information greatly increase the amount of perceived risk associated with the purchase of services over the risk associated with the purchase of goods. In an attempt to combat the higher levels of perceived risk, some service firms have spent a great deal of effort, time, and money in developing a nationally known organizational image. A well-known and respected corporate image lowers the level of perceived risk experienced by potential customers and, in some instances, lowers the reliance upon personal sources of information when making service provider choices. As an example, the consumer who is moving into a new town may bypass personal referrals and automatically seek out the nearest State Farm Insurance agent for home and auto insurance needs based on the firm's organizational image. In this case, the national firm, through image development and subsequent brand awareness, has developed a differential advantage over small, regionally local firms of which the consumer is unaware.

INSEPARABILITY

One of the most intriguing characteristics of the service experience involves the concept of inseparability. **Inseparability** refers to (1) the service provider's physical connection to the service being provided; (2) the customer's involvement in the service production process; and (3) the involvement of other customers in the service production process. Unlike the goods manufacturer, who may seldom see an actual customer while producing the good in a secluded factory, service providers are often in constant contact with their customers and must construct their service operations with the customer's physical presence in mind. This interaction between customer and service provider defines a **critical incident.** Critical incidents represent the greatest opportunity for both gains and losses in regard to customer satisfaction and retention.

critical incident

A specific interaction between a customer and a service provider.

MARKETING PROBLEMS CAUSED BY INSEPARABILITY

Physical Connection of the Service Provider to the Service For many services to occur, the service provider must be physically present to deliver the service. For example, dental services require the physical presence of a dentist or hygienist, medical surgery requires a surgeon, and in-home services such as carpet cleaning require a service provider to complete the work. Because of the intangibility of services, the service provider becomes a tangible clue upon which at least part of the customer's evaluation of the service experience becomes based.

As tangible clues, service providers are particularly evaluated based on their use of language, clothing, personal hygiene, and personal interaction skills. Many service firms have long appreciated the impact that public contact personnel have upon the firm's overall evaluation. For example, wearing uniforms or conforming to dress codes is often required of service employees to reflect professionalism. Other service firms such as restaurants often place their most articulate and attractive personnel in public contact positions such as wait staff, host/hostess, and bartender. Personnel who do not have these skills and traits are often employed in areas that are invisible to the consumer, such as the kitchen and dish room areas.

Face-to-face interactions with customers makes employee satisfaction crucial. Dissatisfied employees are often visible to customers, and their unhappiness often translates into lower consumer perceptions of the firm's performance. The importance of employee satisfaction within service firms cannot be over-emphasized. Employees should be viewed and treated as internal customers of the firm. This issue is discussed in much greater detail in Chapter 9.

Involvement of the Customer in the Production Process The second defining characteristic of inseparability is that the customer is involved in the production process. The customer's involvement in the production process may vary from (1) a requirement that the customer be physically present to receive the service, such as in dental services, a haircut, or surgery; (2) a need for the customer to be present only to start and stop the service, such as in dry cleaning and auto repair; and (3) a need for the customer to be only mentally present, such as in participation in college courses that are transmitted via television to the consumer's home or place of work.

Unlike goods, which are produced, sold, and then consumed, services are first sold and then produced and consumed simultaneously because of inseparability. For example, a box of cornflakes is produced in a factory, shipped to a store where it is sold, and then consumed by customers at a place and time of the customer's choosing. In contrast, services are produced and consumed simultaneously, so consumption takes place inside the service factory. As a result, service firms must design their operations to accommodate the customer's presence. Inseparability makes the service factory become another tangible clue that consumers consider when making service quality evaluations.

Overall, as customer contact increases, the efficiency of the operation decreases. The customer's involvement in the production process creates uncertainties in the scheduling of production. More specifically, the customer has a direct impact on the type of service desired, the length of the service delivery process, and the cycle of service demand. Attempting to balance consumer needs with efficient operating procedures is a delicate art.

Regarding the cycle of demand, restaurants would be more efficient if consumers would smooth their demands for food throughout the day as opposed to eating primarily during breakfast, lunch, and dinner hours. As one frustrated, senior-citizen McDonald's employee told a customer, "These people would get better service if they all didn't show up at the same time!" Further complications arise as consumers also dictate the nature or type of service needed. This is particularly frustrating for health-care workers who provide services to waiting emergency-room patients. Every consumer has a different need, some needs are more immediate than others, and you never know what the next ambulance will deliver. Obviously, this scenario is frustrating for waiting patients as well as for the health-care providers. Finally, even when consumer needs are the same, some consumers ask more questions and/or need more attention than others, thereby affecting the length of demand. As a result, fixed schedules are difficult to adhere to without delays.

During the customer's interaction with the service provider, the customer provides inputs into the service production process. As such, the customer often plays a key role in the successful completion of the service encounter. For example, a patient who feels ill must be able to accurately describe his or her symptoms to a physician to receive proper treatment. Not only must the symptoms be described accurately, but the patient must also take the recommended dosage of medicines prescribed. In this case, the customer (the patient) becomes a key player in the service production process and can directly influence the outcome of the process itself. Failure of the patient to follow recommended instructions will likely lead to a dissatisfactory service experience. The customer will probably blame the service provider, even though the service provider fulfilled his or her part of the transaction.

Another issue directly related to the consumer's presence in the service factory concerns the appearance of the service factory itself. Service factories must be built with consumers' presence in mind. Consequently, the service factory not only provides the service, but in and of itself becomes a key tangible clue in the formation of consumer perceptions regarding service quality. The design and management of the service factory is discussed in much greater detail in Chapter 8.

Involvement of Other Customers in the Production Process The presence of other customers during the service encounter is the third defining characteristic of inseparability. Because production and consumption occur simultaneously, several customers often share a common service experience. This "shared experience" can be negative or positive.

The marketing challenges presented by having other customers involved in the production process generally reflect the negative aspects of their involvement. Restaurants once again provide an ideal setting for examples of negative events, including smokers violating the space of nonsmokers and vice-versa, families with young children sharing the same space with adult couples seeking a quiet dining experience, drunk customers interacting with sober ones, and the occasional lovers' quarrel that spills over into the aisles. Overall, the primary challenge concerns effectively managing different market segments with different needs within a single service environment.

The impact of "other customers" is not always negative. On the positive side, audience reaction in the form of laughter or screams of terror often enhances the show at a movie theater, a crowded bar may facilitate the opportunity for social interaction, and a happy crowd may make a concert an even more pleasurable event. As social creatures, humans tend to frequent places of business and feel more comfortable in places that have other customers in them. In fact, the lack of "other customers" may act as a tangible clue that the impending experience may be less than satisfactory. Given the choice, would you rather eat at an unfamiliar restaurant that had no cars in the parking lot, or would you choose to eat at a restaurant down the street with a full parking lot?

Special Challenges in Mass Production of Services One final obstacle presented by inseparability is how to successfully mass produce services. The problems pertaining to mass production are twofold. First, because the service provider is directly linked to the service being produced, an individual service provider can produce only a limited supply. Consequently, the question arises: How does one provide enough service product to meet the demand of the mass market? The second problem directly relates to the consumer's involvement in the production process. If goods were constrained by inseparability, every consumer in the world who was interested in purchasing a Chevrolet Corvette would have to travel to Bowling Green, Kentucky, to purchase the vehicle. Hence, as a result of the inseparability characteristic inherent in the production of services, the problem for service firms becomes how to sell to a geographically widespread target market.

POSSIBLE SOLUTIONS TO INSEPARABILITY PROBLEMS

Emphasis on Selecting and Training Public Contact Personnel Just as customers are part of the service process, contact personnel are part of the service experience as well. Contact personnel, unlike goods, are not inanimate objects, and being human, they exhibit variations in behavior that cannot be controlled by the service process. Moreover, the attitudes and emotions of contact personnel are apparent to the customer and can affect the service experience for better or worse. Surly or unhappy employees can affect both customers with whom they come into direct

selection and training
A strategy that minimizes the impact of inseparability by hiring and educating employees in such a way that the customer's service experience is positive and the employees are properly equipped to handle customers and their needs.

consumer management
A strategy service personnel can implement that minimizes the impact of inseparability, such as separating smokers from nonsmokers in a restaurant.

multisite locations
A way service firms that mass produce combat inseparability, involving multiple locations to limit the distance the consumers have to travel and staffing each location differently to serve a local market.

factories in the field
Another name for multisite locations.

contact and other employees. On the other hand, a bright, highly motivated employee can create a more pleasant service experience for everyone who comes into contact with that person.[3]

Due to the frequency and the depth of interactions between service providers and consumers, **selection** of service personnel with superior communication and public relations skills is a must. In addition, **training** personnel once they are on the job is also necessary. Too often, newly hired employees are often left to fend for themselves. A large percentage of consumer complaints about service focuses on the action or inaction of employees. Critics of service quality have focused on "robotic" responses by staff and on staff who have been trained in using the technology associated with the business but not in dealing with different types of customers. Experts in service quality believe that employees must also be trained in "soft" management skills such as reliability, responsiveness, empathy, assurance, and managing the tangibles that surround the service.

Consumer Management   The problems created by inseparability can also be minimized through effective **consumer management.** Separating smokers from nonsmokers is an example of one way to minimize the impact of other customers. Sending a patient insurance forms and information about office procedures before the patient arrives may help control the length of the service encounter. Reservation systems may help smooth out demand created by traditional cycles. Providing delivery services may eliminate the need for many consumers to be physically present within a service factory, thereby increasing the firm's operating efficiencies. Finally, isolating the technical core of the business from the consumer allows for consumer involvement but limits the customer's direct impact upon the firm's operations. For example, the typical dry cleaning firm is designed so that customers are attended to at the front counter and the core operation is located in an area of the building where customer contact is not permitted. The management of service consumers is discussed in much greater detail in Chapter 10.

Use of Multisite Locations   To offset the effects of inseparability on centralized mass production, service firms that mass produce do so by setting up multiple locations. Typical examples include H & R Block, Hyatt Legal Services, LensCrafters, and various nationally known insurance firms such as Prudential, State Farm, and Allstate. **Multisite locations** serve at least two purposes. First, because the consumer is involved in the production process, multisite locations limit the distance the consumer must travel to purchase the service. Second, each multisite location is staffed by different service providers, each of whom can produce their own supply of services to serve their local market. Multisite locations act as **factories in the field.** Without them, every consumer who desired legal services would have to travel to a single location that housed all the lawyers in the country plus all their clients for that day. Obviously, this is not practical or realistic.

Multisite locations such as this LensCrafters limit the distance the consumer has to travel to purchase the service and provide their own staff to serve the local market.

© 1995 PhotoDisc, Inc. Image no. 21214.

The use of multisite locations is not without its own set of special challenges. Each site is staffed by different service providers who have their own personalities and their own sets of skills. For example, every H & R Block representative does not have the same personality and same set of skills as the founder, Henry Block. The differences in personnel are particularly troublesome for service firms attempting to establish a consistent image by providing a standardized product. The variability in performance from one multisite location to another and even from one provider to another within a single location leads us to the next special characteristic of services . . . heterogeneity.

HETEROGENEITY

One of the most frequently stressed differences between goods and services is the lack of ability to control service quality before it reaches the consumer. Service encounters occur in realtime, and consumers are already involved in the factory, so if something goes wrong during the service process, it is too late to institute quality-control measures before the service reaches the customer. Indeed, the customer (or another customer) may be part of the quality problem. If, in a restaurant, something goes wrong during a meal, that service experience for a customer is bound to be affected; the manager cannot logically ask the customer to leave the restaurant, re-enter, and start the meal again.

Heterogeneity, almost by definition, makes it impossible for a service operation to achieve 100 percent perfect quality on an ongoing basis. Manufacturing

heterogeneity

A distinguishing characteristic of services that reflects the variation in consistency from one service transaction to the next.

operations may also have problems achieving this sort of target, but they can iso-late mistakes and correct them over time, as mistakes tend to reoccur at the same points in the process. In contrast, many errors in service operations are one-time events; the waiter who drops a plate of food in a customer's lap creates a service failure that can be neither foreseen nor corrected ahead of time.[4]

Another challenge heterogeneity presents is that not only does the consistency of service vary from firm to firm and among personnel within a single firm, but it also varies when interacting with the same service provider on a daily basis. For example, some McDonald's franchises have helpful and smiling employees, while other franchises employ individuals who act like robots. Not only can this be said for different franchises, but the same is true within a single franchise on a daily basis because of the mood swings of individuals.

MARKETING PROBLEMS CAUSED BY HETEROGENEITY

The major obstacles presented by hetero-geneity translate into the fact that service standardization and quality control are difficult to achieve. Why is this so? Because of the inseparability characteristic previously discussed, you now know that in many instances, the service provider must be present to provide the service. Firms such as McDonald's employ a multitude of front-line service providers. As an individual, each employee has a different personality and inter-acts with customers differently. In addition, each employee may act differently from one day to the next due to mood changes as well as numerous other factors. As an example, many students who work as wait staff in restaurants frequently admit that the quality of interaction between themselves and customers will vary even from table to table.

The marketing problems created by heterogeneity are particularly frustrating. A firm could produce the best product in the world, but if an employee is having a "bad day," a customer's perceptions may be adversely affected, and the firm may never have another opportunity to serve that customer. Returning to our McDonald's example, the franchisee may pay $500,000 for the franchise and the right to sell a "proven product." However, the real secret to each individual fran-chise's success is the sixteen-year-old behind the counter who is interacting with customers and operating the cash register. Can you imagine the franchisee who has just spent $500,000 for the franchise trying to sleep at night while thinking that his or her livelihood depends upon the "kid" behind the counter?

POSSIBLE SOLUTIONS TO HETEROGENEITY PROBLEMS

customize

Taking advantage of the variation inherent in each service encounter by developing services that meet each customer's exact specifications.

Customization One possible solution to the problems created by heterogeneity is to take advantage of the variation inherent in each service encounter and **customize** the service. Producers of goods typically manufacture the good in an environment that is isolated from the customer. As such, mass produced goods do not meet individual customer needs. Since both the customer and the service provider are involved in the service delivery process, however, it is easier to customize the service based on the customer's specific instructions.

Note that there are tradeoffs associated with a customized service. On one hand, if everything is provided exactly to the customer's specifications, the customer ends up with a service that meets his or her specific needs. Consequently, the provider can obtain higher prices, which lead to higher profit margins for the provider. Providers pursuing a customization strategy focus on profit margins on a per-customer basis as opposed to achieving profits through a mass volume or turnover strategy.

The downside of providing customized services is threefold. First, customers may not be willing to pay the higher prices associated with customized services. Second, the speed of service delivery may be an issue. Customized services take extra time to provide and deliver. Finally, customers may not be willing to face the uncertainty associated with customized services. Each customized service is different, so the customer is never sure exactly what the final product will be until it is delivered. So, do customers prefer customized services over standardized services? The answer is, "It depends." If price, speed of delivery, and consistency of performance are issues, then the customer will probably be happier with a standardized service.

Standardization Standardizing the service is a second possible solution to the problems created by heterogeneity. Service firms can attempt to standardize their service through intensive training of their service providers. Training certainly helps reduce extreme variations in performance. However, despite all the training in the world, employees ultimately will continue to vary somewhat from one transaction to the next. One way to eliminate this variance is to replace human labor with machines.

An automatic teller machine (ATM) and an automated car wash are prime examples of standardized services that appeal to consumers' convenience-oriented needs. Taco Bell is now experimenting with a system that allows its customers to enter their own orders from one of several computer screens. This type of system minimizes the amount of customer contact and variations in quality during the ordering process.

On the positive side, standardization leads to lower consumer prices, consistency of performance, and faster service delivery. However, some consumer groups believe that standardization sends the message that the firm does not really care about individual consumer needs and is attempting to distance itself from the customer.

PERISHABILITY

Perishability also distinguishes goods from services and refers to the trait that services cannot be inventoried. Unlike goods that can be stored and sold at a later date, services that are not sold when they become available cease to exist. For example, hotel rooms that go unoccupied for the evening cannot be stored and used at a later date; airline seats that are not sold cannot be inventoried and added

standardizing

Reducing variability in service production through intensive training of providers and/or replacing human labor with machines.

perishability

A distinguishing characteristic of services in that they cannot be saved, their unused capacity cannot be reserved, and they cannot be inventoried.

on to aircraft during the holiday season, when airlines seats are scarce; and service providers such as dentists, lawyers, and hairstylists cannot regain the time lost from an empty appointment book.

Some service firms find it possible to inventory part of their service process. McDonald's, for example, can inventory hamburgers for a limited period of time. However, a McDonald's outlet cannot inventory the entire service experience. Spare capacity in the system on a Thursday evening cannot be saved for the Friday evening peak, nor can the hamburgers.

The inability to inventory creates profound difficulties for marketing services. In goods, the ability to create an inventory of the good that eventually will be purchased by the consumer means that production and consumption of the good can be separated in time and space. A good can be produced in one locality in the United States and transported for sale in another; a good can be produced in January and not released into the channels of distribution until June. Most services, however, are consumed at the point of production. From a goods-marketing manager's point of view, concerns about when and where the consumer consumes the product are important in understanding consumer behavior and motivation but largely irrelevant in day-to-day operations.

The existence of inventory also greatly facilitates quality control in goods-producing organizations. Statistical sampling techniques can be used on warehouse stock to select individual items for testing, to the point of destruction if necessary. The sampling process can be set up to ensure minimum variability in the quality of product released for distribution. Quality-control systems also provide numerical targets against which managers can work. It is thus possible for Procter & Gamble to produce tens of millions of packages of Tide that are essentially identical. In contrast, when you purchase a room at a hotel, you are likely to experience a wide range of factors that may influence your good night's sleep.

Finally, in goods-producing businesses, inventory performs the function of separating the marketing and the production departments. In many organizations, stock is actually sold at a transfer price from one department to another. The two parts of the firm have what amounts to a contract for quality and volumes. Once this contract has been negotiated, each department is able to work relatively independently of the other. In service firms, however, marketing and operations constantly interact with each other—because of the inability to inventory the product.[5]

MARKETING PROBLEMS CAUSED BY PERISHABILITY

Without the benefit of carrying an inventory, matching demand and supply within most services firms is a major challenge. In fact, due to the unpredictable nature of consumer demand for services, the only way that supply matches demand is by accident. For example, as a manager, try to imagine scheduling cashiers at a grocery store. Although we can estimate the times of the day that the store will experience increased demand, that demand may fluctuate widely within any 15- minute interval. Simply stated, consumer demand for many services at any given point in time is very unpredictable. Hence, due to the lack of inventories and the need for the service provider to provide the service, which adds additional time to the transaction, several demand and supply scenarios arise. In contrast to their service-producing counterparts, manufacturers of goods could more easily adapt to these scenarios through selling or creating inventories.

Higher Demand than Maximum Available Supply Within this scenario, consumer demand simply outpaces what the firm can supply, which results in long waiting periods and, in many cases, unhappy customers. Business may be lost to competitors as waiting times become too excessive for consumers to endure. Ironically, in cases of consistent excess consumer demand, consumers may continue to attempt to patronize a firm out of curiosity and/or the social status obtained by telling others of their experience . . . "We finally got in to see the show."

Higher Demand than Optimal Supply Level In many instances, the consequences associated with demand exceeding optimal supply may be worse than when demand exceeds maximum available capacity. By accepting the customer's business, the firm implicitly promises to provide the same level of service that it always provides, regardless of the quantity demanded. However, when demand exceeds optimal levels, the service provided is generally at inferior levels. As a result, customer expectations are not met, and customer dissatisfaction and negative word-of-mouth publicity results.

When demand exceeds optimal supply levels, the temptation is to accept the additional business. However, in many instances, the firm's personnel and operations are not up to the task of delivering service effectively beyond optimal demand levels. For example, suppose that a landscaper became very successful in a short period of time by providing high-quality services to upscale customers. As the word spread to other potential clients, demand for the landscaper's time dramatically increased. As the landscaper's firm expanded to serve new clients via the purchase of new equipment and the hiring of new personnel, the landscaper quickly found that he was losing control over the quality of service delivered by his firm. His new personnel simply did not provide the same level of service that his customers had grown accustomed to receiving. Over time, the landscaper lost his new clients as well as his old clients, and he eventually filed for bankruptcy. In this case, the service traits of perishability, inseparability, and heterogeneity all took their toll on the business.

Lower Demand than Optimal Supply Level As we discussed earlier, providing the exact number of grocery store cashiers needed at any given time is a challenge for most store managers. One solution would be to staff each line with a full-time cashier. However, this strategy would result in an inefficient deployment of the firm's resources. During times when demand is below optimal capacity, resources are underutilized (e.g., cashiers are standing around), and operating costs are needlessly increased.

Demand and Supply at Optimal Levels The optimal scenario is to have demand match supply. This scenario describes the situation in which customers do not wait in long lines and in which employees are utilized to their optimal capacity. Since services cannot be stored, a buffer to ease excess demand cannot be developed. Moreover, service providers are not machines and cannot produce a limitless supply. Consequently, service demand and supply rarely balance. Customers do at times experience lengthy waits, and service providers are sometimes faced with no one to serve.

POSSIBLE SOLUTIONS TO PERISHABILITY PROBLEMS[6]

Because service demand and supply balance only by accident, service firms have developed strategies that attempt to adjust supply and demand to achieve a balance between the two. The strategies to be discussed are possible solutions to overcome the difficulties associated with the perishability of services. The first group of strategies concerns the management of the firm's demand. This discussion is followed by a second group of strategies that focus on managing supply.

Demand Strategy: Creative Pricing **Creative pricing** strategies are often used by service firms to help smooth demand fluctuations. For example, offering price reductions in the form of "earlybird specials" and "matinees" have worked well for restaurants and movie theaters, respectively. Price-conscious target markets, such as families with children, are willing to alter their demand patterns for the cost savings. At the same time, service firms are willing to offer price reductions to attract customers during nonpeak hours, thereby making their operations more efficient. Moreover, by shifting demand to other periods, the firm can accommodate more customers and provide better service during periods in which demand in the past has been (1) turned away due to limited supply, and (2) not served as well as usual due to demand surpassing optimal supply levels.

Creative pricing has also been utilized to target specific groups such as senior citizens, children and their parents, and college students. This type of pricing strategy has not only helped smooth fluctuating demand but has also aided in separating diverse target markets from sharing the same consumption experience at the same time. For example, by providing family-type specials during late-afternoon and early evening hours, a restaurant significantly reduces the amount of potential conflict between its "family customers" and its "adult customers," who generally dine later in the evening.

Demand Strategy: Reservation Systems Another common strategy used to reduce fluctuations in demand is to implement a **reservation system** by which consumers

creative pricing
Pricing strategies often used by service firms to help smooth demand fluctuations, such as offering "matinee" prices or "earlybird specials" to shift demand from peak to nonpeak periods.

reservation systems
A strategy to help smooth demand fluctuations in which consumers ultimately request a portion of the firm's services for a particular time slot.

ultimately reserve a portion of the firm's services for a particular time slot. Typical service firms that utilize reservation systems include restaurants, doctors of all varieties, golf courses (tee times), and tanning salons. On the plus side, reservations reduce the customer's risk of not receiving the service and minimize the time spent waiting in line for the service to be available. Reservation systems also allow service firms to prepare in advance for a known quantity of demand. Consequently, the customer and the firm benefit from improved service.

Despite the advantages of a reservation system, a host of disadvantages also accompanies this strategy. First, someone must maintain the reservation system, which adds additional cost to the operation. Next, customers do not always show up on time or sometimes fail to show up at all. As a result, the operation ends up with unutilized service and lost revenues. For example, a common strategy for some golfers (particularly young and single) is to reserve a tee time at two or three different golf courses at two or three different times on the same day. Depending on their whims and which golf course they decide to play that particular day, the golfers choose which tee time to use, leaving the other two golf courses holding the tee for a foursome that is not going to show up. Given that the greens fee for an 18-hole round averages at least $25, the golf course has just lost $100 that it could have otherwise collected by filling the spot with another foursome.

Another drawback of reservation systems is that they offer to the customer an implied guarantee that the service will be available at a specified time, thereby increasing the customer's expectation. All too often, this implied guarantee is not met. For example, customers with early appointments may show up late, causing a chain reaction of delayed appointments for the rest of the day; the rate at which restaurant tables turn over is difficult to determine and is further compounded by the size of the party sitting at a table compared with the size of the party waiting for a table; and medical doctors often schedule as many as four patients at the same appointment time in an attempt to serve patient demand. Hence, in many instances, despite the reservation system, customers may still end up waiting and become even more unhappy (compared with a "first-come-first-serve" system) due to the implied promise made by the reservation system.

Demand Strategy: Development of Complementary Services The trials and tribulations associated with perishability can also be buffered by developing **complementary services** that directly relate to the core service offering. A lounge in a restaurant is a typical example of a complementary service that not only provides the space to store customers while they wait but also provides the restaurant with an additional source of revenue. Similarly, golf courses often provide putting greens for their customers as a form of complementary service. Although free of charge to customers, the putting green occupies the customers' time, thereby minimizing their perceived waiting time. The result is more satisfied customers. Other

complementary services
Services provided for consumers to minimize their perceived waiting time, such as driving ranges at golf courses, arcades at movie theaters, or reading materials in doctors' offices.

complementary services that have been developed to help manage demand include driving ranges at golf courses, arcades at movie theaters, reading materials in doctors' offices, and televisions in the waiting areas of hospital emergency rooms.

nonpeak demand development

A strategy in which service providers utilize their downtime by marketing to a different segment that has a different demand pattern than the firm's traditional market segment.

Demand Strategy: Development of Nonpeak Demand   The effects of perishability can also be modified by **nonpeak demand development.** This strategy can reduce the effects of perishability in two ways. First, the supply of service demanded during peak periods can be increased by utilizing nonpeak periods to prepare for high-demand periods. For example, employees can be cross-trained to perform a variety of other duties to assist fellow personnel (e.g., dishwashers may trained to set up and clear tables) during peak demand periods. In addition, although services cannot be stored, the tangibles associated with the service (such as salads at a restaurant) can be prepared and ready prior to the service encounter. Advance preparation activities such as these free personnel to perform other types of service when needed.

Nonpeak demand can also be developed to generate additional revenues. Many fast-food restaurants such as McDonald's and Wendy's did not always serve breakfast. The restaurants were simply closed to the public while personnel prepared for the lunch and dinner crowds. By offering a breakfast menu, the fast-food industry significantly increased its revenues.

Nonpeak demand is generally generated by marketing to a market segment that has a different demand pattern than the firm's traditional segment. For example, golf courses have filled nonpeak demand by marketing to housewives, senior citizens, and shift workers (e.g., factory workers, nurses, students, and teachers) who use the golf course during the morning and afternoon hours, which are traditionally slow periods during weekdays. These groups exhibit different demand patterns than traditional golfers, who work from 8:00 to 5:00 and demand golf course services in the late afternoon and early evening and on weekends.

As another example of marketing to different market segments with different demand patterns, one golf course struggled for many years to find a league that was willing to play on Friday evenings and large enough (profitable enough) to justify reserving a space for. After an examination of the problem, it became clear that many of the course's current customers spent Friday evenings with their significant others. As a result, a couples league was started and became so successful that a waiting list to join the league now exists. In fact, the couples league has become so popular that it holds parties during the off-season, when the golf course is closed due to inclement weather.

part-time employees

Employees who typically assist during peak demand periods and who generally work fewer than 40 hours per week.

Supply Strategy: Part-time Employee Utilization   In addition to managing consumer demand, the effects of perishability can also be lessened through strategies that make additional supply available in times of need. One such supply strategy is the utilization of **part-time employees** to assist during peak demand periods.

Retailers have successfully utilized part-time employees to increase their supply of service during the holidays for years.

The advantages of employing part-time workers as opposed to adding additional full-time staff include lower labor costs and a flexible labor force that can be employed when needed and released during nonpeak periods. On the negative side, utilizing part-time employees sometimes causes consumers to associate the firm with lower job skills and lack of motivation and organizational commitment. Such traits subsequently lead to dissatisfied customers. However, these disadvantages appear most commonly in organizations who staff their operations with part-time workers on a full-time basis as opposed to employing part-time employees only during peak demand periods.

Supply Strategy: Capacity Sharing Another method of increasing the supply of service is **capacity sharing,** forming a type of service co-op with other service providers, which permits the co-op to expand its supply of service as a whole. For example, many professional service providers are combining their efforts by sharing the cost and storage of expensive diagnostic equipment. By sharing the cost, each service firm is able to supply forms of service it may not otherwise be able to provide due to the prohibitive costs associated with such equipment. In addition, the funds saved through cost sharing are freed to spend on additional resources such as equipment, supplies, and or additional personnel, thereby expanding the supply of service to consumers even further.

capacity sharing
A strategy to increase the supply of service by forming a type of co-op among service providers that permits co-op members to expand their supply or service as a whole.

Supply Strategy: Advance Preparation for Expansion Although the strategy of **expansion preparation** does not provide a "quick-fix" to the supply problems associated with perishability, it may save months in reacting to demand pressures, not to mention thousands of dollars in expansion costs. In the effort to prepare in advance for expansion, many service firms are taking a long-term orientation with regard to constructing their physical facilities.

expansion preparation
Planning for future expansion in advance and taking a long-term orientation to physical facilities and growth.

For example, one local airport was built with future expansion in mind. This facility was built on a isolated portion of the airport property, where no adjoining structure would interfere with future growth. All plumbing and electrical lines were extended to the ends on both sides of the building and capped, making "hook-ups" easier when expansion becomes a reality. Even the road leading to the terminal is curved in the anticipation that new terminal additions will follow along this predetermined pattern.

In contrast, one Lowe's hardware store apparently failed to keep expansion in mind. Only four and a half years after a new Lowe's was built, another Lowe's superstore was built directly next to the existing facility. However, the relatively new "old Lowe's" had to be torn down to provide adequate parking for the new store due to the proximity of other store locations. The Lowe's superstore turned out to be a great facility that supplies its customers with additional services despite the puzzling manner in which the new store was built. In fact, billboards advertising the new store, as you might expect, do not stress the vast amounts of lumber and hardware available. Instead, the billboards promote, "Lowe's . . . Check Out All of Our New Services."

third parties

A supply strategy in which a service firm utilizes an outside party to service customers and thereby save on costs, personnel, etc.

Supply Strategy: Utilization of Third Parties A service firm can also expand its supply of a service through utilizing **third parties.** Travel agencies are a typical example. Travel agents provide the same information to customers as an airline's own representatives. This third-party arrangement, however, enables the airline to reduce the number of personnel it employs to make flight reservations and lets it redirect the efforts of existing personnel to other service areas. The cost savings associated with utilizing third parties is evidenced by the airlines' willingness to pay commissions to travel agencies for booking flights.

Note that although the use of third parties increases the supply of service, this type of arrangement may expose customers to competitive offerings as well. Hence, a tradeoff does exist. Many third parties, such as travel agents, represent a variety of suppliers. A customer who intended to book a flight on USAir may end up taking a Delta flight due to a more compatible flight schedule and/or a cheaper fare. This type of competitive information would not have been available if the customer had called USAir directly to make the flight reservation.

customer participation

A supply strategy that increases the supply of service by having the customer perform part of the service, such as providing a salad bar or dessert bar in a restaurant.

Supply Strategy: Increase in Customer Participation Another method for increasing the supply of service available is to have the customer perform part of the service. For example, in many fast-food restaurants, **customer participation** means giving customers a cup and expecting them to fill their own drink orders. In other restaurants, customers make their own salads at a "salad bar," dress their own sandwiches at the "fixings bar," prepare plates of food at the "food bar," and make their own chocolate sundaes at the "dessert bar."

Without a doubt, we are performing more and more of our own services every day. We pump our own gas, complete our own bank transactions at automatic teller machines, and bag our own groceries at wholesale supermarkets. However, while self-service does free employees to provide other services, a number of advantages and disadvantages are associated with customer participation. The willingness of customers to provide their own service is generally a function of convenience, price, and customization. For example, automatic teller machines offer the customer the convenience of 24-hour banking, bagging groceries is generally accompanied by lower grocery prices, and self-service food preparation provides customers the opportunity to prepare food to their own individual specifications.

In contrast, customer participation may also be associated with a number of disadvantages that predominantly concern loss of control. In many instances, the more the customer becomes a major player in the production of the service, the less control the service firm is able to maintain over the quality of the service provided. For example, the physician who instructs a patient to administer his own medicine relinquishes control over the outcome of the prescribed care. Quality control may also suffer as a result of confused customers who decrease the efficiency of the operating system. Customer confusion in a self-service environment is likely to affect not only the outcome of the confused customer's service, but also the delivery process of other customers who are sharing that customer's experience.

The loss of quality control may also be accompanied by the loss of control over operating costs. Self-service, particularly in the food industry, is associated with waste due to abuse of the system. Customers may take more food than they would normally order and then consume or share food with nonpaying friends.

Finally, increasing customer participation may be interpreted by some customers as the service firm's attempt to distance itself from the customer. As a result, the image of an uncaring, unresponsive, and out-of-touch firm may develop, driving many customers away to full-service competitors. Hence, the trade-off is apparent. While increasing customer participation frees service providers to provide additional services and may provide the customer with increased convenience, opportunities for customization, and reduced prices, this strategy may leave some unhappy customers who are forced to fend for themselves.

THE ROLE OF MARKETING IN THE SERVICE FIRM

This chapter has outlined some of the factors that characterize services marketing in general, and some of the problems that service marketers face. Because of the effects of intangibility, inseparability, heterogeneity, and perishability, marketing plays a very different role in service-oriented organizations than it does in pure goods organizations. This chapter has shown how closely interwoven the different components of the service organization are; the invisible and visible parts of the organization, the contact personnel and the physical environment, the organization and its customers, and, indeed, the customers themselves are all bound together by a complex series of relationships. Consequently, the marketing department must maintain a much closer relationship with the rest of the service organization than is customary in many goods businesses. The concept of operations being responsible for producing the product and marketing being responsible for selling it cannot work in a service firm.

SUMMARY

The major differences between the marketing of goods and the marketing of services are most commonly attributed to four distinguishing characteristics—intangibility, inseparability, heterogeneity, and perishability. This chapter has discussed the marketing challenges presented by these four characteristics and possible solutions that minimize their impact on service firms.

Intangibility means that services lack physical substance and, therefore, cannot be touched or evaluated like goods. The marketing challenges associated with intangibility include difficulties in communication of the properties of services to consumers, pricing decisions, patent protection, and storage of services for future use. Strategies developed to offset the challenges posed by intangibility include the use of tangible clues, organizational image development, and the development of personal sources of information that consumers access when selecting service providers.

Inseparability reflects the interconnection between service providers and their customers. Unlike the producers of goods, service providers engage in face-to-face interactions with their customers, who are directly involved in the service production process. Strategies developed to minimize the challenges of inseparability include the selective screening and thorough training of customer contact personnel, the implementation of strategies that attempt to manage customers throughout the service experience, and the use of multisite facilities to overcome the inseparability difficulties associated with centralized mass production.

Heterogeneity pertains to the variability inherent in the service delivery process. The primary marketing problem associated with heterogeneity is that standardization and quality control are difficult for a service firm to provide on a regular basis. Service firms typically react to heterogeneity in two diverse directions. Some firms try to standardize performance by replacing human labor with machines. In contrast, other firms take advantage of the variability by offering customized services that meet individual customer needs. Neither strategy is universally superior, as customer preference for customization versus standardization is dependent upon price, speed of delivery, and consistency of performance.

Perishability refers to the service provider's inability to store or inventory services. Services that are not used at their appointed time cease to exist. Moreover, because services cannot be inventoried, the few times that supply matches demand often occur by accident. A variety of strategies have been developed to try and offset the potential problems created by perishability. Some strategies attack the problems by attempting to manage demand, while others attempt to manage supply. Demand management strategies include creative pricing strategies, reservation systems, staging demand through complementary services, and developing nonpeak demand periods. Supply management strategies include utilizing part-time employees, capacity sharing, third-party utilization, increasing customer participation in the production process, and preparing in advance for future expansion to reduce the response time in reaction to demand increases.

Because of the challenges posed by intangibility, inseparability, heterogeneity, and perishability, marketing plays a very different role in service-oriented organizations than it does in pure goods organizations. Traditional management practices, which work under the premises that operations is solely responsible for producing the product and that marketing is solely responsible for selling it, cannot work in a service firm. The four characteristics presented in this chapter that distinguish the marketing of goods from the marketing of services provide ample evidence that the invisible and visible parts of the organization, the contact personnel, the physical environment, and the organization and its customers are bound together by a complex set of relationships. As a result, marketing must maintain a much closer relationship with the rest of the service organization than is customary in a traditional goods manufacturing plant.

KEY TERMS

intangibility	customization
physical evidence/tangible clues	standardization
nonpersonal sources	perishability
personal sources	creative pricing
organizational image	reservation system
inseparability	complementary services
critical incident	nonpeak demand development
selection and training	part-time employees
consumer management	capacity sharing
multisite locations	expansion preparation
factories in the field	third parties
heterogeneity	customer participation

DISCUSSION QUESTIONS

1. Discuss the ordering of the following terms as they relate to goods and services: consumption, production, and purchase.

2. Why is the pricing of services particularly difficult in comparison with the pricing of goods?

3. What strategies has the insurance industry utilized in its attempt to minimize the effects of intangibility?

4. Discuss the implications of having the customer involved in the production process.

5. Discuss the reasons that centralized mass production of services is limited.

6. Why are standardization and quality control difficult to maintain throughout the service delivery process?

7. Which is better for consumers: (1) a customized service, or (2) a standardized service? Explain.

8. What are the limitations associated with a service firm's inability to maintain inventories?

NOTES

1. The framework for this chapter was adapted from Figures 2 and 3 in Valerie A. Zeithaml, A. Parasuraman, and Leonard L. Berry, "Problems and Strategies in Services Marketing," *Journal of Marketing* 49 (Spring 1985), pp. 33–46. For a more

in-depth discussion of each of the problems and strategies associated with services marketing, consult Figures 2 and 3 in this article for the appropriate list of references.

2. Adapted from John E. G. Bateson, *Managing Services Marketing,* 3rd ed. (Fort Worth, TX: The Dryden Press, 1995), p. 9.

3. Bateson, *Managing Services Marketing,* p. 17.

4. Bateson, *Managing Services Marketing,* p. 18.

5. Bateson, *Managing Services Marketing,* pp. 11–13.

6. The framework and materials for this section were adapted from W. Earl Sasser, "Match Supply and Demand in Service Industries," *Harvard Business Review* (November–December 1976).

AN OVERVIEW OF THE SERVICES SECTOR

"Recognizing that the products of service organizations previously considered as 'different' actually face similar problems or share certain characteristics in common can yield valuable managerial insights. Innovation in marketing, after all, often reflects the manager's ability to seek out and learn from analogous situations in other contexts."

Christopher H. Lovelock, "Classifying Services to Gain Strategic Marketing Insights," *Journal of Marketing* (Summer 1983), 9–20

CHAPTER OBJECTIVES

This chapter provides an overview of the service sector and focuses on changes taking place within the sector, the industries experiencing the most substantial changes, and criticisms of the emerging service economy. After reading this chapter, you should be able to

▶ Provide an overview of the service economy based on economic impact, the consequences of deregulation, the impact on labor, and the effects of changing consumer needs.

  ▶ *Discuss the changes taking place within the most dynamic segments of the service sector.*

▶ Discuss the commonalities and predicted keys to success within the service sector.

  ▶ *Discuss the various criticisms leveled against the growth of the service sector.*

LEARNING FROM OTHERS THROUGH BENCHMARKING

Over the years, many of the most successful companies have learned to look beyond their own borders for sources of innovative ideas by using benchmarking. Benchmarking examines why some companies perform some functions much better than other companies do. The goal of benchmarking is to duplicate or improve upon the practices of other companies and was perfected by the Japanese during the post-World War II period.

The practice of benchmarking involves seven steps: (1) Identify the functions of the business to be benchmarked; (2) identify the methods by which key performance variables are measured; (3) identify companies to benchmark that excel in these activities; (4) measure the performance of the "best" companies on selected processes; (5) measure the company's own performance; (6) develop strategies that narrow the gaps between performance levels; and (7) implement strategies and monitor results.

The art of benchmarking has evolved over the years through a series of corporate attitudes that started with, "If we didn't invent it, then it's not any good," progressed to "reverse engineering," which involved examining how competitive products were constructed, and has now evolved to a process referred to as "best practices." While some companies prefer to examine the practices of competitors within their own industries, other companies have gone beyond standard competitive analysis by examining the "best practices" in the world.

"Best practices" represents a fundamental change in philosophy from focusing on "what gets done" to "how things get done." Thus far, "best practices" have taught corporations three lessons. First, other companies outside industry lines have much to teach one another. For example, Xerox has redesigned (1) its warehouse and software systems based on lessons learned through L.L. Bean; (2) its billing systems through the help of American Express; and (3) its production scheduling through benchmarking Cummins Engine. The second lesson is the value associated with continuously improving processes, even in small ways, rather than in making large overall improvements. Finally, "best practices" has indicated that someone needs to take ownership of the process and transcend traditional functional boundaries. An individual needs to be able to integrate the processes produced by the various departments.

Overall, "best practices" has become one the most productive ideas for improving quality and competitive performance. Moreover, as noncompetitors, many of the "best practice" companies are happy to share ideas with other industries. The advances made by companies who practice benchmarking provide the proof that different industries really can learn from one another.

Sources: Thomas A. Stewart, "G.E. Keeps Those Ideas Coming," *Fortune*, August 12, 1991, pp. 41–49; Robert C. Camp, *Benchmarking: The Search for Industry-Best Practices That Lead to Superior Performance* (White Plains, NY: Quality Resources, 1989); Michael J. Spendolini, *The Benchmarking Book* (New York: AMACOM, 1992); Jeremy Main, "How to Steal the Best Ideas Around," *Fortune*, October 19, 1992; and A. Steven Walleck et al., "Benchmarking World Class Performance," *Mckinsey Quarterly* 1 (1990), pp.3–24.

INTRODUCTION

*T*his chapter provides an overview of the service sector and highlights the similarities and differences among various service industries. The chapter promotes the stance that services industries should not be studied solely as separate entities. Many service industries share common service delivery challenges and, therefore, would benefit from sharing their knowledge with one another. Unfortunately, many service firms look only to firms within their own industry for guidance. For example, banks look to other banks, insurance companies to other insurance companies, and so on. This myopic approach slows the progress of truly unique service innovations within each of the respective industries. One needs only to consider the advances that hospitals could make if they borrowed concepts from restaurants and hotels instead of constantly rely on other hospitals for innovative service ideas.

This chapter is constructed in three sections. The first section provides an overview of service economy and focuses on a variety of issues that reflect the tremendous growth of the service sector. The second section features service industries undergoing the most significant periods of change throughout the 1990s, the characteristics they share with one another, and their keys to success. The last section of the chapter discusses criticisms that have been leveled at the service sector. Some experts believe that the dominance of the service economy without a healthy goods economy will ultimately be detrimental to people's standard of living and way of life.

An Overview of the Service Sector

Economic Impact

The demand for service knowledge by businesses around the world is directly related to the growth of the service sector in many world economies. Service and service-related industries clearly dominate the U.S. economy and will continue to do so in the foreseeable future. Similarly situated, other nations once known for their industrial might are also becoming predominantly service economies (see Figure 3.1). Countries such as Great Britain, Canada, France, Italy, Japan, and Germany have service economies that account for more than 50 percent of their **Gross Domestic Products (GDP).**[1]

According to the U.S. Bureau of Labor Statistics, the private service sector has increased its contribution to the GDP by more than 300 percent over the past 30 years. As a result, the private service sector now accounts for more than 70 percent of the GDP. In contrast, since 1970, GDP attributed to the manufacturing of goods

Gross Domestic Product (GDP)

The total value of a nation's annual output of goods and services.

AN OVERVIEW OF THE
SERVICES SECTOR

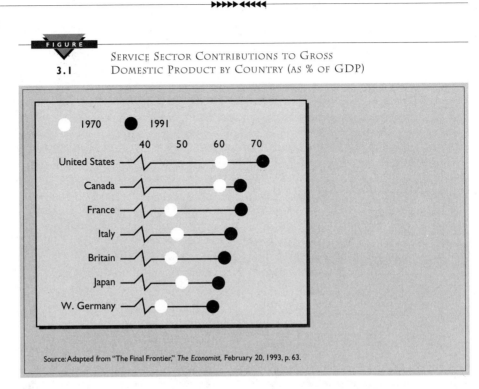

FIGURE

3.1

SERVICE SECTOR CONTRIBUTIONS TO GROSS
DOMESTIC PRODUCT BY COUNTRY (AS % OF GDP)

Source: Adapted from "The Final Frontier," *The Economist,* February 20, 1993, p. 63.

has fallen from 26 percent to 19 percent. This means that for the first time in U.S. history, the majority of industries in our economy do not produce—they perform.

THE IMPACT OF DEREGULATION

deregulation

The act or process of removing government restrictions and regulations.

The growth of the service economy is not the only reason that the demand for services marketing knowledge has increased. Over the past 15 years, interest has been increasing in the marketing problems of service organizations, paralleling the emergence of competition in many parts of the service sector. The late emergence of services marketing as an academic field could then rightly be explained by the lack of a need for it in times when demand exceeded supply and competitive pressures were few. **Deregulation** has certainly changed the competitive situation in many industries.

During the 1980s, deregulation forced many traditional service industries such as airlines, financial services, telecommunications, and trucking into the competitive arena for the first time. These industries were forced to be competitive not only with existing firms within their industry but also with new firms that were permitted to enter the industry as a result of deregulation. The new firms were leaner, more focused, and extremely competitive.

As competitive pressures increased within the deregulated industries, the need for services marketing knowledge became apparent. In addition to facing new competitors, the deregulated industries found themselves with excess supply and engaged in price wars with the competition. The effect of deregulation on the various industries resulted in a dramatic decrease in the number of competitive firms.[2] From 1980 to 1992, U.S. commercial airline operators declined from 36 to 11. The number of trucking companies that failed during the 1980s was more than during the previous 45 years combined, and the number of commercial banks declined by 14 percent.

It quickly became apparent that competing on pricing alone was leading to devastating results. Services marketing knowledge was needed in nonprice strategy areas such as customer service, customer retention, service differentiation, service quality, image enhancement, and the transformation of public contact employees into marketing-oriented personnel. Service industries such as the health-care industry, which in its recent past had considered marketing a "dirty word" and beneath the dignity of its personnel, now embraced marketing techniques as a means for individual firms' survival.

IMPACT ON LABOR

Throughout the world, the shifting of economies from agricultural, through industrial manufacturing, and on to services is evident.[3] In 1900, both Great Britain and the United States already had more jobs in the service sector than in the manufacturing sector. Today, manufacturing employs only 1 out of every 6 persons in the United States, 1 out of every 5 in Great Britain, and 1 out of every 3 in Germany and Japan.

From 1970 to 1993, the U.S. labor force employed by manufacturing fell from 27 percent to 16 percent. Great Britain's labor force experienced a similar decline in manufacturing employment at a rate of 37 percent to 20 percent. In contrast, labor employed in the service sector has risen to 57 percent in Germany, 62 percent in Japan, 73 percent in Great Britain, and 78 percent in the United States. From 1970 to 1993, employment in the service sector rose from 66 percent to 78 percent in the United States and from 50 percent to an astounding 73 percent in Great Britain (see Figure 3.2).

The increase in service employment is directly related to new service jobs. Between 1980 and 1990, 80 percent of all new jobs were developed in service industries.[4] Estimates suggest that 90 percent of all new jobs between 1990 and 2000 will also be service related. Experts project that by 2005, only 12 percent of U.S. workers will have manufacturing jobs and that this number will decrease to 10 percent by the year 2020.[5]

FUELED GROWTH OF SERVICE SECTOR BY DEMOGRAPHIC CHANGES

A type of chain reaction is occurring that facilitates the growth of the service sector. As a group, consumers have less time than ever to accomplish their various

AN OVERVIEW OF THE
SERVICES SECTOR

THE TRANSFORMATION OF U.S. EMPLOYMENT FROM
3.2   FARMING TO INDUSTRY TO SERVICES

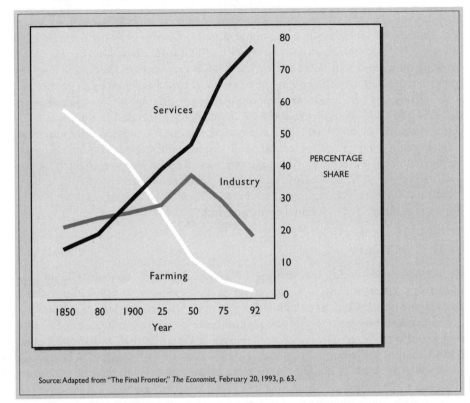

Source: Adapted from "The Final Frontier," *The Economist*, February 20, 1993, p. 63.

woofs

Stands for "well-off older folks,"
that segment of the population
that controls 77 percent of the
nation's assets and 50 percent
of its discretionary income.

roles. The growth in the number of time-pressured consumers has led to an increase in time-saving services such as restaurants, housekeeping services, laundry services, hairstyling shops, and tax preparation services. Subsequently, the time saved through the use of these services is now being spent on entertainment, travel, and recreation services.[6]

On average, the population of the United States is becoming older. The oldest "baby boomers" only recently turned 50, and advances in health care combined with more health-conscious consumers has led to a dramatic growth in "older" market segments. Although the immediate implication is an increase in demand for health-care services, other service industries stand to benefit from an aging population. The over-50 age group controls 77 percent of the nation's assets and 50 percent of the country's discretionary income.[7] In fact, the term **woofs** which stands for "well-off older folks," has been coined to represent this group's purchasing power. It has also been noted that this particular group is engaged in

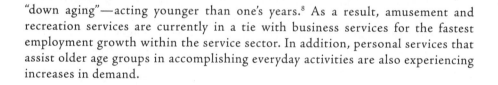

More services are being provided to older market segments due to the aging of the population. Entertainment and recreation services such as tennis, golf, and other activities are now being offered to older Americans.

© 1995 PhotoDisc, Inc. Image no. 15134.

"down aging"—acting younger than one's years.[8] As a result, amusement and recreation services are currently in a tie with business services for the fastest employment growth within the service sector. In addition, personal services that assist older age groups in accomplishing everyday activities are also experiencing increases in demand.

CORPORATE DOWNSIZING

Despite CEO claims that "employees are the firm's most important assets," we find to be true that when it comes to becoming cost efficient, "employees are the firm's most expendable asset." **Corporate downsizing** has led to a boom in the consulting area and to dramatic growth in business services. Ironically, because of downsizing, most new consultants' first clients are their former employers.[9]

corporate downsizing
Reduction in the number of corporate workers in order for a corporation to become more cost efficient.

AN OVERVIEW OF THE MOST DYNAMIC SERVICE INDUSTRIES[10]

BUSINESS SERVICES

Business services is the fastest growing service sector in terms of sales and establishments. In particular, Las Vegas has seen the largest establishment increase in terms of new startups. Businesses relocating from California and the tremendous revenues generated from tourism have been noted as the sources

business services
Service sector that provides "outsourced" services such as advertising, credit reporting and collection, and building maintenance to businesses.

of the growth. Throughout the country, business services experiencing the most dramatic increases in growth include

- Advertising
- Credit reporting and collections
- Mail and copying
- Building maintenance
- Equipment rental
- Temporary help services
- Computer services
- Detective agencies
- Security guards

HEALTH CARE

health-care services

Services such as hospitals, physicians, group practices, and home health care, that provide physical care to consumers.

Business services, along with health-care and professional services, account for two-thirds of all service firms. The **health-care service** sector is undergoing significant changes in terms of daily operation and the competitive structure of the sector. Independent hospitals are being swallowed by hospital systems that enjoy the cost savings of economies of scale. Likewise, independent physicians are moving into group practices, which allow them to share overhead costs with other physicians plus provide them the opportunity to have a more independent life-style. Group practices share on-call duties, allowing each individual physician more personal time.

Other physicians are leaving hospitals and focusing on niches within the health-care sector. Independent surgery centers and corner "doc-in-a-box" diagnostic centers have created leaner and meaner niche players with whom traditional health-care delivery systems must contend. Other health-care services that are predicted to see dramatic growth include outpatient care and home health care. Due to the aging population and an increase in insurance coverage for home health-care services, its future growth is predicted to be particularly explosive. Health services expected to experience the most dramatic increases in growth include

- Physicians
- Dentists
- Nursing and personal-care homes
- Hospitals
- Medical labs
- Home health services
- Kidney dialysis centers
- Outpatient clinics

professional services

Services such as accounting, engineering, research, and management consulting, provided by firms traditionally classified as "professionals."

PROFESSIONAL SERVICES

Over the years, the competitive area of **professional services** has also experienced significant change. Court rulings and the utilization of marketing techniques have led to easier entry into some professions, more freedom to compete on price, the removal of geographic competitive restrictions, the incentive to differentiate services, and the ability to use mass media. Accounting, engineering, research, and management consulting firms alone have created an $18 billion-a-year industry. As was the case with health-care services, many professional services are also finding profitable niches in the marketplace. Attorneys, for example, are creating "boutique firms" that specialize in areas of litigation such as intellectual property, labor law, and trusts and estates.

THE HOSPITALITY INDUSTRY

The hospitality industry has experienced tremendous growth over the past several decades. In the past, many of the services offered by the industry were available only to the privileged few. Fortunately for the industry, times have changed. In many countries, the standard of living is higher, consumers are living longer and have increased leisure time, education is improving, and opportunities for individuals to improve themselves and their standard of living are increasing as society continues to rapidly advance. In short, the hospitality industry has advanced with society.[11]

The hospitality industry comprises a variety of segments including food service, lodging, travel and tourism, and meeting and convention planning. The hospitality industry is the world's largest industry and largest generator of jobs, with an estimated 338 million people to be employed in 2005, up from 212 million in 1995. The industry generates more than $300 billion in revenues and employs 6 million people in the United States alone.

The Food Service Industry The food service segment is the largest and most diverse segment of the hospitality industry. Table 3.1 provides an overview of the different types of food service establishments in operation. One out of every three meals is now eaten outside the home, and food service operations provide nearly half of all meals eaten in the United States today.

Competition in the $200 billion-a-year food industry is intense. In addition to traditional competitors, nontraditional competitors such as convenience stores and grocery stores have modified their product offering to include meals that were at one time available only in restaurants. Meanwhile, traditional competitors are constantly altering their marketing strategies to adapt to changes in consumer demands. For example, some fast-food restaurants are now offering table service to compete with more traditional family restaurants, gourmet restaurants are now offering take-out services, and a great deal of product bundling is occuring to create "value meals" that are sold at discounted prices.

Other changes in the industry reflect consumers' changing tastes in what they want to eat and drink. Sales of ethnic foods, chicken, and turkey are up, while the

AN OVERVIEW OF THE
SERVICES SECTOR

TABLE 3.1   TYPES AND CHARACTERISTICS OF FOOD SERVICE ESTABLISHMENTS

Restaurant	Size (in seats)	Location	Service
Full service	75–200	Urban and suburban with high-traffic locations	Sit-down table service, often French service
Theme	100–400	Moderate traffic and shopping centers	Table service and beverage service
Coffee shop	35–300	Moderate to heavy traffic areas	Service to table, booth, or counter
Cafeteria	100–400	Moderate traffic and shopping centers	Line service with limited beverage table service
Buffet	100–400	Free-standing near high traffic	Self-serve from buffet line
Quick service	0–100	High-traffic locations with good accessibility	Inside counter service and drive-through
Lodging dining room	75–200	In first-class hotels, resorts; on main floor or rooftop	Sit-down table service, often French service
Lodging coffee shop	100–300	In hotels, motor hotels, resorts	Casual table service; informal
Lodging banquet	10–200	In hotels, motor hotels, resorts	Entire room served at one time— sit-down buffet service
Room service	N/A	Food and beverage delivered to guest room	Convenience; food stored in warmer box; extended hours of service
Institutional/Contract	10–500	Integral part of larger organization	Very limited; self-service predominates; cafeteria or buffet
Industrial/Contract	Highly dependent on facility	Integral part of larger organization	Cafeterias, table service, vending, and snack bars
Clubs	50–300	Part of larger facility	Formal dining room, banquet services, beverage and snack bars
Catering	N/A	Food and beverage served on and off premises	Varied meals and functions

Source: Robert A. Brymer and Lynn M. Huffman, "Overview of the Hospitality Industry," in *Hospitality Management*, 7th ed., Robert A. Brymer, ed. (Dubuque, IA: Kendall/Hunt Publishing Company, 1995), pp. 6–7.

consumption of beef is down. Additionally, coffee bars and wine have become increasingly popular as people have become more aware of the problems associated with drinking traditional alcoholic beverages. Moreover, despite claims that Americans are eating healthier, sales of gourmet ice cream, cookies, and pastries are increasing.

TABLE 3.1 *(CONTINUED)*

Price	Consumer	Menu	Management
High average check	Special occasion dinner crowd and business luncheons	Full range of items from appetizers to elaborate desserts	Independent or chain affiliated
Higher to moderate average check due to service and menu	Leisure dinner crowd and business luncheons and singles	Steaks, seafood, and ethnic specialties	Chain operation or franchise
Moderate average check varies due to location, service and menu	Casual breakfast, luncheon, and dinner crowds	Wide range of items from appetizers to desserts	Chain operation or franchise
Moderate average check due to lesser services; a la carte pricing	Family; convenient; price-conscious consumer shoppers	Wide range of items on serving line	Chain operation
One price for entire meal, all you can eat	Price conscious	More limited than cafeteria but similar layout	Individual ownership or partnership
Lower average check because of limited service	Convenient and quick service with broad appeal	Limited to a few specialty items	Chain operation or franchise
High average check	In-house and local clientele	Limited to finely prepared items; often French cuisine	Under supervision of hotel food and beverage director
Moderate average check	In-house guests—breakfast and lunch	Wide range of items prepared for quick service	Under supervision of hotel food and beverage director
Moderate price on a per-person basis	Group functions and special occasions	Wide range of items— selected in advance	Under supervision of food and beverage director
Higher average check; 10–20% higher than the hotel restaurant	Weary traveler or those seeking privacy and convenience of room	Full range of items prepared for delivery	Under supervision of hotel food and beverage director
Often prepaid; daily, weekly, and monthly prices available	Captive, consumer has limited or no choice	Limited to a few items per meal, cycle menu	Professional management, contract company, or government
Moderate average check	Captive, consumer has limited or no choice	Limited to a few items per serving	Professional management, contract company
Highly variable; good value for money	Members and other guests who expect high quality	Full range	Professional manager, hired by club members; or club management company
High average check; depends on menu and services	Serves special function needs of client	Full range—items selected in advance of meal	Individual proprietor or management company

The Lodging Industry The primary service offering of hotels and lodging facilities is overnight accomodations for guests. Similar to the food industry, consumers have a wide array of lodging choices that serve a variety of market segments, such as luxury hotels, bed and breakfast inns, and economy motels. Table 3.2 provides an overview of the **lodging industry** to enable you to more fully understand how

hotel and lodging services

Services that provide temporary residences for a nonresident market such as tourists.

AN OVERVIEW OF THE
SERVICES SECTOR

TABLE 3.2	TYPES AND CHARACTERISTICS OF LODGING ESTABLISHMENTS		
Type	**Size**	**Location**	**Service**
Luxury/Hotel upscale	Small to midsize; 100–400 rooms	Large city with strong economic base	Extensive and very high quality; well-trained staff cater to all needs
Hotel/Convention Hotel business/Convention	Larger; 400 rooms and more, up to 2,000 rooms	Urban; downtown in large cities	Wide range of services available; doorman, room service, concierge, and more; full-service staff
All-suite hotel	Small to midsize; 100–400 suites	Large city with transient population	Mid-range level of services; used by some guests as temporary housing
Motor hotel— mid-priced	Midsized; 150–400 rooms	Suburban; in and near large cities; often at major interstate exits	Mid-range service available; fewer staff required
Economy/Budget	Smaller; 10–150 rooms	Rural and suburban, or near major highways or interstate roads	Limited range of service available; limited staff required
Bed and breakfast inn	Smaller; 10–150 rooms	Suburban and rural locations	Continental breakfast and early evening appetizers served in a casual central location
Resort/Gambling	100–500 rooms (can vary a great deal)	Isolated locations; usually near geographical highlight (mountains, ocean, or lake)	Full range of services available; more than hotel because of isolated locations
Condominium hotel/ Time-sharing	50–250 rooms (can vary a great deal); units often in smaller 4–5 unit clusters	Similar to resorts; rely on geographical highlight	Similar to resorts; optional housekeeping and other services
Institutional housing	Larger; no normal range in number of rooms	Integral part of larger organization—military, college, or hospital	Very limited services available, self-serve predominates

Source: Robert A. Brymer and Lynn M. Huffman, "Overview of the Hospitality Industry," in *Hospitality Management,* 7th ed., Robert A. Brymer, ed. (Dubuque, IA: Kendall/Hunt Publishing Company, 1995), pp. 10–11.

TABLE 3.2 *(CONTINUED)*

Price	Consumer	Menu	Management
Very high room rate to cover additional services offered	Corporate officers, professionals, and upscale small meetings	Formal and very expensive decor, emphasis on tasteful appointments, quiet and sophisticated atmosphere	Professional management company
Higher average room rate; due in part to location, service, and facilities offered	Individual transient business traveler, group meetings and conventions; expense account business and meeting travelers	Elaborate and highly priced furniture and fixtures; large and attractive lobby; fine restaurants; extensive meeting space	Professional management company
Nightly, weekly, or monthly rates available	Business and family travelers; temporary residents	Similar to an apartment and nicely decorated	Professional management company
Mid-priced average room rate, between hotel and economy/budget motel	Same as hotel except less affluent, also some leisure travel	Nicely appointed but not as elaborate or expensive as hotel; smaller lobby; coffee shop and dining room	Professional contract company, individual proprietor, or franchise
Lower average room rate, this is often primary attraction for customer	Overnight leisure travelers en route to other destinations	Modest appointments to serve guests quickly and with no frills; little or no lobby; coffee shop or no food service	Individual proprietor or franchise
Mid-range price includes breakfast and appetizers	Business and leisure travelers seeking a more personal environment	Nicely appointed, often a converted plantation or new facility designed specifically for this market	Individual proprietor or chain affiliation
Higher average room rate due in part to location, service, and facilities; package prices available (American Plan); casino hotels may have lower than average rates	Individual and family leisure destination point; group meetings and conventions	Elaborate and extensive development of recreation facilities; large and attractive lobby; fine restaurants and meeting facilities; may have casino	Independent or professional management company
Units are sold to individual owners who live in and/or rent out; transient guests' prices similar to resorts	Individuals who purchase seek investment and vacation housing; transient guests seek as primary guest destination	Recreation facilities similar to resorts; smaller lobby; restaurant and meeting facilities; rooms are apartmentlike	Same as resort
Package price usually includes meals, often prepaid	Captive; individuals using other services of the organization; convenience and price conscious	Very modest; necessities provided for basic accomodations in a comfortable environment	Federal, state, local government; professional management company

the various establishments operate. Within the service industry as a whole, hotels and lodging facilities account for 3 percent of service establishments and 6 percent of sales.

The lodging industry has recently undergone significant change. In the early 1990s, an oversupply of hotel rooms existed, and too few customers were available to fill them. Consumer demand had dropped off during the recession of the early 1990s, and many hotels were forced to close due to their debt load. In 1993, the average occupancy rate was barely above 60 percent. This means that four out of every ten rooms were vacant every evening. The oversupply of rooms forced many hotels to cut room rates to the point that the average daily rate is now between $55 and $60.

The success stories in the lodging industry today include those firms that are creative in how they conduct business. Marriott, for example, operates Marriott Hotels and Resorts, Courtyard by Marriott, Fairfield Inn, Residence Inn by Marriott, and Marriott Suites to appeal to a variety of market segments. Hence, the many corporations in the industry are competing not only against one another but also against themselves. Competition in the United States has also increased due to the rise in international hotel companies who now have properties in the United States. In turn, U.S.-based companies continue to expand overseas with particular interest in the Pacific Rim and Eastern Europe. Finally, for some hotels and for some customers, the room itself is only a small part of the lodging experience. Hotels such as the MGM Grand and the Mirage in Las Vegas and the Taj Mahal in Atlantic City provide an atmosphere that caters to the customer's entertainment as well as lodging needs.

The Travel and Tourism Industry   Like many of the other hospitality industries, the specific components of travel and tourism are difficult to define and are often divided into the areas of travel and recreation. The travel segment of the industry involves the physical movement of people from one place to another and includes services associated with automobiles, airlines, bus lines, railroads, passenger ships, sightseeing companies, travel agencies, and tour companies.

In comparison, the recreation segment provides recreation and relaxation to the public and includes attractions, clubs, and public parks. More specifically, attractions include theme parks, sporting events, scenic attractions, and special activities such as the Olympics or Mardi Gras in New Orleans. Clubs include civic clubs, fraternal clubs, and country clubs to name a few. The first and best known public park in the United States is Central Park in New York City.

The travel and tourism industry generates $2 trillion in worldwide revenues. In 1992, 476 million travelers generated 7 percent of world trade and 100 million jobs. In the United States, tourism ranks as the first, second, or third largest industry in 47 states and directly employs 4.7 million Americans, who

▶▶▶▶ ◀◀◀◀

receive more than $50 billion in wages and salaries. Tourism destinations such as Las Vegas and other gaming destinations are experiencing tremendous growth. In fact, the location experiencing the most recent growth in hotel and lodging facilities is Dubuque, Iowa, due to the introduction of riverboat gambling.

Meeting and Convention Planning A meeting planner must be well acquainted with all areas of the hospitality industry. Typically, the planner works with the convention group and the meeting site to coordinate all the activities involved, such as booking hotel rooms, arranging for meals, and securing travel arrangements. The meeting and convention industry in the United States generates approximately $56 billion annually and hosts meetings ranging in size from a few people to the 100,000 who regularly attend the Consumer Electronics Show usually held in Las Vegas.

What Can Service Firms Learn from Each Other?

One of the major objectives of this text is to convey the message that fields of services marketing should not be studied as separate entities (such as banking, health-care, and food service firms). This book focuses on the commonalities and challenges firms face across the service spectrum. One method of analyzing commonalities across industries is the development of classification schemes.

Service Classification Schemes

Marketing has traditionally developed classification schemes to facilitate an understanding of how different products share similar characteristics. For example, the product classification of convenience, shopping, and specialty products has aided in the understanding of how consumers spend their time shopping for various products and has eventually led to the development of new types of retail stores. Similarly, the classification of consumer and industrial products has led to numerous implications concerning promotion mix strategies, types of goods purchased, evaluation processes, usage behavior, and purchasing procedures, to name a few.

Classification schemes applied solely to services have also been developed to facilitate our understanding of what different types of service operations have in common. Typical classification categories include those presented in Table 3.3. Tables 3.4 through 3.8 expand upon these categories and provide examples of service industries that fit within each scenario. Your services marketing class may want to discuss each of these classification schemes and their marketing implications.

AN OVERVIEW OF THE
SERVICES SECTOR

TABLE **3.3**   TRADITIONAL SERVICE CLASSIFICATIONS

Degree of Tangibility

- Owned goods
- Rented goods
- Nongoods

Skill Level of the Service Provider

- Professional
- Nonprofessional

Labor Intensiveness

- People-based
- Equipment-based

Degree of Customer Contact

- High
- Low

Goal of the Service Provider

- Profit
- Nonprofit

TABLE **3.4**   UNDERSTANDING THE NATURE OF THE SERVICE

WHAT IS THE NATURE OF THE SERVICE ACT?	WHO OR WHAT IS THE DIRECT RECIPIENT OF THE SERVICE?	
	People	**Things**
Tangible Actions	Services directed at people's bodies: • Health care • Passenger transportation • Beauty salons • Exercise clinics • Restaurants • Haircutting	Services directed at goods and other physical possessions: • Freight transportation • Industrial equipment repair and maintenance • Janitorial services • Laundry and dry cleaning • Landscaping/lawn care • Veterinary care
Intangible Actions	Services directed at people's minds: • Education • Broadcasting • Information services • Theaters • Museums	Services directed at intangible assets: • Banking • Legal services • Accounting • Securities • Insurance

Source: Christopher H. Lovelock, "Classifying Services to Gain Strategic Marketing Insights" *Journal of Marketing* 47 (Summer 1983), pp. 9–20. Reprinted by permission of the American Marketing Association.

TABLE 3.5   RELATIONSHIPS WITH CUSTOMERS

NATURE OF SERVICE DELIVERY	TYPE OF RELATIONSHIP BETWEEN THE SERVICE ORGANIZATION AND ITS CUSTOMERS	
	"Membership" Relationship	No Formal Relationship
Continuous Delivery of Service	Insurance Telephone subscription College enrollment Banking American Automobile Association	Radio station Police protection Lighthouse Public highway
Discrete Transactions	Long-distance phone calls Theater series subscriptions Commuter ticket or transit pass	Car rental Mail service Toll highway Pay phone Movie theater Public transportation Restaurant

Source: Christopher H. Lovelock, "Classifying Services to Gain Strategic Marketing Insights" *Journal of Marketing* 47 (Summer 1983), pp. 9–20. Reprinted by permission of the American Marketing Association.

TABLE 3.6   CUSTOMIZATION AND JUDGMENT IN SERVICE DELIVERY

EXTENT TO WHICH CUSTOMER CONTACT PERSONNEL EXERCISE JUDGMENT IN MEETING INDIVIDUAL CUSTOMER NEEDS	EXTENT TO WHICH SERVICE CHARACTERISTICS ARE CUSTOMIZED	
	High	Low
High	Legal services Health care/surgery Architectural design Executive search firm Real-estate agency Taxi service Beautician Plumber Education (tutorials)	Education (large classes) Preventive health programs
Low	Telephone service Hotel services Retail banking (excluding major loans) Good restaurant	Public transportation Routine appliance repair Fast-food restaurant Movie theater Spectator sports

Source: Christopher H. Lovelock, "Classifying Services to Gain Strategic Marketing Insights" *Journal of Marketing* 47 (Summer 1983), pp. 9–20. Reprinted by permission of the American Marketing Association.

AN OVERVIEW OF THE
SERVICES SECTOR

TABLE 3.7   WHAT IS THE NATURE OF DEMAND FOR THE SERVICE RELATIVE TO SUPPLY?

EXTENT TO WHICH SUPPLY IS CONSTRAINED	EXTENT OF DEMAND FLUCTUATIONS OVER TIME	
	Wide	**Narrow**
Peak Demand Can Usually Be Met without a Major Delay	Electricity Natural gas Telephone Hospital maternity unit Police and fire emergencies	Insurance Legal services Banking Laundry and dry cleaning
Peak Demand Regularly Exceeds Capacity	Accounting and tax preparation Passenger transportation Hotels and motels Restaurants Theaters	Services similar to those directly above but that have insufficient capacity for their base level of business

Source: Christopher H. Lovelock, "Classifying Services to Gain Strategic Marketing Insights" *Journal of Marketing* 47 (Summer 1983), pp. 9–20. Reprinted by permission of the American Marketing Association.

TABLE 3.8   METHOD OF SERVICE DELIVERY

NATURE OF INTERACTION BETWEEN CUSTOMER AND SERVICE ORGANIZATION	AVAILABILITY OF SERVICE OUTLETS	
	Single Site	**Multiple Site**
Customer goes to service organization	Theater Barbershop	Bus service Fast-food chain
Service organization comes to customer	Lawn care service Pest control service Taxi	Mail delivery AAA emergency repairs
Customer and service organization transact at arm's length (mail or electronic communications)	Credit card co. Local TV station	Broadcast network Telephone co.

Source: Christopher H. Lovelock, "Classifying Services to Gain Strategic Marketing Insights" *Journal of Marketing* 47 (Summer 1983), pp. 9–20. Reprinted by permission of the American Marketing Association.

PREDICTED KEYS TO SUCCESS WITHIN THE SERVICE SECTOR

niche marketing

Strategies that focus on marketing to particular consumer groups as opposed to the broad population of consumers.

Several guidelines to success become clear when examining the growth and dominance of the service sector. First, many of the successful firms excel at niche marketing. **Niche marketing** strategies include focusing on particular consumer groups and on filling voids in specific locations. For example, the areas currently experiencing the fastest service firm growth are the small southern metro areas, where competition is scarce and the population base is rapidly expanding.

The second key to success seems to be directly related to the firm's ability to master **technological change.** Firms that view technology as a source of innovation as opposed to a "necessary evil" are particularly successful. Improvements in technology have enabled successful service firms to open new avenues of communication between them and their customers. Other technological innovations have led to improved services that permit more customer involvement in the service delivery process, offering the dual advantages of decreasing customer-handling costs while providing customers with convenient services. Automatic teller machines (ATMs) and a variety of "online services" are prime examples.

technological change

Changes in the area of automation that help progress and enhance service experiences.

Another key to success is the firm's ability to blow away the competition when it comes to **customer service.** Due to the absence of a tangible product, successful service firms must look to their customer service delivery systems to differentiate themselves from competitors. In 1898, Caesar Ritz, the founder of "Ritz" hotels, became the manager of the struggling Savoy Hotel in London. Ritz understood men and women and their desire for beautiful things, and he went to great lengths to achieve the atmosphere he desired. First, he turned the Savoy into a center of cultural activity by introducing an orchestra to the dining room and extending the dining period. Proper evening attire was made compulsory, and unescorted women were prohibited from the premises. Ritz also understood his guests' need for romance. For a period of time, the lower dining room of the Savoy was converted into a Venetian waterway, complete with gondolas and gondoliers who sang Italian love songs. So it seems that regardless of the industry involved, one common thread connects all service firms that are successful—service excellence, the ability to continuously provide courteous, professional, and caring service to customers.[12]

customer service

Providing a customer with a better service experience by focusing on technology and serving niche consumers.

The final key to success, which also differentiates successful service firms from mediocre ones, is an understanding of the value of **customer retention** strategies. Businesses commonly lose 50 percent of their customers every five years.[13] However, most companies have no idea how many customers are lost or the reasons for their defections. Consequently, companies that do not excel at customer retention are destined to make the same mistakes over and over.

customer retention

The strategy of retaining existing customers instead of always seeking new ones.

The lack of attention paid to customer retention can be explained by the time-honored tradition of conquest marketing—the pursuit of new customers as opposed to the retention of existing ones. Successful service firms understand the value of retaining existing customers: (1) the marketing costs associated with retaining customers are much lower than the costs associated with acquiring new customers; (2) existing customers tend to purchase more services more frequently; (3) current customers are more familiar with the firm's personnel and procedures and are therefore more efficient in their service transactions; and (4) reducing customer defections by 5 percent in some industries can increase profits by as much as 50 percent.

SERVICE INDUSTRY CRITICISMS

The dramatic growth in the service sector has been accompanied by a resounding groan from those who believe that a strong service economy represents the end of an era in which the United States dominated many of the world's markets. In addition, some believe that the marketing of services is no different from the marketing of goods; therefore, services marketing should not be a field of study at all.

SHOULD SERVICES MARKETING BE A SEPARATE FIELD IN MARKETING?

No introductory part in a services marketing textbook would be complete without a mention of the various criticisms that are lodged against the service sector and services marketing in general, the first being that services marketing is no different from goods marketing and should not be considered a separate field of marketing. This criticism was particularly troublesome in the early days of services marketing research because most of the researchers were young, untenured, assistant professors who had to convince senior professors that their work in services marketing was legitimate.

Although several articles that attempted to legitimize the field were written by academics in the late 1970s, the article that made the biggest impact was written by Lynn Shostack, a vice-president at Citibank at that time. Basically, Shostack informed the marketing community that the reason many service industries were slow to adopt marketing in their decision-making processes was simply because traditional "marketing offers no guidance, terminology, or practical rules that are clearly relevant to services."[14] Because Shostack was a practitioner and not an academic, her article became the cornerstone upon which the services marketing field flourished.

MATERIALISMO SNOBBERY

materialismo snobbery
Belief that without manufacturing, there will be less for people to service and so more people available to do less work.

Although the service economy is growing in leaps and bounds, not everyone is rejoicing about the transformation of the United States from an industrial economy to a service economy.[15] **Materialismo snobbery** reflects the attitude that only manufacturing can create real wealth and that all other sectors of the economy are parasitic and/or inconsequential. Materialismic individuals believe that without manufacturing, there will be little for people to service. As a result, more people will be available to do less work. Consequently, the abundance of labor will drive wages down and subsequently decrease the standard of living in the United States. Ultimately, these individuals believe that the shift to a service economy will jeopardize the American way of life.

Similar concerns were voiced in the United States more than 140 years ago, when the economy was shifting from agriculture to manufacturing. In 1850, 50 years after industrialization, 65 percent of the population was connected to farming (Figure 3.2). During this period, many experts voiced great concern over workers leaving the farms to work in the factories. The concerns centered on the same type of logic: If the vast majority of the population left the farms, what would the people eat? Today, 3 percent of the U.S. labor force is involved in farming operations. This 3 percent provides such a surplus of food that the federal government provides price supports and subsidies to keep the farms in business. Apparently, the concerns regarding the shift to manufacturing were unwarranted. In fact, the shift lead to economic growth.

Similarly, with advances in technology and new management practices, the need no longer exists to have as many people in manufacturing as we had in the mid 1900s. Manufacturing is not superior to services. The two are interdependent. In fact, half of all manufacturing workers perform service-type jobs.[16]

DICHOTOMIZATION OF WEALTH

Another criticism of the service economy pertains to the distribution of wealth among service workers. In the United States, 60 percent of the population has experienced a decrease in real income over the past 15 years. In contrast, the wealthiest 5 percent has seen an increase of 50 percent, and the top 1 percent has seen a doubling in income.[17] Although experts disagree, some believe that because of the poor wages paid by some service industries, the shift of the economy away from manufacturing will lead to a further **dichotomization of wealth.** In other words, the rich will get richer and the poor will get poorer.

Without a doubt, the service sector has a lot of low-paying jobs.[18] For men under the age of 30, service jobs pay 25 percent less than manufacturing jobs. The average hourly wage for a factory worker in 1993 was $11.75. In comparison, the average retail employee earned $7.29 a hour. Some experts believe that as the manufacturing sector continues to decline, the supply of labor available for service jobs will increase, driving wages even lower.

However, not everyone in services is poorly paid. For example, in the finance and wholesale trade, the 1993 hourly wages reported at $11.32 and $11.71, respectively, were much closer to manufacturing wages. Moreover, an increasing number of service personnel are highly skilled and employed in knowledge-based industries. In fact, more than half the U.S. labor force is currently employed in either the production, storage, retrieval, or dissemination of knowledge. Furthermore, the fastest growing service-sector employment opportunities are in finance, insurance, property, and business services, occupations that require educated personnel.[19] Overall, service wages seem to be catching up with wages obtained via manufacturing employment (see Figure 3.3)

The concern over wages associated with service employment is real, and continued acceptance of the industrial model within service industries will do nothing but perpetuate the problem. "Most service enterprises consist of a well-paid brain trust and poorly paid support staff—$500-an-hour lawyers and $5-an-hour secretaries."[20] Due to the democratic election process in most service economies, a multitude of workers unable to feed and support their families could substantially alter the makeup and direction of future governments. Future demands for major wealth redistribution programs could make the current U.S. welfare system look like a local charity drive.

dichotomization of wealth

Theory that the service sector's low wages will lead to further polarization in the distribution of wealth.

FIGURE 3.3

SERVICE WAGES ARE CATCHING UP!

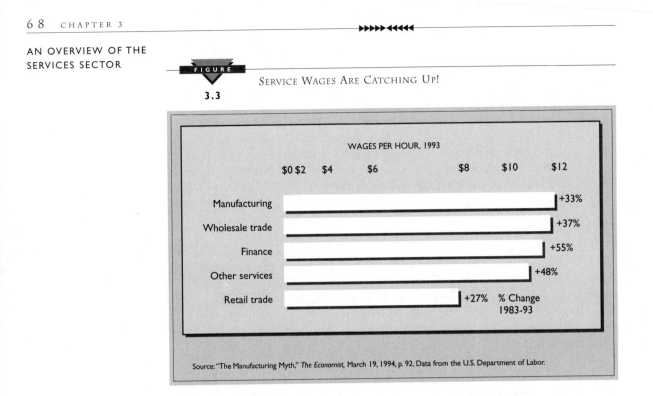

WAGES PER HOUR, 1993

	$0 $2	$4	$6	$8	$10	$12	
Manufacturing							+33%
Wholesale trade							+37%
Finance							+55%
Other services							+48%
Retail trade				+27%			% Change 1983-93

Source: "The Manufacturing Myth," *The Economist*, March 19, 1994, p. 92. Data from the U.S. Department of Labor.

SLOWNESS ADOPTING NEW TECHNOLOGY

The service sector has also been criticized for its inability to exploit new technology and revitalize the economy.[21] Truth to tell, computerization actually decreased the efficiency of the service sector during its early stages of implementation. At first, due to the lack of trust and computer-based knowledge, computers and the old manual systems were kept simultaneously. The net effect of maintaining two systems and paying for training to get the new system up and running cut into company profits.

The other problem when technology was introduced into service firms was that most companies had no master plan for what the new technology was supposed to accomplish. Most firms used the technology piecemeal and failed to integrate a firm's efforts through one system. Today, service firms are thriving with the assistance of advanced technology. However, it was not the technology alone that made the difference. As managers were having to quickly adapt to new competitive situ-ations, changes in managerial philosophy enabled these firms to utilize the technology for the right reasons as opposed to the wrong ones. Technology is used now as a resource and support, not as an answer in and of itself.

Successful service firms, such as those in the hospitality industry, utilize technology as a resource for front-line personnel by providing up-to-date information on everything from past consumer purchases and current inventory holdings to individual store performance measures. Such instant feedback enables the service worker to better serve the customer. The traditional philosophy that technology should be used to control and monitor employee efforts is out of date and out of touch.

INCREASING PRICES IN SERVICES

As this book is being written, the price inflation of goods is currently under control, whereas the prices of services are rising rapidly (see Figure 3.4). Experts believe that this price inflation is not particularly unreasonable. First, many believe that as the United States attempts to rebound from the recession of the early 1990s, **service productivity** has grown at a much slower rate compared with manufacturing productivity. However, wages for manufacturing and services have grown at the same rate, resulting in higher per-unit wage costs for services, which is reflected in consumer prices.

service productivity
The amount of output and growth experienced by the service industry.

Another plausible explanation is that the service sector may be less sensitive to recession than is the manufacturing sector. Services are not inventoried; consequently, surpluses that must be sold at discounted rates to make room for new inventory do not develop during recessions. Furthermore, unique characteristics inherent in the service production process make services less susceptible to foreign competition than manufactured goods are. As a result, consumer prices are unaffected.

Consumer behavior issues also play a role in the pricing of services. As a consumer's income increases, the demand for better and expensive services also increases. Hence, it makes intuitive sense that as the economy and consumer confidence improve, the demand and subsequent prices for services will also rise. Finally, the consumer behavior issue of brand loyalty may also play a role in the increasing prices of services. Compared with consumers of manufactured goods, consumers of services are more brand loyal and are willing to pay more to reduce the uncertainty associated with unfamiliar service providers.

WEAK SERVICE PRODUCTIVITY

A leading indicator of economic revitalization is productivity. Many experts have noted that in terms of its contribution to the economy, worker productivity grows at a much slower rate in service sector jobs than it does in manufacturing jobs. For example, between 1980 and 1991, manufacturing productivity rose by 2.9 percent. In comparison, service productivity figures hardly budged.[22]

However, most agree that service productivity is underestimated due to the complicated task of obtaining real measures of service output. "To estimate productivity growth, statisticians have to split changes in firms' sales into changes in output and changes in prices."[23] Although productivity is fairly easy to calculate for the manufacturing sector, the difficulty in measuring service sector output makes the productivity calculation more difficult. For example, measuring the

AN OVERVIEW OF THE
SERVICES SECTOR

FIGURE

3.4

INFLATIONARY TRENDS: GOODS VERSUS SERVICES

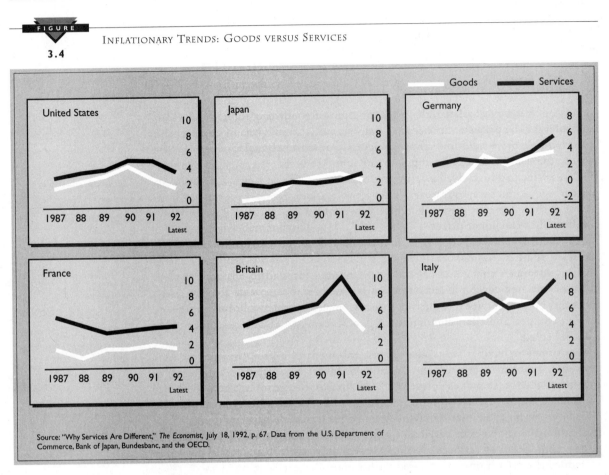

Source: "Why Services Are Different," *The Economist*, July 18, 1992, p. 67. Data from the U.S. Department of Commerce, Bank of Japan, Bundesbanc, and the OECD.

output of law firms, universities, and consulting firms are typical challenges when attempting to calculate service productivity.

Most of the increases in service productivity are in the shape of improved quality. However, improved quality dimensions such as increased convenience, fewer employee mistakes, and improved technology have not had an impact on traditional output measures. The problem with measuring service productivity (and this is a good problem to have) is that firms play "follow the leader" and improve their services after one innovation is successful. For example, when some banks started installing automatic teller machines, the rest of the industry quickly followed. Hence, as is the case with most technology that becomes easily available, the ATM's use as a long-term differential advantage was futile. As a result, no single bank had much chance to increase its prices and subsequent profit margins. The subsequent increase in customer convenience and service provided by the ATM, then, had little impact on traditional productivity measures.

FIGURE
3.5

THE RISING TIDE OF SERVICE EXPORTS

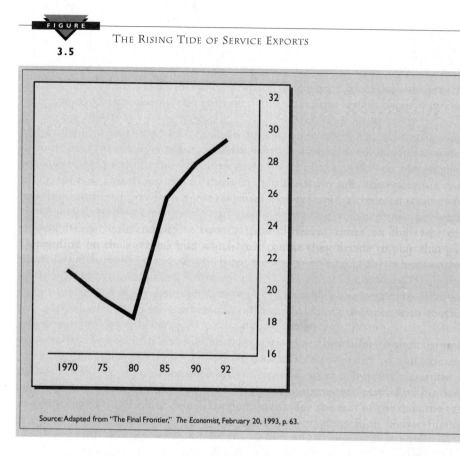

Source: Adapted from "The Final Frontier," *The Economist*, February 20, 1993, p. 63.

FOREIGN TRADE

Finally, the service sector is criticized for its lack of export content in comparison with the manufacturing sector. Materialismic individuals believe that as the size of the manufacturing sector continues to dwindle, the trade deficit will magnify. While it is true that some services, such as haircuts, hotel rooms, and lawn care, cannot be exported, many other services, such as finance, telecommunications, consultancy, and tourism, can be traded. In fact, U.S. service exports are huge, and they give the United States a tremendous competitive advantage over foreign competitors.

Even the nonbelievers are beginning to take notice of services' increasing contribution to international trade.[24] Over the past ten years, the percentage of total U.S. exports attributed to services has risen from 20 percent to 30 percent (see Figure 3.5).[25] Tourism alone accounts for 7 percent of total U.S. exports.[26] In 1992, the U.S trade surplus in private, nongovernmental services hit a record $59 billion, a trade surplus, not a deficit! In fact, services' trade surplus cuts the often-cited $96 billion U.S. trade deficit to a more manageable $37 billion. In terms of world trade, services' share has risen from 17 percent in 1980 to 22 percent in 1992.

SUMMARY

This chapter has provided an overview of the service industry by focusing on changes taking place in the sector, the industries experiencing the most substantial change, the characteristics they share with one another, and their keys to success.

The service sector has experienced phenomenal growth. The service sector in the United States accounts for more than 70 percent of the GDP and employs more than 70 percent of the U.S. workforce. Other countries, such as Japan, Great Britain, Canada, France, Italy, and West Germany are experiencing similar service-related economic and employment growth. In addition, deregulation has created a demand for services marketing knowledge in service areas where demand traditionally exceeded supply and competitive pressures were few. Demographic changes and corporate downsizing have also influenced the growth of the service sector.

Specific industries leading the growth of the service sector include business services, health care, professional services, and hospitality. Many service industries share common service delivery challenges and therefore would benefit from sharing their knowledge with one another. One method for analyzing commonalities across industries is the use of classification schemes. Service classification schemes include (1) the degree of tangibility, which further classifies services as owned goods, rented goods, and nongoods; (2) the skill level of the provider, which includes professional and nonprofessional providers; (3) the amount of labor intensiveness, which pertains to people-based as opposed to equipment-based services; (4) the degree of customer contact, which varies from high to low; and (5) the goal of the service provider, be it profit or nonprofit. Additional methods for classifying services are presented in Tables 3.4 to 3.8.

Several guidelines to success become clear when examining the growth and dominance of the service sector across industries. These strategies include (1) excelling at niche marketing; (2) providing customer service far superior to that offered by competitors; (3) mastering technological change; and (4) excelling at customer retention.

The growth of the service sector has not received unanimous support. Broad criticisms have been voiced regarding the economy's shifting from an industrial base to a services base. These criticisms include the following: (1) services marketing is no different from goods marketing and should not be considered a different field; (2) materialismo snobbery—the belief than only manufacturing can create real wealth; (3) the dichotomization of income in service industries among personnel and the possible political backlash associated with this inequitable distribution of wealth; (4) the service sector's inability to quickly exploit new technology;

(5) inflation in services is not as easily controlled as in goods; (6) productivity gains in services are historically low; and (7) service exports are minimal.

KEY TERMS

Gross Domestic Product (GDP)	niche marketing
deregulation	technological change
woofs	customer service
corporate downsizing	customer retention
business services	materialismo snobbery
health-care services	dichotomization of wealth
professional services	service productivity
lodging industry	international trade

DISCUSSION QUESTIONS

1. Discuss the impact of the service sector on the worldwide economy and employment.

2. Discuss the impact of deregulation upon service industries.

3. Discuss the latest trends in the hospitality industry.

4. Service firms can learn a great deal from other firms in other industries. What strategies appear to be linked with success across the service spectrum?

5. Discuss the marketing implications of Table 3.4, "Understanding the Nature of the Service Act."

6. Define the term *materialismo snobbery.*

7. Discuss the comparisons of changing from an agricultural economy to an industrial economy as they relate to the changes associated with moving from an industrial economy to a service economy.

8. Discuss the possible political consequences associated with the dichotomization of wealth in the United States.

9. Why are productivity gains generally slower in services than in goods?

10. Discuss the possible reasons that inflation is under control for goods but not necessarily for services.

NOTES

1. "The Final Frontier," *The Economist,* February 20th, 1993, p. 63.

2. Leonard L. Berry and A. Parasuraman, "Building a New Academic Field—The Case of Services Marketing," *Journal of Retailing* 69 (Spring 1993), pp. 1, 13.

3. "The Manufacturing Myth," *The Economist,* March 19th, 1994, p. 91.

4. Stephen Keopp, "Pul-eeze! Will Somebody Help Me?," *Time*, February 2, 1987, pp. 28–34.

5. "The Manufacturing Myth," p. 91.

6. Fanglan Du, Paula Mergenhagen, and Marlene Lee, "The Future of Services," *American Demographics*, (November 1995). Web site: http://www.marketingtools.com

7. Michael Levy and Barton A. Weitz, *Retail Management*, 2nd ed. (Chicago: Irwin, 1995), p. 68.

8. Philip Kotler, *Marketing Management*, 8th ed. (New York: Prentice-Hall, 1995).

9. "The Future of Services," Web site.

10. This section was adapted from "The Future of Services," Web site.

11. The hospitality industry section was developed from the following sources: Richard L. Brush and Teresa M. Schulz, "Pioneers and Leaders of the Hospitality Industry," pp. 24–34; Robert A. Brymer and Lynn M. Huffman, "Overview of the Hospitality Industry," pp. 3–15; Leland L. Nichols, "Introduction to Travel and Tourism Management," pp. 307–322; and Sheryl Fried, "Casino Hotel Operations and Management," pp. 370–385 in *Hospitality Management*, 7th ed., Robert A. Brymer, ed. (Dubuque, IA: Kendall/Hunt Publishing Company, 1995); and Rocco M. Angelo and Andrew N. Vladimir, *Hospitality Today* (East Lansing, MI: The Educational Institute of the American Hotel & Motel Association, 1991).

12. Frederick F. Reichheld, "Learning from Customer Defections," *Harvard Business Review* (March–April 1996), pp. 56–69.

13. Richard L. Brush and Teresa Schulz, "Pioneers and Leaders in the Hospitality Industry," in *Hospitality Management*, 7th ed., Robert A. Brymer, ed. (Dubuque, IA: Kendall/Hunt Publishing Company, 1995), pp. 24–34.

14. Raymond P. Fisk, Stephen W. Brown, and Mary Jo Bitner, "Tracking the Evolution of the Services Marketing Literature," *Journal of Retailing* 69 (Spring 1993), pp. 1, 60.

15. Michael E. Raynor, "After Materialismo . . .," *Across the Board* (July–August 1992), pp. 38–41.

16. "Wealth in Services," *The Economist*, February 20th, 1993, p. 16.

17. Raynor, "After Materialismo . . .," p. 41.

18. "The Manufacturing Myth," p. 92.

19. "The Final Frontier," p. 63.

20. Raynor, "After Materialismo . . .," p. 41.

21. "The Manufacturing Myth," p. 92.

22. "The Manufacturing Myth," p. 91.

23. "The Manufacturing Myth," p. 92.

24. Myron Magnet, "Good News for the Service Economy," *Fortune*, May 3, 1993, pp. 47–48.

25. "Wealth in Services," p. 16.

26. "The Manufacturing Myth," p. 92.

4

CONSUMER DECISION PROCESS ISSUES IN SERVICES MARKETING

"The competitor that best understands the consumer wins."

John E. G. Bateson, *Managing Services Marketing: Text and Readings*, 2nd ed. (Fort Worth: The Dryden Press, 1992), p. 103

CHAPTER OBJECTIVES

In this chapter we discuss consumer decision process issues as they relate to the purchase of services. After reading this chapter, you should be able to

▶ Describe the steps involved in the consumer decision process model.

> ▶ *Discuss the factors that influence the consumer decision-making process.*

▶ Discuss the special considerations about services during the prepurchase stage.

> ▶ *Discuss the special considerations about services during the consumption stage.*

▶ Discuss the special considerations about services during the postpurchase stage.

> ▶ *Describe models that attempt to explain the consumer's postpurchase evaluation.*

RIVERSIDE METHODIST HOSPITAL

Hospitals are unique among service providers in that they provide services that most people need but don't necessarily want. Relatively few people use the services of a hospital out of pure choice.

A number of factors set hospitals apart from other services. In the first place, hospitals' levels of risk are higher—a poor service can endanger health or life, not just create an unpleasant impression of the experience. Second, because many patients lack proper knowledge about how a hospital functions and the nature of the treatment they are receiving, even a merely unpleasant service experience can be genuinely frightening.

Riverside Methodist Hospital in Columbus, Ohio, is part of U.S. Health Corporation, a small for-profit hospital chain. A key aspect of Riverside's competitive strategy centers on changing the image of the hospital and the service experience in the eyes of patients and potential patients. Reducing patients' concerns can change the nature of the patients' evaluation of the service before, during, and after the hospital visit.

Understanding patient demands is an important part of this strategy, which recognizes that not all patients are the same and that the needs of different groups can become important points of differentiation. For example, the presence of a large Honda automobile plant nearby means that the hospital regularly takes in Japanese-speaking patients and visitors. On a different note, Riverside Methodist has developed the Elizabeth Blackwell Center, a separate facility dealing specifically with women's needs for health care.

Once patients have been admitted to the hospital, the principal objective is to reduce patient anxiety and insecurity. The physical facilities of the hospital, the attitude and demeanor of the nursing and medical staff, and the perceived quality and frequency of care can all have an impact, as can more peripheral factors such as frequency and duration of family visits to patients. The question is not one of improving patient care but of improving patient perceptions of care by making an otherwise unpleasant experience as comfortable as possible.

One area where this policy has been put into practice is the hospital emergency ward. In most emergency wards, the patient is first met by an admitting clerk, whose primary function is to take information about the patient and get the patient to wait until a doctor is available. Riverside has put nursing staff directly into the emergency ward. First, the patient is met immediately by a senior nurse, who determines the severity of his or her condition; serious cases are taken immediately for treatment. Less serious cases are assigned a primary nurse, who looks after the patient until a doctor is available. Because patients receive at least basic attention immediately, patient uncertainty is reduced.

Source: John E. G. Bateson, *Managing Services Marketing: Text and Readings*, 2nd ed. (Fort Worth, TX: The Dryden Press, 1992), p. 103. © 1992 by The Dryden Press. Reprinted by permission of the publisher.

INTRODUCTION

Consumer orientation lies at the heart of the marketing concept.[1] As marketers, we are required to understand our consumers and to build our organizations around them. This requirement is particularly important for services, which in many instances still tend to be operations dominated rather than customer oriented (see Figure 4.1). Hence, today it is more important than ever to understand consumers, how they choose among alternative services offered to them, and how they evaluate these services once they have received them.

Throughout the prepurchase choice and postpurchase evaluation, the consumer must be using a process or model to make his or her decision. Although a variety of models have been developed and are discussed in this chapter, it is important to point out that no model is wholly accurate. The consumer's mind is still closed to us; it is a "black box" that remains sealed. We can observe inputs to the box and the decisions made as a result, but we can never know how the process truly happens.

Why, then, bother with such models? Whether marketing managers like it or not, every time they make marketing decisions, they are basing their decisions on some model of how the consumer will behave. Quite often these models are implicit and seldom shared with others, representing, in effect, the marketing manager's own experience. However, every time a price is changed, a new product is launched, or advertising appears, some assumption has been made about how the consumer will react.

The purpose of this chapter is to discuss the consumer decision process as it relates to the purchase of services. Due to the unique characteristics of services, differences exist between the way consumers make decisions regarding services versus goods. This chapter has been constructed in two sections. The first section is a broad overview of the consumer decision-making process. It provides a summary of the process and its applications to marketing decisions. The second section of the chapter is dedicated to specific considerations about the consumer decision-making process as it relates to services.

THE CONSUMER DECISION PROCESS: AN OVERVIEW

To market services effectively, marketing managers need to understand the thought processes used by consumers during each of the three stages of the **consumer decision process:** the prepurchase choice among alternatives, the consumer's reaction during consumption, and the postpurchase evaluation of satisfaction (see Figure 4.2). Although we can never truly know the thought process used by

consumer decision process
The three-step process consumers use to make purchase decisions; includes the prepurchase stage, the consumption stage, and the postpurchase evaluation stage.

CONSUMER DECISION PROCESS ISSUES
IN SERVICES MARKETING

FIGURE 4.1 EXAMPLE OF OPERATIONS-DOMINATED COMMUNICATIONS

CP&L

1700 EASTWOOD RD
PO BOX 1110
WILMINGTON NC 28402

00011606 1 AC 0.230 00 **AUTOCR **C064

Customer Bill
page 1 of 2

Account	872 675 5229
Date mailed	Oct 3, 1996
Usage period	Sep 4 - Oct 2
Payment received - Sep 30	$197.22
Total due	**$146.86**
Payment due	Oct 28

Thank you for your last payment!

Hurricane Fran has made things tough for many of us by bringing financial hardship and inconvenience. In addition to restoring your power, we are here to answer billing questions and to find a payment option that will work for you. If you have questions, or face a financial hardship due to Fran, please call 1-800-228-8485.

Usage

Meter number		R71133
Readings: Oct 2		60947
Sep 4		- 58872
Kwh usage		2075

Total Peak Registration

On-peak KW	Sep 11 at 8:15 pm	13.35
On-peak KW	Oct 1 at 8:00 am	7.50
Off-peak KW	Sep 29 at 7:30 pm	13.72
Off-peak KW	Oct 1 at 10:15 pm	5.98

Billing
Residential-
Time of Use
Demand rate

			28 Days
Basic customer charge			9.85
Summer, September 04 - September 30			
On-peak KWH	777 kwh x $0.04301		33.4188
Off-peak KWH	1,226 kwh x $0.02927		35.8850
On-peak KW at .9361 proration	13.35 kw x $5.02000		62.7346
Non-summer, October 1 - October 02			
On-peak KWH	53 kwh x $0.04301		2.2795
Off-peak KWH	19 kwh x $0.02927		0.5561
On-peak KW at .0639 proration	7.50 kw x $3.73000		1.7876
Energy conservation discount			-6.8331
Total R-TOUD Rate Billing			139.68

On-peak kw proration factor

Non-summer	on-peak kwh	53 kwh /	830 kwh	.0639
Summer	on-peak kwh	777 kwh /	830 kwh	.9361
Total on-peak kwh		830		

SLR rate

			28 Days
Sodium vapor lights, 8 kwh, 9500 lumens, enclosed			
Residential lighting	1 Light x	$2.90	2.90
3% North Carolina sales tax			4.28
Total due			$146.86

The first page of a typical electric bill is dominated by operations-oriented information. Company bills are often the only form of communication with customers, yet most fail to communicate with customers effectively.

▼ FIGURE
4.2   CONSUMER DECISION PROCESS

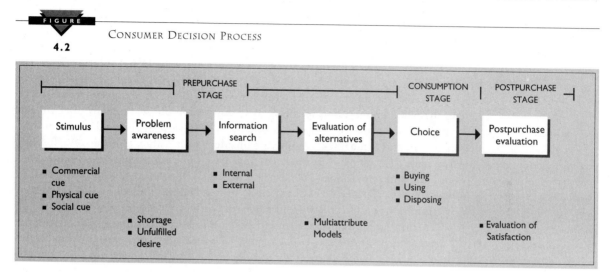

the individual when making that choice, the consumer decision process helps to structure our thinking and to guide our marketing research regarding consumer behavior. Let's begin this discussion by focusing on the prepurchase stage.

THE PREPURCHASE STAGE

The Stimulus The **prepurchase stage** of the consumer decision process refers to all consumer activities occurring before the acquisition of the service. This stage begins when an individual receives a **stimulus** that may incite the person to consider a purchase.[2] The stimulus may be a commercial cue, a social cue, or a physical cue. **Commercial cues** are the result of promotional efforts. For example, a consumer may be exposed to a commercial about a local college. As a result, the individual may begin to assess his or her current situation and the possibility of enrolling at a university to pursue a degree. Similarly, **social cues** are obtained from the individual's peer group or from significant others. For example, watching friends leave for college in the fall may incite an individual to consider furthering his or her own education. The stimulus may also be the result of a **physical cue** such as thirst, hunger, or various other biological cues.

Problem Awareness Once the consumer has received the stimulus, the next phase of the process is **problem awareness.** During the problem awareness phase, the consumer examines whether a need exists for the product. The need may be based on **a shortage** or on an **unfulfilled desire.** For example, if the consumer is incited by a commercial cue for a university and is not currently enrolled in any other university, then a shortage exists. In contrast, if the consumer is currently enrolled in

prepurchase stage

All consumer activities occurring before and leading up to the acquisition of the service.

stimulus

The thought, action, or motivation that incites a person to consider a purchase.

commercial cue

An event or motivation that provides a stimulus to the consumer and is a promotional effort on the part of the company.

social cue

An event or motivation that provides a stimulus to the consumer, obtained from the individual's peer group or from significant others.

physical cue

A motivation, such as thirst, hunger, or another biological cue that provides a stimulus to the consumer.

problem awareness

The second phase of the prepurchase stage, in which the consumer determines whether a need exists for the product.

shortage

The need for a product or service due to the consumer's not having that particular product or service.

unfulfilled desire

The need for a product or service due to a consumer's dissatisfaction with a current product or service.

information search

The phase in the prepurchase stage in which the consumer collects information on possible alternatives.

evoked set

The limited set of "brands" that comes to the consumer's mind when thinking about a particular product category from which the purchase choice will be made.

internal search

A passive approach to gathering information in which the consumer's own memory is the main source of information about a product.

a college but in one that he or she no longer values, then an unfulfilled desire exists. If the consumer does not recognize a shortage or unfulfilled desire the decision process stops at this point.

Information Search The recognition of a problem demands a solution from the individual, and it usually implies a potential purchase. The individual searches for alternatives during the **information search** phase of the prepurchase stage. As the name implies, during the information search phase, the consumer collects information regarding possible alternatives. It is clear that in all consumer decision making, consumers seldom consider all feasible alternatives. Instead, they have a limited list of options chosen on the basis of past experience, convenience, and knowledge. This list is often referred to by theorists as the **evoked set**—the set of "brands" that comes to the consumer's mind when thinking about a particular product category and from which the choice will be made.

Returning to our college selection example, when considering alternatives, the consumer may first engage in an **internal search.** An internal search accesses the consumer's own memories about possible alternative colleges. In this example, the previous knowledge may be based on the proximity to a local college, information obtained while watching local sporting events, or listening to older family members reminisce about their own college experiences. An internal search is a passive approach to gathering information.

The internal search may be followed by an **external search,** which would involve the collection of new information obtained via campus visits, talking to friends, and/or reading *U.S. News & World Report,* which rates universities on an annual basis.

Evaluation of Alternatives Once relevant information has been collected from both internal and external sources, the consumer arrives at a set of alternative solutions to the recognized problem. The possible solutions are considered in the **evaluation of alternatives** phase of the consumer decision process. This phase may consist of a **nonsystematic evaluation** of alternatives, such as the use of intuition—simply choosing an alternative by relying on a "gut-level feeling"—or it may involve a **systematic evaluation** technique, such as a multiattribute model. Such systematic models utilize a set of formalized steps to arrive at a decision.

Marketing theorists have made extensive use of multiattribute models to simulate the process of evaluating products.[3] According to these models, consumers employ a number of salient attributes or dimensions as basic references when evaluating a service. For example, consumers may compare alternative colleges based on entrance requirements, tuition, academic reputation, and location. Consumers compute their preference for the service by combining the scores of the service on each individual attribute.

Within the evaluation of alternatives phase of the decision process, consumers are assumed to create a matrix similar to the one shown in Table 4.1 to compare alternatives. The example in the table is the choice of a college for an undergraduate degree. Across the top of the table are two types of variables. The first is the

TABLE 4.1 ▼ A TYPICAL MULTIATTRIBUTE CHOICE MATRIX

Attributes	EVOKED SET OF BRANDS				Importance Weights
	UNT	ETU	SCSU	SCG	
Location	10	10	10	9.9	10
Tuition	10	10	9	9	9
Admission requirements	10	10	10	10	8
Academic reputation	8	9	9	9	7
Degree programs	10	8	8	10	6

evoked set of brands to be evaluated. As previously mentioned, this evoked set will, for various reasons, be less than an exhaustive list of all possible choices; in this example it includes UNT, ETU, SCSU, and SCG. The second type of variable is the importance rating with which the consumer ranks the various attributes that constitute the vertical axis of the table. For example, in Table 4.1, the consumer rates location as the most important attribute, followed by tuition, and so on. To complete the table, the consumer rates each brand on each attribute based on his or her expectations of each attribute. For example, this particular consumer gives UNT top marks for location, tuition, and admission requirements but perceives the university to be not as strong on academic reputation.

Given such a table, various choice processes have been suggested with which the consumer can use the table to make a decision. The **linear compensatory approach** proposes that the consumer creates a global score for each brand by multiplying the rating of the brand on each attribute by the importance attached to the attribute and adding the scores together. UNT would score 10×10 (location) plus 10×9 (tuition) plus 10×8 (admission requirements), and so on. The university with the highest score, in this example UNT, is then chosen.

Another type of multiattribute approach that has been suggested is the **lexicographic approach.** This approach describes lazy decision makers who try to minimize the effort involved. They look at each attribute in turn, starting with the most important, and try to make a decision. The individual whose preferences are shown in Table 4.1 would look first at location and rule out SCG. Next, tuition would rule out SCSU. At this stage, the choice is reduced to UNT and ETU, but admission requirements produces a tie in the scoring. Finally, the choice would be made in favor of ETU based on the next attribute, academic reputation. Thus, a different decision rule results in a different choice: ETU under the lexicographic model and UNT under the liner compensatory model.

Given the popularity of multiattribute models, it is no surprise that they have been used to describe and explain the consumer's service decision processes. The merit of these models lies in their simplicity and explicitness. The attributes identified cover a wide range of concerns related to the service experience, and they are easily understood by service managers.

external search

A proactive approach to gathering information in which the consumer collects new information from sources outside the consumer's own experience.

evaluation of alternatives

The phase of the prepurchase stage in which the consumer places a value or "rank" on each alternative.

nonsystematic evaluation

Choosing among alternatives in a random fashion or by a "gut-level feeling" approach.

systematic evaluation

Choosing among alternatives by using a set of formalized steps to arrive at a decision.

linear compensatory approach

A systematic model that proposes that the consumer creates a global score for each brand by multiplying the rating of the brand on each attribute by the importance attached to the attribute and adding the scores together.

lexicographic approach

A systematic model that
proposes that the consumer
makes a decision by examining
each attribute, starting with the
most important, to rule out
alternatives.

consumption stage

The stage of the consumer
decision process in which the
consumer purchases and uses
the product or service.

store choice

The decision to purchase from
a particular outlet or store.

nonstore choice

The decision to purchase from
a catalog, the Internet, or
through mail order.

consumption process

The activities of buying, using,
and disposing of a product.

postpurchase evaluation

The stage of the consumer
decision-making process during
which the consumer determines
whether the correct purchase
decision was made.

cognitive dissonance

Doubt in the consumer's mind
regarding the correctness of the
purchase decision.

The tasks for management when using these models are relatively straightforward. For example, advertising can be used to stress a particular attribute on which the firm's service appears to be weak in the mind of consumers. A college may have had a poor academic reputation in the past, but advertising may change consumer perceptions by featuring the school's accomplishments. If necessary, competitive advertising can also be used to try and reduce the attribute scores obtained by competitors. For example, many regional universities are attracting students by comparing the student/instructor ratio of large universities to their own ratios.

THE CONSUMPTION STAGE

Thus far, we have discussed the prepurchase stage of the consumer decision process, which described the stimulus, problem awareness, information search, and evaluation of alternatives phases. An important outcome of the prepurchase stage is a decision to buy a certain brand of the product category. During this **consumption stage,** the consumer may make a **store choice**—deciding to purchase from a particular outlet—or a **nonstore choice**—deciding to purchase from a catalog, the Internet, or a variety of mail-order possibilities. This decision is accompanied by a set of expectations about the performance of the product. In the case of goods, the consumer then uses the product and disposes of any solid waste remaining. The activities of buying, using, and disposing are grouped together and labeled the **consumption process.**[4]

THE POSTPURCHASE EVALUATION STAGE

Once a choice has been made and as the product is being consumed, **postpurchase evaluation** takes place. During this stage, consumers may experience varying levels of **cognitive dissonance**—doubt that the correct purchase decision has been made. Marketers often attempt to minimize the consumer's cognitive dissonance by reassuring the customer that the correct decision has been made. Strategies to minimize cognitive dissonance include aftersale contact with the customer, providing a reassuring letter in the packaging of the product, providing warranties and guarantees, and reinforcing the consumer's decision through the firm's advertising. For example, learning through the college's advertising that the school has been nationally recognized by *U.S. News & World Report* would positively reinforce the consumer's enrollment decision. Simply stated, postpurchase evaluation is all about customer satisfaction, and customer satisfaction is the key outcome of the marketing process. Customer satisfaction is achieved when consumers' perceptions meet or exceed their expectations. Customer satisfaction is an end in itself, but is also the source of word-of-mouth recommendations and can thus stimulate further purchases.

During the evaluation process of the postpurchase stage, multiattribute models can once again be utilized. For this process, the choices of schools are replaced

TABLE 4.2	COLLEGE SELECTION: A POSTPURCHASE EVALUATION FOR UT		
Attributes	Expected Score (from Table 4.1)	Perceived Score	Importance Weights
Location	10	10	10
Tuition	10	9.5	9
Admission requirements	10	10	8
Academic reputation	8	6	7
Degree programs	10	10	6

by two columns. The first is the score expected by the consumer on each attribute. The second is the perceived score on each attribute obtained by the consumer after enrollment. The satisfaction score is then derived by creating a global score of the comparisons between perceptions and expectations weighted by the importance of each attribute. This is shown in Table 4.2.

In this example, the customer chose UNT by using the multiattribute choice matrix shown in Table 4.1 and based on the linear compensatory approach. The expected levels on each attribute are, therefore, taken from that matrix. In reality, the tuition was increased, and the school did not live up to its academic reputation. The consumer, therefore, downgraded his evaluation on those attributes. The smaller the gap between expectations and perceptions, the more positive the postpurchase evaluation.

SPECIAL CONSIDERATIONS PERTAINING TO SERVICES

Although the consumer decision process model applies to both goods and services, unique considerations arise with respect to services. The considerations addressed in this part of the chapter help in developing a deeper understanding of the challenges faced when marketing services.

PREPURCHASE STAGE CONSIDERATIONS

Perceived Risk and the Purchase of Consumer Services In comparison with goods consumers, consumers of services tend to perceive a higher level of risk during the prepurchase decision stage. The concept of perceived risk as an explanation for customer purchasing behavior was first suggested in the 1960s.[5] The central theory is that consumer behavior involves risk in the sense that any action taken by a consumer will produce consequences that he or she cannot anticipate with any certainty, and some of which are likely to be unpleasant. Perceived risk is proposed to consist of two dimensions:

▶▶▶▶ ◀◀◀◀

▲ **Consequence,** the degree of importance and/or danger of the outcomes derived from any consumer decision.
▲ **Uncertainty,** the subjective possibility of the occurrence of these outcomes.

consequence

The degree of importance and/or danger of the outcomes of any consumer decision.

uncertainty

The subjective possibility of occurrence of consequences.

financial risk

The possibility of a monetary loss if the purchase goes wrong or fails to operate correctly.

performance risk

The possibility that the item or service purchased will not perform the task for which it was purchased.

physical risk

The possibility that if something does go wrong, injury could be inflicted on the purchaser.

social risk

The possibility of a loss in personal social status associated with a particular purchase.

psychological risk

The possibility that a purchase will affect an individual's self-esteem.

Surgery provides an excellent example of how consequence and uncertainty play a major role in service purchases. With respect to uncertainty, the consumer may have never undergone surgery before. Moreover, even though the surgeon has performed the operation successfully in the past, the patient is not guaranteed that this particular surgery will end with the same successful outcome. In addition, uncertainty is likely to increase if the patient lacks sufficient knowledge prior to the operation concerning details of the surgery and its aftereffects. The consequences of a poor decision regarding surgery could be life threatening.

Types of Risk As the idea of consumer perceived risk developed, five types of perceived risk were identified, based on five different kinds of outcomes: financial, performance, physical, social, and psychological.[6] **Financial risk** assumes that financial loss could occur if the purchase goes wrong or fails to operate correctly. **Performance risk** relates to the idea that the item or service purchased will not perform the task for which it was purchased. The **physical risk** of a purchase can emerge if something does go wrong and injury is inflicted on the purchaser. **Social risk** suggests that there might be a loss of personal social status associated with a particular purchase (e.g., a fear that one's peer group will react negatively—"Who bought this?"). **Psychological risk** pertains to the influence of the purchase upon the individual's self-esteem. For example, you will not consider wearing certain clothes, or you will refuse to own certain cars because they are not consistent with your self-image.

Risk and Standardization Much of the heightened level of perceived risk can be attributed to the difficulty in producing a standardized service product. Because a service is an experience involving highly complex interactions, it is, not surprisingly, very difficult to replicate the experience from customer to customer or from day to day.[7] As a result, the customer may find it difficult to predict precisely the quality of service he or she will be buying. The fact that Brown's Auto Repair Shop did a good tune-up for your neighbor does not mean that it will perform on the same level for you. Perceived risk, therefore, tends to be higher for purchasing services in contrast to the purchase of goods.

Co-producer Risk The involvement of the consumer in the "production process of services" is another source of increased perceived risk. Once again, surgery is a good example of the consumer's involvement in the production process. Unlike goods, which can be purchased and taken away, services cannot be taken home and used in private, where the buyer's mistakes will not be visible. Instead, the consumer must take part in the ritual of the service itself. To be part of such a process and not to know exactly what is going on clearly increases the uncertainty about the consequences, particularly the physical consequences of being involved in a service encounter such as surgery, or the social consequences of doing the "wrong" thing, such as wearing the wrong type of clothing to an important dinner party.

Information and Risk   Others have argued that the higher risk level associated with services purchasing is due to the limited information available before the purchase decision is made. For example, economics literature suggests that goods and services possess three different types of attributes:[8]

- **Search attributes**—attributes that can be determined prior to purchase.
- **Experience attributes**—attributes that can be evaluated only during and after the production process.
- **Credence attributes**—attributes that cannot be evaluated confidently even immediately after receipt of the good or service.

Because of the intangible nature of services, it is often extremely difficult for consumers to objectively evaluate a service before it is bought. Services thus have very low search attributes. In contrast, goods can be touched, seen, smelled, heard, and, in some instances, tasted prior to purchase and are therefore predominantly characterized by search attributes.

A large proportion of the properties possessed by services (e.g., the friendliness of the flight attendants of a particular airline or the skill level of a hairstylist) can be discovered by consumers only during and after the consumption of the service; these are thus experience attributes. Moreover, some of the properties of many services (e.g., how well a car has been repaired by a body shop or how well your doctor performs services) cannot be assessed even after the service is completed; these are called credence attributes. In sum, due to the properties of intangibility, inseparability, and the variation in quality provided by service personnel, services tend to be characterized by experience and credence attributes.

Brand Loyalty Among Service Consumers   If we start with the premise that consumers do not like taking risks, then it would seem obvious that they will try, whenever possible, to reduce risk during the purchase process. One strategy is to be brand- or store-loyal.[9] Brand loyalty is based on the degree to which the consumer has obtained satisfaction in the past. If consumers have been satisfied in the past with their supplier of service, they have little incentive to risk trying someone or something new.

Having been satisfied in a high-risk purchase, a consumer is less likely to experiment with a different purchase. Maintaining a long-term relationship with the same service provider, in and of itself, helps to reduce the perceived risk associated with the purchase. This is why it is common to observe consumers acquiring services from the same physician, dentist, and hairstylist over long periods of time.

search attributes
Attributes that can be determined prior to purchase.

experience attributes
Attributes that can be evaluated only during and after the production process.

credence attributes
Attributes that cannot be evaluated confidently even immediately after receipt of the good or service.

CONSUMER DECISION
PROCESS ISSUES IN
SERVICES MARKETING

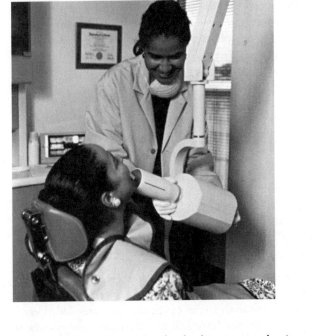

Maintaining a long-term relationship with the same service provider, such as going to the same dentist every time you need dental work, reduces the perceived risk associated with the purchase. In a sense, customers are "brand loyal" to their service providers as well as to the products they buy.

© Mary Kate Denny/PhotoEdit

switching costs

The costs that accrue when changing from one service provider to another.

search costs

The time it takes to seek out new alternatives.

transaction costs

The costs associated with first-time visits.

learning costs

The costs associated with learning new systems.

loyal customer discounts

Discounts that are given for maintaining the same service over time and that are lost when switching from one supplier to another.

Brand loyalty may also be higher in purchasing services due to the limited number of alternative choices available. This is particularly true of professional services, where acceptable substitutes may not be available. In contrast, consumers of goods generally have more substitutes available. Moreover, purchasing alternative goods does not represent the same level of increased risk as purchasing alternative services.

Finally, brand loyalty may also be higher for services due to the **switching costs** that can accrue when changing from one service provider to another. A wide array of switching costs can be accrued, depending on the product involved. Consider, for example, the switching costs involved in changing from one brand of green beans to another compared with the costs involved in changing banks. Typical switching costs include:

▲ **Search costs**—the time it takes to seek out new alternatives.
▲ **Transaction costs**—the costs associated with first-time visits, such as new x-rays when changing dentists.
▲ **Learning costs**—costs such as time and money that are associated with learning new systems, such as new versions of software packages.
▲ **Loyal customer discounts**—discounts that are given for maintaining the same service over time, such as accident-free auto insurance rates. Such discounts are sacrificed when switching from one supplier to the next.
▲ **Customer habit**—costs associated with changing established behavior patterns.

▲ **Emotional costs**—emotional turmoil that one may experience when severing a long-term relationship with a provider. Emotional costs are particularly high when a personal relationship has developed between the client and the provider.

▲ **Cognitive costs**—costs in terms of the time it takes simply thinking about making a change in service providers.

customer habit

Costs associated with changing established behavior patterns.

emotional costs

Emotional turmoil that can be experienced when severing a long-term relationship with a provider.

cognitive costs

Costs associated with thinking about changing providers.

The Importance of Personal Sources of Information Another special consideration during the prepurchase stage is the importance of personal sources of information. Research has shown that in the area of communications, personal forms such as word-of-mouth references and information from opinion leaders often is given more importance than company-controlled communications. A reference from a friend becomes more important when the purchase to be made has a greater risk. For example, a visit to a new hairdresser can be stressful since the outcome of the service will be highly visible. That stress can be reduced by a recommendation from someone whose judgment the consumer trusts. The consumer will then feel more confident about the outcome.

Similarly, evidence suggests that opinion leaders play an important role in the purchase of services. An opinion leader in a community is an individual who is looked to for advice. Within the perceived-risk framework, an opinion leader can be viewed as a source of reduced social risk. A woman who visits a hairdresser for the first time may feel uncertain about the quality of the outcome. However, she might be reassured by the fact that the friend who recommended the service is widely known to have good judgment in such matters and will convey this to others in their mutual social group. In this way, the opinion leader's judgment partially substitutes for the consumer's own.

In addition to reducing perceived risk, the importance of personal sources of information to service consumers is relevant for a number of other reasons. Due to the intangibility of services, mass media is not as effective in communicating the qualities of the service compared with personal sources of information. For example, would you feel comfortable purchasing services from a surgeon who is featured in television advertising? Moreover, would it be feasible for the physician to adequately describe the clinic's services during a 30-second television spot? Overall, personal sources of information become more important as objective standards for evaluation decrease and as the complexity of the product being marketed increases.

Other reasons that consumers rely to such a great extent on personal sources of information is that nonpersonal sources may simply not be available because of professional restrictions or negative attitudes regarding the use of advertising. Many service providers are small and may lack the resources or knowledge to advertise. How many marketing or communications classes do you suppose your dentist or physician enrolled in while attending college? Regardless of their training and subsequent status, professional service providers are operating businesses and must effectively compete in order to maintain their livelihoods. The bottom line is that many professional service providers either lack the knowledge or feel uncomfortable marketing their services.

Fewer Alternatives to Consider In comparison with goods, consumers of services tend to evaluate a smaller number of alternative sources of supply during the prepurchase stage for a variety of reasons. First, each service provider tends to offer only one brand. For example, State Farm sells only State Farm insurance, and your personal dentist provides only one brand of dental care. In contrast, consumers shopping for a blender generally have many brands to consider at each retail location.

The second reason the evoked set tends to be smaller pertains to the number of establishments providing the same service. The tendency in services is to have a smaller number of outlets providing the same service. For example, a market area can support only so many psychologists, dentists, and medical doctors. In comparison, similar goods tend to be available in many locations. The difference between the distribution of goods and services relates directly to the diversification of the product mix. Retailers of goods sell many products under many brand names, thereby earning their revenues through many different sources. Due to the diversified product mix, the same goods are available at many locations. In contrast, the survival of the service firm is dependent upon selling only one brand of service.

A third reason consumers consider fewer service alternatives relates to the lack of available prepurchase information. Consumers of services simply are not aware of as many service substitutes and/or choose not to undertake the time-consuming task of obtaining information from competing service providers. In contrast, consumers of goods often simply look at what is on the store's shelves and are able to compare prices as well as a number of other factors such as ingredients, construction quality, feel, and scent.

Self-Service as a Viable Alternative Another difference between goods and services in the prepurchase choice stage of the consumer decision process is that self-provision often becomes a viable alternative for such services as lawn care, fence installation, housekeeping, painting, and a number of other services. In comparison, consumers rarely consider building a toaster over purchasing one from a local retailer. For obvious reasons, many professional service providers are not generally competing against the self-service alternative.

CONSUMPTION STAGE CONSIDERATIONS

The consumption of goods can be divided into three activities: buying, using, and disposing. The three activities occur in a definite buy-use-dispose order and have clear boundaries between them. The customer buys a box of detergent at a supermarket, uses it at home in the washing machine, and disposes of the empty box after the detergent is used up.

This scenario does not apply to the consumption of services, however. First of all, no clear-cut boundary or definite sequence exists between the acquisition and the use of services because there is no transfer of ownership. Because of the prolonged interactions between the customer and the service provider, the production, acquisition, and use of services become entangled and appear to be a single process.[10] Furthermore, the concept of disposal is irrelevant because of the intangibility and experiential nature of services.

Without a doubt, the consumption stage is more complex for services in comparison with that of goods. The servuction system concept introduced in Chapter 1 suggests that the benefits bought by a customer consist of the experience that is delivered through an interactive process. Even when a service is rendered to something that the consumer owns, such as a car, rather than to the individual's person, the service production/consumption process often involves a sequence of personal interactions (face-to-face or by telephone) between the customer and the service provider.[11]

Interactions between the customer and the company's facilities and personnel are inevitable. It is from these interpersonal and human-environment interactions that the service experience is acquired.[12] Perhaps the most important outcome of these interactions is the contradiction of the idea that postchoice evaluation occurs only at a certain point in time after use.[13] The *use* of goods is essentially free from any kind of direct marketer influence. For example, the manufacturer of the raisin bran you ate this morning for breakfast had no interaction with you whatsoever. Hence, consumers of goods can choose when, where, and how they will use a good. On the other hand, service firms play an active role in customer consumption activities because services are produced and consumed simultaneously.

No service can be produced or used with either the consumer or the service firm absent. Due to the extended service delivery process, many believe that the consumer's postchoice evaluation occurs both during and after the use of services rather than only afterward. In other words, consumers evaluate the service while they are experiencing the service encounter during the consumption stage as well as during the postpurchase stage.

From a marketer's point of view, this opens up the prospect of being able to directly influence that evaluation. Hence, the restaurant manager who visits diners' tables and asks, "How is the meal?" is able to catch problems and change evaluations in a way that the manufacturer of a packaged good cannot.

POSTCHOICE CONSIDERATIONS

The postpurchase evaluation of services is a complex process. It begins soon after the customer makes the choice of the service firm he or she will be using and continues throughout the consumption and postconsumption stages. The evaluation is influenced by the unavoidable interaction of a substantial number of social, psychological, and situational variables. Service satisfaction relies not only on the properties of the four elements of the servuction system—contact personnel, inanimate environment, other customers, and internal organization systems—but also on the synchronization of these elements in the service production/consumption process.

The success or failure of a service firm can be at least partly attributed to management's ability or inability to manipulate the customer experience as the output of a collection of interpersonal interactions (client versus client, client versus employee) and human-environment interactions (employee versus working environment and supporting facilities, customer versus service environment and supporting facilities). A number of proposed models attempt to describe the process by which consumers evaluate their purchase decisions.

**expectancy
disconfirmation model**

The model in which consumers
evaluate services by comparing
expections with perceptions.

The Expectancy Disconfirmation Model How does service satisfaction arise during the consumption and postpurchase stages? A number of approaches have been suggested, but perhaps the simplest and most powerful is the **expectancy disconfirmation model.** The concept of this model is straightforward. Consumers evaluate services by comparing expectations with perceptions. If the perceived service is better than or equal to the expected service, then consumers are satisfied. Hence, ultimately customer service is achieved through the effective management of customer perceptions and expectations.

It is crucial to point out that this entire process of comparing expectations with perceptions takes place in the mind of the customer. It is the perceived service that matters, not the actual service. One of the best examples that reinforces this issue involves a high-rise hotel. The hotel was receiving numerous complaints concerning the time guests had to wait for elevator service in the lobby. Realizing that from an operational viewpoint, the speed of the elevators could not be increased, and that attempting to schedule the guests' elevator usage was futile, management installed mirrors in the lobby next to the elevator bays. Guest complaints were reduced immediately—the mirrors provided a means for the guests to occupy their waiting time. Guests were observed using the mirror to observe their own appearance and that of others around them. In reality, the speed of the elevators had not changed; however, the perception was that the waiting time was now acceptable.

It is also feasible to manage expectations in order to produce satisfaction without altering in any way the quality of the actual service delivered. Motel Six, for example, by downplaying its service offering in its cleverly contrived advertising, actually increases consumer satisfaction by lowering customer expectations prior to purchase. The firm's advertising effectively informs consumers of both what to expect and what not to expect: "A good clean room for $19.99 . . . a little more in some places . . . a little less in some others . . . and remember . . . we'll leave the light on for you." Many customers simply do not use services such as swimming pools, health clubs, and full-service restaurants, which are associated with the higher-priced hotels. Economy-minded hotels, such as Motel Six, are carving out a niche in the market by providing the basics. The result is that customers know exactly what they will get ahead of time and are happy not only with the quality of the service received but also with the cost savings.

The Perceived-Control Perspective Another model that assists in describing the post-purchase stage is the **perceived-control perspective.** The concept of control has drawn considerable attention from psychologists. They argue that in modern society, in which people no longer have to bother about the satisfaction of primary biological needs, the need for control over situations in which one finds oneself is a major force driving human behavior.[14] Rather than being treated as a service attribute, as implied by multiattribute models, perceived control can be conceptualized as a superfactor—a global index that summarizes an individual's experience with a service. The basic premise of this perspective is that during the service experience, the higher the level of control over the situation perceived by consumers, the higher their satisfaction with the service will be. A similar positive relationship is proposed between service providers' experience of control and their job satisfaction.

In a slightly different way, it is equally important for the service firm itself to maintain control of the service experience. If the consumer gets too much control, the economic position of the firm may be affected as consumers tip the value equation in their favor, even to an extent that the firm may begin to lose money. On the other hand, if the service employees take complete control, consumers may become unhappy and leave. Even if this does not happen, the operational efficiency of the firm may be impaired. This three-cornered struggle among the service firm, its employees, and consumers is described in Figure 4.3.

Services can be thought of as a consumer's giving up cash and control in exchange for benefits, with each party seeking to gain as much advantage as possible. But it would appear that no one can truly win in such a "contest." In fact, the concept of control is much broader than implied. Behavioral control, the ability to control what is actually going on, is only part of the idea. Research shows that cognitive control is also important. Thus, when consumers perceive that they are in control, or at least that what is happening to them is predictable, the effect can be the same as that achieved by behavioral control. In other words, it is the perception of control, not the reality, that is important.

Managerially, this concept raises a number of interesting ideas. The first idea raised is the value of the information given to consumers during the service experience in order to increase their sense that they are in control and that they know what will happen next. This is particularly important for professional service firms, which often assume that simply doing a good job will make their clients happy—they forget that their clients may not have heard from them for more than a month and might be frantic because of lack of information. It is equally important to an airline that delays a flight after boarding the passengers but fails to let them know what is happening.

Similarly, if a firm is due to make changes in its operation that will have an impact on consumers, it is important that those consumers be forewarned. If they

perceived-control perspective
A model in which consumers evaluate services by the amount of control they have over the perceived situation.

CONSUMER DECISION
PROCESS ISSUES IN
SERVICES MARKETING

FIGURE 4.3   THE PERCEIVED BEHAVIORAL CONTROL CONFLICTS
IN THE SERVICE ENCOUNTER

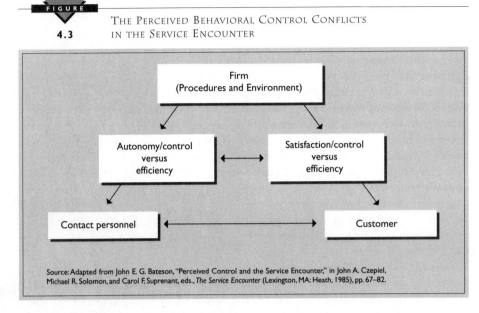

Source: Adapted from John E. G. Bateson, "Perceived Control and the Service Encounter," in John A. Czepiel, Michael R. Solomon, and Carol F. Suprenant, eds., *The Service Encounter* (Lexington, MA: Heath, 1985), pp. 67–82.

are not, they may perceive themselves to be "out of control" and become dissatisfied with the service received to the extent that they change suppliers.

The control perspective raises interesting issues about the trade-off between predictability and choice. Operationally, one of the most important strategic issues is the amount of choice to give the consumer. Because both choice and predictability (standardization) can contribute to a sense of control, it is crucial to determine which is the more powerful source of control for the consumer.

The Script Perspective—All the World's a Stage and All the People Players A number of theories in psychology and sociology can be brought together in the ideas of a script and a **role.** A role is defined as "a set of behavior patterns learned through experience and communication, to be performed by an individual in certain social interaction in order to attain a maximum effectiveness in goal accomplishment."[15] The principle idea proposed is that in a service encounter, customers perform roles, and their satisfaction is a function of **role congruence**—whether the actual behaviors by customers and staff are consistent with the expected roles.

This role congruence thus focuses on the postpurchase phases of a service encounter. The described interaction is two-way, so role congruence is expected to exert an impact on the customer as well as on the service provider. In other words, satisfaction of both parties is likely when the customer and the service provider engage in behaviors that are consistent with each other's role expectation; otherwise, both performers may be upset by the interaction.

role
Behavior patterns learned through experience and communication, to be performed in social interaction to attain a maximum effectiveness in goal accomplishment.

role congruence
The property of actual behaviors by customers and staff being consistent with their expected roles.

The key managerial tasks implied by role theory perspectives are (1) to design roles for the service encounter that are acceptable and capable of ful-filling the needs of both the customers and the service providers and (2) to communi-cate these roles to both customers and employees so that both have realistic perceptions of their roles as well as those of their partners in their inter-actions.

Role is assumed to be **extra-individual.** Hence, every individual is expected to display the same predetermined set of behaviors when he or she takes up a certain role, either as a customer or as a service provider. Because role theory originally was not directly concerned with the perception of participants in the service encounter, it is incompatible with the concepts of service evaluation and customer satisfaction. For example, consider that two customers, one an introvert and one an extrovert, may have completely different perceptions and evaluations of inter-actions with the same chatty provider. In this case, **intra-individual** variables must be employed in order to explain the differences in customer evaluation and satisfaction.

The role idea can, however, be adapted for use in service situations. This adap-tation draws on the psychological idea of a **script.** The script theory and role theory perspectives appear on the surface to be similar. Script theory argues that rules, mostly determined by social and cultural variables, exist to facilitate inter-actions in daily repetitive events, including a variety of service experiences.[16] These rules shape the participants' expectations in these types of interactions. Furthermore, the rules must be acknowledged and obeyed by all participants if satisfactory outcomes are to be generated; if one participant deviates from the rules, the other co-actors will be uncomfortable. Therefore, a satisfied customer is unlikely given a dissatisfied service provider, and a dissatisfied customer is unlikely given a satisfied service provider.

Despite the similarity of the role theory and script theory perspectives, basic differences exist between them. First, the script theory perspective has a wider range of concerns (e.g., the impact of the service setting) and hence is concerned with the whole service experience rather than with only the inter-personal service encounter. Second, scripts are by definition intra-individual and are a function of an individual's experience and personality. Finally, consumer scripts can be revised by service providers who educate consumers about the service process.

The expectancy disconfirmation model, the perceived-control perspective, and the script perspective may not totally reflect reality, but because they are the re-sult of much research in marketing and psychology, they at least allow us to make logical deductions about consumer behavior when making marketing decisions. Moreover, since all the models to be described have both strengths and weak-nesses, they should be considered complementary rather than mutually exclusive. Managerial insights can be developed more effectively through a combination of these various perspectives as we continue to learn about consumer decision processing.

extra-individual

Term used to describe roles that theorizes that every individual is expected to display the same set of behaviors in certain roles.

intra-individual

Term used to describe scripts that are a function of an individual's experience and personality and that can therefore differ among individuals.

script

A learned sequence of behavior patterns that consumers and service providers follow during service transactions; can be modified via training and experience.

S U M M A R Y

This chapter has presented consumer decision process issues as they relate to service consumers. The consumer decision process model consists of three main stages: the prepurchase stage, the consumption stage, and the postpurchase stage. The prepurchase stage consists of the events that occur prior to the consumer's acquisition of the service and includes stimulus reception, problem awareness, information search, and evaluation of alternatives. The outcome of the prepurchase stage is a choice that takes place during the consumption stage. The consumption stage includes the activities of buying, using, and disposing of the product. The postpurchase stage refers to the process by which the consumer evaluates his or her level of satisfaction with the purchase.

Although the consumer decision process model applies to both goods and services, unique considerations arise with respect to services in each of the three stages. Compared with their considerations when purchasing goods, consumers of services during the prepurchase stage of the decision process (1) perceive higher levels of risk to be associated with the purchase; (2) tend to be more brand loyal; (3) rely more on personal sources of information; (4) tend to have fewer alternatives to consider; and (5) often include self-provision as a viable alternative.

The consumption stage is more complex for services in comparison with that of goods as the production, acquisition, and use of services become entangled in a single process. Moreover, due to the extended service delivery process, many believe that the consumer's postchoice evaluation occurs both during and after, rather than only after, the use of services. From a marketer's point of view, this provides the opportunity to directly influence the consumer's evaluation during the service delivery process. Because of the client–company interface, the service provider is able to catch problems and change evaluations in a way that the manufacturer of a packaged good cannot.

Similarly, the postpurchase evaluation of services is also a complex process. The evaluation process begins soon after the customer makes the choice of the service firm he or she will be using and continues throughout the consumption and postconsumption stages. The evaluation is influenced by the unavoidable interaction of a substantial number of social, psychological, and situational variables. Service satisfaction relies not only on the technical quality of the service and the four elements of the servuction system—contact personnel, inanimate environment, other customers, and internal organizational systems—but also on the synchronization of these elements in the service production/consumption process.

Models that assist in our understanding of the consumer's postpurchase evaluation process include the expectancy disconfirmation model, the perceived-control perspective, and the script perspective. In short, the expectancy disconfirmation model defines satisfaction as meeting or exceeding customer expectations. The perceived-control perspective proposes that during the service experience, the higher the level of control over the situation perceived by consumers, the stronger will be their satisfaction with the service. The script perspective proposes that in a service encounter, customers perform roles, and their satisfaction is a function of "role congruence"—whether or not the actual behaviors by customers and staff are consistent with the expected roles. Models such as these help us understand how consumer evaluations are processed and indicate areas where service marketers can focus their efforts in pursuit of the ultimate goal of providing customer satisfaction.

KEY TERMS

consumer decision process	uncertainty
prepurchase stage	financial risk
stimulus	performance risk
commercial cue	physical risk
social cue	social risk
physical cue	psychological risk
problem awareness	search attributes
shortage	experience attributes
unfulfilled desire	credence attributes
information search	switching costs
evoked set	search costs
internal search	transaction costs
external search	learning costs
evaluation of alternatives	loyal customer discounts
nonsystematic evaluation	customer habit
systematic evaluation	emotional costs
linear compensatory approach	cognitive costs
lexicographic approach	expectancy disconfirmation model
consumption stage	perceived-control perspective
store choice	role
nonstore choice	role congruence
consumption process	extra-individual
postpurchase evaluation	intra-individual
cognitive dissonance	script
consequence	

REVIEW QUESTIONS

1. In general terms, discuss the value of consumer behavior models.

2. Why do consumers of services perceive higher levels of risk associated with their purchases?

3. Discuss the different types of risk.

▶▶▶▶ ◀◀◀◀

4. Define and discuss the following terms: search attributes, experience attributes, and credence attributes. Which type(s) of attributes most accurately apply to services? Explain.

5. Regarding multiattribute models, what is the difference between the linear compensatory approach and the lexicographic approach?

6. Explain why consumers of services tend to be more brand loyal.

7. Why do personal sources of information tend to be more important for consumers of services?

8. Discuss the managerial implications of the client–company interface during the consumption stage.

9. What is the difference between a role and a script?

10. Explain the relevance of the perceived-control model as it relates to the postconsumption stage.

NOTES

1. John E. G. Bateson, *Managing Services Marketing: Text and Readings*, 2nd ed. (Fort Worth, TX: The Dryden Press, 1992), p. 93.

2. Adapted from Michael Levy and Barton A. Weitz, *Retailing Management* (Homewood, IL: Irwin, 1992), pp. 117–154.

3. Adapted from John E. G. Bateson, *Managing Services Marketing*.

4. F. Nicosia and R. N. Mayer, "Toward a Sociology of Consumption," *Journal of Consumer Research* 3,2 (1976), pp. 65–75.

5. D. Guseman, "Risk Perception and Risk Reduction in Consumer Services," in *Marketing of Services*, eds. J. Donnelly and William R. George (Chicago: American Marketing Association, 1981), pp. 200–204; and R. A. Bauer, "Consumer Behavior as Risk Taking," in *Dynamic Marketing for a Changing World*, ed. R. S. Hancock (Chicago: American Marketing Association, 1960), pp. 389–398.

6. L. Kaplan, G. J. Szybilo, and J. Jacoby, "Components of Perceived Risk in Product Purchase; A Cross-Validation," *Journal of Applied Psychology* 59 (1974): pp. 287–291.

7. D. Guseman, "Risk Perception," pp. 200–204.

8. Adapted from John E. G. Bateson, *Managing Services*.

9. Zeithaml, Valerie A., "How Consumer Evaluation Processes Differ between Goods and Services," in *Marketing of Services*, eds. J. Donnelly and William R. George (Chicago: American Marketing Association, 1981), pp. 191–199.

10. Bernard Booms and Jody Nyquist, "Analyzing the Customer/Firm Communication Component of the Services Marketing Mix," in *Marketing of Services*, eds. J. Donnelly and W. George (Chicago: American Marketing Association, 1981), p. 172; and Raymond Fisk, "Toward a Consumption/Evaluation Process Model for Services," in *Marketing of Services*, eds. J. Donnelly and W. George (Chicago: American Marketing Association, 1981), p. 191.

11. Christopher H. Lovelock, "Classifying Services to Gain Strategic Marketing Insights," *Journal of Marketing* 47 (Summer 1983), pp. 9–20.

12. Alan Andrasen, "Consumer Research in the Service Sector," in *Emerging Perspectives on Services Marketing*, eds. L. Berry, G. L. Shostack, and G. Upah (Chicago: American Marketing Association, 1982), pp. 63–64.

13. Raymond Fisk, "Toward a Consumption/Evaluation Process Model for Services," in *Marketing of Services*, eds. J. Donnelly and W. George (Chicago: American Marketing Association, 1981), p. 191.

14. John E. G. Bateson, "Perceived Control and the Service Encounter," in *The Service Encounter*, eds. John A. Czepiel, Michael R. Solomon, and Carol F. Suprenant (Lexington, MA: Lexington Books, 1984), pp. 67–82.

15. Michael R. Solomon, Carol F. Suprenant, John A. Czepiel, and Evelyn G. Gatman, "A Role Theory Perspective on Dyadic Interactions: The Service Encounter," *Journal of Marketing* 1, 49 (Winter 1985), pp. 99–111.

16. Ruth A. Smith and Michael Houston, "Script-Based Evaluations of Satisfaction with Services," in *Emerging Perspectives in Services Marketing*, eds. L. Berry, G. L. Shostack, and G. Upah (Chicago: American Marketing Association, 1982), pp. 59–62.

5

Ethical Issues in Services Marketing

> "*Always do right. This will gratify some people, and astonish the rest.*"
>
> Mark Twain

CHAPTER OBJECTIVES

The primary purpose of this chapter is to introduce students to a variety of ethical issues as they relate to services marketing. After reading this chapter, you should be able to

▸ Define the difference between ethical decisions and ordinary decisions.

    ▸ *Discuss the reasons that consumers are particularly vulnerable to ethical misconduct within the service sector.*

▸ Describe the moral philosophies upon which individuals base their ethical decisions.

    ▸ *Discuss the types of ethical issues that often arise in the business sector.*

▸ Discuss factors, other than moral philosophies, that may influence ethical decision making.

    ▸ *Describe the consequences of ethical misconduct.*

▸ Discuss strategies that attempt to control ethical behavior.

SEARS AUTO CENTERS: PREVENTIVE MAINTENANCE
OR ETHICAL MISCONDUCT?

The marketing concept states that the goal of the organization is to recognize and satisfy customer needs while making a profit. Such was the goal of Edward Brennan, chairman of Sears, Roebuck and Company. Under his leadership, market research studies were conducted on customer automotive repair needs. Subsequently, Sears established a preventive maintenance program that instructed the auto repair centers to recommend repair/replacement of parts based on the mileage indicated on the odometer. Concurrently, sales quotas were established for Sears's 850 auto repair centers. Meeting or exceeding these quotas earned bonus money for the service personnel and provided management with an objective means of evaluating employee performance.

The new sales incentive program required the sale of a certain number of repairs or services—including alignments, springs, and brake jobs—every eight hours. Service employees were also able to qualify for bonus money by selling a specified number of shock absorbers or struts for every hour worked. The objective of this program was to meet customer needs while increasing the profits of the auto service centers.

After the program was put into place, the automotive unit became the fastest growing and most profitable unit in recent Sears history. However, a growing number of consumer complaints were lodged against Sears. These complaints sparked investigations by the states of California, New Jersey, and Florida into practices at Sears auto service centers. The state of California alleged that Sears consistently overcharged its customers an average of $223 for unnecessary repairs or work that was never done.

Sears now faces a hearing in California on charges of fraud, making false and misleading statements, false advertisement, and willful departure from accepted trade practices. Based on the outcome of this hearing, Sears may face revocation of its license to operate repair centers in California. Legal action in other states is pending. Sears contends that its auto centers were merely servicing vehicles based on the manufacturer's suggested maintenance schedule. Moreover, Sears maintains that its failure to make these suggestions for improvements would neglect the safety of the consumer.

Sources: Lawrence M. Fisher, "Sears Auto Centers Halt Commissions After Flap," *The New York Times*, 1992, pp. D1, D2; Gregory A. Patterson, "Sear's Brennan Accepts Blame for Auto Flap," *The Wall Street Journal*, 1992, p. B1; "Systematic Looting," *Time*, June 22, 1992, pp. 27, 30; and Tung Yin, "Sears Is Accused of Billing Fraud at Auto Centers," *The Wall Street Journal*, June 12, 1992, pp. B1, B5.

INTRODUCTION

Within the past decade, integrating ethics into the business curriculum has become a common topic of discussion among marketing educators and practitioners. Originally, business ethics was generally taught as a single course; however, many business schools now believe that business ethics should be taught across the curriculum and that ethical issues as they relate to each topic area should be discussed.[1]

Because of the unique opportunities that exist for ethical misconduct in service fields, students of the services marketing course in particular should be made aware of the issues surrounding ethical decision making. Although the majority of service providers fulfill their duties ethically, infamous service providers such as Jim Bakker, Leona Helmsley, Ivan Boesky, and Sears Auto Centers have given recent evidence that not all service providers may be trustworthy.

Unique circumstances occur in the service sector that create an ethical environment worth examination and discussion. This chapter presents a variety of ethics-related topics as they pertain to the service sector. More specifically, these topics include (1) methods of ethical decision making, (2) issues that create ethical conflict, (3) factors influencing ethical decision making, (4) the effects of ethical misconduct, and (5) strategies for controlling ethical behavior.

Note that in this chapter, we do not intend to "preach" to you what we think is right or wrong. Such a decision is left to the discretion of the individual student. Unfortunately, as you will live to learn, the appropriateness and/or public acceptance of your decision is usually decided on "Oprah" or "Donahue." Our objective is primarily to provide you with food for thought and to facilitate class discussions about an important subject that is often overlooked. Overall, we hope that the information provided in this chapter will aid in your understanding of ethics and perhaps have an impact on the decisions with which you will be faced as you pursue your career.

WHAT ARE ETHICS?

In general, **ethics** are commonly defined as: (1) "a branch of philosophy dealing with what is good and bad and with moral duty and obligation;" and (2) "the principles of moral conduct governing an individual or group."[2] **Business ethics** comprises moral principles and standards that guide behavior in the world of business.[3] The distinction between an ordinary decision and an ethical one is that values and judgments play a critical role in ethical decisions. In contrast, ordinary decisions are generally decided utilizing a set of preordained acceptable rules.

The field of business ethics is particularly intriguing. On one hand, businesses must make a profit in order to survive. The survival of the firm provides employ-

---

ethics

A branch of philosophy dealing with what is good and bad and with moral duty and obligations; the principles of moral conduct governing an individual or group.

business ethics

The principles of moral conduct that guide behavior in the business world.

ees salaries with which employees feed their families and educate their children, thereby leading to the betterment of society. In addition, company profits and employee salaries are taxed, the funds from which furnish the support for various governmental programs. On the other hand, business profits should not be obtained by *any* means necessary. A trade-off must exist between the firm's desire for profits and what is good for individuals and society.

ETHICS AND BUSINESS

How does the public feel about business when it comes to ethical behavior? Not very positive.[4] According to a *Business Week/Harris* poll, 46 percent of respondents believed that the ethical standards of businesspeople were only average. In addition, 90 percent of respondents believed that white-collar crime was somewhat or very common.

Another survey reported that the majority of Americans believe that many businesspeople regularly engage in ethical misconduct. In fact, 76 percent of respondents in yet another study believe that the decline in moral standards in the United States is a direct result of the lack of business ethics practiced daily. Perhaps even more damaging are the results of a survey of business practitioners themselves: 66 percent of executives surveyed believe that businesspeople will occasionally act unethically during business dealings, while another 15 percent believe that ethical misconduct occurs often in the business sector.

THE OPPORTUNITY FOR ETHICAL MISCONDUCT IN SERVICES MARKETING

Opportunities for ethical misconduct within the service sector can be attributed predominantly to the intangibility, heterogeneity, and inseparability dimensions inherent in the provision of services.[5] Intangibility complicates the consumer's ability to objectively evaluate the quality of service provided; heterogeneity reflects the difficulty in standardization and quality control; and inseparability reflects the human element involved in the service delivery process. All three dimensions contribute to consumer vulnerability to and reliance upon the service provider's ethical conduct during the service encounter.

In more specific terms, consumer vulnerability to ethical misconduct within the service sector can be attributed to several sources explained in the following sections.[6]

FEW SEARCH ATTRIBUTES

As discussed in Chapter 4 (on consumer behavior), search attributes can be determined prior to purchase and include such attributes as touch, smell, visual cues, and taste. However, due to the intangibility of services, consumers lack the opportunity to physically examine a service before purchasing it. Consequently, consumers have little prepurchase information available to help them make an informed, intelligent decision. Hence, consumers of services often must base their purchase decisions on information provided by the service provider.

Using Sears Auto Centers as an example, the dilemma a consumer faces due to the lack of search attributes is clear. The car may look fine on the outside, but the mechanic provides information about parts and systems that may not be visible to the consumer. The consumer now must rely on the advice of the mechanic. In addition, even though price is a search attribute that can be obtained prior to purchasing an auto repair service, the price is only an estimate. The final price is not calculated until after the service is performed.

Technical and Specialized Services

Many services are not easily understood and/or evaluated; consequently, the opportunity exists to easily mislead consumers. Evaluating the performance of professional service providers is particularly intriguing. As a consumer, how do you know whether your doctor, lawyer, broker, priest, or minister is competent at his or her job? Often, our evaluations of these people are based on their clothing, the furniture in their offices, and whether they have pleasant social skills.

The auto repair industry is also characterized by services that are technical, specialized, and not easily understood or evaluated by the average consumer. Again, the consumer must rely on the service provider for guidance. As a result, unethical service providers can easily mislead consumers, perform unnecessary services, or charge for services that are never performed. Do you check your oil when it's changed? How do you know that the mechanic really did rotate and balance your tires?

Time Lapse between Performance and Evaluation

The final evaluation of some services such as insurance and financial planning is often conducted only at a time in the distant future. For example, the success or failure of retirement planning may not be realized until 30 years after the original service transaction is conducted. Hence, service providers may not be held accountable for their actions in the short run. This could lead to a scenario where unethical service providers may maximize their short-term gains at the expense of consumers' long-term benefits.

Unethical auto mechanics may also benefit from the time lapse between service performance and service evaluation. The discovery of low-quality work may happen via mechanical problems 30 days after repairs have been made or by having a future mechanic question the previous mechanic's work. In either case, the consumer is left to deal with the situation and generally experiences little success in convincing the original mechanic that the inferiority of past efforts is at the root of present problems.

THE OPPORTUNITY
FOR ETHICAL
MISCONDUCT IN
SERVICES MARKETING

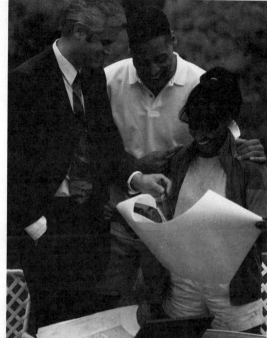

An example of a specialized
service is architecture. Here
an architect is showing a
couple his designs for their
new house. The time lapse
between the blueprints and
the actual building of the
house is a characteristic of
this specialized service.

© 1995 PhotoDisc, Inc. Image no. 14294.

SERVICES SOLD WITHOUT GUARANTEES AND WARRANTIES

Another opportunity for ethical misconduct in the service sector results from few
meaningful guarantees and warranties. Consequently, when the consumer experiences difficulties with an unscrupulous provider, there are few or no means of
seeking quick retribution. For example, what are your options if you get a bad
haircut—glue, a new hat?

Although the auto repair industry is famous for its 90-day guarantee on all parts,
the guarantee generally fails to cover the labor required to reinstall the part that
failed. Moreover, the 90-day guarantee does little to calm the consumer that experiences failure 120 days after the repair. One of the authors had the experience of paying more than $400 to replace the rear-window motor of a Chrysler LeBaron twice
within a 16-month period. The 90-day guarantee did little but indicate that the company that built the replacement motor had little faith in its product—and rightly so!

SERVICES PERFORMED BY BOUNDARY-SPANNING PERSONNEL

Many service providers deliver their services outside their firm's physical facilities.
In doing so, these types of service providers expand the boundary of a firm beyond

ETHICAL ISSUES IN
SERVICES MARKETING

**boundary-spanning
personnel**

Personnel who provide their
services outside the firm's
physical facilities.

the firm's main office. Service providers such as painters, lawn-care specialists, paramedics, and carpet cleaners are typical examples.

Because of the physical distance from the main office inherent in the role of **boundary-spanning personnel,** these particular service providers often are not under direct supervision and may act in a manner inconsistent with organizational objectives. Hence, the opportunity to engage in ethical misconduct without repercussions from upper management arises.

ACCEPTED VARIABILITY IN PERFORMANCE

Another opportunity for ethical misconduct within the service sector is provided via the heterogeneity inherent in the provision of services. Due to heterogeneity, standardization and quality control are difficult to maintain throughout each individual service delivery transaction. Many services are customized, requiring different skills of the service provider, and often consumers are exposed to different providers within the same firm. Variability in performance is unavoidable.

Variability in performance is evident in the auto repair industry. Automobiles develop a variety of problems that require an array of skills from the service provider, who may not be equivalently skilled to undertake each task. Moreover, consumers often receive services from a number of different mechanics. Each mechanic's performance is likely to vary from the next. Due to consumer acceptance of variability in service performance, unethical service providers may attempt to broaden the window of acceptable performance through slightly increasing gaps in performance quality.

OUTCOME-BASED REWARD SYSTEMS

The reward system of an organization often dictates the behavior of its employees, and it does not take employees long to figure out the shortest route to the most money. Hence, the reward system of an organization may encourage, albeit unintentionally, the unethical conduct of its employees.

Straight commissions and quotas reinforce activities that are directly linked to making the sale while discouraging nonselling activities such as maintaining the store, stocking shelves, and spending an inordinate amount of time fielding customer questions.

Looking at the reward structure at Sears Auto Centers, the impact that it likely had on employee behavior is clear. Employees were rewarded for making repairs regardless of whether they were needed or not.

CONSUMER PARTICIPATION IN PRODUCTION

On the surface, one would think that the more the consumer is involved in the service encounter, the less the opportunity exists for the service provider to engage in ethical misconduct. However, service exchanges may be jeopardized by coercive influence strategies used by the service provider.

The consumer's involvement in the service delivery process enables a service provider to try to influence the consumer through fear or guilt to agree to a purchase the consumer would otherwise decline. An auto mechanic who makes a statement such as, "I wouldn't want my family riding around in a car that has brakes like these," is a typical example of the type of influence a service provider can have on a customer. Moreover, due to the consumer's input into the production process, the consumer often accepts much of the responsibility for less-than-satisfactory service transactions. This situation further removes service providers from taking responsibility for their own actions and provides yet another opportunity to engage in unethical behavior.

METHODS FOR ETHICAL DECISION MAKING

The behavior of service providers engaged in ethical decision making reflects the **moral philosophies** in which they believe.[7] Moral philosophies are the principles or rules service providers use when deciding what is right or wrong. For example, if for economic reasons a company is forced to lay off workers, does it notify the workers ahead of the actual layoff? On one hand, notifying employees provides them with time to seek other employment before they are out of a job. On the other hand, disgruntled employees, after learning of the layoff, may not work as hard, and the quality of subsequent service delivery suffers.

As you review the opening vignette about Sears Auto Centers, you should ponder the moral philosophies and decision-making processes embraced by the parties involved. Methods for ethical decision making include teleology, deontology, and relativism. Again, note that we are not proposing that one moral philosophy is better than another. We are merely providing you with alternative schools of thought regarding the way decisions are made.

TELEOLOGY

Teleologists believe an act is morally right or acceptable if the act produces some desired result. **Teleology** is referred to as a type of **consequentialism.** As such, followers of teleology assess the morality of their decisions based on the consequences. If the decision leads to some desired result, such as increased pay, promotion, or recognition, then the decision is acceptable.

As an example, consider the following. Most persons would agree that robbery is an unethical behavior. Let's say that a drug is available at the drugstore, and the pharmacist is charging $1000 for it. Meanwhile, you have a family member who desperately needs the drug in order to survive. A problem arises when you have only $900 and the pharmacist refuses to sell you the drug. Would you steal from the drugstore in order to save a family member? If your answer is yes, then the consequences of your behavior are dictating the morality of your actions.

moral philosophies

The principles or rules service providers use when deciding what is right or wrong.

teleology

A type of ethical decision making in which an act is deemed morally acceptable if it produces some desired result.

consequentialism

A type of ethical decision making that assesses the morality of decisions based on their consequences.

ETHICAL ISSUES IN
SERVICES MARKETING

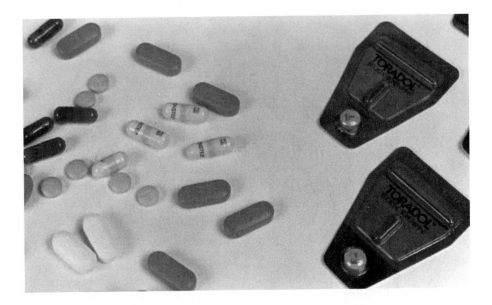

What if a family member
desperately needed drugs
such as these to survive, and
the pharmacy refused to sell
them to you? Would theft be
a viable option? Would it be
a morally correct option?

HB Photo/Annette Coolidge

egoism

A subclass of teleology in which
acceptable actions are defined
as those that benefit the
individual's self-interest as
defined by the individual.

utilitarianism

A subclass of teleology in which
acceptable behavior is defined
as that which maximizes total
utility—the greatest good for
the greatest number of people.

Teleology is further broken down into two subclasses, **egoism** and **utilitarianism,** which reflect the beneficiary of the decision's consequences. Egoists define acceptable actions as those that benefit an individual's self-interest as defined by that individual. Benefits can take the form of fame, personal wealth, recognition, and other self-gratifying consequences. Egoists believe that they should "do the act that promotes the greatest good for oneself."[8]

Returning to the example of Sears Auto Centers, employees who act as egoists may choose alternative behaviors. If the employee wants to increase his own personal wealth, he may engage in activities that lead to greater commissions, such as suggesting repairs that do not need to be made. On the other hand, if the employee believes that reporting the unethical behavior of others would lead to a promotion, the egoist may notify upper management of a problem. Further, an egoist who notifies the press of the problem may be looking for personal recognition.

In contrast to the egoist, the utilitarianist defines acceptable behavior as that which maximizes total utility—the greatest good for the greatest number of people. This philosophy of promoting "the needs of the many over the needs of the few" has led to some interesting decisions. Cuba, for example, isolates all its HIV-positive citizens in a type of asylum. The decision was made to sacrifice the personal freedoms of these people for the health and well-being of the remainder of the Cuban population. (Incidentally, reports tend to support the notion that this decision has led to control of the spread of AIDS in Cuba.)

Using the Sears example, the mechanic who engages in ethical misconduct to make a sale in order to benefit the company, so that all concerned can keep their jobs, may be classified as a utilitarianist. The utilitarianist may also believe that

although not every customer's car may need a specific type of repair, many will benefit from the repairs made over time.

DEONTOLOGY

A deontologist believes that the inherent rightness or wrongness of an act should guide behavior regardless of the outcome. Hence, **deontology** is not a form of consequentialism since it does not focus on the consequences of an action. In contrast, deontology focuses on individual rights and the intentions associated with a particular behavior. Deontologists believe that the rights of the individual should prevail over what is better for society as a whole, thereby differentiating itself from the utilitarian philosophy.

Deontologists believe that there are some things people should never do, regardless of the consequences. If recalling a product to save lives means bankrupting the company, then the company should go bankrupt. Deontologists further believe that moral standards are permanent, do not alter over time, and are based on a so-called categorical imperative. "Simply put, if you feel comfortable allowing everyone in the world to see you commit an act and if your rationale for acting in a particular manner is suitable to become a universal principle guiding behavior, then committing that act is ethical."[9]

Returning again to the Sears example, a deontological mechanic would probably never make repairs that were not needed. Making an unnecessary repair would be a form of lying, and based on the deontological perspective, lying is inherently wrong. On the other hand, it could also be argued based on the deontological perspective that Sears felt it was inherently wrong *not* to do the preventive maintenance as suggested by manufacturers. The deontological mechanic might believe that not conducting the maintenance as suggested by the manufacturer could possibly lead to the harm of an individual customer.

deontology

A type of ethical decision making in which the inherent rightness or wrongness of an act guides behavior, regardless of the outcome.

RELATIVISM

In contrast to deontology, people practicing **relativism** are prone to believe that the correctness of ethical decisions may change over time. Relativists evaluate ethical decisions subjectively on a case-to-case basis based on past individual or group experiences. As such, relativists observe the actions of their relevant group to determine the consensus of opinion concerning decisions. The consensus reflects whether the decision is "right" or "wrong."

Because relativists use themselves or the people around them to judge the ethicality of decisions, they may follow one set of ethical guidelines at work and a different set at home. Consequently, service providers, as relativists, working within an unethical work environment (from an outsider's viewpoint) may eventually come to adopt these behaviors as their own. Sears mechanics who made unnecessary repairs may have simply adopted the actions of their co-workers and supervisors. Co-worker and supervisor opinions can particularly influence the decisions made by new employees. An overview of methods for ethical decision making is presented in Table 5.1.

relativism

A type of ethical decision making in which the correctness of ethical decisions is thought to change over time.

ETHICAL ISSUES IN
SERVICES MARKETING

TABLE 5.1	METHODS FOR ETHICAL DECISION MAKING
Teleology	Acts are morally right or acceptable if they provide some desired result.
Egoism	Acceptable actions are those that maximize a particular person's self-interest as defined by the individual. Egoism is a form of teleology.
Utilitarianism	Acceptable actions are those that maximize total utility—the greatest good for the greatest number of people. Utilitarianisn is a form of teleology.
Deontology	Acceptable actions are those that focus on the preservation of individual rights and on the intentions associated with a particular behavior rather than on its consequences.
Relativism	Acceptable actions are determined by the actions of some relevant group. A relativist evaluates ethicalness on the basis of individual and group experiences.

ISSUES THAT CREATE ETHICAL CONFLICT

The types of ethical issues service providers encounter are not always unique to the service sector. This can be accounted for by the mix of products and customer service involved in a multitude of different businesses. Table 5.2 contains a sample of the many types of ethical issues that are encountered in the business world. Through surveying their personnel, individual companies can determine the specific ethical issues that pertain to their firm. The discussion below focuses on the most typical issues that managers and/or employees will face while conducting business.[10]

CONFLICT OF INTEREST

conflict of interest

The situation in which a service provider feels torn between the organization, the customer, and/or the service provider's own personal interest.

Service providers are often in close proximity to customers during the provision of services. Consequently, the service provider may experience **conflicts of interest** as the service provider–customer relationship develops and friendships are formed. In such a situation, the service provider may feel torn between the organization, the customer, and/or the service provider's own personal interest.

For example, insurance personnel may coach friends and family members on how to complete the necessary forms in order to obtain a less expensive rate. In this situation, the customer benefits (via lower rates), the employee benefits (via "the sale"), but the organization suffers (by failing to obtain the proper premium amount). Likewise, Sears employees may have felt torn between what was best for the customer, what was best for the company, and what was best for their own personal finances.

ORGANIZATIONAL RELATIONSHIPS

organizational relationships

Working relationships formed between service providers and various role partners such as customers, suppliers, peers, subordinates, supervisors, and others.

Service providers form working **organizational relationships** with a variety of role partners, including customers, suppliers, peers, subordinates, supervisors,

TABLE 5.2 TYPES OF ETHICAL ISSUES ENCOUNTERED BY BUSINESSES

Honesty	Accuracy of books, records
Conflict of interest	Privacy of employee records
Marketing, advertising issues	Political activities and contributions
Environmental issues	Misuses of company assets
Discrimination by age, race, or sex	Corporate governance
Product liability and safety	Issues
Codes of ethics and self-governance	Ethical theory
Relations with customers	Ethics in negotiation
Bribery	Relations with local communities
Rights of and responsibilities to shareholders	Plant closing and layoffs
Whistleblowing	Employee discipline
Kickbacks	Use of others' proprietary information
Insider trading	Relations with U.S. government representatives
Antitrust issues	Relations with competitors
Issues facing multinationals	Employee benefits
Relations with foreign governments	Mergers and acquisitions
Ethical foundations of capitalism	Drug and alcohol abuse
Workplace health and safety	Drug and alcohol testing
Managing an ethical environment	Intelligence gathering
Relations with suppliers and subcontractors	Leveraged buyouts
Use of company proprietary information	

Source: Adapted from Lynn Sharp Paine, "Report on Ethics Issues Covered in the Undergraduate Curriculum," in *Ethics Education in American Business Schools* (Washington, D.C.: Ethics Resource Center, Inc., 1988), p. 17. © 1988 Ethics Resource Center, Inc. All Rights Reserved. Reprinted with permission from Ethics Resource Center, Inc., Washington, D.C.

and others. The information gained via these relationships is often highly sensitive. For example, most people would not want their priest to reveal the contents of their confession or their doctor telling others of their medical problems. Because of the sensitivity of information, ethical service providers are required to maintain confidentiality in relationships to meet their professional obligations and responsibilities. In contrast, unethical service providers may use the information acquired from organizational relationships for their own personal gain. The old adage that "knowledge is power" is often embraced by those who engage in ethical misconduct.

The liberties taken with information gained through organizational relationships is addressed in "The Case of Ivan Boesky," which is presented in Part 4 of this book. Boesky, one of Wall Street's top arbitragers, was charged with insider trading activities by the Securities and Exchange Commission (SEC) in 1986. Boesky allegedly made millions from obtaining information concerning company takeovers before the public announcements of the takeovers were made. Once Boesky learned of a takeover, he would purchase large blocks of stock that he later sold at huge profits. In exchange for the names of other inside traders, Boesky plead guilty to one charge of criminal activity and agreed to pay $100 million in penalties. He also served three years in jail.

The structure of the organizational relationship may also provide an opportunity for an unethical firm to place undue influence on its employees. In particular, the relationship between supervisor and subordinate comes to mind. Regarding the Sears example, the mechanics could argue that they felt they would lose their jobs or suffer large decreases in pay if they did not make the repairs required by the quota system that was put into place by upper management.

HONESTY

honesty
The characteristics of truthfulness, integrity, and trustworthiness.

Honesty is a partner of truthfulness, integrity, and trustworthiness. Examples of dishonesty in customer service include promising to do something for a customer but having no intention of delivering on the promise or stating that a service has been performed when, in fact, it has not. Honesty issues may also cover selected business strategies utilized by service firms to manage consumer expectations. For example, a typical practice at some restaurants today is to purposely estimate waiting times in excess of the actual expected waiting times. If customers are seated before expected, they feel they are getting better service. Do you think this practice is ethical?

Other honesty issues involve (1) respecting the private property of clients while services are provided in the clients' homes and places of business; (2) performing services as promised at the designated time; (3) providing accurate billing for services delivered; and (4) providing clients accurate information even if it means the loss of a sale.

The honesty issue certainly applies to the Sears example. According to reports, repairs were often made based on odometer readings, not necessarily on actual need. Hence, the honesty of the firm's actions is in question.

FAIRNESS

fairness
The characteristics of just treatment, equity, and impartiality.

Fairness is an outcome of just treatment, equity, and impartiality. Clients should be treated equitably, and deals based on favoritism should be avoided. In addition, service discrimination issues should also be addressed. Do men receive better service compared with women, or vice versa? Are well-dressed persons served better than blue jean-clad clients? Does a client's race or general appearance affect the level of service provided?

In the Sears example, the just treatment of its customers is in question. The state of California alleged that Sears consistently overcharged its customers an average of $223 for unnecessary repairs or work that was never done. However, discrimination was apparently not a problem—charges allege that Sears took advantage of everyone.

COMMUNICATION

Ethical issues also arise through the communication that the service organization releases to the public. Communication may range from mass advertising to warranty information to interpersonal communication between the service provider and the customer. Ethical misconduct stemming from communication may include making false claims about the superiority of the company's services, making false claims about competitive offerings, and/or making promises the company knowingly understands it cannot keep.

Returning to the Sears example, it seems that Sears also engaged in unethical activities regarding its communications. The state of California brought charges against Sears pertaining to specific allegations of fraud, making false and misleading statements, and false advertising.

Factors That Influence Ethical Decision Making

Different people make different decisions in similar ethical situations. Some individuals make consistent ethical decisions over time, while others evaluate each ethical decision on a case-by-case basis. The reasons that we make different ethical decisions are functions of a variety of factors that may influence our judgments. This section is devoted to an overview of these factors.[11]

Cognitive Moral Development

The model of **cognitive moral development** proposes that individuals progress through six stages of ethical development. As the individual develops, ethical decisions are evaluated differently. In the first stage, the stage of punishment and obedience, a person defines what is right based on rules and authority. Consequently, when faced with an ethical decision, the individual bases it on a set of rules or instructions provided by an authority figure. In the second stage, the stage of individual instrumental purpose and exchange, decisions are based on fulfilling one's own needs or another's in terms of what is fair. During the third stage, the stage of mutual interpersonal expectations, relationships, and conformity, the individual focuses more on others as opposed to personal gains.

As the individual progresses to the fourth stage, the stage of social system and conscience maintenance, the individual defines what is right based on his or her duty to society. In the fifth stage, the stage of prior rights, social contract, or utility, the individual begins to more narrowly define what is right based on basic rights, values, and legal contracts. The sixth and final stage, the stage of universal ethical principles, reflects the individual's belief that right is determined by a set of universal ethical principles that everyone should adhere to when confronted with ethical decisions.

cognitive moral development
A model of ethical development that proposes individuals progress through six stages of ethical development.

Personal Values

Ethical decisions are also influenced by an individual's **personal values.** In general, personal values are not necessarily static. Hence, as the person matures, personal values may change. Furthermore, individuals may apply one set of personal values to their personal life and another set to their business life. Incidentally, this

personal values
The standards by which each person lives in both a personal and professional life.

ETHICAL ISSUES IN
SERVICES MARKETING

explains why, when television tabloids interview the neighbors of a accused embezzler, the neighbors always say: "He was just a regular guy, a good family man, and a great neighbor . . . we had no idea he was a crook!"

CORPORATE CULTURE

corporate culture

The general philosophy of a company that guides decisions, actions, and policies of the company.

Another factor that impacts individual ethical decision making is the **corporate culture** within the firm. Corporate cultures guide decisions, actions, and policies of organizations and are functions of (1) the personal values of those employed by the organization, (2) the procedures used to carry out the daily business, and (3) the policies that are put in place to guide decision making. Overall, procedures and policies play a more important role in corporate culture than do personal values.

CULTURAL DIFFERENCES

cultural differences

Differences in standards of behavior from one culture to another.

In addition to corporate cultures, service firms may have **cultural differences** because of their own nationality-based cultures.[12] For example, although considered unethical in the United States, bribes are common business practice in some countries. Some further argue that ethical behaviors should not be regionally generalized. Accordingly, Asian countries, such as Japan and South Korea, should not be viewed as a single, homogeneous entity with respect to business conduct.[13] Hence, service firms who engage in international operations should consider developing policies that help guide ethical decision making in different cultural climates.

ORGANIZATIONAL STRUCTURE

organizational structure

The way an organization is set up regarding hierarchy of authority and decision making.

The **organizational structure** of a service firm may also impact the ethical decision making of its employees. Traditional organizational structures are characterized as centralized or decentralized. Service providers employed by decentralized firms, where authority is spread throughout the firm, have more latitude when making decisions. In contrast, centralized firms, where authority is concentrated in one area, tend to place stricter controls over employees. Past studies have proposed that centralized organizations tend to be more ethical due to the development and implementation of rigid controls such as codes of ethics and other similar corporate policies.[14] Service firms wishing to implement the concept of empowerment need to consider and discuss with front-line personnel the decentralizing effects of this philosophy as it may create new opportunities for ethical misconduct.

OPPORTUNITY

opportunity

An occasion in which a chance for unethical behavior exists.

As discussed earlier in the chapter, service organizations often operate within a business environment, where ethical misconduct is not easily detected. Hence, the **opportunity** to engage and benefit from unethical behavior within the service sector is fairly prevalent. Opportunity acts as temptation and has been proposed to be a better predictor of behavior than an individual's own personal moral beliefs.[15] Moreover, opportunity is said to increase along with title and status. Recent history has taught us via savings and loan scandals, insider trading schemes, and corrupt ministries that professional service providers may be particularly tempted by the opportunities that arise with a higher title and status.

REWARD SYSTEMS

Ethical misconduct may further be encouraged if rewarded (or not punished) by a firm's **reward system.** As with many types of employees, service providers are often rewarded according to outcome-based control measures (e.g. sales, number of calls handled, etc.). The major problem associated with outcome-based control systems is that employees are evaluated and compensated based on results (outcomes) rather than on behaviors utilized to achieve results. Hence, under this system, if a behavior (ethical or unethical) leads to outcomes valued by the organization (sales), then the employee should be rewarded (salary plus commissions). Thus, outcome-based control systems tend to focus employee efforts on activities with immediate payoffs rather than on behaviors that build long-term relationships between the service provider and the client.

Service firms wishing to enhance the ethical behavior of their employees should consider implementing a behavior-based control system that monitors employees' activities and evaluates employees on the aspects of their jobs in which they exercise control.[16] Compared with outcome-based reward systems, behavior-based reward systems are more harmonious with a long-term relationship marketing approach.

reward systems
The methods used by an organization to evaluate and compensate employees.

SIGNIFICANT OTHERS

As proposed by the theory of differential association, ethical decision making is greatly influenced by **significant others** (e.g., supervisors, peers, subordinates, and customers) with whom the service provider interacts. The more frequent the contact with the significant other, the more likely the employee will adopt similar ethical (or unethical) beliefs. "Association with others who are unethical, combined with the opportunity to act unethically oneself, is a major influence on ethical decision making."[17]

significant others
Supervisors, peers, subordinates, customers, and others who influence a service provider's behavior.

COMPETITIVE ENVIRONMENT

Past research also indicates that the competitive environment in which the individual operates has an impact upon ethical behavior.[18] Pressures from business superiors and ethical climate in the industry are cited as reasons for ethical conflict. Furthermore, it has been suggested that when individuals feel the pressure to succeed and realize what must be done in order to compete, they tend to compromise their own personal standards to reach corporate goals.

CHANGES IN TECHNOLOGY

As science has advanced, many products and services have been developed that carry with them an array of ethical considerations (e.g., abortion, euthanasia, cigarettes, camcorders, etc.). And in handling consumer information, advances in direct marketing techniques (e.g., database technology that allows greater storage and access to consumer information and purchase histories) have given service marketers powerful tools to "identify" their optimal customer profiles and track customer purchase/service histories.[19] For example, when a customer calls Sears to check a catalog order, the service representative has instant access (via an order number) to the customer's previous sales/service transactions. This data can be used to sell other products and service warranties as well as enable more efficient order processing. However, the availability of this information and ease of access to it creates the opportunity to utilize the data in a unethical manner and may violate the customer's right to privacy.

FACTORS CONTRIBUTING TO SEARS EMPLOYEE BEHAVIOR

Returning to the Sears example, factors contributing to the decisions made by Sears Auto Center employees may have included the following: (1) corporate culture—employees were apparently following company procedures and policies; (2) opportunity—due to the difficulty involved in consumer evaluation of service quality, the situation existed where consumers could be easily misled; (3) reward systems—the quota/bonus system rewarded outcomes (sales) rather than ethical behavior; (4) significant others—supervisors and co-workers were engaging in and/or encouraging the method of operation; (5) competitive environment— employees may have felt the pressure to succeed and tended to compromise their own personal standards to reach corporate goals; and (6) technology—the technological advances in the production of automobiles makes it very difficult these days to be one's own mechanic. Hence, technology contributed to the consumer's vulnerability.

THE EFFECTS OF ETHICAL MISCONDUCT

Service organizations should stress the importance of ethical conduct by employees for several reasons. First, in terms of social responsibility, service organizations should be required to act in a manner that is in the best interest of society. Secondly, employees forced to deal with ethical issues on a continuing basis frequently suffer from job-related tension, frustration, anxiety, ineffective performance (i.e., reduced sales and reduced profits), turnover intentions, and lower job satisfaction.[20]

In addition to the personal effects of ethical misconduct, the organization as a whole suffers. Ethical improprieties have also been linked to customer dissatisfaction (loss of sales), unfavorable word-of-mouth publicity for the organization, and a negative public image for the entire industry.[21]

The effects of the Sears Auto Centers policies have been damaging. Some of the consequences have included loss of consumer trust, lost sales due to the publicity surrounding the charges, and an increase in legal actions filed against the company. It could also be argued that employees suffered as well, via increased anxiety, job-related tensions, and low job satisfaction.

CONTROLLING ETHICAL DECISION MAKING

The adverse effects of unethical decision making may lead service firms to try to control the ethical behavior of their employees in a number of ways. The following are some suggestions that might help guide managers in promoting an ethical business environment.[22]

EMPLOYEE SOCIALIZATION

Employee socialization refers to the process through which an individual adapts and comes to appreciate the values, norms, and required behavior patterns of an organization. Ethical issues such as cheating, payment of bribes, and lying may be defined through socialization of organizational values and norms. These values and norms may be transmitted via new employee orientation sessions and subsequent formal meetings to additional sessions and reinforce sessions.

Service organizations can communicate organizational values and norms through communications such as company newsletters and ads. For example, Delta Airlines has been commended for its advertising that depicts very helpful, friendly, and happy employees. Not only do these ads help attract the airline's customers. The ads not only attract customers but also help picture for Delta employees their role within the company and the type of behavior the company expects and rewards.

using ads to help employees recognise behaviour.

STANDARDS OF CONDUCT

As part of the socialization process, standards of conduct are often presented to service employees through a code of ethics. Research suggests that service employees desire codes of ethics to help them understand proper behavior, thereby reducing role conflict and role ambiguity.[23] Although developing a code of ethics does not guarantee subsequent employee ethical behavior, it is an important early step in the process of controlling ethical decision making.

CORRECTIVE CONTROL

For the service firm's code of ethics to be effective, the conditions set forth in it must be enforced. Enforcement of the code of ethics may be accomplished through **corrective control,** the use of rewards and punishments. Service

employee socialization
The process through which an individual adapts and comes to appreciate the values, norms, and required behavior patterns of an organization.

code of ethics
Formal standards of conduct that assist in defining proper organizational behavior.

corrective control
The use of rewards and punishments to enforce a firm's code of ethics.

providers who are rewarded (or not punished) for unethical behavior will continue practicing it. Interestingly, research indicates that employees of firms that have codes of ethics are more prone to believe that violators of ethical codes should be punished.

LEADERSHIP TRAINING

Due to the apparent effects of differential association upon ethical decision making, service organizations need to stress to their leaders the importance of those leaders' own behavior and its influence upon subordinates. Leaders must be examples of the standards of ethical conduct. They need to understand that employees faced with ethical decision making often emulate the behavior of their supervisors. This is particularly true of young employees, who tend to comply with their supervisors to demonstrate loyalty.

SERVICE/PRODUCT KNOWLEDGE

Service firms need to constantly train all employees concerning the details of what the service product can and cannot provide. Due to the complex nature of many service offerings and an ever-changing business environment, service firms cannot afford to assume that employees completely understand the ramifications of new service/product developments. A few service industries understand the social responsibility of keeping employees informed. For example, the insurance industry now requires continuing education of its sales agents.[24]

MONITORING OF EMPLOYEE PERFORMANCE

Another possible method of controlling ethical decision making is the measurement of employee ethical performance. This approach involves comparing behaviors utilized in obtaining performance levels against organizational ethical standards. Service firms may monitor employee performance by either observing employees in action or by utilizing employee questionnaires regarding ethical behavior. Results obtained from monitoring should be discussed with the employees to alleviate any ambiguities in the employees' minds about the appropriate actions to take when questionable situations arise.

STRESS ON LONG-TERM CUSTOMER RELATIONSHIPS

Service providers must build trusting relationships between themselves and their customers to promote a long-term, mutually beneficial relationship.[25] Ethical marketing practices provide the basis from which such trust-based relationships are formed. Many unethical decisions that are made emphasize the short-run benefits that the decision provides. For example, a service provider may mislead a customer in order to make a quick sale. Service firms who properly socialize their employees should stress the importance of building long-term relationships. Service firms whose employees are oriented toward a long-term customer relationship should be able to minimize the frequency of unethical decision making.

STRATEGIES FOR CONTROLLING THE ETHICAL BEHAVIOR AT SEARS AUTO CENTERS

Strategies for controlling the future ethical behavior of Sears Auto Centers employees might include the following: (1) employee socialization—orientation sessions regarding ethics for new employees; (2) standards of conduct—a code of ethics needs to be developed or reviewed; (3) corrective control—violations of the code of ethics need to be enforced; (4) leadership training—supervisors need to understand that subordinates emulate their behavior and that they are role models, particularly to new employees; (5) service/product training—all employees must be required to have adequate skills so that mechanical problems are not misdiagnosed or unnecessary repairs made; (6) monitor employee performance—assess and discuss behavior utilized to obtain results as well as the results themselves; (7) stress long-term customer relationships—emphasize that long-term satisfaction is more important than meeting the company's short-term (monthly) sales quota.

SUMMARY

This chapter has presented an overview of ethics as they apply to the service sector. Service consumers are particularly vulnerable to ethical misconduct for a variety of reasons. For example, services possess few search attributes and therefore are difficult to evaluate before the purchase decision has been made; services are often technical and/or specialized, making evaluation by the common consumer even more difficult; many services are sold without warranties and/or guarantees and are often provided by unsupervised boundary-spanning personnel. In addition, reward systems that compensate service personnel are often based on results as opposed to the behaviors utilized to achieve those results. Other factors contributing to consumer vulnerability include the time lapse that occurs for some services between service performance and customer evaluation (e.g., financial planning, life insurance, etc.), the inherent variation in service performance, and the consumer's willingness to accept the blame for failing to effectively communicate his or her wishes to the service provider.

The most common ethical issues involve conflict of interest, confidentiality in organizational relationships, honesty, fairness, and the integrity of the firm's communications efforts. The behavior of service providers engaged in ethical decision making reflects the moral philosophies in which they believe. Moral philosophies are the principles or rules service providers use when deciding what

▶▶▶▶ ◀◀◀◀

is right or wrong and include philosophies such as teleology, deontology, and relativism.

Different service personnel may make different decisions under similar ethical situations due to their cognitive moral development and a variety of other factors, including personal values, cultural differences, corporate culture, organizational structure, opportunity, reward systems, significant others, and the pressures of conducting business in a competitive environment.

Employees forced to deal with ethical issues on a continuous basis frequently suffer from job-related tension, frustration, anxiety, ineffective performance, turnover intention, and low job satisfaction.

In addition to the personal effects of ethical misconduct, the organization as a whole is likely to suffer as well. Ethical improprieties have been linked to customer dissatisfaction, unfavorable word-of-mouth publicity, and negative public images for an entire industry.

Organizations have utilized a number of strategies that attempt to control the ethical behavior of employees, including employee socialization, the development and enforcement of codes of ethics, leadership training, service/product knowledge training, monitoring employee performance, and education of employees regarding the benefits of long-term customer relationships.

KEY TERMS

ethics	fairness
business ethics	cognitive moral development
boundary-spanning personnel	personal values
moral philosophies	corporate culture
teleology	cultural differences
consequentialism	organizational structure
egoism	opportunity
utilitarianism	reward systems
deontology	significant others
relativism	employee socialization
conflict of interest	code of ethics
organizational relationships	corrective control
honesty	

REVIEW QUESTIONS

1. Discuss the difference between ethics and social responsibility.

2. How does the public feel about the ethical behaviors of businesspeople?

3. What are boundary-spanning personnel? What provides these employees with the opportunity to engage in ethical misconduct?

4. Does consumer participation in the service delivery process increase or decrease the service provider's opportunity to engage in unethical behavior? Explain.

5. Which moral philosophies best describe your own personal ethical behavior? Explain.

6. Discuss the difference between an egoist and a utilitarianist.

7. Discuss the primary difference between a teleologist and a deontologist.

8. Discuss the theory of differential association.

NOTES

1. Mary L. Nicastro, "Infuse Business Ethics into Marketing Curriculum," *Marketing Educator* 11, 1 (1992), p. 1.

2. *Webster's New Ideal Dictionary* (Springfield, MA: G. & C. Merriam Co., 1973), p. 171.

3. O. C. Ferrell and John Fraedrich, *Business Ethics* (Boston, MA: Houghton Mifflin, 1991), p. 5.

4. Gene R. Laczniak and Patrick E. Murphy, *Ethical Marketing Decisions* (Needham Heights, MA: Allyn and Bacon, 1993), p. 3.

5. Valerie A. Zeithaml, A. Parasuraman, and Leonard L. Berry, "Problems and Strategies in Services Marketing," *Journal of Marketing* 49, 2 (1985), pp. 33–46.

6. K. Douglas Hoffman and Judy A. Siguaw, "Incorporating Ethics into the Services Marketing Course: The Case of the Sears Auto Centers," *Marketing Education Review* 3,3 (1993), pp. 26–32.

7. Ferrell and Fraedrich, *Business Ethics*, pp. 40–48.

8. Ferrell and Fraedrich, *Business Ethics*, p. 42.

9. Ferrell and Fraedrich, *Business Ethics*, p. 45.

10. Ferrell and Fraedrich, *Business Ethics*, pp. 22–29.

11. Ferrell and Fraedrich, *Business Ethics*, pp. 68–133.

12. David J. Fritzsche and Helmet Becker, "Linking Management Behavior to Ethical Philosophy—An Empirical Investigation," *Academy of Management Journal* 27 (1984), pp. 166–175.

13. Alan J. Dubinsky, Marvin A. Jolson, Masaaki Kotabe, and Chae Un Lim, "A Cross-National Investigation of Industrial Salespeople's Ethical Perceptions," *Journal of International Business Studies* 4 (1990), pp. 651–671.

14. Sandra Pelfrey and Eileen Peacock, "Ethical Codes of Conduct Are Improving," *Business Horizons* (Spring 1991), pp. 14–17.

15. O. C. Ferrell and Larry G. Gresham, "A Contingency Framework for Understanding Ethical Decision Making in Marketing," *Journal of Marketing* (Summer 1985), pp. 87–96.

16. Gilbert A. Churchill, Jr., Neil M. Ford, Steven W. Hartley and Orville C. Walker, Jr., "The Determinants of Salesperson Performance: A Meta-Analysis," *Journal of Marketing Research* 22, 2 (1985), pp. 103–118.

17. Ferrell and Fraedrich, *Business Ethics*, p. 110.

18. K. Douglas Hoffman, Vince Howe, and Don Hardigree," Selling of Complex Others and Competitive Pressures," *Journal of Personal Selling and Sales Management* 11, 4 (1991), pp. 13–25.

19. David Shepard, *The New Direct Marketing: How to Implement a Profit-Driven Database Marketing Strategy* (Homewood, IL: Business One Irwin, 1990).

20. Orville C. Walker, Gilbert A. Churchill, and Neil M. Ford, "Where Do We Go from Here: Selected Conceptual and Empirical Issues Concerning the Motivation and Performance of the Industrial Sales Force," in *Critical Issues in Sales Management: State-of-the-Art and Future Research Needs*, G. Albaum and G. A. Churchill, eds. (Eugene, OR: College of Business Administration, University of Oregon, 1979).

21. Ronald W. Vinson, "Industry Image Stuck in Downcycle," *National Underwriter Property & Casualty-Risk & Benefits Management*, January 7, 1991, pp. 25–29.

22. Ferrell and Fraedrich, *Business Ethics*, pp. 137–150.

23. Sandra Pelfrey and Eileen Peacock, "Ethical Codes of Conduct are Improving," *Business Horizons* (Spring 1991), pp. 14–17.

24. C. King, "Prof. Challenges Industry to Face Ethical Issues," *National Underwriter Life & Health-Financial Services*, August 16, 1990, pp. 15–16.

25. Lawrence A. Crosby, Kenneth R. Evans, and Deborah Cowles, "Relationship Quality in Services Selling: An Interpersonal Influence Perspective," *Journal of Marketing* (July 1990), pp. 68–81.

PART 2

SERVICE STRATEGY: MANAGING THE SERVICE EXPERIENCE

Part 2 is dedicated to managing the service encounter. Due to consumer involvement in the production of services, many challenges for management occur that rarely, if ever, need to be considered in the production of goods. In this part, you will learn about the strategic issues that affect both the marketing mix and the components of the servuction model.

6

S ERVICE D ELIVERY P ROCESS

" C *ustomers cannot be satisfied until after*

they are not dissatisfied. Your first service priority should be to eliminate all the opportunities

for dissatisfying customers, because they are what cause customers to leave.

Then you can invest in satisfying and delighting them."

Jim Donnelly, Jr., *Close to the Customer* (Homewood, IL: Business One Irwin, 1992)

C H A P T E R   O B J E C T I V E S

The main objective in this chapter is to familiarize you with operations
concepts and explain the importance of balancing operations and
marketing functions in service operations.
After reading this chapter, you should be able to

► Discuss the relationship between operations and marketing as it pertains to developing service delivery systems.

    ► *Discuss the type of operation that would typify peak efficiency.*

► Describe the difficulties associated with applying efficiency models to service organizations.

    ► *Describe alternative strategies available to facilitate the balance of supply and demand.*

► Discuss the fundamental components of a service blueprint.

    ► *Understand the necessary calculations for determining the service cost per output.*

► Discuss the strategies available for new service development.

SOMETIMES IT'S WHAT THEY CAN'T SEE
THAT DRIVES CUSTOMERS AWAY

When moving to North Carolina several years ago, a customer rented the largest moving truck that U-Haul offered, which cost approximately $1,200. He also purchased several U-Haul boxes, some masking tape, and other moving accessories. With the help of many friends, the customer loaded the truck and began the 600 mile trip to the east coast. The truck worked like a charm. It was clean, the air conditioning and radio worked, the cab of the truck was immaculate, and all in all, it was relatively easy to handle on the highway.

Everything was great until the customer went to return the truck after he reached his destination. The peculiar thing is that the problem did not have anything to do with the truck. The problem occurred when he wanted to return a $3.95 dish box. It seemed that U-Haul had implemented a new inventory control system that required customers to provide receipts with any items they wished to return. The objective of the new system was to identify any box's original place of purchase so that it could be taken out of inventory at that location and then re-entered into inventory where the return was taking place.

Unfortunately, the customer had not kept his receipt for the $3.95 dish box. Why keep it? The box had "U-Haul" plastered all over its outside, so it was fairly obvious from whom the box had been purchased. Second, the customer knew exactly which U-Haul distribution center from which he had purchased the box. He offered that information to the U-Haul representative, but she informed him of the new inventory control system and insisted that he needed the receipt in order for her to process the refund.

The customer's next problem was that he was not able to get upset with the U-Haul representative. She was obviously doing what she was told to do. In fact, when he reminded her that he had just spent $1,200.00 on one of her company's trucks and yet it was refusing his return of a $3.95 dish box, she responded with, "Yeah, it's just crazy, isn't it!" The funny thing was that she really meant it—she offered to give him the "800" number for U-Haul customer service so that he could complain.

The lesson learned from this experience is that someone, somewhere within the confines of U-Haul's headquarters, someone who probably has little, if any, contact with customers developed what he or she thought was an efficient method of monitoring inventory levels throughout the company. However, U-Haul failed to recognize how this change, which took place in the invisible organization and systems component of the servuction model, would affect the customer, not to mention U-Haul's own representatives, who would now have to field customer complaints about the new procedures. It was ludicrous to turn away a customer who just spent more than $1,000 for a $3.95 return. However, the new "process" had accomplished exactly that.

INTRODUCTION

The purpose of this chapter is to highlight the fact that operations management problems in services cannot be solved by the operations function alone. The search for operations efficiency can be crucial to long-term competitiveness. However, efficiency must be balanced against the effectiveness of the system from the customer's point of view. Table 6.1 provides a quick glimpse into the major trade-offs between efficiency and customer service when developing operations for low-customer-contact versus high-customer-contact services.

Frequently, it is too easy to view the customer as a constraint: "If we could get rid of all these customers, we could run a good service operation!" Such a negative perspective ignores a golden opportunity. Customers in a service operation can be used to help operations. Such a positive view, does, however, require that operations personnel recognize the importance of their marketing counterparts.

More importantly, such a view also requires that marketing personnel have an intimate knowledge of the operations system and its problems. It is not enough to propose new products that can be delivered through the system. The impact of such products on the whole system must be considered.[1] For example, consider the newly constructed, multi-billion-dollar Denver International Airport and its ill-fated automated luggage system that caused huge delays in the opening of the facility. The airport's opening was postponed so often that locals started referring to DIA as "Done in April . . . Ugh, Done in August, Done in Awhile, and Doesn't Include Airplanes."[2]

THE CUSTOMER'S INVOLVEMENT IN THE PRODUCTION PROCESS

The servuction model presented in Chapter 1 clearly demonstrates that consumers are an integral part of the service process. Their participation may be active or passive, but they are always there. If the consumer is in the factory, it is clear that if the factory is changed, consumer behavior will have to be changed. Clearly, changes to the visible part of the service firm will be apparent to the consumer. Moreover, the changes frequently demand that the consumer change his or her behavior to adapt to the new procedures.

For example, when convenience stores first opened, gasoline was not part of the product offering. The introduction of gasoline to the product mix presented two new challenges to consumers. First, from a psychological standpoint, the initial thought of buying gasoline at the same location as food products was resisted. Gasoline stations at the time were generally dirty, grimy places staffed by burly men who had years of grit built up under their fingernails. A gasoline station was hardly the place one wanted to buy food. The second challenge, having customers pump their own gas, created a change in operations that required a change in

TABLE 6.1 MAJOR DESIGN TRADE-OFFS IN HIGH- AND LOW-CONTACT SYSTEMS

Decision	High-Contact System	Low-Contact System
Facility location	Operations must be near the customer.	Operations may be placed near supply, transportation, or labor.
Facility layout	Facility should accomodate the customer's physical and psychological needs and expectations.	Facility should enhance production.
Product design	Environment as well as the physical product define the nature of the service.	Customer is not in the service environment so the product can be defined by fewer attributes.
Process design	Stages of production process have a direct immediate effect on the customer.	Customer is not involved in the majority of processing steps.
Scheduling	Customer is in the production schedule and must be accomodated.	Customer is concerned mainly with completion dates.
Production planning	Orders cannot be stored, so smoothing production flow will result in loss of business.	Both backlogging and production smoothing are possible.
Worker skills	Direct work force makes up a major part of the service product and so must be able to interact well with the public.	Direct work force need have only technical skills.
Quality control	Quality standards are often in the eye of the beholder and, hence, variable.	Quality standards are generally measurable and, hence, fixed.
Time standards	Service time depends on customer needs, so time standards are inherently loose.	Work is performed on customer surrogates (e.g., forms), and time standards can be tight.
Wage payment	Variable output requires time-based wage systems.	"Fixable" outputs permits output-based wage systems.
Capacity planning	To avoid lost sales, capacity must be set to match peak demand.	Storable output permits setting capacity at some average demand level.
Forecasting	Forecasts are short term, time oriented.	Forecasts are long term, output oriented.

Source: Richard C. Chase, "Where Does the Customer Fit in a Service Operation?" *Harvard Business Review* (November–December 1978), pp. 137–142. Reprinted by permission of *Harvard Business Review*. Copyright © 1978 by the President and Fellows of Harvard College.

consumer behavior. Consumers had to learn how to work a gas pump, and the convenience store and gasoline pump manufacturers had to develop gas pumps and monitoring procedures for this new type of self-service operation.

It can be argued that a decision to change the benefit concept developed for the consumer, such as providing self-service operations, has a far greater impact on a service firm than on a goods firm. Both types of firms will probably have to change their factory procedures. However, many of the changes made in the service firm will be directly visible to the consumer, including the customer service disasters that are likely to occur during the startup of the operation.

Managers of service firms must understand the interactive nature of services and the involvement of the consumer in the production process. As we discussed in Chapter Four, consumers appear to develop a script for frequently used services. This script is similar to a theatrical script in that it helps guide the consumer through the service experience. Changes in the service factory process will imply changes in the consumer script—the way in which the consumer participates in the process.

SERVICE DELIVERY PROCESS

Pumping your own gasoline at a convenience station is a commonly accepted practice today. The change in operations also required a change in consumer behavior.

Source: © 1995 PhotoDisc, Inc. Image no. 2112.

New developments coming from either the service factory or the consumer imply major changes in the consumer script as well as changes in the scripts of contact personnel. This chapter highlights the trade-offs between the search for operational efficiency and the need to create marketing effectiveness. In the service factory, many of the traditional methods for increasing operational effectiveness cannot be implemented behind closed doors. In fact, changes made to increase the service operation's efficiency can often downgrade the final service product, as was the customer's experience with U-Haul. This chapter focuses on the positive things marketing can achieve to help improve the efficiency of the servuction system.

MARKETING AND OPERATIONS: BALANCE IS CRITICAL

In a broad sense, one way of viewing the task of marketing is to think of it as the marrying of consumers' needs with the technology and manufacturing capabilities of the firm. Such a marriage will obviously involve compromises since the consumers' needs can seldom be met completely and economically. In a goods firm, this marriage requires marketing's understanding of the capabilities of manufacturing and of research and development. The task of marketing goods is made somewhat easier because the different functions can be separated by means of an inventory.

In a service firm, this marketing problem is magnified. Significant aspects of the operation *are* the product since they create the interactive experience that delivers the bundle of benefits to the consumer. For example, a restaurant experience is not based solely on the quality of the food. The physical environment and interactions with contact personnel throughout the experience also affect consumer perceptions of the quality of service delivered. A successful compromise between operations efficiency and marketing effectiveness is, therefore, that much more difficult to achieve. Success in services marketing demands a much greater understanding of the constraints and opportunities posed by operations.

To introduce these complexities, in this chapter we first adopt the perspective of an operations manager and ask, "What would be the ideal way to run the system from an operations perspective?" The impact on marketing and the opportunities for marketing to assist in the creation of this ideal are then developed.

As pointed out in Chapter One, the key distinctive characteristic of services is that the product is an experience. That experience is created by the operating system of the firm's interaction with the customer. Thus, the operating system of the firm, in all its complexity, is the product. For a marketing manager, this imposes constraints on the strategies that can be employed, but it also presents new and challenging opportunities for improving the profitability of the firm.

Chapter Four provided one base on which to build an understanding of the product design problem for services. An understanding of consumer behavior has always been a necessary condition for successful marketing. One way of viewing the product design process is to think of it as the process of combining such an understanding with the technological and manufacturing skills of the organization. To be an effective services marketer, a knowledge of consumer behavior is not sufficient in itself to produce economically successful products.

As we discussed in Chapter Two, in a goods firm it is possible to separate the problems of manufacturing and marketing by the use of inventory. Even so, there are many areas of potential conflict, as can be viewed in Table 6.2. Although the issues are characterized as conflicts, they can be reconceptualized as opportunities. In each area it is clear that a better integration of marketing and manufacturing plans could yield a more efficient and profitable organization. For example, the determination of the extent of the product line should be seen as a compromise between the heterogeneous demands of consumers and the manufacturing demand of homogeneity. If marketing managers have their way, too many products will probably be developed, and the operation will become inefficient. As long as this is compensated for by higher prices, then a successful strategy can be implemented. In contrast, if the operations people have their way, everyone would be driving the same model of car, painted the same color, which is less attractive for consumers. As long as this is compensated for by lower costs and hence lower prices, a successful strategy can emerge.

Marketing and operations are in a tug-of-war that should be resolved by compromise. In the service sector, the possible areas of conflict or compromise are much broader because the operation itself is the product. Again, there is no single solution since operational efficiency and marketing effectiveness may push in opposite directions.

TABLE 6.2	SOURCES OF COOPERATION/CONFLICT BETWEEN MARKETING AND OPERATIONS	
Problem Area	**Typical Marketing Comment**	**Typical Manufacturing Comment**
1. Capacity planning and long-range sales forecasting	"Why don't we have enough capacity?"	"Why didn't we have accurate sales forecasts?"
2. Production scheduling and short-range sales forecasting	"We need faster response. Our lead times are ridiculous."	"We need realistic customer commitments and sales forecasts that don't change like wind direction."
3. Delivery and physical distribution	"Why don't we ever have the right merchandise in inventory?"	"We can't keep everything in inventory."
4. Quality assurance	"Why can't we have reasonable quality at reasonable costs?"	"Why must we always offer options that are too hard to manufacture and that offer little customer utility?"
5. Breadth of product line	"Our customers demand variety."	"The product line is too broad—all we get are short, uneconomical runs."
6. Cost control	"Our costs are so high that we are not competitive in the marketplace."	"We can't provide fast delivery, broad variety, rapid response to change, and high quality at low cost."
7. New product introduction	"New products are our lifeblood."	"Unnecessary design changes are prohibitively expensive."
8. Adjunct services such as spare parts, inventory support, installation, and repair	"Field service costs are too high."	"Products are being used in ways for which they weren't designed."

Source: Reprinted by permission of the *Harvard Business Review*. An exhibit from "Can Marketing and Manufacturing Coexist?" by Benson P. Shapiro (September/October 1977), p. 105. Copyright © 1977 by the President and Fellows of Harvard College; all rights reserved.

By its very nature, this chapter is meant to be operations oriented rather than marketing oriented. To polarize the issues, the perspective adopted in this chapter is that of the operations manager, just as in Chapter Four the consumer's position was presented. The focus is on the requirements for operational efficiency and the ways that marketing can help achieve those requirements. We stress that in the drive for competitive advantage in the marketplace, marketing demand may in the end mean less operational efficiency. As the amount of customer contact increases, the likelihood that the service firm will operate efficiently decreases. Customers determine the type of demand, the cycle of demand, and the length of the service experience; meanwhile, the service firm loses more and more control over its daily operations. It's the nature of the service business.

IN A PERFECT WORLD, SERVICE FIRMS WOULD BE EFFICIENT

THOMPSON'S PERFECT-WORLD MODEL

technical core

The place within an organization where its primary operations are conducted.

The starting point for this discussion is the work of J. D. Thompson.[3] Thompson, who started from an organizational perspective, introduced the idea of a **technical core**—the place within the organization where its primary operations are conducted. In the service sector, the technical core consists of kitchens in restaurants, garages in gasoline stations, work areas at dry cleaners, and surgical suites in a hospital. Thompson proposed in his **perfect-world model** that to operate efficiently, a firm must be able to operate "as if the market will absorb the single kind of product at a continuous rate and as if the inputs flowed continuously at a steady rate and with specified quality." At the center of his argument was the idea that uncertainty creates inefficiency. In the ideal situation, the technical core is able to operate without uncertainty on both the input and output side, thereby creating many advantages for management.

The absence of uncertainty means that decisions within the core can become programmed and that individual discretion can be replaced by rules; the removal of individual discretion means that jobs are "de-skilled" and that a lower quality of labor can be used. Alternatively, the rules can be programmed into machines and labor replaced with capital. Because output and input are fixed, it is simple to plan production and to run at the high levels of utilization needed to generate the most efficient operations performance.

A system without uncertainty is easy to control and manage. Performance can be measured using objective standards. And since the system is not subject to disturbances from the outside, the causes of any problems are also easy to diagnose.

THE FOCUSED FACTORY CONCEPT

Obviously, such an ideal world as proposed by Thompson is virtually impossible to create, and even in goods companies the demands of purchasing the inputs and marketing's management of the outputs have to be traded off against the ideal operations demands. In goods manufacturing, this trade-off has been accomplished through the **focused factory**.[4] The focused factory focuses on a particular job; once this focus is achieved, the factory does a better job because repetition and concentration in one area allow the work force and managers to become effective and experienced in the task required for success. The focused factory broadens Thompson's perfect-world model in that it argues that focus generates effectiveness as well as efficiency. In other words, the focused factory can meet the demands of the market better whether the demand is low cost through efficiency, high quality, or any other criterion.

THE PLANT-WITHIN-A-PLANT-CONCEPT

The idea of a focused factory can be extended in another direction by introducing the **plant-within-a-plant (PWP)** concept. Because there are advantages to having production capability at a single site, the plant-within-a-plant strategy introduces the concept of breaking up large, unfocused plants into smaller units buffered from one another so that they can each be focused separately.

perfect-world model
J. D. Thompson's model of organizations proposing that operations' "perfect" efficiency is possible only if inputs, outputs, and quality happen at a constant rate and remain known and certain.

focused factory
An operation that concentrates on performing one particular task in one particular part of the plant; used for promoting experience and effectiveness through repetition and concentration on one task necessary for success.

plant within a plant
The strategy of breaking up large, unfocused plants into smaller units buffered from one another so that each can be focused separately.

SERVICE DELIVERY PROCESS

buffering

Surrounding the technical core with input and output components to buffer environmental influences.

smoothing

Managing the environment to reduce fluctuations in supply and/or demand.

anticipating

Mitigating the worst effects of supply and demand fluctuations by planning for them.

rationing

Direct allocations of inputs and outputs when the demands placed on a system by the environment exceed the system's ability to handle them.

In goods manufacturing, the concept of **buffering** is a powerful one. "Organizations seek to buffer environmental influences by surrounding their technical core with input and output components."[5] A PWP can thus be operated in a manner close to Thompson's perfect-world model if buffer inventories are created on the input and output sides. On the input side, the components needed in a plant can be inventoried and their quality controlled before they are needed; in this way, it can appear to the PWP that the quality and flow of the inputs into the system are constant. In a similar way, the PWP can be separated from downstream plants or from the market by creating finished goods inventories.

The alternatives proposed by Thompson to buffering are smoothing, anticipating, and rationing. Smoothing and anticipating focus on the uncertainty introduced into the system by the flow of work; **smoothing** involves managing the environment to reduce fluctuations in supply and/or demand, and **anticipating** involves mitigating the worst effects of those fluctuations by planning for them. Finally, **rationing** involves resorting to triage when the demands placed on the system by the environment exceed its ability to handle them.

APPLYING THE EFFICIENCY MODELS TO SERVICES

The application of operations concepts to services is fraught with difficulty. The problem can be easily understood by thinking about the servuction model presented in Chapter One. From an operational point of view, the key characteristics of the model are that the customer is an integral part of the process and that the system operates in realtime. Because the system is interactive, it can be (and often is) used to customize the service for each individual.

The servuction system itself is an operations nightmare since it is impossible to use inventories and impossible to decouple production from the customer. Instead of receiving demand at a constant rate, the system is linked directly to a market that frequently varies from day to day, hour to hour, and even minute to minute. This creates massive problems in capacity planning and utilization.

It is clear from this simplified model that services, by their very nature, do not meet the requirements of the perfect-world model. The closest the servuction model comes to this ideal state is the part of the system that is invisible to the customer. Even here, however, the customization taking place may introduce uncertainty into the system. Providing that all customization can take place within the servuction system itself, then the part invisible to the customer can be run separately. It can often be located in a place different from the customer contact portion of the model.[6] However, when customization cannot be done within the servuction system, uncertainty can be introduced into the back office.

Instead of "the single kind of product" desired by the perfect-world model, the service system can be called upon to make a different "product" for each customer. Indeed, one could argue that since each customer is different and is an integral part of the process, and since each experience or product is unique, the uncertainty about the next task to be performed is massive.

The Thompson model specifies inputs that flow continuously, at a steady rate, and at a specified quality. Consider the inputs to the servuction system: the physical environment, contact personnel, other customers, and the individual customer. The environment may remain constant in many service encounters, but the other three inputs are totally variable, not only in their quality, but also in their rate of arrival into the process.

Moreover, contact personnel are individuals, not inanimate objects. They have emotions and feelings and, like all other people, are affected by things happening in their lives outside work. If they arrive in a bad mood, this can influence their performance throughout the day. And that bad mood directly affects the customer, since the service worker is part of the experience being purchased.

Customers can also be subject to moods that can affect their behavior toward the service firm and toward one another. Some moods are predictable, like the mood when a home team wins and the crowds hit the local bars. Other moods are individual, specific, and totally unpredictable until after the consumer is already part of the servuction system.

Finally, customers arrive at the service firm at unpredictable rates, making smoothing and anticipation of incoming demand difficult. One minute a restaurant can be empty, and in the next few minutes, it can be full. One need only consider the variability of demand for cashiers in a grocery store to understand the basics of this problem. Analysis of demand can often show predictable peaks that can be planned for in advance; but even this precaution introduces inefficiency into the firm since the firm would ideally prefer the customers to arrive in a steady stream. Worse still are the unpredictable peaks. Planning for these peaks would produce large amounts of excess capacity at most times. The excess would strain the entire system, undermining the experience for customer and contact personnel alike.

POTENTIAL SOLUTIONS TO SERVICE OPERATIONS PROBLEMS

Within the operations management literature of the past decade is a growing body of ideas about how to overcome some of the problems of service operations. These ideas can be classified into four broad areas: isolating the technical core; minimizing the servuction system; production-lining the whole system (including the servuction system); and creating flexible capacity. Other solutions, such as moving the time of demand and increasing customer participation, have been suggested in the marketing literature.

ISOLATING THE TECHNICAL CORE AND MINIMIZING THE SERVUCTION SYSTEM

The Operations Perspective Isolating the technical core of the service firm and minimizing the servuction system have been combined because they are closely related from an operations viewpoint and because their marketing implications are similar.

SERVICE DELIVERY PROCESS

Unpredictable arrivals of customers can make it difficult to meet the needs of consumers. When an unexpected flow of customers descends upon a service provider such as this coffee bar, the contact personnel may experience the same anger and frustration as the consumer.

Source: © 1995 PhotoDisc, Inc. Image no. 21013.

This approach proposes the clear separation of the servuction system, which is characterized by a high degree of customer contact, from the technical core. Once separation is achieved, different management philosophies should be adopted for each separate unit of operation.

In the servuction system, management should focus on optimizing the experience for the consumer. Conversely, once the technical core has been isolated, it should be subjected to traditional production-lining approaches.[7] In sum, high-contact systems should sacrifice efficiency in the interest of the customer, but low-contact systems need not do so.[8]

Isolating the technical core argues for minimizing the amount of customer contact with the system. "Clients . . . pose problems for organizations . . . by disrupting their routines, ignoring their offers for service, failing to comply with their procedures, making exaggerated demands and so forth."[9] Operating efficiency is thus reduced by the uncertainty introduced into the system by the customer.[10]

decoupling

Disassociating the technical core from the servuction system.

Examples of **decoupling** the technical core from the servuction system include suggestions from operations experts such as handling only exceptions on a face-to-face basis, with routine transactions as much as possible being handled by telephone or, even better, by mail—mail transactions have the great advantage of being able to be inventoried.[11] In addition, the degree of customer contact should be matched to customer requirements, and the amount of high-contact service offered should be the minimum acceptable to the customer.[12] Overall, operational efficiency always favors low-contact systems, but effectiveness from the customer's point of view may be something completely different.

The Marketing Perspective At this point, the need for marketing involvement in the approach becomes clear, as a decision about the extent of customer contact favored by the customer is clearly a marketing issue. In some cases, a high degree of customer contact can be used to differentiate the service from its competitors; in such cases, the operational costs must be weighed against the competitive benefits.

Conversely, in some situations, the segment of the firm that the operations group views as the back office is not actually invisible to the customer. For example, in some financial services, the teller operation takes place in the administrative offices. Operationally, this means that staff members can leave their paperwork to serve customers only when needed. Unfortunately, customers view this operationally efficient system negatively. A customer waiting to be served can see a closed teller window and observe staff who apparently do not care because they sit at their desks without offering to assist the customer. However, the reality is that these tellers may be very busy, but the nature of the administrative work is such that they may not give this impression to customers.

Even if it is decided that part of the system can be decoupled, marketing has a major role in evaluating and implementing alternative approaches. Any change in the way in which the servuction system works implies a change in the behavior of the customer. A switch from a personal service to a combined mail and telephone system clearly requires a massive change in the way the customer behaves in the system.

Sometimes decoupling the system to become more efficient does not go over well with customers. For example, in its effort to make its tellers use their time more efficiently, First National Bank of Chicago made national news when it started charging customers with certain types of accounts a $3.00 fee for speaking with a bank teller. The bank's Chicago competition had a field day with promotions, featuring "live tellers" and giving away "free" money at their teller windows. Even Jay Leno, from NBC's "The Tonight Show" got in on the act: "Nice day isn't it? . . . That'll be $3.00 please. Huh?, What? Who? . . . That'll be another $9.00 please."[13]

Production-Lining the Whole System

The **production-line approach** involves the application of hard and soft technologies to both the "front" and "back" of the service operation.[14] **Hard technologies** involve hardware to facilitate the production of a standardized product. Similarly, **soft technologies** refer to rules, regulations, and procedures that should be followed to produce the same result. This kind of approach to increasing operational efficiency is relatively rare, and, indeed, fast-food firms provide a classic example in which customization is minimal, volume is large, and customer participation in the process is high.

Generating any kind of operational efficiency in such a servuction system implies a limited product line. In the case of fast-food, the product line is the

production-line approach
The application of hard and soft technologies to a service operation in order to produce a standardized service product.

hard technologies
Hardware that facilitates the production of a standardized product.

soft technologies
Rules, regulations, and procedures that facilitate the production of a standardized product.

menu. Moreover, customization must be kept to a minimum since the whole operating system is linked straight through to the consumer. The primary problem is how to provide efficient, standardized service at some acceptable level of quality while simultaneously treating each customer as unique.[15] Past attempts to solve this problem illustrate its complexity. Attempts at forms of routine personalization such as the "have-a-nice-day" syndrome have had positive effects on the perceived friendliness of the service provider but have had adverse effects on perceived competence. Consequently, an apparently simple operations decision can have complex effects on customer perceptions.

The servuction system applied to fast food also depends for its success on a large volume of customers being available to take the food that is produced. Since the invisible component is not decoupled and food cannot be prepared to order, the operating system has to run independently of individual demand and assume that, in the end, aggregate demand will absorb the food produced.

Such an operating system is extremely demanding of its customers. They must preselect what they want to eat. They are expected to have their order ready when they reach the order point. They must leave the order point quickly and carry their food to the table. Finally, in many cases, these same customers are expected to bus their own tables.

Creating Flexible Capacity

As pointed out in Chapter Two, the few times that supply matches demand during service encounters occur primarily by accident. One method used to minimize the effects of variable demand is to create flexible capacity (supply).[16] However, even in this area, strategies that start as common-sense operational solutions have far-reaching marketing implications as these new initiatives come face-to-face with the service firm's customer base. For example, a few of the strategies to create flexible capacity mentioned in Chapter Two included (1) using part-time employees; (2) cross-training employees so that the majority of employee efforts focus on customer-contact jobs during peak hours; and (3) sharing capacity with other firms.

Although these strategies are fairly straightforward from an operational point of view, consider their marketing implications. Part-time employees appear to be a useful strategy since they can be used to provide extra capacity in peak times without increasing the costs in off-peak times. There are, however, a number of marketing implications. For example, part-time employees may deliver a lower-quality service than full-time workers; their dedication to quality may be less, as will probably be their training. They are used at times when the operation is at its busiest, such as Christmas or during tourist seasons, when demand is fast and furious, and this may be reflected in their attitudes of frustration, which can be highly visible to customers and negatively influence customer perceptions of the quality of service delivered.[17]

In a similar way, the other two possible solutions for creating flexible capacity also have major marketing implications. First, focusing on customer contact jobs during peak demand presupposes that it is possible to identify the key part of the service from the customer's point of view. Secondly, the dangers of sharing capacity are numerous. For example, the television show "Cheers" provided ample examples of the problems associated with the upscale and upstairs customers of Melville's Restaurant as they mixed with Cheers everyday clientele such as Norm and Cliff. Confusion may be produced in the customer's mind over exactly what the service facility is doing, and this could be particularly critical during changeover times when customers from two different firms are in the same facility, each group with different priorities and different scripts.

INCREASING CUSTOMER PARTICIPATION

The essence of increasing customer participation is to replace the work done by the employees of the firm with work done by the customer.[18] Unlike the other strategies discussed, which focus on improving the efficiency of the operation, this approach primarily focuses on reducing the costs associated with providing the service to the customer. This strategy, too, has its trade-offs.

Consider for a moment our earlier discussions about consumer scripts. Increasing consumer participation in the service encounter requires a substantial modification of the consumer's script. Moreover, the customers are called upon to take greater responsibility for the service they receive. For example, the automatic teller machine is seen by many operations personnel as a way of saving labor. In fact, the substitution of human labor with machines is a classic operations approach, and the ATM can definitely be viewed in that light. From a customer's point of view, such ATMs provide added convenience in terms of the hours during which the bank is accessible. However, it has been shown that for some customers, an ATM represents increased risk, less control of the situation, and a loss of human contact.[19]

Such a switching of activities to the customer clearly has major market implications since the whole nature of the product received is changing. Such changes in the customer's script, therefore, require much customer research and detailed planning.

MOVING THE TIME OF DEMAND TO FIT CAPACITY

Finally, yet another strategy utilized to optimize the efficiency of service operations is the attempt to shift the time of demand to smooth the peaks and valleys associated with many services. Perhaps the classic example of this problem is the mass transit system that needs to create capacity to deal with the rush hour and, as a consequence, has much of its fleet and labor idle during nonrush hours. Many mass transit authorities have attempted to reduce the severity of the problem by inducing customers through discounts and give-aways to travel during nonrush periods. Once again, operations and marketing become intertwined. Smoothing demand is a useful strategy from an operations point of view; however, this strategy fails to recognize the change in consumer behavior needed to make the strategy effective. Unfortunately, because much of the travel on the mass transit system is derived from demand based on consumer work schedules, little success in the effort to reallocate demand can be expected.[20]

The Art of Blueprinting

blueprinting
The flowcharting of a service operation.

One of the most common techniques used to analyze and manage complex production processes in pursuit of operational efficiency is flowcharting. Flowcharts identify the directions in which processes flow, the time it takes to move from one process to the next, the costs involved with each process step, the amount of inventory build-up at each step, and the bottlenecks in the system. The flowcharting of a service operation, commonly referred to as **blueprinting,** is a useful tool not only for the operations manager but for the marketing manager as well.[21]

Because services are delivered by an interactive process involving the consumer, the marketing manager in a service firm needs to have a detailed knowledge of the operation. Blueprinting provides a useful systematic method for acquiring that knowledge. Blueprints enable the marketing manager to understand which parts in the operating system are visible to the consumer and hence part of the servuction system—the fundamental building blocks of consumer perceptions.

Identifying the components of an individual firm's servuction system turns out to be more difficult than it first appears. Many firms, for example, underestimate the number of points of contact between them and their customers. Many forget or underestimate the importance of telephone operators, secretarial and janitorial staff, or accounting personnel. The material that follows describes the simple process of flowcharting these numerous points of contact. Service flowcharts, in addition to being useful to the operations managers, allow marketing managers to better understand the servuction process.

The heart of the service product is the experience of the consumer, which takes place in realtime. This interaction can occur in a building or in an environment created by the service firm, such as the complex environments that are created at Disney World, Epcot Center, and Universal Studios. In some instances, such as lawncare, the service interaction takes place in a natural setting. It is the interactive process itself that creates the benefits desired by the consumer. Designing that process, therefore, becomes key to the product design for a service firm.

The interactive process that is visible to consumers develops consumers' perceptions of reality and defines the final service product. However, as the servuction model discussed in Chapter One demonstrated, the visible part of the operations process, with which the consumer interacts, must be supported by an invisible process.

The search for operational efficiency is not unique to service firms, but it does pose some interesting problems. A change in the service operation may be more efficient, but it may also change the quality of interaction with the consumer. For example, students at many universities are now able to register for classes through automated telephone services. This type of operation offers increased efficiency but sometimes minimizes the quality of the student/advisor interaction. A detailed blueprint provides a means of communications between operations and marketing and can highlight potential problems on paper before they occur in realtime.

AN EXAMPLE OF A SIMPLE BLUEPRINT[22]

Figure 6.1 shows a simple process in which, for now, it is assumed that the entire operation is visible to the customer. It represents the blueprint of a cafeteria-style restaurant and specifies the steps involved in getting a meal. In this example, each process activity is represented by a box. In contrast to a goods manufacturer, the "raw materials" flowing through the process are the customers. Due to the intangibility of services, there are no inventories in the process, but clearly, inventories of customers form at each step in the process while they wait their turn to proceed to the next counter. A restaurant run in this manner would be a single long chain of counters with customers progressing along the chain and emerging after paying, such as a Western Sizzlin' or Golden Corral. In Figure 6.1, the cost figure by each stage represents the cost of providing personnel to service each counter.

To calculate the **service cost per meal,** or the labor costs associated with providing the meal on a per-meal basis, the following calculations are made. First, the **process time** is calculated by dividing the **activity time** (the time required to perform the activity) by the number of **stations,** or locations performing the activity. In our example, the process and activity times are the same because only one station is available for each activity.

Second, the **maximum output per hour** for each location is calculated based on the process time. Simply stated, the maximum output per hour is the number of people that can be served at each station in an hour's time. For example, the process time at the salad counter is 30 seconds. This means that two people can be processed in a minute, or 120 people (2 people × 60 minutes) in an hour. Another easy way to calculate the maximum output per hour is to use the formula: 60(60/process time). In our example, the salad counter calculation would be 60(60/30)=120.

Finally, to calculate the service cost per meal, total labor costs per hour of the entire system are divided by the maximum output per hour for the system (total labor costs/maximum output per hour). Total labor costs per hour are calculated by simply adding the hourly wages of personnel stationed at each counter. In our example, total labor cost per hour equals $32.00 (5 + 5 + 5 + 5 + 5 + 7). Maximum output per hour is determined by selecting the lowest maximum output calculated in the second step. Hence, the service cost per meal in our example is $32.00/60 customers, or $0.53 per meal.

Why would you use the lowest maximum output per hour? This step is particularly confusing for some students. The lowest maximum output in the system is

service cost per meal

The labor costs associated with providing a meal on a per-meal basis (total labor costs/maximum output per hour).

process time

Calculated by dividing the activity time by the number of locations at which the activity is performed.

activity time

The time required to perform one activity at one station.

stations

A location at which an activity is performed.

maximum output per hour

The number of people that can be processed at each station in one hour.

SERVICE DELIVERY PROCESS

BLUEPRINT FOR CAFETERIA-STYLE RESTAURANT

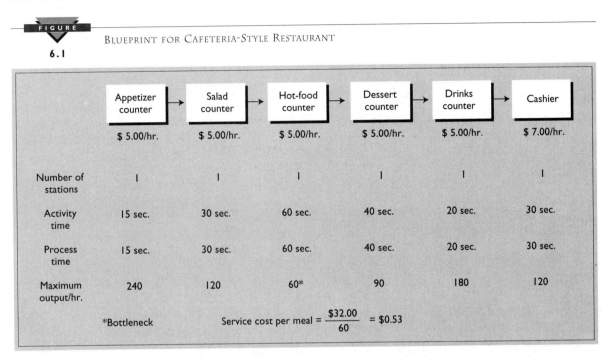

	Appetizer counter	Salad counter	Hot-food counter	Dessert counter	Drinks counter	Cashier
	$ 5.00/hr.	$ 5.00/hr.	$ 5.00/hr.	$ 5.00/hr.	$ 5.00/hr.	$ 7.00/hr.
Number of stations	1	1	1	1	1	1
Activity time	15 sec.	30 sec.	60 sec.	40 sec.	20 sec.	30 sec.
Process time	15 sec.	30 sec.	60 sec.	40 sec.	20 sec.	30 sec.
Maximum output/hr.	240	120	60*	90	180	120

*Bottleneck   Service cost per meal = $\dfrac{\$32.00}{60}$ = $0.53

the maximum number of people who can be processed through the entire system in a hour's time. In our example, 240 customers can be processed through the appetizer counter in an hour; however, only 120 customers can be processed through the salad counter in the same amount of time. This means that after the first hour, 120 customers (240 − 120) are still waiting to be processed through the salad counter. Similarly, only 60 customers can be processed through the hot-food counter in an hour's time. Since 60 is the lowest maximum output per hour for any counter in the system, only 60 customers can actually complete the entire system in an hour.

THE SERVICE OPERATIONS MANAGER'S PERSPECTIVE

The first thing the blueprint does is provide a check on the logical flow of the whole process. Clearly, a service blueprint makes it immediately apparent if a task is being performed out of sequence. At this point, we shall place a constraint on our example system that the cashier's station is fixed and cannot be moved to another point in the process. All other stations can be moved and resequenced.

Once the different steps have been identified, it is relatively easy to identify the potential **bottlenecks** in the system. Bottlenecks represent points in the system where consumers wait the longest periods of time. In Figure 6.1, the hot-food counter is an obvious bottleneck since it represents the longest process time—the

bottlenecks

Points in the system at which consumers wait the longest periods of time.

time to process one individual through that stage. A balanced production line is one in which the process times of all the steps are the same and inventories or, in our case, consumers flow smoothly through the system without waiting for the next process.

To solve this particular bottleneck problem, we could consider adding one extra station, in this case an extra counter, to the hot-food stage. The process time would drop to 30 seconds (60 seconds divided by 2). The bottleneck would then become the dessert counter, which has a process time of 40 seconds and a maximum turnover rate of 90 persons per hour. Costs would go up by $5.00 per hour; however, the service cost per meal would go down to $0.41 per meal. These changes are illustrated in Figure 6.2.

The creative use of additional counters and staff may produce a model such as that shown in Figure 6.3, which combines certain activities and uses multiple stations. This particular layout is capable of handling 120 customers per hour compared with the original layout presented in Figure 6.1. Although labor costs rise, the service cost per meal falls because of the increase in number of consumers that are processed through the system in a shorter period of time. Further changes to this particular setup would be fruitless. Adding counters at the bottlenecks created by both the dessert/drinks and cashier counters would actually increase the service cost per meal from $0.31 ($37.00/120 meals) to $0.36 ($49.00/137.14 meals).

THE SERVICE MARKETING MANAGER'S PERSPECTIVE

A marketing manager dealing with the process illustrated in Figure 6.1 has some of the same problems as the operations manager. The process as defined is designed to operate at certain production levels, and these are the service standards that customers should perceive. But if the process is capable of processing only 60 customer per hour, there may be a problem. For example, lunch customers who need to return to work quickly might purchase their lunches at a competing restaurant that serves its customers more efficiently. Also, it is clear that the bottleneck at the hot-food counter will produce lengthy, possibly frustrating, waits within the line.

The marketing manager should immediately recognize the benefits of changing the system to process customers more effectively. However, the blueprint also shows the change in consumer behavior that would be required in order for the new system to operate. In Figure 6.1, the consumer goes from counter to counter, has only one choice at each counter, will probably have to wait in line at each counter, and will definitely have to wait longer at the hot-food counter. Moreover, the wait at each stage will certainly exceed the time spent in each activity. In the process proposed in Figure 6.3, the consumer visits fewer stations but is frequently faced with a choice between different stations. Clearly, depending on the format chosen, the script to be followed by consumers will be different. In addition, the restaurant itself will look completely different.

SERVICE DELIVERY PROCESS

FIGURE

6.2

MODIFIED BLUEPRINT FOR CAFETERIA-STYLE RESTAURANT

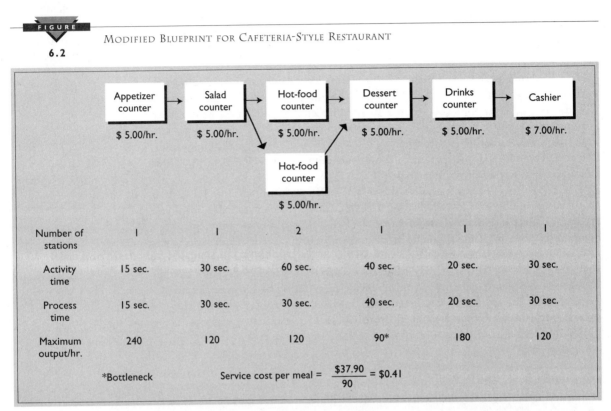

The use of the blueprinting approach allows the marketing and operations personnel to analyze in detail the process that they are jointly trying to create and manage. It can easily highlight the types of conflict between operations and marketing managers and provide a common framework for their discussion and a basis for the resolution of their problems.

USING SERVICE BLUEPRINTS TO IDENTIFY THE SERVUCTION PROCESS

Blueprints may also be used for a different purpose. Consider Figure 6.4, which shows a much more detailed blueprint for the production of a discount brokerage service. This chart is designed to identify the points of contact between the service firm and the customer. The points above the line are visible to the consumer, and those below are invisible. In assessing the quality of service received, according to the servuction model, the customer refers to the points of contact when developing perceptions regarding the value of service quality received.

To illustrate, consider the customers to be proactive rather than reactive. Consider them as worried individuals looking for clues that they have made the

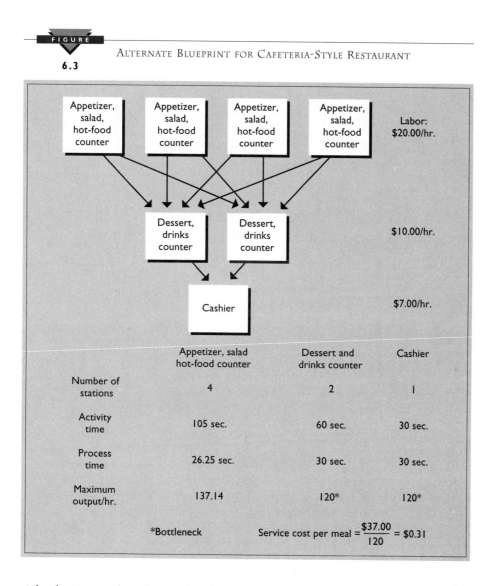

FIGURE 6.3 ALTERNATE BLUEPRINT FOR CAFETERIA-STYLE RESTAURANT

right decision rather than as inanimate raw materials to which things are done. The points of contact are the clues that develop the servuction process.

Besides illustrating a more complicated process, Figure 6.4 has a number of added features. First, each of the main features is linked to a target time. In the top right corner, for example, the time to mail a statement is targeted as five days after the month's end. In designing a service, these target times should initially be set by marketing, and they should be based on the consumers' expected level of service. If the service is to be offered in a competitive marketplace, it may be necessary to set standards higher than those of services currently available. Once the

FLOWCHART OF A DISCOUNT BROKERAGE SERVICE

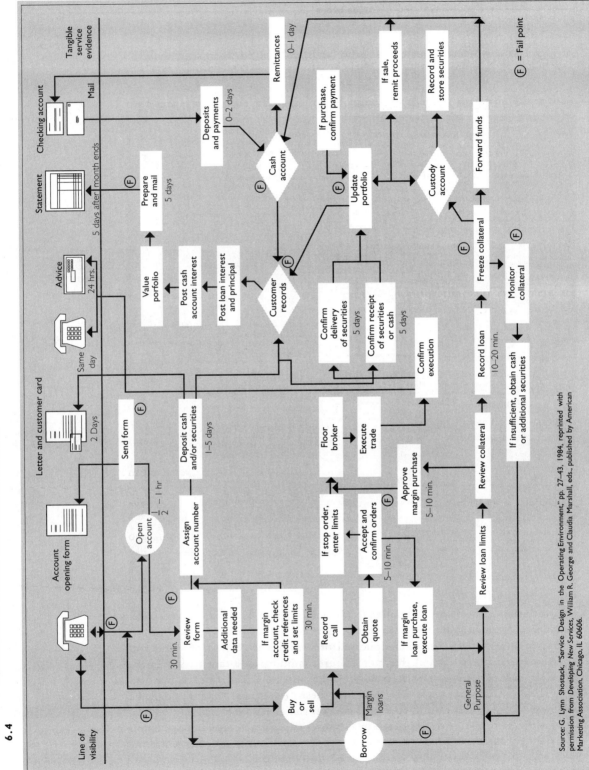

Source: G. Lynn Shostack, "Service Design in the Operating Environment," pp. 27–43, 1984, reprinted with permission from *Developing New Services*, William R. George and Claudia Marshall, eds., published by American Marketing Association, Chicago, IL 60606.

standards have been set, however, the probability of achieving them must be assessed. If the firm is prepared to invest enough, it may be feasible to meet all of the standards developed by marketing; doing so, however, affects the costs and, therefore, the subsequent price of the service. The process should, then, be an interactive one.

Figure 6.4 also highlights the potential **fail points,** "F." Fail points have three characteristics: (1) the potential for operations malfunction is high; (2) the result of the malfunction is visible to consumers; and (3) a system malfunction is regarded by consumers as particularly significant.

fail points
Points in the system at which the potential for malfunction is high and at which a failure would be visible to the customer and regarded as significant.

A Marketing or an Operations Blueprint?

Although the idea of a blueprint is attractive to both marketing and operations, it may well be that a marketing blueprint should be prepared in a different way. The blueprints we have discussed so far have an internal focus—although they identify clearly the tangible points of contact with the client, they start from the organization and look outward.

An alternative way to develop a blueprint would be to start from consumer scripts. Consumers, individually or in groups, would be asked to describe the process or steps they follow in using a service. Obviously, such an approach cannot cover the invisible part of the service firm, but it can provide a much better understanding of the points of contact. The process as described by the consumer may differ greatly from that perceived by the firm.

Consumers asked to describe a flight on USAir, for example, might start with their experience with the travel agent. They might then describe the process of getting to the airport, parking, and entering the terminal. If the signs for USAir and the entrance to its specific terminal are confusing, this will be reflected in consumers' perceptions of the airline. A parking lot that is littered, poorly lit, and inhabited by vagrants will also deter customers. Although the airline may not have direct control over these points of contact, it could be a wise investment for the airline to use its own staff to improve the parking lot. McDonald's long ago learned the value of removing the litter not only from its own property but also from the adjoining roadways.

Constructing the Service Blueprint[23]

The first step in the design of a service blueprint is to elicit scripts from both employees and consumers. The primary objective of this task is to break down the service system into a sequence of events followed by both parties. Too often, management makes the mistake of developing a **one-sided blueprint** based on its own perception of how the sequence of events should occur. This one-sided approach fails to recognize that consumer perceptions, not management's, define the realities of the encounter. Similarly, employee scripts are equally important in identifying those parts of the service system not observable to the consumer. Hence, both scripts are necessary to develop a successful blueprint.

one-sided blueprint
An unbalanced blueprint based on management's perception of how the sequence of events *should* occur.

SERVICE DELIVERY PROCESS

convergent scripts

Employee/consumer scripts that are mutually agreeable and enhance the probability of customer satisfaction.

divergent scripts

Employee/consumer scripts that "mismatch" and point to areas in which consumer expectations are not being met.

two-sided blueprint

A blueprint that takes into account both employee and customer perceptions of how the sequence of events actually occurs.

script norms

Proposed scripts developed by grouping together events commonly mentioned by both employees and customers and then ordering those events in their sequence of occurence.

Script theory suggests that consumers possess purchasing scripts that guide their thinking and behavior during service encounters. The scripts contain the sequence of actions that consumers follow when entering a service interaction. Experts believe that "these action sequences, or cognitive scripts, guide the interpretation of information, the development of expectations, and the enactment of appropriate behavior routines."[24]

Similarly, service employees also have scripts that dictate their own behavior during interactions with the customer. **Convergent scripts,** those that are mutually agreeable, enhance the probability of customer satisfaction and the quality of the relationship between the customer and the service operation. **Divergent scripts** point to areas that need to be examined and corrected because consumer expectations are not being met and evaluations of service quality could decline.

Obtaining consumer and employee scripts is a potentially powerful technique for analyzing the service encounter. Scripts provide the dialogue from which consumer and employee perceptions of the encounter can be analyzed and potential or existing problems identified. Overall, scripts provide the basis for planning service encounters, setting goals and objectives, developing behavioral routines that maximize the opportunities for a successful exchange, and evaluating the effectiveness of current service delivery systems.

The procedure used to develop **two-sided blueprints** is to present employees and customers with a script-relevant situation, such as the steps taken to proceed through a cafeteria-type restaurant. Respondents are requested to note specific events or activities expected in their involvement in the situation. In particular, employees and consumers are asked to pay special attention to those contact activities that elicit strong positive or negative reactions during the service encounter. **Script norms** are then constructed by grouping together commonly mentioned events and ordering the events in their sequence of occurrence.

To facilitate the process of identifying script norms, the blueprint designer can compare the frequency of specific events mentioned by each of the groups. The value of this process is the potential recognition of gaps or discrepancies existing between employee and consumer perceptions. For example, consumers may mention the difficulties associated with parking, which employees may not mention since many report to work before the operation is open to customers.

The second step of the blueprint development process is to identify steps in the process at which the system can go awry. By asking employees and customers to further focus on events that are important in conveying service dis/satisfaction, fail points can be isolated. The consequences of service failures can be greatly reduced by analyzing fail points and instructing employees on the appropriate response or action when the inevitable failure occurs.

After the sequence of events/activities and potential fail points have been identified, the third step in the process involves specifying the timeframe of service execution. The major cost component of most service systems relates to the time required to complete the service; consequently, standard execution time norms must be established.

Once the standard execution times of the events that make up the service encounter have been specified, the manager can analyze the profitability of the system, given the costs of inputs needed for the system to operate. The resulting blueprint allows the planner to determine the profitability of the existing service delivery system as well as to speculate on the effects on profitability when changing one or more system components. Consequently, the service blueprint allows a company to test its assumptions on paper and to minimize the system's shortcomings before the system is imposed on customers and employees. The service manager can test a prototype of the delivery system with potential customers and use the feedback to modify the blueprint before testing the procedure again.

BLUEPRINTING AND NEW-PRODUCT DEVELOPMENT: THE ROLES OF COMPLEXITY AND DIVERGENCE

Blueprints may also be used in new-product development. Once the process has been documented and a blueprint has been drawn, choices can be made that will produce "new" products. Although the processes in Figures 6.1, 6.2 and 6.3 are for the same task, from the consumer's point of view they are very different. The two blueprints define alternatives that are operationally feasible; the choice between which of the two to implement is for marketing.

Strategically, the decision may be to move the line separating visibility and invisibility. Operationally, arguments have been made for minimizing the visible component by isolating the technical core of the process. From a marketing point of view, however, more visibility may create more differentiation in the mind of the consumer. For example, a restaurant can make its kitchen into a distinctive feature by making it visible. This poses constraints on the operational personnel, but it may add value in the mind of the consumer.

New-product development within service firms can be implemented through the introduction of complexity and divergence.[25] **Complexity** is a measure of the number and intricacy of the steps and sequences that constitute the process—the more steps, the more complex the process. **Divergence** is defined as the degrees of freedom service personnel are allowed when providing the service. As an example, Figures 6.5 and 6.6 illustrate the blueprints for two florists who differ dramatically in their complexity and divergence. Although they perform equivalent tasks from an operations viewpoint, they can be very different from a marketing viewpoint and, therefore, constitute new products.

Figure 6.5 presents a traditional florist. The process, as in our restaurant example in Figure 6.1, is linear and involves a limited number of steps and so is low in complexity. However, the generation of flower arrangements under such a system calls for considerable discretion or degrees of freedom to be allowed the florist at each stage—in the choice of vase, flowers, and display—and produces a heterogeneous final product. The system is, therefore, high in divergence.

complexity

A measure of the number and intricacy of the steps and sequences that constitute a process.

divergence

A measure of the degrees of freedom service personnel are allowed when providing a service.

SERVICE DELIVERY PROCESS

FIGURE

6.5

PARK AVENUE FLORIST

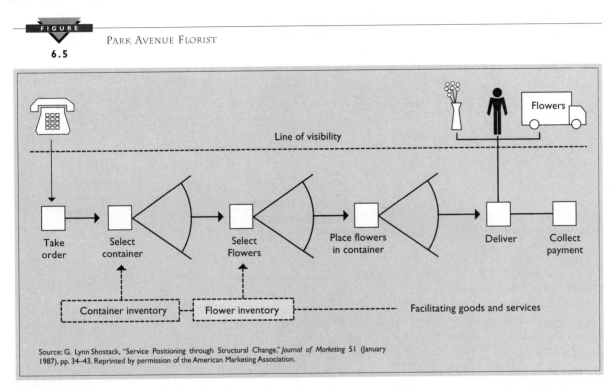

Source: G. Lynn Shostack, "Service Positioning through Structural Change," *Journal of Marketing* 51 (January 1987), pp. 34–43. Reprinted by permission of the American Marketing Association.

Figure 6.6 provides the blueprint for a second florist that has attempted to standardize its final product. Because the objective of this system is to deskill the job, the system is designed to generate a limited number of standardized arrangements. The divergence of the system is therefore reduced, but to achieve this, the complexity of the process is increased significantly.

In developing products in the service sector, the amount of manipulation of the operation's complexity and divergence are the two key choices. Reducing divergence creates the uniformity that can reduce costs, but it does so at the expense of creativity and flexibility in the system. Companies that wish to pursue a **volume-oriented positioning strategy** often do so by reducing divergence. For example, a builder of swimming pools who focuses on the installation of prefabricated vinyl pools has greatly reduced the divergence of his operations. In addition to lowering production costs, reducing divergence increases productivity and facilitates distribution of the standardized service. From the customer's perspective, reducing divergence is associated with improved reliability, availability, and uniform service quality. However, the downside of reduced divergence is the lack of customization that can be provided individual customers.

On the other hand, increasing divergence creates flexibility in tailoring the experience to each customer, but it does so at increased expense, and consumer prices are subsequently higher. Companies wishing to pursue a **niche positioning strategy** do so

volume-oriented positioning strategy

A positioning strategy that reduces divergence to create product uniformity and reduce costs.

niche positioning strategy

A positioning strategy that increases divergence in an operation to tailor the service experience to each customer.

FIGURE 6.6

FLORIST SERVICES: ALTERNATIVE DESIGN

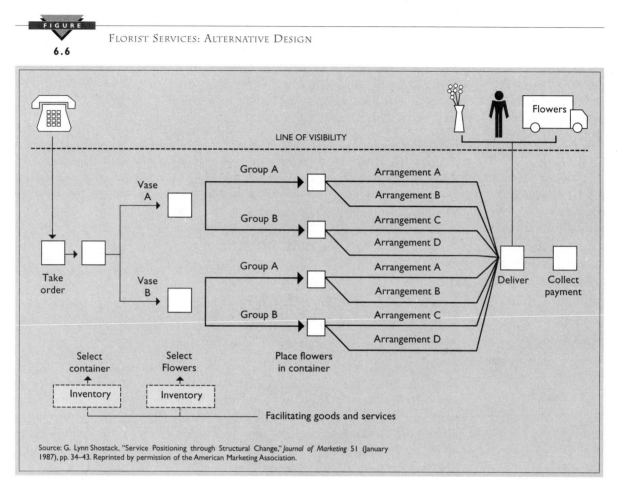

Source: G. Lynn Shostack, "Service Positioning through Structural Change," *Journal of Marketing* 51 (January 1987), pp. 34–43. Reprinted by permission of the American Marketing Association.

through increasing the divergence in their operations. For example, our pool builder may increase the divergence of his operation by specializing in the design and construction of customized pools and spas that can be built to resemble anything from a classical guitar to an exclamation point! Profits, under this scenario, depend less on volume and more on margins on each individual purchase. The downside of increasing divergence is that the service operation becomes more difficult to manage, control, and distribute. Moreover, customers may not be willing to pay the higher prices associated with a customized service.

Reducing complexity is a **specialization positioning strategy** often involving the **unbundling** of the different services offered. Hence, our hypothetical pool builder may restrict himself to the installation of a single type of prefabricated pool and divest operations that were focused on maintenance and repair as well as the design of pools and spas. The advantages associated with reduced complexity include improved control over the final product and improved distribution.

specialization positioning strategy

A positioning strategy that reduces complexity by unbundling the different services offered.

unbundling

Divesting an operation of different services and concentrating on providing only one or a few services in order to pursue a specialization positioning strategy.

penetration strategy

A positioning strategy that increases complexity by adding more services and/or enhancing current services to capture more of a market.

However, risks are involved if full-service competitors, offering one-stop convenience, continue to operate. The full-service competitor appeals to consumers wishing to work with a provider that offers a number of choices.

Increasing complexity is utilized by companies that pursue a mass market or **penetration strategy.** Increasing complexity translates into the addition of more services to the firm's offering as well as the enhancement of current ones. Within this scenario, our pool builder would offer customized pools and spas and a wide variety of prefabricated vinyl pools. In addition to installation, other services such as general pool maintenance and repair would be offered. Firms pursuing a penetration strategy often try to be everything to everybody and often gloss over individual consumer needs. Moreover, when providing such a broad range of services, the quality of the provider's skills are bound to vary depending upon the task being performed, leaving some customers less than satisfied. Hence, firms that increase complexity of their operations by offering enhanced and/or additional services run the risk of becoming vulnerable to companies that pursue more specialized types of operations.

SUMMARY

The primary objective of this chapter was to highlight the idea that for a service firm to be successful, its marketing and operations departments must work together. In a broad sense, one could view the functions of marketing and operations as the marriage of consumers' needs with the technology and manufacturing capabilities of the firm. This marriage entails many compromises that attempt to balance operational efficiency with the effectiveness of the system from the consumer's point of view. To be effective, operations personnel must recognize the importance of their marketing counterparts, and vice versa.

Firms operating at peak efficiency are free from outside influences and operate as if the market will consume the firm's production at a continuous rate. Uncertainty creates inefficiency. Hence, in an ideal situation, the technical core of the firm is able to operate without uncertainty on either the input or output side.

Although the attempt to operate at peak efficiency is a worthy goal, it likely represents an unrealistic objective for most service firms. The production of most services is an operations nightmare. Instead of receiving demand at a constant rate, service firms are often linked directly to a market that frequently varies from day to day, hour to hour, and even minute to minute. Service customers frequently affect the time of demand, the cycle of demand, the type of demand, and the duration of many service transactions.

Plans to operate at peak efficiency must be altered to cope with the uncertainties inherent in service operations. Strategies that attempt to increase the efficiency of the service operation by facilitating the balance of supply and demand include minimizing the servuction system by isolating the technical core; production-lining the whole system utilizing hard and soft technologies; creating flexible capacity; increasing customer participation; and moving the time of demand to fit capacity. In addition, service blueprints can be developed that identify the directions in which processes flow and parts of a process that may both increase operational efficiency and enhance the customer's service experience.

Operational changes made to the service blueprint often require changes in consumer behavior and, in some instances, lead to new service products. New-service development is achieved through the introduction of complexity and divergence. Reducing divergence standardizes the service product and reduces production costs, whereas increasing divergence enables service providers to tailor their products to individual customers. Similarly, reducing complexity is consistent with a specialization positioning strategy, while increasing complexity is appropriate for firms pursuing a penetration strategy.

KEY TERMS

technical core	stations
perfect-world model	maximum output per hour
focused factory	bottlenecks
plant within a plant (PWP)	fail points
buffering	one-sided blueprint
smoothing	convergent scripts
anticipating	divergent scripts
rationing	two-sided blueprint
decoupling	script norms
production-line approach	complexity
hard technologies	divergence
soft technologies	volume-oriented positioning
blueprinting	niche positioning strategy
service cost per meal	specialization positioning strategy
process time	unbundling
activity time	penetration strategy

REVIEW QUESTIONS

1. Explain how the inability to store services affects the operational efficiency of most service firms.

2. Compare Thompson's perfect-world model to the focused factory and plant-within-a-plant concepts.

3. What is buffering? How do the strategies of anticipating, smoothing, and rationing relate to buffering?

4. Discuss some specific examples of how the customer's involvement in the service encounter influences the operational efficiency of the average service firm.

5. What does it mean to isolate the technical core of a business?

6. Provide examples of hard and soft technologies and explain their relevance to this chapter.

7. Discuss the steps for developing a meaningful blueprint.

8. What are the trade-offs associated with increasing/decreasing divergence and increasing/decreasing complexity?

NOTES

1. Much of this chapter is adopted from Chapters 3 and 4 of John E. G. Bateson, *Managing Services Marketing,* 2nd ed. (Fort Worth, TX: The Dryden Press, 1992), pp. 156–169, 200–207.

2. Mathew Wiseman, "Denver Offers a Host of New Attractions," *Travel News* (July 1995), p. 1.

3. J. D. Thompson, *Organizations in Action* (New York: McGraw-Hill, 1967).

4. W. Skinner, "The Focused Factory," *Harvard Business Review* 52, 3 (May–June 1974), pp. 113–121.

5. Thompson, *Organizations in Action,* p. 69.

6. R. J. Matteis, "The New Back Office Focuses on Customer Service," *Harvard Business Review* 57 (1979), pp. 146–159.

7. Matteis, "The New Back Office."

8. These extensions of the customer contact model are developed in Richard B. Chase, "The Customer Contact Approach to Services: Theoretical Base and Practical Extensions," *Operations Research* 29, 4 (July–August 1981), pp. 698–706; and Richard B. Chase and David A. Tansik, "The Customer Contact Model for Organization Design," *Management Service* 29, 9 (1983), pp. 1037–1050.

9. B. Danet, "Client-Organization Interfaces," in *Handbook of Organization Design,* 2nd ed., P. C. Nystrom and W. N. Starbuck, eds. (New York: Oxford University Press, 1984), p. 384.

10. These studies employed the critical incident technique to look at service encounters that fail. See Mary J. Bitner, Jody D. Nyquist, and Bernard H. Booms, "The Critical Incident Technique for Analyzing the Service Encounter," in *Service Marketing in a Changing Environment,* Thomas M. Block, Gregory D. Upah, and Valerie A. Zeithaml, eds. (Chicago: American Marketing Association, 1985), pp. 48–51.

11. Chase, "The Customer Contact Approach."

12. For a detailed description, see Richard B. Chase and Gerrit Wolf, "Designing High Contact Systems: Applications to Branches of Savings and Loans," Working Paper, Department of Management, College of Business and Public Administration, University of Arizona.

13. Chad Rubel, "Banks Should Show that They Care for Customers," *Marketing News*, July 3, 1995, p. 4.

14. T. Levitt, "Production-line Approach to Services," *Harvard Business Review* 50, 5, (September–October 1972), pp. 41–52.

15. Carol F. Suprenant and Michael Solomon, "Predictability and Personalization in the Service Encounter," *Journal of Marketing* 51 (April 1987), pp. 86–96.

16. W. Earl Sasser, "Match Supply and Demand in Service Industries," *Harvard Business Review* 54, 5 (November–December 1976), pp. 61–65.

17. Benjamin Schneider, "The Service Organization: Climate is Crucial," *Organizational Dynamics* (Autumn 1980), pp. 52–65.

18. See also J. E. G. Bateson, "Self-Service Consumer: An Exploratory Study," *Journal of Retailing* 61, 3 (Fall 1986), pp. 49–79.

19. Ibid.

20. Christopher H. Lovelock and Robert F. Young, "Look to Consumers to Increase Productivity," *Harvard Business Review* (May–June 1979), pp. 168–178.

21. G. Lynn Shostack, "Service Positioning through Structural Change," *Journal of Marketing* 51 (January 1987), pp. 34–43.

22. Bateson, *Managing Services*, pp. 200–207.

23. K. Douglas Hoffman and Vince Howe, "Developing the Micro Service Audit via Script Theoretic and Blueprinting Procedures," in *Marketing Toward the Twenty-First Century*, Robert L. King, ed. (University of Richmond: Southern Marketing Association, 1991), pp. 379–383.

24. Thomas W. Leigh and Arno J. Rethans, "Experience with Script Elicitation within Consumer Making Contexts," in *Advances in Consumer Research*, Volume Ten, Alice Tybout and Richard Bagozzi, eds. (Ann Arbor, MI: Association for Consumer Research, 1983) pp. 667–672.

25. Shostack, "Service Positioning," pp. 34–43.

7

THE PRICING OF SERVICES

"*The real price of anything is the toil and the trouble of acquiring it.*"

Adam Smith

CHAPTER OBJECTIVES

The purpose of this chapter is to familiarize you with the special considerations needed when pricing services. After reading this chapter, you should be able to

▸ Discuss how consumers relate value and price.

    ▸ *Discuss pricing decisions from the provider's perspective.*

▸ Discuss the various types of costs involved in pricing decisions.

    ▸ *Discuss the circumstances under which price segmentation is most effective.*

▸ Discuss typical price segmentation approaches.

    ▸ *Discuss satisfaction-based, relationship, and efficiency approaches to pricing.*

WHICH PRICE WOULD YOU BE WILLING TO PAY?

As we warned you at the beginning of the text, by now you are probably noticing a lot of strange occurrences at the service establishments with which you conduct business. In fact, many past students have noted that it becomes increasingly difficult to finish a meal at a restaurant without thinking about how the various components of the servuction system are affecting their own personal experiences. By the end of the semester, the class tends to hear a lot of stories from classmates concerning particularly good and particularly poor service, and, as is often the case with life in general, fact is stranger than fiction.

After finishing my bachelor's degree, I remained in the Columbus, Ohio, area to work for Volkswagen of America, Inc. My co-workers and I would often go to lunch at various places in the area. One day we tried a restaurant that we had not visited before in search of a departure from our weekly routine. Although the food was fairly routine, our checks were a little on the peculiar side. Each of us had received a separate check containing the following instructions:

Circle the amount that you wish to pay:

> $4.25
>
> $4.50
>
> $4.75

We all glanced at one another with confused looks, started laughing, and then began discussing the appropriate course of action. As the customer, if you circled $4.25, you felt like the person at the cash register would think that you were "cheap." If you circled $4.75, you felt foolish for not circling a less expensive amount. Finally, if you circled $4.50, you felt both "cheap" and foolish. To say the least, we felt confused. The waitress offered no explanation other than shrugging her shoulders and repeating the message on the check: "Just circle the price you want to pay."

To this day, we still are not sure whether the restaurant was attempting to run a pricing experiment or simply attempting to be unique in its pricing strategy. After our third trip to the restaurant, we did not return. It was too much pressure! As customers, we felt like we were placed in a "no-win" situation: we either felt like we were "cheap" or like we were "chumps." Which price would you be willing to pay?

THE PRICING OF SERVICES

monetary price

The actual dollar price paid by the consumer for a product..

time costs

The time the customer has to spend to acquire the service.

energy costs

The physical energy spent by the customer to acquire the service.

psychic costs

The mental energy spent by the customer to acquire the service.

product value

The worth assigned to the product by the customer.

service value

The worth assigned to the service by the customer.

personnel value

The worth assigned to the service-providing personnel by the customer.

image value

The worth assigned to the image of the service or service provider by the customer.

cost

The amount of sacrifice relative to the amount of value perceived by the customer.

benefit

The customer-perceived advantages to buying or using a product or service.

INTRODUCTION

*I*n the area of pricing, many of the concepts developed for goods apply equally to services. This chapter focuses on how the pricing approaches apply and on how, to a greater or lesser extent, service pricing policies differ from those of goods.[1]

The Consumer's Perspective

Buyers' perceptions of value represent a trade-off between the perceived benefits of the service to be purchased and the perceived sacrifice in terms of the costs to be paid (Figure 7.1). Total customer costs include more than simply the **monetary price** paid for the service. Other costs include **time costs, energy costs,** and **psychic costs,** which reflect the time and trouble the customer has to endure to acquire the service. Similarly, total customer value extends beyond **product value** and includes **service value, personnel value,** and **image value.**[2]

For example, a customer who wishes to purchase an 18-inch satellite dish system must pay the monetary price for the dish and receiver plus the monthly charges for the video services received. In this example, the customer chose a Sony system due to its hardware and software advantages (product value) over those of competitors and the quality associated with the Sony name (image value). In addition, Sony's warranty (service value) was competitive with leading alternatives. The customer bought the system at Sears because of the sales representative's superior product knowledge (personnel value) compared with the dismal quality of information received at alternative purchase locations.

In addition to the monetary cost, the customer incurred time and energy costs while shopping at various locations and questioning sales representatives about the various brands of satellite systems. Additional time costs were incurred waiting for the installer to actually install the system. The installation, which should have taken two hours, took six hours. In addition, the installer's truck leaked vast amounts of oil onto the customer's driveway, the installer's ladder scraped paint off the outside of the house, and the installer accidentally dropped the satellite receiver from the large screen TV onto the floor. Each of these events added to the psychic cost of the whole experience.

Overall, if the signal sent by total customer **cost** is an indicator of sacrifice relative to value, then price will have a negative or repelling effect and may reduce demand. If the signal sent by the price is an indicator of **benefit** or value, then price will be an attractor and may increase demand. Because of the perceived con-

FIGURE
7.1

BUYER'S PERCEPTION OF VALUE

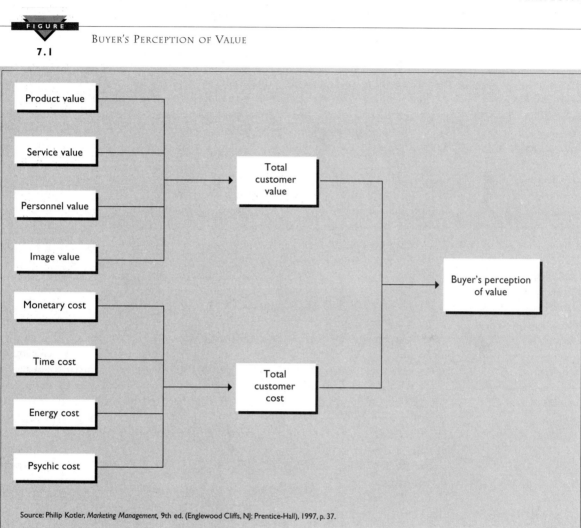

Source: Philip Kotler, *Marketing Management*, 9th ed. (Englewood Cliffs, NJ: Prentice-Hall), 1997, p. 37.

nection between cost and benefit, buyers have both **lower** and **upper price thresholds.** For example, buyers might be discouraged from buying when the price is perceived to be too low simply because they see a low price as an indicator of inferior quality.

Consumers exchange their money, time, and effort for the bundle of benefits the service provider offers. Economic theory suggests that consumers will have a **reservation price** that captures the value they place on these benefits. As long as the total cost to the consumer is less than the reservation price, he or she will

lower price threshold
The minimum price that consumers will accept due to their perception of low price equaling low quality.

THE PRICING OF SERVICES

upper price threshold

The maximum price that consumers will accept because of the perceived connection between price and value.

reservation price

The price a consumer considers to capture the value he or she places on the benefits.

consumer's surplus

The money left over if a consumer purchases the service for less than the reservation price.

price ceiling

The consumer demand consideration that dictates a ceiling to the price that may be charged.

price floor

The provider cost consideration that dictates the lowest price possible that a service can charge.

fixed costs

Costs that are planned and accrued during the operating period regardless of the level of production and sales.

direct variable costs

Costs that are directly associated with increases in production and sales.

be prepared to buy. If the consumer can purchase the service for less than the reservation price, a **consumer's surplus** will exist.

THE SERVICE PROVIDER'S PERSPECTIVE

When deciding on a pricing policy, the seller must be aware of the range of pricing options that are available. Consumer demand considerations provide a **price ceiling,** an upper limit to the price that may be charged, while provider cost considerations create a **price floor.** The difference between what buyers are willing to pay and what sellers can afford to charge creates a vital price discretion.

The price discretion is narrowed at both ends. Sellers must consider corporate objectives as well as costs when setting the price floor. Merely covering costs is insufficient since the firm needs to meet its financial objectives and generate a profit. At the other end, competitive factors usually reduce the price ceiling and can often prevent the firm from charging the full value that customers would be willing to pay if no other sources were available.

COST CONSIDERATIONS

Costs play an important role in the pricing of services. Costs together with corporate objectives provide a price floor below which the service firm cannot make an acceptable return. To thrive as a profitable service firm, service managers are under constant pressure to remain competitive by cutting operating costs while at the same time improving the quality of the service delivered. Hence, the understanding of costs and cost structures involved in providing a quality service is critical to the firm's competitiveness and long-term survival in the marketplace. Developing such an understanding requires knowledge of the different types of costs, how they relate to one another, and how they affect a firm's profitability. Figure 7.2 provides an overview of these relationships.

Fixed costs are planned and accrued during the operating period regardless of the level of production and sales. Examples of fixed costs include research and development, depreciation of the physical facility, rent, insurance, advertising, administrative overheads, and employee health benefits.

Direct variable costs include costs that are directly associated with increases in production and sales. Typical examples include component and raw materials, direct labor, royalties, distribution costs, and sales commissions. Total direct variable costs (TVC) are a function of the quantity sold and produced. Although the TVC increases with production and sales, it does so at a decreasing rate as a firm achieves economies of scale in the areas of buying, producing, and selling at various levels of output. Profits begin to accumulate when the firm is able to cover its fixed and variable costs and the **break-even point**

FIGURE

7.2 THE RELATIONSHIP BETWEEN COSTS, PROFIT,
AND GROSS CONTRIBUTION

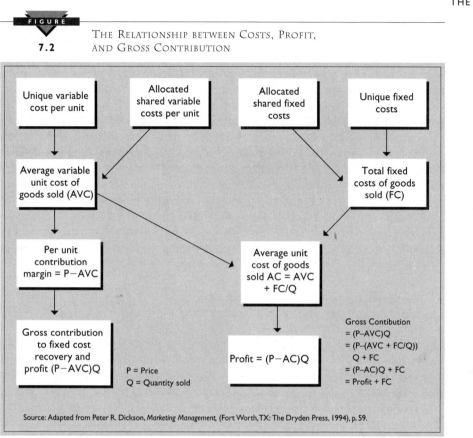

Source: Adapted from Peter R. Dickson, *Marketing Management*, (Fort Worth, TX: The Dryden Press, 1994), p. 59.

is realized. The most basic method for calculating the break-even point is as follows:

Sales = Variable Costs × (Sales) + Fixed Costs

Let: Y = sales in dollars needed to break even
        Fixed costs = $6,000
        Variable costs = .80

Hence: Y = .80Y + $6,000
        .20Y = $6,000
        Y = $30,000

break-even point
The point at which profit begins, when the firm is able to cover its fixed and variable costs.

Shared costs are calculated by isolating both fixed and variable costs that are shared among products. Calculating the costs for services is particularly troublesome since several costs are shared among services provided. Shared

shared costs
An isolation of both fixed and variable costs that are shared among products.

THE PRICING OF SERVICES

costs can be both fixed and variable. "The traditional way of allocating shared costs by a percentage of direct labor cost involved in making a product can create serious cost and pricing distortions, particularly when shared costs, such as factory support operations, engineering, design, distribution, marketing, and other overheads, make up a significant portion of the firm's cost structure."[3]

average costs

A cost figured by adding together all the fixed and variable costs and dividing the amount by the quantity of product produced.

Average costs are calculated by simply adding together all the fixed and variable costs and dividing this amount by the quantity of product produced. In many service industries that are characterized by a high fixed cost-to-variable cost ratio, average costs fall quickly as the quantity produced and sold increases. This occurs for two reasons: (1) the economies of scale that occur in purchasing, manufacturing, distribution, and marketing; and (2) a **learning curve** effect that tends to exert a downward pressure on costs over time. In service industries where the fixed cost-to-variable cost ratio is high, price wars often erupt as firms within the industry try to wrestle market share away from one another in order to lower average costs.

learning curve

A contributing factor to lowering costs; exerts a downward pressure on costs over time.

marginal costs

The costs involved in producing one more unit of output.

Marginal costs refer to the costs involved in producing one more unit of output. Marginal costs are typically lower than the costs of producing and selling what has already been sold. Typical examples of marginal costs include: materials, direct processing, transportation, and sales commissions. In times of capacity underutilization, new sales at any rate above marginal costs is worthwhile as long as the rate does not affect past sales. In periods of full capacity, selling at levels just above marginal cost makes little sense since major investment may be necessary to expand existing capacity.

future costs

The estimate of probable increases or decreases in costs; used to calculate future prices.

Future costs involve the anticipation of increasing or decreasing costs and are used to calculate future prices. Future costs are subjectively based and difficult to effectively estimate. They may also be the source of conflict among different departments within the organization, each of which is trying to accomplish a separate goal.

contribution margin (CM)

The difference between the final asking price and the average variable cost; the amount of money left to cover fixed costs.

The contribution margin (CM) is calculated by taking the difference between the final asking price and average variable cost. The contribution margin stated in dollars represents the amount of money left over to cover fixed costs. Amounts that remain are profits. Similarly, the contribution margin expressed as a percentage is calculated by dividing the contribution margin in dollars by the asking price. Firms wishing to achieve benchmark levels of a contribution margin percentage have two choices: (1) decreasing variable costs, and/or (2) increasing the price of the service.

ELASTICITY CONSIDERATIONS

price elasticity

The relationship of price to demand.

In addition to cost considerations, service provider pricing strategy is commonly influenced by consumer **price elasticity.** Price elasticity of demand measures the responsiveness of the demanded quantity of a product or service to any change in price. This responsiveness is measured as a percentage change in the quantity demanded of a service relative to a change in price. If the change in price is greater than the change in quantity demanded, then consumer **demand** is **inelastic.** Conversely, if the change in price is less than the change in quantity demanded, **demand** is **elastic.** Equal changes in demand and price result in **unitary demand.**

Price elasticity of demand can have an important effect on a seller's revenues. An increase in the sales volume will create marginal revenue, which, depending on the type of elasticity present, can be either positive or negative. Marginal revenue is created when prices are increased, and it is measured by taking the total increased revenue generated from all continuing services and subtracting the total lost revenue from all orders lost as a result of the price increase. For example, a cable television service with 20,000 customers increases its price from $10 to $12 per month and loses 4,000 customers as a result. Its marginal revenue consists of a revenue gain of $2 for each of the 16,000 remaining customers, or $32,000, less the revenue lost from 4,000 customers at the original $10 price, or $40,000. In this case, the demand for cable television service was elastic, and total revenues decreased by $8,000.

Two other measures of elasticity are important when deciding on a price ceiling. Each concerns the impact of price on the total size of the market. **Income elasticity** of demand is the percentage change in quantity of demand of a service relative to the change in personal income. If income elasticity is negative, less service is demanded as income goes up. For example, the demand for welfare services such as food stamp programs and a variety of other social services are characterized by negative income elasticity. If income elasticity is positive, demand increases as income increases. For example, as many households move from earning single incomes to earning dual incomes, the demand for housekeeping services may also see an increase. In general, the demand for many personal services is characterized by positive income elasticity.

Cross-price elasticity of demand measures the responsiveness of demand for a service relative to a change in price for another service. If this relationship is negative, then the two services are said to be **complementary,** and the consumption of one is unlikely to affect the consumption of the other, such as lawn care and housekeeping. If the relationship is positive, however, then the two services may be **substitutes,** and consumption of one is at the expense of the consumption of the other. For example, new parents may give up their housekeeping and lawn services to help pay for child-care services.

INFORMATION CONSIDERATIONS

The consumer's sensitivity to price depends on the number of alternatives considered for the purchase. The fewer the number of alternatives considered, the more inelastic the demand curve will be. The number of alternatives considered, however, depends on the number of alternatives about which the consumer is knowledgeable. The consumer's ability to obtain knowledge of alternatives

inelastic demand
The type of market demand when a change in price of service is greater than a change in quantity demanded.

elastic demand
The type of market demand when a change in quantity demand is greater than a change in price of service.

unitary demand
The type of market demand characterized by equal changes in both demand and price.

income elasticity
A percentage change in quantity of demand of a service relative to a change in personal income.

cross-price elasticity
A measure of the responsiveness of demand for a service relative to a change in price for another service.

complementary
The effect of cross-price elasticity in which the consumption of one service is unlikely to affect the consumption of the other.

substitutes
The effect of cross-price elasticity in which the consumption of one service is likely to be at the expense of consumption of another service.

depends on whether the service is characterized by search, experience, or credence attributes.

Demand is likely to be more elastic for services that can be evaluated on the basis of search attributes. Consumers will be aware of more alternatives since such information is easier to collect. On the other hand, demand for services characterized by experience and credence attributes tends to be more inelastic. If service personnel themselves dictate the quality or nature of the service, and if the service can be customized, consumers will be less able to evaluate the service and thus less sensitive to price differences among alternatives.

COMMUNICATING QUALITY THROUGH PRICE

Service providers must also consider the message the service price sends to customers. Much work has been devoted to understanding whether price can be an indicator of quality. Some studies that have been performed seem to imply that consumers can use price to infer the quality of the good or service they are considering; conflicting studies seem to indicate that they cannot. For example, classic studies in this field have presented customers with identical products, such as pieces of carpet, priced at different levels. The respondents' judgment of quality seemed to indicate that quality followed price. However, very similar studies later found little relationship between price and perceived quality. The subtle difference in these studies that led to such different results seems to suggest that price will indicate quality only in the absence of other information.

Considering our earlier discussion of information considerations, these findings are not particularly surprising. Price is a search attribute, and it is often the most visible characteristic. In the absence of other information, as is the case for services characterized by experience and credence attributes, we would expect high price elasticity. However, dissonance theory would suggest that after making a choice based on a single attribute (price), consumers would then rationalize their choice by suggesting that price indicated quality, thereby reducing the levels of perceived cognitive dissonance and increasing the consumers' willingness to pay a higher price.

PRICE SEGMENTATION

Up to this point, we have assumed that consumers' reservation price is fixed and homogenous across the market. Segmentation theory would argue that it is more likely that the market will be heterogeneous and that different groups of consumers will put different valuations or reservation prices on a service. For example, when considering the reservation price for an airline shuttle ticket between Boston and New York City, the value placed on that ticket can vary even with the same individual. One reservation price applies to business travel, but when the traveler is paying for the ticket out of his or her own pocket, there will be a different valuation. For the airline, on the other hand, the cost of operating a particular flight will not vary because of who its passengers are. Where different groups of customers are willing to pay different prices, **price segmentation** strategies can be utilized.

Effective price segmentation benefits consumers and providers alike. Consumers often benefit from options that offer lower prices, and providers are often able to manage demand and increase capacity utilization. The interaction that creates the service experience, which is what the consumer buys, takes place in realtime. Since consumers must, in most cases, come to the service setting to be part of the experience, capacity utilization depends on when they arrive. For most services, consumers tend to arrive unevenly and unpredictably, such as at a grocery store or restaurant. The result is often periods of low utilization of capacity because of the impossibility of matching capacity to demand.

Capacity, in turn, represents the bulk of the costs for a service. The restaurant has to be open, staffed, and resourced even at times when it has no customers. The result is a very low level of variable costs for services and a high value attributable to incremental customers, even at discount prices. As a result, pricing is called upon to try to smooth demand in two ways:

▲ Creating new demand in off-peak, low-capacity utilization periods.
▲ Flattening peaks by moving existing customers from peaks to less busy times.

CRITERIA FOR EFFECTIVE PRICE SEGMENTATION

1. **Different groups of consumers must have different responses to price.** If different groups of consumers have the same response to price changes, then the price segmentation strategy becomes counterproductive. For example, for years movie theaters have offered afternoon matinees at a reduced fee. This strategy helped the theater create demand for unused capacity during the day and also helped to smooth demand during the evening shows. Moreover, this approach has attracted market segments such as families with children and individuals on fixed incomes, who may not otherwise attend the higher-priced evening shows. This strategy has been effective because the price change did not create the same response for everyone. If most consumers had shifted their demand to the afternoon shows at lower rates, the movie theater would have overutilized capacity in the afternoons and would be generating lower total revenues for the firm.

2. **The different segments must be identifiable, and a mechanism must exist to price them differently.** Effective price segmentation requires that consumer segments with different demand patterns be identifiable based on some readily apparent common characteristic such as age, family-life cycle stage, gender, and/or educational status. Discriminating based on a convoluted segmentation scheme confuses customers and service providers, who must implement the strategy. Common forms of

price segmentation
A pricing policy in which different prices for the same service are set, depending on different market segments interested in a purchase.

segmentation identification include college ID card holders, AARP card holders, and drivers' licensees.

3. **No opportunity should exist for individuals in one segment who have paid a low price to sell their tickets to those in other segments.** For example, it does the movie theater little good to sell reduced-price seats in the afternoon to buyers who can turn around and sell those tickets that evening in the parking lot to full-paying customers. Sometimes you just can't win! A local municipal golf course was trying to do "the right thing" by offering its senior citizen customers coupon books for rounds of golf priced at a reduced rate. Soon after the promotion began, some senior citizen customers were seen in the parking lot selling their coupons at a profit to the golf course's full-price customers.

4. **The segment should be large enough to make the exercise worthwhile.** The time and effort involved in offering a price segmentation scheme should be justified based on the return it brings to the business. Having little or no response to the firm's effort signals that either consumers are uninterested, eligible customers are few, or the firm's price segmentation offer is off its mark.

5. **The cost of running the price segmentation strategy should not exceed the incremental revenues obtained.** The objectives of engaging in price segmentation efforts may be to reduce peak demand, fill periods of underutilized capacity, increase overall revenues, or achieve nonprofit issues, such as making your service available to individuals who otherwise may not be able to take advantage of the services the firm offers. If the cost of running the price segmentation strategy exceeds the returns produced, management needs to reconsider the offering.

6. **The customers should not be confused by the use of different prices.** Phone companies and electric utilities often offer customers reduced rates that are based on the time of usage. Frequently, however, these time-related discounts change as new promotions arise. Customers caught unaware of the change often end up paying higher rates than expected, which negatively impacts customer satisfaction. Other pricing strategies such as the one discussed in the opening vignette may simply frustrate the customer. Recently, phone companies such as AT&T have attempted to utilize "simple pricing" as a point of differentiation in their advertising. Other firms are offering higher-priced "peak rates" and lower-priced "nonpeak" rates that vary throughout the day, and customers must be aware at all times which rate they will be paying in order to take advantage of this particular type of pricing strategy.

PRICE SEGMENTATION APPROACHES

Discrimination by Time of Usage Effective price segmentation for services can frequently be met through the time-based nature of demand. Segmentation can be

practiced by time of usage of the service or by time of reservation or ticket purchase. A number of obvious examples of **time-based pricing** come to mind. To return to the airline ticket example, it is clearly impossible to identify the business and the leisure travelers separately as they approach the ticket counter. Even if they were identifiable, it would be impossible to then offer them differential prices at the same time. The fact that a Hawaiian shirt guaranteed a low ticket price would soon produce a rash of such shirts. Clearly, the second criterion for effective price segmentation would be violated.

A good solution exists, however. Business travelers are unlikely to want to travel at awkward hours, but leisure travelers may be willing to do so. Hence, airlines can offer inexpensive late-night flights to attract leisure demand without risking the possibility that everyone will want to fly during these discounted times.

Segmentation by Time of Reservation or Ticket Purchase The hotel industry has long utilized price discrimination by time of reservation or ticket purchase. Conference or group bookings offer the hotel the advantage of guaranteed demand but usually require cheaper prices. The lone traveler arriving at 6 P.M. without a reservation

time-based pricing

Price discrimination based on the time of usage of the service or by time of reservation or ticket purchase.

has, by comparison, little bargaining power and will quite happily pay the full rate. Profitable hotel management, therefore, depends on a balancing act between capacity utilization and revenues generated. Filling the hotel with low-rate guests who have booked six months in advance precludes higher-priced, same-day sales. On the other hand, keeping rooms unfilled until the last moment runs the risk that capacity will be unused.

The airline industry uses time of reservation to tap into the leisure and business segments. Few business travelers can risk booking flights weeks in advance, and most of them often need to book tickets on the day of departure. Leisure travelers, by comparison, plan their trips in advance and are willing to buy tickets in advance. Discrimination is, therefore, possible, and airlines can offer low prices for early booking while minimizing the impact of revenues generated by the business traveler.

Both airlines and hotels have an advantage in that tickets are not interchangeable, so that cross-selling of tickets by different segments is impossible. Confusion in the consumer's mind is avoided because the strategies follow an economic logic, which is consistent with the nature of service costs.

The complexity of airline pricing becomes apparent when you realize that airlines use both of the above forms of price discrimination simultaneously. Fares between a single pair of cities vary both by time of day and time of booking. Airline pricing schemes have been made even more complex by the introduction of the standby flight. This idea taps into yet another segment by providing very low fares but without any guarantee of a seat. As in many other service businesses, these types of strategies are driven by the nature of costs as well as by demand considerations.

Segmentation by Self-Service It is possible to reduce costs of providing a service by having the consumer do part of the work. The issue then arises as to whether it is necessary to change the price to reflect the added cost of that effort to the consumer. Is it necessary for self-service gas stations to be cheaper than full-service stations?

At first, it would appear that a price cut is necessary in order to balance the consumer's value equation. However, considerable evidence suggests that this may not be the case. Research suggests that consumers' response to such do-it-yourself offerings is variable. One segment of consumers would prefer to "do it themselves" even if no price incentive were offered. Conversely, another segment would not use these kinds of services even for large price discounts.

The do-it-yourself consumers attach a high value to perceived control and time. They perceive that increasing their participation increases their value through a greater sense of control over the situation and lower time costs. Members of the second group of consumers see these services as equal to full-service options on control and time but lacking in "human contact." The value of these services is reduced for them because of the lack of contact with service personnel.

▶▶▶▶ ◀◀◀◀

Emerging Service Pricing Strategies

Traditional pricing strategies such as penetration pricing, competitive pricing, and premium pricing offer little benefit to service customers or service providers. For example, competitive pricing has led to disappearing profit margins in industries such as car rental and health insurance and to customer confusion and mistrust in industries such as long distance telephone service. At the core of the pricing problem is a lack of understanding of the special considerations in the pricing of intangibles and how consumers use and benefit from the services they are purchasing. Service marketers should create pricing strategies that offer a compromise between the overly complex (see Table 7.1) and the too simplistic, both of which neglect the variations in consumer needs.[4]

To effectively price services, the service firm must first understand what its target market truly values. Three alternative pricing strategies that convey value to the customer include satisfaction-based, relationship, and efficiency pricing (see Table 7.2).[5]

Satisfaction-Based Pricing

The primary goal of **satisfaction-based pricing** is to reduce the amount of perceived risk associated with the service purchase and appeal to target markets that value certainty. Satisfaction-based pricing can be achieved through offering guarantees, benefit-driven pricing, and flat-rate pricing.

Service guarantees are quickly becoming a popular way of attracting customers.[6] The guarantee assures customers that if they are less than satisfied with their purchase, they can invoke the guarantee, and a partial or full refund will occur. Offering guarantees signals to customers that the firm is committed to delivering quality services and confident in its ability to do so. In instances where competing services are priced similarly, the service guarantee offers a differential advantage.

Benefit-driven pricing focuses on the aspects of the service that customers actually use. The objective of this approach is to develop a direct association between the price of the service and the components of the service that customers value. For example, online computer services typically do not use benefit-driven pricing strategies. This is evident by their practice of charging customers for the amount of time spent online as opposed to billing for services they actually use. Innovative online services, such as ESA-IRS and its "pricing for information" program, have introduced benefit-driven pricing and have shifted their marketing focus from keeping customers online to marketing information that is beneficial to their customers.

The concept of **flat-rate pricing** is fairly straightforward. Its primary objective is to decrease consumer uncertainty about the final price of the service by agreeing to a fixed price before the service transaction occurs. With flat-rate pricing, the provider assumes the risk of price increases and overruns. Flat-rate pricing

satisfaction-based pricing
Pricing strategies that are designed to reduce the amount of perceived risk associated with a purchase.

benefit-driven pricing
A pricing strategy that charges customers for services actually used as opposed to overall "membership" fees.

flat-rate pricing
A pricing strategy in which the customer pays a fixed price and the provider assumes the risk of price increases and cost overruns.

THE PRICING OF SERVICES

TABLE 7.1	THE RELENTLESS STREAM OF LONG DISTANCE CALLING PLANS

AT&T's "True USA Savings" Program
10 percent discount to customers spending $10 to $24.99
20 percent discount to customers spending $25 to $74.99
30 percent discount to customers spending $75 or more

AT&T 's "True Rewards" Program
Allows frequent callers to accumulate points, which can be exchanged for frequent flyer miles, savings bonds, free calling time, and a variety of other products.

MCI's "Friends & Family" Program
20 percent discount to preset group of MCI customers

MCI's "Friends & Family II/Sure Savings" Program
40 percent discount to MCI customers
20 percent discount to non-MCI customers

MCI's "Personal Thanks" Program
Similar program to AT&T's "True Rewards" program

Sprint's "The Most" Program
20 percent discount on calls made to the most-called number, as well as to other Sprint customers
36 percent discount if the most-called number is a Sprint customer

Sprint's "The Most II" Program
Tiered discounts based on level of long-distance calling

Sprint's "Priority Rewards" Program
Similar to AT&T's "True Rewards" and MCI's "Personal Thanks" programs

Source: "Reach Out and Confuse Someone," *Services Marketing Today* (June 1995), p. 4.

makes the most sense when the price is competitive, the firm offering the flat rate has its costs under control and operates an efficient operation, and the opportunities to engage in a long-term relationship and to generate additional revenues with the customer is possible.

RELATIONSHIP PRICING

relationship pricing
Pricing strategies that encourage the customer to expand his/her dealings with the service provider.

The primary objective of **relationship pricing** is to enhance the firm's relationship with its targeted consumers. For example, in the banking industry, relationship pricing strategies can be utilized to further nurture the relationship between the bank and its existing checking account customers by offering special savings accounts, deals on safe-deposit boxes, and special rates on certificates of deposit. Two types of relationship pricing techniques include long-term contracts and price bundling.

EMERGING SERVICE
PRICING STRATEGIES

TABLE 7.2	SATISFACTION-BASED, RELATIONSHIP, AND EFFICIENCY PRICING STRATEGIES	
Pricing Strategy	**Provides Value by . . .**	**Implemented as . . .**
Satisfaction-based pricing	Recognizing and reducing customers' perceptions of uncertainty, which the intangible nature of service magnifies.	Service guarantees Benefit-driven pricing Flat-rate pricing
Relationship pricing	Encouraging long-term relationships with the company that customers view as beneficial.	Long-term contracts Price bundling
Efficiency pricing	Sharing with customers the cost savings that the company has achieved by understanding, managing, and reducing the costs of providing the service.	Cost-leader pricing

Source: Leonard L. Berry and Manjit S. Yadav, "Capture and Communicate Value in the Pricing of Services," *Sloan Management Review* (Summer 1996), pp. 41–51.

Long-term contracts offer prospective customers price and nonprice incentives for dealing with the same provider over a number of years. UPS recently entered into long-term shipping contracts with Land's End and Ford Motor Company. Because of its customers' long-term commitments, UPS has been able to transform its business with these clients from discrete to continuous transactions. UPS now has operations and personnel dedicated solely to providing services to these specific customers. Since transactions are now continuous, economies of scale have developed, and cost savings that can be passed to the customer plus opportunities for improving the firm's profit performance have emerged.

Since most service organizations provide more than one service, the practice of bundling services has become more common.[7] **Price bundling,** broadly defined, is the practice of marketing two or more products and/or services in a single package at a single price. Common examples include hotels putting together weekend packages that include lodging, meals, and sometimes entertainment at an inclusive rate. Airlines routinely price vacation packages that include air travel, car rental, and hotel accommodations.

Price bundling flows logically from the issues discussed earlier in the chapter. Individual services have low marginal costs and high shared costs. Moreover, the services offered by most businesses are generally interdependent in terms of demand. For example, the demand for the hotel's food service is directly related to the demand for hotel rooms.

Generally, services are concerned with **mixed bundling,** which enables consumers to either buy Service A and Service B together or purchase one service separately. The simplest argument for bundling is based on the idea of consumer surplus: Bundling makes it possible to shift the consumer surplus from one service to another service that otherwise would have a negative surplus (i.e., would not be purchased). Thus, the combined value of the two services is less

price bundling
The practice of marketing two or more products and/or services in a single package at a single price.

mixed bundling
Price-bundling technique that allows consumers to either buy Service A and Service B together or purchase one service separately.

than the combined price, even though separately, only one service would be purchased.

Three reasons have been suggested for why the sum of the parts would have less value than the whole. First, information theory would argue that the consumer finds value in easy access to information: Consumers of one financial service institution have a lower information cost when buying another service from the same institution than when buying that service from a different institution. A second case argues that the bundling of Service B with Service A can enhance a consumer's satisfaction with Service A, for example, a ski resort that offers a ski-rental-and-lessons package. The reservation price for the lessons is likely to be the same whether or not the skis are rented because the value of the lessons depends on the skills and needs of the skier. However, the reservation price of the ski rental will be enhanced, at least for novices, by lessons. The final argument is that the addition of Service B to Service A can enhance the total image of the firm. A financial-planning service offering both investment advice and tax advice enhances its credibility in both services.

EFFICIENCY PRICING

efficiency pricing

Pricing strategies that appeal to economically minded consumers by delivering the best and most cost-effective service for the price.

The primary goal of **efficiency pricing** is to appeal to economically minded consumers who are looking for the best price. "Efficiency pricers almost always are industry heretics, shunning traditional operating practices in search of sustainable cost advantages."[8] Southwest Airlines and its relentless efforts to reduce costs is one such example. Southwest reduces costs by flying shorter, more direct routes to less congested, less expensive airports. No meals are served, passengers are seated on a first-come, first-served basis, and the airline was the first to offer "ticketless" travel on all flights.

Efficiency pricing is focused on delivering the best and most cost-effective service available for the price. Operations are streamlined, and innovations that enable further cost reduction become part of the operation's culture. The leaner the cost structure, the more difficult it is for new competitors to imitate Southwest's success.

Understanding and managing costs are the fundamental building blocks of efficiency pricing. Unfortunately, traditional cost accounting practices, which were designed to monitor raw material consumption, depreciation, and labor, offer little in helping service managers understand their own cost structures. A more useful approach, activity-based costing (ABC), focuses on the resources consumed in developing the final product.

activity-based costing (ABC)

Costing method that breaks down the organization into a set of activities, and activities into tasks, which convert materials, labor, and technology into outputs.

Activity-based costing (ABC) has a great deal to offer service firms and represents the latest innovation in management accounting.[9] Traditionally, overhead in most service firms has been allocated to projects based on the amount of direct labor charged to complete the customer's requirements. However, this method of charging overhead has frustrated managers of specific projects for years. Consider the following example:

Let's say that ABC company charges $2.00 for overhead for every dollar of direct labor charged to customers. As the manager of ABC company, you have just negotiated with a customer to provide architectural drawings of a deck for $1,000. The customer wants the drawing in three days. Realizing that using your best architect, whom you pay $20 an hour, will result in a loss for the project, you assign the architect's apprentice, who makes $7 an hour. The results of the project are as follows:

Time Required	40 hours
Apprentice's Rate	$7 per hour
Direct Labor	$280
Overhead @ $2	$560
Project Cost	$800
Revenue	$1000
Profit	$200

If the firm's best architect had completed the job, the following results would have been submitted:

Time Required	20 hours
Architect's Rate	$20 per hour
Direct Labor	$400
Overhead @ $2	$800
Project Cost	$1200
Revenue	$1000
Profit	($200)

This traditional approach used in service firms makes little sense. Intuitively, it does not make sense that a job that took a shorter period of time should be charged more overhead. Moreover, this type of system encourages the firm to use less-skilled labor, who produce an inferior product in an unacceptable period of time as specified by the customer. The firm produces a profit on paper but will most likely never have the opportunity to work for this customer again (or his/her friends, for that matter). Even more confusing is that raises and promotions are based on profits generated, so the manager is rewarded for using inferior labor. Something is definitely wrong with this picture!

Activity-based costing focuses on the cost of activities by breaking down the organization into a set of activities and activities into tasks, which convert materials, labor, and technology into outputs. The tasks are thought of as "users" of overhead and identified as **cost drivers.** The firm's past records are used to arrive at cost-per-task figures that are then allocated to each project based on the activities required to complete the project. In addition, by breaking the overall overhead figure into a set of activities that are driven by cost drivers, the firm can now concentrate its efforts on reducing costs and increasing profitability.

For example, one activity in the firm's overall overhead figure is ordering materials. Ordering materials is driven by the number of purchase orders submitted. Company records indicate that overhead associated with ordering materials cost the firm $10,400 during the period. During this same period, 325 purchase orders

cost drivers

The tasks in activity-based costing that are considered to be the "users" of overhead.

THE PRICING OF SERVICES

TABLE 7.3 ACTIVITY-BASED COSTING

Activity Pools	Cost Driver
General administration	Direct Labor $
Project costing	No. of timesheet entries
Accounts payable/receiving	No. of vendor invoices
Accounts receivable	No. of client invoices
Payroll/mail sorting and delivery	No. of employees
Recruiting personnel	No. of new hires
Employee insurance processing	Insurance claims processed
Proposals/RFPs	No. of proposals
Client sales meeting/sales aids	Sales $
Shipping	No. of project numbers
Ordering	No. of purchase orders
Xeroxing	No. of xeroxes
Blueprinting	No. of blueprints

Cost Driver	Fixed Overhead Cost	Total Base	Cost per Driver
Direct labor $	73	1,016,687	0.07
No. of time entries	10	13,300	0.78
No. of vendor invoices	29	2,270	12.60
No. of client invoices	10	1,128	9.22
No. of employees	18	67	271.64
No. of new hires	8	19	410.53
Insurance claims filed	3	670	3.88
No. of proposals	29	510	56.08
Sales $	42	3,795,264	0.01
No. of project numbers	5	253	20.55
No. of purchase orders	10	325	32.00
No. of xeroxes	16	373,750	0.04
No. of blueprint sq. ft.	8	86,200	0.09
	260		

Source: Beth M. Chapman and John Talbott, "Activity-Based Costing in a Service Organization," *CMA Magazine* (December 1990/January 1991), pp. 15–18.

were submitted. Hence, the activity cost associated with each purchase order is $32.00. Similar calculations are made for other overhead items. Overhead is then allocated to each project based on the activities undertaken to complete the project. Table 7.3 presents examples of overhead items and their cost drivers.

SOME FINAL THOUGHTS ON PRICING SERVICES

Pricing services is a difficult task. Consumers are purchasing an experience and often feel uneasy about or do not understand what they are paying for. Similarly, service providers do not have a cost of goods sold figure upon which to base their prices. Confused and bewildered, many providers simply look to what the competition is charging, regardless of their own cost structures and competitive advantage. In contrast, successful service providers tend to abide by the following pricing guidelines:[10]

1. The price should be easy for customers to understand.
2. The price should represent value to the customer.
3. The price should encourage customer retention and facilitate the customer's relationship with the providing firm.
4. The price should reinforce customer trust.
5. The price should reduce customer uincertainty.

S U M M A R Y

Successful service pricing depends on recognizing the value that a customer places on a service and pricing that service accordingly. Customer peceptions of value represent a trade-off between the perceived benefits obtained from purchasing the product and the perceived sacrifice in terms of cost to be paid. Total customer costs extend beyond monetary costs and include time, energy, and psychic costs. Similarly, total customer value extends beyond product value and includes service, personnel, and image value.

Costs play an important role in the pricing of services. Sellers must consider corporate objectives as well as costs when setting prices. Merely covering costs is insufficient since the firm needs to meet its financial objectives and generate a profit. Understanding costs and the cost structure involved in producing a quality service is critical to the firm's competitiveness. Types of costs to be considered include fixed costs, direct variable costs, shared costs, average costs, marginal costs, and future costs.

In addition to cost considerations, service provider pricing strategy is commonly influenced by consumer price elasticity. Price elasticity of demand measures the responsiveness of the quantity demanded of a product to any change in price. When developing service pricing strategies, managers should consider consumer demand elasticity, income elasticity, and cross-price elasticity.

Consumers' sensitivity to price depends on the number of alternatives considered for the purchase. In general, the fewer the number of alternatives considered, the less elastic demand will be. Demand is likely to be more elastic for services characterized by search attributes and less elastic for services characterized by experience and credence attributes.

Segmentation theory supports the notion that different groups of consumers will place different values on a service. As a result, price segmentation strategies such as segmenting by the time of purchase, the time of usage, and self-service have been successful. For price segmentation schemes to be effective, a number of criteria discussed in the chapter must be met.

Overall, traditional pricing strategies and cost accounting approaches offer little benefit to either service consumers or service providers. Three alternative pricing strategies that convey value to the customer include satisfaction-based, relationship, and efficiency pricing. The primary goal of satisfaction-based pricing is to reduce the perceived risk associated with the purchase of services and to appeal to target markets that value certainty. Satisfaction-based pricing strategies include offering guarantees, benefit-driven pricing, and flat-rate pricing. The goal of relationship pricing is to enhance the firm's relationship with its targeted consumers. Relationship pricing techniques include offering long-term contracts and price bundling. In comparison, efficiency pricing appeals to economically-minded consumers and focuses on delivering the best and most cost-effective service for the price. Understanding and managing costs are the fundamental building blocks of efficiency pricing. Activity-based costing appears to offer service marketers more assistance than traditional cost accounting approaches when implementing price strategies.

Key Terms

monetary price	marginal costs
time costs	future costs
energy costs	contribution margin (CM)
psychic costs	price elasticity
product value	inelastic demand
service value	elastic demand
personnel value	unitary demand
image value	income elasticity
cost	cross-price elasticity
benefit	complementary
lower price threshold	substitutes
upper price threshold	price segmentation
reservation price	time-based pricing
consumer's surplus	satisfaction-based pricing
price ceiling	benefit-driven pricing
price floor	flat-rate pricing
fixed costs	relationship pricing
direct variable costs	price bundling
break-even point	mixed bundling
shared costs	efficiency pricing
average costs	activity-based costing (ABC)
learning curve	cost drivers

REVIEW QUESTIONS

1. Define the following terms: elastic demand, inelastic demand, unitary demand, income elasticity, cross-price elasticity, complements, and substitutes.

2. Discuss the role of price as an indicator of quality to consumers.

3. Describe the trade-offs associated with taking hotel reservations from customers who pay lower rates than same-day customers.

4. Discuss the differences between traditional methods of allocating overhead expenses and activity-based costing.

5. Explain what is meant by the term *time dependent capacity.*

6. Under what conditions is price segmentation most effective?

7. Discuss the basic concepts behind satisfaction-based, relationship, and efficiency pricing.

NOTES

1. Adapted from John E. G. Bateson, *Managing Services Marketing,* 2nd ed. (Fort Worth, TX: The Dryden Press, 1992), pp. 357–365.

2. Philip Kotler, *Marketing Management,* 8th ed. (Englewood Cliffs, NJ: Prentice-Hall, 1994), p. 38.

3. Peter R. Dickson, *Marketing Management* (Fort Worth, TX: The Dryden Press, 1995), p. 59.

4. Leonard L. Berry and Manjit S. Yadav, "Capture and Communicate Value in the Pricing of Services," *Sloan Management Review* (Summer 1996), pp. 41–51.

5. Ibid.

6. Christopher W. L. Hart, Leonard A. Schlesinger, and Dan Maher, "Guarantees Come to Professional Service Firms," *Sloan Management Review* (Spring 1992), pp. 19–29.

7. Joseph P. Guiltinan, "The Price Bundling of Services: A Normative Framework," *Journal of Marketing* (April 1987), pp. 51, 74–85.

8. Berry and Manjit, "Capture and Communicate Value," p. 49.

9. Beth M. Chaffman and John Talbott, "Activity-Based Costing in a Service Organization," *CMA Magazine* (December 1990/January 1991), pp. 15–18.

10. Berry and Manjit, "Capture and Communicate Value," p. 50.

A P P E N D I X

A COMPREHENSIVE PRICING MODEL: THE DIFFERENTATION PREMIUM APPROACH[1]

differentiation premium approach
A competitive-oriented pricing model based on the concept of a differentiation premium derived from the factors of availability, testability, commitment, and price sensitivity.

The pricing of services has traditionally been dominated by cost, competitive, and premium pricing strategies. Although these approaches to pricing can be quite helpful and currently dominate the service sector, their simplistic nature often causes them to lose their effectiveness as environmental conditions become more dynamic and complex. The **differentiation premium approach** focuses on developing a competitive-oriented pricing model based on the concept of a differentiation premium. The calculated differentiation premium results from combining the evaluation of a set of differentiation factors. Individually, the categories of differentiation factors exert upward or downward pressure on the price a service provider can charge.

DIFFERENTIATION FACTORS

The differentiation premium model incorporates four categorical factors upon which the professional service provider can differentiate the service firm from its competitors. These factors are availability, testability, commitment, and price sensitivity.

AVAILABILITY

availability
The number of sources from which consumers can acquire comparable services at comparable effort and cost.

Availability refers to the number of sources from which consumers can acquire a comparable service at comparable effort and cost. The number of sources as well as the type of source will vary, depending on the service sought. For example, some services may be readily available from competing service providers, or they may be performed in-house by the customer if he or she so chooses. Hence, regardless of the source, a readily available service must be priced competitively with in-house or other alternatives.

TESTABILITY

testability
The degree to which the service performance can be objectively evaluated before the actual purchase transaction.

Evaluating the degree of testability that can be assigned to a service performance is an important step in formulating a pricing policy. **Testability** refers to the degree to which the service performance can be objectively evaluated before the actual purchase transaction has been consummated. Services that are vulnerable to high performance variability and/or customized to meet individual customer specifications are generally untestable. Consequently, potential clients for these types of services assume an element of risk when selecting a service provider from a number of alternatives.

A service provider well established in his or her field can substitute reputation for testability. Although reputation does not guarantee a flawless performance on every occasion, it does provide a basis for differentiation among service professional alternatives. To illustrate, an attorney who has never lost a case in court still cannot guarantee the outcome of the next jury decision. However, the past success would lend the attorney a higher degree of testability and a reputation that could command higher fees than an attorney with a lower success rate.

Because reputation depends heavily on service quality, a rating for this component can be derived from surveying consumers and analyzing the key determinants of perceived service quality. Determinants of service quality include reliability, responsiveness, assurance, empathy, and tangible indicators such as physical facilities and appearance of personnel. These factors are not included separately in the differentiation premium model because they are encompassed in other factors and are a critical portion of the service firm's reputation.

COMMITMENT INCENTIVES

The relationship between profitability and duration of the service provider/ customer relationship can also have a major influence on developing a pricing strategy. When opportunities exist for the service provider to build a loyal clientele, it may be very advantageous for the provider to pursue a strategy that includes **commitment incentives** to reward those clients who appear to be committed to the service organization. Thus, due to lower retention costs, it may be more profitable over the long run for some service providers to forego the full markup generally charged customers who patronize the service provider sporadically (short-term commitment) and reward those current customers who purchase services on a regular basis (long-term commitment).

Conversely, some service providers may charge a premium price if consumer costs (i.e., monetary, time, energy, and psychic) associated with switching to a competitor are high. For example, dentists who require a full set of X-rays upon the admission of a new client illustrate some of the economic and physical switching costs involved when changing doctors. Thus, due to varying degrees of the duration of the service provider/customer relationship, the service provider must sometimes design alternative pricing strategies to reflect the separate commitment arrangements of different target markets.

commitment incentives
The strategy that offers price incentives to reward clients who appear to be committed to the service organization.

PRICE SENSITIVITY

According to information theory (or search theory), an individual's sensitivity to changes in price depends on the number of alternatives about which the consumer is aware. Moreover, the number of alternatives known to the consumer is based on what it costs to acquire the information relative to the benefits gained.

THE PRICING OF SERVICES

X-rays for new patients illustrate some of the economic and physical costs involved when changing physicians. Premiums can be high when switching to a competitor.

Source: © 1995 PhotoDisc, Inc. Image no. 7092.

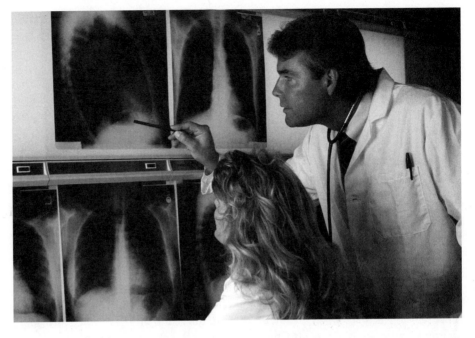

price sensitivity

Consumers' levels of reaction to prices of services.

Thus, the less costly it is to acquire the information, the greater the number of alternatives known to the consumer, and the more **price sensitivity** the consumer develops.

The cost of acquiring information about alternatives is based on whether the benefits produced by the alternatives can be examined through search, experience, or credence attributes. These three categories have important pricing implications for service providers. First, if the salient attributes of the service category are search attributes, consumers will tend to be sensitive to price changes. Consequently, it appears that providers of standardized services, which tend to be characterized by search attributes, need to be very competitive in their pricing. Moreover, since the costs of switching to a competitor are low in this case, failure to be price competitive would mean an almost certain loss in revenues.

Second, higher degrees of customization and personal judgment increase the difficulty of evaluating alternatives and, thus, imply that the salient attributes are experience/credence oriented. Consequently, producers of services whose salient service attributes are experience/credence oriented appear much less subject to consumer price sensitivity and can procure a fee for their services based on factors other than competitive.

MECHANICS OF THE MODEL

The differentiation premium model incorporates four factors upon which the professional service provider can differentiate the service firm from its competitors:

availability, testability, commitment, and price sensitivity. Each factor is designed to be subjectively evaluated and then scored from (0) to (+1) or from (−1) to (+1), depending on the factor's impact on price. The score assigned to a factor provides two indications regarding the potential pricing differential relative to competitor's prices. First, the sign (+ or −) indicates the direction of the differential. Second, the absolute value indicates the amount or degree of the differentiation. The model is designed so that positive values exert an upward influence on the service provider's price (relative to the average competitive price) and negative values exert downward pressure.

AVAILABILITY

Availability is incorporated into a service provider's pricing strategy through an availability premium (Ap), which ranges in value from (0) to (+1). Services that can be easily handled in-house by most consumers or easily obtained through a competing service provider should be priced competitively. Thus, Ap would be factored into the equation at a level approaching zero to reflect the highly competitive nature of the service. Conversely, services not readily available from other providers can be priced higher; Ap could, therefore, be factored into the formula at a level approaching (+1).

TESTABILITY

Incorporating testability into the service professional's pricing strategy can be accomplished through a reputation testability premium (RTp). RTp ranges in value from (−1) to (+1). The upper range (+1) reflects the idea that a superior, testable reputation generally justifies charging a higher price than "average" competitors. Conversely, the lower range is set at (−1) because a relatively poor reputation can exert downward pressure on prices.

COMMITMENT INCENTIVE PREMIUMS

Financial considerations designed to stimulate repeat business and customer loyalty are commitment incentive premiums (CIp). Services that yield perishable and repeatable benefits may be priced so as to encourage repeat business. These incentives may take the form of initial discounts or long-run volume savings for the client. Thus, in these types of cases, CIp would be factored into the formula as a negative value approaching (−1.0), which would reflect the downward pressure on the pricing arrangement. In cases where switching costs are high and consumers have "committed" themselves to the service firm through their initial purchase, the firm may be able to charge a premium (up to the cost of switching). Hence, CIp would be factored into the formula as a positive value approaching (+1), which would reflect an upward pressure on the price. In cases in which price incentives are unnecessary and/or inappropriate, CIp would be factored into the formula as zero. The exact size of the incentive would depend upon the caliber of customer and relative competitive offerings.

PRICE SENSITIVITY

The sensitivity of consumers to prices is incorporated into the pricing formula through a price sensitivity premium (PSp). Providers of services whose salient attributes are search attributes would factor PSp into the formula at a level approaching zero to reflect increasing consumer price sensitivity and the downward pressure on price associated with the competitive nature of the market's pricing structure. Conversely, providers of services whose salient attributes are experience/credence oriented would be free to factor PSp into the pricing formula at a level greater than zero and approaching ($+1$) to reflect decreasing consumer price sensitivity and the absence of downward pressure on the price for the service. Ideally, the provider of services whose offerings' salient attributes are experience/credence is looking for the optimal price at which consumer price sensitivity changes from insensitive to sensitive and total revenue is maximized.

Table 7A.1 reviews the range of scores for each of the differentiation factors.

THE DIFFERENTIATION PREMIUM MODEL

Upon evaluation of each factor included in the model, scores are summed and divided by 4 to calculate the differentiation premium as follows:

$$DP = \frac{(Ap) + (RTp) + (Clp) + (PSp)}{4}$$

where:

DP = differentiation premium
Ap = availability premium
RTp = reputation testability premium
Clp = commitment incentive premium
PSp = price sensitivity premium

Because of the rating system, DP can range from $+1.00$ (4/4) to $-.50$ ($-2/4$). Once the differentiation premium has been calculated, the differentiation premium-based price for a service is derived by using the following formula:

$$Pdp(SL) = (1 + DP) \times (ACP)$$

where:

Pdp = service price based on differentiation premium
(SL) = standard limits
DP = differentiation premium
ACP = average competitor's price

TABLE 7A.1 DIFFERENTIATION PREMIUM FACTOR RANGES	
Factor	**Range**
Availability	(0) to (+1)
Testability	(-1) to (+1)
Commitment	(-1) to (+1)
Price Sensitivity	(0) to (+1)

Thus, a differentiation premium of zero indicates that the firm is highly comparable with its competitors and that an average competitive price is appropriate. A differentiation premium between zero and (+1.00) indicates that the service firm has successfully differentiated itself from its competitors and can command a higher-than-average fee for services rendered. Finally, a differentiation premium less than zero and approaching (−.50) tends to indicate that the firm offers less than average value. Firms in this group would charge lower-than-average prices.

STANDARD LIMITS

Within a given market, the prices charged for each type of service fall within a certain price range or **standard limit (SL).** How the standard limit is set depends on the type of service examined. In many cases, the lowest prices within the range generally represent a "price floor" or minimum price that covers the cost of providing the service plus some minimum markup percentage. Conversely, the highest prices within the range represent a "price ceiling" or maximum price that reflects the highest level consumers are willing to pay for the service. In other instances, the standard limit is dictated by government regulation or professional association guidelines. Regardless of how the standard limit is set, the professional service provider must price within the standard limit range.

Due to the constraint of the standard limit, special consideration needs to be given to the extreme values that are derived through the differentiation premium price (Pdp) formula. In its current state, the minimum value for the differentiation premium is (−.50). This translates into a Pdp of one-half the average competitor's price. However, if this minimum Pdp is less than the lower standard limit, the latter of the two values must be accepted as the final service price. Conversely, the maximum value for the differentiation premium is (1.00). This value translates into a Pdp 100 percent greater than the average competitor's price. If this maximum Pdp is greater than the upper standard limit, the upper standard limit must be accepted as the professional service price. Hence, regardless of Pdp, the professional service price cannot exceed the upper limit or fall below the lower limit.

standard limits (SL)
The lowest and highest prices consumers are willing to pay for a given service.

THE DIFFERENTIATION PREMIUM APPROACH: AN EXAMPLE

A service provider with an average reputation produces a service that is readily available at a large number of competitors. Due to the competitive situation, demand for this service is highly elastic. However, due to the nature of the service, switching costs are very high. The standard limits for this type of service range from $45 to $95. If the average competitive price is $50, what price should the service provider charge according to the differentiation premium model?

Because the range of the reputation/testability premium is (-1) to $(+1)$, a service provider with an average reputation would score (0). Likewise, since the service is readily available, the availability premium would also be (0). Due to the elastic nature of consumer demand, consumers are very price sensitive. Consequently, the price sensitivity premium would also be (0). Finally, this particular service provider incurs high switching costs upon consumers, which permits the service provider to assign the value of $(+1)$ to the commitment premium.

Based on the assigned scores, the differentiation premium would equal:

$$DP = \frac{(Ap) + (RTp) + (Clp) + (PSp)}{4}$$
$$= \{(0+0+0+1)/4\}$$
$$= 1/4$$
$$= .25$$

The price for the service based on the differentiation premium model would then be calculated as follows:

$$Pdp(SL) = (1 + DP) \times (ACP)$$
$$=$$
$$Pdp(\$45 – \$95) = (1 + .25) \times (\$50)$$
$$= \$75$$

Since $75 is within the standard limits of $45 to $95, the differentiation premium model suggests that the service provider can price his/her service at $75, or 50 percent higher than the average competitive price.

CONCLUDING REMARKS

The differentiation premium model does not eliminate subjectivity; rather, it adds some objectivity and, most importantly, strives to achieve greater organized subjectivity. Hence, the true value of the model lies in breaking a general subjective decision into smaller, more manageable components. For example, service providers are typically forced into logic such as "I am a little better than average, so I can charge a little more than my competition." The differentiation approach enhances the service provider's ability to determine "how much more" by focusing specific attention on differentiation factors.

The model incorporates the firm's ability to differentiate from competitors into the firm's pricing strategy through the use of differentiation premiums. Based on the discussion concerning differentiation premiums, the following conclusions can be drawn: (1) The more unavailable the service is to the consumer, the higher the price the service provider can command, (2) the more testable the service, the lower the risk consumers perceive concerning the purchase, and the higher the price consumers are willing to pay for it, (3) the more standardized the service, the greater the level of consumer price sensitivity, (4) the more customized the service, the lower the level of consumer price sensitivity, and (5) the greater the need to obtain a long-term commitment from customers, the lower the price the service firm will charge its customers.

KEY TERMS

differentiation premium approach
availability
testability

commitment incentives
price sensitivity
standard limit

NOTES:

1. Danny R. Arnold, K. Douglas Hoffman, and James McCormick, "Service Pricing: A Differentiation Premium Approach," *Journal of Services Marketing*, 3,3 (Summer 1989), pp. 25–33.

Developing the Service Communication Mix

"It is what you say and how you say it!"

Service Providers Who Stay in Business

CHAPTER OBJECTIVES

The purpose of this chapter is to provide an overview of communication mix strategies as they apply to the marketing of services.

After reading this chapter, you should be able to

▸ Discuss factors that influence the development of the firm's communication mix.

  ▸ *Discuss the goals of the communication mix during prepurchase, consumption, and postpurchase stages.*

▸ Describe the special problems associated with developing the service communication mix.

  ▸ *Discuss the basic guidelines for advertising services.*

▸ Describe the special problems encountered by professional service providers.

UNIQUE COMMUNICATION STRATEGY:
TACO BELL "CRACKS" A JOKE THAT FOOLS THE COUNTRY

*I*n an effort to help the U.S. government reduce the federal budget deficit, Taco Bell recently announced that its corporation had purchased the Liberty Bell. The announcement was made in seven major newspapers in New York, Chicago, Los Angeles, Washington D.C., Philadelphia, Dallas, and in *USA Today.* The announcement further explained that the bell would be renamed the "Taco Liberty Bell" and rotated between the bell's traditional home of Philadelphia and Taco Bell's home headquarters in Irvine, California. Concerned citizens who were fed up with corporate sponsorship of anything and everything these days lit up phones across the country. Taco Bell's service hotline received 2,000 calls alone, and radio talk shows had a field day with their listeners. However, what most of these people overlooked was the day the announcement was made—April 1—April Fools Day!

In an era of dull corporate pronouncements, Taco Bell made a bold move that caught the country's attention. Later in the day, Taco Bell issued a press release confessing to the carefully contrived and professionally executed communications gag and announced a $50,000 contribution to the fund to assist in the restoration of the aging national treasure. The final result was a publicity gold mine for Taco Bell.

The cost of the communication campaign was approximately $300,000; however, the value of the publicity generated by the campaign far exceeded Taco Bell's out-of-pocket costs. So far, the company believes that the ploy generated more than 400 TV mentions, thousands of newspaper stories and radio mentions, and perhaps the crowning glory, a full news story by Tom Brokaw of "NBC Nightly News" that evening. Experts figure that the total exposure for Taco Bell was worth several million dollars.

Source: Bob Lamons, "Taco Bell Rings in New Age of Publicity Stunts," *Marketing News* 30,11 (1996), p. 15.

Reprinted by permission of the American Marketing Association.

**DEVELOPING THE SERVICE
COMMUNICATION MIX**

INTRODUCTION

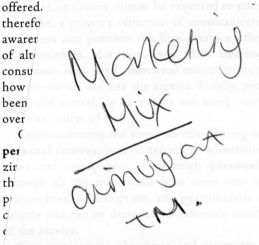

Communications strategy is one of the key components of the service marketing mix.[1] In general, the primary role of a service firm's communication strategy is to inform, persuade, or remind consumers about the service being offered. Consumers cannot be expected to use a service they do not know about; therefore, a primary objective of communication strategy is to create consumer awareness and position the firm's service offering in the consumer's evoked set of alternatives. Moreover, even when awareness of the service product exists, consumers may need additional encouragement to try it and information about how to obtain and use the service. Finally, people forget. Just because they have been told something once does not mean that they will necessarily remember it over the course of time.

Communicating the basic service offering may be accomplished through **non-personal sources**, such as television advertising or printed information in magazines and newspapers, or through personal sources on a face-to-face basis through all the individuals who come into contact with the consumer in the prepurchase, consumption, and postpurchase stages. In addition, the communications mix can be designed to influence customer expectations and perceptions of the service.

Communications objectives and strategies vary, depending upon the nature of the target audience. Separate communications strategies are necessary for current users of a service in order to influence or change their patterns of service use, and for nonusers in order to attract them to the service. In addition, the communications mix can be designed to influence customer expectations and perceptions of the service. Service firms also need to understand the effects that communications have on their own employees.

DEVELOPING A COMMUNICATIONS STRATEGY

SELECTING TARGET MARKETS

Developing a communications strategy follows a common pattern whether the firm is producing goods or services. The service firm must first analyze the needs of consumers and then categorize consumers with similar needs into market segments. Each market segment should then be considered based on profit and growth potential and the segment's compatibility with organizational resources and objectives. Segments that become the focus of the firm's marketing efforts become **target markets**.

---

nonpersonal sources
Communication channels that are considered impersonal, such as television advertising or printed information.

personal sources
Communication channels that are considered personal, such as a face-to-face encounter.

target markets
The segments of potential customers that become the focus of a firm's marketing efforts.

DEVELOPING THE FIRM'S POSITIONING STRATEGY

Once the target market is selected, successful service firms establish a **positioning strategy,** which differentiates them from competitors in consumers' eyes. Effective positioning is particularly critical for service firms where intangibility clouds the consumer's ability to differentiate one service provider's offering from the next. For example, competing airlines that fly the same routes may stress operational elements such as the percentage of "on-time" arrivals, while others stress service elements such as the friendliness and helpfulness of the flght crew and the quality of the food served.

Ultimately, positioning involves a strategic manipulation of the firm's marketing mix variables: product, price, promotion, place, physical facilities, people, and processes. Each of these marketing mix variables is controllable. When effectively combined, the marketing mix can offset the effects of the uncontrollable factors that exist in every firm's operating environment such as technological advances, consumer needs, new and existing competitors, governmental regulations, economic conditions, and the effects of seasonality that are constantly changing the environment in which the firm operates. Firms that fail to alter their positioning strategy to reflect environmental changes in order to differentiate themselves from competitors often falter in the long run (see Table 8.1).[2]

DEVELOPING THE COMMUNICATIONS BUDGET AND MIX

The firm's promotion, or **communications mix,** communicates the firm's positioning strategy to its relevant markets, including consumers, employees, stockholders, and suppliers. The term *communications mix* describes the array of communications tools available to marketers. Just as marketers need to combine the elements of the marketing mix (including communications) to produce a marketing program, they must also select the most appropriate communication vehicles to convey their message.

The elements of the communications mix fall into four broad categories: **personal selling; media advertising; publicity and public relations,** and **sales promotions**—promotional or informational activities at the point of sale. Only personal selling is a two-way form of communication. The remainder are one-way communications, going only from the marketer to the customer. Using more than one communications tool or using any one tool repeatedly increases the chances that existing and potential customers will be exposed to the firm's message, associate it with the firm, and remember it. By reinforcing its message, the firm can ensure that existing customers as well as potential ones become more aware of "who" the firm is and what it has to offer. The firm's communications mix often lays the foundation for subsequent contact with potential consumers, making discussions with consumers easier for the provider and more comfortable for the consumers.

positioning strategy
The plan for differentiating the firm from its competitors in consumers' eyes.

communications mix
The array of communications tools available to marketers.

personal selling
The two-way element of the communications mix in which the service provider influences a consumer via direct interaction.

media advertising
A one-way communications tool that utilizes such media as television and radio to reach a broadly defined audience.

publicity/public relations
A one-way communications tool between an organization and its customers, vendors, news media, employees, stockholders, the government, and the general public.

sales promotions
A one-way communications tool that utilizes promotional or informational activities at the point of sale.

DEVELOPING THE SERVICE
COMMUNICATION MIX

TABLE 8.1 — DIFFERENTIATION APPROACHES FOR EFFECTIVE POSITIONING

Product Differentiation	Personnel Differentiation
Features	Competence
Performance	Courtesy
Conformance	Credibility
Durability	Reliability
Reliability	Responsiveness
Repairability	Communication
Style	
Design (integrates the above)	
Image Differentiation	**Service Differentiation**
Symbols	Delivery (speed, accuracy)
Written, audio/visual media	Installation
Atmosphere	Customer training
Events	Consulting service
	Repair
	Miscellaneous service

Source: Adapted from Philip Kotler, *Marketing Management*, 9th ed. (Englewood Cliffs, NJ: Prentice-Hall, 1997), p. 283.

It is important at this stage of developing the firm's communications mix to determine the communications budget. Budget-setting techniques typically covered in most introductory marketing classes include the percentage-of-sales technique, the incremental technique, the all-you-can-afford approach, competitive parity, and the objective-and-task method.[3] After the budget has been established, the target audience or audiences, objectives, and budgets are divided among the different areas of the communications mix. Each area does not have to be assigned the same task or audience as long as together, they meet the overall objectives of the firm's communications strategy. Once they do, information delivery can be planned and executed and the results monitored.

DEFINING COMMUNICATIONS OBJECTIVES

The objectives of a firm's communications mix often relate directly to the service offering's stage within the product life cycle (see Table 8.2). In general, the major communication objectives within the introduction and growth stages of the PLC are to inform the customer. Informational communications introduce the service offering and create brand awareness for the firm. Informational communications also encourage trial and often prepare the way for personal selling efforts to be conducted later.

TABLE 8.2 COMMUNICATION CONTENT AND OBJECTIVES		
PRODUCT LIFE CYCLE STAGE	**Communication Content**	**Communication Objectives**
Introduction	Informational	Introduce the service offering Create brand awareness Prepare the way for personal selling efforts Encourage trial
Growth and maturity	Informational and persuasive	Create a positive attitude relative to competitive offerings Provoke an immediate buying action Enhance the firm's image
Maturity and decline	Persuasive and reminder	Encourage repeat purchases Provide ongoing contact Express gratitude to existing customer base Confirm past purchase decisions

As professional service providers slowly begin to advertise, informational communications objectives tend to be the first step. Informational communications tend to be less obtrusive than other forms of communication, and in many ways, the information being conveyed often provides a public service to consumers who otherwise might not have access or knowledge of the range of services available. Legal and medical referral services that advertise are typical examples. Many of the clients who contact these services are lower-income, lower-educated clients who, by their own admission, have stated that if it were not for the referral services, they would not know where to turn.[4]

Communications objectives during the growth and maturity stages of the PLC tend to lean toward informational and persuasive content. Objectives during this stage include creating a positive attitude toward the service offering relative to competitive alternatives, attempting to provoke an immediate purchase action, and enhancing the firm's image. Professional service organizations often discourage the use of persuasive advertising among their members as it often pits one professional member of the organization against another. Many in professional organizations believe that members engaged in persuasive communications ultimately cheapen the image of the entire industry.

Finally, communications objectives during the maturity and decline stages of the PLC tend to utilize persuasive and reminder communications. The communications objectives during this phase of the PLC are to influence existing customers to purchase again, to provide ongoing contact with the existing client base in order to remind clients that the firm still values their relationship, and to confirm clients' past purchase decisions, thereby minimizing levels of felt cognitive dissonance. As with informational communications, reminder communications tend to be less obtrusive and more acceptable to professional organizations than persuasive communications.

DIVIDING THE COMMUNICATIONS OBJECTIVES AND TARGET AUDIENCES

Once the overall objectives and target audiences for the entire communications mix have been set, it is necessary to divide the tasks among advertising, selling, publicity and public relations, and sales promotions. This is a process of matching the tasks to the capabilities of the different communications channels.

TARGETING NONUSERS

If the objective is to reach nonusers of the service, then the choice of communications channel is reduced to media advertising, selling performed by a sales force rather than a service provider, and publicity and public relations.

One way of assigning tasks across the array of communications channels is to consider the degree to which the message can be targeted at specific audiences. Media advertising itself varies along this dimension. At the broadcast, "shotgun" level, television can reach a very wide audience but is not especially selective except in the variation of audiences across channels by time of day. National print media such as newspapers and magazines offer more selective focus, as they themselves tend to be targeted at more specific segments of consumers. Trade magazines are even more specific in their readership. Direct mail offers the most focused of the impersonal media.

The choice among these media must be based on the cost per thousand members of the target audience and the risk and cost of reaching the wrong segments.

When the service provider has a broadly defined audience and little to lose in reaching the wrong segments, television advertising may work out to be the least expensive vehicle. However, television and other forms of mass media are unlikely to be efficient for a specialty service such as an upscale restaurant with a tightly defined target audience and a high cost associated with attracting the wrong segment.

Public relations and publicity can be either broad or tightly focused, depending on how they are used. Editorial comment can be solicited in broad or narrow media. Public relations carries with it the advantages and disadvantages of not being paid advertising. On the positive side, it is given more credence by the consumer; on the negative side, it is much more difficult to control. The content may not be designed, or the coverage may be limited.

Both media advertising and public relations and publicity are one-way forms of communication. They cannot respond to consumers' inquiries or tailor the message to the particular characteristics of the receiver. Personal or telemarketing is far more expensive per member of the target audience, but it does offer the flexibility of altering the message during the presentation. If the message is difficult to communicate or a great deal of persuasion is needed, personal communication may be most appropriate. A sales force can be highly targeted and trained to make complex arguments interactively, responding to the inputs of consumers during the process.

Targeting Users

Users can be reached through all the channels discussed above, and they can be further reached by communications through the service provider. The role of the service provider is multifaceted. Different providers are called upon to perform different communication functions. These providers and functions have been classified along the following lines:[5]

Type 1 service staff are required to deal with customers quickly and effectively in "once only" situations where large numbers of customers are present. The exchanges consist of simple information and limited responses to customer requests. Effective communication requires the ability to establish customer relationships very quickly, deal efficiently with customer problems, and convey short, rapid messages that customers can easily understand. Typical examples include front-line personnel at fast-food restaurants or dry cleaners and patient representatives whose job is to obtain and process insurance information.

Type 2 service staff deal with numerous, often repeat customers in restricted interactions of somewhat longer duration. The information provided is mixed— partly simple and partly more complex—and requires some independent decision making on the part of the staff member. Communication in this category requires effective listening skills, the ability to establish trust, interpreting customer information, and making decisions in customer relationships that are often ongoing over a period of time. Communications are generally more intense than in Type 1 situations. Typical examples include relationships with suppliers or customer relationships such as with a customer who requests floral designs from a florist on a regular basis, a loyal customer of a seamstress/tailor, or an effective wait staff person at a fine dining establishment.

Type 3 service staff are required to have more complex communication skills. Interactions with consumers are repeated over time, extensive flow of communication is required, and communication tasks are complicated and often non-repeatable. Effective communication requires the ability to listen and process complicated information, to think creatively in face-to-face interactions with consumers, and to provide information in a clear and understandable manner. Typical examples include staff members who are likely to be qualified as professionals.

Any service organization may have employees in one, two, or all three of the above categories. Thus, a bank may have tellers performing type 1 communications, a loan officer engaged in type 2, and a commercial loan officer engaged in type 3. A travel company may have an agent engaged in both type 2 (when writing tickets and booking arrangements) and type 3 communications (when planning trips) and a receptionist handling type 1 communications.

Each type of communication requires a different set of skills from the providers and places different levels of stress on them. It is clearly important that

type 1 staff
Service staff that are required to deal with customers quickly and effectively in "once only" situations where large numbers of customers are present.

type 2 staff
Service staff that deal with numerous, often repeat customers in restricted interactions of somewhat longer duration.

type 3 staff
Service staff required to have more highly developed communication skills because of more extended and complex interactions with customers.

the correct communications role be assigned to the correct person within the organization. Type 1 is predominantly an operations role, whereas type 3 is a mixed selling and operations role.

When a communications mix that includes the service provider is developed, the final objectives for the staff will probably fall within one of the above categories. However, it is important to recall the position of the employee providing the service. The service provider is not simply a salesperson; he or she is an integral part of the operations process and a part of the experience purchased by the customer. An apparently simple decision—for example, to have a bank teller sell services—can have profound negative consequences. It could well be that the decision produces role conflict for the teller. Role/self-conflict could be caused by the tellers' wanting to see themselves not as salespeople but as bankers. Direct conflict between the two roles can arise when the operations role demands fast service and minimization of the time spent with each customer but the selling role demands the opposite. In addition, the script may break down for both the service provider and the customer as the teller tries to do something new. The customer may be expecting a brisk, businesslike transaction when suddenly, the teller wants to build rapport by talking about the weather (before starting the sell).

Potentially, such a decision can also diminish operational efficiency as the transaction time per customer rises. This problem is illustrated by the experiences of FedEx before it centralized its telephone customer contact system. In times of peak demand, especially if those times were unpredicted, everyone in the FedEx depots answered telephones, including the field salespersons based at the depots. The result was that the various depot employees changed the service communication from type 1 to type 3. It also meant that calls took much longer than usual, and the telephone bottleneck consequently worsened.

THE COMMUNICATIONS MIX AS IT RELATES TO CONSUMER BEHAVIOR CONSIDERATIONS[6]

Consumer behavior is important because it imposes constraints on the objectives set for services. It is perhaps best to consider behavior during the three phases discussed in Chapter Four—prepurchase, consumption, and postpurchase.

THE PRECONSUMPTION CHOICE STAGE

Consumers will try to minimize risk taken in the purchase phase. Risk is some combination of consequences and uncertainty, so these are the two dimensions along which advertising can operate. In each case, the objective must be to ensure that the company's service is the one perceived to be the least risky alternative.

Communication can obviously impart information that is a key factor in reducing the uncertainty in all risky decisions. It can also offer reassurance. Consequences are generally of three basic types: **financial, social,** and **performance.** Financial consequences can be reduced by communications that ensure that

---

financial consequences

The perceived monetary consequences of a purchase decision by a consumer.

social consequences

The perceived consequences of a consumer's purchase decision among the consumer's peers or the public in general.

performance consequences

The perceived consequences of a consumer's purchase decision should the service perform less than 100 percent effectively.

FedEx improved its communications mix when it centralized its telephone customer contact system. Now employees can interact with customers and accomplish mailouts without having to worry about answering the phone during peak periods.

Source: HB Photo/Annette Coolidge.

consumers correctly understand the likely financial consequences of a purchase, particularly if a money-back guarantee is offered. Concerns about social consequences can be reduced by highlighting for consumers that other people are using the service and that it would not be embarrassing for them to use it. Performance consequences need to be made explicit and clearly communicated to ensure that consumers understand what would happen if the performance were not 100 percent successful. Clearly, most services are perceived as more risky on the social and performance dimensions, and communications have a key role to play in reassuring customers.

The communications mix can, for example, be based on generating positive word-of-mouth references. This key communications area for services can be managed using public relations and publicity. It has also been shown to be a key method in reducing consumers' perceived risk.

The **rational mathematician model** assumes that consumers are rational decision makers using a choice matrix of attributes, brand or company scores, and importance weights like those described in the airlines example presented in Chapter Four. Services in the evoked set are scored using the matrix, and the one with the highest score is chosen. Communications can be used to try to influence the choice in the following ways:

▲ To alter the weights consumers attach to different attributes to favor those in which the company is strong.

rational mathematician model

A model that assumes consumers are rational decision makers using a choice matrix of attributes, brand or company scores, and importance weights.

▶▶▶▶ ◀◀◀◀

- To alter the score on a given attribute for the company, particularly if a gap exists between performance and consumer's perceptions.
- To alter the score on a given attribute given to a competitor, again, particularly if a gap exists between performance and consumers' perceptions.
- If the company is not in the evoked set, to build enough awareness of the offering to stimulate inclusion.

It is important to remember the difference between tangible performance and perceived performance. If actual performance is higher than perceived performance, communications may be more effective than if the reverse were the case. Alternatively, advertising can be used to maintain a situation that is favorable to the firm. Consumers need to be reminded that a firm does well on particular attributes and that those attributes are important.

THE CONSUMPTION STAGE

During the consumption stage, the service consumer is more or less an active participant in the production process. It is important that consumers perform that production role successfully. From the firm's point of view, successful performance will improve the efficiency of the operation and the satisfaction of other customers. From the consumer's point of view, successful performance will ensure a high level of perceived control and, in all probability, a high level of satisfaction in the postconsumption phase.

Communications, in the broadest sense, can be used to ensure successful performance by giving the consumer a clear script. Although this can be done through advertising, the presence of the consumer in the actual service setting gives the opportunity for a much broader range of communications channels. Point-of-sale signs, service providers, and the environment itself can all be used to teach the consumer the script.

In times of operational change, managing the consumer's script takes on even more importance. An example can be seen in a bank that is changing from multiple-line queuing to single-line queuing. No longer may consumers wait in front of a specific teller window. Instead, they must form a single line and go to the first free window available to them when they arrive at the head of the line. Operationally, this offers shorter and more predictable waiting times.

However, such a shift requires a script change. Arriving at the bank without prior warning of the change, the consumer finds a new experience, one that no longer conforms to the existing script. Because it is not immediately obvious how the new system works, the customer may feel a loss of control. The line seems to be extremely long, and worse still, it is no longer possible to choose a specific, favorite teller. Clearly, the script needs to be modified.

It is fairly obvious how elements of the communications mix can be used to achieve script modification. The bank can use media advertising or leaflets to describe the new process. "Salespeople" outside the bank can explain the new system to customers before they enter. Public relations can be used to generate consumer comment about the benefits of the new system. Inside the building, the layout and signs displayed can clearly signal the desired customer behavior. Finally, service providers can personally reassure customers and reinforce the new script.

The Postconsumption Evaluation Stage

Chapter Four also introduced the disconfirmation model of consumer satisfaction. This model hypothesizes that consumers determine satisfaction by comparing their prior expectations of performance with the perceived actual performance.

Consumer expectations come from a number of sources, some within the control of the service firm, and some beyond its control. Expectations arise either from previous experience with the firm and/or its competitors or from some form of communication. The latter can encompass all aspects of the communications mix. Advertising, designed to influence prepurchase choice behavior, can set expectations in the customer's mind about the quality of service that will be received. Indeed, setting such expectations may be a key aspect of a firm's advertising strategy.

In Chapter Four, you learned that, based on studies of consumer behavior, word-of-mouth communication can be expected to have an increased role in the service industry because of the high levels of perceived risk associated with the purchase of many services. Such word-of-mouth communication can be random, or it can be orchestrated through the public relations component of the communications mix.

Special Problems of the Service Communications Mix[7]

Mistargeted Communications

Segmentation is one of the basic concepts of marketing. In essence, it suggests that a firm's marketing efficiency can be improved by targeting marketing activities at discrete groups of consumers who behave differently in some way toward the firm. Although segmentation is applied in both goods and service companies, the consequences of reaching an inappropriate segment with a part of the communication mix are far less serious for goods companies than for services. If the wrong group of consumers buys a particular brand of detergent, for example, it does not really affect the company making the detergent; sales are still being generated. Or a product may have been developed for the youth market, but through some quirk of the advertising execution, the product has attracted some senior citizens. For example, take the Pepsi advertisement that portrayed the youthful effects of Pepsi being delivered to a senior citizens' home by error instead of to the college fraternity house. Let's say that the ad is interpreted by senior citizens that Pepsi will make them feel young again. Clearly, this was not Pepsi's (who targets the younger generation) original intent. Members of this group that misinterpreted the message visit the supermarket, buy the product, and use it in their homes. The negative consequences associated with the elderly's use of the product are few.

Suppose, however, that some of the wrong segment decides to buy the services of a restaurant. An upscale concept has been developed, but to launch the restaurant, management decides to have a price promotion, and the advertising agency develops inappropriate advertising. Or, through poor management, publicity activity is unfocused and produces feature articles in the wrong media. The result is that the restaurant gets two types of customers: upscale, middle-aged couples and price-conscious groups of students. The former were the original target, and the latter were attracted by inappropriate marketing tactics. Unfortunately for the restaurant and for many other services, the other customers are part of the product. The result is that neither segment enjoys the experience because of the presence of the other, and neither type of customer returns. Hence, the consequences of **mistargeted communications** for service firms, because of the shared consumption experience, are clearly more significant than the consequences experienced by traditional goods-producing firms.

mistargeted communications

Communications methods that affect an inappropriate segment of the market.

MANAGING EXPECTATIONS[8]

The service firm can play a key role in formulating customer expectations about its services. These are realtime expectations created during the service experience itself. Firms may reinforce pre-existing ideas or they may dramatically alter those ideas. Expectations can be set by something as explicit as a promise ("Your food will be ready in five minutes") or as implicit as a behavior pattern that sets a tone. Often such expectations are created unwittingly, as when a server promises to "be right back." Such a statement can be viewed both as a binding contract by a customer and as a farewell salutation by the service provider.

Perceived service also has many service sources. **Technical service quality** is an objective level of performance produced by the operating system of the firm. It is measurable with a stopwatch, temperature gauge, or other measuring instrument. Unfortunately, this is not the level of performance the customer perceives. Perception acts as a filter that moves the perceived service level up or down.

technical service quality

An objective, measurable level of performance produced by the operating system of the firm.

Perception is itself influenced by the same factors that dictate expectations. For example, communications can create warm feelings toward the organization that raises perceived service levels. Inappropriately dressed and ill-behaving staff can deliver high-quality service but be poorly perceived by the consumer, who will downgrade the perceived service level.

Many sources of expectations are under the direct control of the firm. Only past experience and competitors' activities cannot be directly influenced in one way or the other. Given such control, the firm must determine what the objectives of the communications mix should be.

In the absence of competition, reduced expectations will result in higher satisfaction levels, provided that levels of perceived service are maintained. One strategy would, therefore, be to reduce expectations as much as possible. Regardless of the service actually delivered, the customer would then be satisfied.

Unfortunately, communications must also play the more traditional role of stimulating demand. It is inconsistent to think of achieving this by promising bad service, even if doing so might minimize customers' expectations (for the few customers who use the service!).

In competitive terms, firms make promises and strive to build expectations that will differentiate them in the marketplace and cause customers to come to them and not to their competitors. The temptation is, therefore, to promise too much and to raise expectations to an unrealistic level. It is perhaps fortunate that the variability in services is well known to most consumers and that they, therefore, discount many of the promises made by services. When the promises are taken seriously, however, the result is often dissatisfied customers.

It is probably more effective to attempt to match customers' expectations to the performance characteristics of the servuction system. In such a scenario, the behavior of the customer is most likely to conform to the script required by the operating system. There is little point, for example, in encouraging McDonald's customers to specify how well they want their hamburgers done. Not only would the customers be disappointed, but any attempt to meet their demands would destroy the efficiency of the operating system.

ADVERTISING TO EMPLOYEES

The staff frequently _____ sing campaign. Clearly, comm_____ it, can be highly motivating. H_____ ut a clear understanding of th_____ rformance levels that are techn_____ set expectation levels unreal_____ on the staff since (1) it shows t_____ marketing department) did _____ prospects that customers wi_____ and the staff will have to tell t_____ ice portrayed in the firm's com_____ egative influence on staff m_____ nce customer satisfaction.

The bottom l_____ y must first sell the service job _____ customer.[9] For years, communicatio_____ mployees going through great lengths to please the cus_____ munications are clearly targeted toward customers, they also send a messag_____ nployees regarding appropriate role behavior. In the end, service communications not only provide a means of communicating with customers, but also serve as a vehicle to communicate, motivate, and educate employees.[10]

SELLING/OPERATION CONFLICTS

Another consideration unique to the service sector is that the individuals who sell the service are often the same people who provide the service. In many instances, the service provider is much more comfortable providing the service than marketing his or her own abilities. However, in some cases, providers become so involved in the communications aspects of their firm that they no longer actively participate in the operations end of the business.

The conflicts associated with marketing versus operations are at least twofold. First are the economic considerations. Typically, service providers are paid for providing services and are not paid for time spent on communications activities. Clearly, the provider must engage in marketing activities in order to generate future customers, but the time spent on marketing does not generate revenues for the provider at that particular moment. Moreover, the time spent on communications activities is often while an ongoing project is being conducted. This means that the time dedicated to communications activities must be considered when estimating completion dates to customers. Often the firm's communications efforts must occur while previously sold services are being processed in order to avoid shut-down periods between customer orders.

The second conflict that arises is often role related. Many professional service providers believe that communications activities such as personal selling are not within their areas of expertise. Consequently, some providers feel uncomfortable with communications activities, and, even more disturbing, some providers feel that this type of activity is beneath them. The health-care field in particular has been plagued by this problem through the years. However, increased competition in the health-care arena has lead to a recognition of the need for marketing training directed at technical specialists. Many health-care institutions, particularly the good ones, now embrace the importance of the firm's communication efforts.

GENERAL GUIDELINES FOR DEVELOPING SERVICE COMMUNICATIONS

After a review of the literature that directly examines the specifics of advertising services, several common themes emerge that create guidelines for advertising services. Many of these guidelines have developed directly as a result of the intangibility, inseparability, heterogeneity, and perishability inherent in service products.

DEVELOP A WORD-OF-MOUTH COMMUNICATIONS NETWORK

Consumers of services often rely on personal sources of information more than nonpersonal sources to reduce the risk associated with a purchase. Given the importance of nonpersonal sources, communications should be developed that facilitate the development of a word-of-mouth network. Advertising that features satisfied customers and promotional strategies that encourage current customers to recruit their friends are typical. Other communication strategies such as presentations for community and professional groups and sponsorship of community and professional activities have also been effective in stimulating word-of-mouth communications.

PROMISE WHAT IS POSSIBLE

In its most basic form, customer satisfaction is developed by customers' comparing their expectations to their perceptions of the actual service delivery process. In times of increasing competitive pressures, firms may be tempted to overpromise. Making promises the firm cannot keep initially increases customer expectations and then subsequently lowers customer satisfaction as those promises are not met.

Two problems are associated with overpromising. First, customers leave disappointed, and a significant loss of trust occurs between the firm and its customers. Moreover, disappointed customers are sure to tell others of their experience, which increases the fallout from the experience. The second problem directly affects the service firm's employees. Working for firms who make false promises places employees in compromising and often confrontational positions. Front-line personnel are left to repeatedly explain to customers why the company cannot keep its promises. Given the link between employee satisfaction and customer satisfaction, creating expectations that cannot be met can have devastating long-term effects.

TANGIBILIZE THE INTANGIBLE[11]

In Chapter One, we discussed that the distinction between goods and services is unclear and presented the scale of market entities—a continuum that assesses the tangible properties of the market entity, ranging from tangible dominant to intangible dominant. Interestingly, tangible dominant market entities such as perfume utilize image development in their advertising schemes. From a basic viewpoint, perfume is simply liquid scent in a bottle. The customer can pick it up, try it on, and smell the perfume's fragrance. Hence, the perfume is tangible dominant. As with many tangible dominant products, the advertising tends to make them more abstract in order to differentiate one product from another.

In contrast, services are already abstract. Hence, one of the principle guidelines for advertising a service is to make it more concrete. This explains why insurance companies utilize tangible symbols to represent their companies. The product of insurance is already abstract, so it becomes the advertisement's objective to explain the service in simple and concrete terms. In addition to tangible symbols, other firms have tangibilized their service offerings by using numbers in their advertisements, such as, "We've been in business since 1925," or "Nine out of ten customers would recommend us to a friend."

In tangiblizing the intangible, the scale of market entities should be turned on its ends (see Figure 8.1). The advertising of tangible dominant products tends to make them more abstract in order to differentiate them from one another. In contrast, the advertising of intangible dominant products should concentrate on making them more concrete through the use of physical cues and tangible evidence. The advertising of products in the middle of the continuum often utilizes both approaches. McDonald's, for example, promotes "food, folks, and fun" in its advertisement. Food and folks are concrete, and fun is abstract.

FEATURE THE WORKING RELATIONSHIP BETWEEN CUSTOMER AND PROVIDER

As you should well understand by now, service delivery is an interactive process between the service provider and the customer. Because of inseparability, it is appropriate in the firm's advertising to feature a company representative and a customer working together to achieve a desired outcome. H&R Block advertising commonly shows a company representative and a customer interacting in a friendly and reassuring manner. The advertising of services, in particular, must concentrate not only on encouraging customers to buy, but also on encouraging employees to perform. Clearly, advertising that illustrates the inseparability of the service delivery process should target both the customer and the firm's service providers.

REDUCE CONSUMER FEARS ABOUT VARIATIONS IN PERFORMANCE

The firm's advertising can also minimize the pitfalls of heterogeneity in the customer's mind. To enhance the perception of consistent quality, the firm's advertising should provide some form of documentation that reassures the customer. Typical examples include stating the firm's performance record through numbers as opposed to qualitative testimonials. The use of "hard" numbers in advertisements reduces the consumer's fear of variability and also tangibilizes the service, as mentioned earlier.

DETERMINE AND FOCUS ON RELEVANT SERVICE QUALITY DIMENSIONS

The reasons customers choose among competing services are often closely related to the five dimensions of service quality—reliability, responsiveness, assurance, empathy, and the quality of the tangibles associated with the service. However, it is common that some features are more salient to customers than others. For example, 30 percent of today's airline customers list "safety" as one of their top five considerations when choosing an airline.[12] Consequently, it would be appropriate for airlines to emphasize the assurance dimension of service quality by featuring the airline's safety record, maintenance and training programs, as well as any certified aspects of their particular airline operation. One advertising campaign that

FIGURE
8.1

THE IMPACT OF INTANGIBILITY:
DIFFERENT COMMUNICATION STRATEGIES FOR DIFFERENT PRODUCTS

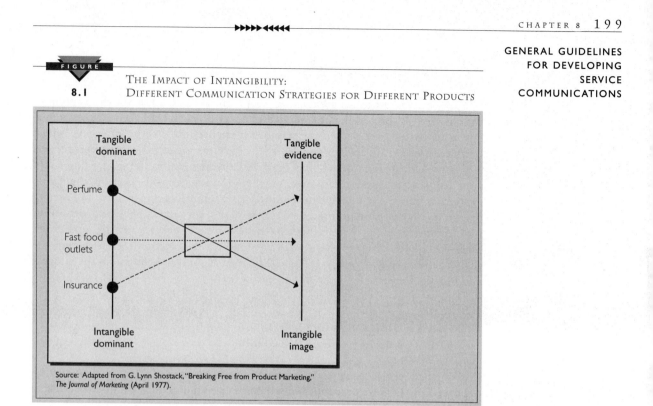

Source: Adapted from G. Lynn Shostack, "Breaking Free from Product Marketing,"
The Journal of Marketing (April 1977).

backfired promoted a hotel as one of the tallest hotels in the world. Although this reinforced the tangible dimension of service quality, this particular tangible component was not very important to customers in choosing hotels. In fact, many customers who had even the slightest fear of heights avoided the hotel and the risk of being placed on an upper floor.

DIFFERENTIATE THE SERVICE PRODUCT FROM SERVICE DELIVERY

A dramatic difference exists between what the service provides and how it is provided. Identifying the various inputs into the process, which contributes to a competitive or quality advantage, and stressing these inputs in the firm's advertising is likely to be a successful approach. On the surface, it appears somewhat difficult to differentiate one tax accountant from the next. However, if we consider the process of obtaining a consultation, which consists of calling to make an appointment, interacting with staff at the front desk, the appearance of the office in the reception area where the client is waiting, the appearance of the accountant's office, the interaction between the client and the accountant, and the payment procedures, several potential areas for differentiation arise. Outlining the various inputs within the service delivery process may indicate key competitive and/or quality advantages that traditionally have been overlooked.

MAKE THE SERVICE MORE EASILY UNDERSTOOD

Services can be more fully explained to potential customers via the communications mix by presenting the service as a series of events. When questioned, consumers often break down the service experience into a series of events, which permits the service provider to view the service from the customer's perspective. For example, bank customers may first view the external building, parking facilities, landscaping, and cleanliness of the grounds. When entering the bank, customers notice the interior furnishings, odors, music, temperature, and service personnel. While conducting bank transactions, the appearance and demeanor of specific contact personnel become issues. Hence, perceptions of quality are assessed at each stage of the service encounter. Advertising developed from the sequence-of-events perspective considers the customer throughout the process and highlights the firm's strengths in each area.

SPECIAL CONSIDERATIONS OF PROFESSIONAL SERVICE PROVIDERS

Professional service providers often experience distinct challenges that may be tempered by the development of an effective communications program.[12] Specifically, the ten most frequent problems encountered include:

1. *Third-Party Accountability.* Investors, insurance companies, banks, governmental agencies, and even members of their own professions often hold professional service providers accountable for their actions or at least monitor those actions. Creating credibility and projecting the image of a quality firm to third parties can be accomplished through the firm's communications mix, thereby minimizing excessive scrutiny by outside parties. Communication strategies that come to mind include conducting business seminars, giving speeches, and writing articles.[13]

   Business seminars in the professional's area of specialization demonstrate the provider's expertise not only to potential and existing clients, but also to interested third parties, particularly other industry members. Speeches to local civic organizations as well as national conventions spotlight the firm's talents and further enhance the firm's image. Reprints of articles should be included in company newsletters and sent to appropriate audiences.

2. *Client Uncertainty.* Many professional services are costly, are associated with danger or importance, and are, in some cases, technical and specialized, making them difficult for the customer/client to understand. Effective communications can communicate the procedures involved, show the likely outcomes (which manages consumer expectations), answer consumers' common questions, and/or minimize consumers' areas

of concern. Communications featuring customer testimonials by local well-known clientele are particularly effective in easing uncertainty.

3. *Experience Is Essential.* Communications must be effective in attracting and maintaining the customer base. The opening of a new doctor's office is not greeted with nearly the enthusiasm as that of a new restaurant. Once again, the value of offering seminars, membership in local organizations, speaking at civic funcions or on talk-radio programs, and writing articles for local consumption are great ice breakers.

4. *Limited Differentiability.* As the level of competition increases among professional service providers, differentiation among providers decreases as they match one another's offerings with comparable alternatives. Communications that differentiate the provider on factors beyond the mere service product itself, such as personnel, customer service, and image, must be communicated to the marketplace to set the provider apart from the crowd (see Table 8.1)

5. *Maintaining Quality Control.* Because the consumer is part of the service production process, he or she ultimately has a large amount of control over the quality of the final outcome. Communications that stress the importance of following the professional's advice and its relationship to positive outcomes educates the consumer about the importance of his or her own role in the service delivery system.

6. *Turning Doers into Sellers.* In many instances, the employment of outside sales representatives to push professional services to clientele is inappropriate and ineffective. Client uncertainty dictates that the professional provider him/herself must become actively involved in the sales process to reassure clients and minimize their fears. Ultimately, no one should be able to sell the available service better than the provider. However, while some providers thrive on making sales, many other providers feel uncomfortable when thrust into the sales spotlight.

7. *The Challenge of Dividing the Professional's Time between Marketing and Providing Services.* Directly related to the previous point are the problems associated with the professional's becoming too involved in the personal selling component of the firm's communications mix. Professionals generate revenues by billing for the time that they are servicing existing customers. Marketing activities not only consume a portion of the professional's billable hours, but the professional does not get paid directly for the time spent conducting marketing efforts. As a result, the professional must make decisions about how much personal time to allocate to marketing activities and also how to divide that time among cultivating new prospects, maintaining relationships with existing clients, and involvement in more general public relations work.

8. *Tendencies to Be Reactive Rather than Proactive.* The pressure of everyday business cuts into the amount of time the professional can devote to marketing activities. Existing customers demand the attention of the

provider in the short-run by expecting services to be delivered in an expedient manner. As a result, many professionals find themselves in a reactive mode as they search out new business while existing business transactions end. This creates the unenviable position of attempting to run a business while moving from one client to the next. Often, slack time develops between clients, which negatively affects the cash flow of the operation, not to mention placing increased pressure on the desperate provider looking for new clients.

The communications mix should not be based solely on the professional's personal selling efforts. Ongoing communications must work for the provider in a proactive manner while the provider performs everyday activities with existing clientele. The professional can make better use of the time devoted to marketing efforts by focusing on closing the sale, not starting from scratch.

9. *The Effects of Advertising Are Unknown.* In the not-so-distant past, many professional organizations such as those for lawyers forbid their members to engage in marketing communication activities. However, in 1978, the courts ruled that the ban on marketing communications was unconstitutional, based on the case *Bates v The State Bar of Arizona.* Despite the ruling, some members of professional societies still frown upon the use of certain communication methods such as traditional advertising.

Consumer groups are particularly advocating that professional service providers engage in active marketing communications. Consumer advocates believe that an increase in communication efforts will provide consumers with much-needed information and increase the level of competition among providers. They also believe that as a result of the increase in competition, prices will fall, and the quality of service will improve. However, service providers such as those in the health-care arena do not agree. Health-care providers quickly point to the legal profession and state that increasing communications will likely have a negative impact on their profession's image, credibility, and dignity. In addition, health-care professionals believe that customer benefits created by increased communications efforts are unlikely. In fact, some state that if consumers believe that health-care is expensive now . . . just wait until the profession has to start covering the costs of its communications efforts. Needless to say, the jury is still out on who is correct. However, as time has passed and as competitive pressures among professional service providers have mounted, the use of marketing communications seems to be becoming more acceptable in general.

10. *Professional Providers Have a Limited Marketing Knowledge Base.* As business students, many of the terms you take for granted, such as market segments, target markets, marketing mix variables, and differentiation and positioning strategies, are totally foreign terms to

many service providers. Professional service providers are trained to effectively perform their technical duties. Lawyers attend law schools, medical doctors attend medical schools, dentists attend dental schools, and veterinarians attend veterinary schools. What do all these professional providers have in common when they go into practice for themselves? They all run businesses yet have no formal business educational backgrounds.

Due to a limited marketing knowledge base, their temptation is to develop the firm's communications mix in isolation, without regard to the firm's overall marketing strategy. Ultimately, the firm's communications mix should be consistent with targeted consumer expectations and synergistic with other elements in the marketing mix.

COMMUNICATIONS TIPS FOR PROFESSIONALS[14]

Turning Current Clients into Company Spokespersons Too often, service firms lose sight of their existing clients as they develop a communications mix with the sole purpose of attracting new business. A firm's existing client base is the heart of its business and represents a vast potential for additional revenue. Existing clients are a rich resource of further revenue and offer opportunities for business that can be generated without substantial promotional expenditures, without additional overhead, and frequently, without hiring additional personnel. By being constantly on the alert for suggestions and ideas and by discovering the clients' needs and responding to them in a professional and timely manner, professional service providers essentially win over clients, who, in turn, become a perpetual advertisement for the firm. Given the importance of personal sources of information in choosing among service alternatives, having existing clients who sing the praises of your firm to others is an invaluable resource.

First Impressions Are Everything Because of the **halo effect,** early stages of the service encounter often set the tone for consumer evaluations made throughout the service experience. As a result, providers must pay special attention to the initial interactions in the encounter because they are often the most important. For example, telephone calls need to be answered promptly and politely. During a speech about service excellence, Tom Peters of *In Search of Excellence* fame reported his personal experience with telephone contact personnel at FedEx. Mr. Peters reported that in 27 of 28 cases, FedEx operators answered the phone on or before the first ring. In fact, Mr. Peters admitted that the mail service may be 28 for 28 since he assumes that he misdialed and hung up the phone on the twenty-eighth event.

Communication cues on which consumers base initial impressions include "yellow-page" advertisements, signage, and an easily accessible place of business. Once the client actually arrives, the firm's reception area should be a showplace, complete with tangible clues that reinforce the firm's quality image. Possible

halo effect
An overall favorable or unfavorable impression based on early stages of the service encounter.

tangible clues in the reception area include the name of the firm and its service providers prominently displayed, furnishings that reflect the personality of the business, fresh flowers, a "brag book" that includes letters from happy customers, past company newsletters, provider profiles, and indications of the firm's involvement in the community. Finally, the reception area should be staffed by professional and pleasant customer contact personnel. Despite the importance of first impressions, many firms simply view their reception areas as waiting rooms, making little effort to enhance the aesthetics of these areas. In many cases, these areas are equipped with uncomfortable and unappealing furnishings and staffed by low-paid, poorly trained personnel.

Create Visual Pathways that Reflect the Firm's Quality The firm's printed image includes all printed communication to clients such as correspondence, annual reports, newsletters, and billings. It also includes printed material of general use, such as firm brochures, letterhead, envelopes, and business cards, as well as internal communications—from agendas to checklists, from memos to manuals. Printed materials create a **visual pathway** through which the professional image of the firm can be consistently transmitted.

visual pathway

Printed materials through which the professional image of the firm can be consistently transmitted, including firm brochures, letterhead, envelopes, and business cards.

From the first time the firm's business card is put into a prospective client's hand, through the first letter the client receives, and on through finished reports delivered to the client and final billings, the presentation of printed material is making an impression. With every piece of material the client receives, he or she subconsciously reacts to the quality of paper, reproduction, and binding with which the firm has produced it. And most of all, he or she is responding to the visual images the professional provider has chosen to represent the firm, starting with the logo.

Effective communication of the firm's logo assists the firm in establishing familiarity throughout the region in which it operates. In addition to identifying the firm, other primary goals of logo development are to simplify and explain the purpose of the organization. In essence, logo development can be viewed as creating a form of hieroglyphic symbol that enables others to quickly identify the professional firm. The logo is the service firm's brand.

Given the lack of a substantial marketing knowledge base, professional service providers should seriously consider engaging the advice of a communications professional. Graphic artists, ad agencies, and public relations firms are typical examples of communications specialists who work with a client to produce the kind of image that will give the firm the individual yet professional identity that successfully positions it in the marketplace. When a logo is designed, it can be printed in various sizes and in reverse. The various forms of the logo can then be easily applied to all manner and style of printed materials. Finally, the firm's choice of stock (paper), typeface, and kind of printing (engraving, offset, or thermograph) will complete the highly professional image of its printed material and create a visual pathway that consistently communicates quality to the client.

Printed materials such as a company's logo create a visual pathway through which the professional image of the firm can be consistently transmitted.

Source: HB Photo/Annette Coolidge.

Establish Regular Communications with Clients Every letter sent to a client or a colleague is a potential promotional opportunity. Experts suggest taking advantage of this potential from the very beginning of the relationship with the client. Every new client should receive a special letter of welcome to the firm and a sample newsletter that conveys the firm's service concept. The use of standardized letters embossed with the firm's logo, which can be adapted for different circumstances such as welcome letters, thank yous for referrals, and reminder letters of upcoming appointments, is also effective. Better yet, handwritten, personalized messages on the firm's notecards provide a personal touch.

The most important piece of regular communication with clients should be the firm newsletter. It can be as simple as an $8\frac{1}{2}$-by-11 sheet, typed at the office and photocopied, or as elaborate as a small booklet, typeset and printed in color on quality stock. Some firms choose to make their newsletters informal bulletins; others prefer to make them polished publications. Regardless of the technique, the newsletter should always have a clean, professional appearance and be filled with information valuable to clientele.

Develop a Firm Brochure The firm's brochure is a menu of the firm's service offering and should be *the* written showpiece. In addition to providing an overview of available services, firm brochures typically include the firm's history, philosophy, and profiles of personnel. To add to its flexibility, the brochure may be developed with flaps on the inside front and/or back covers for holding supplemental materials or other information that changes from time to time. Personnel profiles featuring printed photographs and biographies are likely candidates for materials that frequently change as employees move from firm to firm. The flaps for supplemental materials also provide the option to customize each brochure for particular clients who desire specific services and who will be dealing with specific personnel. The firm brochure is a prime opportunity for the professional service firm to project its uniqueness. Ultimately, the firm brochure should be the kind of product the firm can enthusiastically present to existing and prospective clients.

An Informed Office Staff Is Vital Last, but definitely not least, engendering respect and pride in the firm's capability does not stop with external promotion. In fact, it starts internally, and generating a professional image for the benefit of firm staff can be as important as promoting that image to clients. Remember, the staff is in constant, direct contact with clients. Failure to effectively communicate with the firm's staff is readily apparent and quickly erases all other communication efforts to project a quality program.

SUMMARY

This chapter has provided an overview of communications mix strategies as they apply to the marketing of services. Communication strategy is one of the key components of a firm's overall marketing mix. Its role is to inform, persuade, and/or remind consumers about the services being offered. The components of the communications mix include personal selling, media advertising, publicity and public relations, and sales promotion. The service firm's budget is allocated among each component of the communications mix. Depending on the target audience and the firm's objectives, some communication components will be utilized more often than others.

The objectives of a firm's communications mix often relate directly to the service offering's stage within the product life cycle. For instance, the content of communications during the introduction stage tends to be informational to create consumer awareness. As the service moves into the growth and maturity stages of its life cycle, the content of the communication tends to be informational and persuasive to help position the service among competing alternatives. The content of the communication mix switches to persuasive and reminder as the firm progresses through the maturity stage and into the decline stage.

A variety of special considerations that pertain to services must be addressed when developing the communication mix. These issues include mistargeted communications, the role of communications in managing consumer expectations, the effects of the communications mix on employees, and the conflicts many professional service providers face when attempting to allocate their time to marketing activities while being directly involved in the day-to-day operations of the firm.

KEY TERMS

nonpersonal sources
personal sources
target markets
positioning strategy
communications mix
personal selling
media advertising
publicity/public relations
sales promotions
Type 1 staff

Type 2 staff
Type 3 staff
financial consequences
social consequences
performance consequences
rational mathematician model
mistargeted communications
technical service quality
halo effect
visual pathway

REVIEW QUESTIONS

1. Discuss the options available for positioning and differentiating service firms.

2. Describe the strategic differences among the four elements of the communications mix.

3. Compare the communication skills necessary to conduct Type 1, Type 2, and Type 3 transactions.

4. What is the relevance of the rational mathematician model as it relates to developing communications strategy?

5. What problems are associated with mistargeted communications? Why do they occur?

6. Why should service employees be considered when developing communications materials?

7. Discuss how insurance companies make their services more easily understood.

8. What problems arise in turning professional service providers into proactive marketing personnel?

9. Discuss the concept of "visual pathways."

NOTES

1. This section is adapted from John E. G. Bateson, *Managing Services Marketing*, 2nd ed. (Fort Worth, TX: The Dryden Press, 1992), pp. 393–401.

2. Adapted from Philip Kotler, *Marketing Management*, 9th ed. (Englewood Cliffs, NJ: Prentice Hall, 1997), pp. 279–305.

3. See, for instance, Louis E. Boone and David L. Kurtz, *Contemporary Marketing*, 8th ed. (Fort Worth, TX: The Dryden Press, 1995).

4. Based on a customer satisfaction study conducted by K. Douglas Hoffman for Rainmaker Marketing's North Carolina Lawyer Referral Service.

5. Bernard H. Booms and Jody L. Nyquist, "Analyzing the Customer/Firm Communication Component of the Services Marketing Mix," in *Marketing of Services*, James H. Donelly and William R. George, eds. (Chicago: American Marketing Association, 1981), pp. 172–177.

6. This section is adapted from John E. G. Bateson, *Managing Services Marketing*, 3rd ed. (Fort Worth, TX: The Dryden Press, 1995), pp. 338–341.

7. This section has been modified from William R. George and Leonard L. Berry, "Guidelines for the Advertising of Services," *Business Horizons*, 24,4 (July–August 1981): pp. 52–56.

8. This section is adapted from John E. G. Bateson, *Managing Services Marketing*, 2nd ed. (Fort Worth, TX: The Dryden Press, 1992), pp. 397–399.

9. W. Earl Sasser and Stephen P. Albeit, "Selling Jobs in the Service Sector," *Business Horizons* (June 1976), p. 64.

10. George and Berry, "Guidelines for the Advertising of Services."

11. Donna H. Hill and Nimish Gandhi, "Service Advertising: A Framework to Its Effectiveness," *The Journal of Services Marketing* 6,4 (Fall 1992), pp. 63–77.

12. This section adapted from Philip Kotler and Paul N. Bloom, *Marketing Professional Services* (Englewood Cliffs, NJ: Prentice-Hall, 1984), pp. 9–13.

13. Cyndee Miller, "Airline Safety Seen as New Marketing Issue," *Marketing News*, July 8, 1991, pp. 1, 11.

14. This section adapted from Jack Fox, *Starting and Building Your Own Accounting Business* (New York: John Wiley & Sons, 1994).

9

Managing the Firm's Physical Evidence

"*From the customer's point of view, if they can see it, walk on it, hold it, step in it, smell it, carry it, step over it, touch it, use it, even taste it, if they can feel it or sense it, it's customer service.*"

SuperAmerica Training Program, from Kristen Anderson and Ron Zemke,
Delivering Knock Your Socks Off Service (New York: AMACOM), 1991

CHAPTER OBJECTIVES

This chapter's purpose is to provide you with an understanding of the importance of the service firm's physical evidence regarding customer perceptions of the quality of services provided. After reading this chapter, you should be able to

▶ Define the various elements that make up the firm's physical evidence.

    ▶ *Discuss the strategic role of physical evidence as it relates to the marketing of service firms.*

▶ Explain the stimulus-organism-response (SOR) model.

    ▶ *Discuss the major components of the servicescapes model.*

▶ Discuss the use of sensory cues when developing tactical design strategies.

    ▶ *Discuss design considerations for low-contact versus high-contact firms.*

WHAT SIGNALS ARE YOUR BANK'S PHYSICAL FACILITIES SENDING?

*I*nterviewing for faculty positions often becomes an interesting experience. For example, some candidates have spent the night alone in the Dodge family mansion on the campus of Oakland University, while others have slept in the Quaker Square Hilton, a hotel that has been converted from grain silos originally operated by The Quaker Oats Company, near the University of Akron. Just as intriguing is the involvement in the interview process of two local banks that serve the students, faculty, and staff of Mississippi State University.

Although several other banks were located in the area, Deposit Guaranty and the National Bank of Commerce were particularly involved in recruiting new faculty to the area. The banks funded and attended recruiting dinners and lunches for the opportunity to establish relationships with the recruits should they be hired and move to the area. New faculty often bought homes, needed car loans, and had a variety of other banking needs that were attractive to the bank's marketing personnel and, thus, were the motives behind the bank's involvement.

As is the case with many types of services, banking services are difficult to differentiate from competitive offerings. Checking accounts, savings accounts, home mortgages, and car loans are essentially the same from one bank to the next. As a result, banks are faced with the task of differentiating themselves based on factors other than their core business functions. What was particularly striking about these two banks was their use of tangibles to differentiate their services.

The National Bank of Commerce was built to project the image of security. The outside of the building was attractive, yet it looked like a cement vault. The building itself was square in shape, built with a smooth concrete exterior, and had small windows lining the upper second storey of the building. Inside the bank was red carpeting, nice offices, lots of plants, and banking personnel who were sure to remember your name and always greeted you with a warm smile. The bank's marketing personnel ensured that every prospective client left with note cubes and pens bearing the National Bank of Commerce name and logo.

Directly across the street, Deposit Guaranty projected a totally different image. White pillars, fountains, and two-storey-tall windows adorned the front of the bank. In contrast to the vault across the street, the Deposit Guaranty building projected an image of Southern charm and hospitality. The bank's personnel were very personable and accommodating. On the second floor, the bank offered its customers a lounge where they could get a free cup of coffee or a soft drink while reading the day's newspaper. The lounge itself was decorated with mahogany panelling, large heavy chairs, and large windows overlooking the city's downtown area. The bank's lounge was so popular it had become a morning meeting place for the town's retired citizens. After recruits had been offered a job and accepted it, Deposit Guaranty mailed the local newspaper to their current homes for six months prior to their move as a courtesy. One recruit, who had not opened an account and was earning $8,000 a year as a graduate student, was stunned and amazed by the caliber of treatment that he received from both banks prior to and after moving to the Mississippi State community.

Unfortunately, his Mississippi banking experience set expectations that were not met when he later selected a bank in his new home at a new school. The first bank he walked into was a branch bank located in the parking lot of a shopping center. A woman yelled over the counter, inquiring whether she could help him with something. When he told her he would like to open a checking and savings account, she told him to "sit down over there somewhere and someone [would] get with [him] as soon as they [could.]" As he sat and waited, he noticed the worn veneer on the walls in front of the tellers. The carpet was equally worn and dirty, and the couch on which he was sitting looked like a leftover from somebody's college days. The longer he sat and waited, the more he thought about how ugly the bank's physical facilities were. He knew that it probably had nothing to do with how they would take care of his money, but after a few minutes he simply walked out of the bank and drove down the street to a much nicer looking bank. Two years later, the branch bank was closed to due lack of customer transactions, so apparently he was not the only one who took his business elsewhere. Overall, the firm's physical facilities affected (1) his impressions on how qualified the bank was to handle his banking affairs; (2) his impressions of what the firm must think of its customers and employees to make them conduct business in such a dismal place; and (3) his impression that the bank simply did not project an image that made him want to claim, "This is my bank."

INTRODUCTION

Managing the firm's physical evidence includes everything tangible, from the firm's physical facilities, to brochures and business cards, to the firm's personnel. A firm's physical evidence affects the consumer's experience throughout the duration of the service encounter. Consider the average consumer's restaurant experience.[1]

Prior to entering the restaurant, customers begin to evaluate it based on advertising they may have seen on television or in the phone book. As the consumer drives to the restaurant, the location of the restaurant, the ease with which the location can be found, the restaurant's sign, and the building itself all enter into the consumer's evaluation process. Similarly, the availability of parking spaces, the cleanliness of the parking lot, and the smells that fill the air once the customer steps out of the car affect consumer expectations and perceptions.

Upon entering, the restaurant's furnishings, cleanliness, and overall ambience provide further evidence regarding the quality of the ensuing experience. The appearance and friendliness of the firm's personnel and the ease with which customers can move about and find telephones and restrooms without asking also enters into the consumer's mind.

When seated at a table, the customer notices the stability and quality of the table and chairs, and the cleanliness of napkins, silverware, and the table itself. Additional evaluations occur as well: Is the menu attractive? Is it readable or crumbled and spotted with food stains from past customers? How are the waitstaff interacting with other customers? What do the other customers look like?

Once the meal is served, the presentation of the food is yet another indicator of the restaurant's quality. Consumers will make comparisons of the food's actual appearance and the way it is pictured in advertisements and menus. Of course, how the food tastes also enters into the customer's evaluation.

Upon completing the meal, the bill itself becomes a tangible clue. Is it correct? Are charges clearly written? Is the bill clean, or is it sopping wet with spaghetti sauce? Are the restrooms clean? Did the waitstaff personnel say thank you and really mean it?

THE STRATEGIC ROLE OF PHYSICAL EVIDENCE

facility exterior
The physical exterior of the service facility; includes the exterior design, signage, parking, landscaping, and the surrounding environment.

Due to the intangibility of services, service quality is difficult for consumers to objectively evaluate. As a result, consumers often rely on the tangible evidence that surrounds the service to help them form their evaluations. Physical evidence can fall into three broad categories: (1) facility exterior; (2) facility interior; and (3) other tangibles. Examples of the elements that compose the **facility exterior** include the exterior design, signage, parking, landscaping, and the surrounding environment. For example, the facility may be built on a mountainside, over-looking a lake. The **facility interior** includes elements such as the interior design, equipment used to serve the customer directly or used to run the business, signage, layout, air quality, and temperature. Other **tangibles** that are part of the firm's physical evidence include such items as business cards, stationery, billing statements, reports, employee appearance, uniforms, and brochures.[2]

The extensive use of physical evidence varies by the type of service firm (see Figure 9.1). Service firms such as hospitals, resorts, and child-care facilities often make extensive use of physical evidence in facility design and other tangibles associated with the service. In contrast, service firms such as insurance and express mail drop-off locations use limited physical evidence. Regardless of the variation in usage, all service firms need to recognize the importance of managing their physical evidence in its role of (1) packaging the service; (2) facilitating the flow of the service delivery process; (3) socializing customers and employees alike in terms of their respective roles, behaviors, and relationships; and (4) differentiating the firm from its competitors.[3]

facility interior

The physical interior of the service facility; includes the interior design, equipment used to serve customers, signage, layout, air quality, and temperature.

tangibles

Other items that are part of the firm's physical evidence, such as business cards, stationery, billing statements, reports, employee appearance, uniforms, and brochures.

PACKAGING

The firm's physical evidence plays a major role in packaging the service. The service itself is intangible and, therefore, does not require a package for purely functional reasons. However, utilizing the firm's physical evidence to package the service does send quality cues to consumers and adds value to the service in terms of image development. Image development, in turn, improves consumer perceptions of service while reducing both levels of perceived risk associated with the purchase and levels of cognitive dissonance after the purchase.

The firm's exterior, interior elements, and other tangibles create the package that surrounds the service. The firm's physical facility forms the customer's initial impression concerning the type and quality of service provided. For example, Mexican and Chinese restaurants often utilize specific types of architectural designs that communicate to customers their firms' offerings. The firm's physical evidence also conveys expectations to consumers. Consumers will have one set of expectations for a restaurant with dimly lit dining rooms, soft music, and linen tablecloths and napkins and a different set of expectations for a restaurant that has cement floors, picnic tables, and peanut shells on the floor.

FACILITATING THE SERVICE PROCESS

Another use of the firm's physical evidence is to facilitate the flow of activities that produce the service. Physical evidence can provide information to customers on how the service production process works. Examples include signage that specifically instructs customers, menus and brochures that explain the firm's offerings and facilitate the ordering process for consumers and providers, physical

MANAGING THE FIRM'S
PHYSICAL EVIDENCE

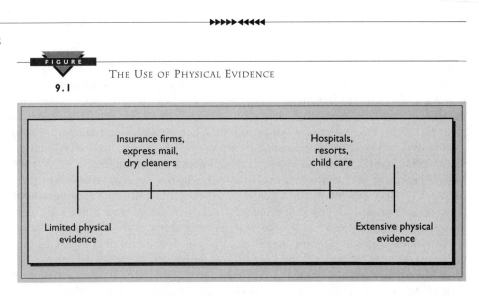

FIGURE
9.1

THE USE OF PHYSICAL EVIDENCE

structures that direct the flow of consumers while waiting, and barriers, such as counters at a dry cleaners, that separate the technical core of the business from the part of the business in which customers are involved in the production process.

SOCIALIZING EMPLOYEES AND CUSTOMERS

socialization

The process by which an individual adapts to the values, norms, and required behavior patterns of an organization.

Organizational **socialization** is the process by which an individual adapts to and comes to appreciate the values, norms, and required behavior patterns of an organization.[4] The firm's physical evidence plays an important part in the socialization process by conveying expected roles, behaviors, and relationships among employees and between employees and customers. The purpose of the socialization process is to project a positive and consistent image to the public. However, the service firm's image is only as good as the image each employee conveys when interacting with the public.[5]

Physical evidence, such as the use of uniforms, facilitates the socialization of employees toward accepting organizational goals and affects consumer perceptions of the caliber of service provided. Studies have shown that the use of uniforms aids in identifying the firm's personnel, presents a physical symbol that embodies the group's ideals and attributes, implies a coherent group structure, facilitates the perceived consistency of performance, provides a tangible symbol of an employee's change in status (e.g., military uniforms change as personnel move through the ranks), and assists in controlling the behavior of errant employees.[6]

One classic example of how tangible evidence affects the socialization process of employees involves women in the military. Pregnant military personnel were originally permitted to wear civilian clothing when pregnant in lieu of their traditional military uniforms. However, the military soon noticed discipline and morale problems with these servicewomen as they began to lose their identification with their roles as soldiers. "Maternity uniforms are now standard issue in the Air Force, Army, and Navy, as well as at US Air, Hertz, Safeway, McDonald's, and the National Park Service."[7]

A MEANS FOR DIFFERENTIATION

As discussed in the opening vignette, service firms such as banks often experience difficulties in differentiating themselves from competitive offerings. The firm's physical evidence provides a means for service differentiation. The appearance of personnel and facilities often have a direct impact on how consumers perceive that the firm will handle the service aspects of its business. Numerous studies have shown that well-dressed individuals are perceived as more intelligent, better workers, and more pleasant to engage in interactions.[8] Similarly, nicely designed facilities are going to be perceived as having the advantage over poorly designed and decorated alternatives.

Differentiation can also be achieved by utilizing physical evidence to reposition the service firm in the eyes of its customers. Upgrading the firm's facilities often upgrades the image of the firm in the minds of consumers and may also lead to attracting more desirable market segments, which further aids in differentiating the firm from its competitors. On the other hand, note that too elaborate of a facility upgrade may alienate some customers who believe that the firm may be passing on the costs of the upgrade to consumers through higher prices.

A FRAMEWORK FOR UNDERSTANDING THE USE OF PHYSICAL EVIDENCE IN CREATING SERVICE ENVIRONMENTS

The use of physical evidence to create service environments and its influence on the perceptions and behaviors of individuals is referred to as **environmental psychology.** The **stimulus-organism-response (SOR) model** presented in Figure 9.2 was developed by environmental psychologists to help explain the effects of the service environment on consumer behavior.[9] The SOR model consists of three components: a set of **stimuli,** an **organism** component, and a set of **responses** or **outcomes.** In a service context, the different elements of the firm's physical evidence, such as exterior, interior design, lighting, and so on, compose the set of stimuli.

The organism component, which describes the recipients of the set of stimuli within the service encounter, includes employees and customers. The responses of employees and customers to the set of stimuli are influenced by three basic emotional states: pleasure-displeasure, arousal-nonarousal, and dominance-submissiveness. The **pleasure-displeasure** emotional state reflects the degree to which consumers and employees feel satisfied with the service experience. The **arousal-nonarousal** state reflects the degree to which consumers and employees feel excited and stimulated. The third emotional state, **dominance-submissiveness,** reflects feelings of control and the ability to act freely within

---

environmental psychology
The use of physical evidence to create service environments and its influence on the perceptions and behaviors of individuals.

SOR (stimulus-organism-response) model
A model developed by environmental psychologists to help explain the effects of the service environment on consumer behavior; describes environmental stimuli, emotional states, and responses to those states.

stimuli
The various elements of the firm's physical evidence.

organism
The recipients of the set of stimuli in the service encounter; includes employees and customers.

responses (outcomes)
Consumers' reaction or behavior in response to stimuli.

pleasure-displeasure
The emotional state that reflects the degree to which consumers and employees feel satisfied with the service experience.

arousal-nonarousal
The emotional state that reflects the degree to which consumers and employees feel excited and stimulated.

MANAGING THE FIRM'S
PHYSICAL EVIDENCE

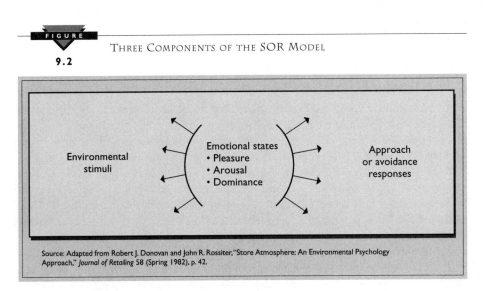

FIGURE 9.2   THREE COMPONENTS OF THE SOR MODEL

Source: Adapted from Robert J. Donovan and John R. Rossiter, "Store Atmosphere: An Environmental Psychology Approach," *Journal of Retailing* 58 (Spring 1982), p. 42.

dominance-submissiveness

The emotional state that reflects the degree to which consumers and employees feel in control and able to act freely within the service environment.

the service environment. Ideally, service firms should utilize physical evidence to build environments that appeal to pleasure and arousal states and avoid creating atmospheres that create submissiveness.

Consumer and employee responses to the set of environmental stimuli are characterized as **approach behaviors** or **avoidance behaviors.** Consumer approach and avoidance behaviors and outcomes can be demonstrated in any combination of four ways (employees exhibit similar behaviors):[10]

approach/avoidance behaviors

Consumer responses to the set of environmental stimuli that are characterized by a desire to stay or leave an establishment, explore/interact with the service environment or ignore it, or feel satisfaction or disappointment with the service experience.

1. A desire to stay (approach) or leave (avoid) the service establishment.
2. A desire to further explore and interact with the service environment (approach) or a tendency to ignore it (avoidance).
3. A desire to communicate with others (approach) or to ignore the attempts of service providers to communicate with customers (avoid).
4. Feelings of satisfaction (approach) or disappointment (avoidance) with the service experience.

THE DEVELOPMENT OF SERVICESCAPES[11]

servicescapes

The use of physical evidence to design service environments.

The framework presented in Figure 9.3 is a more comprehensive SOR model that directly applies to the influence of the service firm's physical evidence on consumers' and employees' subsequent behaviors. The term **servicescapes** refers to the use of physical evidence to design service environments. Due to inseparability, the model recognizes that the firm's environment is likely to affect consumers and

FIGURE
9.3

THE SERVICESCAPES MODEL

BEHAVIOR

**PHYSICAL
ENVIRONMENTAL
DIMENSIONS**

Ambient conditions

• Temperature
• Air quality
• Noise
• Music
• Odor
• Etc.

Space/Function

• Layout
• Equipment
• Furnishings
• Etc.

Signs, symbols,
and artifacts

• Signage
• Personal artifacts
• Style of decor
• Etc.

HOLISTIC
ENVIRONMENT

Perceived
servicescape

INTERNAL
RESPONSE
MODERATORS

Employee
response
moderators

Customer
response
moderators

Cognitive

• Beliefs
• Catagorization
• Symbolic
  meaning

Emotional

• Mood
• Attitude

Physiological

• Pain
• Comfort
• Physical fit

INTERNAL
RESPONSES

Employee
responses

Customer
responses

Cognitive

• Beliefs
• Catagorization
• Symbolic
  meaning

Emotional

• Mood
• Attitude

Physiological

• Pain
• Comfort
• Movement
• Physical fit

Individual behaviors
approach

• Affiliation
• Exploration
• Stay longer
• Commitment
• Carry out plan

Avoid

(Opposites of
approach)

Social Interactions

(Between and
among customers
and employees

Individual behaviors
approach

• Affiliation
• Stay/explore
• Spend money
• Return
• Carry out plan

Avoid

(Opposites of

approach)

Source: Mary J. Bitner, "Servicescapes: The Impact of Physical Surroundings on Customers and Employees," *Journal of Marketing* 56,2 (April 1992), p. 60. Reprinted with permission of the American Marketing Association.

A framework for understanding environment-user relationships in service organizations

▶▶▶▶ ◀◀◀◀

MANAGING THE FIRM'S PHYSICAL EVIDENCE

remote services

Services in which employees are physically present while customer involvement in the service production process is at arm's length.

self-services

Service environments that are dominated by the customer's physical presence, such as ATMs or postal kiosks.

interpersonal services

Service environments in which customers and providers interact.

ambient conditions

The distinctive atmosphere of the service setting that includes lighting, air quality, noise, music, and so on.

space/function

Environmental dimensions that include the layout of the facility, the equipment, and the firm's furnishings.

signs, symbols, artifacts

Environmental physical evidence that includes signage to direct the flow of the service process, personal artifacts to personalize the facility, and the style of decor.

holistic environment

Overall perceptions of the servicescape formed by employees and customers based on the physical environmental dimensions.

employees alike. However, the facility should be designed to meet the needs of those individuals who spend the most time within the confines of the facility.

REMOTE, SELF-SERVICE, AND INTERPERSONAL SERVICES

Figure 9.4 presents a continuum of facility usage by service type. Some services, such as mail order, coupon-sorting houses, and telephone and utility services are described as **remote services.** In remote services, employees are physically present while customer involvement in the service production process is at arm's length. Consequently, facility design should facilitate the employees' efforts and enhance motivation, productivity, and employee satisfaction.

At the other end of the spectrum are services that customers can acquire on their own—**self-services.** Self-service environments are dominated by the customer's physical presence and include services such as ATMs, miniature golf courses, postal kiosks, and self-service car washes. The environment of self-service establishments should be constructed to enhance customer attraction and satisfaction.

In contrast to remote and self-service environments, many services such as restaurants, hospitals, hotels, banks, and airlines are **interpersonal services,** where the physical space is shared jointly by consumers and employees. The environments of interpersonal services should be developed with the needs of both parties involved and should facilitate the social interaction between and among customers and employees.

PHYSICAL ENVIRONMENTAL DIMENSIONS

The servicescapes model depicted in Figure 9.3 begins by recognizing the set of stimuli that are commonly utilized when developing service environments. In broad terms, the set of stimuli include **ambient conditions, space/function,** and **signs, symbols,** and **artifacts.** Ambient conditions reflect the distinctive atmosphere of the service setting and include elements such as lighting, air quality, noise, music, and so on. Environmental dimensions that pertain to the use of space/function include elements such as the layout of the facility, equipment, and the firm's furnishings. Signs, symbols, and artifacts include signage that directs the flow of the service process, personal artifacts, which lend character and individuality that personalize the facility, and the style of decor, such as southwestern, contemporary, or traditional, to name a few.

HOLISTIC ENVIRONMENT

The **holistic environment** portion of the servicescapes model pertains to the perceptions of the servicescape that employees and customers form based on the physical environmental dimensions. In other words, the holistic environment is a perceived overview or image of the firm based on the physical evidence, which is

▶▶▶▶ ◀◀◀◀

FIGURE
9.4

FACILITY USAGE

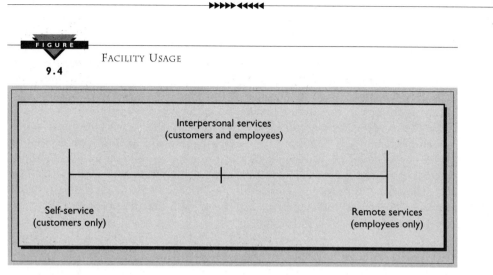

referred to in the model as the **perceived servicescape.** The perceived servicescape is difficult to precisely define, and perceptions of the same establishment will vary among individuals. Essentially, the perceived servicescape is a
composite of mental images of the service firm's physical facilities.

Strategically managing the perceived servicescape aids in establishing a positioning strategy that differentiates the firm from competitors and ultimately
influences the customer decision process when choosing among competing alternatives. The firm should develop the servicescape with its target market in mind.
Economic customers, who make purchase decisions based on price, will avoid
service establishments that appear too fancy or plush based on the perception that
such an establishment will be a high-priced provider. Economic customers tend to
be attracted to environments that are simple yet reflect quality and those that
are clean and modern. Oil-change specialists such as Jiffy Lube use this type of
environment. In contrast, **personalized customers** desire to be pampered and
attended to and are much less price sensitive when choosing among alternative providers. Firms catering to personalized shoppers create environments that
reflect the status their customers seek by investing more in items such as marble
foyers, glass and brass fixtures, and furnishings that encourage customers to shop
at a leisurely pace. Similarly, firms that service **apathetic customers,** who seek
convenience, and **ethical customers,** who support smaller or local as opposed to
larger or national service providers should create their servicescapes accordingly.

INTERNAL RESPONSE MODERATORS

The **internal response moderators** of the servicescapes model simply pertain to
the three basic emotional states of the SOR model discussed earlier: pleasure-
displeasure, arousal-nonarousal, and dominance-submissiveness. The three response moderators mediate the reaction between the perceived servicescape and

perceived servicescape
A composite of mental images
of the service firm's physical
facilities.

economic customers
Consumers who make purchase
decisions based primarily on
price.

personalized customers
Consumers who desire to be
pampered and attended to and
who are much less price
sensitive.

apathetic customers
Consumers who seek
convenience over price and
personal attention.

ethical customers
Consumers who support
smaller or local firms as
opposed to larger or national
service providers.

MANAGING THE FIRM'S
PHYSICAL EVIDENCE

**internal response
moderators**
The three basic emotional
states of the SOR model that
mediate the reaction between
the perceived servicescape and
customers' and employees'
responses to the service
environment.

customers' and employees' responses to the service environment. For example, if a customer desires to remain in a state of nonarousal and spend a nice, quiet evening with someone special, that customer will avoid bright, loud, and crowded service establishments and will be attracted to environments that are more peaceful and conducive to conducting conversation. Similarly, the employees' responses to the firm's environment will also be affected by their own emotional states. Sometimes employees look forward to engaging in conversations with customers. Other days, employees would just as soon minimize conversations and process customers as raw materials on a production line. Response moderators help explain why services are characterized by heterogeneity as the service varies from provider to provider, and even from day to day with the same provider.

INTERNAL RESPONSES TO THE ENVIRONMENT

Theory asserts that once customers and employees are exposed to the set of stimuli that make up the firm's perceived servicescape and the responses to these stimuli are moderated by emotional states. Customers and employees internally respond to the firm's environment at different levels—cognitively, emotionally, and physiologically.

cognitive responses
The thought processes of
individuals that lead them to
form beliefs, categorize, and
assign symbolic meanings to
elements of their physical
environment.

beliefs
Consumers' opinions about the
provider's ability to perform the
service.

Cognitive Responses **Cognitive Responses** are the thought processes of individuals and, according to the model, include beliefs, categorization, and symbolic meaning. In the formation of **beliefs,** the firm's environment acts as a form of nonverbal communication and influences a consumer's beliefs about the provider's ability to perform the service. For example, if a professor's lectures are difficult to follow in class, a student may attribute this difficulty to the professor's inability to teach or may blame him/herself for an inability to learn the subject. Studies have shown that faced with this type of scenario, the physical environment influences consumers when they are attributing blame.[12] If the provider's office is messy and smells bad, consumers are more likely to attribute poor service to the provider. Hence, physical evidence assists customers with beliefs about the provider's success, price for services, and competence. Employees form similar types of beliefs about the firm based on the physical evidence.

categorization
Consumer assessment of the
physical evidence and a quick
mental assignment of a firm to a
known group of styles or types.

Categorization is the second type of cognitive response. Bars and nightclubs operate within a number of environments. Some are high-class establishments, and others cater strictly to local clientele or specific market segments. The process of categorization facilitates human understanding at a quicker pace. Consumers assess the physical evidence and often quickly categorize new service establishments with existing types of operations. They then access the appropriate behavior script for the type of operation and act accordingly.

symbolic meaning
Meaning inferred from the firm's
use of physical evidence.

Individuals also infer **symbolic meaning** from the firm's use of physical evidence. For example, if a nightclub features portraits of James Dean, Jimi Hendrix, Janice Joplin, Kurt Cobain, and others who have followed similar paths, the club evokes a symbolic meaning to its employees and customers. In this instance, the physical evidence may translate into a number of symbols, such as individuality, youthful success, shattered dreams, or other meanings, depending on individual interpretation. Symbolic meaning through the use of physical evidence aids in differentiation and positioning.

Emotional Responses In addition to forming beliefs, individuals will also respond to the firm's physical environment on an emotional level. **Emotional responses** do not involve thinking, they simply happen, often unexplainably and suddenly. Specific songs, for example, may make individuals feel happy, feel sad, or recreate other past feelings that were associated with the particular piece of music. Scents have similar effects on individuals. Having grown up actively involved in the golf course business, some individuals claim that the smells found on any golf course, such as cut grass, wet grass, fertilizer, and the sounds of the course's water irrigation systems, recall feelings of home. Obviously, the goal of effective physical evidence management is to stimulate positive emotions that create atmospheres in which employees love to work and customers want to spend their time and money.

emotional responses
Responses to the firm's physical environment on an emotional level instead of an intellectual or social level.

Physiological Responses In contrast to cognitive and emotional responses, **physiological responses** are often described in terms of physical pleasure or discomfort. Typical physiological responses involve pain and comfort. Environments in which music is played very loudly may lead to employee and customer discomfort and movement away from the source of the noise. The lack of a nonsmoking section may cause some customers difficulty in breathing and further discomfort. Instead of being arousing, environments that are brightly lit may cause eye discomfort. In contrast, a dimly lit restaurant may cause eye strain as customers struggle to read their menus. All these responses determine whether a customer will approach and explore the firm's offerings or avoid and leave the premises to minimize the amount of physiological discomfort. Because of the duration of time spent in the firm's facility, employees might find the physical environment particularly harmful if mismanaged. Adequate work space, proper equipment to get the job done, and appropriate ambient conditions such as temperature and air quality are directly related to employees' willingness to continue to work, their productivity while at work, their job satisfaction, and their positive interactions with co-workers.

physiological responses
Responses to the firm's physical environment based on pain or comfort.

BEHAVIORAL RESPONSES TO THE ENVIRONMENT

Individual Behaviors As stated in the section on the fundamentals of the stimulus-organism-response (SOR) model, individual responses to environmental stimuli are characterized as approach and avoidance behaviors. In retail settings, the store's environment influences approach behaviors such as shopping enjoyment, repeat visits, favorable impressions of the store, money spent, time spent shopping, and willingness of consumers to stay and explore the store. In other instances, convenience stores have cleverly used "elevator music" outside their stores to repel unwelcome neighborhood gangs that "hang out" in the store's parking lot and deter desired clientele from entering the store.

Social Interactions Due to the inseparability inherent in interpersonal services, the firm's servicescape should encourage interactions between employees and customers, among customers, and among employees. The challenge in creating such an environment is that often, what the customer desires, employees would prefer to forego so that they can complete their tasks with a minimum of customer involvement. Environmental variables such as physical proximity, seating arrangements, facility size, and flexibility in changing the configuration of the servicescape define the possibilities and place limits on the amount of social interaction possible.[13]

Consider the seating arrangements of a Japanese steakhouse, which combines different groups of customers at one table as opposed to traditional seating arrangements in which each party has its own table. Obviously, for better or worse, "community seating" at a Japanese steakhouse encourages interaction among customers. In addition, each table is assigned its own chef who actively interacts with the customers during the production process. Similar strides have been made in increasing consumer interaction at Max's and Erma's restaurants. Tables are numbered overhead and equipped with phones that enable customers to call one another. . . . "Are you really with that loser, or is he your brother or something?" Oversized booths at Outback Steakhouse permit the waitstaff to actually sit at the customer's table while explaining the menu and taking dinner orders. This type of approach, while bothersome to some customers who are not familiar with the practice (a modification to the traditional restaurant script), facilitates the amount of interaction between the waitstaff and their customers and yet permits them to stay within the traditional boundary of simply taking and delivering orders.

SPECIFIC TACTICS FOR CREATING SERVICE ATMOSPHERES

When developing the facility's atmosphere, the service firm must consider the physical and psychological impact of the atmosphere on customers, employees, and the firm's operations. Just as the firm cannot be all things to all people, the atmosphere developed will likely not appeal to all consumers. Therefore, firms should develop facilities with a particular target market in mind. Experts suggest answering the following questions before implementing an atmosphere development plan:[14]

1. Who is the firm's target market?
2. What does the target market seek from the service experience?
3. What atmospheric elements can reinforce the beliefs and emotional reactions that buyers seek?

4. How do these same atmospheric elements affect employee satisfaction and the firm's operations?

5. Does the suggested atmosphere development plan compete effectively with competitors' atmospheres?

Ultimately, individuals base their perceptions of a firm's facilities on their interpretation of sensory cues. The following section discusses how firms can utilize the senses of sight, sound, scent, touch, and taste in creating sensory appeals that enhance customer and employee attraction responses.[15]

Sight Appeals

The sense of sight conveys more information to consumers than any other sense and, therefore, should be considered as the most important means available to service firms when developing the firm's atmosphere. **Sight appeals** can be defined as the process of interpreting stimuli, resulting in perceived visual relationships.[16] On a basic level, the three primary visual stimuli that appeal to consumers are **size, shape,** and **colors.** Consumers interpret visual stimuli in terms of visual relationships, consisting of perceptions of harmony, contrast, and clash. **Harmony** refers to visual agreement and is associated with quieter, plusher, and more formal business settings. In comparison, **contrast** and **clash** are associated with exciting, cheerful, and informal business settings. Hence, based on the size, shape, and colors of the visual stimuli utilized and the way consumers interpret the various visual relationships, extremely differing perceptions of the firm emerge. For example, consider how different target markets might respond to entering a "Chucky Cheese" restaurant for the first time. Some segments would find the environment inviting, while others might be completely overwhelmed by too much stimuli.

Size Perceptions The actual size of the firm's facility, signs, and departments conveys different meanings to different markets. In general, the larger the size of the firm and its corresponding physical evidence, the more consumers associate the firm with importance, power, success, security, and stability. For many consumers, the larger the firm, the lower the perceived risk associated with the service purchase. Such consumers believe that larger firms are more competent and more likely to engage in service recovery efforts when problems do arise. Still other customers enjoy the prestige often associated with conducting business with a larger, well-known, firm. On the flip side, other customers may view large firms as impersonal and uncaring and seek out smaller, niche firms that they view as more personal, intimate, and friendly. Hence, depending on the needs of the firm's target market, size appeals differently to different segments.

Shape Shape perceptions of a service firm are created from a variety of sources, such as the use and placement of shelves, mirrors, and windows, and even the design of wallpaper if applicable. Studies show that different shapes arouse

sight appeals
Stimuli that result in perceived visual relationships.

size/shape/colors
The three primary visual stimuli that appeal to consumers on a basic level.

harmony
Visual agreement associated with quieter, plusher, and more formal business settings.

contrast/clash
Visual effects associated with exciting, cheerful, and informal business settings.

different emotions in consumers. Vertical shapes or vertical lines are perceived as "rigid, severe, and lend[ing] a masculine quality to an area. It expresses strength and stability . . . gives the viewer an up-and-down eye movement . . . tends to heighten an area, gives the illusion of increased space in this direction."[17] In contrast, horizontal shapes or lines evoke perceptions of relaxation and restfulness. Diagonal shapes and lines evoke perceptions of progressiveness, proactiveness, and movement. Curved shapes and lines are perceived as feminine and flowing. Utilizing similar and/or dissimilar shapes in facility design will create the desired visual relationship of harmony, contrast, or clash. For example, the use of several different shapes in one area might be utilized to distinguish an area of emphasis.[18]

Color Perceptions The color of the firm's physical evidence often makes the first impression, whether seen in the firm's brochure, the business cards of its personnel, or the exterior or interior of the facility itself. The psychological impact of color upon individuals is the result of three properties: hue, value, and intensity. **Hue** refers to the actual family of the color, such as red, blue, yellow, or green. **Value** defines the lightness and darkness of the colors. Darker values are called **shades,** and lighter values are called **tints. Intensity** defines the brightness or the dullness of the hue.

Hues are classified into warm and cool colors. Warm colors include red, yellow, and orange hues, while cool colors include blue, green, and violet hues. Warm and cool colors symbolize different things to different consumer groups, as presented in Table 9.1. In general, warm colors tend to evoke consumer feelings of comfort and informality. For example, red commonly evokes feelings of love and romance, yellow evokes feelings of sunlight and warmth, and orange evokes feelings of openness and friendliness. Studies have shown that warm colors, particularly red and yellow, are a better choice than cool colors for attracting customers in retail settings. Warm colors are also said to encourage quick decisions and work best for businesses where low-involvement purchase decisions are made.

In contrast to warm colors, cool colors are perceived as aloof, icy, and formal. For example, the use of too much violet may dampen consumer spirits and depress employees who have to continuously work in the violet environment. Although cool colors do not initially attract customers as well as warm colors, cool colors are favored when the customer needs to take time to make decisions, such as the time needed for high-involvement purchases. Despite their different psychological effects, when used together properly, combinations of warm and cool colors can create relaxing, yet stimulating atmospheres.

The value of hues also psychologically affects the firm's customers. Offices painted in lighter colors tend to look larger, while darker colors may make large, empty spaces look smaller. Lighter hues are also popular for fixtures such as electrical face plates, air conditioning vents, and overhead speaker systems. The lighter colors help the fixtures blend in with the firm's environment. On the other hand, darker colors can be used to grab consumer's attention. Retailers are often faced with the problem that only 25 percent of their customers ever make it more

hue

The actual color, such as red, blue, yellow, or green.

value

The lightness and darkness of the colors.

shades

Darker values.

tints

Lighter values.

intensity

The brightness or the dullness of the colors.

TABLE 9.1 PERCEPTIONS OF COLORS

WARM COLORS			COOL COLORS		
Red	**Yellow**	**Orange**	**Blue**	**Green**	**Violet**
Love	Sunlight	Sunlight	Coolness	Coolness	Coolness
Romance	Warmth	Warmth	Aloofness	Restfulness	Shyness
Sex	Cowardice	Openness	Fidelity	Peace	Dignity
Courage	Openness	Friendliness	Calmness	Freshness	Wealth
Danger	Friendliness	Gaiety	Piety	Growth	
Fire	Gaiety	Glory	Masculinity	Softness	
Sin	Glory		Assurance	Richness	
Warmth	Brightness		Sadness	Go	
Excitement	Caution				
Vigor					
Cheerfulness					
Enthusiasm					
Stop					

Source: Dale M. Lewison, *Retailing*, 4th ed. (New York: Macmillan, 1991), p. 277.

than halfway into the store. Some retailers have had some success in attracting more customers farther into the store by painting the back wall in a darker color that attracts the customer's attention.

The intensity of the color also affects perceptions of the service firm's atmosphere. For example, bright colors make objects appear larger than do duller colors. However, bright colors are perceived as harsher and "harder," while duller colors are perceived as "softer." In general, children appear to favor brighter colors, and adults tend to favor softer tones.

The Location of the Firm The firm's location is dependent upon the amount of customer involvement necessary to produce the service. While low-contact services should consider locating in remote sites that are less expensive and closer to sources of supply, transportation, and labor, high-contact services have other concerns. Typically, when evaluating locations for the firm, three questions need to addressed:

First, how visible is the firm? Customers tend to shop at places of which they are aware. The firm's visibility is essential in creating awareness. Ideally, firms should be visible from major traffic arteries and can enhance their visibility by facing the direction of traffic that maximizes visibility. If available, sites that are set back from the street (which permit customers to gain a broad perspective) while still remaining close enough to permit customers to read the firm's signs are preferable.

The second question about a location under consideration pertains to the compatibility of the site being evaluated with its surrounding environment. Is the size of the site suitable for the size of the building being planned? More importantly, what other types of businesses are in the area? For example, it would make sense for a law office specializing in health-care matters to locate close to a major hospital, which is generally surrounded by a number of private medical practices as well.

The third question concerns whether the site is suited for customer convenience. Is the site accessible? Does it have ample parking or alternative parking options nearby? Do customers who use mass transit systems have reasonable access to the firm?

The Firm's Architecture   The architecture of the firm's physical facility is often a three-way trade-off among the type of design that will attract the firm's intended target market, the type of design that maximizes the efficiency of the service production process, and the type of design that is affordable. The firm's architecture conveys a number of impressions as well as communicates information to its customers, such as the nature of the firm's business, the firm's strength and stability, and the price of the firm's services.

The Firm's Sign   The firm's sign has two major purposes: to identify the firm and to attract attention. The firm's sign is often the first "mark" of the firm the customer notices. All logos on the firm's remaining physical evidence, such as letterhead, business cards, and note cards, should be consistent with the firm's sign to reinforce the firm's image. Ideally, signs should indicate to consumers the who, what, where, and when of the service offering. The sign's size, shape, coloring, and lighting all contribute to the firm's projected image.

The Firm's Entrance   The firm's entrance and foyer areas can dramatically influence customer perceptions about the firm's activities. Worn carpet, scuffed walls, cheap-looking artwork, torn and outdated reading materials, and unskilled and unkempt personnel form one impression, while neatly appointed reception areas, the creative use of colors, distinctive furnishings, and friendly and professional staff create a much different, more positive impression. Other tactical considerations include lighting that clearly identifies the entrance, doors that are easy to open, flat entryways that minimize the number of customers who might trip, nonskid floor materials for rainy days, and doors that are wide enough to accommodate customers with disabilities as well as large materials being transported in and out of the firm.

Lighting   The psychological effects of lighting on consumer behavior are particularly intriguing. Our response to light may have started when our parents put us to bed, turned out the lights, and told us to be quiet and go to sleep. Through repetitive conditioning, most individuals' response to dimly lit rooms is that of a calming effect. Lighting can set the mood, tone, and pace of the service encounter. Consumers talk more softly when the lights are low, the service environment is perceived as more formal, and the pace of the encounter slows. In contrast, brightly lit service environments are louder, communication exchanges among customers and between customers and employees are more frequent, and the overall environment is perceived as more informal, exciting, and cheerful.

SOUND APPEALS

Sound appeals have three major roles: mood setter, attention grabber, and informer.

sound appeals
Appeals associated with certain sounds, such as music or announcements.

Music Studies have shown that background music affects sales in at least two ways. First, background music enhances the customer's perception of the store's atmosphere, which in turn influences the consumer's mood. Second, music often influences the amount of time spent in stores.[19] In another study, firms that played background music in their facilities were thought to care more about their customers.[20]

Studies have shown that in addition to creating a positive attitude, music directly influences consumer buying behavior. Playing faster tempo music increases the pace of consumer transactions. Slowing down the tempo of the music encourages customers to stay longer. Still other studies have indicated that consumers find music distracting when considering high-involvement purchases yet found that listening to music during low-involvement purchases made the choice process easier. Moreover, employees tend to be happier and more productive when listening to background music, which in turn leads to a more positive experience for customers.

Table 9.2 displays the impact of background music on consumer and provider behavior in a restaurant setting. As can be concluded by the figures, the pace of service delivered and the pace of consumer consumption is affected by the tempo of the music. Although the estimated gross margin was higher when the restaurant played slow music, the restaurant should also consider the additional number of tables that would turn if faster-paced music was played throughout the day.

Announcements Another common sound in service establishments is the announcements made over intercom systems, such as to alert restaurant patrons when their tables are ready, to inform airline passengers of their current location, and to page specific employees within the firm. The professionalism in which announcements are made directly influences consumer perceptions of the firm. An example of a bizarre announcement made in a grocery store setting involved a male who over the intercom requested: "Red, what's the price on a box of so and so?" A female then responded for everyone in the store to hear: "Red, my ass!" If this type of announcement had been made in a doctor's or lawyer's office, consider how it would have reflected on the competence of the firm. Speaking of such incidents, now is probably a good time to discuss sound avoidance.

MANAGING THE FIRM'S
PHYSICAL EVIDENCE

TABLE 9.2 THE IMPACT OF BACKGROUND MUSIC ON RESTAURANT PATRONS		
Variables	Slow Music	Fast Music
Service time	29 min.	27 min.
Customer time at table	56 min.	45 min.
Customer groups leaving before seated	10.5%	12.0%
Amount of food purchased	$55.81	$55.12
Amount of bar purchases	$30.47	$21.62
Estimated gross margin	$55.82	$48.62

Source: R. E. Milliman, "The Influences of Background Music on the Behavior of Restaurant Patrons," *Journal of Consumer Research* 13 (September 1986), p. 288; see also R. E. Milliman, "Using Background Music to Affect the Behavior of Supermarket Shoppers," *Journal of Marketing*, Summer 1982, pp. 86–91.

Sound Avoidance When planning the firm's facilities, it is as important to understand the avoidance of undesirable sounds as it is to understand the creation of desirable sounds. Desirable sounds attract customers, and undesirable sounds distract from the firm's overall atmosphere. Within a restaurant setting, sounds that should be strategically masked include kitchen, dish room, and restroom noises. Obviously, listening to a toilet flush throughout dinner does little to add to the enjoyment of the customer's dining experience. Other tactics for eliminating unwanted noise include installing durable hallway carpets to eliminate the distracting sounds of clicking heels, strategically placing loud central air conditioning units in areas away from those where the firm conducts the majority of its business, and installing lower ceilings and sound-absorbing partitions so that unwanted sounds can be reduced even further.

SCENT APPEALS

scent appeals

Appeals associated with certain scents.

The atmosphere of the firm can be strongly affected by scents, and the service manager should be aware of this fact. When considering **scent appeals,** as was the case with sound appeals, service managers should pay as much attention to scent avoidance as to scent creation. Stale, musty, foul odors affect everyone and are sure to create negative impressions about the firm. Poor ventilation systems that fail to remove odors and poorly placed trash receptacles are common contributors to potential odor problems.

On the other hand, pleasurable scents often induce customers to make purchases and can affect the perception of products that don't naturally have their own scent. For example, in one study conducted by Nike, customers examined pairs of gym shoes in two different rooms. One room was completely odor free, and the other was artificially permeated with a floral scent. Results of the study indicated that the floral scent had a direct positive effect on the desirability of the sneakers

CHAPTER 9 229

DESIGN
CONSIDERATIONS
FOR HIGH- VERSUS
LOW-CONTACT
SERVICE FIRMS

to 84 percent of the participants.[21] Although this particular example is related to a tangible product, it does seem to indicate that scents do influence consumer perceptions regarding products such as services that do not naturally smell on their own. Experts in scent creation note that a firm should smell like it's supposed to, according to target market expectations. Hospitals should smell clean and antiseptic, and perhaps older, entrenched law firms should even smell a little musty.

TOUCH APPEALS

The chances of a product's selling increases substantially when the consumer handles the product. But how does one touch an intangible product? Service firms such as mail order retailers have a tangible component that can be shipped to customers. One of the reasons that nonstore retailing now accounts for 10 percent of all retail sales and is increasing is the liberal return policies that were implemented to increase **touch appeals.** Spiegel, for example, will send the customer the merchandise for inspection, and if the customer does not want it, the customer simply picks up the phone, notifies Spiegel, and places the returning product outside the door. Spiegel notifies UPS to pick up the package and pays for all costs associated with the return.

> **touch appeals**
> Appeals associated with being able to touch a tangible product or physical evidence of a service, such as shaking hands with service providers.

For purer services with a smaller tangible component, touch appeals can be developed through the use of "open houses" where the public has a chance to meet the people providing the service. Shaking hands and engaging in face-to-face communications with potential and existing customers is definitely a form of touch appeal. Clearly, firms engaged in creating touch appeals are perceived as more caring, closer to their customers, and genuinely concerned and interested in their customers' welfare.

TASTE APPEALS

Taste appeals, the final sensory cue, are the equivalent of providing the customer with samples. Within the service sector, the usefulness of taste appeals when developing service atmospheres is dependent upon the tangibility of the service. Service firms such as car washes, dry cleaners, and restaurants may use taste appeals to initially attract customers. While sampling the firm's services, the customer will have the opportunity to observe the firm's physical evidence and form perceptions regarding the firm and its performance capabilities. Consequently, firms that use samples should view this process as an opportunity rather than as catering to a bunch of customers who want something for free.

> **taste appeals**
> The equivalent of providing the customer with free samples.

DESIGN CONSIDERATIONS FOR HIGH- VERSUS LOW-CONTACT SERVICE FIRMS[22]

One final topic that deserves special attention is the design considerations for low-contact versus high-contact firms. High-customer-contact firms include self-service and interpersonal services, while low-contact firms include remote services. Depending on the level of contact, strategic differences exist regarding facility location, facility design, product design, and process design.

FACILITY LOCATION

The choice location for the firm's service operation depends upon the amount of customer contact that is necessary during the production process. If customers are an integral part of the process, convenient locations located near customers' homes or workplaces will offer the firm a differential advantage over competitors. For example, with all other things being equal, the most conveniently located car washes, dry cleaners, and hairstylists are likely to obtain the most business.

In contrast, low-contact businesses should consider locations that may be more convenient for labor, closer to sources of supply, and closer to major transportation routes. For example, mail-order facilities have little or no customer contact and can actually increase the efficiencies of their operations by locating closer to sources of supply and major transportation alternatives, such as close to interstate highways for trucking purposes or airports for overnight airline shipments. In many cases, these types of locations are less expensive to purchase or rent since they are generally in remote areas, where the cost of land and construction is not as expensive as it is inside city limits where other businesses are trying to locate close to their customers.

FACILITY LAYOUT

In regard to the layout of the service operation, high-contact service firms should take the customers' physical and psychological needs and expectations into consideration. When a customer enters a high-contact service operation, that customer expects the facility to look like something other than a dusty, musty, old warehouse. Attractive personnel, clearly marked signs explaining the process, enough room to comfortably move about the facility, and a facility suited to bring friends and family to are among consumer expectations. In contrast, low-contact facility layouts should be designed to maximize employee expectations and production requirements. Clearly, designing facilities for high-contact services is often more expensive than designing for their low-contact counterparts.

PRODUCT DESIGN

Since the customer is involved in the production process of high-contact services, the customer will ultimately define the product differently from one produced by a low-contact service. In services such as restaurants, which have a tangible product associated with their service offering, the customer will define the product by the physical product itself as well as by the physical evidence that surrounds the product in the service environment. High-contact services that produce purely intangible products such as education and insurance are defined almost solely by the physical evidence that surrounds the service and by the thoughts and opinions of others.

In low-contact services, the customer is not directly involved in the production process, so the product is defined by fewer attributes. Consider our mail-order operation in which the customer never physically enters the facility. The customer will define the end product by the physical product itself (a pair of boots), the conversation that took place with personnel when ordering the boots, the quality of the mail-order catalog that featured the boots, the box in which the boots were packaged, and the billing materials that request payment.

PROCESS DESIGN

In high-contact operations, the physical presence of the customer in the process itself must also be considered. Each stage in the process will have a direct and immediate effect on the customer. Consequently, a set of mini service encounters and the physical evidence present at each encounter will contribute to the customer's overall evaluation of the service process. For example, a hotel guest is directly involved in the reservation process, the check-in process, the consumption process associated with the use of the hotel room itself, the consumption processes associated with the use of hotel amenities such as the restaurant, pool, and health club, and the check-out process. In contrast, since the customer is not involved with many of the production steps in low-contact services, their evaluation is based primarily on the outcome itself.

SUMMARY

The effective management of physical evidence is particularly important to service firms. Due to the intangibility of services, consumers lack objective sources of information when forming evaluations. As a result, customers often look to the physical evidence that surrounds the service when forming evaluations.

A firm's physical evidence includes, but is not limited to, facility exterior design elements such as the architecture of the building, the firm's sign, parking, landscaping, and the surrounding environment of the firm's location; interior design elements such as size, shape, and colors, the firm's entrance and foyer areas, equipment utilized to operate the business, interior signage, layout, air quality, and temperature; and other physical evidence that forms customer perceptions, including business cards, stationery, billing statements, reports, the appearance of personnel, and the firm's brochures.

From a strategic perspective, the importance of managing the firm's physical evidence stems from the firm's ability to: (1) package the service; (2) facilitate the flow of the service delivery process; (3) socialize customers and employees alike in terms of their respective roles, behaviors, and relationships; and (4) differentiate the firm from its competitors.

From a theoretical perspective, the firm's environment influences the behavior of consumers and employees alike due to the inseparability of many services. When designing the firm's facilities, consideration needs to be given to whether the firm is a remote service, an interpersonal service, or a self-service. The subsequent design should reflect the needs of the parties who are dominating the service production process. Decisions about facility location, layout, product design, and process design in particular may result in different outcomes, depending on whether the customer is actively involved in the production process or not. Figure 9.3 illustrates the theoretical framework that helps us to further understand how individuals are affected by the firm's environmental dimensions, which ultimately leads to approach and/or avoidance behaviors.

Finally, numerous tactical decisions must be made when designing the firm's environment. Individuals base perceptions of the firm's services on sensory cues that exist in the firm's environment. Specific tactical decisions must be made about the creation and sometimes the avoidance of scent appeals, sight appeals, sound appeals, touch appeals, and taste appeals. The design and management of the firm's sensory cues are critical to the firm's long-term success.

KEY TERMS

facility exterior	personalized customers
facility interior	apathetic customers
tangibles	ethical customers
socialization	internal response moderators
environmental psychology	cognitive responses
SOR model	beliefs
stimuli	categorization
organism	symbolic meaning
response (outcome)	emotional responses
pleasure-displeasure	physiological responses
arousal-nonarousal	sight appeals
dominance-submissiveness	size/shape/colors
approach behaviors	harmony
avoidance behaviors	contrast/clash
servicescapes	hue
remote services	value
self-services	shades
interpersonal services	tints
ambient conditions	intensity
space/function	sound appeals
signs, symbols, artifacts	scent appeals
holistic environment	touch appeals
perceived servicescape	taste appeals
economic customers	

REVIEW QUESTIONS

1. Discuss the strategic role of physical evidence.

2. Discuss the relevance of remote, self-service, and interpersonal services to facility design.

3. How should the servicescape of a firm that targets ethical shoppers be designed?

4. Discuss how internal response moderators relate to the characteristic of heterogeneity.

5. Discuss internal responses to the firm's environment.

6. What is the impact of music on customer and employee behavior?

7. Develop strategies for a service firm that would enhance the firm's touch and taste appeals.

8. Discuss the use of employee uniforms as physical evidence.

9. What are the major design differences between high-customer-contact and low-customer-contact services?

NOTES

1. Kristen Anderson and Ron Zemke, *Delivering Knock Your Socks Off Service* (New York: AMACOM, 1991), pp. 27–30.

2. Mary Jo Bitner, "Servicescapes: The Impact of Physical Surroundings on Customers and Employees," *Journal of Marketing* 56 (April 1992), pp. 57-–71.

3. Ibid.

4. Edgar Schein, "Organizational Socialization and the Profession of Management," *Industrial Management Review* 9 (Winter 1968), pp. 1–16.

5. Michael R. Solomon, "Packaging the Service Provider," in Christopher H. Lovelock, *Managing Services Marketing, Operations, and Human Resources* (Englewood Cliffs, NJ: Prentice-Hall, 1988), pp. 318–324.

6. Ibid.

7. Ibid.

8. Ibid.

9. Avijit Ghosh, *Retail Management*, 2nd ed. (Fort Worth, TX: The Dryden Press, 1994), pp. 522–523.

10. Ibid.

11. Valerie A. Zeithaml and Mary Jo Bitner, *Services Marketing* (New York: McGraw Hill, 1996), p. 528.

12. Ibid, p. 531.

13. Ibid.

14. Philip Kotler, "Atmospherics as a Marketing Tool," *Journal of Retailing* (Winter 1973–1974), p. 48.

15. Dale M. Lewison, *Retailing*, 4th ed. (New York: MacMillan, 1991), pp. 273–283.

16. Ibid.

17. Kenneth H. Mills and Judith E. Paul, *Applied Visual Merchandising* (Englewood Cliffs, NJ: Prentice-Hall, 1982), p. 47.

18. Kenneth H. Mills and Judith E. Paul, *Create Distinctive Displays* (Englewood Cliffs, NJ: Prentice-Hall, 1974), p. 61.

19. J. Barry Mason, Morris L. Mayer, and J. B. Wilkinson, *Modern Retailing: Theory and Practice*, 6th ed. (Homewood, IL: Irwin, 1993), pp. 642–643.

20. Ronald E. Milliman, "Using Background Music to Affect the Behavior of Supermarket Shoppers," *Journal of Marketing* 46,3 (Summer 1982), pp. 86–91; see also Douglas K. Hawse and Hugh McGinley, "Music for the Eyes, Color for the Ears: An Overview," in *Proceedings of the Society for Consumer Psychology*, David W. Schumann, ed. (Washington, DC: Society for Consumer Psychology, 1988), pp. 145–152.

21. J. Barry Mason, Morris L. Mayer, and Hazel F. Ezell, *Retailing*, 5th ed. (Homewood, IL: Irwin), 1994.

22. Richard B. Chase, "Where Does the Customer Fit in a Service Operation?" *Harvard Business Review* (November–December 1978), pp. 137–142.

P EOPLE I SSUES: M ANAGING
E MPLOYEES AND C USTOMERS

" H *ere's your food, and I hope you choke on it!"*

Fast-food server to a customer who complained about waiting 10 minutes for his food

" T *here are no bad customers; some are just*
harder to please than others."

Someone who never waited on a customer in their life

Kristen Anderson and Ron Zemke, *Delivering Knock Your Socks Off Service*, (New York: AMACOM, 1991)

C H A P T E R   O B J E C T I V E S

The purpose of this chapter is to discuss the key issues that will help you understand the many challenges associated with managing employees and customers within the service experience. Service business, by its very definition, is a people business and requires talented managers who can navigate the thin line between the needs of the organization, its employees, and its customers. After reading this chapter, you should be able to

- ▶ Discuss the importance of contact personnel as boundary spanners.
  - ▶ *Describe sources of conflict in boundary-spanning roles.*
- ▶ Explain the consequences of role stress.
  - ▶ *Discuss methods for reducing role stress through marketing activities.*
- ▶ Describe the concepts of empowerment and enfranchisement.
  - ▶ *Explain the contingency approach to empowerment.*
- ▶ Discuss the principles of waiting.
  - ▶ *Discuss factors for consideration in the effective management of consumer participation.*
- ▶ Discuss strategies for dealing with difficult customers.

SERVICE PROVIDERS FROM YOU-KNOW-WHERE

Within the service experience, it often seems that customers and providers are in pursuit of different goals. Inevitably, clashes occur that have profound long-term effects on how customers view the organization and how the service providers view customers in subsequent transactions. It is a self-perpetuating nightmare. Cynical service providers turn their clientele into "customers from hell," and nightmarish customers return the favor by eventually wearing down even the best service providers.

In a recent *Wall Street Journal* survey, approximately 1,000 customers were asked what irritated them the most about service personnel. Answers most frequently mentioned on customer lists included:

1. Service personnel who say that they will show up at a particular time and fail to show up at all (40 percent).

2. Poorly informed personnel (37 percent).

3. Contact personnel who continue their personal phone calls while they wait on the customer (25 percent).

4. Personnel who pass customers off by saying "It's not my department" (25 percent).

5. Personnel who talk down to the customer (21 percent).

6. Personnel who can't explain how products work (16 percent).

Similarly, in the book *At America's Service,* service personnel behaviors that irk customers the most have been classified into seven categories.

1. Apathy: What comedian George Carlin refers to as DILLIGAD—Do I look like I give a damn?

2. Brush-off: Attempts to get rid of the customer by dismissing the customer completely . . . the "I want you to go away" syndrome.

3. Coldness: Indifferent service providers who could not care less what the customer really wants.

4. Condescension: The "you are the client/patient, so you must be stupid" approach.

5. Robotism: Where the customers are treated simply as inputs into a system that must be processed.

6. Rulebook: Providers who live by the rules of the organization even when those rules do not make good sense.

7. Runaround: Passing the customer off to another provider, who will simply pass them off to yet another provider.

Unfortunately, customers experience service providers from you-know-where almost everyday, and anecdotal evidence continues to mount indicating that dramatic improvements in the customer/provider relationship are slow in coming. For example, a colleague recently relayed the story of his attempt to order a ham and cheese sandwich with mayonnaise from the deli department of a local grocery store. The employee informed him that she could not fulfill his request because the deli was out of mayonnaise. (Gee whiz, lady, do you think you could get a new jar on aisle 2?)

Source: Ron Zemke and Kristen Anderson, "Customers from Hell,"
Training (February 1990), pp. 25–29.

PEOPLE ISSUES:
MANAGING EMPLOYEES
AND CUSTOMERS

INTRODUCTION

[handwritten note: differentiation — service level → right back to Walt being disappointed when taking his kids to a theme park.]

The public face of a service firm is its contact personnel. Partly workers, part administrators, part servants, service personnel often perform a complex and difficult job.[1] Despite their importance and the complexity of their activities, service personnel are often the least trained and least respected individuals in most companies, and often in society. For example, in the health-care community, the individuals most responsible for patient care and patient perceptions of service quality received are ... the nurses? No, the nurses are the lowest paid and least respected individuals in the health-care community? The nurses? In the education system, who is most responsible for day-to-day communication and interaction with students? The classroom teachers. Yet, in the education system, the least paid and least respected individuals? The classroom teachers. The list goes on and on. Consider any service industry, and look to the individuals who are the most responsible for customer interactions and customer perceptions of quality delivered, and you will most likely see the lowest paid and least respected individuals in the company. It makes no sense!

It is little wonder, therefore, that service jobs often have extremely high levels of staff turnover. In 1989, 119,000 sales jobs turned over within the retail network of the Sears Merchandise Group. The cost of hiring and training each new sales assistant was $900, or more than $110 million in total, a sum that represented 17 percent of Sears's 1989 income.[2]

Today, more than 45 million people representing 42 percent of the U.S. workforce are employed in selling food; selling merchandise in retail stores; performing clerical work in service industries; cleaning hospitals, schools, and offices; or providing some other form of personal service. These are occupations that accounted for most of the U.S. job growth in the 1980s, a pattern that will continue at least until the turn of the century. Yet, for the most part, these jobs are poorly paid, lead nowhere, and provide little, if anything, in the way of health, pension, and other benefits.[3] Is it any wonder that the service provider behaviors discussed in the opening vignette are experienced by most customers every day?

THE IMPORTANCE OF CONTACT PERSONNEL

This first section of the chapter highlights the importance of contact personnel to the firm and explains their particular role in creating customer satisfaction. This section also attempts to explain the pressures and tensions on service workers as they perform their **boundary-spanning roles.** As boundary spanners, contact personnel perform the dual functions of interacting with both the firm's external environment and its internal organization and structure.

boundary-spanning roles
The various parts played by contact personnel who perform dual functions of interacting with the firm's external environment and internal organization.

Strategically, contact personnel are an important source of product differentiation. One way to consider the problem of product differentiation is to break the
service firm into three parts: the benefit concept, the servuction system, and the
service level. The benefit concept is the bundle of benefits received by the customer, and it can be measured only in the mind of the customer. The basis of the
service-level idea is that the service delivery system itself should be separated
from the way it operates, a rather arbitrary separation of systems design from the
actual operating performance of that design.

It is often challenging for a service organization to differentiate itself from
other similar organizations in the benefit bundle it offers or its delivery servuction system. For example, one extreme view is that many airlines offer similar
bundles of benefits and fly the same types of aircraft from the same airports.
Their only hope of a competitive advantage is, therefore, from the service level—
the way things are done. Some of this differentiation can come from staffing
levels or the physical systems designed to support the staff. Often, however, the
deciding factor that distinguishes one airline from another is the poise and attitude of the service providers.[4] Singapore Airlines, for example, enjoys an excellent
reputation due in large part to the beauty and grace of their flight attendants.
Other firms that hold a differential advantage over competitors based on personnel include the Ritz Carlton, IBM, and Disney.[5]

THE BOUNDARY-SPANNING ROLE

The boundary-spanning role has been defined as one that links an organization
with the outside world.[6] Employees in boundary-spanning roles create these
links for the organization by interacting with nonmembers of the organization.
Boundary-spanning personnel have two main purposes: information transfer and
representation. Boundary spanners collect information from the environment
and feed it back into the organization, and they communicate with the environment on behalf of the organization. Boundary-spanning personnel are also the
organization's personal representatives.

Individuals who occupy boundary-spanning roles can be classified along a
continuum that ranges from **subordinate service roles** to **professional service
roles** (see Figure 10.1).[7] At one end of the continuum are the subordinate service
roles that traditionally exist at the bottom of an organization. People who work
in these roles work for service firms where the customers' purchase decision is
entirely discretionary. They are subordinate to the organization and to the customer. Examples of subordinate service roles include waiters, bellmen, drivers,
and others who operate at the very base of the organization and yet are the organization's contact personnel with the outside world.

Professional service roles occupy the position at the other end of the continuum. Professionals are also boundary spanners; however, their status is quite
different from that of the subordinate provider. Due to their professional qualifications, professional service providers have a status that is independent of their

subordinate service roles
The parts played by personnel
who work in firms where
customers' purchase decisions
are entirely discretionary, such
as waitresses, bellmen, and
drivers.

professional service roles
The parts played by personnel
who have a status independent
of their place in an organization
due to their professional
qualifications.

PEOPLE ISSUES:
MANAGING EMPLOYEES
AND CUSTOMERS

FIGURE 10.1 RANGE OF BOUNDARY-SPANNING ROLES

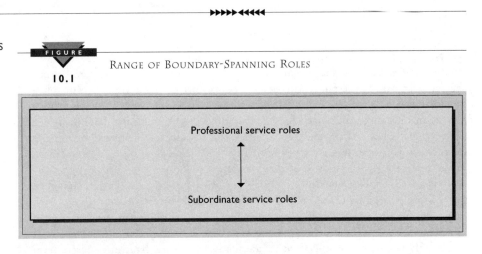

place in the organization. Customers, or as they are more often called, clients, are not superior to professionals because clients acknowledge the professionals' expertise on which they wish to draw.

SOURCES OF CONFLICT IN BOUNDARY-SPANNING ROLES

Employees who occupy boundary-spanning roles are often placed in situations that produce conflict and stress.

Person/Role Conflicts For services to operate successfully, both customers and contact personnel must conform to a script or role. Each must play his or her part. A **person/role conflict** indicates that playing such a role may be inconsistent with an individual's self-perception. Some customers may wish boundary spanners to be subservient, a role that an employee normally would not desire to play, especially with certain types of customers. Boundary-spanning personnel often are called on to subordinate personal feelings to their role, to smile and be helpful while feeling miserable and aggressive; this is particularly the case for low-level staff.[8] Professionals are much more likely to be able to operate within their own self-image and to feel less obligated to maintain a "bedside manner."

person/role conflict
A bad fit between an individual's self-perception and the specific role the person must play in an organization.

Organization/Client Conflicts Conflicts between the demands of the organization and those of the client are the most common source of conflict for boundary-spanning personnel. Conflicts of this type arise when the client or customer requests services that violate the rules of the organization. Such a violation can be as simple as a request for a second bread roll in a restaurant or as complex as a request that a bus driver leave the established route to drop off a passenger at home.[9]

The reaction to the **organization/client conflict** is often related to the employee's role within the organization. Subordinate service personnel are often unable to change the rules and regulations of the company. Moreover, they are unable to explain why the rules and regulations exist in the first place. However, subordinate

organization/client conflicts
Disagreements that arise when a customer requests services that violate the rules of the organization.

Some service roles, such as that of a taxi driver, may operate at the base of the organization but are its contact point with the outside world and, thus, are instrumental in maintaining a positive relationship with the consumer in the service experience.

©1995 PhotoDisc, Inc. Image no. 14106.

service personnel appear to be well aware of the rules and regulations that prevent them from giving good service. In many cases, when faced with an organization/client conflict, subordinate service personnel will side with the client and away from the organization to resolve the conflict. In contrast, professional service personnel, with their higher status and clearer understanding of the purpose of specific rules and regulations, are more able to control what happens.

Interclient Conflicts Conflicts between clients, or **interclient conflicts,** arise because many service delivery systems have a number of other clients who influence one another's experiences. Because different clients are likely to have different needs, they tend to have completely different scripts for themselves, the contact personnel, and other customers. When customers do conflict, it is usually the boundary-spanning personnel who are asked to resolve the confrontation. For example, it is the waiter who is generally requested to ask another diner not to smoke in a nonsmoking section. Attempts to satisfy all of the clients all of the time can escalate the conflict or bring the boundary-spanning personnel into the battle. For example, a restaurant customer requesting speedy service and receiving it can cause complaints from other tables about the inequitable levels of service.

Employee reaction and effectiveness in resolving interclient conflicts appear to be once again related to the employee's role within the organization. Employees in subordinate roles start from the weakest position since they have low status with clients. Clients may simply disregard responses made by subordinate service providers. Professionals may face the same problems; for example, consider the

interclient conflicts
Disagreements between clients that arise because of the number of clients who influence one another's experience.

patient in the hospital waiting room, demanding preferential treatment. In a case such as this, however, the professional can invoke his or her status and expertise to resolve the situation.

THE IMPLICATIONS OF ROLE STRESS FOR BOUNDARY-SPANNING PERSONNEL

The consequences of conflict and stress produce dissatisfaction, frustration, and turnover intention in personnel. When faced with potential conflict and stress in their jobs, employees attempt a variety of strategies to shield themselves. The simplest way of avoiding conflict is to avoid the customers. This is exemplified by the waiter who refuses to notice a customer who wishes to place an order. This strategy allows the employee to increase his or her personal sense of control over the encounter. An alternative strategy is to move into a people-processing mode,[10] where customers are treated as inanimate objects to be processed rather than as individuals. This reduces the requirement of the boundary-spanning personnel to associate or empathize with an individual.

Boundary-spanning personnel also employ other strategies to maintain a sense of control of the encounter. Physical symbols and furniture are often used to boost the employee's status and, hence, his or her sense of control.[11] In an extreme case, the employee may overact the role and force the customer into a subservient role, as is the case with many waiters and waitresses. Interestingly, a national restaurant franchise called Dick's Last Resort encourages employees to be overly demanding as part of their overall theme.

An alternative strategy employees use to reduce organization/client conflict is to side completely with the customer. When forced to obey a rule with which they disagree, boundary-spanning personnel will proceed to list for the customer all the other things about the organization with which they disagree. In this way, employees attempt to reduce stress by seeking sympathy from the customer.

REDUCING ROLE STRESS WITH MARKETING

Traditionally, marketing can either cause or reduce role stress. Marketing can, without making major strategic changes, help to reduce service employee stress levels, and it's in the firm's best interest to do so. Clearly, unhappy, frustrated, and disagreeing contact personnel are visible to customers and will ultimately affect consumer perceptions of service quality.[12] Strategies such as ignoring the customer or simply processing the customer as a raw material through the service delivery system will most likely generate negative customer perceptions. Customers obviously do not like being ignored by waiters or treated as if they were inanimate objects. If contact personnel attempt to maximize their sense of control over their encounters, it will most likely be at the expense of the amount of control felt by customers. In addition, although customers may sympathize with a service provider's explanation that the organization stops them from providing excellent service, customers will still develop negative perceptions about the organization.

Reducing Person/Role Conflicts Marketing can reduce the conflict between the individual and the assigned role by simply being sensitive and by actively seeking input from employees about the issue. A promotional gimmick dreamed up at the head office may look great on paper. A medieval-theme day in the hotel almost certainly will have great public relations value, but how will the staff feel when they are called upon to wear strange and awkward (not to mention uncomfortable) costumes? How will these costumes affect the employees' relationships with customers during the service encounter?

To improve the quality of service, a change in operating procedure may be needed. However, it is important to ensure that service providers are well trained in the new script. Should they not be, they may well become extremely embarrassed in the presence of customers. This situation can be aggravated if the new service is advertised in such a way that the customers are more aware of the new script than the staff.

Reducing Organization/Client Conflicts Similarly, marketing can help reduce conflicts between the organization and its clients. It is crucial, for example, that customer expectations be consistent with the capabilities of the service system. Customers should not ask for services the system cannot provide. Advertising is one of the main causes of inflated expectations as the temptation is to exaggerate claims in advertising to maximize the impact. Consider, for example, the advertisement that depicted a flight attendant reading a young child a story while the plane was in flight. A number of passengers took the advertisement literally, either because they believed it or because they could not resist the temptation, and called upon the flight attendants to read stories to their children.

Reducing Interclient Conflicts Conflicts between clients can be avoided if the clients are relatively homogeneous in their expectations. Due to the inseparability of services, customers often share their service experiences with other customers. Hence, successful service firms recognize the importance of effective segmentation, which minimizes the chances that two or more divergent groups will share the encounter simultaneously. As long as all the clients share the same script and expect the same standard of service. the chances of interclient conflicts are much reduced.

The Importance of Human Resources for Service Firms

Personnel constitutes the bulk of the product of most service firms. However, marketing theory is ill equipped to provide insights into the problem of where contact personnel fit into the hierarchy of the service firm. Human resources, by comparison, is a field of study focused on this and similar problems. Human

climate

Employee perceptions of their
employer's passion for service.

resource policies are associated with the outcomes experienced by customers and
the culture created within the service firm.[13]

Because service firms often involve the customer as a co-producer, they operate open systems, where the effects of human resource practices and policies
as well as the organization's **climate** are visible to customers. Climate is defined
as employee perceptions of one or more strategic imperatives. For example, a
passion for service within the organization would lead to a climate that sets
service as the key strategic imperative (see, for example, Tables 10.1 and 10.2).
When service commitment is high, the service firm displays a passion for doing
things directly related to the provision of service. Employees speak often and favorably about the service delivery process and the product offered to consumers,
as well as about the concern for and/or responsiveness of the firm to customer
opinions. In addtion, when service passion is strong, employees speak favorably
about performance feedback, internal equity of compensation, training, and staff
quality, which is communicated to customers throughout the service delivery
process.

CREATING THE RIGHT TYPE OF ORGANIZATION

Human resource management practices are the key drivers available to senior
management for creating the type of organization that can be a source of sustainable competitive advantage. Often, however, front-line customer contact jobs
are designed to be as simple and narrow as possible so that they can be filled by
anyone—in other words, "idiot-proof" jobs. Employers place few demands on
employees, selection criteria are minimal, and wages are low.

The result is the classic cycle of failure of the industrial model as discussed
in Chapter One. Fewer and less-knowledgeable contact personnel are available,
and hence, the customer gets less and lower-quality help. Customers vent their
feelings of impatience and dissatisfaction on the staff, which, in turn, demotivates
the employees, especially the most conscientious ones, since they are already
aware of the poor service they are being forced to give. The best staff leave and are
replaced with poorly trained recruits—and the cycle continues. Current human
resource theory is looking for ways to break out of the industrial model mindset,
and, in particular, how to use empowerment and enfranchisement to break the
the cycle of failure.

empowerment

Giving discretion to front-line
personnel to meet the needs of
consumers creatively.

enfranchisement

Empowerment coupled with a
performance-based
compensation method.

EMPOWERMENT AND ENFRANCHISEMENT

One of the most powerful tools for breaking free of the old logic is the use of
employee empowerment and enfranchisement. **Empowerment** means giving
discretion to contact personnel to "turn the front-line loose." Empowerment is
the reverse of "doing things by the book." **Enfranchisement** carries this logic even
further by first empowering individuals and then coupling this with a compensation method that pays people for their performance.

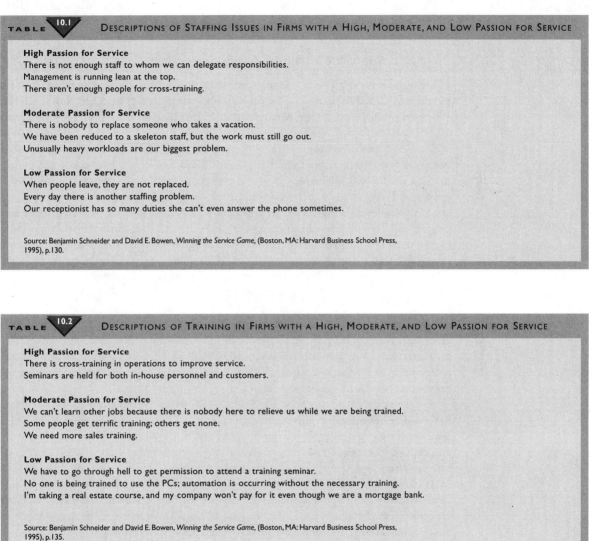

TABLE 10.1   DESCRIPTIONS OF STAFFING ISSUES IN FIRMS WITH A HIGH, MODERATE, AND LOW PASSION FOR SERVICE

High Passion for Service
There is not enough staff to whom we can delegate responsibilities.
Management is running lean at the top.
There aren't enough people for cross-training.

Moderate Passion for Service
There is nobody to replace someone who takes a vacation.
We have been reduced to a skeleton staff, but the work must still go out.
Unusually heavy workloads are our biggest problem.

Low Passion for Service
When people leave, they are not replaced.
Every day there is another staffing problem.
Our receptionist has so many duties she can't even answer the phone sometimes.

Source: Benjamin Schneider and David E. Bowen, *Winning the Service Game,* (Boston, MA: Harvard Business School Press, 1995), p.130.

TABLE 10.2   DESCRIPTIONS OF TRAINING IN FIRMS WITH A HIGH, MODERATE, AND LOW PASSION FOR SERVICE

High Passion for Service
There is cross-training in operations to improve service.
Seminars are held for both in-house personnel and customers.

Moderate Passion for Service
We can't learn other jobs because there is nobody here to relieve us while we are being trained.
Some people get terrific training; others get none.
We need more sales training.

Low Passion for Service
We have to go through hell to get permission to attend a training seminar.
No one is being trained to use the PCs; automation is occurring without the necessary training.
I'm taking a real estate course, and my company won't pay for it even though we are a mortgage bank.

Source: Benjamin Schneider and David E. Bowen, *Winning the Service Game,* (Boston, MA: Harvard Business School Press, 1995), p.135.

The most significant and successful enfranchisement programs have occured in the field of retailing. Here, advocates argue that it can improve sales and earnings dramatically while at the same time require less supervision from corporate management. Perhaps the most commonly used example is Nordstrom, which pays salespeople a commmission not only on what they sell but also on the extent to which they can exceed their superior's projected sales forecasts. At the same time,

Nordstrom's management frees salespeople of normal constraints and publicly celebrates "associates'" outstanding service accomplishments.

When to Empower and Enfranchise

No single solution exists to the problems encountered in managing contact personnel. Empowerment and enfranchisement do not always win out over the industrial-based models of management. Consider the examples of FedEx and UPS.

In 1990, FedEx became the first service organization to win the coveted Malcolm Baldrige National Quality Award. Behind the blue, white, and red planes and uniforms are self-managed work teams, garnishing plans, and empowered employees seemingly concerned with providing flexible and creative service to customers with varying needs. In contrast, at UPS, we find turned-on people and profits, but we do not find empowerment. Instead we find controls, rules, a detailed union contract, and carefully studied work methods. UPS makes no promises that its employees will bend over backward to meet individual customer needs. However, what we *do* find are rigid operational guidelines, which help guarantee the customer reliable, low-cost service.[14]

The Benefits Empowerment clearly brings benefits. Empowered employees are more customer focused and are much quicker in responding to customer needs. They will customize the product or remix it in realtime.[15] Empowered employees are more likely to respond in a positive manner to service failures and to engage in effective service recovery strategies.

Employees who are empowered tend to feel better about their jobs and themselves. This is automatically reflected in the way they interact with customers. They will be genuinely warmer and friendlier. Empowerment, therefore, not only can reduce unnecessary service recovery costs, but also can improve the quality of the product.

If close to the front line, an empowered employee is in a position continuously exposed to both the good and the bad aspects of the service delivery system. This employee can be the key to new service ideas and often be a cheaper source of market research than going to the customer directly.

The Costs Unfortunately, empowerment and enfranchisement do carry costs. The balance between benefits and costs determines the appropriateness of the approach. Empowerment increases the costs of the organization. A greater investment is need in remuneration and recruitment to assure that the right people are empowered. A low-cost model of using inexpensive and/or part-time labor cannot cope with empowerment, so the basic labor costs of the organization will be higher.

If costs are higher, marketing implications also arise. By defintion, an empowered employee will customize the product. This means that the service received will vary from one encounter to the next, depending on the employee. The delivery is also likely to be slower because the service is customized. Moreover, since customers are treated differently, other customers may perceive that some customers are receiving preferential treatment. Finally, empowered employees, when attempting to satisfy customers, sometimes give away too much and make bad decisions. For example, a bellman who notices that a businessman forgot his briefcase at the front desk should make every attempt to return the briefcase to its owner. However, tracking the owner to the airport and hopping on the next available flight to the owner's destination is far beyond the call of duty and worlds beyond what is economically feasible.

The balance of empowerment and enfranchisement, therefore, comes down to the benefit concept of the organization. A branded organization that guarantees consistency of product and service dare not empower for fear of the inconsistency that doing so would produce. For example, McDonald's would lose one of its key differential advantages if it empowered its employees.

An organization that competes on the basis of value driven by a low cost base cannot afford to empower because of the costs involved. Equally, a high-cost service organization using a nonroutine and complex technology almost certainly has to empower because its ability to use an industrial approach is severely limited.

LEVELS OF EMPOWERMENT

As evidenced by the UPS and FedEx examples, empowerment is not for every firm. Firms can indeed be successful without fully empowering their employees. However, empowerment approaches vary by degree and include suggestion involvement, job involvement, and high involvement. Each of the three levels of empowerment fall along a continuum that ranges from control-oriented to involvement-oriented approaches (see Figure 10.2).

Suggestion involvement falls near the control-oriented point of the empowerment continuum. Suggestion involvement empowers employees to recommend suggestions for improving the firm's operations. Employees are not empowered to implement suggestions themselves but are encouraged to suggest improvements for formal review. Firms that utilize suggestion involvement typically maintain formal suggestion programs that proactively solicit employee suggestions. **Quality circles,** which often involve small groups of employees from various departments in the firm, are also utilized as brainstorming sessions to generate additional suggestions. Typical success stories of suggestion involvement programs include McDonald's, whose employees recommended the development of products such as the "Big Mac," "Egg McMuffin," and "McDLT."

Job involvement typically falls in the middle of the empowerment continuum, between control-oriented and involvement-oriented approaches. Job involvement allows employees to examine the content of their own jobs and to define their role within the organization. Firms engaged in job involvement use teams of employees extensively for the betterment of the firm's service delivery system. In

suggestion involvement
Low-level empowerment that allows employees to recommend suggestions for improvement of the firm's operations.

quality circles
Empowerment involving small groups of employees from various departments in the firm who use brainstorming sessions to generate additional improvement suggestions.

job involvement
Allows employees to examine the content of their own jobs and to define their role within the organization.

FIGURE
10.2

LEVELS OF EMPOWERMENT

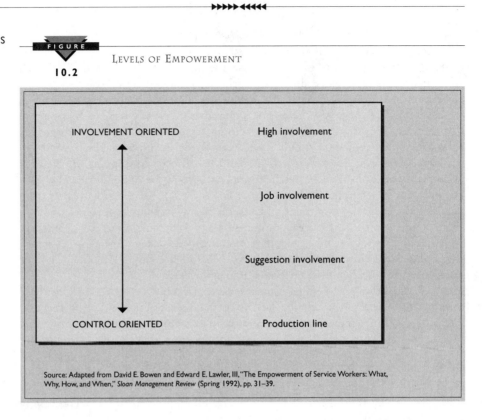

Source: Adapted from David E. Bowen and Edward E. Lawler, III, "The Empowerment of Service Workers: What, Why, How, and When," *Sloan Management Review* (Spring 1992), pp. 31–39.

contrast to suggestion involvement, employees engaged in job involvement use a variety of skills, have considerably more freedom, and receive extensive feedback from management, employees, and customers. However, higher-level decisions and reward allocation decisions remain the responsibility of the firm's upper management.

high involvement

Allows employees to eventually learn to manage themselves, utilizing extensive training and employee control of the reward allocation decisions.

High involvement falls at the involvement-oriented end of the empowerment continuum. Essentially, the goal of high involvement is to train people to manage themselves. Extensive training is utilized to develop skills in teamwork, problem solving, and business operations. Moreover, employees control the majority of the reward allocation decisions through profit sharing and employee ownership of the firm. In sum, virtually every aspect of a high-involvement firm is different from those of a control-oriented firm.

HOW MUCH TO EMPOWER: A CONTINGENCY APPROACH

When deciding among suggestion involvement, job involvement, and high-involvement empowerment strategies, the firm must consider several factors in order to select the correct strategy. Table 10.3 provides a rating system to help managers assess their particular situations. According to the table, managers

TABLE 10.3   THE CONTINGENCIES OF EMPOWERMENT

Contingency	Production-Line Approach		Empowerment
Basic business strategy	Low cost, high volume	1 2 3 4 5	Differentiation, customized, personalized
Tie to the customer	Transaction, short time period	1 2 3 4 5	Relationship, long time period
Technology	Routine, simple	1 2 3 4 5	Nonroutine, complex
Business environment	Predictable, few surprises	1 2 3 4 5	Unpredictable, many surprises
Types of people	Theory X managers, employees with low growth needs, low social needs, and weak interpersonal skills	1 2 3 4 5	Theory Y managers, employees with high growth needs, high social needs, and strong interpersonal skills

Source: David E. Bowen and Edward E. Lawler, III, "The Empowerment of Service Workers: What, Why, How, and When," *Sloan Management Review* (Spring 1992), pp. 31–39.

should rate their firms on five contingencies: the firm's basic business strategy, its tie to the customer, technology, the business environment, and types of leadership.

The **basic business strategy** of the firm pertains to whether the firm produces a standardized, low-cost, high-volume product or whether it produces a differentiated, customized, personalized product. As the product becomes more standardized, lower levels of empowerment are suggested. Production lining the service delivery system will make the system more efficient, thereby controlling costs and increasing the standardization of product produced.

The firm's **tie to the customer** refers to the type of relationship the firm has with its customers. If the relationship involves discrete transactions that occur over a short time period, control-oriented approaches should dominate. In contrast, if the customer-client relationship is long-term, such as that with an insurance agent, broker, or CPA, employees should be empowered to meet the individual needs of clients.

Similarly, if the **technology** utilized to carry out the firm's operations is simple and routine and the **business environment** within which the firm operates is predictable, then the costs associated with empowered employees outweigh the benefits. If, on the other hand, the technology is nonroutine and complex and the business environment is volatile, empowered employees are necesary for coping with client concerns and the constantly changing environment.

Finally, empowered employees need different kinds of leadership. Theory Y managers, who coach and facilitate rather than control and manipulate, are needed to work with employees who have high growth needs and strong interpersonal skills . . . the needs and skills of empowered employees. In contrast, firms governed by Theory X managers believe that employees are working primarily to collect a paycheck. Theory X managers work best with employees who have low growth needs, low social needs, and weak interpersonal skills. Theory X managers fit best with control-oriented organizations.

basic business strategy
A firm's fundamental approach as to whether it produces a standardized, low-cost, high-volume product or a differentiated, customized, personalized product.

tie to the customer
The degrees of involvement the firm has with its customers.

technology
The level of automation a firm utilizes.

business environment
The social, technological, and financial environment in which a firm operates and markets.

The contingency approach, presented in Table 10.3, rates each of the five factors (basic business strategy, tie to the customer, technology, business environment, and types of people) on a scale from 1 to 5, where lower numbers favor a control-oriented approach and higher numbers favor an empowerment approach. Upon adding the scores of the five factors together, firms scoring in the 5–10 range are recommended to pursue a very control-oriented, production-line approach. Firms scoring 11–15 are recommended to implement a suggestion involvement strategy. Firms rating 16–20 are urged to utilize a job involvement approach, and firms that score 21–25 are suggested to implement a high-involvement empowerment approach. Ultimately, the selection of empowerment strategy should be dependent upon the firm and the market in which it operates. Different types of firms have different needs.

PEOPLE ISSUES: MANAGING CUSTOMERS

This second section of the chapter focuses on another important "people issue" in the service encounter—the management of consumers. As mentioned in previous chapters, the service encounter can be viewed as a three-way fight for control between the customer, the employee, and the organization itself.[16] An early study of restaurants, for example, found that waitresses coped with the pressures of their jobs by managing their customers. They were able to wrestle control away from the customers by suggesting menu items and telling customers how long they would have to wait.[17] This is precisely the strategy employed by many professionals who use their status, and the fact that the client is not in a postion to leave, to take control.

Because the fight for control is not simply a two-way fight, the organization also wants to establish control of the encounter. The procedures and systems established by the organization are not created to simply add to the bureaucracy of the encounter but are primarily put into place for economic reasons to ensure profitability.

STRATEGIES FOR MANAGING CONSUMERS

Service firms have attempted to manage consumers using a variety of strategies over the years. Typical examples include reservation systems that attempt to control the flow of consumers into the system, separate seating sections for smokers and nonsmokers to control consumer interactions, and price discounts for families who are willing to dine early so that families with young children do not disrupt the dining experience of older segments, who generally dine later in the evening. The focus of the remainder of this chapter is on three areas of particular importance: the management of consumer waiting periods, the management of consumer participation in the service process, and dealing with difficult customers—managing to keep your cool while those around you are losing theirs.

Managing Consumer Waits

Due to the unpredictablity of consumer demand inherent in many service operations, the only cases in which the supply of available service and consumer demand balance exactly is by accident. As a result, consumers of services often find themselves waiting for service. Effectively managing consumer waits is particularly crucial due to the importance of first impressions on consumer perceptions of the service experience. First impressions are often long lasting and can dramatically affect customer evaluations of the total experience, regardless of how good the service was after the wait. A dental patient waiting until 4:00 P.M. for an appointment that was supposed to be at 2:00 P.M. will most likely care little about how friendly the staff and the dentist are by the time the appointment actually begins.

Over the years, through trial and error, eight principles of waiting have developed to help service firms effectively manage consumer waits.[18] Service firms sensitive to these principles have developed strategies to deal with consumer waits and minimize the negative affects associated with delays. In fact, in some instances, effective management of consumer waits has actually led to increased profit opportunities.

Unoccupied Waits Feel Longer Than Occupied Waits Waiting around with nothing to do makes every minute seem so much longer. Successful service firms have learned to manage consumer waits by occupying the consumer's time. Restaurants can occupy consumer waits by offering to let the consumer wait in the lounge area, which also increases the profit-making opportunity for the firm. Similarly, golf courses offer driving ranges, and the medical community tends to offer reading materials. Ideally, tactics utilized to occupy consumers should be related to the ensuing service encounter. Trivial attempts to occupy consumer waits, such as forcing the customer to listen to Muzak when placed on hold during a phone call, are sometimes met with customer resistance.

Preprocess Waits Feel Longer than In-Process Waits—Postprocess Waits Feel Longest of All The waiting period before the service starts feels longer to customers than waiting while the service is in process. For example, doctors often move waiting patients into empty examining rooms to convey the sense that the service has started. Realistically, the physician has simply changed the location of the wait. Effective techniques to manage preprocess waits include simply acknowledging the customer. Waitstaff are often too busy to serve customers as soon as they are seated. Phrases such as "I'll be with you as soon as I can" acknowledges the customer's presence and conveys the message that the service has started. Other phrases such as "Your order is being processed" are also effective in keeping the customer informed of the status of the order.

Postprocess waits feel the longest of all waits. In many instances, the service has been delivered, and now the customer is simply waiting for the check or bill. It's baffling to customers to be subjected to delays when the customer simply wants to give the service establishment money. Another example of customer impatience regarding postprocess waits can be experienced during deplaning procedures at the airport. On your next flight, listen to the sounds of passengers releasing their seatbelts as soon as the plane comes to a full stop. The door to the plane is not open, no one is leaving the plane, yet people are literally fighting for positions to get themselves off the plane as quickly as possible.

Anxiety Makes the Wait Seem Longer Have you ever noticed how much longer traffic lights take to change when you are in a hurry? This is because anxiety expands consumer perceptions of time. Effective service firms manage the anxiety levels of their customers by attempting to identify and then removing anxiety-producing components of the service encounter. The use of focus groups is particularly helpful in effectively identifying anxiety producers because many consumer fears may be irrational and/or overlooked by providers who fully understand the service delivery process. Often, information is one of the most effective tools in relieving consumer anxiety. For example, informing delayed airline passengers that connecting flights are being held for them, notifying waiting movie-goers that seats are available, and assisting new students in finding the right lines during registration will remove much of the anxiety felt by these consumer groups.

Uncertain Waits Are Longer than Known, Finite Waits While waiting in a doctor's office, the time before the appointment is due passes much more quickly than the time spent waiting beyond the appointment time. Restaurants have learned this lesson the hard way. In the not-so-distant-past, it seemed that restaurants would purposely underestimate their wait-times to encourage patrons not to leave the restaurant to dine at a competitor's establishment. This strategy resulted in angry, frustrated customers who felt they had been purposely misled and lied to for the sake of greed. By the time the customers were seated, they were so consumed with anger that the food, service, and atmosphere of the encounter became irrelevant, regardless of their quality. Moreover, many of these patrons would vow never to return. Today, it seems that restaurants overestimate their waits to provide consumers with a realistic time frame from which to develop expectations. Other service providers simply make and keep appointments, which eliminates the customer's wait altogether. Even other providers, such as Disney, provide finite waiting times from certain points within a line (e.g., 10 minutes from this point).

Unexplained Waits Are Longer than Explained Waits It is human nature to want an explanation. You can almost see the disappointment in people's faces when the slow speed during a traffic jam on the highway resumes its normal pace without an explanation. Customers want to know why they have to wait, and the earlier the information is provided, the more understanding the consumer becomes, and the less long the wait seems to take.

Due to the inseparability of services, customers sometimes have a difficult time understanding why all the service providers in the factory are not serving customers. Banks are a good example. Bank tellers must sometimes perform operational duties, such as balancing the cash drawer, which prohibits them from serving customers. However, since all bank teller stations are visible to the customers, customers often question why all the bank tellers are not actively serving the bank's customers.

Effective management may try to minimize this problem in one of two ways. First, management may consider educating consumers about the realities of the bank teller's duties, which extend beyond interactions with customers. Second, management may consider developing a physical facility where the teller is out of sight when performing noncustomer-related duties. This type of problem extends beyond the banking industry. Airlines, grocery stores, and other businesses that grant their employees rest breaks that are visible to the customer face similar challenges.

Unfair Waits Are Longer than Equitable Waits Effective consumer management should strive to provide a level playing field that is fair for all consumers. The majority of consumers are not unreasonable. Most restaurant consumers understand that larger parties will wait longer than smaller parties and that parties with reservations will be seated sooner than those who arrive unannounced. However, probably nothing will ignite a serious confrontation faster than consumers who feel they have been passed over by other customers who entered the service experience at a later time under the same set of circumstances.

Lines such as those found at McDonald's, Hardee's, and drive-through banks are classic examples of why consumers become frustrated. In each instance, the customer must pick the line he or she thinks will move fastest. Inevitably, the other lines move faster, and customers who entered the lines at a later time are served first, out of order. From a fairness perspective, methods that form a single line, such as those used at Wendy's, Burger King, and many banks, are preferable. Customers are served in the order in which they enter the service process.

Another classic example of unfair service is the priority that telephone calls receive over customers who are physically standing in line. The person on the telephone usually takes priority, which is the equivalent of that person's walking up to the front of the line. Management needs to consider the costs of having employees returning the phone calls at the appropriate time versus the cost of alienating customers and placing employees in awkward and often indefensible positions.

The More Valuable the Service, the Longer the Customer Will Wait Why else would you wait in a doctor's office for two hours? Is it any wonder that the word *patient* is a form of the word *patience?* The amount of time customers are willing to wait is often situational. When the service is considered valuable and few alternatives exist, customers will be willing to wait much longer than if the reverse were true.

Perceived value of the service tends to increase with the title and status of the provider. Students will tend to wait longer for a full professor who is late for class than they will wait for an assistant professor, and they will wait for a dean or chancellor of the unviersity even longer. Similarly, customers are willing to wait much longer for their meals at upscale restaurants than at fast-food establishments. When managing consumer waits, the firm must understand the value its customers place on its services and the time they consider to be a reasonable wait.

Solo Waits Are Longer than Group Waits It is amusing to consider the amount of customer interaction typically displayed in a grocery store line. Generally, there is none at all, even though we are standing within inches of one another. However, watch what happens when a delay occurs, such as a price check on an item or a customer who takes too long to fill out a check . . . the rest of the line quickly bonds together like old friends! Group waits serve the function of occupying customers' time and reduces the perceived wait. When managing consumer waits, the practicality of actively encouraging consumers to interact may be considered.

MANAGING CONSUMER PARTICIPATION

Increasing consumer participation in the service delivery process has become a popular strategy to increase the supply of service available to the firm and to provide a form of service differentiation. By allowing consumers to produce at least part of their own service, contact personnel are freed to perform other duties, such as serving other customers or engaging in noncustomer-related activities (such as completing paperwork). Increasing customer participation is associated with a number of advantages and disadvantages. The primary advantage to the customer and the service firm is that customers can customize their own service and produce it faster and less expensively than if the firm had produced it. Customers who pump their own gas, make their own salads, and pick their own strawberries are classic examples. On the other hand, increased levels of customer participation are also associated with the firm's losing control of quality, increased waste, which increases operating costs, and customer perceptions that the firm may be attempting to distance itself from its customers.

When making the transition from a full-service to a self-service operation, the firm needs to be sensitive to the reasons the customer may prefer one format over another. Guidelines have evolved that help facilitate this transition and avoid insensitivity.[19]

Develop Customer Trust Efforts to increase customer participation throughout the production process should not be interpreted as the firm's way of distancing itself from the customer. The firm should provide information to the customer that explains why self-service opportunities are being provided and the potential customer benefits. When it is readily apparent that the only reason the firm is offering self-service options is to benefit the firm, customers will quickly flock to full-service competitors.

An automatic teller machine enables a bank to provide 24-hour service to its customers and extend the bank's services to hundreds of convenient locations. What is another advantage of providing an ATM?

Source: © 1995 PhotoDisc, Inc. Image no. 21091.

Promote the Benefits and Stimulate Trial The typical benefits associated with self-service are convenience, customization, and cost savings to the customer. Self-service gas stations provide a cost savings, self-service salad and dessert bars allow customers to customize their own salads and ice cream sundaes, and automatic teller machines provide 24-hour service and extend the bank's services to hundreds of convenient locations.

To promote new self-service options, customers may need an incentive to stimulate trial. For example, one bank rigged its new automatic teller machine to sporadically distribute more cash than its customers requested to stimulate trial of the machine. The cash was used as a promotional tool and was free to the customer. The strategy was originally intended to make customers aware of the new ATM's location and to encourage older clientele, who traditionally resist change, to use the ATM. Soon after the promotion started, clever college students began withdrawing and redepositing their money over and over again to increase their chances to win extra cash. A grand prize of $500 was randomly distributed to an elderly gentleman, who believed the ATM had made a mistake and attempted to return the money to the bank. It took bank employees several attempts to convince the man that this was his money to take and that it had not been withdrawn from his account.

Understand Customer Habits Part of the problem when transfering from full-service to self-service is that we tend to forget why customers might prefer using full-service options in the first place. Despite the convenience of ATMs, many customers like the personalization of dealing with a particular teller. Friendships and trust develops that cannot be replaced by machinery. In addition, many bank customers will use an ATM for withdrawals, but refuse to make deposits through the same ATM. The thought of handing over checks and cash to a machine seems to be too much.

Pretest New Procedures All new self-service options should be thoroughly pretested, not only by the firm's employees but particularly by customers who do not have the advantage of full information. For example, the British postal system attempted to enlist the help of its customers by requesting them to use extremely long zip codes when addressing envelopes. The plan was a disaster. The zip codes were far too long to remember, and the public basically vetoed any further development of the project by simply refusing to participate.

Pretesting helps in identifying and correcting potential problems before new procedures are fully introduced. In many instances, the company may have only one or two chances to prove to customers the benefits of self-service alternatives. However, if the procedures themselves are flawed and/or difficult to understand, the firm may lose its chance to convince customers of the advantages. For example, more customers might use ATMs if the screens did not face the sun and were easier to read, if the machines had not initally frequently "eaten" the customer's ATM cards, and if customers did not have to be gymnasts to use drive-through ATMs from their vehicles.

Understand the Determinants of Consumer Behavior When considering consumer benefits of self-service alternatives, firms should understand the determinants of consumer behavior. Why would a customer use an ATM instead of a bank teller? Or why would customers like to select and cook their own steaks in a fine dining restaurant? The consumer benefits promoted by the firm should be defined by the customer. For example, customers who work shifts other than the traditional 8-to-5 slot enjoy the 24-hour accessibility of ATMs. Other customers may simply be in a hurry, and the ATM provides a faster means of service. At self-service cookeries, the experience of selection and preparation may facilitate social interaction and/or be ego driven.

Teach Consumers How to Use Service Innovations Many of today's self-service options are technology driven, and in many cases, customers are left to fend for themselves in attempts to use these new alternatives. An "on your own" approach does not exactly encourage customers to try new self-service methods. For customers to be taught, employees must first know how and what to teach. Nothing will turn off customers faster than employess who have no idea how to use the new systems themselves.

Monitor and Evaluate Performance Finally, if a firm's self-service option enjoys an initial success, it should be continuously monitored and evaluated throughout

the year. Does demand fluctuate? What are the possible causes? Has demand increased, decreased, or leveled off? What other services do consumers want self-service access to? Customer surveys and focus groups will not only define satisfaction with today's services but also tomorrow's needs.

MANAGING UNCOOPERATIVE CUSTOMERS

Customers are not always saints, and despite words to the contrary, they are not always right. However, few companies ever sit down with employees to discuss how to deal with difficult customers. The lack of discussion about dealing with difficult customers may be a result of the lack of attention paid to the subject in institutions of higher learning. Despite the importance of the customer as the central theme that runs throughout the field of marketing, little discussion, if any, occurs on how to interact with a real, live customer in most colleges and universities. Here's your chance to be part of the cutting edge.

Five customer profiles have been developed, representing the worst that customers have to offer.[20] In reality, the worst customer of all is a little of all five types. The characteristics of each of the five "customers from hell" and suggestions for ways to deal with them are discussed below.

Egocentric Edgar is the guy Carly Simon had in mind when she wrote the song, "You're So Vain." Edgar doesn't believe he should stand in line for any reason. He'll push his way to the front and demand service on a variety of things that demand little immediate attention. If your company's creed is "We are here to serve," Edgar interprets that message as, "Your company exists to serve my needs and my needs alone, and right now!"

Another of Edgar's nasty characteristics is that he will walk over front-line employees to get to who he'll call "the man in charge." Edgar treats front-line employees as well-worn speed bumps that deserve just that much consideration.

Egocentric Edgar

The type of customer who places his or her needs above all other customers and service personnel.

PEOPLE ISSUES:
MANAGING EMPLOYEES
AND CUSTOMERS

Once he gets to the top, Edgar uses the chance to belittle upper management and prove he knows how things should be done.

Dealing with Edgar is particularly troublesome for providers who are new on the job, unsure of their own abilities, and easily pushed around. The key to dealing with Edgar is to not let his ego destroy yours, while at the same time appealing to his ego. Because Edgar believes you are incapable of performing any function, take action that demonstrates your ability to solve his problem. This will surprise Edgar. In addition, never talk policy to Edgar. Edgar thinks he is special and that the rules that apply to everyone else should not apply to him. Policy should still apply to Edgar, but just don't let him know that you are restating policy. Phrases such as, "For you Edgar, I can do the following. . . ." where "the following" is simply policy, will appeal to Edgar's ego while still managing him within the policies of the organization.

Bad-Mouth Betty

The type of customer who becomes loud, crude, and abusive to service personnel and other customers alike.

Bad-Mouth Betty lets you know in no uncertain terms exactly what she thinks of you, your organization, and the heritage of both. If she cannot be right, she will be loud, vulgar, and insensitive. She is crude not only to service employees but also to other customers who are sharing her unpleasant experience.

selective agreement

A method of dealing with a dissatisfied customer by agreeing on minor issues in order to show that the customer is being heard.

Dealing with Betty consists of at least four options. First, since Betty is polluting the service environment with her foul mouth, attempt to move her "off-stage" so as to not further contaminate the service environment of your other customers. Once isolated, another option is to ignore her foul language and listen to determine the core of the problem and take appropriate action. This is a difficult option to undertake, particularly if her language is excessively abusive and personal in nature. Another option is use **selective agreement** in an attempt to show Betty that you are listening and possibly on her side. Selective agreement involves agreeing with Betty on minor issues such as, "You're right, waiting 10 minutes for your Egg McMuffin is a long time." However, agreeing with Betty that your boss really is an "SOB" is not advisable since Betty is likely to use this to her advantage at a later date. The last option that every good service firm should take is to force the issue. Let Betty know that you would be more than willing to help her solve her problem but that you don't have to

Source: Ron Zemke and Kristin Anderson,
"Customers from Hell," *Training* 26 (February
1990), pp. 25–31. Reprinted with permission from
TRAINING Magazine. © 1990, Lakewood
Publications, Minneapolis, MN. All rights reserved.
Not for Resale.

listen to her language. If Betty continues to be crude, hang up, walk away, or do whatever is necessary to let her know she is on her own. In most cases, she will return the call, walk over and apologize, and let you get on with your job.

Hysterical Harold is a screamer. If he doesn't get his way, his face will turn colors and veins will literally pop out from his neck. "Harold demonstrates the dark side . . . of the child inside all of us. He is the classic tantrum thrower, the adult embodiment of the terrible twos. Only louder. Much louder."[21]

Dealing with Harold is much like dealing with Betty in many ways. These two occupy the "other customers" slot of the servuction model and negatively affect everyone else's service experience. Consequently, move Harold offstage and give your other customers a chance to enjoy the remainder of their encounter. When Harold has a problem, Harold has to vent. When offstage, let him vent and get it off his chest. This is when you can finally get to the heart of the matter and begin to take action. Finally, take responsibility for the problem. Do not blame the problem on fellow employees, upper management, or others who may ultimately be responsible. Offer an apology for what has occurred and, more importantly, a solution to Harold's problem.

Dictatorial Dick is claimed to be Egocentric Edgar's evil twin. Dick likes to tell everyone exactly how they are supposed to do their jobs because he has done it all before. Just so you don't get confused, Dick will provide you a written copy of his instructions, which is copied to your boss, your boss's boss, and his lawyer. Dick will most likely make you sign for your copy.

If his brilliant instructions do not produce the desired outcome, then it's your company's fault, or, more likely, your fault because you were too incompetent to fully understand Dick's brilliance. Or perhaps Dick's paranoia will set in, which

Hysterical Harold
The type of customer who reverts to screaming and tantrums to make his or her point.

Dictatorial Dick
The type of customer who assumes superiority over all personnel and management.

PEOPLE ISSUES:
MANAGING EMPLOYEES
AND CUSTOMERS

makes him believe that you deliberately sabotaged his plan to make him look bad. You wouldn't do that, would you?

Dealing with Dick would test anyone's patience. The main key is to not let him push you around. Employees should stick to their game plans and provide service in the manner they know is appropriate and equitable for all concerned. Since other customers are likely to be present, employees need to be consistent in how they deal with individual customers. Dick should not be treated as the "squeaky wheel" who always gets the grease. The best strategy for dealing with Dick is to tell him in a straightforward fashion exactly what you can do for him. If reasonable to do so, fulfilling his request will break up Dick's game plan and resolve the conflict.

Freeloading Freda

The type of customer who uses "tricks" or verbal abuse to acquire services without paying.

Freeloading Freda wants it all for free. Give her an inch and she'll take the plates, the silverware, and everything else that's not nailed down. Freda will push your return policy to the limits. If her kids' shoes begin to wear out in a year or two, she'll return them for new ones. In need of a cocktail dress, Freda will buy one on Thursday and return it bright and early Monday morning, punch stains and all. Question her credibility, and Freda will scream bloody murder to anyone and everyone who will listen . . . including the news media and the Better Business Bureau.

Dealing with Freda, in many cases, involves biting your tongue and giving her what she wants. Despite popular beliefs, the Fredas of the world probably represent only 1 to 2 percent of your customers, if that. Most customers are honest and believe that they should pay for the goods and services they consume. Another possibility is to track Freda's actions and suggest possible legal action to persuade her to take her business elsewhere. Managers of competing firms often share information regarding the Fredas of the world to avoid their excessive abuses. Finally, recognize that Freda is the exception and not the common customer. Too often, new policies are developed for the sole purpose of defeating Freda and her

comrades. These new policies add to the bureaucratization of the organization and penalize the customers who follow the rules. The filing of lengthy forms to return merchandise or invoke service guarantees is a common example of penalizing the majority of customers by treating them as suspected criminals rather than as valued customers.

Some Other Thoughts   When dealing with "customers from hell," it is difficult for employees not to take these sorts of confrontations personally. The consumer profiles introduced above should help employees prepare for the various types of difficult customers and provide strategies for minimizing the amount of conflict that actually occurs. Viewing customers as distinct profile types helps depersonalize the situation for the employee—"Oh, it's just Edgar again." This is not to say that each customer shouldn't be treated as an individual, but simply that customer complaints and behavior shouldn't be taken overly personally. In closing, one word of warning: Employees who truly master the art of dealing with difficult customers are rewarded by becoming these customers' favorite provider, the one they request by name time after time. No good deed goes unpunished.

SUMMARY

This chapter focused on some of the "people issues" that must be considered when marketing services. Much has been written about the fact that, for many service firms, personnel constitute the bulk of their product. It is thus important that the place of personnel within the organization be understood. By drawing on the concepts of organizational behavior and, in particular, the concepts of boundary-spanning roles, empowerment, and enfranchisement, this chapter has provided a solid framework on which to develop the marketing implicatons of personnel as a key component of the firm's overall product offering.

This chapter has also focused on the importance of managing the consumer's involvement in the service production process. Developing skills in managing consumer waits, managing consumer participation, and effectively managing difficult customers are crucial for all service firm employees. Given the importance of consumer expectations and perceptions and the flow of word-of-mouth communication, expertise in managing customers is ultimately related to perceptions of customer satisfaction and overall service quality views.

KEY TERMS

boundary-spanning roles

subordinate service roles

professional service roles

person/role conflict

organization/client conflicts

interclient conflicts

climate

empowerment

enfranchisement

suggestion involvement

quality circles

job involvement

high involvement

basic business strategy

tie to the customer

technology

business environment

Egocentric Edgar

Bad-Mouth Betty

selective agreement

Hysterical Harold

Dictatorial Dick

Freeloading Freda

REVIEW QUESTIONS

1. Relate the concepts of intangibility, inseparability, heterogeneity, and perishability to the importance of personnel in the service firm.

2. What are boundary-spanning personnel? What three types of conflict do they generally encounter?

3. How can marketing be utilized to reduce the amount of stress and conflict experienced by boundary-spanning personnel?

4. In what types of organizations would it be best to avoid empowerment approaches?

5. In what type of organization would it be best to implement a job involvement empowerment approach?

6. Discuss the benefits and costs associated with empowerment and enfranchisement.

7. Why is the management of consumer waits and customer participation particularly important for service firms?

8. Select one of the profiles of "customers from hell." Describe the profile of this customer and offer suggested methods for dealing with this type of individual.

9. What types of employee behaviors tend to upset customers the most?

NOTES

1. The first section of this chapter is based on Chapters 4 and 6 of John E. G. Bateson, *Managing of Services Marketing*, 3rd ed. (Fort Worth, TX: The Dryden Press, 1995).

2. Dave Ulrich et al., "Employee and Customer Attachment: Synergies for Competetive Advantage," *Human Resource Planning* 14,3 (1991), p. 89(15).

3. Leonard A. Schlesinger and James L. Heskett, "The Service-Driven Service Company," *Harvard Business Review* (September–October, 1991), pp. 71–81.

4. This idea was originally suggested in a slightly different form in W. Earl Sasser, P. Olsen, and D. Daryl Wycoff, *Management of Service Operations: Text, Cases, and Readings* (Boston: Allyn and Bacon, 1978).

5. Philip Kotler, *Marketing Management*, 8th ed. (Englewood Cliffs, NJ: Prentice-Hall, 1994), p. 303.

6. J. D. Thompson, "Organization and Output Transactions," *American Journal of Sociology* 68 (1967), pp. 309–324.

7. Boas Shamir, "Between Service and Servility: Role Conflict in Subordinate Service Roles," *Human Relations* 33,10, pp. 741–756.

8. See Arlie Hochshild, *The Managed Heart* (Berkeley, CA: University of California Press, 1983).

9. For example, see Jody D. Nyquist, Mary Jo Bitner, and Bernard Booms, "Identifying Difficulties in the Service Encounter: A Critical Incident Approach," in John Czepiel, Michael R. Solomon, and Carol F. Suprenant, eds., *The Service Encounter* (Lexington, MA: Heath, 1985), pp. 195–212.

10. Peter Klaus, "The Quality Epiphenomenon," in John Czepiel, Michael R. Solomon, and Carol F. Suprenant, eds., *The Service Encounter* (Lexington, MA: Heath, 1985), p. 15.

11. Charles T. Goodsell, "Bureaucratic Manipulation of Physical Symbols: An Empirical Investigation," *American Journal of Political Science* XXI (February 1977), pp. 79–91.

12. Benjamin Schneider, Jill K. Wheeler, and Jonathan F. Cox, "A Passion for Service: Using Content Analysis to Explicate Service Climate Themes," *Journal of Applied Psychology* Vol. 77, No. 5 (1992), pp. 705–716.

13. See Benjamin Schneider, "The Service Organization: Climate Is Crucial," *Organizational Dynamics* (Autumn 1980), pp. 52–65; and Benjamin Schneider and

David E. Bowen, "The Service Organization: Human Resource Management is Crucial," *Organizational Dynamics* (Spring 1993), pp. 39–52.

14. David E. Bowen and Edward E. Lawler, III, "The Empowerment of Service Workers: What, Why, How, and When," *Sloan Management Review* (Spring 1992), pp. 31–39.

15. Martin L. Bell, "Tactical Services Marketing and the Process of Remixing," in *Marketing of Services*, W. R. George and J. M. Donnelly, eds. (Chicago: American Marketing Association, 1986), pp. 162–165.

16. John E. G. Bateson, "Perceived Control and the Service Encounter," in John Czepiel, Michael R. Solomon, and Carol F. Suprenant, eds., *The Service Encounter* (Lexington, MA: Heath, 1985), pp. 67–82.

17. See W. Foote Whyte, *Men at Work*, Dorsey Series in Behavioral Sciences (Homewood, IL: Dorsey Press and Irwin, 1949).

18. D. H. Maister, "The Psychology of Waiting in Lines" (Boston: Harvard Business School Note 9-684-064, Rev. May 1984), pp. 2–3.

19. Christopher Lovelock and Robert F. Young, "Look to Consumers to Increase Productivity in Services," *Harvard Business Review* (May/June, 1979), pp. 168–178.

20. Ron Zemke and Kristen Anderson, "Customers from Hell," *Training* 26 (February 1990), pp. 25–31.

21. Bateson, *Managing Services Marketing*, p. 121.

PART 3

ASSESSING AND IMPROVING SERVICE DELIVERY

*P*art Three, **Assessing and Improving Service Delivery,** *focuses on customer satisfaction and service quality issues. Methods for tracking service failures and employee recovery efforts as well as customer retention strategies are presented. Ideally, assessing and improving the service delivery system will lead to "seamless" service—provided without interruption, confusion, or hassle to the customer.*

11

Defining and Measuring Customer Satisfaction

"*If you can't measure it, goes the old cliché,
you can't manage it. In fact, if you can't measure it, managers seem unable to pay attention to it.*"

Fortune, September 19, 1994, p. 218

CHAPTER OBJECTIVES

The major objectives of this chapter are to introduce you to the importance and benefits of customer satisfaction and the special factors to consider in measuring customer satisfaction.
After reading this chapter, you should be able to:

► Define customer satisfaction.

    ► *Discuss the benefits associated with satisfied customers.*

► Discuss various methods for measuring customer satisfaction.

    ► *Discuss the limitations of customer satisfaction measurements.*

► Discuss factors to consider when investing in customer satisfaction improvements.

    ► *Discuss the three types of expectations and their relationships to customer satisfaction and service quality measurement.*

► Discuss the factors that influence customer expectations.

TRACKING CONSUMER SATISFACTION IN THE UNITED STATES

*T*racking customer satisfaction in the United States is a highly complex task that has recently been undertaken through the joint efforts of the American Society for Quality Control and the University of Michigan's business school. The two groups have developed the American Customer Satisfaction Index (ACSI), which is based on 3,900 products representing more than two dozen manufacturing and services industries. Companies included in the study are selected based on size and U.S. market share and together represent about 40 percent of the United States' Gross Domestic Product. Government services are also included in the index.

The ACSI consists of 17 questions rated on a scale from 1 to 10, regarding issues such as consumer perceptions of service, quality, value, the performance of the product compared with expectations, how the product compares with an ideal product, and how willing consumers would be to pay more for the product. Consumer responses are gathered via telephone surveys to approximately 30,000 people. The products of each company included in the survey are assessed roughly 250 times.

Results from the latest ACSI indicate that, as a whole, customer satisfaction in the United States is headed slightly downward with the exception of manufactured goods. On a scale of 0 to 100, the national satisfaction average is 73.7, down 1.1 percent from the previous year's national average. Dole Food's canned pineapple topped the satisfaction list with a score of 90, while the Internal Revenue Service came in dead last with a score of 54.

Other notable trends included good news, such as increases in customer satisfaction with domestically produced automobiles, and bad news, such as a large decrease in consumer satisfaction with computers, which fell 3.8 percent last year. An overview of the specific companies included in the ACSI and their satisfaction ratings are presented in Table 11.1.

Upon analyzing ACSI results, businesses often make three common mistakes that lead to lower levels of customer satisfaction. First, many firms continue to view customer service as a cost rather than as an investment. Second, firms tend to forget that customer satisfaction is a constantly rising bar. During the 1980s, automobile consumers demanded technical excellence from manufacturers. Now consumers are looking beyond technical excellence and demanding better ways to purchase and service their vehicles. These areas are the new battlefields on which fights for future customer satisfaction will be won or lost. Finally, the third most common mistake is a firm's inability to link customer satisfaction to its bottom line. Some firms still do not see (or fail to appreciate) the connection. However, others, like those in the advertising industry, realize that a 5 percent increase in customer retention rate translates into a 95 percent increase in customer net present value.

Source: Thomas A. Stewart, "After All You've Done for Your Customers, Why Are They Still NOT HAPPY," *Fortune*, December 11, 1995, pp. 178–181; and Jacklyn Fierman, "Americans Can't Get No Satisfaction," *Fortune*, December 11, 1995, pp. 186–194.

DEFINING AND MEASURING CUSTOMER SATISFACTION

TABLE 11.1 — AMERICAN CUSTOMER SATISFACTION INDEX RESULTS

Product Category / Company	1995 Score	% Change from '94
Soft Drinks	86	None
PepsiCo	87	1.2
Coca-Cola	85	None
Cadbury Schweppes	85	N.A.
Food Processing	84	None
Dole Food	90	None
Mars	89	2.3
Hershey Foods	88	2.3
CPC International	88	N.A.
H.J. Heinz	87	−2.2
Borden	86	None
Nestlé	86	−2.3
Pillsbury (Grand Metropolitan)	86	−2.3
Kellogg	84	None
Kraft Foods (Philip Morris)	84	None
Nabisco	84	−3.4
ConAgra	83	None
Quaker Oats	82	None
Sara Lee	82	−4.7
Campbell Soup	81	−2.4
General Mills	81	−2.4
Tyson Foods	80	−3.6
Ralston Purina	79	−3.7
Personal Care and Cleaning	84	None
Clorox	88	None
Procter & Gamble	87	2.4
Colgate-Palmolive	86	2.4
Dial	85	−1.2
Unilever	83	−1.2
Household Appliances	82	−3.5
Maytag	87	2.4
General Electric	84	3.7
Whirlpool	82	−5.7
Cigarettes	82	1.2
American Tobacco[1]	87	None[1]
Philip Morris	81	1.3
R.J. Reynolds Tobacco	81	None
Long Distance	82	None
Sprint	83	5.1
AT&T	83	−2.4
MCI Communications	75	None
Apparel	81	−1.2
Levi Strauss Associates	83	−1.2
Sara Lee[2]	81	−2.4[2]
Liz Claiborne	81	−3.6
Fruit of the Loom	80	−3.6
VF	80	−3.6
Parcel Delivery— Express Mail	81	None
FedEx	85	None
United Parcel Service	83	1.2
U.S. Postal Service	See Mail Delivery	
Consumer Electronics— TV and VCR	81	−2.4
Sony	84	−2.3
Zenith Electronics	84	−4.5
Mitsubishi Electronics	82	1.2
General Electric	82	−1.2
Emerson Electric	81	1.3
Philips Electronics	81	−3.6
Panasonic (Matsushita El. Ind.)	80	None
Sanyo Electric	79	−6.0
JVC (Matsushita El. Ind.)	78	1.3
Beer	81	−2.4
Adolph Coors	84	3.7
Miller Brewing (Philip Morris)	82	2.5
Anheuser-Busch	80	−4.8
Automobiles	80	1.3
Honda Motor	86	1.2
Mercedes-Benz (Daimler-Benz)	86	1.2
Lincoln, Mercury (Ford Motor)	84	6.3
Volvo	84	2.4
Buick, Olds, Cadillac (GM)	84	1.2
Toyota Motor	84	−2.3
Saturn (GM)	83	−1.2
Chrysler (Chrysler)	82	1.2
Nissan Motor	82	−1.2
BMW	81	−1.2
Ford (Ford Motor)	79	5.3
Pontiac (GM)	79	3.9
Chevrolet, GEO (GM)	79	2.6
Subaru (Fuji Heavy Ind.)	79	−1.3
Jeep, Eagle (Chrysler)	77	−1.3
Mazda Motor	77	−1.3
Dodge, Plymouth (Chrysler)	77	−3.8
Volkswagen	76	2.7
Hyundai	68	None
Gas Service Stations	80	2.6
Chevron	81	3.8
Amoco	81	None
Phillips Petroleum	81	None
Exxon	80	2.6
Texaco	80	2.6
Shell Oil (Royal Dutch/Shell)	80	None
Unocal	80	N.A.
Mobil	79	−1.3
Atlantic Richfield	78	4.0
Athletic Shoes	79	None
Reebok International	80	6.7
Nike	78	−4.9
Telecommunication— Local	78	−1.3
BellSouth	83	None
Bell Atlantic	81	1.3
SBC Communications	80	None
Nynex	79	None
Ameritech	79	−2.5
Pacific Telesis Group	78	−3.7
US West	76	−1.3
GTE	72	−5.3
Motion Pictures	72	None
Walt Disney	80	−4.8
Paramount (Viacom)	79	9.7
20th-Century Fox (News Corp.)	79	None
Warner Bros. (Time Warner)	77	−1.3
TriStar/Columbia (Sony)	74	4.2
Universal (Seagram)	74	−3.9
Broadcasting—TV	76	−1.3
Turner Broadcasting	81	−1.2
ABC	77	1.3
CBS	75	−5.1
NBC	74	−2.6
Personal Property Insurance	76	−6.2
State Farm Group	78	None
Allstate	75	1.4
Farmers Insurance Group (BAT)	73	−3.9
Personal Computers	75	−3.8
Hewlett-Packard	80	2.6
IBM	78	None
Compaq Computer	77	−1.3
Apple Computer	75	−2.6
Life Insurance	75	−2.6
Travelers Group	N.A.	N.A.
Prudential Ins. of America	76	5.6
Metropolitan Life Insurance	74	5.1
Aetna Life & Casualty	69	−5.5
Utilities— Electric Service	74	−1.3
Central & South West	82	6.5
American Electric Power	80	2.6
Public Service Enterprise Group	80	1.3
Duke Power	80	−2.4
General Public Utilities	79	2.6
Detroit Edison	78	None
Southern	78	None
FPL Group	77	None
Entergy	76	1.3
Consolidated Edison of N.Y.	76	−1.3
CMS Energy	76	−3.8
Dominion Resources	75	1.3
Texas Utilities	74	1.4
SCEcorp	74	−2.6
Niagara Mohawk Power	73	5.8
PECO Energy	72	N.A.
Pacific Gas & Electric	71	−2.7
Northeast Utilities	70	None
Commonwealth Edison (Unicom)	68	−4.2

N.A. Not applicable.
[1] Sold by American Brands to BAT Industries, December 1994.
[2] Brands include Hanes, Bali, Leggs.

| TABLE 11.1 | (CONTINUED) |

PRODUCT CATEGORY COMPANY	1995 SCORE	% CHANGE FROM '94						
Supermarkets	**74**	**−2.6**	**Hotels**	**73**	**−2.7**	**Airlines**	**69**	**−4.2**
Publix Super Markets	81	−1.2	Promus	80	−2.4	Southwest Airlines	76	−2.6
Meijer	77	None	Marriott International	76	−5.0	Delta Air Lines	72	−6.5
Supervalu	77	None	Hilton Hotels	75	None	Northwest Airlines	71	2.9
Food Lion	76	−2.6	Hyatt	75	−1.3	American Airlines (AMR)	71	1.4
Kroger	76	−2.6	Best Western International	70	−5.4	United Airlines (UAL)	67	−5.6
Albertson's	74	−1.3	Holiday Inn Worldwide (Bass)	69	None	USAir Group	67	−6.9
Winn-Dixie Stores	74	−2.6	Ramada	69	−1.4	Continental Airlines	64	−4.5
American Stores	72	1.4						
Safeway	72	None	**Department Stores**	**73**	**−5.2**	**Newspapers**	**68**	**−5.6**
A&P	69	1.5	Nordstrum	81	−3.6	Dow Jones	76	1.3
			May Department Stores	76	2.7	Knight-Ridder	70	2.9
Banks	**74**	**None**	Dillard Department Stores	76	1.3	Tribune	70	None
Chemical Banking Corp.	N.A.	N.A.	J.C. Penney	76	−3.8	New York Times	70	−5.4
Norwest Corp.	76	−1.3	Federated Department Stores	71	None	Times Mirror	67	−1.5
First Union Corp.	75	−1.3	Montgomery Ward	71	−1.4	Gannett	66	−12.0
Banc One Corp.	75	−2.6	Sears Roebuck	71	−2.7			
NationsBank Corp.	74	−1.3	R.H. Macy[5]	70	1.4[5]	**Mail Delivery**	**N.A.**	**N.A.**
Citicorp	71	−2.7				U.S. Postal Service—Express		
First Interstate Bancorp	70	−1.4	**Restaurants—Fast Food—**			Mail, package delivery	70	1.4
Wells Fargo & Co.	69	−2.8	**Pizza—Carry Out**	**70**	**1.4**	U.S. Postal Service—first-		
BankAmerica Corp.	68	−5.9	Wendy's International	71	−1.4	class mail, counter services	69	13.0
			Little Caesar Enterprises	70	−2.8			
Discount Stores	**74**	**−3.9**	KFC (PepsiCo)	69	3.0	**Public Administration**	**N.A.**	**N.A.**
Wal-Mart Stores	80	None	Pizza Hut (PepsiCo)	69	None	Local garbage—suburban	78	5.4
Dayton Hudson	75	−2.6	Domino's Pizza	67	None	Local garbage—city	75	1.4
Meijer	74	N.A.	Burger King (Grand Met)	66	None	Local police—suburban	66	1.5
Kmart	70	−5.4	McDonald's	65	3.2	Local police—central	59	−3.3
			Taco Bell (PepsiCo)	65	−1.5	Internal Revenue Service	54	−1.8
Hospitals	**74**	**None**						
American Medical Holdings[3]	73	N.A.[3]				**National Average**	**73.7**	**−1.1**
Columbia/HCA Healthcare	73	−6.4						
HealthTrust[4]	70	4.5[4]						

[3]Merged with National Medical Enterprises to form Tenet Healthcare, March 1995.
[4]Acquired by Columbia/HCA Healthcare, April 1995.
[5]Acquired by Federated Department Stores, December 1994.

INTRODUCTION

Customer satisfaction is one of the most studied areas in marketing. Over the past 20 years, more than 15,000 academic and trade articles have been published on the topic.[1] In fact, *The Journal of Advertising Research* has suggested that customer satisfaction surveys may be the fastest growing area in market research. Such devotion to the subject is certainly understandable given that satisfaction is a central theme of the marketing concept and is frequently included in the mission statements and promotional campaigns of American corporations.

From a historical perspective, a great deal of the work in the customer satisfaction area began in the 1970s, when consumerism was on the rise. The rise of the consumer movement was directly related to the decline in service felt by many consumers. The decline in customer service and resulting customer dissatisfaction can be attributed to a number of sources. First, skyrocketing inflation during this period forced many firms to slash service in the effort to keep prices down. In some industries, deregulation led to fierce competition among firms who had never had to compete before. Price competition quickly became the attempted means of differentiation, and price wars quickly broke out. Firms once again slashed costs associated with customer service to cut operating expenses.

As time went on, labor shortages also contributed to the decline in customer service. Service workers who were motivated were difficult to find, and who could blame them? The typical service job included low pay, no career path, no sense of pride, and no training in customer relations. Automation also contributed to the problem. Replacing human labor with machines indeed increased the efficiency of many operating systems, but often at the expense of distancing customers from the firm and leaving customers to fend for themselves. Finally, over the years, customers have become tougher to please. They are more informed than ever, their expectations have increased, and they are more particular about where they spend their discretionary dollars.

Researchers in the field of consumer satisfaction clearly recognized the connection between the study of satisfaction and the consumer movement. The connection between the marketing concept, satisfaction, and consumerism continues to be one of the driving forces behind the study of consumer satisfaction.

The Importance of Customer Satisfaction

The importance of customer satisfaction cannot be overstated. Without customers, the service firm has no reason to exist. Every service business needs to proactively define and measure customer satisfaction. Waiting for customers to complain in order to identify problems in the service delivery system or gauging the firm's progress in customer satisfaction based on the number of complaints received is naïve. Consider the following figures gathered by the Technical Assistance Research Program (TARP):[2]

- The average business does not hear from 96 percent of its unhappy customers.
- For every complaint received, 26 customers actually have the same problem.
- The average person with a problem tells 9 or 10 people. Thirteen percent will tell more than 20.
- Customers who have their complaints satisfactorily resolved tell an average of five people about the treatment they received.

▲ Complainers are more likely to do business with you again than noncomplainers: 54–70 percent if resolved at all, and 95 percent if handled quickly.

The TARP figures demonstrate that customers do not actively complain to service firms themselves. Instead, consumers voice their dissatisfaction with their feet, by defecting to competitors, and with their mouths, by telling your existing and potential customers exactly how they were mistreated by your firm. Based on the figures, a firm that serves 100 customers per week and boasts a 90-percent customer satisfaction rating will be the object of thousands of negative stories by the end of a year. For example, if 10 dissatisfied customers per week tell 10 of their friends of the poor service received, by the end of the year (52 weeks), 5,200 negative word-of-mouth communications will have been generated.

The TARP figures are not all bad news. Firms that effectively respond to customer complaints are the objects of positive word-of-mouth communications. Although positive news travels at half the rate of negative news, the positive stories can ultimately translate into customer loyalty and new customers. A firm should also learn from the TARP figures that complainers are the firm's friends. Complainers are a free source of market information, and the complaints themselves should be viewed as opportunities for the firm to improve its delivery systems, not as a source of irritation.

What Is Customer Satisfaction/Dissatisfaction?

Although a variety of alternative definitions exist, the most popular definition of customer satisfaction/dissatisfaction is that it is a comparison of customer expectations to perceptions regarding the actual service encounter. (Alternative definitions are provided in Table 11.2).[3] Comparing customer expectations with their perceptions is based on what marketers refer to as the **expectancy disconfirmation model.** Simply stated, if customer perceptions meet expectations, the expectations are said to be **confirmed,** and the customer is satisfied. If perceptions and expectations are not equal, then the expectation is said to be **disconfirmed.**

Although the term *disconfirmation* sounds like a negative experience, it is not necessarily so. There are two types of disconfirmations. If actual perceptions were less than what was expected, the result is a **negative disconfirmation,** which results in customer dissatisfaction and may lead to negative word-of-mouth publicity and/or customer defection. In contrast, a **positive disconfirmation** exists when perceptions exceed expectations, thereby resulting in customer satisfaction, positive word-of-mouth publicity, and customer retention.

Every day, consumers utilize the disconfirmation paradigm by comparing their expectations with perceptions. While we recently were dining at a resort restaurant on the west coast of Florida, our waiter not only provided everything we requested but also was very good at anticipating needs. My three-year-old niece had had enough fun and sun for the day and went to sleep in a booth located

expectancy disconfirmation model
Model proposing that comparing customer expectations to their perceptions leads customers to have their expectations confirmed or disconfirmed.

confirmed expectations
Customer expectations that match customer perceptions.

disconfirmed expectations
Customer expectations that do not match customer perceptions.

negative disconfirmation
A nonmatch because customer perceptions are lower than customer expectations.

positive disconfirmation
A nonmatch because customer perceptions exceed customer expectations.

DEFINING AND MEASURING
CUSTOMER SATISFACTION

TABLE 11.2 ALTERNATIVE SATISFACTION DEFINITIONS

Normative deficit definition	Compares actual outcomes to those that are culturally acceptable.
Equity definition	Compares gains in a social exchange— if the gains are inequal, the loser is dissatisfied.
Normative standard definition	Expectations are based on what the consumer believes he/she *should* receive— dissatisfaction occurs when the actual outcome is different from the standard expectation.
Procedural fairness definition	Satisfaction is a function of the consumer's belief that he/she was treated fairly.

Source: Keith Hunt, "Consumer Satisfaction, Dissatisfaction, and Complaining Behavior," *Journal of Social Issues* 47,1 (1991), pp. 109–110.

directly behind our table. The waiter, noticing her absence from our table and on his own initiative, provided a white tablecloth for her to use as a blanket. This particular incident combined with other incidents throughout the evening lead to a positive disconfirmation of our expectations. That evening's great service reinforced our notion that with so much poor service all around, customers really do notice when the service is excellent.

THE BENEFITS OF CUSTOMER SATISFACTION

Although some may argue that customers are unreasonable at times, little evidence can be found of extravagant customer expectations.[4] Consequently, satisfying customers is not an impossible task. In fact, meeting and exceeding customer expectations may reap several valuable benefits for the firm. Positive word-of-mouth generated from existing customers often translates into more new customers. In addition, satisfied current customers often purchase more products more frequently and are less likely to be lost to competitors than are dissatisfied customers.

Companies who command high customer satisfaction ratings also seem to have the ability to insulate themselves from competitive pressures . . . particularly price competition. Customers are often willing to pay more and stay with a firm that meets their needs than to take the risk associated with moving to a lower-priced service offering. Finally, firms that pride themselves on their customer satisfaction efforts generally provide better environments in which to work. Within these positive work environments, organizational cultures develop where employees are challenged to perform and rewarded for their efforts.

In and of themselves, customer satisfaction surveys also provide several worthwhile benefits. Such surveys provide a formal means of customer feedback to the firm, which may identify existing and potential problems. Satisfaction surveys also convey the message to customers that the firm cares about their well-being and values customer input concerning its operations.[5]

Other benefits are derived directly from the results of the satisfaction surveys. Satisfaction results are often utilized in evaluating employee performance for merit and compensation reviews and for sales management purposes, such as the development of sales training programs. Survey results are also useful for comparison purposes to determine how the firm stacks up against the competition. When ratings are favorable, many firms utilize the results in their corporate advertising.[6]

MEASURING CUSTOMER SATISFACTION

Measures of customer satisfaction are derived via indirect and direct measures. Indirect measures of customer satisfaction include tracking and monitoring sales records, profits, and customer complaints. Firms that rely solely on indirect measures are taking a passive approach to determining whether customer perceptions are meeting or exceeding customer expectations. Moreover, if the average firm does not hear from 96 percent of its unhappy customers, it is losing a great many customers while waiting for the other 4 percent to speak their minds.

Direct measures of satisfaction are not standardized among firms. For example, the scales used to collect the data vary (e.g., 5-point to 100-point scales), questions asked of respondents vary (e.g., general to specific questions), and data collection methods vary (e.g., personal interviews to self-administered questionnaires). The following section focuses on the use of various scales.

THE SCALE OF 100 APPROACH

Some firms request customers to rate the firm's performance on a scale of 100. In essence, the firm is asking customers to give the firm a grade. However, the problems with this approach are readily apparent. Let's say that the firm scores an average of 83. What does the 83 mean—the firm received a B−? Does an 83 mean the same thing to all customers? Not likely. More importantly, what should the firm do to improve its satisfaction rating? The 83 does not provide specific suggestions for improvements that would lead to an increased customer satisfaction rating.

THE "VERY DISSATISFIED/VERY SATISFIED" APPROACH

Other firms present customers with a 5-point scale, which is typically labeled utilizing the following format:

1—Very Dissatisfied

2—Somewhat Dissatisfied

3—Neutral

4—Somewhat Satisfied

5—Very Satisfied

Firms utilizing this format generally combine the percentage of "somewhat satisfied" and "very satisfied" responses to arrive at a satisfaction rating. Similarly, firms that utilize a 10-point scale with anchor points of "very dissatisfied" and "very satisfied" define customer satisfaction as the percentage of customers rating their satisfaction higher than 6. Although this approach provides more meaning to the satisfaction rating itself, it still lacks the diagnostic power to indicate areas of improvement.

THE COMBINED APPROACH

The combined approach utilizes the quantitative scores obtained by the "very dissatisfied/very satisfied" approach and adds a qualitative analysis of feedback obtained from respondents who indicated that they were less than "very satisfied." Customers who indicate that they are less than "very satisfied" are informing the firm that the delivery system is performing at levels lower than customer-expected levels. By prompting customers to suggest how the firm could do better, the firm can then categorize and prioritize the suggestions for continuous improvement efforts.

The combined approach provides two valuable pieces of information. The quantitative satisfaction rating provides a benchmark against which future satisfaction surveys should be compared. In addition, the quantitative rating provides the means of comparing the firm's performance against its competition. Complementing the quantitative rating, the qualitative data provides diagnostic information and pinpoints areas for improvement. Combining the qualitative and quantitative data outperforms either approach used alone.

UNDERSTANDING CUSTOMER SATISFACTION RATINGS

After a consultant conducted a customer satisfaction survey for a regional engineering firm, the results were revealed to upper management that the firm commanded an 85 percent customer satisfaction rating. Immediately, upper management wanted to know whether 85 percent was a "good" satisfaction rating or not. To effectively utilize customer satisfaction ratings, it is necessary to understand the factors that may influence customer responses.

Despite the lack of standardization among satisfaction studies, they share one common characteristic. "Virtually all self-reports of customer satisfaction possess a distribution in which a majority of the responses indicate that customers are satisfied and the distribution itself is negatively skewed."[7] Figure 11.1 depicts the negatively skewed distribution of customer satisfaction results.

CONCEPTUAL DISTRIBUTION OF SATISFACTION MEASUREMENTS

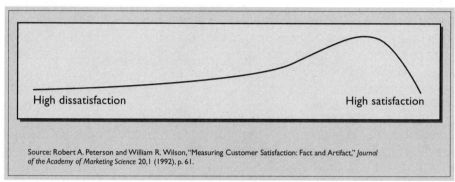

Source: Robert A. Peterson and William R. Wilson, "Measuring Customer Satisfaction: Fact and Artifact," *Journal of the Academy of Marketing Science* 20,1 (1992), p. 61.

Typically, customer satisfaction ratings are fairly high. Table 11.3 displays a sample of customer satisfaction results across various industries. As can be viewed from the table, it is not unusual to see results in the 80-90 percent range. Repeated findings such as these have led some researchers to conclude that "to feel above average is normal."

The truth of the matter is that satisfaction ratings may be influenced by numerous confounding factors that occur during the data collection process. The following section provides explanations for inflated satisfaction results and reinforces the notion that obtaining accurate measures of customer satisfaction is not an easily accomplished task.

FACTORS INFLUENCING CUSTOMER SATISFACTION RATINGS

Customers Are Genuinely Satisfied One possible reason for high satisfaction scores is simply that customers are satisfied with the goods and services they typically purchase and consume—that's why they buy these products from the firm in the first place! Intuitively, this makes good sense. If the majority of customers were neutral or dissatisfied, they would most likely defect to the competitor's offering of goods and services. Of course, this explanation assumes that competitors in the market are better at providing goods and services than the original supplier.

Response Bias Another possible explanation for inflated satisfaction results may be **response bias.** Some experts argue that the reason ratings are so high is that companies hear from only satisfied customers. In contrast, dissatisfied customers do not believe that the firm's survey will do them any good; therefore, the questionnaire is thrown away, or the customer hangs up on the interviewer.

Other experts discount this explanation. Their argument is that it makes more sense for highly dissatisfied customers to express their opinion than it does for

response bias

A bias in survey results because of responses' being received from only a limited group among the total survey participants.

DEFINING AND MEASURING
CUSTOMER SATISFACTION

TABLE 11.3 SAMPLING OF SATISFACTION RESULTS	
Sample	**Percentage Satisfied**
British Airways Customers	85
HMO Enrollees	92
Sear's Customers	84
Children's Instructional Programs/Parents	82
Medical Care	84
Clothing/and White Goods/Adults	82
Shoes/Students	83

Source: Robert A. Peterson and William R. Wilson, "Measuring Customer Satisfaction: Fact and Artifact," *Journal of the Academy of Marketing Science* 20,1 (1992), p. 61.

highly satisfied customers to do so. This position is supported by prior research, which indicates that dissatisfaction itself is more action oriented and emotionally intense than satisfaction.[8] Others argue that it is possible that highly dissatisfied customers and highly satisfied customers are more likely to respond than are those who are more neutral. Although these additional explanations are intriguing, they fail to explain the traditional response distribution depicted in Figure 11.1.

data collection method

The method used to collect information, such as questionnaires, surveys, and personal interviews.

Data Collection Method A third explanation for inflated satisfaction scores is the **data collection method** used to obtain results. Prior research suggests that higher levels of satisfaction are obtained via personal interviews and phone surveys compared with results from mail questionnaires and/or self-administered interviews. In fact, studies indicate that as much as a 10 percent difference exists between questionnaires administered orally and self-administered questionnaires. The reason is that respondents to personal interviews and phone surveys may feel awkward expressing negative statements to other "live" individuals as opposed to expressing them anonymously on a self-administered questionnaire.

Research on data collection modes' effects on satisfaction ratings has produced some interesting results. The data collection mode does indeed appear to influence the level of reported satisfaction; however, the negatively skewed distribution of the satisfaction ratings remains unchanged, regardless of the data collection mode.

question form

The way a question is phrased, i.e., positively or negatively.

Question Form The way the question is asked on the questionnaire, or the **question form,** has also been posited as a possible explanation for inflated satisfaction ratings. It does appear that the question's being asked in positive form ("How satisfied are you?") as opposed to negative form ("How dissatisfied are you?")

One method of data collection is that of verbal surveys. This individual is talking to a group of young women to find out their views on different products and services.

Source: © Michael Newman/PhotoEdit.

does have an impact on satisfaction ratings. Asking a question in the positive form appears to lead to greater reported levels of satisfaction than does posing the question in a negative form.

Table 11.4 presents results from a study about the effects of stating the same question in two forms. In one version, the question asked respondents "how satisfied" they were, and in the other version, the question asked "how dissatisfied" they were. Results reveal that 91 percent of respondents reported feeling "very" or "somewhat satisfied" when the question was stated in its positive form but only 82 percent when stated in the negative form. Similarly, 9 percent of respondents expressed that they were somewhat or very dissatisfied when asked in the positive form, compared with nearly 18 percent when asked in the negative form.

Context of the Question   The **question context** may also affect the satisfaction rating. Question-context effects pertain to the ordering of questions and whether questions asked earlier in a questionnaire influence answers to subsequent questions. For example, in a study concerning satisfaction with vehicles, asking a general satisfaction question (e.g., "In general, how satisfied are you with the products in your house?") prior to a specific vehicle satisfaction question (e.g., "How satisfied are you with your Saturn?") increased the tendency toward a "very satisfied" response for the specific question.

question context

The placement and tone of a question relative to the other questions asked.

DEFINING AND MEASURING
CUSTOMER SATISFACTION

TABLE 11.4 RESPONSES BY QUESTION FORM		
	QUESTION FORM	
Response Category	**"Satisfied"**	**"Dissatisfied"**
Very Satisfied	57.4%	53.4%
Somewhat Satisfied	33.6%	28.7%
Somewhat Dissatisfied	5.0%	8.5%
Very Dissatisfied	4.0%	9.4%

Source: Robert A. Peterson and William R. Wilson, "Measuring Customer Satisfaction: Fact and Artifact,"
Journal of the Academy of Marketing Science 20,1 (1992), p. 65.

question timing

The length of time after the date of purchase that questions are asked.

Timing of the Question Satisfaction ratings may also be influenced by the **timing of the question** relative to the date of purchase. Customer satisfaction appears to be highest immediately after a purchase and then begins to decrease over time. Again, regarding automobile purchases, researchers have noted a 20 percent decline in satisfaction ratings over a 60-day period. It's not clear whether the initial ratings are inflated to compensate for feelings of cognitive dissonance or the latter ratings are deflated. Some consideration has been given that there may be different types of satisfaction measured at different points in time.

Another possible explanation is that satisfaction rates may decay over time as customers reflect upon their purchase decision. Prior research indicates that the influence of negative events, which are more memorable than positive events, carries more weight in satisfaction evaluations over time. Consequently, satisfaction surveys distributed longer after purchases provide respondents the opportunity to take retribution as they recall such negative events.

social desirability bias

A bias in survey results because of respondents' tendencies to provide information they believe is socially appropriate.

Social Desirability Bias **Social desirability bias** describes a respondent's tendency to provide information that the respondent believes is socially appropriate. In satisfaction surveys, some researchers argue that respondents tend to withhold critical judgment because to do otherwise would be socially inappropriate. This would explain high satisfaction ratings and the shape of the distribution of results. Although the explanation is intriguing, widespread empirical support is lacking.

Mood One more factor that could possibly influence customer satisfaction ratings is the mood of the customer while completing the survey. An abundance of research demonstrates the influence of positive mood states toward prosocial behaviors.[9] More specifically, prior research has shown that respondents in positive mood states make more positive judgments, rate products they own more favorably, tend to see the brighter side of things, and are more likely to rate strangers favorably. Hence, consumers in positive moods should give higher marks to service personnel and service firms than their neutral- or negative-mood counterparts.

Are Customer Satisfaction Surveys Worth It?

Customer satisfaction ratings may fall under the category of the Hawthorne effect, that is, in and of themselves, satisfaction surveys might increase customer satisfaction regardless of the good or service being evaluated. Due to the already high levels of customer satisfaction, it may not make sense to attempt to increase satisfaction levels across the board. Two areas of satisfaction that do deserve special attention are (1) company attempts to maintain satisfaction over time to counter the decay effect, and (2) concentration on the tail of the satisfaction distribution—those customers who are dissatisfied. In and of themselves, satisfaction ratings cannot be interpreted with much meaning. Consequently, **benchmarking** with past performance and comparisons with competition provides some norm or standard.

Despite all the possible complications and given the benefits derived from customer satisfaction, when firms use satisfaction surveys in conjunction with other measures, such as those described later in this chapter, the information provided is invaluable.

benchmarking
Setting standards against which to compare future data collected.

Customer Satisfaction: How Good Is Good Enough?

How much satisfaction is enough? At 98 percent, a company that completes 1,000 transactions per week upsets 20 customers per week, who tell 9 or 10 of their friends. Given this scenario, the bottom line translates into 200 negative stories per week and 10,400 negative stories per year. Although these numbers are convincing when trying to increase customer satisfaction ratings, we tend to forget that for every percentage of satisfaction improvement, very real investment costs are involved.

If your firm currently boasts a 95 percent customer satisfaction rating, is it worth a $100,000 investment to improve satisfaction to 98 percent?[10] It depends. Pete Babich, the quality manager for the San Diego division of Hewlett-Packard, was faced with this exact question. Hewlett-Packard defines customer satisfaction as the customer's willingness to refer Hewlett-Packard products to friends. Hewlett-Packard has found that 70 percent of its purchases are made because of previous positive experiences with the product or referrals from others.

Although Babich found an abundance of anecdotal evidence that retaining customers was much less expensive than seeking out new customers, this information failed to answer his original question. Consequently, Babich proceeded to develop a **customer satisfaction model** that would predict market share changes over time as they related to customer satisfaction ratings.

The model is based on an algorithm that can easily be converted into a spreadsheet and that is built upon a number of assumptions. First, in this particular

customer satisfaction model
A model that predicts market share changes over time as they relate to customer satisfaction ratings; developed by Peter Babich.

DEFINING AND
MEASURING CUSTOMER
SATISFACTION

example, the model assumes a closed market of three firms that begin at period 0 with equal market shares. The three firms offer comparable products and prices and compete for a growing customer base. Next, the model assumes that satisfied consumers will continue to buy from the same firm and that dissatisfied customers will defect to other firms in the market. For example, dissatisfied customers of Firm A will buy at Firm B or Firm C during the next time period. The length of the time period varies, depending on the product (e.g., eye exam versus lawn care).

The direction of customer defection depends upon the firm's market share. In other words, if Firm C's market share is higher than Firm B's market share, Firm C will obtain a higher share of Firm A's dissatisfied customers. This logic is based on the premise that dissatisfied customers will be more particular the next time around and will conduct more research and seek out referrals from others. In this case, due to Firm C's higher market share, Firm C would be the beneficiary of more positive referrals.

Results generated from the customer satisfaction model when given three different scenarios are presented in Figure 11.2. Panel (a) illustrates the scenario of how a firm with a 95 percent customer satisfaction rating would stack up against firms commanding 90 percent and 91 percent customer satisfaction ratings. Clearly, the firm with 95 percent satisfaction dominates the market after 12 time periods. Panel (b) of the figure illustrates how that same firm with a 95 percent satisfaction rating would compete with firms commanding 98 percent and 99 percent ratings. In this scenario, the 95 percent firm controls less than 10 percent of the market after 24 time periods. This scenario dramatically illustrates the impact of the competition's satisfaction ratings.

Finally, Panel (c) illustrates the effect of customer satisfaction on market share at lower customer satisfaction levels. In this scenario, Firms A, B, and C command satisfaction ratings of 90 percent, 82 percent, and 80 percent respectively. In essence, this panel illustrates the effect of increasing the dissatisfaction levels of Panel (a) by 2. In this scenario, Firm A once again achieves market dominance, but at a much faster rate.

What does Peter Babich's customer satisfaction model tell us? First, firms with higher customer satisfaction ratings make the firm more resistant to competitor's efforts to improve their market share. Secondly, if the firm knows what a 1-percent improvement in market share does for its bottom line, then comparing the 1 percent increase in market share to the investment needed to improve customer satisfaction gives the firm the necessary information to make a business decision. Finally, the model points out the necessity of knowing not only your own firm's satisfaction rating, but also your competitors'.

Should a firm invest $100,000 to improve customer satisfaction ratings from 95 percent to 98 percent? It depends upon the satisfaction ratings of the firm's competitors, the dollar investment necessary to increase customer satisfaction relative to the impact of increasing the firm's market share, the number of time

FIGURE

11.2

CUSTOMER SATISFACTION MODEL: THREE SCENARIOS

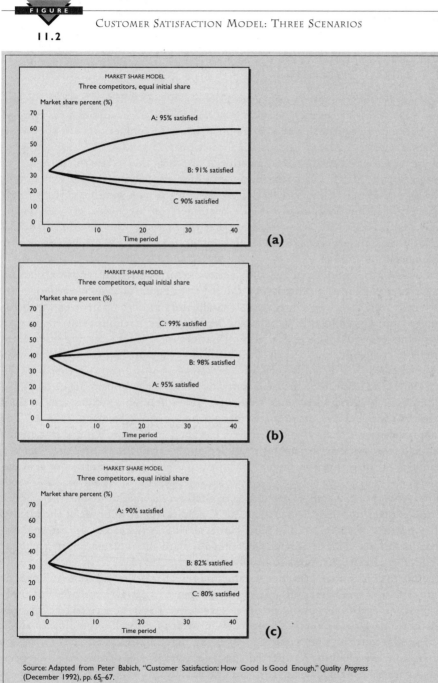

Source: Adapted from Peter Babich, "Customer Satisfaction: How Good Is Good Enough," *Quality Progress* (December 1992), pp. 65–67.

▶▶▶▶ ◀◀◀◀

periods required to recoup the investment, and the opportunity costs associated with other uses of the $100,000.

DOES CUSTOMER SATISFACTION TRANSLATE INTO CUSTOMER RETENTION?

High satisfaction ratings do not necessarily mean that a firm is going to retain a customer forever.[11] In fact, according to one group of consultants, on average, 65 percent to 85 percent of customers who defect to competitors say they were "satisfied" or "very satisfied" with their former providers.

Five criticisms of customer satisfaction research as they relate to customer retention provide insights into why firms with high satisfaction ratings may potentially lose customers. First, satisfaction research focuses on whether current needs are being met but fails to investigate customers' future needs. As customers' needs change, they will seek out a firm that best satisfies this new set of needs. Consequently, the progressive service firm must proactively engage in assessing its customers' future needs.

Another criticism of customer satisfaction research is that it tends to focus on registered complaints. According to the TARP figures presented earlier, many customers who defect never relay their complaints to an employee or the firm's management. Consequently, satisfaction research that examines only registered complaints overlooks a great deal of information. In addition, limiting research to registered complaints most likely also overlooks many of the problems that need to be remedied in order to lower defection rates.

A third criticism is that customer satisfaction research tends to focus on global attributes and ignore operational elements. Firms often phrase questions in their customer satisfaction questionnaires using broad, global statements such as "The firm provides good service" and "The firm has good employees." Global statements such as these overlook the operational elements that make up these statements. Examples of operational elements that measure employee performance may include such items as eye contact, product knowledge, courteous actions, and credibility. Operational elements pertaining to good service might include the amount of time it takes to check in and check out at a hotel, the cleanliness of the facility, and the hours of operation. Utilizing global attributes instead of operational elements in surveys fails to provide the company with the information it needs for developing effective solutions to problems.

A fourth criticism of customer satisfaction research is that it often excludes the firm's employees from the survey process. Employee satisfaction drives customer loyalty. Employees' perceptions of the service delivery system need to be compared with customers' perceptions. This process provides feedback to employees about the firm's performance and assists in ensuring that employees and customers are on the same wavelength. As internal customers, employees often contribute valuable suggestions for improving the firm's operations.

Finally, a fifth criticism is that some firms are convinced that customers may not know what they want and that sometimes ignoring the customer is the best strategy to follow, particularly when it comes to new product innovation.[12] Some believe that firms can go overboard listening to customers, thereby becoming slaves to demographics, market research, and focus groups. And, in fact, listening to customers often does discourage truly innovative products. As evidence, 90 percent of so-called new products are simply line extensions of existing products.

Listening to customers does have its faults. As stated earlier, customers often focus on current needs and have a difficult time projecting their needs into the future. In addition, consumers sometimes pick up cues from the person asking questions and attempt to answer questions in a direction that will please the interviewer. Other problems include the consumer's being in a hurry, not fully understanding what is being asked, not wanting to be rude and so cheerfully agreeing with whatever is being asked, and most importantly, not making decisions using real money.

The list of products consumers initially rejected that went on to be huge successes is impressive. Products such as the Chrysler minivan, fax machines, VCRs, FedEx, CNN, Compaq PC servers, cellular phones, personal digital assistants, microwave ovens, and even Birdseye frozen foods were all rejected by customers during initial survey attempts. In contrast, products that surveyed customers indicated would be great successes, such as McDonald's McLean, KFC's skinless fried chicken, Pizza Hut's low-calorie pizza, and New Coke, among others, turned out to be flops (see Figure 11.3).

The problem is not so much listening to what customers have to say as it is companies' feeling paralyzed to make strategic moves without strong consumer support. Of course, customers should not be completely ignored. However, some marketers argue that the best consumer information is obtained through detached observation instead of through traditional survey techniques—"Ignore what your customers say; pay attention to what they do."[13]

CUSTOMER SATISFACTION: A CLOSER LOOK

The first half of this chapter provided a broad overview of customer satisfaction. The following section takes a closer look at customer expectations and how they relate to customer satisfaction and service quality assessments. This section further defines customer satisfaction and provides the transition into the next chapter, which focuses solely on service quality issues.

TYPES OF CUSTOMER EXPECTATIONS

At first glance, comparing expectations with perceptions when developing customer satisfaction evaluations sounds fairly straightforward. Expectations serve as benchmarks against which present and future service encounters are compared. However, this relatively simple scenario becomes a bit more confusing when you realize that there exist at least three different types of expectations.[14]

Predicted service is a **probability expectation** that reflects the level of service customers believe is likely to occur. For example, bank customers tend to conduct

predicted service

The level of service quality a customer believes is likely to occur.

DEFINING AND
MEASURING CUSTOMER
SATISFACTION

FIGURE

11.3

OOPS! NEVER MIND . . .

OOPS! NEVER MIND ...

■ Consumer research can be downright misleading. Just because customers say they want something doesn't mean they'll buy it.

■ **New Coke beat out the old formula in tests with 190,000 consumers. Beat Pepsi too. But its launch fizzled.**

■ **Schwarzenegger's** *Junior* **did well in screenings. Still, a pregnant Arnold! It grossed just $36 million.**

■ **People asked for diet burgers, but a greasy one still holds the allure. Sales of McDonald's McLean have been, well, lean.**

■ **In tests, sluggers thought pump baseball gloves a great idea. In stores, a snugger fit didn't justify a $100 pricetag.**

Source: Justin Martin, "Ignore Your Customer," *Fortune*, May 1, 1995, pp. 121–126. © 1995 Time Inc. All rights reserved.

Consumer research can be downright misleading. Just because customers say they want something doesn't mean they'll buy it.

probability expectation

A customer expectation based on the customer's opinion of what will be most likely when dealing with service personnel.

their banking business at the same location over time. Customers become accustomed to dealing with the same bank personnel and, over time, begin to anticipate certain performance levels. *It is generally agreed that customer satisfaction evaluations are developed by comparing predicted service to perceived service received* (see Figure 11.4).

FIGURE

11.4 Comparison between Customer Evaluation of Service Quality and Customer Satisfaction

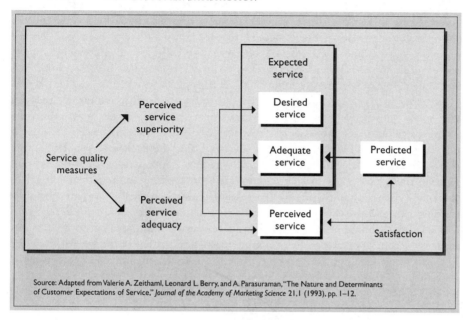

Source: Adapted from Valerie A. Zeithaml, Leonard L. Berry, and A. Parasuraman, "The Nature and Determinants of Customer Expectations of Service," *Journal of the Academy of Marketing Science* 21,1 (1993), pp. 1–12.

Desired service is an **ideal expectation** that reflects what customers actually want compared with predicted service, which is what is likely to occur. Hence, in most instances, desired service reflects a higher expectation than predicted service. For example, our bank customer's desired service is that he not only receive his predicted service but that the tellers call him by his first name and enthusiastically greet him as he enters the bank. Comparing desired service expectations to perceived service received results in a measure of **perceived service superiority** (see Figure 11.4).

In contrast, **adequate service** is a **minimum tolerable expectation** and reflects the level of service the customer is willing to accept. Adequate service is based on experiences or norms that develop over time. For example, most adult consumers have dined at hundreds, if not thousands, of restaurants. Through these experiences, norms develop that consumers expect to occur. Hence, one factor that influences adequate service is predicted service. Encounters that fall below expected norms fall below adequate service expectations. Comparing adequate service with perceived service produces a measure of **perceived service adequacy** (see Figure 11.4).

THE ZONE OF TOLERANCE

Because services are characterized by heterogeneity, consumers learn to expect variation in service delivery from one location to the next and even in the same

desired service

The level of service quality a customer actually wants from a service encounter.

ideal expectation

A customer's expectation of what a "perfect" service encounter would be.

perceived service superiority

A measure of service quality derived by comparing desired service expectations and perceived service received.

adequate service

The level of service quality a customer is willing to accept.

▶▶▶▶ ◀◀◀◀

**minimum tolerable
expectation**

A customer expectation based
on the absolute minimum
acceptable outcome.

**perceived service
adequacy**

A measure of service quality
derived by comparing adequate
service and perceived service.

zone of tolerance

Level of quality ranging from
high to low and reflecting the
difference between desired
service and adequate service;
expands and contracts across
customers and within the same
customer, depending on the
service and the conditions
under which it is provided.

**enduring service
intensifiers**

Personal factors that are stable
over time and increase a
customer's sensitivity to how a
service should be best provided.

derived expectations

Expectations appropriated from
and based on the expectations
of others.

**personal service
philosophies**

A customer's own internal
views of the meaning of service
and the manner in which
service providers should
conduct themselves.

provider from one day to the next. Consumers who accept this variation develop a **zone of tolerance,** which reflects the difference between desired service and adequate service (see Figure 11.5). The zone of tolerance expands and contracts across customers and within the same customer depending on the service and the conditions under which the service is provided. Other factors, such as price, for example, may influence the zone of tolerance. Typically, as the price increases, the customer's zone of tolerance decreases as desired service needs begin to dominate, and the customer becomes less forgiving for sloppy service.

Another interesting characteristic of the zone of tolerance is that desired service is less subject to change than adequate service. One way to picture the zone of tolerance is to compare it with a projector screen located at the top of a blackboard. The metal canister bolted to the wall that holds the screen represents the desired service level. The desired service level represents what the customer believes the ideal service firm *should* provide to its customers. Its movement is less subject to change than the rest of the screen. The screen itself represents the zone of tolerance, and the metal piece with the handle at the bottom of the screen represents the adequate service level. Adequate service fluctuates based on circumstances surrounding the service delivery process and changes the size of the zone of tolerance accordingly. In contrast, desired service levels tend to be fairly stable.

FACTORS INFLUENCING SERVICE EXPECTATIONS: DESIRED SERVICE

Desired expectations are developed as a result of six different sources (see Figure 11.6). The first source, **enduring service intensifiers,** are personal factors that are stable over time and that increase a customer's sensitivity to how the service should be best provided. Two types of enduring service intensifiers include the customer's derived expectations and personal service philosophies. **Derived expectations** are created from the expectations of others. For example, if your boss requests that you find someone to pressure-wash the office building, your expectations of the provider performing the job will most likely be higher than if you had hired the provider on your own initiative. In the attempt to satisfy your boss's expectations, your sensitivity to the caliber of service significantly increases.

Similarly, the customer's **personal service philosophies,** or personal views of the meaning of service and the manner in which service providers should conduct themselves, will also heighten his or her sensitivities. Customers who work in the service sector are particularly sensitive to the caliber of service provided. These customers hold their own views regarding exactly how service should be provided . . . they want to be treated the way they believe they treat their customers.

The second factor influencing desired service expectations is the customer's own **personal needs,** including physical, social, and psychological needs. Simply stated, some customers have more needs than others. Some customers are very particular about where they are seated in a restaurant, while others are happy to

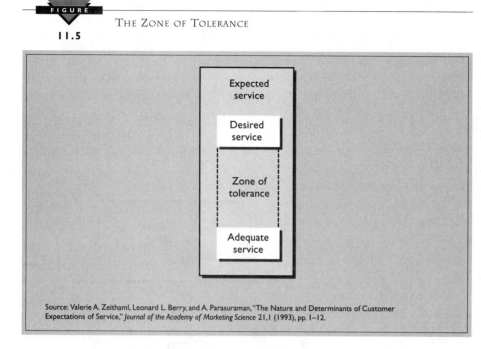

**FIGURE
11.5**

THE ZONE OF TOLERANCE

Expected
service

Desired
service

Zone of
tolerance

Adequate
service

Source: Valerie A. Zeithaml, Leonard L. Berry, and A. Parasuraman, "The Nature and Determinants of Customer Expectations of Service," *Journal of the Academy of Marketing Science* 21,1 (1993), pp. 1–12.

sit nearly anywhere. In a hotel, some customers are very interested in the hotel's amenities, such as the pool, sauna, dining room, and other forms of available entertainment, while others are simply looking for a clean room. This is one of the reasons that managing a service firm is particularly challenging. Customers have a variety of needs, and no two customers are alike in every way.

personal needs

A customer's physical, social, and psychological needs.

FACTORS INFLUENCING SERVICE EXPECTATIONS: DESIRED SERVICE AND PREDICTED SERVICE

The other four factors that influence desired service expectations also influence predicted service expectations and include (1) explicit service promises; (2) implicit service promises; (3) word-of-mouth communications; and (4) past experience (see Figure 11.6).

Explicit service promises encompass the firm's advertising, personal selling, contracts, and other forms of communication. Due to the lack of a tangible product, consumers of services base their evaluations of the service on various forms of information available. The more ambiguous the service, the more customers rely on the firm's advertising when forming expectations. If a hotel stresses modern and clean rooms, customers expect the rooms to be exactly the way they were pictured in the advertisement. Similarly, if a builder states that a customer's new house will be completed in December, the customer takes this as

explicit service promises

Obligations to which the firm commits itself via its advertising, personal selling, contracts, and other forms of communication.

DEFINING AND
MEASURING CUSTOMER
SATISFACTION

FIGURE
11.6

FACTORS INFLUENCING EXPECTED SERVICE

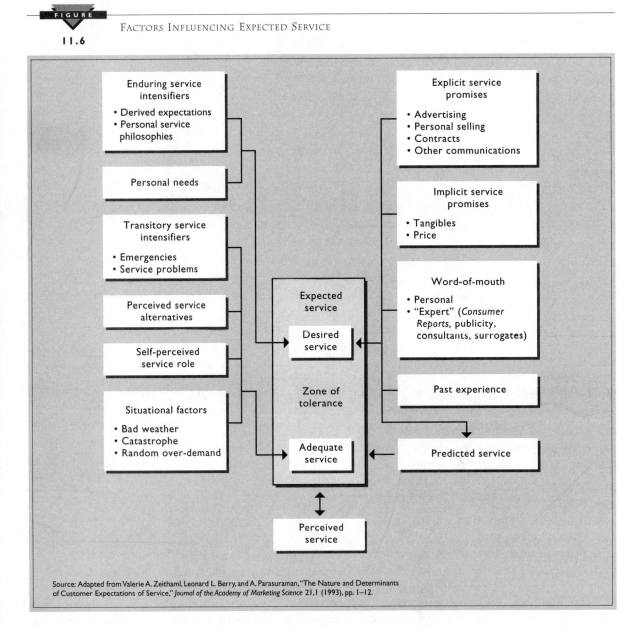

Source: Adapted from Valerie A. Zeithaml, Leonard L. Berry, and A. Parasuraman, "The Nature and Determinants of Customer Expectations of Service," *Journal of the Academy of Marketing Science* 21,1 (1993), pp. 1–12.

Some guests like the amenities of a hotel to include swimming pool, sauna, and workout facilities, while others simply want a clean room and a quiet place to rest. This is why managing a service firm is particularly challenging—consumers have different expectations.
© Jeff Greenberg/PhotoEdit.

the builder's promise, and the standard is established on which the customer will base subsequent evaluations.

Implicit service promises also influence desired service and predicted service. The tangibles surrounding the service and the price of the service are common types of implicit service promises. As the price increases, customers expect the firm to deliver higher-quality services. In the absence of a tangible product, the price becomes an indicator of quality to most consumers. For example, customers would probably have higher expectations for service at a higher-priced hair salon than they would for "Cheap Charley's Barber Shop." Similarly, if the tangibles surrounding a service are plush, customers interpret those tangibles as a sign of quality. In general, the nicer the furnishings of the service establishment, the higher customer expectations become.

Word-of-mouth communications also play an important role in forming customer expectations. As discussed in Chapter Four, customers tend to rely more on personal sources of information than on nonpersonal ones when choosing among service alternatives. Since services cannot be evaluated fully before purchase, customers view word-of-mouth information as unbiased information from someone who has been through the service experience. Sources of word-of-mouth information range from friends and family to consultants and *Consumer Reports.*

implicit service promises

Obligations to which the firm commits itself via the tangibles surrounding the service and the price of the service.

word-of-mouth communications

Unbiased information from someone who has been through the service experience, such as friends, family, or consultants.

▶▶▶▶ ◀◀◀◀

DEFINING AND MEASURING CUSTOMER SATISFACTION

past experience

The previous service encounters a consumer has had with a service provider.

Past experience also contributes to customer expectations of desired and predicted service. Service evaluations are often based on a comparison of the current service encounter to other encounters with the same provider, other providers in the industry, and other providers in other industries. In the education system, student desired and predicted service expectations of instructors are likely to be based on past experience in other classes with the same instructor and on other classes with other instructors.

FACTORS INFLUENCING SERVICE EXPECTATIONS: ADEQUATE SERVICE

Adequate service reflects the level of service the consumer is willing to accept and is influenced by five factors: (1) transitory service intensifiers; (2) perceived service alternatives; (3) customer self-perceived service roles; (4) situation factors; and (5) predicted service (see Figure 11.6).

transitory service intensifiers

Personal, short-term factors that heighten a customer's sensitivity to service.

Transitory Service Intensifiers In contrast to enduring service intensifiers, **transitory service intensifiers** are individualized, short-term factors that heighten the customer's sensitivity to service. For example, customers who have had service problems in the past with specific types of providers are more sensitive to the quality of service delivered during subsequent encounters. Another example is the need for service under personal emergency situations. Typically, consumers are willing to wait their turn to see a physician. However, under personal emergency conditions, consumers are less willing to be patient and expect a higher level of service in a shorter period of time. Hence, the level of adequate service increases, and the zone of tolerance becomes more narrow.

perceived service alternatives

Comparable services customers believe they can obtain elsewhere and/or produce themselves.

Perceived Service Alternatives The level of adequate service is also affected by the customer's **perceived service alternatives.** The higher the number of perceived service alternatives, the higher the level of adequate service expectations, and the more narrow the zone of tolerance. Customers who believe that they can obtain comparable services elsewhere and/or that they can produce the service themselves expect higher levels of adequate service than those customers who believe they are not able to receive sufficiently better service from another provider.

self-perceived service role

The input a customer believes he or she is required to present in order to produce a satisfactory service encounter.

Self-Perceived Service Role As has been discussed on numerous occasions, the service customer is often involved in the production process and can directly influence the outcome of the service delivery system. When customers have a strong **self-perceived service role,** that is, when they believe that they are doing their part, their adequate service expectations are increased. However, if customers willingly admit that they have failed to complete forms or provide the necessary information to produce a superior service outcome, then their adequate service expectations decrease, and the zone of tolerance increases.

Situational Factors As a group, customers are not unreasonable. They understand that from time to time **situational factors** beyond the control of the service provider will lower the quality of service. If the power goes out in one part of town around dinner time, restaurants in other parts of town will be overrun by hungry patrons. As a result, lengthy waits will develop as the service delivery system becomes backed up. Similarly, after a hurricane, tornado, or other natural disaster occurs, the customer's insurance agent may not be as responsive as under normal circumstances. When circumstances occur beyond the control of the provider and the customer has knowledge of those circumstances, adequate service expectations are lowered, and the zone of tolerance becomes wider.

Predicted Service The level of service consumers believe is likely to occur, is the fifth and final factor which influences adequate service expectations. **Predicted service** is a function of the firm's explicit and implicit service promises, word-of-mouth communications, and the customer's own past experiences. Taking these factors into consideration, customers form judgments regarding the predicted service that is likely to occur and set adequate service expectations simultaneously.

The Link between Expectations, Customer Satisfaction, and Service Quality

Now that we have introduced the concepts of predicted, adequate, and desired service, you may wonder what all the fuss is about. It is actually simple and straightforward. When evaluating the service experience, consumers compare the three types of expectations (predicted service, adequate service, and desired service) to the perceived service delivered. Customer satisfaction is calculated by comparing predicted service and perceived service. Perceived service adequacy, which compares adequate service and perceived service, and perceived service superiority, which compares desired service and perceived service, are measures of service quality (refer to Figure 11.4). Other major differences between service quality and customer satisfaction as well as issues related to service quality measurement are discussed in greater detail in Chapter Twelve.

SUMMARY

Customer satisfaction research is one of the fastest growing areas in market research today. Defined as a comparison of perceptions and predicted service expectations, customer satisfaction has been associated with such benefits as repeat sales, more frequent sales, increased sales per transaction, positive word-of-mouth communications, insulation from price competition, and pleasant work environments for employees. Customer satisfaction questionnaires send the signal to consumers that the firm cares about its customers and wants their input. In addition, data collected from questionnaires facilitates the development of employee training programs, identifies strengths and weaknesses in the firm's service delivery process, and provides information to be used in employee performance reviews and compensation decisions.

Firms use a variety of methods to track customer satisfaction. Moreover, a number of factors can dramatically increase or decrease the firm's satisfaction ratings. The main lessons to be learned are that (1) customer satisfaction surveys that collect qualitative and quantitative data are better than those that collect either qualitative or quantitative data alone; and (2) regardless of the methods used, such as the timing of the questions, the context of the questions, the data collection method, and a variety of other research issues, the firm must be consistent in its approach in order to make comparisons over time meaningful. Overall, customer satisfaction ratings tend to be negatively skewed, and responses indicating above-average performance tend to be the norm.

Despite its problems, customer satisfaction assessment is a valuable management exercise. However, firms should not attempt to increase their satisfaction ratings without carefully considering (1) the satisfaction ratings of competing firms; (2) the cost of an investment in increasing market share relative to the impact on the firm's bottom line; (3) the number of time periods it takes to recoup such an investment; and (4) the opportunity costs associated with the use of the firm's funds.

Finally, one of the driving forces behind customer satisfaction is the customer's expectations. Three types of expectations and the factors influencing each type were presented. The three types of expectations form the bases for both customer satisfaction and service quality assessments, which are discussed in Chapter Twelve.

KEY TERMS

expectancy disconfirmation model	probability expectation
confirmed expectations	desired service
disconfirmed expectations	ideal expectation
negative disconfirmation	perceived service superiority
positive disconfirmation	adequate service
response bias	minimum tolerable expectation
data collection method	perceived service adequacy
question form	zone of tolerance
question context	enduring service intensifiers
question timing	derived expectations
social desirability bias	personal service philosophies
benchmarking	personal needs
customer satisfaction model	explicit service promises
predicted service	implicit service promises

word-of-mouth communications   self-perceived service role
past experience   situational factors
transitory service intensifiers   predicted service
perceived service alternatives

REVIEW QUESTIONS

1. Discuss the differences among a confirmation, a positive disconfirmation, and a negative disconfirmation.

2. What is meant by the description that most satisfaction scores are negatively skewed? Why does this score distribution occur?

3. Discuss how the form of a question may influence satisfaction scores.

4. Should a company always attempt to achieve 100 percent customer satisfaction?

5. Discuss the relationship between customer satisfaction and customer retention.

6. What are the drawbacks of listening to customers and assessing customer satisfaction?

7. Define and explain the relevance of the terms *predicted service, desired service,* and *adequate service* as they pertain to customer satisfaction and service quality.

8. What are the factors that influence customer expectations?

NOTES

1. Robert A. Peterson and William R. Wilson, "Measuring Customer Satisfaction: Fact and Artifact," *Journal of the Academy of Marketing Science* 20,1 (1992), p. 61.

2. Karl Albrecht and Ron Zemke, *Service America! Doing Business in the New Economy* (Homewood, IL: Business One Irwin, 1985), p. 6.

3. Keith Hunt, "Consumer Satisfaction, Dissatisfaction, and Complaining Behavior," *Journal of Social Issues* 47,1, (1991), pp. 109–110.

4. Leonard L. Berry, A. Parasuraman, and Valerie A. Zeithaml, "Improving Service Quality in America: Lessons Learned," *Academy of Management Executive* 8,2 (1994), p. 36.

5. Peterson and Wilson, "Measuring Customer Satisfaction," p. 61.

6. Peterson and Wilson, "Measuring Customer Satisfaction," p. 61.

7. Peterson and Wilson, "Measuring Customer Satisfaction," p. 62.

8. Marsha L. Richins, "Negative Word-of-Mouth by Dissatisfied Consumers: A Pilot Study," *Journal of Marketing* 47 (Winter 1983), pp. 68–78.

9. K. Douglas Hoffman, "A Conceptual Framework of the Influence of Positive Mood States on Service Exchange Relationships," in *Marketing Theory and Applications,* Chris T. Allen et al., eds. (San Antonio, TX: American Marketing Association Winter Educator's Conference), p. 147.

10. Adapted from Peter Babich, "Customer Satisfaction: How Good Is Good Enough," *Quality Progress* (December 1992), pp. 65–67.

11. Adapted from Michael W. Lowenstein, "The Voice of the Customer," *Small Business Reports* (December 1993), pp. 57–61.

12. Justin Martin, "Ignore Your Customer," *Fortune*, May 1, 1995, pp. 121–126.

13. Ibid, p. 126.

14. This section adapted from Valerie A. Zeithaml, Leonard L. Berry, and A. Parasuraman, "The Nature and Determinants of Customer Expectations of Service," *Journal of the Academy of Marketing Science* 21,1 (1993), pp. 1–12.

12

Defining and Measuring Service Quality

> "*It's just the little touches after the average man would quit that makes the master's fame.*"

Orison Swett Marden, founder, *Success* magazine

CHAPTER OBJECTIVES

The major objectives of this chapter are to introduce you to the concepts of service quality, service quality measurement, and service quality information systems.
After completing this chapter, you should be able to

▸ Define service quality as it relates to customer satisfaction.

▸ *Identify and discuss the gaps that influence consumer perceptions of service quality.*

▸ Discuss factors that influence the size of each of the service quality gaps.

▸ *Discuss the basic concepts of SERVQUAL.*

▸ Describe the components of a service quality information system.

MEASURING SERVICE QUALITY: THE FEDEX APPROACH

"*We believe that service quality must be mathematically measured.*"

—Frederick W. Smith, Chair and CEO, FedEx

When Federal Express first opened its doors on April 17, 1973, it shipped eight packages, seven of which were trial runs addressed from one Federal Express employee to another. No one had any idea that this event marked the birth of an entire industry—overnight mail or parcel delivery. Particularly inspiring to college students is that Fred Smith, the CEO of FedEx, had sketched out the early details of the operation in an undergraduate paper at Yale University. The paper was given a grade of "C." By 1990, the company was generating $7 billion in annual sales revenue and controlled 43 percent of the air express mail market.

FedEx has two ambitious goals: 100 percent customer satisfaction with every interaction and transaction, and 100 percent performance on every package handled. In its early days, Federal Express defined service quality as the percentage of packages delivered on time. After cataloging complaints for many years, it had become apparent that percentage of on-time delivery was an internal measure of service quality and did not necessarily reflect absolute service quality by customer standards.

The customer's definition of service quality, which included eight service failures to be avoided, became known as the "Hierarchy of Horrors" and included (1) wrong-day delivery; (2) right day, late delivery; (3) pick-up not made; (4) lost package; (5) customer misinformed by FedEx; (6) billing and paperwork mistakes; (7) employee performance failures; and (8) damaged packages. Based on these categories generated by customer complaints, it was readily apparent that on-time delivery was not the only measure important to FedEx customers.

In addition to categorizing customer complaints, FedEx measures service quality by tracking 12 service quality indicators every day, both individually and in total. Moreover, the firm conducts numerous customer research studies each year in five major categories: (1) service quality studies, conducted quarterly, of four market segments: base business that is phoned to FedEx, U.S. export customers, manned-center customers, and drop-box customers; (2) 10 targeted customer studies, conducted semi-annually, that contact customers who have had an experience with one of 10 specific FedEx processes such as customer service, billing, and invoice adjustments; (3) FedEx center comment cards, which are collected and tabulated twice a year and used as feedback to the managers of each center; (4) customer automation studies of FedEx's 7,600 largest customers, representing 30 percent of the company's total package volume, who are equipped with automated systems that permit package tracking and a variety of other self-service activities; and (5) the Canadian customer study conducted yearly, which is the single most frequent point of destination for FedEx packages shipped outside the United States.

How successful is FedEx? In monetary terms, its success has been history making. FedEx was the first company in U.S. history to top $1 billion in revenues within its first 10 years of existence. Customer satisfaction ratings at FedEx are also legendary. The highest quarterly rating of customer satisfaction achieved thus far has been a 94 percent "completely satisfied" rating from customers on a 5-point scale that ranges from "completely dissatisfied" to "completely satisfied." Most firms combine "somewhat satisfied" and "completely satisfied" responses when calculating customer satisfaction ratings, but not at FedEx. Due to achievements such as these and many others, FedEx is a recipient of the Malcolm Baldrige National Quality Award.

Source: Briefing Staff, *Blueprints for Service Quality: The Federal Express Approach*, AMA Management Briefing (American Management Association: New York, 1991). Reprinted by permission of the publisher. © 1991 American Marketing Association.

INTRODUCTION

One of the few issues on which service quality researchers agree is that service quality is an elusive and abstract concept that is difficult to define and measure.[1] This particular problem is challenging for academicians and practitioners alike. For example, traditional measures of productivity such as Gross Domestic Product (GDP) do not account for increases in service quality delivered. In fact, providing poor quality can actually increase the country's GDP.[2] If a mail-order company sends you the wrong product, the dollars spent on phone calls and return mailings to correct the mistake will add to the GDP.

Other governmental institutions, such as the Bureau of Labor Statistics (BLS), have attempted to account for increases in quality by adjusting the consumer price index. For example, if a car costs more this year than last but includes quality improvements such as an air bag, better gas mileage, and cleaner emissions, the BLS will subtract the estimated retail value of the improvements before calculating the consumer price index. However, the BLS does this for only a few industries and without the help of customers—the true evaluators of quality improvements. Efficiency measures are also of no help. A retail store, which stocks lots of merchandise, may please more customers and make more money while decreasing the firm's efficiency rating.

The productivity of education and government services is notoriously difficult to measure. Increases in quality, such as improving the quality of education and training governmental employees to be more pleasant throughout their daily interactions with the pubic, do not show up in productivity measures. However, it is readily apparent that increases in quality can have a dramatic impact on a firm's or industry's survival. As evidence, Japan did not simply bulldoze its way into U.S. markets by offering lower prices alone—superior quality relative to the competition at that time ultimately won customers over.

WHAT IS SERVICE QUALITY?

Perhaps the best way to begin a discussion of service quality is to first attempt to distinguish service quality measurement from customer satisfaction measurement. Most experts agree that customer satisfaction is a short-term, transaction-specific measure, whereas **service quality** is an attitude formed by a long-term, overall evaluation of a performance.

service quality
An attitude formed by a long-term, overall evaluation of a firm's performance.

Without a doubt, the two concepts of customer satisfaction and service quality are intertwined. However, the relationship between these two concepts is unclear. Some believe that customer satisfaction leads to perceived service quality, while others believe that service quality leads to customer satisfaction. In addition, the relationship between customer satisfaction and service quality and the way these two concepts relate to purchasing behavior remains largely unexplained.[3]

One plausible explanation is that satisfaction assists consumers in revising service quality perceptions.[4] The logic for this position consists of the following: (1) Consumer perceptions of the service quality of a firm with which he or she has no prior experience is based on the consumer's expectations; (2) subsequent encounters with the firm lead the consumer through the disconfirmation process and revise perceptions of service quality; (3) each additional encounter with the firm further revises or reinforces service quality perceptions; and (4) revised service quality perceptions modify future consumer purchase intentions toward the firm.

To deliver a consistent set of satisfying experiences that can build into an evaluation of high quality requires the entire organization to be focused on the task. The needs of the consumer must be understood in detail, as must the operational constraints under which the firm operates. Service providers must be focused on quality, and the system must be designed to support that mission by being controlled correctly and delivering as it was designed to do.

THE DIFFERENCE IN QUALITY PERSPECTIVES BETWEEN GOODS AND SERVICES

Service quality offers a way of achieving success among competing services.[5] Particularly, where a small number of firms that offer nearly identical services are competing within a small area, such as banks might do, establishing service quality may be the only way of differentiating oneself. Service quality differentiation can generate increased market share and ultimately mean the difference between financial success and failure.

Ample evidence suggests that the provision of quality can deliver repeat purchases as well as new customers. The value of retaining existing customers is discussed in much greater detail in Chapter Fourteen. Briefly, repeat customers yield many benefits to the service organization. The cost of marketing to them is lower than that of marketing to new customers. Once customers have become regulars of the service, they know the script and are efficient users of the servuction system. As they gain trust in the organization, the level of risk for them is reduced, and they are more likely to consolidate their business with the firm. For example, insurance customers tend to move current policies to and purchase new policies from the one provider they feel serves their needs the best.

Goods manufacturers have already learned this lesson over the past decade and have made producing quality goods a priority issue. Improving the quality of manufactured goods has become a major strategy for both establishing efficient, smoothly running operations and increasing consumer market share in an atmosphere in which customers are consistently demanding higher and higher quality. Goods quality improvement measures have focused largely on the quality of the products themselves, and specifically on eliminating product failure. Initially, these measures were based on rigorous checking of all finished products before they came into contact with the customer. More recently, quality control has focused on the principal of ensuring quality during the manufacturing process, on "getting it right the first time," and on reducing end-of-production-line failures to zero. The final evolution in goods manufacturing has been to define quality as delivering the right product to the right customer at the right time, thus extending quality beyond the good itself and using external as well as internal measures to assess overall quality.

However, service quality cannot be understood in quite the same way. The servuction system depends on the customer as a participant in the production process, and normal quality-control measures that depend on eliminating defects before the consumer sees the product are not available. Consequently, service quality is not a specific goal or program that can be achieved or completed but must be an ongoing part of all management and service production.

Diagnosing Failure Gaps in Service Quality

Many difficulties are inherent in implementing and evaluating service quality. In the first place, perceptions of quality tend to rely on a repeated comparison of the customer's expectation about a particular service. If a service, no matter how good, fails repeatedly to meet a customer's expectations, the customer will perceive the service to be of poor quality. Second, unlike goods marketing, where customers evaluate the finished product alone, in services, the customer evaluates the process of the service as well as its outcome. A customer visiting a hairdresser, for example, will evaluate service not only on the basis of whether he or she likes the haircut, but also on whether the hairdresser was friendly, competent, and personally clean.

Conceptually, the service quality process can be examined in terms of gaps between expectations and perceptions on the part of management, employees, and customers (see Figure 12.1).[6] The most important gap, **the service gap,** is between customers' expectations of service and their perception of the service actually delivered. Ultimately, the goal of the service firm is to close the service gap or at least narrow it as far as possible. Consequently, examining service quality gaps is much like the disconfirmation of expectations model discussed in Chapter Eleven. However, remember that service quality focuses on the customer's cumulative attitude toward the firm, which is collected by the consumer from a number of successful or unsuccessful service experiences.

Before the firm can close the service gap, it must close or attempt to narrow four other gaps:

The knowledge gap, or the difference between what consumers expect of a service and what management perceives the consumers to expect.

The standards gap, or the difference between what management perceives consumers to expect and the quality specifications set for service delivery.

---

service gap

The distance between a customer's expectation of a service and perception of the service actually delivered.

knowledge gap

The difference between what consumers expect of a service and what management perceives the consumers to expect.

standards gap

The difference between what management perceives consumers to expect and the quality specifications set for service delivery.

FIGURE

12.1

CONCEPTUAL MODEL OF SERVICE QUALITY

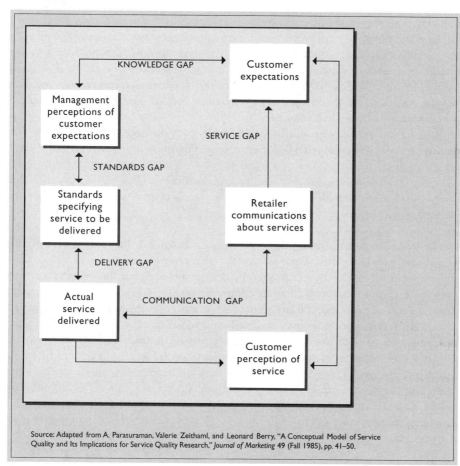

Source: Adapted from A. Parasuraman, Valerie Zeithaml, and Leonard Berry, "A Conceptual Model of Service Quality and Its Implications for Service Quality Research," *Journal of Marketing* 49 (Fall 1985), pp. 41–50.

The delivery gap, or the difference between the quality specifications set for service delivery and the actual quality of service delivery. For example, do employees perform the service as they were trained?

The communications gap, or the difference between the actual quality of service delivered and the quality of service described in the firm's external communications such as brochures and mass media advertising.

Hence, the service gap is a function of the knowledge gap, the specifications gap, the delivery gap, and the communications gap. As each of these gaps increases or decreases, the service gap responds in a similar manner.

delivery gap

The difference between the quality standards set for service delivery and the actual quality of service delivery.

communications gap

The difference between the actual quality of service delivered and the quality of service described in the firm's external communications.

DEFINING AND
MEASURING SERVICE
QUALITY

THE KNOWLEDGE GAP

The most immediate and obvious gap is usually between what customers want and what managers think customers want. Briefly, many managers think they know what their customers want but are, in fact, mistaken. Banking customers may prefer security to a good interest rate. Some restaurant customers may prefer quality and taste of food over an attractive arrangement of the tables or a good view from the window. A hotel may feel that its customers prefer comfortable rooms, when, in fact, the majority of them spend little time in their rooms and are more interested in on-site amenities.

When a knowledge gap occurs, a variety of other mistakes tend to follow. The wrong facilities may be provided, the wrong staff may be hired, and the wrong training may be given to them. Services may be provided that customers have no use for, while the services they *do* desire are not offered. Closing this gap requires minutely detailed knowledge of what customers desire and then building that response into the service operating system.

research orientation

A firm's attitude toward conducting consumer research.

upward communication

The flow of information from front-line personnel to upper levels of the organization.

levels of management

The complexity of the organizational hierarchy and the number of levels between top management and the customers.

Factors Influencing the Knowledge Gap   Three main factors influence the size of the knowledge gap. First, the firm's **research orientation,** which reflects its attitude toward conducting consumer research, can dramatically influence the size of the gap. Information obtained from consumer research defines consumer expectations. As the firm's research orientation increases, the size of the knowledge gap should decrease. The amount of **upward communication** is a second factor that influences the size of the knowledge gap. Upward communication refers to the flow of information from front-line personnel to upper levels of the organization. Front-line personnel interact with customers on a frequent basis, so they are often more in touch with customer needs than is top management. Consequently, as the flow of upward communication increases through the organization, the smaller the knowledge gap should become. Finally, the **levels of management** in the organization can also influence the size of the knowledge gap. As the organizational hierarchy becomes more complex and more levels of management are added, higher levels of management tend to become more distant from customers and the day-to-day activities of the organization. As a result, when the levels of management increase, the size of the knowledge gap tends to increase.

THE STANDARDS GAP

Even if customer expectations have been accurately determined, the standards gap may open between management's perception of customer expectations and the actual standards set for service delivery, such as order processing speed, the way cloth napkins are to be folded, or the way customers are to be greeted. When developing standards, the firm should use a flowchart of its operations to identify all points of contact between it and its customers. Detailed standards can be written for (1) the way the system should operate, and (2) the behavior of contact personnel at each point in the system. Hotel front-desk personnel, for example, may be trained to perform to specification in such areas as acknowledging the customer upon arrival, establishing eye contact, smiling, completing the proper paperwork, reviewing with the customer the available amenities, and providing the customer with keys to the room.

Factors Influencing the Standards Gap In many cases, management does not believe it can or should meet customer requirements for service. For example, overnight delivery of mail used to be thought of as an absurd possibility before Fred Smith and FedEx proved that, in fact, it could be done.

Sometimes management has no commitment to the delivery of service quality. Corporate leadership may set other priorities that interfere with setting standards that lead to good service. For example, a company's orientation toward implementing cost-reduction strategies that maximize short-term profits is often cited as a misguided priority that impedes the firm's progress in delivering quality services. Personal computer companies whose automated service hotlines reduce the number of customer service representatives employed are typical examples. In some instances, customers in need of service have been forced to remain on hold for hours before they could actually speak to a "real person." Hotlines were originally named to reflect the speed with which the customer could talk to the manufacturer. Now the name more appropriately reflects the customer's temper by the time he or she talks to someone who can actually help.

Sometimes there is simply no culture of service quality, and management genuinely fails to understand the issues involved. In other cases, management may wish to meet customer requirements but feel hampered by insufficient methods of measuring quality or by converting those measurements into standards. Because of the difficulties in attempting to write specifications for particular employee behaviors, some managers feel that quality measurement is not worth the effort.

THE DELIVERY GAP

The delivery gap occurs between the actual performance of a service and the standards set by management. The existence of the delivery gap depends on both the willingness and the ability of employees to provide the service according to specification. For example, do employees wear their name tags, do they establish eye contact, and do they thank the customer when the transaction is completed?

Factors Influencing the Delivery Gap One factor that influences the size of the delivery gap is the employee's **willingness to perform** the service. Obviously, employees' willingness to provide a service can vary greatly from employee to employee and in the same employee over time. Many employees who start off working to their full

willingness to perform
An employee's desire to perform to his/her full potential in a service encounter.

DEFINING AND
MEASURING SERVICE
QUALITY

Every service firm must maintain certain standards in order to give customers a pleasant experience. For hotel employees, it may be acknowledging the customer on arrival, establishing eye contact, smiling, answering questions, and providing keys to the hotel room.

Source: © Don Couch Photography, Houston.

potential often become less willing to do so over time because of frustration and dissatisfaction with the organization. Furthermore, a considerable range exists between what the employee is actually capable of accomplishing and the minimum the employee must do in order to keep his/her job. Most service managers find it difficult to keep employees working at their full potential all the time.

Other employees, no matter how willing, may simply not be able to perform the service to specification. Hence, a second factor that influences the size of the delivery gap is the **employee–job fit.** Individuals may have been hired for jobs they are not qualified to handle or to which they are tempermentally unsuited, or they may not have been provided with sufficient training for the roles expected of them. Generally, employees who are not capable of performing assigned roles are less willing to keep trying.

Another common factor influencing the size of the delivery gap is **role conflict.** Whether or not the knowledge gap has been closed, service providers may still see an inconsistency between what the service manager expects employees to provide and the service their customers actually want. A waiter who is expected to promote various items on the menu may alienate some customers who prefer

employee–job fit

The degree to which employees are able to perform a service to specifications.

role conflict

An inconsistency in service providers' minds between what the service manager expects them to provide and the service they think their customers actually want.

to make their own choices undisturbed. For example, how long does it take a McDonald's employee to finally realize that most customers really don't want an apple pie with their meal and are annoyed by the constant prompting? In some instances, customers even finish relaying their order by saying, "And no, I don't want an apple pie with that."

In more formal settings, persistent waiters may find customers retaliating by not leaving a tip. In other cases, the service provider may be expected to do too many kinds of work, such as simultaneously answering telephones and dealing with customers face to face in a busy office. If this kind of conflict continues to occur, employees become frustrated, gradually lose their commitment to providing the best service they can, and/or simply quit altogether.

Another cause of the delivery gap is **role ambiguity.** Role ambiguity results when employees, due to poor employee–job fit or inadequate training, do not understand the roles of their jobs or what their jobs are intended to accomplish. Sometimes, too, they are even unfamiliar with the service firm and its goals. Consequently, as role ambiguity increases, the delivery gap widens.

A further complication for employees is the **dispersion of control,** the situation in which control over the nature of the service being provided is removed from employees' hands. When employees are not allowed to make independent decisions about individual cases without first conferring with a manager, they may feel alienated from the service and less a part of their job. Furthermore, when control over certain aspects of the service is moved to a different location, such as control over credit being removed from individual bank branches, employee alienation is bound to increase. Employees experience **learned helplessness** and feel unable to respond to customer requests for help. Consequently, as the dispersion of control increases, the delivery gap becomes wider.

Finally, the delivery gap may also suffer due to **inadequate support,** such as not receiving personal training and/or technological and other resources necessary for employees to perform their jobs in the best possible manner. Even the best employees can be discouraged if they are forced to work with out-of-date or faulty equipment, especially if the employees of competing firms have superior resources and are able to provide the same or superior levels of service with far less effort. Failure to properly support employees leads to a lot of wasted effort, poor employee productivity, unsatisfied customers, and an increase in the size of the delivery gap.

THE COMMUNICATIONS GAP

The communications gap is the difference between the service the firm promises it will deliver through its external communications and the service it actually delivers to its customers. If advertising or sales promotions promise one kind of service and the consumer receives a different kind of service, the communications gap becomes wider. External communicators are essentially promises the firm makes to its customers. When the communications gap is wide, the firm has

role ambiguity

Uncertainty of employees' roles in their jobs and poor understanding of the purpose of their jobs.

disperson of control

The situation in which control over the nature of the service being provided is removed from employees' hands.

learned helplessness

The condition of employees who, through repeated dispersion of control, feel themselves unable to perform a service adequately.

inadequate support

A management failure to give employees personal training and/or technological and other resources necessary for them to perform their jobs in the best possible manner.

broken its promises, resulting in a lack of future customer trust. A customer who orders a bottle of wine from a menu only to be told it is out of stock may feel that the offer held out on the menu has not been fulfilled. A customer who is promised delivery in three days but who then has to wait a week will perceive service quality to be lower than expected.

overpromising
A firm's promise of more than it can deliver.

horizontal communication
The flow of internal communication between a firm's headquarters and its service firms in the field.

Factors Influencing the Communications Gap The communications gap is influenced primarily by two factors. The first, the propensity of the firm to **overpromise,** often occurs in highly competitive business environments as firms try to outdo one another in the name of recruiting new customers. The second factor pertains to the flow of **horizontal communication** within the firm. In other words, "Does the left hand know what the right hand is doing?" All too often, communications are developed at the firm's headquarters without conferring with service firms in the field. In some instances, new service programs are announced to the public by corporate headquarters before the local service firms are aware that the new programs exist. A lack of horizontal communication places an unsuspecting service provider in an awkward position when a customer requests the service promised and the provider has no idea what the customer is talking about.

Measuring Service Quality: SERVQUAL

Although measurements of customer satisfaction and service quality are both obtained by comparing perceptions to expectations, subtle differences between the two concepts are seen in their operational definitions. While satisfaction compares consumer perceptions to what consumers *would* normally expect, service quality compares perceptions to what a consumer *should* expect from a firm that delivers high-quality services. Given these definitions, service quality appears to measure a higher standard of service delivery.

SERVQUAL
A 44-item scale that measures customer expectations and perceptions regarding five service quality dimensions.

A frequently used and highly debated measure of service quality is the **SERVQUAL** scale.[7] According to its developers, SERVQUAL is a diagnostic tool that uncovers a firm's broad weaknesses and strengths in the area of service quality. The SERVQUAL instrument is based on five service quality dimensions that were obtained through extensive focus group interviews with consumers. The five dimensions include tangibles, reliability, responsiveness, assurance and empathy, and they provide the basic "skeleton" underlying service quality.

The SERVQUAL instrument consists of two sections: a 22-item section that records customer expectations of excellent firms in the specific service industry, and a second 22-item section that measures consumer perceptions of a particular company in that service industry (i.e., the firm being evaluated). Results from the two sections are then compared to arrive at "gap scores" for each of the five dimensions. The larger the gap, the farther consumer perceptions are from expectations, and the lower the service quality evaluation. In contrast, the smaller the gap, the higher the service quality evaluation. Customer expectations are measured on a 7-point scale with the anchor labels of "not at all essential" and "absolutely essential."[8] Similarly, customer perceptions are measured on another 7-point scale with anchor labels of "strongly agree" and "strongly disagree." Hence, SERVQUAL is a 44-item scale that measures customer expectations and perceptions regarding five service quality dimensions.

THE TANGIBLES DIMENSION

Because of the absence of a physical product, consumers often rely on the tangible evidence that surrounds the service in forming evaluations. The **tangibles dimension** of SERVQUAL compares consumer expectations and the firm's performance regarding the firm's ability to manage its tangibles. A firm's tangibles consist of a wide variety of objects such as carpeting, desks, lighting, wall colors, brochures, daily correspondence, and the appearance of the firm's personnel. Consequently, the tangibles component in SERVQUAL is two-dimensional—one focusing on equipment and facilities, the other focusing on personnel and communications materials.

tangibles dimension
The SERVQUAL assessment of a firm's ability to manage its tangibles.

The tangibles component of SERVQUAL is obtained via four expectations questions (E1–E4) and four perception questions (P1–P4). Keep in mind that the expectation questions apply to excellent firms within a particular industry, while the perception questions apply to the specific firm under investigation. Comparing the perception scores to the expectation scores provides a numerical variable that indicates the tangibles gap. The smaller the number, the smaller the gap, and the closer consumer perceptions are to their expectations. The questions that pertain to the tangibles dimension are as follows:[9]

TANGIBLES EXPECTATIONS:

E1.   Excellent companies will have modern-looking equipment.
E2.   The physical facilities at excellent companies will be visually appealing.
E3.   Employees of excellent companies will be neat in appearance.
E4.   Materials associated with the service (such as pamphlets or statements) will be visually appealing in an excellent company.

TANGIBLES PERCEPTIONS:

P1.   XYZ has modern-looking equipment.
P2.   XYZ's physical facilities are visually appealing.
P3.   XYZ's employees are neat in appearance.
P4.   Materials associated with the service (such as pamphlets or statements) are visually appealing at XYZ.

THE RELIABILITY DIMENSION

In general, reliability reflects the consistency and dependability of a firm's performance. Does the firm provide the same level of service time after time, or does quality dramatically vary with each encounter? Does the firm keep its promises, bill its customers accurately, keep accurate records, and perform the service correctly the first time? Nothing can be more frustrating for customers than unreliable service providers.

A constantly amazing observation is the number of businesses that fail to keep their promises. In many instances, the consumer is ready to spend money if only the service provider will show up and conduct the transaction as promised. As students, you may have experienced the reliability gap while attempting to have the local cable company install its services in your new apartment. Typically, the cable company will approximate the time at which the installer will come to your apartment in four-hour increments (e.g., morning or afternoon). In many cases, you may miss class or work waiting for the cable installer to arrive. All too often, the installer fails to show up during this time period and you must reschedule . . . missing yet more classes and/or time at work. Further aggravating this process is that you, the customer, must initiate the rescheduling process. Often the cable company offers no apology and provides little explanation other than, "Our installers are very busy."

reliability dimension
The SERVQUAL assessment of a firm's consistency and dependability in service performance.

Consumers perceive the **reliability dimension** to be the most important of the five SERVQUAL dimensions. Consequently, failure to provide reliable service generally translates into an unsuccessful firm. The questions used to assess the reliability gap are as follows:

RELIABILITY EXPECTATIONS:

E5.   When excellent companies promise to do something by a certain time, they will do so.

E6.   When customers have a problem, excellent companies will show a sincere interest in solving it.

E7.   Excellent companies will perform the service right the first time.

E8.   Excellent companies will provide their services at the time they promise to do so.

E9.   Excellent companies will insist on error-free records.

RELIABILITY PERCEPTIONS:

P5.   When XYZ promises to do something by a certain time, it does so.

P6.   When you have a problem, XYZ shows a sincere interest in solving it.

P7.   XYZ performs the service right the first time.

P8.   XYZ provides its services at the time it promises to do so.

P9.   XYZ insists on error-free records.

THE RESPONSIVENESS DIMENSION

**responsiveness
dimension**
The SERVQUAL assessment of a firm's commitment to providing its services in a timely manner.

Responsiveness reflects a service firm's commitment to provide its services in a timely manner. As such, the **responsiveness dimension** of SERVQUAL concerns the willingness and/or readiness of employees to provide a service. Occasionally, customers may encounter a situation in which employees are engaged in their own conversations with one another while ignoring the needs of the customer. Obviously, this is an example of unresponsiveness.

Responsiveness also reflects the preparedness of the firm to provide the service. Typically, new restaurants do not advertise their "opening night" so that the service delivery system can be fine-tuned and prepared to handle larger crowds, thereby minimizing service failures and subsequent customer complaints. The SERVQUAL expectation and perception items that address the responsiveness gap are as follows:

RESPONSIVENESS EXPECTATIONS:

E10. Employees of excellent companies will tell customers exactly when services will be performed.
E11. Employees of excellent companies will give prompt service to customers.
E12. Employees of excellent companies will always be willing to help customers.
E13. Employees of excellent companies will never be too busy to respond to customer requests.

RESPONSIVENESS PERCEPTIONS:

P10. Employees of XYZ tell you exactly when service will be performed.
P11. Employees of XYZ give you prompt service.
P12. Employees of XYZ are always willing to help you.
P13. Employees of XYZ are never too busy to respond to your requests.

THE ASSURANCE DIMENSION

SERVQUAL's **assurance dimension** addresses the competence of the firm, the courtesy it extends its customers, and the security of its operations. Competence pertains to the firm's knowledge and skill in performing its service. Does the firm possess the required skills to complete the service on a professional basis?

Courtesy refers to how the firm's personnel interact with the customer and the customer's possessions. As such, courtesy reflects politeness, friendliness, and consideration for the customer's property (e.g., a mechanic who places paper floormats in a customer's car so as to not soil the car's carpet).

Security is also an important component of the assurance dimension. Security reflects a customer's feelings that he or she is free from danger, risk, and doubt. Recent robberies at ATM locations provide ample evidence of the possible harm that may arise at service locations. In addition to physical danger, the security component of the assurance dimension also reflects financial risk issues (e.g., will the bank fail?) and confidentiality issues (e.g., are my medical records at the school's health center kept private?). The SERVQUAL items utilized to address the assurance gap are as follows:

assurance dimension
The SERVQUAL assessment of a firm's competence, courtesy to its customers, and security of its operations.

ASSURANCE EXPECTATIONS:

E14. The behavior of employees of excellent companies will instill confidence in customers.

E15. Customers of excellent companies will feel safe in their transactions.
E16. Employees of excellent companies will be consistently courteous with customers.
E17. Employees of excellent companies will have the knowledge to answer customer questions.

ASSURANCE PERCEPTIONS:

P14. The behavior of employees of XYZ instills confidence in customers.
P15. You feel safe in your transactions with XYZ.
P16. Employees of XYZ are consistently courteous with you.
P17. Employees of XYZ have the knowledge to answer your questions.

THE EMPATHY DIMENSION

Empathy is the ability to experience another's feelings as one's own. Empathetic firms have not lost touch of what it is like to be a customer of their own firm. As such, empathetic firms understand their customer needs and make their services accessible to their customers. In contrast, firms that do not provide their customers individualized attention when requested and that offer operating hours convenient to the firm and not its customers fail to demonstrate empathetic behaviors.

empathy dimension
The SERVQUAL assessment of a firm's ability to put itself in its customers' place.

The SERVQUAL **empathy dimension** addresses the empathy gap as follows:

EMPATHY EXPECTATIONS

E18. Excellent companies will give customers individual attention.
E19. Excellent companies will have operating hours convenient to all their customers.
E20. Excellent companies will have employees who give customers personal attention.
E21. Excellent companies will have the customer's best interest at heart.
E22. The employees of excellent companies will understand the specific needs of their customers.

EMPATHY PERCEPTIONS:

P18. XYZ gives you individual attention.
P19. XYZ has operating hours convenient to all its customers.
P20. XYZ has employees who give you personal attention.
P21. XYZ has your best interests at heart.
P22. Employees of XYZ understand your specific needs.

CRITICISMS OF SERVQUAL

Since the development of the SERVQUAL instrument, it has received its share of criticism.[10] The major criticisms of the instrument involve the length of the questionnaire, the validity of the five service quality dimensions, and the predictive power of the instrument in regard to subsequent consumer purchases. The following discussion focuses on each of these issues and their respective importance to interpreting SERVQUAL results.

Length of the Questionnaire Combining the expectation and perception items of SERVQUAL results in a 44-item survey instrument. Opponents of the SERVQUAL instrument argue that the 44 items are highly repetitive and unnecessarily increase the questionnaire's length. Opponents further argue that the expectations section of the instrument is of no real value and that the perceptions (actual performance) section should be utilized alone to assess service quality.[11]

In response, the developers of SERVQUAL effectively argue that including the expectations section enhances the managerial usefulness of the scale as a diagnostic tool due to the gap scores developed for each dimension. Perception scores alone merely rate whether the respondent agrees or disagrees with each question. For example, Table 12.1 provides a set of perception scores and SERVQUAL scores for a hypothetical firm. Utilizing this information for diagnostic purposes, perception scores alone would suggest placing an equal emphasis on improving the reliability and empathy dimensions. Incorporating expectations into the SERVQUAL score indicates that improving the reliability dimension should be the firm's top priority. Given that implementing service quality improvements requires a financial investment from the firm, maintaining the expectation section becomes valuable.

Creative suggestions have been made for maintaining the expectations component while at the same time reducing the questionnaire's length by 22 questions. Three approaches have been suggested: (1) On a single scale, ask respondents where they would rate a high-quality company and then where they would rate the firm under investigation; (2) utilize the scale's midpoint as the expected level of service from a high-quality company, and then rate the specific firm in relation to the midpoint—above expectation or below; and (3) utilize the end point (e.g., 7 on a 7-point scale) as the expected level of a high-quality company, and rate the specific company relative to the high-quality company on the same scale. All three approaches provide alternatives for assessing customer perceptions and expectations while reducing the questionnaire's length.

The Validity of the Five Dimensions Another frequent criticism of the SERVQUAL instrument is that the five proposed dimensions of service quality—reliability, responsiveness, assurance, empathy, and tangibles—do not hold up under statistical scrutiny. Consequently, opponents of SERVQUAL question the validity of the specific dimensions in the measurement instrument.

SERVQUAL's developers argue that although the five dimensions represent conceptually distinct facets of service quality, they are interrelated. Hence, some overlap may exist (as measured by correlations) among items that measure specific dimensions. In particular, the distinction among the responsiveness,

TABLE 12.1	THE DIAGNOSTIC ADVANTAGE OF SERVQUAL SCORES	
Dimension	Perception Scores	SERVQUAL Scores
Tangibles	5.3	0.0
Reliability	4.8	−1.7
Responsiveness	5.1	−1.0
Assurance	5.4	−1.5
Empathy	4.8	−1.1

assurance, and reliability dimensions tends to blur under statistical scrutiny. However, when respondents are asked to assign importance weights to each dimension, results indicate that consumers do indeed distinguish among the five dimensions, as exhibited in Table 12.2. According to the developers of SERVQUAL, this ranking provides additional evidence of the dimensions' distinctiveness. For the statistical enthusiast, a variety of articles offering additional evidence and rationale supporting the viability of the five-dimensional framework is cited in the "Notes" section located at the end of the chapter.[12]

The Predictive Power of SERVQUAL The third major criticism of SERVQUAL pertains to the instrument's ability to predict consumer purchase intentions. Research has indicated that the performance (perceptions) section alone of the SERVQUAL scale is a better predictor of purchase intentions than the combined expectations-minus-perception instrument. As such, opponents of the SERVQUAL instrument conclude that satisfaction has a more significant effect on purchase intentions than does service quality. Consequently, they assert that managers need to emphasize customer satisfaction programs over strategies focusing solely on service quality.

The developers of SERVQUAL once again take issue with the preceding objections based on a variety of conceptual, methodological, analytical, and practical issues. Consequently, the jury is still out regarding this particular objection. From a managerial standpoint, perhaps the SERVQUAL proponents' most important counterpoint is the diagnostic value of the expectations-minus-perceptions approach. Based on information provided earlier, the developers of SERVQUAL make a convincing argument that incorporating customer expectations provides richer information than does examining the perceptions scores alone.

SERVQUAL: SOME FINAL THOUGHTS

The Importance of Contact Personnel The SERVQUAL instrument highlights several points that service providers should consider when examining service quality. First, customer perceptions of service are heavily dependent on the attitudes and

TABLE 12.2	RELATIVE IMPORTANCE OF SERVQUAL DIMENSIONS AS REPORTED BY CONSUMERS

SERVQUAL Dimension	Importance (%)*
Reliability	(32%)
Responsiveness	(22%)
Assurance	(19%)
Empathy	(16%)
Tangibles	(11%)

*Consumers were asked to allocate 100 points among the five dimensions. The Importance (%) reflects the mean point allocation for each dimension.

Source: Leonard L. Berry, A. Parasuraman, and Valerie A. Zeithaml, "Improving Service Quality in America: Lessons Learned," *Academy of Management Executive* 8,2 (1994), pp. 32–52.

performance of contact personnel. Of the five dimensions measured, responsiveness, empathy, and assurance directly reflect the interaction between customers and staff. Even tangibles depend partly on the appearance, dress, and hygiene of the service staff.

Process Is as Important as Outcome Second, the ways in which customers judge a service depends as much on the service process as on the outcome. How the service is delivered is as important as the frequency and nature of the service. Customer satisfaction depends on the production of services as well as their consumption.

Viewing services as a process raises considerable difficulties for management when trying to write service quality standards. Standards can be examined either from the perspective of the consumer or from that of the operating system. Thus, a specification can be written based on consumers' ratings of the responsiveness of the organization. Unfortunately, although this is a quantitative measure, it does little to guide the behavior of operations managers and contact personnel.

Consumer Perceptions Are Unpredictable Ratings of service quality dimensions may be influenced by factors outside the control of the organization that may not be readily apparent to managers. For example, consumer moods and attitudes may influence ratings. Studies have shown that when rating services, consumers use a diverse variety of clues. A recent study shows that, even if a service firm generates a negative disconfirmation for a consumer, it may not be judged as delivering a poor level of satisfaction. Since they are part of the process, consumers may attribute failures to themselves or to factors outside the control of the firm. Such attributions are shown to depend on the physical characteristics of the service firm. For example, a tidy office setting leads negative attributions away from the firm, while a messy office generates attributions of dissatisfaction toward the firm.[13]

▶▶▶▶ ◀◀◀◀

Assessing the Criticisms of SERVQUAL Finally, the criticisms of SERVQUAL should not be taken lightly. As is the case with most measurement scales, constructive criticisms assist in the further development of improved measurement instruments. Moreover, concerns regarding measurement instruments should remind practitioners that firms should not "live or die" and make drastic decisions based solely on *one* measurement instrument's results. The value of measurement tools is that they provide management the opportunity to make a more informed decision.

Despite its opponents, SERVQUAL remains a frequently utilized instrument to assess service quality. From the beginning, its developers have claimed that SERVQUAL is a useful starting point for measuring service quality and was never presented as "the final answer." The developers of SERVQUAL further contend that when used in conjunction with other forms of measurement, both quantitative and qualitative, SERVQUAL provides a valuable diagnostic tool for evaluating the firm's service quality performance. Overall, as was the case with satisfaction measures, SERVQUAL is most valuable when compared with a firm's own past service quality trends and when compared with measures of competitive service quality performance.

SERVICE QUALITY INFORMATION SYSTEMS

**service quality
information system**
An ongoing research process
that provides relevant data on a
timely basis to managers, who
use the data in decision making.

A **service quality information system** is an ongoing research process that provides relevant data on a timely basis to managers, who utilize the data for decision-making purposes.[14] More specifically, service quality information systems utilize service quality and customer satisfaction measures in conjunction with other measures obtained at various points to assess the firm's overall performance. Components of a service quality information system include (1) reports on solicitation of customer complaints; (2) after-sales surveys; (3) customer focus group interviews; (4) mystery shopping results; (5) employee surveys; and (6) total market service quality surveys.

customer research
Research that examines the
customer's perspective of a
firm's strengths and weaknesses.

In general, service quality information systems focus on two types of research: customer research and noncustomer research. **Customer research** examines the customer's perspective of a firm's strengths and weaknesses and includes such measures as customer complaints, after-sales surveys, focus group interviews, and service quality surveys. In contrast, **noncustomer research** focuses on employee perspectives of the firm's strengths and weaknesses and employee performance (e.g., employee surveys and mystery shopping). In addition, noncustomer research examines how competitors perform on service (via total market service quality surveys) and serves as a basis for comparison.

noncustomer research
Research that examines how
competitors perform on service
and how employees view the
firm's strengths and weaknesses.

SOLICITATION OF CUSTOMER COMPLAINTS

The primary objectives of soliciting customer complaints are twofold. First, customer complaints identify unhappy customers. The firm's follow-up efforts may enable it to retain many of these customers before they defect to competitors. The second objective of soliciting customer complaints is to identify weaknesses in the firm's service delivery system and take the corrective actions necessary to minimize future occurrences of the same problem. Customer complaints should be solicited on a continuous basis.

The value of continuous customer feedback cannot be understated. Unfortunately, many firms address one complaint at a time and fail to analyze the content of the complaints as a group. The Chicago Marriott took 15 years to figure out that 66 percent of the calls to its customer service line concerned requests for an iron or ironing board.[15] As a result of learning this, the hotel redesignated $20,000 that had been earmarked for color televisions in guest bathrooms to purchase irons and ironing boards for the hotel. Interestingly, few, if any, customers had ever complained about the black-and-white televisions in the bathrooms. If the color televisions had been installed, we would have seen a classic example of a firm defining service quality on its own as opposed to listening to the voice of the customer. Chapter Thirteen takes an in-depth look at analyzing customer complaints and developing effective recovery strategies for use when service failures do occur.

AFTER-SALES SURVEYS

As part of the service quality information system, **after-sales surveys** should also be conducted on a continuous basis. Since after-sales surveys pertain to discrete transactions, they are a type of satisfaction survey and, as such, are subject to the advantages and disadvantages of all customer satisfaction surveys discussed in Chapter Eleven. For example, after-sales surveys address customer satisfaction while the service encounter is still fresh in the customer's mind. Consequently, the information reflects the firm's recent performance but may be biased by the customer's inadvertent attempt to minimize cognitive dissonance.

Although after-sales surveys can also identify areas for improvement, after-sales surveys are a more proactive approach to assessing customer satisfaction than is soliciting customer complaints. Many firms wait for customers to complain and then take action based on those complaints. Given the average customer's reluctance to complain, waiting for customer complaints does not provide the firm a "true" picture of its performance. The after-sale survey attempts to contact every customer and take corrective action if a customer is less than satisfied with his or her purchase decision.

CUSTOMER FOCUS GROUP INTERVIEWS

Another important component of the service quality information system involves customer **focus group interviews**.[16] Focus group interviews are informal discussions with eight to twelve customers that are usually guided by a trained moderator. Participants in the group are encouraged to express their views and to

after-sales surveys
A type of satisfaction survey that addresses customer satisfaction while the service encounter is still fresh in the customer's mind.

focus group interviews
Informal discussions with eight to twelve customers that are usually guided by a trained moderator; used to identify areas of information to be collected in subsequent survey research.

▶▶▶▶ ◀◀◀◀

comment on the suggestions made by others in the group. Because of the group interaction, customers tend to feel more comfortable, which motivates them to talk more openly and honestly. Consequently, researchers feel that the information obtained via focus group interviews is richer than data that reflects the opinions of a single individual.

Focus groups are probably the most widely used market research method. However, their primary purpose is to identify areas of information to be collected in subsequent survey research. Although the information provided by the group is considered very valuable, other forms of research are generally necessary to confirm that the groups' ideas reflect the feelings of the broader segment of customers. Advocates of service quality information systems believe that customer focus groups should be conducted on a monthly basis.

MYSTERY SHOPPING

mystery shopping

A form of noncustomer research that consists of trained personnel who pose as customers, shop at the firm unannounced, and evaluate employees.

Mystery shopping is a form of noncustomer research that measures individual employee service behavior. As the name indicates, mystery shoppers are generally trained personnel who pose as customers and who shop at the firm unannounced. The idea is to evaluate an individual employee during an actual service encounter. Mystery shoppers evaluate employees on a number of characteristics, such as: the time it takes for the employee to acknowledge the customer, eye contact, appearance, and numerous other specific customer service and sales techniques promoted by the firm.

Mystery shopping is a form of observation research and is recommended to be conducted on a quarterly basis. Results obtained from mystery shoppers are used as constructive employee feedback. Consequently, mystery shopping aids the firm in coaching, training, evaluating, and formally recognizing its employees.

EMPLOYEE SURVEYS

Another vital component of the service quality information system is employee research. When the product is a performance, it is essential that the company listen to the performers. Too often, employees are forgotten in the quest for customer satisfaction. However, the reality is that employee satisfaction with the firm directly corresponds with customer satisfaction. Hence, the lesson to be learned by service firms is that if they want the needs of their customers to come first, they cannot place the needs of their employees last.

employee surveys

Internal measures of service quality concerning employee morale, attitudes, and perceived obstacles to the provision of quality services.

Conducted quarterly, **employee surveys** provide an internal measure of service quality concerning employee morale, attitudes, and perceived obstacles to the provision of quality services. Often employees would like to provide a higher level of quality service but feel that their hands are tied by internal regulations and policies. Employee surveys provide the means to uncover these obstacles so that they can be removed when appropriate. Moreover, employees are customers of internal service and assess internal service quality. Because of their direct involvement in

Focus groups can provide
invaluable feedback to
service firms. A roundtable
format with participants and
a facilitator helps identify
areas that need to be
improved, ways the service
firm best meets the
customers' needs, and other
valuable information.

Source: © 1995 PhotoDisc, Inc. Image no. 14119.

providing service delivery, employee complaints serve as an early warning system; that is, employees often see the system breaking down before customers do.

TOTAL MARKET SERVICE QUALITY SURVEYS

Total market service quality surveys not only measure the service quality of the firm sponsoring the survey but also assess the perceived service quality of the firm's competitors. When service quality measures such as SERVQUAL are used in conjunction with other measures, a firm can evaluate its own performance compared with previous time periods and with its competitors. Service quality surveys provide a firm with information about needed improvements in the service delivery system, plus measure the progress in making needed improvements that have been previously identified.

Advocates of the service quality information system recommend that total market service quality surveys be conducted three times a year. However, as is the case with all the components of the service quality information system, the recommended frequencies are dependent upon the size of the customer base. Too frequent contact with the same customers can be an annoyance to them. On the other hand, conducting surveys too infrequently may ultimately cost the business its existence.

Overall, the service quality information system provides a comprehensive look at the firm's performance and overcomes many of the shortcomings of individual

**total market service
quality surveys**
Surveys that measure the
service quality of the firm
sponsoring the survey *and* the
service quality of the firm's
competitors.

measures used in isolation. As with all measures, the information system's true value lies in the information it gives managers to help in their decision making. The measures should serve as a support system for decisions but not be the only inputs into the decision process. Managerial expertise and intuition remain critical components of every business decision. Ultimately, the key components that need to be built into every service quality system include the following:[17]

Listening: Quality is defined by the customer. Conformance to company specifications is not quality; conformance to customers' specifications is. Spending wisely to improve service comes from continuous learning about expectations and perceptions of customers and manufacturers.

Reliability: Reliability is the core of service quality. Little else matters to a customer when the service is unreliable.

Basic Service: Forget the frills if you cannot deliver the basics. American service customers want the basics; they expect fundamentals, not fanciness, performance, not empty promises.

Service Design: Reliably delivering the basic service that customers expect depends, in part, on how well various elements function together in a service system. Design flaws in any part of a service system can reduce the perception of quality.

Recovery: Research shows that companies consistently receive the most unfavorable service quality scores from customers whose problems were not resolved satisfactorily. In effect, companies that do not respond effectively to customer complaints compound the service failure, thereby failing twice.

Surprising Customers: Exceeding customers' expectations requires the element of surprise. If service organizations can not only be reliable in output but also surprise the customer in the way the service is delivered, then they are truly excellent.

Fair Play: Customers expect service companies to treat them fairly and become resentful and mistrustful when they perceive they are being treated otherwise.

Teamwork: The presence of "teammates" is an important dynamic in sustaining a server's motivation to serve. Service team building should not be left to chance.

Employee Research: Employee Research is as important to service improvement as customer research is.

Servant Leadership: Delivering excellent service requires a special form of leadership. Leadership must serve the servers, inspiring and enabling them to achieve.

SUMMARY

This chapter has focused on defining and measuring service quality. The concepts of service quality and customer satisfaction, discussed in Chapter Eleven, are intertwined. In general, customer satisfaction can be defined as a short-term, transaction-specific measure. In turn, service quality is a long-term, overall measure. Another difference is that satisfaction compares perceptions to what consumers *would* normally expect. In comparison, service quality compares perceptions to what a customer *should* expect from a high-quality firm. Customer satisfaction and service quality assessments compliment each other. Satisfaction evaluations made after each service transaction help revise customers' overall service quality evaluations of the firm's performance.

Firms that excel in service quality do so by avoiding potential quality gaps in their delivery systems. Service quality gaps discussed in this chapter include knowledge, standards, delivery, and communication. Numerous managerial, marketing, and operational factors influence the size of each of these gaps. Ultimately, the goal of every firm is to minimize the service gap—the difference between customer perceptions and expectations. The service gap is a function of the knowledge, standards, delivery, and communication gaps and responds accordingly in the combined direction of the four gaps.

One popular method for assessing service quality is the SERVQUAL scale. The original SERVQUAL survey instrument consists of 44 questions that compare consumers' expectations to perceptions along five service quality dimensions— tangibles, responsiveness, reliability, assurance, and empathy. Gap scores for each of the five dimensions can be calculated by comparing consumer expectation and perception ratings. The SERVQUAL gaps indicate specific areas in need of improvement and assist the service firm in its continuous improvement efforts.

SERVQUAL is only one method to assess a firm's service quality. A service quality information system utilizes a variety of continuous measures to assess the firm's overall performance. The major components of such a system collect information about both customer and noncustomer research. Customer research methods include analyzing customer complaints, after-sales surveys, focus group interviews, and service quality surveys. Noncustomer research methods include employee surveys and mystery shopping.

In sum, service quality offers a means of achieving success among competing firms that offer similar products. The benefits associated with service quality include increases in market share and repeat purchases. Ultimately, the keys to delivering service quality are a detailed understanding of the needs of the consumer, service providers who are focused on providing quality, and service delivery systems that are designed to support the firm's overall quality mission.

KEY TERMS

service quality

service gap

knowledge gap

standards gap

delivery gap

communications gap

research orientation

overpromising

horizontal communication

SERVQUAL

tangibles dimension

reliability dimension

responsiveness dimension

assurance dimension

DEFINING AND
MEASURING SERVICE
QUALITY

upward communication
levels of management
willingness to perform
employee–job fit
role conflict
role ambiguity
dispersion of control
learned helplessness
inadequate support

empathy dimension
service quality information system
customer research
noncustomer research
after-sales surveys
focus group interviews
mystery shopping
employee surveys
total market service quality surveys

REVIEW QUESTIONS

1. What are the basic differences between customer satisfaction and service quality?

2. Explain how a manager might use the conceptual model of service quality to improve the quality of his/her own firm.

3. What factors contribute to the size of the knowledge gap?

4. Discuss the basics of the SERVQUAL measurement instrument.

5. Develop specifications for the role of a "good student."

6. What are the criticisms of SERVQUAL? What are its developers' responses to these criticisms?

7. You have been hired by a firm to develop the firm's service quality information system. What are the components of this system?

NOTES

1. J. Joseph Cronin, Jr., and Steven A. Taylor, "Measuring Service Quality: A Reexamination and Extension," *Journal of Marketing* 56 (July 1992), p. 55.

2. Thomas A. Stewart, "After All You've Done for Your Customers, Why Are They Still NOT HAPPY," *Fortune*, December 11, 1995, pp. 178–182.

3. Cronin, Jr., and Taylor, "Measuring Service Quality," pp. 60–63.

4. Ibid.

5. This section was adapted from John E. G. Bateson, *Managing Services Marketing*, 3rd ed. (Fort Worth, TX: The Dryden Press, 1995), pp. 558–565.

6. A. Parasuraman, Valerie A. Zeithaml, and Leonard L. Berry, "A Conceptual Model of Service Quality and Its Implications for Future Research," *Journal of Marketing* 49, (Fall 1985), pp. 41–50.

7. A. Parasuraman, Leonard L. Berry, and Valerie A. Zeithaml, "SERVQUAL: A Multiple-Item Scale for Measuring Customer Perceptions of Service Quality," *Journal of Retailing* 64,1 (1988), pp. 12–40.

8. Parasuraman, Zeithaml, and Berry, "A Conceptual Model."

9. Scale items from A. Parasuraman, Leonard L. Berry, and Valerie A. Zeithaml, "Refinement and Reassessment of the SERVQUAL Scale," *Journal of Retailing* 67 (Winter 1991), pp. 420–450.

10. Cronin, Jr., and Taylor, "Measuring Service Quality," pp. 60–63.

11. A. Parasuraman, Valerie A. Zeithaml, and Leonard L. Berry, "Reassessment of Expectations as a Comparison Standard in Measuring Service Quality: Implications for Future Research," *Journal of Marketing,* 58 (January 1994), pp. 111–124.

12. See A. Parasuraman, Leonard L. Berry, and Valerie A. Zeithaml, "Refinement and Reassessment of the SERVQUAL Scale," *Journal of Retailing,* pp. 420–450; A. Parasuraman, Leonard L. Berry, and Valerie A. Zeithaml, "More On Improving Service Quality Measurement," *Journal of Retailing* 69,1 (Spring 1993) pp. 140+; and A. Parasuraman, Valerie A. Zeithaml, and Leonard L. Berry, "Reassessment of Expectations as a Comparison Standard in Measuring Service Quality: Implications for Future Research," *Journal of Marketing* 58 (January 1994), pp. 111–124.

13. Mary Jo Bitner, "Evaluating Service Encounters: The Effects of Physical Surroundings and Employee Responses," *Journal of Marketing* (April 1990), pp. 42–50.

14. Leonard L. Berry, A. Parasuraman, and Valerie A. Zeithaml, "Improving Service Quality in America: Lessons Learned," *Academy of Management Executive* 8,2 (1994), pp. 32–52.

15. Ibid., p. 33.

16. Adapted from Henry Assael, *Marketing Principles & Strategy,* 2nd ed. (Fort Worth, TX: The Dryden Press, 1993), p. 226; and Michael Levy and Barton Weitz, *Retailing Management,* (Homewood, IL: Irwin, 1992), p. 149.

17. Berry, Parasuraman, and Zeithaml, "Improving Service Quality," pp. 32–52.

13

SERVICE FAILURES AND RECOVERY STRATEGIES

"*Don't fight a battle if you don't gain anything by winning.*"

General George S. Patton, Jr.

CHAPTER OBJECTIVES

The major objectives of this chapter are to introduce the concepts of service failures, consumer complaint behavior, service recovery strategies, and procedures for tracking and monitoring service failures and employee recovery efforts.

After reading this chapter, you should be able to

▶ Specify the different categories of service failures.

▶ *Discuss the reasons customers complain.*

▶ Discuss the reasons customers do not complain.

▶ *Describe tactics that are successful as service recovery efforts.*

▶ Discuss the value of tracking and monitoring service failures and employee recovery efforts.

Is This Any Way to Run an Airline?

The following letters are detailed accounts of an actual service encounter and the company's response to the service failures.

July 23, 199x

Dear Customer Service Manager:

Through the Carolina Motor Club my wife and I booked round-trip first-class and clipper-class seats on the following World Airlines flights on the dates indicated:

1 July	World Airlines	3072	Charlotte to Kennedy
1 July	World Airlines	86	Kennedy to Munich
21 July	World Airlines	87	Munich to Kennedy
21 July	World Airlines	3073	Kennedy to Charlotte

We additionally booked connecting flights to and from Wilmington and Charlotte on Trans Air flights 263 (on 1 July) and 2208 (on 21 July).

The outbound flights 3072 and 86 seemed pleasant enough, especially since World Airlines had upgraded our clipper-class seats on flight 86 to first class. However, midflight on 86 we discovered that we had been food poisoned on flight 3072, apparently by the seafood salad that was served in first class that day (it seemed warm to us and we hesitated to eat it but unfortunately did so anyway). My wife was so ill that, trying to get to the restroom to throw up, she passed out cold, hitting her head and, we discovered over the next few days, apparently damaging her back. The flight attendants were very concerned and immediately tried to help her, but there was nothing they could do except help her clean herself up and get the food off her from the food trays she hit. In addition to the nausea and diarrhea, she had a large knot on her head and headaches for several days. Her lower back has been in constant pain ever since. I, too, was very ill for several days. A nice start for a vacation! But it gets worse.

During the long layover between flights at Kennedy, there was a tremendous rainstorm, and our baggage apparently was left out in it, a situation that we discovered when we arrived at our first night's lodging and discovered ALL of our clothing was literally wringing wet. In addition, four art prints we were bringing as gifts for friends were ruined.

The return flights were better only in that we did not get poisoned; instead we did not get fed! Flight 87 out of Munich was apparently short-handed and due to our seating location, the flight attendant who had to do double duty always got to us last. We had to ask for drinks; there were no hot towels left for us; the meals ran out and we were given no choice but an overdone piece of gray meat with tomato sauce on it—we tasted it, but it was odd tasting and given our experience on flight 3072, we were afraid to eat it.

Flight 87 was delayed in boarding due to the slowness in cleaning the aircraft (according to an announcement made) and also due to the late arrival of the crew. In addition, the flight was further delayed due to a heavy rainstorm, which backed up traffic for takeoff. However, had the flight boarded on time it would have not lost its takeoff priority and could likely have taken off two hours sooner than it did. We might have been able to make our connection in Charlotte. Onboard the flight, the plane was the dirtiest and in the most disrepair of any aircraft I have ever flown on—peeling wall coverings, litter on floor, overhead bins taped shut with duct tape, etc. As a first-class passenger I asked for some cold beer while we were waiting for the rest of the passengers to board; it was warm. We were quite hungry, having not eaten much in the past 12 hours, and asked for some peanuts; there were none; the plane had not been stocked. I asked for a pillow and blanket for my wife; there was none. What a great first-class section! There were only three flight attendants for the whole plane, and I felt sorry for the pregnant one who had to do double duty in first class and the rear cabin. She was very sympathetic to the poor conditions; I don't see how you keep employees when they are treated like that.

Due to the excess delay at Kennedy, flight 87 was very late and we could not make our connection from Charlotte to Wilmington. As it turned out, we would have barely been able to make it if the flight had been on time because World Airlines had changed not only the flight numbers but also the flight times on the Kennedy-Charlotte leg of our journey—AND WE WERE NEVER NOTIFIED OF THIS CHANGE UNTIL WE ARRIVED AT THE AIRPORT! I deplaned in Raleigh to try to alert the people meeting us in Wilmington that we would not be in that night; however, it was too late and they had already gone to the airport. The gate attendant at Raleigh assured me that World Airlines would put us up for the night in Charlotte, so I returned to the plane. However, when we arrived in Charlotte, the World Airlines representative refused to take care of us stating that, since we had not booked the Wilmington-Charlotte portion of our trip through World Airlines, "it is not our problem." Furthermore, he tried to wash his hands of it, saying we had an "illegal connection" due to the times between flights and that he wouldn't provide lodging and meals. After I pointed out to him at least three times that the connection was not illegal when booked and World Airlines changed its flight times without notifying us, and further made it clear that not only was I not going to go away, but that there was going to be a lot more said about the matter, he finally capitulated and gave us a voucher.

After traveling for 24 hours, receiving lousy service, poor food, no amenities, it is a real pleasure to run into an argumentative SOB like your agent in Charlotte. He should be fired!!! As first-class passengers we have been treated like cattle! But, it does not end here.

Upon arriving in Wilmington the next morning, only two of our four bags arrived with us. We had to initiate a baggage trace action. Our missing bags were finally delivered to our house around 3:00 p.m. on 23 July. And SURPRISE, they were left out in the rain at Kennedy again and EVERYTHING was so wet that water poured out of the pockets. I poured water out of the hairdryer. All of our paper purchases, maps, guide books, photos, souvenir brochures, etc. are ruined. I don't know yet if the dryer, radio, electric toothbrush, voltage converters, etc., will work—they are drying out as this is being written. In addition, my brand new bag now has a hole in the bottom of a corner where it was obvious that World Airline baggage handlers dragged it on the tarmac (obviously a water-logged dufflebag-size piece of luggage is too heavy to lift).

As near as I can figure, we have lost at least a roll of color prints (irreplace-able); approximately $100.00 in travel guides and tour books, many souvenir booklets, brochures, menus, etc.; $100.00 in art prints; $50.00 in damage to luggage; an unknown amount in electronics that may not work; a lot of enjoy-ment due to pain and suffering resulting from illness and injury (bill for x-rays enclosed); and all sense of humor and patience for such inexcusable treatment by an airline.

If there is to be any compensation for what we have suffered it should be in monetary form. There is no recapturing the lost time and pleasure on the vacation. The art, books, etc. (except for the photos) can be replaced . . . assuming we should make such a trip again. But if we do, you can be assured we would not choose World Airlines.

In closing, I am particularly angry and adamant about this whole fiasco as we wanted this vacation to be special and treated ourselves to the luxury of first-class treatment . . . which we got everywhere except on World Airlines . . . it is almost unbelievable how poorly we were treated by your airline, almost a perfect negative case study in customer service. I have purposely tried to mention every little nit-picky thing I can recall because I want you to realize just how totally bad this whole experience has been!

In disgust,

J. Q. Customer

WORLD AIRLINE'S RECOVERY STRATEGY

The following is World Airline's actual response, which occurred approxi-mately two and three months following the customer's letter. The first letter was written by the Claims Manager, and the second by the Customer Relations Manager.

September 25, 199x

Dear Mr. and Mrs. Customer:

This letter confirms the settlement agreed upon during our phone conversation just concluded.

Accordingly, we have prepared and enclosed (in duplicate) a General Release for $2,000.00. Both you and your wife should sign in the presence of a Notary Public, have your signatures notarized, and return the Original to this office, keeping the copy for your records.

As soon as we receive the notarized Release, we will forward our draft for $2000.00.

Again, our sincerest apologies to Mrs. Customer. It will be most helpful for our Customer Relations staff if you included with the Release copies of all available travel documents.

Very truly yours,

Manager–Claims

October 12, 199x

Dear Mr. Customer:

Let me begin by apologizing for this delayed response and all of the unfortunate incidents that you described in your letter. Although we try to make our flights as enjoyable as possible, we obviously failed on this occasion.

Our claims manager informs me that you have worked out a potential settlement for the matter regarding the food poisoning. We regret you were not able to enjoy the food service on the other flights on your itinerary because of it. I assure you that such incidents are a rare occurrence and that much time and effort is expended to ensure that our catering is of the finest quality.

Fewer things can be more irritating than faulty baggage handling. Only in an ideal world could we say that baggage will never again be damaged. Still, we are striving to ensure baggage is handled in such a way that if damage should occur, it will be minimized.

Flight disruptions caused by weather conditions can be particularly frustrating since, despite advanced technology, accurate forecasts for resumption of full operations cannot always be obtained as rapidly as one would wish. These disruptions are, of course, beyond the airlines' control. Safety is paramount in such situations and we sincerely regret the inconvenience caused.

We make every reasonable effort to lessen the inconvenience to passengers who are affected by schedule changes. Our practice is, in fact, to advise passengers of such changes when we have a local contact for them and time permits. We also try to obtain satisfactory alternative reservations. We are reviewing our schedule change requirements with all personnel concerned and will take whatever corrective measures are necessary to ensure that a similar problem does not arise in the future.

You made it clear in your letter that the interior of our aircraft was not attractive. We know that aircraft appearance is a reflection of our professionalism. We regret that our airplane did not measure up to our standards since we place great emphasis on cabin maintenance and cleanliness. Please be assured that this particular matter is being investigated by the responsible management and corrective action will be taken.

As tangible evidence of our concern over your unpleasant trip. I have enclosed two travel vouchers, which may be exchanged for 2 first-class tickets anywhere that World Airlines flies. Once again, please accept our humble apology. We hope for the opportunity to restore your faith in World Airlines by providing you with completely carefree travel.

Sincerely,

Customer Relations Manager

Epilogue

World Airlines filed for bankruptcy within 24 months after this incident.

Source: Richard A. Engdahl and K. Douglas Hoffman, "World Airlines: A Customer Service Air Disaster," in Carol A. Anderson, *Retailing: Concepts, Strategy, and Information* (Minneapolis/St. Paul: West, 1993), pp. 215–218.

INTRODUCTION

Despite the service firm's best efforts, service failures are inevitable. Planes are late, employees are rude or inattentive, and the maintenance of the tangibles surrounding the service is not always perfect. Don't give up! Developing an indifferent attitude or accepting service failures as a part of everyday business can be "the kiss of death." The secrets to success are to take a proactive stance to reduce the occurrence of **service failures** and to equip employees with a set of effective recovery tools to repair the service encounter when failures do occur.

service failures
Breakdowns in the delivery of service; service that does not meet customer expectations.

The reasons failures are inherent events in the service encounter are directly related to the unique characteristics that distinguish services from goods. Due to intangibility, customer comparison of perceptions to expectations is a highly subjective evaluation; consequently, not all customers are going to be satisfied. Due to heterogeneity, variations in the service delivery process are going to occur, and not every service encounter is going to be identical. Due to perishability, supply and demand match each other only by accident. Hence, service customers will experience delays from time to time, and service workers will occasionally lose their patience while attempting to appease an overabundance of anxious customers. Finally, inseparability places the service provider face-to-face with the customer, which provides a Pandora's box of failure possibilities.

CRITICAL INCIDENTS

Service failures occur at **critical incidents** in the service encounter. Every service encounter is made up of numerous critical incidents, or "moments of truth," the moments of interaction between the customer and the firm. In the opening vignette, the critical incidents that resulted in service failures included poor food preparation, mishandled luggage, overworked flight attendants, out-of-stock conditions concerning a variety of items, slow service, poorly managed physical facilities, unannounced flight schedule changes, and an unsympathetic and uncooperative company representative. The opening vignette is an excellent example of the variety of "moments of truth" a successful firm needs to effectively manage.

critical incidents
The moments of actual interaction between the customer and the firm.

TYPES OF SERVICE FAILURES

Employee responses to service failures are related directly to customer satisfaction and dissatisfaction. Service failures are generally categorized into one of three main categories: (1) responses to service delivery system failures; (2) responses to customer needs and requests; and (3) unprompted and unsolicited employee actions (see Figure 13.1).[1]

FIGURE 13.1

INCIDENT SORTING PROCESS

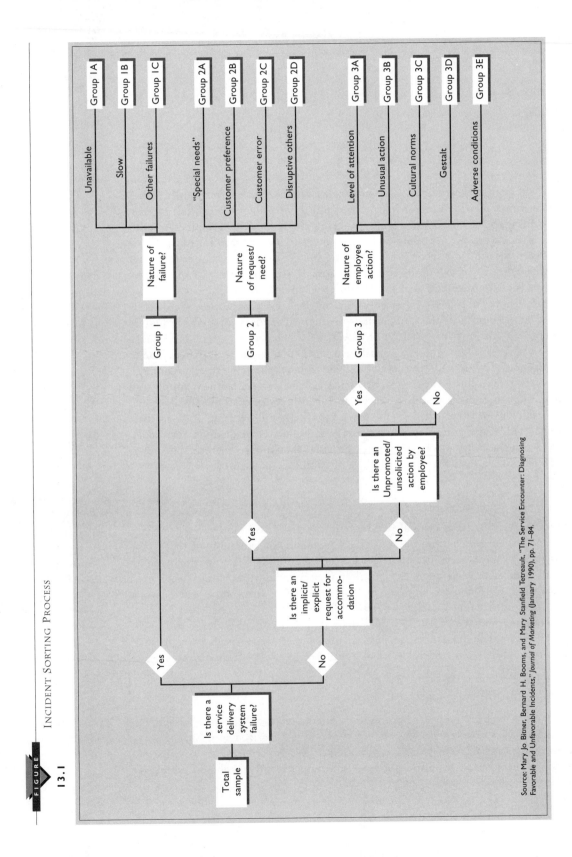

Source: Mary Jo Bitner, Bernard H. Booms, and Mary Stanfield Tetreault, "The Service Encounter: Diagnosing Favorable and Unfavorable Incidents," *Journal of Marketing* (January 1990), pp. 71–84.

Service delivery **system failures** are failures in the core service offering of the firm. In the airline horror story presented in the opening vignette, service delivery system failures included providing spoiled food and warm beer, the mishandling of baggage, the unannounced change in flight schedules, the condition of the plane, the inadequate stock of food supplies, blankets, and pillows, and the shortage in the number of of flight attendants adequate to meet the needs of passengers. All these activities are directly tied to the core service of the airline.

In general, service delivery system failures consist of employee responses to three types of failures: (1) unavailable service, (2) unreasonably slow service, and (3) other core service failures. **Unavailable service** refers to services normally available that are lacking or absent. **Unreasonably slow service** concerns services or employees that customers perceive as being extraordinary slow in fulfilling their function. **Other core service failures** encompass all other core service failures. This category is deliberately broad to reflect the various core services offered by different industries (e.g., the food was cold, the plane was dirty, and the baggage was mishandled).

The second type of service failure, responses to **customer needs and requests,** pertains to employee responses to individual consumer needs and special requests. Consumer needs can be implicit or explicit. **Implicit needs** are not requested. For example, in the opening vignette, when the wife of the airline customer became sick and fainted, her implicit needs were readily apparent. The flight attendants immediately came to her aid to help her clean up and expressed genuine concern for her health. Despite all the failures that occurred, the customer noted and appreciated the employees' response to this particular failure. The airline also failed to meet an implicit need when the flight schedule was changed and the airline failed to notify its customers so that alternative connecting flights could be arranged. In contrast, **explicit requests** are overtly requested. The airline employee in Charlotte who initially refused to provide the couple with vouchers for a night's lodging failed to accommodate the passengers' explicit request.

In general, customer needs and requests consist of employee responses to four types of possible failures: (1) special needs; (2) customer preferences; (3) customer errors; and (4) disruptive others. Employee responses to **special needs** involve complying with requests based on a customer's special medical, dietary, psychological, language, or sociological difficulties. Preparing a meal for a vegetarian would fulfill a "special request." Employee responses to **customer preferences** require the employee to modify the service delivery system in some way that meets the preferred needs of the customer. A customer request for a substitution at a restaurant is a typical example of a customer preference. An employee response to a **customer error** involves a scenario in which the failure is initiated by an admitted customer mistake (e.g., lost tickets, lost hotel key, forgot to tell the waitress to "hold the mustard"). Finally, employee responses to **disruptive others** require employees to settle disputes

system failures

Failures in the core service offering of the firm.

unavailable service

Services normally available that are lacking or absent.

unreasonably slow service

Services or employees that customers perceive as being extraordinarily slow in fulfilling their function.

other core service failures

All remaining core service breakdowns or actions that do not live up to customer expectations.

customer needs and requests

The individual needs and special requests of customers.

implicit needs

Customer needs that are not requested but that should be obvious to service providers.

explicit requests

Customer needs that are overtly requested.

special needs

Requests based on a customer's special medical, psychological, language, or sociological difficulties.

SERVICE FAILURES AND
RECOVERY STRATEGIES

customer preferences

The needs of a customer that
are not due to medical, dietary,
psychological, language, or
sociological difficulties.

customer errors

Service failures caused by
admitted customer mistakes.

disruptive others

Customers who negatively
influence the service experience
of other customers.

**unprompted/unsolicited
actions**

Events and employee behaviors,
both good and bad, totally
unexpected by the customer.

level of attention

Positive *and/or* negative regard
given a customer by an
employee.

unusual action

Both positive and negative
events in which an employee
responds with something out of
the ordinary.

cultural norms

Service personnel actions that
either positively reinforce or
violate the cultural norms of
society.

gestalt

Customer evaluations that are
made holistically and given in
overall terms rather than in
descriptions of discrete events.

between customers, such as requesting patrons to be quiet in movie theaters or requesting that smoking customers not smoke in nonsmoking sections of a restaurant.

The third type of service failure, **unprompted and unsolicited employee actions,** pertains to events and employee behaviors—both good and bad—that are totally unexpected by the customer. These actions are not initiated by the customer via a request, nor are they part of the core delivery system. Subcategories in this group include (1) level of attention, (2) unusual action, (3) cultural norms, (4) gestalt, and (5) adverse condition. In the airline example from the opening vignette, the customer did not note unprompted or unsolicited employee actions as failures. However, if a flight attendant had become abusive or began jumping up and down while singing "My Way" in the aisle, such actions would have qualified as unprompted or unsolicited employee actions.

Within the failure group of unprompted or unsolicited employee action, the subcategory of **level of attention** refers to both positive and negative events. Positive levels of attention would occur when an employee goes out of his or her way to pamper a customer and anticipate the customer's needs. Negative levels of attention pertain to employees who have poor attitudes, employees who ignore a customer, and employees who exhibit behaviors consistent with an indifferent attitude.

The **unusual action** subcategory can also reflect positive and negative events. For example, a Domino's employee happened to see a family's members searching through the burnt-out remains of their house while making a delivery to another customer in the area. The employee reported the event to the manager, and the two immediately prepared and delivered pizzas for the family free of charge. The family was stunned by the action and never forgot the kindness that was extended toward them during their time of need. Unfortunately, an unusual action can also be a negative event. Employee actions such as rudeness, abusiveness, and inappropriate touching would qualify equally as unusual actions.

The **cultural norms** subcategory refers to actions that either positively reinforce cultural norms such as equality, fairness, and honesty, or violate the cultural norms of society. Violations would include discriminatory behavior, acts of dishonesty such as lying, cheating, and stealing, and other activities considered unfair by customers.

The **gestalt** subcategory refers to customer evaluations that are made holistically, that is, the customer does not describe the service encounter as discrete events but uses overall terms such as "pleasant" or "terrible." In our airline example, if the customer had not specified the individual failure events but had commented only, "It is almost unbelievable how poorly we were treated by *the employees* of your airline, almost a perfect negative case study in customer service," the complaint would be categorized as a gestalt evaluation.

Finally, the **adverse conditions** subcategory covers positive and negative employee actions under stressful conditions. If an employee takes effective control of a situation when all others around him/her are "losing their heads," customers

Domino's Pizza provides not only a service, but also goodwill, such as the time a delivery person observed a family searching through the burned remains of their house. The local pizza provider prepared pizzas for the family free of charge, making this unusual action one of social responsibility.

Source: © David Young-Wolff/PhotoEdit.

are impressed by the employee's performance under those adverse conditions. In contrast, if the captain and crew of a sinking ship board the lifeboats before the passengers, this would obviously be remembered as a negative action under adverse conditions.

adverse conditions

Positive and negative employee actions under stressful conditions.

CUSTOMER COMPLAINING BEHAVIOR

In a striking example of the impact of service failures, consumers were asked: "Have you ever gotten so upset at a store (or manufacturer) that you said, 'I'll never go into that store or buy that brand again,' and you haven't?" Researchers found that they had to limit respondents to relating *only* three incidents to keep the interview time reasonable. The oldest incident had happened more than 25 years ago, and 86 percent of the incidents were more than 5 years old.

The consequences of service failures can be dramatic. The vast majority of respondents in the survey (87 percent) indicated that they were still somewhat or very emotionally upset and were more upset about the treatment they received from employees than at the store or product performance. More than three-quarters of respondents indicated that they had engaged in negative word-of-mouth communications regarding the incident (46 percent claimed that they had told "lots of people"). Finally, true to form in what is typical consumer complaint behavior today, only 53 percent had voiced their complaint to the store, even though 100 percent defected to other firms.[2]

Most companies cringe at the thought of customers who complain, while other companies look at complaints as a necessary evil in conducting business. The truth of the matter is that every company should encourage its customers to complain. Complainers are telling the firm that it has some operational or managerial problems that need to be corrected. Hence, complainers are offering the company a free gift, that is, they act as consultants and diagnose the firm's problems—at no fee. Moreover, complainers provide the firm with the chance to reestablish a customer's satisfaction. Complainers are more likely to do business with the firm again than are noncomplainers. Consequently, successful firms view complaints as an opportunity to satisfy unhappy customers and prevent defections and unfavorable word-of-mouth communications.[3]

It's not the complainers the company should worry about, it's the noncomplainers. Customers who do not express their complaints are already gone or ready to leave for the competition at any moment. In fact, 63 percent of dissatisfied customers who do not complain and who have purchased goods or services costing $1.00 to $5.00 will defect to a competitor. Even more disturbing is that as purchases exceed $100, the defection rate approaches 91 percent.[4]

Complaining is defined in *Webster's Third International Dictionary* as "expressing discontent, dissatisfaction, protest, resentment, or regret."[5] Complaining is different from criticism. Complaining expresses a dissatisfaction within the complainer, while criticism may be an objective and dispassionate observation about a person or object.

TYPES OF COMPLAINTS

instrumental complaints

Complaints expressed for the purpose of altering an undesirable state of affairs.

noninstrumental complaints

Complaints expressed without expectation that an undesirable state will be altered.

ostensive complaints

Complaints directed at someone or something outside the realm of the complainer.

reflexive complaints

Complaints directed at some inner aspect of the complainer.

Based on past research in consumer psychology, complaints can be instrumental or noninstrumental.[6] **Instrumental complaints** are expressed for the purpose of altering an undesirable state of affairs. For example, complaining to a waiter about an undercooked steak is an instrumental complaint. In such a case, the complainer fully expects the waiter to correct the situation. Interestingly, research indicates that instrumental complaints make up only a very small number of the complaints that are voiced everyday.

In contrast, **noninstrumental complaints** are voiced without any expectation that the undesirable state will be altered. These kinds of complaints are voiced much more often than are instrumental complaints. For example, complaints about the weather or one's physical appearance such as, "It's too hot!" or "I'm so ugly!" are voiced without any real expectation that conditions will change. Another type of noninstrumental complaint is an instrumental complaint that is voiced to a second party and not to the offending source. For example, complaining to a friend about your roommate being a "slob" is a noninstrumental complaint.

Complaints are also categorized as ostensive or reflexive. **Ostensive complaints** are directed at someone or something outside the realm of the complainer. In contrast, **reflexive complaints** are directed at some inner aspect of the complainer. Typically, complaints tend to be more ostensive than reflexive for two reasons. First, people generally avoid making negative comments about themselves so as not to reinforce negative self-esteem. Second, people seldom want to convey negative attributes about themselves to others.

WHY DO CUSTOMERS COMPLAIN?

In the case of the instrumental complaint, the reason a customer complains is pretty clear. The complainer wants the undesirable state to be corrected. However, the reason is not so clear when it comes to noninstrumental complaints. Experts believe that noninstrumental complaints occur for several reasons. First, complaining serves a function much like the release of a pressure valve—it gives the complainer an emotional release from frustration. Complaints provide people with the mechanism for venting their feelings.

Complaining also serves as a mechanism for the complainer's regaining some measure of control. Control is reestablished if the complainer is able to influence other people's evaluations of the source of the complaint. For example, negative word of mouth spread by the complainer for the purpose of taking revenge on an offending business gives the complainer some measure of control through indirect retribution.

A third reason people complain to others is to solicit sympathy and test for consensus of the complaint, thereby validating the complainer's subjective evaluation of the events that led to the complaint. In other words, the complainer wants to know whether others would feel the same way under similar circumstances. If they would, the complainer then feels justified in having voiced the complaint.

Finally, complainers may complain simply to create an impression. As strange as it may seem, complainers are often considered to be more intelligent and discerning than noncomplainers.[7] The implication is that the complainer's standards and expectations are higher than those of noncomplainers.

WHY DON'T CUSTOMERS COMPLAIN?

A greater percentage of services' problems than goods' problems are not voiced "because potential complainers do not know what to do or think that it wouldn't do any good."[8] This situation is directly attributable to the intangibility and inseparability inherent in the provision of services. Due to intangibility, evaluation of the service delivery process is primarily subjective. Consequently, consumers often lack the security of making an objective observation and may doubt their own evaluations.

Due to inseparability, customers often provide inputs into the process. Hence, given an undesirable outcome, customers may place much of the blame upon themselves for failing to convey to the service provider a satisfactory description of the level and type of service desired. In addition, inseparability encompasses the often face-to-face interaction between the customer and the service provider, and the customer may feel uncomfortable about complaining because of the physical presence of the provider.

Finally, many services are technical and specialized. Customers may not feel adequately qualified to voice a complaint for fear that they lack the expertise to evaluate the quality of the service. For example, do you really know when your auto mechanic has done everything you were billed for?

COMPLAINING OUTCOMES

voice

A complaining outcome in which the consumer verbally communicates dissatisfaction with the store or the product.

In general, complaining behavior results in three outcomes: voice, exit, and retaliation.[9] **Voice** refers to an outcome in which the consumer verbally communicates dissatisfaction with the store or the product. High voice means that the communication is expressed to the manager or someone higher in the structure than the actual provider. Medium voice occurs when the consumer communicates the problem to the person providing the service. Low voice occurs when the consumer does not communicate the problem to anyone associated with the store or product but may be relaying the problem to others outside the store.

exit

A complaining outcome in which the consumer stops patronizing the store or using the product.

Exit, the second type of complaining outcome, describes the situation in which a consumer stops patronizing the store or using the product. High exit occurs when the consumer makes a conscious decision never to purchase from the firm or buy the product again. Medium exit reflects a consumer's conscious decision to try not to use the store or product again if at all possible. Low exit means that the consumer does not change his or her purchasing behavior and continues to shop as usual.

retaliation

A complaining outcome in which the consumer takes action deliberately designed to damage the physical operation or hurt future business.

The third type of complaint outcome is **retaliation,** the situation in which a consumer takes action deliberately designed to either damage the physical operation or hurt future business. High retaliation involves the consumer's physically damaging the store or going out of his or her way to communicate to others negative aspects about the business. In medium retaliation, the consumer creates minor inconveniences for the store or perhaps tells only a few people about the incident. Low retaliation involves no retaliation at all against the store, perhaps consisting of only minor negative word of mouth.

Interestingly, the three complaining outcomes are not mutually exclusive and can be considered as three aspects of one behavior that may occur simultaneously. Experiencing high levels of all three outcomes simultaneously can result in explosive behavior. For example, "In one high-high-high example, the customer shouted his dissatisfaction at the clerk and the store manager, vowed never to buy at the store again, went out of the store, got in his car, and drove it in the front doors of the store through the checkout counter and between two lines of shelving, destroying everything in its path."[10] In contrast, a consumer who displays high-voice, low-exit, and low-retaliation behavior would typify a perpetual complainer who nevertheless continues to shop at the store.

The Art of Service Recovery

Complainers provide the firm with an opportunity to recover from the service failure. When the service is provided incorrectly the first time, an important but often forgotten management tool is the art of **service recovery**.[11] While some companies are great at delivering service until something goes wrong, other companies thrive on recovering from service failures and impressing customers in the process. Customers of service organizations often allow the firm one mistake.[12] Consequently, the customer provides the business with an opportunity to make amends. Unfortunately, many companies still drop the ball and further aggravate the customer in failing to take the opportunity.

When the service delivery system fails, it is the responsibility of contact personnel to react to the complaint. The content and form of the contact personnel's response determines the customer's perceived satisfaction or dissatisfaction with the service encounter.[13] Ironically, customers will remember a service encounter favorably if the contact personnel respond in a positive manner to the service failure. Hence, even though the service encounter included a service failure, the customer recalls the encounter as a positive event. In fact, a **service recovery paradox** is that a customer will rate performance higher if a failure occurs and the contact personnel successfully recover from the failure than if the service had been delivered correctly the first time.

Experts in the area of service recovery recommend that in establishing service recovery as a priority and developing recovery skills, firms should consider the strategies that follow.

service recovery
A firm's reaction to a complaint that results in customer satisfaction and goodwill.

service recovery paradox
Situation in which the customer rates performance higher if a failure occurs and the contact personnel successfully recover from it than if the service had been delivered correctly the first time.

Measure the Costs

The costs of losing and the benefits of keeping existing customers as opposed to chasing new customers are substantial. In short, the costs of obtaining new customers are three to five times greater than those of keeping existing customers; current customers are more receptive to the firm's marketing efforts and are, therefore, an important source of profit for the firm; and existing customers ask fewer questions, are familiar with the firm's procedures and employees, and are willing to pay more for services.

Actively Encourage Complaints

Experts assert that actively encouraging complaints is a good way to "break the silence." Remember that complainers who actually voice their complaints to the source of the problem are the exception—most customers don't speak up. In fact, research indicates that the average company does not hear from 96 percent of its unhappy customers.[14] This doesn't mean that customers don't complain, only that they complain to friends and family rather than to the company. The average unhappy customer voices displeasure with a firm to 11 other people. If these 11 tell 5 other people, the firm has potentially lost 67 customers.[15] Strategies to encourage complaints include customer surveys, focus groups, and active monitoring of the service delivery process to ensure customer satisfaction throughout the encounter, before a customer leaves the premises.

ANTICIPATE NEEDS FOR RECOVERY

Every service encounter is made up of a series of critical incidents, the points in the system where the customer and the firm interact. Firms that are effective in service recovery anticipate in advance the areas in their service delivery process where failures are most likely to occur. Of course, these firms take every step possible to minimize the occurrence of the failure in the first place, but they are prepared for recovery if delivery goes awry. Experts believe that firms should pay special attention to areas in which employee turnover is high. Many high-turnover positions are low-paying customer contact positions, and employees often lack motivation and/or are inexperienced in effective recovery techniques.

A good example of failing to anticipate a need for recovery was provided in this chapter's opening vignette. World Airlines had changed its flight schedule without notifying passengers. The airline should have anticipated that this change would cause passengers problems with connecting flights. The problem was further aggravated by the employee in Charlotte who initially would not provide the passenger and his wife a voucher for a night's lodging. Had World Airlines anticipated the events caused by its flight schedule change and had made alternative arrangements for passengers or hassle-free vouchers for the night's lodging, the magnitude of the failure would have been minimized.

RESPOND QUICKLY

When a service failure does occur, the faster the company responds, the more likely that the recovery effort will result in a successful outcome. In fact, past studies have indicated that if the complaint is handled *promptly*, the company will retain 95 percent of its unhappy customers. In contrast, if the complaint is resolved at all, the firm retains only 64 percent of unhappy customers.[16] Time is of the essence. The faster the firm responds to the problem, the better the message the firm sends to customers about the value it places on pleasing its customers. It took World Airlines two to three months to respond to our unhappy passenger in the opening vignette. What kind of message does that send? In addition, the severity of the failure regarding the voucher for the night's lodging was magnified tremendously due to the delay in response. Why not give customers what they want, when they want it? Is it really worth it to the firm for employees to actively argue with customers?

Another firm that learned this lesson the hard way is a bank in Spokane, Washington. A customer who had millions of dollars in the bank's checking, investment, and trust accounts was denied having his parking validated because he "only" cashed a check as opposed to making a deposit. The customer was at a branch bank that was not his normal bank. After explaining the situation to the teller, who was unimpressed, and more loudly voicing his opinion to the branch manager, the customer drove to his usual bank and threatened to close his accounts if he did not receive a response from the bank's upper management by the end of the day. As incredible as it may seem, the call never came, and the customer withdrew $1 million the first thing next morning. This action did get the bank's attention, and the bank has been trying to recover ever since.[17]

TRAIN EMPLOYEES

Expecting employees to be naturals at service recovery is unrealistic. Most employees don't know what to do when a failure occurs, and many others find making on-the-spot decisions a difficult task. Employee training in service recovery should take place on two levels. First, the firm must work at creating in the employee an awareness of customer concerns. Placing an employee in the shoes of the customer is often enlightening for an employee who has forgotten what it's like to be a customer of his or her own firm. For example, hospitals have made interns and staff dress in hospital gowns and had them rolled around on gurneys to experience some of the hospitals' processes firsthand.

The second level of employee training, beyond developing an appreciation for customer needs, is defining management's expectation toward recovery efforts. What *is* acceptable behavior from management's perspective? Effective recovery often means that management has to let go and allow employees to take risks, a transition that often leads to the empowerment of front-line employees.

EMPOWER THE FRONT LINE

Effective recovery often means that the employee has to bend the firm's rules and regulations—the exact type of activity that employees are trained not to do at any cost. Often the rules and regulations of the firm tie the hands of employees when it comes to effective recovery efforts, particularly in the area of prompt response. In many instances, firms require managerial approval before any effort to compensate a customer is undertaken. However, the manager is often engaged in other duties, which delays the response and adds to the frustration for both customer and employee.

CLOSE THE LOOP

One of the most important activities in service recovery is providing feedback to the customer about how that customer's complaint made a difference. Referring again to the opening vignette, the airline's response letters fail to mention how any of the events that befell the customer will be prevented in the future. The letters

SERVICE FAILURES AND
RECOVERY STRATEGIES

Employees such as this bank teller make up the "front line" in a service encounter. If empowered, these employees can make the appropriate decisions in order to recover effectively from any lapse in the service experience.

Source: © David Young-Wolff/PhotoEdit.

express why the events occur but do not really say what the company is doing to correct the situations. Statements such as, "We will take whatever corrective measures are necessary to ensure that a similar problem does not arise in the future," fail to close the loop and convey the impression that the firm is attempting to push the whole matter aside.

RECOVERY TACTICS

Responses to service failures can be categorized into two types: (1) responses to service failures that are attributed to the firm, and (2) responses to service failures that are attributed to customer error. Both categories are based on the customer's perspective of the service failure. Following are both good and poor responses to service failures attributed to the firm:[18]

GOOD RESPONSES:

1. Acknowledge the problem—customers need to know that their complaints are being heard.
2. Make the customer feel unique or special—convey to customers that their opinions are valued and their business is important to the firm.
3. Apologize when appropriate—when the failure is clearly the fault of the firm, a sincere apology is often an effective form of recovery.

4.   Explain what happened—providing the customer with extra information about events that led to the failure conveys that the firm feels the customer is of value and that his or her understanding of events is important.
5.   Offer to compensate—compensation is often the most desired response by customers, but firms tend to forget the hidden costs associated with the service failure, such as time and frustration.

POOR RESPONSES:

1.   Fail to recognize the seriousness of the problem.
2.   Fail to adequately accommodate the customer.
3.   Act as though nothing is wrong.
4.   Fail to explain why the problem occurred.
5.   Leave the customer to solve the problem on his or her own.
6.   Promise to do something and don't follow through.

Experts also suggest a number of good and poor responses regarding service failures that occur due to customer error. Assisting customers in recovering from their own errors is especially memorable from the customers' perspective and is likely to translate into repeat business.

GOOD RESPONSES:

1.   Acknowledge the customer's problem—listening and being attentive to customer needs conveys the message that the firm is seriously concerned about the customer's well-being, regardless of who committed the error.
2.   Take responsibility—anticipate the errors customers are likely to make (e.g, losing room keys, leaving behind personal items, etc.) and make provisions to accommodate these events when they do occur. Do not avoid responsibility, thereby leaving customers to fend for themselves.
3.   Assist in solving the problem without embarrassing the customer— when solving the problem, avoid making flippant statements that refer to the customer's lack of intelligence and/or unique ability to create the current situation. Chances are the customer is already embarrassed when asking for assistance. Do not further aggravate the situation by laughing or speaking loudly in the presence of other customers or employees regarding the predicament.

POOR RESPONSES:

1.   Laugh and embarrass the customer.
2.   Avoid any responsibility.
3.   Be unwilling to assist the customer in solving the problem.

SERVICE FAILURE AND RECOVERY ANALYSIS: AN EMPIRICAL EXAMPLE IN THE RESTAURANT INDUSTRY[19]

The obvious benefit of service failure and recovery analysis is that management can identify common failure situations, minimize their occurrence, and train employees to recover from failures when they do occur. The example that follows is an actual study of service failures and recovery strategies in the restaurant industry.

THE VALUE OF TRACKING SERVICE FAILURES

As is the case in most service industries today, restaurant managers and service personnel are facing intensive customer service pressures now more than ever.[20] When a service failure does occur, the service provider's reaction can either reinforce a strong customer bond or change a seemingly minor distraction into a major incident. For example, an employee's indifferent reaction to a customer's complaint about cold french fries can cost a restaurant years of that particular customer's business and an abundance of negative word-of-mouth publicity. Consequently, it is imperative that managers have an established service recovery plan to overcome possible service failures.

Analyzing service failures and service recovery strategies is an extremely useful management tool.[21] In general, service failure analysis provides the type, frequency, and magnitude of various failures. By management's systematically categorizing consumer complaints, a hierarchy of criteria evolve that reflect the consumer's perspective of effective performance. This is a very important point. Typically, firms using measures such as FedEx's initial approach to measuring customer satisfaction defined performance based on measures developed internally.[22] However, performance should be measured based on what the customer, not upper management, perceives as important.

THE VALUE OF ANALYZING SERVICE RECOVERY STRATEGIES

In addition to tracking service failures, analyzing service recovery strategies is equally enlightening. Service recovery analysis provides a sometimes frightful insight into how personnel react to service failures, how consumers rate the effectiveness of the employee's recovery efforts, and the relationship between recovery strategies and customer retention rates.

Recent studies suggest that nearly half the responses to customer complaints actually reinforce a customer's negative feeling toward a firm.[23] Effective recovery strategies often require contact personnel to make decisions and to occasionally break company rules—the types of behaviors that many firms prohibit their employees from initiating. Contact personnel are often frustrated by rules and regulations that tie their hands and often prevent them from assisting a customer when needed. Furthermore, due to the lack of training in recovery efforts ex-

SERVICE FAILURE
AND RECOVERY
ANALYSIS: AN
EMPIRICAL EXAMPLE
IN THE RESTAURANT
INDUSTRY

hibited by most firms, many employees simply do not know how to recover from service failures. The result is a poor response or no response to customer complaints.

THE RESTAURANT STUDY

The study was conducted by services marketing students and is a great example of the valuable managerial information that can be obtained by monitoring and tracking service failures. The example is presented in a series of steps that can be easily duplicated. We highly recommend this exercise to services marketing classes as a group project. Different groups may investigate different industries or specific businesses.

STEP 1: DEVELOPING THE QUESTIONNAIRE

An example of the questionnaire used to collect the data for this study is provided in the appendix to this chapter. The main objective of the questionnaire is to (1) identify and classify failures in the restaurant industry, (2) assess customer perceptions of the magnitude of each failure, (3) identify and classify recovery strategies utilized by restaurants to correct failures, (4) assess customer perceptions of the effectiveness of each type of recovery, (5) assess subsequent patronage behaviors that reflect restaurants' customer retention rates, and (6) provide demographic information about respondents.

STEP 2: DATA COLLECTION

The Critical Incident Technique The study utilized a data collection method referred to as the **critical incident technique** (CIT). The purpose of CIT in this study is to examine the sources of customer satisfaction and dissatisfaction regarding restaurant services. In essence, CIT is a qualitative approach to analyzing and categorizing critical incidents. The CIT analyzes the content of the critical incidents described by respondents in story form.

critical incident technique
A method of studying service failures by analyzing critical incidents described in story form by respondents.

The actual critical incidents (or stories) for this study were recorded by students. Respondents were asked to report a restaurant service failure that was associated with a positive service recovery as well as a service failure that was associated with a negative service recovery. Both scenarios were requested in order to identify recovery strategies that were effective as well as responses that were ineffective. Incidents associated with positive recovery strategies accounted for 49.6 percent of the sample, while 50.4 percent of the sample was associated with poor recoveries.

In addition, respondents were asked to do the following: (1) rate the magnitude of the failure on a scale from 1 through 10, which ranges from trivial to serious; (2) rate the effectiveness of the recovery strategy on a scale from 1 through 10, which ranges from poor to good; (3) report changes in shopping behavior subsequent to the service failure attributed to the encounter; and (4) provide demographic information on gender, education, and age. The data collection efforts resulted in the accumulation of 373 critical incidents.

STEP 3: DATA ANALYSIS

The critical incident technique is a qualitative approach to analyzing and categorizing critical incidents. More specifically, the CIT utilized in this study involved three steps:

1. *Identify the Failure Incident.* Initially, each of the 373 critical incidents was systematically categorized through a deductive sorting process into one of the three major failure groups discussed earlier in the chapter, (1) employee responses to service delivery system failures, (2) employee responses to implicit/explicit customer requests, and (3) unprompted and unsolicited employee actions.
2. *Identify Failure Subgroups within the Three Major Groups.* This step involved classifying failures into subgroups within each of the three major failure groups noted above. This process resulted in the identification of 11 unique failure subgroups (five in Group 1; two in Group 2; and four in Group 3).
3. *Classify Recovery Strategies.* This step involved classifying the service recovery strategies within each failure subgroup. This process resulted in eight final service recovery strategies that are applicable to a variety of food service operations.

STEP 4: ESTABLISHING THE RELIABILITY OF THE CATEGORIES

An important procedure when categorizing data is to determine the reliability of the categories. Reliability simply refers to the issue of whether other researchers, given the same set of data, would assign each of the critical incidents to the same set of categories. To assess the reliability of the 11 failure subgroups and eight recovery strategies established through the sorting process in the study, an independent judge (such as a group member not involved in the original categorization) categorized each of the incidents included in the sample.

As a starting point to test for reliability, the critical incidents were presorted into the three main failure categories: (1) employee responses to service delivery system failures, (2) employee responses to implicit/explicit customer requests, and (3) unprompted and unsolicited employee actions. The independent judge was then presented with the 11 previously identified failure subgroups and asked to independently sort each failure incident into one of the 11 categories. In this example, the task resulted in agreement rates of 92 percent, 90 percent, and 90 percent. Typically, agreement rates of 70 percent or higher are regarded as acceptable for establishing reliability.

After establishing the reliability of the service failure categories, the independent judge's next task is to verify the reliability of the service recovery categories.

SERVICE FAILURE
AND RECOVERY
ANALYSIS: AN
EMPIRICAL EXAMPLE
IN THE RESTAURANT
INDUSTRY

Following a procedure similar to the one described above, the independent judge is given the stack of recovery strategies and the names of the eight categories of recovery strategies previously identified. The independent judge then compares his/her categorization efforts with the original results. For this study, the recovery agreement rate was 93 percent, and reliability was established for the recovery categories as well as for the failure categories.

STEP 5: PRESENTING THE RESULTS

Demographic Results Sample demographics revealed 42.5 percent of the respondents were male while 57.5 percent of the respondents were female. Regarding education, 68.2 percent of the respondents did not have college degrees; 21.7 percent had undergraduate degrees; and 10.1 percent had "some" or had completed graduate school. Results concerning the age of respondents revealed that 67.5 percent were 25 years old or younger, 14.1 percent were from 26 to 35, and 18.4 percent were 36 years of age or older.

Statistical tests were used in examining the relationships between demographics and restaurant type, failure type, recovery strategies, failure ratings, recovery ratings, and retention rates. Results revealed no statistically significant findings. These tests provide evidence that the findings, reported across different types of customers and across restaurant types, can be safely generalized.

The Failure Categories: Frequency and Definition After carefully sorting the 373 critical incidents, the following restaurant service failure categories were developed and their reliability established. As described earlier in step 3, the incidents were first sorted into three main failure groups and then into subclass failures within each main failure group.

Group 1, "Employee Responses to Core Service Failures," accounted for 44.4 percent of the critical incidents. Core service failures included the following subclass categories (the frequency of occurrence expressed as a percentage of the total critical incidents is reported in parentheses):

Product Defects (20.9%): Food that was described as cold, soggy, raw, burnt, spoiled, or containing inanimate objects such as hair, glass, bandages, bag ties, and cardboard.

Slow/Unavailable Service (17.9%): Waiting an excessive amount of time and/or not being able to find assistance.

Facility Problems (3.2%): Cleanliness issues such as bad smells, dirty utensils, and animate objects found in food or crawling across the table (e.g., insects).

Unclear Policies (1.6%): Restaurant policies that were perceived as unfair by the customer (e.g., coupon redemption, form of payment).

Out of Stock Conditions (.8%): An inadequate supply of menu items.

Group 2, "Employee Responses to Implicit/Explicit Customer Requests," accounted for 18.4 percent of the critical incidents. Implicit/explicit customer requests included the following subclass categories (the frequency of occurrence expressed as a percentage of the total critical incidents is reported in parentheses):

Food Not Cooked to Order (15.0%): The scenario in which the customer explicitly asks for the food to be prepared in a specific manner (e.g., medium rare, no mustard) and the request is not honored.

Seating Problems (3.4%): Involved seating smokers in nonsmoking sections and vice versa, lost or disregarded reservations, denial of request for special tables, and seating among unruly customers.

Group 3, "Unprompted/Unsolicited Employee Actions, " accounted for 37.2 percent of the total critical incidents. Unprompted/unsolicited employee actions included the following subclass categories (the frequency of occurrence expressed as a percentage of the total critical incidents is reported in parentheses):

Inappropriate Employee Behavior (15.2%): Rudeness, inappropriate verbal exchanges, and poor attitudes that were associated with unpleasant behaviors.

Wrong Orders (12.6%): The delivery of an incorrect food item to the table, or in the case of fast food, packaging an incorrect food item that was not discovered until the customer was no longer on the restaurant premises.

Lost Orders (7.5%): Situations in which the customer's order was apparently misplaced and never fulfilled.

Mischarged (1.9%): Being charged for items that were never ordered, charging incorrect prices for items that were ordered, and providing incorrect change.

The Failure Categories: Magnitude and Recovery In addition to developing the failure categories, we also recorded each respondent's perception of the magnitude of the failure. Respondents rated the magnitude of the failure on a scale from 1 (minor mistake) through 10 (major mistake). In addition, the average effectiveness of recovery for each failure was calculated on a scale from 1 (poor recovery) through 10 (good recovery). Magnitude and recovery rankings presented according to the failures' perceived severity are as follows:

Failure Category	Magnitude	Recovery
1. Seating Problems	8.00	5.61
2. Out of Stock	7.33	6.00
3. Facility Problems	7.25	3.92
4. Inappropriate Employee Behavior	7.12	3.71
5. Slow/Unavailable Service	7.05	5.38
6. Lost Orders	6.71	5.82
7. Product Defects	6.69	6.21

CHAPTER 13 345

SERVICE FAILURE
AND RECOVERY
ANALYSIS: AN
EMPIRICAL EXAMPLE
IN THE RESTAURANT
INDUSTRY

8. Wrong Orders	6.25	6.44
9. Unclear Policy	6.16	6.33
10. Food Not Cooked to Order	6.02	5.80
11. Mischarged	5.86	7.71

The Recovery Categories: Frequency and Definition In addition to categorizing the primary service failures in the restaurant industry, a second objective of this study was to utilize the critical incident technique to categorize employee response (recovery strategies) to the various service failures. The service recovery strategies resulting from the CIT approach are defined below (the frequency of occurrence expressed as a percentage of the total critical incidents is reported in parentheses):

Replacement (33.4%): Replacing the defective order with a new order.

Free Food (23.5%): Providing the meal, desserts, and/or drinks on a complimentary basis.

Nothing (21.3%): No action was taken to correct the failure.

Apology (7.8%): The employee apologized for the failure.

Correction (5.7%): Fixing the existing defective order as opposed to replacing the order with a new one as in *Replacement*.

Discount (4.3%): Discounts were provided to customers for food items at the time of the incident.

Managerial Intervention (2.7%): Management in some way became involved and helped resolve the problem.

Coupon (1.3%): Discounts for food items purchased at the restaurant were provided to customers for use on their next visit.

The Recovery Categories: Perceived Effectiveness and Corresponding Customer Retention Rates Respondents rated the effectiveness of each recovery on a scale from 1 (very poor) through 10 (very good). Recoveries ranked in declining order of effectiveness and their corresponding customer retention rates are as follows:

Recovery Strategy	Effectiveness	Retention Rate
1. Free Food	8.05	89.0%
2. Discount	7.75	87.5%
3. Coupon	7.00	80.0%
4. Managerial Intervention	7.00	88.8%
5. Replacement	6.35	80.2%
6. Correction	5.14	80.0%
7. Apology	3.72	71.4%
8. Nothing	1.71	51.3%

The customer retention rates revealed in this study suggest that it is possible to recover from failures, regardless of the type. Overall, customer retention for the incidents considered was above 75 percent. Even customers experiencing

▶▶▶▶ ◀◀◀◀

less-than-acceptable recoveries were still retained at a rate approaching 60 percent. However, in general, the statistical relationship between failure rating and recovery rating does indicate that as the magnitude of the seriousness of the failure increases, so does the difficulty in executing an effective recovery.

STEP 6: DEVELOPING MANAGERIAL IMPLICATIONS BASED ON RESULTS

This research provides restaurant managers and employees with a list of service failures that are likely to occur in the restaurant industry as well as methods for effectively (and ineffectively) recovering from these failures when they occur. Managers should use this type of information when designing service delivery systems and procedures, establishing policies regarding service recovery, and selecting and training service personnel. Remarkably, approximately 1 out of every 4 service failures (23.5 percent) was met with no response by the offending firm. Unfortunately, other research has indicated that this "no response" rate is typical.[24]

The findings also suggest that it is difficult to recover from two failure types in particular. On a 10-point scale, failures associated with facility problems (failure 3) and employee behavior (failure 8) had mean recovery ratings of only 3.92 and 3.71, respectively. This amplifies the importance of providing the basics of service delivery well, as recovery from facility problems are particularly difficult. In addition, these findings provide evidence indicating the importance of employee training in the restaurant industry, as employee failures were difficult to effectively recover from as well. The mean recovery ratings of all other failure types exceeded the midpoint on the 10-point scale.

The recovery findings provide information concerning the desirability of specific recovery strategies. For example, recoveries involving some form of compensation were rated most favorably. Compensation took the form of free food (recovery 1), discounts (recovery 2), and coupons (recovery 3). On a 10-point scale, these three recovery strategies had mean recovery ratings of 8.05, 7.75, and 7.00, respectively.

Several less effective recovery strategies were also identified. Based on recovery ratings, simply correcting a failure (recovery 6), apologizing (recovery 7), and doing nothing (recovery 8) seem to be less effective, as these recovery strategies had ratings of 5.14, 3.72, and 1.71, respectively.

As a result of this study and others like it that track service failure and recovery strategies, the categorization process reveals enlightening information about the particular industry's "hierarchy of horrors" and its sometimes feeble, sometimes admirable attempts to recover from its failures. Managing service firms is a highly complex task. Exercises like this make this point abundantly clear.

SUMMARY

The benefit of service failure and recovery analysis is that service managers can identify common failure situations, minimize their occurrence, and train employees to recover from them when they do occur. The value associated with developing effective service recovery skills is clear. Two-thirds of lost customers do not defect to competitiors due to poor product quality but due to the poor customer service they receive when problems arise.

Many of today's service firms are great as long as the service delivery system is operating smoothly. However, once kinks develop in the system, many firms are unprepared to face unhappy customers who are looking for solutions to their problems. As evidence, nearly half the responses to customer complaints reinforce customers' negative feelings toward a firm. Consequently, firms that truly excel in customer service equip employees with a set of recovery tools to repair the service encounter when failures occur and customer complaints are voiced.

Customer complaints should be viewed as opportunities to improve the service delivery system and to ensure that the customer is satisfied before the service encounter ends. Customers voice complaints for a number of reasons, including the following: to have the problem resolved, to gain an emotional release from frustration, to regain some measure of control by influencing other people's evaluation of the source of the complaint, to solicit sympathy or test the consensus of the complaint, or to create an impression.

However, it's not the complainers who service firms should worry about, it's the people who leave without saying a word, who never intend on returning, and who inform others, thereby generating negative word-of-mouth information. A number of reasons explain why many consumers do not complain. Most simply, customers of services often do not know who to complain to and/or do not think complaining will do any good. Other reasons consumers fail to complain are that (1) consumer evaluation of services is highly subjective; (2) consumers tend to shift some of the blame to themselves for not clearly specifying to the service provider their exact needs; (3) since many services are technical and specialized, many consumers do not feel qualified to voice their complaints; and (4) due to the inseparability of services, consumers may feel that a complaint is too confrontational.

Service failures generally fall into one of three main categories: (1) employee responses to core service failures such as slow service, unavailable service, and other core service failures; (2) employee responses to implicit/explicit customer requests such as special needs, customer preferences, customer error, and disruptive others; and (3) unprompted/unsolicited employee actions, which include level of attention, unusual actions, cultural norms, gestalt evaluations, and employee actions under adverse conditions.

Service recovery strategies are often industry specific, such as the restaurant example provided in the chapter. However, in general, responses to service failures can be categorized as two types: (1) responses to service failures that are attributed to the firm; and (2) responses to service failures that are attributed to customer error. Successful tactics for recovery from failures attributed to the firm include acknowledging the problem, making the customer feel unique or special, apologizing when appropriate, explaining what happened, and offering to compensate the customer. Successful responses to service failures attributed to customer error include acknowledging the problem, taking responsibility for the problem, and assisting in solving the problem without embarrassing the customer. Successful service recovery efforts such as these play an important role in customer retention.

KEY TERMS

service failures	unusual action
critical incidents	cultural norms
system failures	gestalt
unavailable service	adverse conditions
unreasonably slow service	instrumental complaints
other core service failures	noninstrumental complaints
customer needs and requests	ostensive complaints
implicit needs	reflexive complaints
explicit requests	voice
special needs	exit
customer preferences	retaliation
customer errors	service recovery
disruptive others	service recovery paradox
unprompted/unsolicited actions	critical incident technique
level of attention	

REVIEW QUESTIONS

1. Define and discuss the subclass failures associated with the implicit/explicit request failure category.

2. Discuss the following types of complaints: instrumental, noninstrumental, ostensive, and reflexive.

3. What is the service recovery paradox? Provide an example based on your own personal experience.

4. Discuss the following types of failure outcomes: voice, exit, and retaliation.

5. What are the pros and cons of complaining customers?

6. Give an overview of the steps described in the chapter necessary to track and monitor employee service failures and recovery efforts.

NOTES

1. Mary Jo Bitner, Bernard H. Booms, and Mary Stanfield Tetreault, "The Service Encounter: Diagnosing Favorable and Unfavorable Incidents," *Journal of Marketing* (January 1990), pp. 71–84.

2. H. Keith Hunt, "Consumer Satisfaction, Dissatisfaction, and Complaining Behavior," *Journal of Social Issues* 47,1 (1991), p. 116.

3. Mary C. Gilly, William B. Stevenson, and Laura J. Yale, "Dynamics of Complaint Management in the Service Organization," *The Journal of Consumer Affairs* 25,2 (1991), p. 296.

4. Oren Harari, "Thank Heaven for Complainers," *Management Review* (January 1992), p. 60.

5. Mark D. Alicke et al., "Complaining Behavior in Social Interaction," *Personality and Social Psychology Bulletin* (June 1992), p. 286.

6. Alicke, "Complaining Behavior," p. 287.

7. T. M. Amabile, "Brilliant but Cruel: Perceptions of Negative Evaluators," *Journal of Experimental Social Psychology* 19 (1983), pp. 146–156.

8. Gilly, Stevenson, and Yale, "Dynamics of Complaint Management," p. 297.

9. Hunt, "Consumer Satisfaction," p. 114.

10. Hunt, "Consumer Satisfaction," p. 115.

11. Adapted from Christopher W. L. Hart, James L. Heskett, and W. Earl Sasser, "The Profitable Art of Service Recovery," *Harvard Business Review* (July–August 1990), pp. 148–156.

12. James L. Heskett et al., "Putting the Service-Profit Chain to Work," *Harvard Business Review* (March–April 1994), p. 172.

13. Bitner, Booms, and Tetreault, "The Service Encounter," p. 321.

14. Karl Albrecht and Ron Zemke, *Services America* (Homewood, IL: Dow-Jones Irwin, 1985), p. 6.

15. Donna Partow, "Turn Gripes into Gold," *Home Office Computing* (September 1993), p. 24.

16. Albrecht and Zemke, *Services America*, p. 6.

17. Hart, Heskett, and Sasser, "The Profitable Art," p. 150.

18. Bitner, Booms, and Tetreault, "The Service Encounter," pp. 71–84.

19. Adapted from K. Douglas Hoffman, Scott W. Kelley, and Holly M. Rotalsky, "Tracking Service Failures and Employee Recovery Efforts," *Journal of Services Marketing* 9,2 (1995), pp. 49–61.

20. Eleena De Lisser, "Today's Specials Include Customer Satisfaction," *The Wall Street Journal*, June 7, 1993, p. B1.

21. Terry Vavra, "Learning from Your Losses," *Brandweek* 33,46 (December 7, 1992), p. 20(2).

22. American Management Association, *Blueprints for Service Quality: The Federal Express Approach*, (New York: AMA Membership Publication Division, 1991).

23. Hart, Heskett, and Sasser, "The Profitable Art," p. 150.

24. See Scott W. Kelley, K. Douglas Hoffman, and Mark A. Davis, "A Typology of Retail Failures and Recoveries," *Journal of Retailing* (Winter 1993), pp. 429–445; and K. Douglas Hoffman, Scott W. Kelley, and Laure M. Soulage, "Customer Defection Analysis: A Critical Incident Approach" (1994), working paper.

A P P E N D I X

SAMPLE OF CRITICAL INCIDENT FORM

I. Introduction/Purpose of Study

Have you ever been at a **restaurant** and received poor service?

We are conducting a study on service mistakes or failures made by **restaurants** and how **restaurants** recover when a service failure occurs.

Would you be willing to participate in this study?

II. Think of a time when you had an experience at a **restaurant** where a mistake was made and the **restaurant** tried to correct that mistake but did a POOR job of recovering. Please describe the nature of this service failure.

Where? _____

When? _____

What happened? _____

_____

_____

What did the **restaurant** do to correct the failure? _____

_____

_____

On a scale of 1 to 10, 1 being a MINOR MISTAKE and 10 being a MAJOR MISTAKE, how would you rate the severity of the mistake?

Minor Mistake   Major Mistake

1   2   3   4   5   6   7   8   9   10

On a scale of 1 to 10, 1 being VERY POOR and 10 being a VERY GOOD how would you rate the efforts of the **restaurant** regarding the correction of the mistake?

Very Poor   Very Good

1   2   3   4   5   6   7   8   9   10

Do you still patronize this **restaurant?**

_____ No, due to the service failure

_____ No, due to other reasons

_____ Yes

III. Think of a time when you had an experience at a **restaurant** where a mistake was made and the **restaurant** tried to correct that mistake but did a GOOD job of recovering. Please describe the nature of this service failure.

Where? _____

When? _____

What happened? _____
_____
_____
_____

What did the **restaurant** do to correct the failure? _____
_____
_____
_____

On a scale of 1 to 10, 1 being a MINOR MISTAKE and 10 being a MAJOR MISTAKE, how would you rate the severity of the mistake?

Minor Mistake   Major Mistake
1   2   3   4   5   6   7   8   9   10

On a scale of 1 to 10, 1 being VERY POOR and 10 being VERY GOOD how would you rate the efforts of the **restaurant** regarding the correction of the mistake?

Very Poor   Very Good
1   2   3   4   5   6   7   8   9   10

Do you still patronize this **restaurant?**

_____ No, due to the service failure
_____ No, due to other reasons
_____ Yes

IV. Demographics

Sex (Categorical choices)
Education (Categorical choices)
Age (Categorical choices)

CUSTOMER RETENTION

"*Who will testify to your existence during the last twelve months?*"

Tom Peters

CHAPTER OBJECTIVES

The major objective of this chapter is to introduce you to the concept of customer retention. After reading this chapter, you should be able to

▸ Define customer retention.

    ▸ *Discuss why the concept of customer retention has become increasingly important.*

▸ Discuss the benefits of retaining existing customers.

    ▸ *Explain defection management.*

▸ Describe successful tactics for retaining existing customers.

    ▸ *Discuss the trade-offs associated with unconditional service guarantees.*

THE PROFITABILITY OF CUSTOMER RETENTION EFFORTS AT MBNA

MBNA America, a Delaware-based credit card company, has improved its industry ranking from 38 to 4 and increased its profits by sixteen-fold. How did MBNA do it? Profitability in the credit card industry is directly linked to customer retention.

In general, credit card companies lose money during the first year of a new account because the fees obtained by establishments that honor credit cards do not offset the costs of advertising, setting up new accounts, and printing. Consequently, retaining customers beyond that first year is critical to the profitability of the credit card industry.

The key to developing customer loyalty is to employ measures that monitor the firm's customer retention efforts. If you can measure it, you can manage it! Specific measures provide managers concrete targets on which to focus their efforts. In MBNA's case, the company tracks the average balance per card plus 15 measures of customer satisfaction daily.

MBNA further reinforces to employees the importance of customer retention through its reward structure. MBNA's employees earn up to 20 percent of their salaries in bonuses associated with customer retention efforts. MBNA employees talk with every customer who wishes to drop its services, and by doing so, they retain 50 percent of these customers.

How do MBNA's customer retention efforts affect the bottom line? MBNA's overall customer retention rate is 95 percent, and MBNA keeps its customers twice as long as industry averages. In fact, MBNA's retention rate of profitable customers, those who revolve their balances, is 98 percent. In addition, MBNA's credit losses due to bad debt are one-third to one-half lower than those of other companies. Moreover, MBNA customers use their cards more often and maintain higher balances—$2,500 compared with the industry average of $1,600.

Source: Adapted from Larry Armstrong, "Beyond May I Help You?" *Business Week/Quality* (1991), pp. 100–103; Ron Zemke, "The Emerging Art of Service Management," *Training* (January 1992), pp. 37–42; Frederick F. Reichheld and W. Earl Sasser, Jr., "Zero Defections: Quality Comes to Services," *Harvard Business Review* (September–October 1990), pp. 105–111; and Rahul Jacob, "Why Some Customers Are More Equal than Others," *Fortune*, September 19, 1994, p. 218.

INTRODUCTION

Depending on who you ask within a service operation, you will likely discover that the various managers within the firm evaluate the firm's value differently. The chief financial officer might spout a variety of impressive financial ratios that are great to use at cocktail parties, the operations manager will speak in terms of inventory and equipment, and the human relations manager will focus on the strengths of the firm's employees.[1] Although all these measures are crucial to the firm's success, they all ignore the value of the customer.

This chapter focuses on the important concept of customer retention (see Figure 14.1). Customer retention is a key strategy in today's leading-edge service firms and reflects a more futuristic outlook than does the concept of customer satisfaction. As discussed in Chapter Eleven, satisfaction measures assess the customer's current state of evaluation but fail to tap into the customer's set of changing needs. Consequently, additional measures that assess evolving customer expectations, the probability of future purchases with the firm, and the customer's willingness to conduct business with competitive firms are necessary in order to truly assess the firm's customer retention efforts.

WHAT IS CUSTOMER RETENTION?

customer retention

Focusing the firm's marketing efforts toward the existing customer base.

Simply stated, **customer retention** refers to focusing the firm's marketing efforts toward the existing customer base. More specifically, in contrast to seeking new customers, firms engaged in customer retention efforts work to satisfy existing customers with the intent of developing long-term relationships between the firm and its current clientele.

Many examples of successful customer retention efforts are based on the firm's ability to redefine its existing business. Companies are challenging themselves, now more than ever before, to look at what the product really provides to their customers. Understanding consumer uses of the product and the steps required by consumers to obtain the product often leads to ideas that assist the firm in differentiating itself from its competition. Providing value-added services to the consumer reshapes the traditional and often confrontational supplier–customer relationship into more of a partnership.

After rethinking its business, British Airways no longer viewed itself solely as a provider of air transportation.[2] As a result, the airline has revised its focus on first-class transatlantic customers to include improved services on the ground as well as in the air. Realizing that many of its customers would like to sleep through the night rather than eat huge meals followed by lavish desserts, accompanied

How Much Profit a Customer Generates over Time

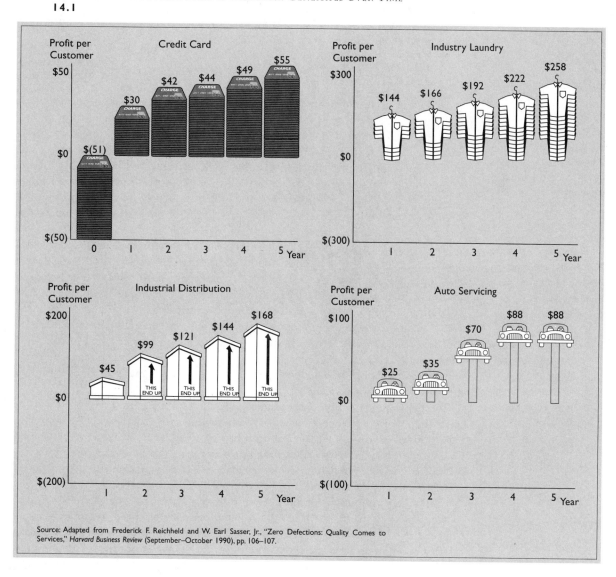

14.1

Source: Adapted from Frederick F. Reichheld and W. Earl Sasser, Jr., "Zero Defections: Quality Comes to Services," *Harvard Business Review* (September–October 1990), pp. 106–107.

with an endless supply of alcohol and bad movies, British Airways now provides its first-class passengers with the option of having dinner on the ground in its first-class lounge. Once on board, passengers are provided British Airway pajamas, real pillows, and a duvet to curl up in.

Once the plane has landed and after a good night's sleep, passengers are provided with breakfast on the ground as well as a shower and dressing room so that they can be fresh for the day's events. British Airways will even have passengers' clothes pressed while they are enjoying their breakfasts. With value-added services such as these, it is not surprising to learn that British Airway's profits were up 61 percent for the year ending March 1994.

THE TREND TOWARD CUSTOMER RETENTION

Today's market is totally different than the ones U.S. marketers have experienced in the past. Competition is intense, and service and goods differentiation among competitors is minimal.[3] Let's face it: There is no great deal of difference today among products, be they insurance companies, banks, or eye exams. Due to the relative parity among brand choices, consumer risk associated with switching brands has been drastically minimized. For example, consumers may be indifferent about the firm that holds their car insurance policy. Consequently, many consumers have forgone brand loyalty and selected the product that offers the best value—the best product at the best price.

Unfortunately, the majority of marketers today have reacted to this new environment of "brand parity" and "nonbrand loyalty" by constantly chasing new customers. Firms that are constantly seeking new customers are engaged in **conquest marketing.** Typical conquest marketing techniques include offering discounts and markdowns and developing promotions that encourage new business. Results obtained from conquest marketing are generally successful in the short run due to customers' lack of brand loyalty. The firm engaged in conquest marketing may even get a repeat purchase or two. However, as soon as the competition offers another "discount special," the firm loses many of the customers it previously obtained.

To this day, many companies spend the bulk of their marketing efforts on attracting new customers instead of on keeping the customers they already have. However, the long-term profitability of firms that utilize conquest marketing techniques is highly questionable. When one considers the cost of a sales promotion to attract customers, followed by sales at a discounted price, profits are minimal.

Even when conquest marketing techniques are successful, they sometimes lead to the demise of the firm. All too often, businesses are tempted to grow as fast as they can in order to increase their sales volume. However, because of the inseparability inherent in services, extensive growth of many service firms is commonly associated with a decrease in the quality of service provided.

As the firm continues to grow, the owner/provider will likely take on more of an administrative role, providing estimates, handling customer complaints, and managing employees. These additional duties result in the owner spending less time in the field attending to the original customer base. Consequently, the owner/provider might have to hire additional help, who may not provide the

conquest marketing

A marketing strategy for constantly seeking new customers by offering discounts and markdowns and developing promotions that encourage new business.

Conquest marketing techniques are used by firms that are constantly seeking new customers. Examples of such a technique are shown here—discounts, markdowns, and sales promotions to encourage new business.

Source: © 1995 PhotoDisc, Inc. Image no. 21325.

same level of service as the owner had. Subsequently, customers may become disgruntled about the poor service and begin to look for other alternatives.

Considering the costs associated with winning new customers, the only way to make a profit and avoid the continuous cycle of price discounts is to increase the lifetime spending of existing customers. "Customer retention is, therefore, far more important than customer attraction."[4] Given today's marketing environment, coddling existing clients makes good economic sense.

The Importance of Customer Retention

Customer retention has become increasingly important because of several changes in the marketing environment.[5] First, in the United States, consumer markets are stagnant. The U.S. population for the next 50 years is predicted to grow at half the rate of the period from 1965 to 1990. Consequently, there are fewer new customers to go around. Concurrent with the decrease in population growth, the gross national product has also slowed substantially to an annual growth rate of less than 3 percent. In sum, there are not as many new customers as there once were, and those customers that exist are spending less.

Another reason customer retention has become important to today's marketers is the increase in competition. Factors contributing to increased competition include the relative parity and lack of differential advantage of goods and services on the market, deregulated industries that now must compete for customers in an open market, and accessible market information that is available to more firms, thereby minimizing informational advantages among competing firms. As a result of the increase in competition and the predominant use of conquest marketing techniques, firms are finding that retaining their current customer base is now more challenging than ever.

Customer retention is also becoming increasingly important because of the rising costs of marketing. In particular, the cost of mass marketing, the primary tool of conquest marketers, has substantially increased. For example, the cost of a 30-second television spot in 1965 was $19,700. In contrast, a 1991 30-second spot sold for $106,400.

Coupled with the increased cost of advertising has been the loss of the advertiser's "share of voice." Due to the shorter time period now allotted for individual commercials (the average length of commercials has decreased from 60 seconds, to 30 seconds, to 15 seconds), the number of commercials has increased by approximately 25 percent over the past ten years. Hence, firms are competing for attention in a medium that is constantly expanding. In addition, new forms of advertising have evolved, and consumer markets have become more fragmented, which further dilutes the chances of an advertiser's message reaching its intended target audience.

Interestingly, the growth of direct mail marketing in the 1980s is directly attributed to the high costs of mass marketing and subsequent heightened importance of customer retention efforts. Marketers became more selective about how and where their advertising dollars were spent. As a result, the databases built for direct marketing provided the means to identify current customers and track purchases. Subsequently, advertising to current customers became much more efficient than mass marketing in reaching the firm's target market.

Changes in the channels of distribution utilized in today's markets are also having an impact on customer retention. In many cases, the physical distance between producer and consumer is increasing. The growth of nonstore retailing is a prime illustration of how the physical distance between the provider of products and the customer is changing. Transactions can be conducted by phone, mail order, or over the Internet, thereby limiting the physical contact between the provider and the customer. Firms engaged in customer retention efforts should beware of the old saying, "Out of sight, out of mind," and realize that separation from the customer does not diminish their obligation to the customer.

Another change in the channel of distribution is the increasing use of market intermediaries, or "third parties," that assist in the transaction between provider and customer. In this scenario, the marketing intermediary becomes a surrogate provider and, as such, represents the firm that produces the product. Although the use of third parties and other market intermediaries increases the firm's market coverage, it can also adversely affect customer retention rates. For example, a travel agent who sells an airline's service may misrepresent the airline (e.g., flight times, seating arrangements, etc.) and damage the relationship between the customer and the airline. Again, firms engaged in customer retention

The use of marketing intermediaries, such as a travel agent who sells an airline's service, has its advantages and disadvantages. The intermediary can become a surrogate provider and, as such, represent the original firm that produces the product or service.

Source: © 1995 PhotoDisc, Inc. Image no. 14167.

efforts must recognize that the physical distance between themselves and their customers does not minimize their responsibility.

Customer retention has also become increasingly important to firms because today's customers have changed. Typical consumers in the 1990s compared with past generations are more informed about purchasing decisions, command more discretionary income, and are increasingly skeptical about the average firm's concern for their business. Consequently, firms that engage in customer retention practices are usually noticed by today's consumers and rewarded for their efforts via repeat sales.

THE BENEFITS OF CUSTOMER RETENTION

Some experts believe that customer retention has a more powerful effect on profits than market share, scale economies, and other variables commonly associated with competitive advantage. In fact, studies have indicated that as much as 95 percent of profits come from long-term customers via profits derived from sales, referrals, and reduced operating costs (see Figure 14.2).[6]

PROFITS DERIVED FROM SALES

One of the key benefits of customer retention is repeat sales. In addition to the base profit derived from sales, profits are also acquired from increased purchase

CUSTOMER RETENTION

FIGURE 14.2

WHY CUSTOMERS ARE MORE PROFITABLE OVER TIME

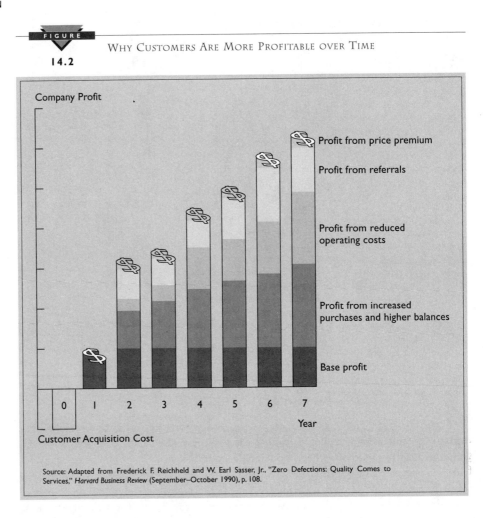

Source: Adapted from Frederick F. Reichheld and W. Earl Sasser, Jr., "Zero Defections: Quality Comes to Services," *Harvard Business Review* (September–October 1990), p. 108.

frequency and interest rates applied to higher balances on charge accounts (for firms that offer credit services). An added bonus of retaining existing customers is that existing customers are willing to pay more for a firm's offering. This occurs because customers become accustomed to the firm, its employees, and the manner in which the service is delivered. Subsequently, a relationship develops that lowers the customer's risk. In essence, repeat customers are willing to pay more for purchase situations in which the uncertainty of the outcome is lessened or removed.

Increasing customer retention rates can have a profound effect on a firm's profitability. For example, past studies have shown that a 5 percent increase in retention rate can translate into 85 percent higher profits for a branch bank,

50 percent higher profits for an insurance broker, and 30 percent higher profits for an auto-service chain.[7]

PROFITS FROM REDUCED OPERATING COSTS

Past research has indicated that it costs three to five times less to keep a customer than to get a new one.[8] The trusting relationship that develops between customers and the firm makes existing customers more receptive to the firm's marketing efforts and, therefore, easier to sell new services to. This, in turn, lowers the cost of the firm's marketing efforts.

Overall, long-term customers tend to have lower maintenance costs. Existing customers become accustomed to the company, employees, and procedures; therefore, they ask fewer questions and have fewer problems. The airline price war that took place in the summer of 1992 presented a few unforeseen problems for the airlines. On one hand, the lower prices did achieve their desired effect—increased sales. Many of these sales, however, were to passengers who had never flown before and who were unfamiliar with ticketing practices, baggage handling, and typical airline behavior. Services such as complimentary beverages had to be explained to new passengers who were unfamiliar with the term *complimentary*. In one instance, a passenger requested instructions on how to "roll down her window." The result of adding new customers to the mix was stressed-out and overworked flight attendants and lower-than-average quality service to existing customers.

PROFITS FROM REFERRALS

Another benefit of customer retention is the positive word-of-mouth advertising generated by satisfied customers. Existing customers are necessary in order for a firm to develop a reputation that attracts new business. Satisfied customers often refer businesses to their friends and family, which, in turn, reinforces their own decision. As discussed in Chapter Four, personal sources of information are particularly important to services consumers because of intangibility and the perception of increased risk associated with service purchases. New business attributed to current customer referrals can be dramatic. For example, a leading home builder in the United States has found that 60 percent of its business is based on referrals from past customers.[9]

CUSTOMER RETENTION TACTICS

Firms that embrace a defection management philosophy engage in customer retention tactics that should be routinely implemented on a per-customer basis. Unfortunately, prior research suggests that two-thirds of customers defect because they feel that companies are not genuinely concerned for their well-being.

CUSTOMER RETENTION

That's the bad news! The good news is that the opportunity exists to demonstrate to customers that the firm really cares about them. Because of the lack of consistent customer service that customers experience, firms that effectively communicate customer retention as a primary goal are noticed. Consequently, a firm's defection management efforts should serve to successfully differentiate the firm from its competitors. Effective tactics for retaining customers include the items discussed next.[10]

MAINTAIN THE PROPER PERSPECTIVE

Managers and employees of service firms need to remember that the company exists to meet the needs and wants of its consumers. Processing customers like raw materials on an assembly line or being rude to customers is incredibly short-sighted. Companies such as USAir employ slogans such as, "The U in USAir starts with you, the passenger." Credos such as this affect customer expectations and reinforce to employees exactly where the firm's priorities lie.

Interacting with the public is not an easy task, and, unfortunately, employees occasionally fail to maintain the proper perspective. The same questions may have to be asked over and over, and not every customer is polite. Maintaining the proper perspective involves a customer-oriented frame of mind and an attitude for service. Employees need to remember that every customer has his or her own personal set of needs and that the customer's, not the employee's, expectations define performance.

REMEMBER CUSTOMERS BETWEEN CALLS

Contacting customers between service encounters is a useful approach in building relationships with the service firm. The key is in making customer contact sincere and personal. Typical approaches include sending birthday, get-well, and/or anniversary cards, writing personal notes congratulating customers for their personal successes, and keeping in touch with consumers concerning the performance of past services rendered and offering assistance if necessary. The goal of this tactic is to communicate to customers that the firm genuinely cares for their well-being.

BUILD TRUSTING RELATIONSHIPS

Trust is defined as a firm belief or confidence in the honesty, integrity, and reliability of another person. In the service environment, three major components of trust are (1) the service provider's expertise, (2) the service provider's reliability, and (3) the service provider's concern for the customer. Strategies for building trust include

- Protecting confidential information.
- Refraining from making disparaging remarks about other customers and competitors.

▴ Telling the customer the truth, even when it hurts.

▴ Providing the customer with full information—the pros and the cons.

▴ Being dependable, courteous, and considerate with customers.

▴ Becoming actively involved in community affairs.

MONITOR THE SERVICE DELIVERY PROCESS

After the service has been requested, monitoring the service delivery process should be a key tactic in the firm's customer retention efforts. Due to the inseparability of services, the customer is involved in the delivery process. Although the customer's involvement may decrease the efficiency of the delivery process, vital information can be obtained regarding satisfaction levels prior to the final result of the service. Consequently, service providers that monitor the service delivery process are able to compensate for service inadequacies and influence customer perceptions of service quality prior to completion. Incidentally, this is not true in the manufacturing sector, where the customer has little or no input into the production process prior to the completed product.

Obvious examples would involve a restaurant that regularly communicates with its customers throughout their meal or the owner of firm who contacts a customer with questions about a recent purchase. Proactively seeking customer feedback throughout the process builds customer perceptions of trust and facilitates maintaining customers for life. Note, however, that asking for too much feedback can become an annoyance to the customer.

PROPERLY INSTALL EQUIPMENT AND TRAIN
CUSTOMERS IN USING THE PRODUCT

Proper installation and training saves a lot of headaches in the long run. Customers should not have to become frustrated over not understanding how to use something or, worse, improperly use the product, which may result in damage and further dissatisfaction. Simply dropping off the product and leaving customers to fend for themselves reinforces the idea that the company is not genuinely concerned for the customer's well-being.

BE THERE WHEN YOU ARE NEEDED MOST

When a customer returns a product that is in need of service and repair, don't crawl under a rock and hide. Every firm should stand behind what it sells and ensure that every transaction is handled to the customer's satisfaction. Most customers are realistic and understand that nothing lasts forever. Many times customers are simply looking for advice and alternative solutions to problems, not looking for someone to blame. Expressing a sincere concern for the customer's situation reinforces the firm's customer retention efforts.

PROVIDE DISCRETIONARY EFFORT

Discretionary effort is behavior beyond the call of duty. It is the Procter & Gamble salesperson who voluntarily bags groceries at the grand opening of new grocery store. It is the hotel that sends items misplaced by customers to their homes at no charge. It is the oil company that recognizes the special needs of its customers during difficult times (see Figure 14.3). Discretionary effort involves countless personal touches, little things that distinguish a discrete business transaction from an ongoing relationship.

IS IT ALWAYS WORTHWHILE TO KEEP A CUSTOMER?

Although saving every customer at any cost is a controversial topic and opinions are divided, some experts believe that the customer is no longer worth saving under the following conditions:[11]

- The account is no longer profitable.
- Conditions specified in the sales contract are no longer being met.
- Customers are abusive to the point that it lowers employee morale.
- Customer demands are beyond reasonable, and fulfilling those demands would result in poor service for the remaining customer base.
- The customer's reputation is so poor that associating with the customer tarnishes the image and reputation of the selling firm.

Other experts believe that although these criteria are valid, a more appropriate strategy is to retreat but keep the lines of communication open. Overall, retention efforts should focus on retaining the most profitable customers. Although zero defection is an admirable goal worth pursuing, the investment in customer retention and service recovery programs may not be economically justified in every case. Moreover, it is argued that focusing too heavily on customer retention efforts can harm the firm in the long run if customer acquisition and development efforts are completely overlooked in the process.[12]

EMERGING CUSTOMER RETENTION PROGRAMS

Several relatively new marketing programs have surfaced that typify the recent interest in customer retention, strategies, such as frequency marketing, relationship marketing, aftermarketing, service guarantees, and defection management. The descriptions that follow illustrate the importance of customer retention within each of these programs.

FIGURE 14.3 AN EXAMPLE OF DISCRETIONARY EFFORT

BP OIL COMPANY
101 PROSPECT AVENUE, WEST
CLEVELAND OH 44115

September 18, 1996

K DOUGLAS HOFFMAN
WILMINGTON NC 28409

RE: 04122

Dear K DOUGLAS HOFFMAN:

We are very concerned about the devastation from the recent hurricane in your
area. We hope you have not been personally affected.

If you have, we know how disruptive and financially burdensome such a loss of
property is. We'll be happy to give you additional time to pay any balance that
may be due on your credit card account with no finance charges or late fees.

Just write a short note at the bottom of this letter to let us know how you wish
to extend payment over the next few months. Or, you may call us toll free at
1-800-883-5527 to work out an arrangement.

We realize this is a small gesture but we wanted to offer a helping hand to you as
one of our valued customers.

BP Oil Company

Credit Card Account Number: 04122

Payment Plan:

_____

_____

_____

_____

_____

_____

_____

FREQUENCY MARKETING

The primary goal of **frequency marketing** is to make existing customers more
productive.[13] Consequently, customer retention is a critical component in frequency marketing efforts. In short, frequency marketing combines the use of
data collection, communications, recognition, and rewards to build lasting relationships.

The first step in implementing a frequency marketing program is to collect data
on the firm's best customers and to determine their level of relationship with the

frequency marketing
Marketing technique that strives
to make existing customers
purchase more often from the
same provider.

firm. The level of relationship pertains to the number of different services the customer purchases. For example, bank customers may be involved with their bank not only through checking accounts, but also through savings accounts, car loans, investments, or a home mortgage.

The next step is to communicate with customers on a personal level. Communications need to be interactive to the point that customers can ask questions and establish a relationship with the firm and action oriented in that the firm's communications incite customers to respond. Personal communications demonstrate to customers that the firm recognizes the importance of their patronage. When reward programs are developed that prompt customers to act, the communica-tions become action oriented. Perhaps the most successful frequency marketing programs of all time are the frequent-flier programs. Airlines such as American, Continental, Delta, Northwest, Southwest, TWA, United, and USAir have de-veloped frequent flyer programs designed to reward passengers for flying with one airline. Passenger loyalty is rewarded with credit for "miles," which can be redeemed for discounted fares, free flights, and upgraded seating from coach to first class.

In addition to appealing to the pleasure traveler, frequent-flier programs are the easiest way for airlines to compete for business travelers who often travel 10 to 12 times a year or more. Due to the nature of their activities, business travelers often book flights at the last minute and pay higher fares than pleasure travelers. To attract the more profitable business flier segment, most airlines now assign their best customers, customers who fly more than 25,000 to 30,000 miles a year, to premium memberships that include reservation hotlines, early boarding, bonus mileage, and frequent upgrade privileges.[14]

The frequent-flier programs have become so popular that they are now referred to as the "Green Stamps of the 1990s." In addition to redeeming miles for airline-associated discounts, miles are increasingly being redeemed for things other than flights, such as free nights at hotels, savings bonds, restaurant meals, cruises, and merchandise from a variety of retailers. This new way to redeem miles has been accompanied with new ways to earn the miles as well. Other businesses, such as credit card and telephone companies, have signed on with the airlines and typically pay an airline 2 cents per mile to help retain their own customers as well as attract new ones. Travel experts report that frequent-flier program members earn, on average, 40 percent of their miles without flying and redeem 10 percent of their miles for things other than free trips.[15]

RELATIONSHIP MARKETING

relationship marketing
Marketing technique based on developing long-term relationships with customers.

Another relatively new marketing term that typifies the newfound interest in customer retention efforts is relationship marketing. **Relationship marketing** is the union of customer service, quality, and marketing. More specifically, the relationship marketing perspective takes place on two levels: macro and micro.[16] At the macro level, firms engaged in relationship marketing recognize that the marketing activity impacts customer markets, employee markets, supplier markets, internal markets, and influencer markets (such as financial and government markets). Simultaneously, at the micro level, relationship marketing recognizes that the focus of marketing is changing from completing the single transaction and other conquest marketing practices to building a long-term relationship with existing customers.

Proponents of relationship marketing believe that their firm's products will come and go; consequently, the real unit of value is the long-term relationship with the customer. For example, construction and agricultural equipment manufacturer John Deere & Co. measures its success in terms of generations of farming families that have used its products. Baxter International, a $9 billion health-care products and services company, has also embraced the relationship marketing concept.[17] Baxter International actually offers to share the business risk with some of its customers by jointly setting sales and cost reduction targets and sharing the savings or extra expenses.[18]

Overall, relationship marketing emphasizes the importance of customer retention and a concern for quality that transcends departmental boundaries. Relationship marketing broadens the definition of the customer from final consumer to all the groups (e.g., suppliers, employees, influencer markets, etc.) that are integral components in bringing the good or service to the marketplace. Efforts to retain the relationship with all these types of customers are at the core of the relationship marketing concept.

AFTERMARKETING

A third marketing concept that embraces customer retention efforts is aftermarketing.[19] **Aftermarketing** emphasizes the importance of marketing efforts after the initial sale has been made. Aftermarketing techniques include the following:

aftermarketing
Marketing technique that emphasizes marketing after the initial sale has been made.

- ▲ Identifying customers and building a customer data base so that customers can be easily contacted after the sale has been completed.
- ▲ Measuring customer satisfaction and continuously making improvements based on customer feedback.
- ▲ Establishing formal customer communication programs, such as newsletters that convey information such as how the company is using customer feedback in its continuous improvement efforts.
- ▲ Creating an aftermarketing culture throughout the firm that reinforces the importance of maintaining a relationship with the customer after the initial sale.

An industry that has made some of the biggest strides in aftermarketing is the automobile industry. Customers are frequently contacted by sales and service personnel after a vehicle has been purchased or after service has been completed on a vehicle. Generally, customers have been very impressed by the dealer's concern in an industry that has historically focused on the quick sell.

CUSTOMER RETENTION

Weyerhaueser, the paper giant, has taken aftermarketing even farther by requiring some of its employees to actually work at their client's operations sites for a week. One aftermarketing success story involved the placement of a bar code on newsprint rolls the company regularly shipped to its consumers. Weyerhaueser employees in the field noticed that the bar code would regularly stick to its customers' high-speed presses. The problem was solved by merely moving the bar code a few inches. Weyerhaueser later found that other customers had experienced similar problems but had never complained. Placing employees in the field to see personally how customers use the company's products has been beneficial for both Weyerhaueser and its customers.[20]

SERVICE GUARANTEES

One of the most innovative and intriguing customer retention strategies to be developed in recent years is the service guarantee.[21] Although guarantees in and of themselves are not particularly new, they are very new with respect to services, particularly professional services. Overall, service guarantees appear to facilitate three worthwhile goals: (1) reinforce customer loyalty, (2) build market share, and (3) force the firm offering the guarantee to improve its overall service quality.

As discussed in Chapter Twelve, service quality consists of five dimensions: reliability, responsiveness, assurance, empathy, and tangibles. Although each dimension is a crucial component of the service delivery process, experts contend that "customers value reliability above all other dimensions." Consequently, a firm's efforts to enhance its reliability may serve to significantly differentiate the firm from its competitors.

In theory, the offering of a service guarantee to customers should ensure customers that the firm is reliable. Simply stated, reliability is "the ability to perform the service dependably and accurately." The service guarantee lowers the risk generally assumed by service customers by "overcoming client concerns about the highest value for the money."

Characteristics of Successful Guarantees   In general, successful guarantees are unrestrictive, stated in specific and clear terms, meaningful, hassle free when invoked, and quick to be paid out. On the other hand mistakes to avoid when constructing a guarantee include (1) promising something that is trivial and normally expected, (2) specifying an inordinate number of conditions as part of the guarantee, and (3) making the guarantee so mild that it is never invoked.

Types of Guarantees   In general, there are three types of guarantees: (1) the implicit guarantee, (2) the specific result guarantee, and (3) the unconditional guarantee. The discussion that follows briefly describes each type of guarantee and the trade-offs associated with it.

The **implicit guarantee** is essentially an unwritten, unspoken, guarantee that establishes an understanding between the firm and its customers. Although the

implicit guarantee

An unwritten, unspoken guarantee that establishes an understanding between the firm and its customers.

guarantee is not specified, customers of firms that offer implicit guarantees are ensured that the firm is dedicated to complete customer satisfaction. Consequently, a partnership spirit is developed between the firm and its customers based on mutual trust and respect.

The trade-offs associated with an implicit guarantee strategy are intriguing. On the positive side, because the guarantee is implicit, no explicit specifications state exactly what the firm will do should the guarantee need to be invoked. Consequently, the service firm can tailor the payout of the guarantee to fit the magnitude of the service failure. Hence, an implicit guarantee may not result in an all-or-nothing type of arrangement. Other benefits associated with the implicit guarantee strategy are that (1) it avoids the appearance of a tacky marketing ploy compared with an explicit guarantee; and (2) it avoids stating publicly the possibility that the firm on occasion may not fulfill its promises. In sum, an implicit guarantee is thought to be the "classy" way of pursuing a guarantee strategy.

An implicit guarantee also has its drawbacks. Since an implicit guarantee is unspoken and unwritten, "a firm pursuing an implicit guarantee strategy has to earn its reputation by repeated acts of goodwill communicated to potential clients via word of mouth, a time-consuming process."[22] Hence, an implicit guarantee does little to differentiate a firm early in its business life cycle. In addition, because the guarantee is implicit, new customers may be unaware of the firm's stance on customer satisfaction and may not bring problems to the firm's attention.

Another type of guarantee is a specific result guarantee. A **specific result guarantee** is considered milder than an explicit unconditional guarantee as "the conditions for triggering the guarantee are narrower and well defined, and the payouts are less traumatic."[23] In contrast to an unconditional guarantee, which covers every aspect of the service delivery process, a specific result guarantee applies only to specific steps or outputs.

On the positive side, specific result guarantees are most easily applied to quantitative results. For example, FedEx guarantees overnight delivery. Moreover, by guaranteeing a specific result as opposed to an overall guarantee, the firm may be able to state its commitment to a particular goal more powerfully. On the negative side, a specific result guarantee may appear weak compared with an unconditional guarantee, and customers may perceive this as the firm's lack of confidence in its own abilities.

An **unconditional guarantee** is the most powerful of the three types of guarantees. The unconditional guarantee "in its pure form promises complete customer satisfaction, and, at a minimum, a full refund or complete, no-cost problem resolution for the payout."[24] In general, offering unconditional guarantees benefits the firm in two ways. First, the firm benefits from the effect that the guarantee has upon customers. More specifically, customer-directed benefits associated with unconditional guarantees include the following:

1. Customers perceive they are getting a better value.
2. The perceived risk associated with the purchase is lower.

specific result guarantee
A guarantee that applies only to specific steps or outputs in the service delivery process.

unconditional guarantee
A guarantee that promises complete customer satisfaction, and at a minimum, a full refund or complete, no-cost problem resolution.

3. The consumer perceives the firm to be more reliable.
4. The guarantee helps consumers decide when comparing competing choices; consequently, the guarantee serves as a differential advantage.
5. The guarantee helps in overcoming customer resistance toward making the purchase.
6. The guarantee reinforces customer loyalty, increases sales, and builds market share.
7. A good guarantee can overcome negative word-of-mouth advertising.
8. The guarantee can lead to brand recognition and differentiation; consequently, a higher price can be commanded.

The second benefit of the unconditional guarantee is directed at the organization itself. A necessary condition for a firm to offer an unconditional guarantee is that it must first have its own operations in order. If not, the payouts associated with an unconditional guarantee will eventually bankrupt the firm. Organization directed benefits of offering unconditional guarantees include the following:

1. The guarantee forces the firm to focus on the customer's definition of good service as opposed to the firm's own definition.
2. In and of itself, the guarantee states a clear performance goal that is communicated to employees and customers.
3. Guarantees that are invoked provide a measurable means of tracking poor service.
4. Offering the guarantee forces the firm to examine its entire service delivery system for failure points.
5. The guarantee can be a source of pride and provide a motive for team building within the firm.

As with the other types of guarantees, a number of risks worth discussing are associated with unconditional guarantees. First, guarantees may send a negative message to some customers, thereby tarnishing the image of a firm that offers a guarantee. Some customers may ponder why the firm needs to offer the guarantee in the first place. For example, customers may consider whether the guarantee is because of failures in the past or out of desperation for new business. Another drawback to unconditional guarantees involves the actual payout when the guarantee is invoked. Customers may be too embarrassed to invoke the guarantee; consequently, the guarantee may actually motivate customers not to complain. Other potential problems associated with the payout involve the amount of documentation the firm requires in order to invoke the guarantee and the time it takes for the actual payout to be completed.

Minimizing the Risk of a Payout Obviously, the primary purpose of a guarantee is to communicate to customers that the firm believes in what it provides and that it is committed to customer satisfaction. Ideally, firms that employ a guarantee strategy will seldom have the guarantee invoked. Firms implementing a guarantee strategy can minimize the event of a payout by (1) fully understanding the customer's needs prior to service delivery; (2) tracking and monitoring the firm's performance throughout the service delivery process; (3) limiting the payout so that it pertains to the key activities and not to minor details (e.g., the firm is refunding the entire amount of the project because the doughnuts were stale at one of the meetings); (4) specifying up front who has the authorization to approve a payout (i.e., upper management or contact personnel); and (5) specifying prior to service delivery the amount involved in the payout.

The Payout When a guarantee is invoked, the question then turns to the amount of the **payout.** While a full refund or double the customer's money back in some instances may make sense, these types of refunds may be out of proportion for small mistakes. In general, the amount of the payout ultimately should depend upon the cost of the service, the magnitude of the service failure, and the customer's perception of what is fair.

payout

The amount of money or resolution a service firm spends in order to fulfill an invoked guarantee.

In 1989, the Hampton Inn chain offered an unconditional guarantee to its customers.[25] "The policy states that any guest who has a problem and is not satisfied by the end of the stay will receive one night's stay at no charge." Incidentally, the guarantee is paid out when the guest settles the account and is not a voucher for a future stay. The impact of the guarantee has been overwhelmingly positive. Employees immediately took notice and responsibility for correcting potential service problems. Moreover, overall quality standards in the hotel have noticeably changed. As a result, employee morale has increased, and employee turnover has decreased.

During the first few months of the program, fewer than $1/10$ of 1 percent of customers invoked the guarantee. By 1991, only 7,000 guests, representing $350,000 in sales, had used the guarantee. Of the guests who have invoked the guarantee, 86 percent say they will return, and 45 percent have already done so. The CEO of Hampton Inn believes that these numbers prove that most guests will not take unfair advantage of the guarantee, and this fact coupled with the impact on employee morale has meant that the guarantee has had a very positive effect on the firm's bottom line.

Professional Service Guarantees As a final note, guarantees as they relate to professional services deserve special consideration.[26] Experts in the area of guarantees believe that guarantees are most effective for professional service providers under the following conditions:

1. Prices are high. Professional service prices easily approach the five- and six-figure range. Guarantees may alleviate some of the risk associated with such costly decisions.
2. The costs of a negative outcome are high. Simply stated, the more important the decision and the more disastrous a negative outcome, the more powerful the guarantee.

3. The service is customized. As opposed to standardized services, where outcomes are fairly certain, customized services are accompanied by a degree of uncertainty. The guarantee helps to alleviate some of the risk associated with the uncertainty.
4. Brand recognition is difficult to achieve. It is difficult to successfully differentiate professional services. For example, an eye exam or dental services are fairly consistent from one provider to the next. In cases like these, the unconditional service guarantee may successfully differentiate the service from the competition.
5. Buyer resistance is high. Due to the expense of many professional services and the uncertainty of the outcome, buyers of professional services are highly cautious. An unconditional guarantee may help in overcoming customer reservations and making the sale.

DEFECTION MANAGEMENT

defection management
A systematic process that actively attempts to retain customers before they defect.

Another way of increasing the customer retention rate is by reducing customer defections. The concept of defection management has its roots in the total quality management (TQM) movement. **Defection management** is a systematic process that actively attempts to retain customers before they defect. Defection management involves tracking the reasons that customers defect and using this information to continuously improve the service delivery system, thereby reducing future defections. Cutting defections in half doubles the average company's growth rate. Moreover, reducing the defection rate by even 5 percent can boost profits 25 percent to 85 percent, depending on the industry (see Figure 14.4).[27]

ZERO DEFECTS VERSUS ZERO DEFECTIONS

zero defects model
A model used in manufacturing that strives for no defects in goods produced.

Since the acceptance of total quality management by the manufacturing sector, the guide to follow has been the **zero defects model.** Although appropriate within the manufacturing sector, where specifications can be identified well ahead of production, the zero defects model does not work well in the service sector.[28]

Service customers carry specifications in their minds and can only approximate their desires to a service provider. For example, customers often show hairstylists a picture of a another person's hairstyle and request a similar style for themselves. The picture is an approximation of a desired result—it does not specify exact lengths to be cut nor specific degree of curve for curls.

Another obstacle to applying the zero defects model in the service sector is that each consumer has his or her own set of expectations and corresponding specifications. As one hairstylist stated, "They [some consumers] come in here with two spoonfuls of hair and expect to leave here looking like Diana Ross!" Consequently, specifications that *are* available in the service sector frequently can not be stan-

DEFECTION MANAGEMENT

FIGURE

14.4

REDUCING DEFECTIONS 5 PERCENT BOOSTS PROFITS 25 TO 85 PERCENT

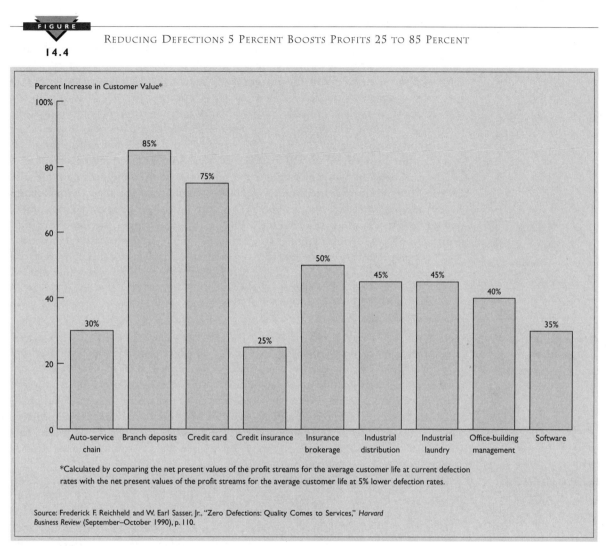

Percent Increase in Customer Value*

*Calculated by comparing the net present values of the profit streams for the average customer life at current defection rates with the net present values of the profit streams for the average customer life at 5% lower defection rates.

Source: Frederick F. Reichheld and W. Earl Sasser, Jr., "Zero Defections: Quality Comes to Services," *Harvard Business Review* (September–October 1990), p. 110.

dardized for all customers. As a result, the service provider must be able to adapt to each set of expectations on the spot.

Because of the unique properties of the service delivery system, the zero defects model used in the manufacturing sector is out of touch with the realities of the service sector. A more appropriate philosophy for service firms would be **zero defections.** In contrast to the "defect pile" of unsellable goods for the manufacturing sector, the "defect pile" in the services sector consists of customers who will not come back.

zero defections

A model used by service providers that strives for no customers defections to competitors.

CUSTOMER RETENTION

The Importance of Defection Management

Businesses commonly lose 15 percent to 20 percent of their customers each year.[29] In some industries, the rate is much higher. For example, the cable television industry loses in excess of 50 percent each year,[30] the cellular phone industry experiences turnover at a rate of 30 percent to 45 percent per year,[31] and customer defections in the pager industry range from 40 percent to 70 percent annually.[32] Reducing customer defections is associated with immediate payoffs. In the credit card industry, for example, a 2 percent decrease in defections has the same net effect on the bottom line as a 10 percent decrease in cost (see Figure 14.5).[33]

Another reason that monitoring customer defections is important is the disturbing possibility that customer defection rates may not be directly associated with customer satisfaction ratings.[34] One would think that satisfied customers would be easily retained. Although the idea is intuitively appealing, receiving high satisfaction marks from current customers does not necessarily translate into undying customer loyalty. On average, 65 to 85 percent of defectors say they were satisfied or very satisfied with their former provider.[35] Why, then, do customers defect?

Defector Types

price defectors
Customers who switch to competitors for lower priced goods and services.

Customers defect for a variety of reasons.[36] **Price defectors** switch to competitors for lower priced goods and services and are probably the least loyal of any customer type. Many businesses that pursue a customer retention philosophy are willing to sacrifice price defectors to avoid constantly discounting their own products and services. In particular, firms that differentiate themselves from competitors based on factors such as reliability, responsiveness, empathy, assurance, and the effective management of the tangible evidence that surrounds the service are generally able to retain customers without constantly discounting their products.

product defectors
Customers who switch to competitors who offer superior goods and services.

Product defectors switch to competitors who offer superior goods and services. As such, product defectors are the most difficult to bring back to the fold once they leave. For example, it is difficult to imagine returning to a provider of inferior service once a superior provider is found. The secret to minimizing product defectors is to not become complacent with today's successes and ignore the changing needs of customers. Innovations and continuous improvement are critical in the battle of retaining product defectors.

service defectors
Customers who defect due to poor customer service.

Service defectors defect due to poor customer service. Contrary to other defector types, firms that are plagued by service defectors are actually providing existing customers with reasons to take their business elsewhere. Inadequately informed personnel, unfulfilled promises, and unacceptable employee behavior are typical reasons customers flee to the competition. Service failures like these combined with inadequate employee responses to those failures can lead to service defections. While other defector types are primarily externally driven, service defectors leave as a result of problems with the internal operations of the firm.

FIGURE
14.5

A CREDIT CARD COMPANY'S DEFECTION CURVE

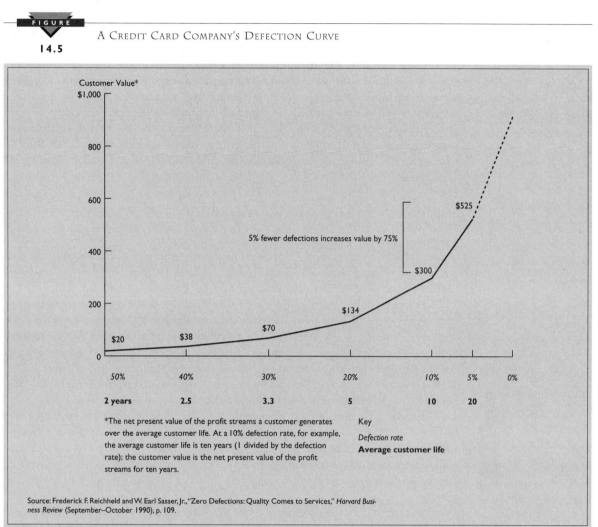

*The net present value of the profit streams a customer generates over the average customer life. At a 10% defection rate, for example, the average customer life is ten years (1 divided by the defection rate); the customer value is the net present value of the profit streams for ten years.

Key

Defection rate
Average customer life

Source: Frederick F. Reichheld and W. Earl Sasser, Jr., "Zero Defections: Quality Comes to Services," *Harvard Business Review* (September–October 1990), p. 109.

Market defectors exit the market because of relocation or business failure reasons. Customers, both individuals and businesses, who move out of the market area would be considered market defectors. Similarly, companies that go out of business and are no longer in the market for goods and services are market defectors.

Technological defectors switch to products outside the industry. Typical examples of technological defections include the switch from lamp oil to electricity and from rail to air transportation. As is the case with product defections, technological defections may occur due to the complacency of the firm. Successful firms are often lulled into a false sense of security and fail to react to technological developments

market defectors
Customers who exit the market due to relocation or business failure.

technological defectors
Customers who switch to products outside the industry.

outside their own industry. For example, the manufacturers of vinyl albums who were caught off guard by the development and consumer acceptance of the compact disk lost much of their business through technological defections.

Organizational defectors result from political considerations inside the firm. In some instances, organizational defections will occur due to reciprocal buying arrangements. For example, an engineering firm may switch its paper products purchasing to a firm that sells the brand of paper products marketed by the pulp and paper mill that retains the engineering firm's services. In other instances, organizational defections may occur as the result of friendships that develop through civic clubs, country clubs, and a variety of other social and business gatherings.

organizational defectors
Customers who leave due to political considerations inside the firm, such as reciprocal buying arrangements.

THE DEFECTION MANAGEMENT PROCESS

Although customer defections are frustrating for many firms, defection rates are measurable and manageable.[37] Defections indicate where profits are heading as well as specific reasons that customers are leaving. Information obtained by analyzing defections can assist firms in reaching the goal of continuous improvement.

The key to defection management is the creation of a zero defections culture within the firm. Everyone in the firm must understand that zero defection is a primary goal of the organization. To establish this primary goal, the firm's first step in the defection management process is communicating to its employees the importance of retaining current customers and the benefits obtained by reducing defections. The earlier discussions in this chapter outline the importance and benefits of customer retention that should be conveyed to employees.

The zero defections goal communicated to employees must have supporters at all levels, starting at the top of the organization. It is critical that upper management lead by example and that managers "walk what they talk." Managers who talk customer service in employee meetings and then bad-mouth customers in the backroom will never successfully implement a zero defections culture within their firm.

The second step in creating a zero defections culture is to train employees in defection management. Defection management involves (1) gathering customer information; (2) providing specific instructions about what to do with the information; (3) instructing employees in how to react to the information; and (4) encouraging employees to respond to the information.

The third and perhaps most critical step in the defection management process is to tie incentives to defection rates. Simply stated, if the firm truly values reducing defections, the reward structure should reinforce customer retention efforts. Firms such as MBNA, as mentioned in the opening vignette, are dedicated to customer retention and have developed reward systems consistent with their customer retention efforts. It is MBNA's policy to talk with every customer who wishes to drop its services. MBNA's employees earn up to 20 percent of their salaries in bonuses associated with customer retention efforts. As a result of the reward structure and these extra communication efforts with customers, MBNA retains 50 percent of customers who call with an intent to end the relationship.[38] Another example is State Farm Insurance. State Farm agents receive the same commission for securing renewals as they do for signing up new customers.[39] As a company, State Farm recognizes the value of customer retention and rewards employees for their customer retention efforts.

Finally, firms successful in defection management also carefully consider creating switching barriers that discourage defections.[40] A customer switching banks is subjected to the time-consuming task of closing one account at the old bank, opening a new account at the new bank, and sometimes paying for new checks to be printed. Switching to a new dentist may require the cost of new x-rays, and switching to a new physician may translate into completing extensive patient information forms and enduring an extensive physical exam. The key to successfully implementing switching barriers is to develop low entry barriers and nonmanipulative yet high exit barriers.

Overall, the key to defection management is the realization that customer defections are measurable and manageable. Too often, firms simply write off customers who no longer request their services. Defection management focuses on retaining customers before they defect and determining the reasons for defections when they do occur. In sum, defectors are a valuable source of information regarding the firm's operations, its employees, and its future.

S U M M A R Y

Due to stagnant markets, increased competition, the rising costs of marketing, changes in channels of distribution, and the ever-changing needs of consumers, the concept of customer retention has increased in importance. Customer retention refers to focusing the firm's marketing efforts toward its existing customer base. Hence, in contrast to seeking new customers, firms engaged in customer retention efforts work to satisfy existing customers in hope of further developing the customer-provider relationship.

Customer retention is associated with a wide variety of benefits, including the profits derived from initial and repeat sales, the profits from reduced operating costs, and the profits from referrals. Typically, existing customers make more efficient use of the supply of service available and often prefer to stay with one provider over long periods of time to reduce the risk associated with service purchases.

A number of effective customer retention tactics were presented in this chapter. These strategies include maintaining the proper perspective and remembering that the company exists to serve the needs of its customers; maintaining contact with customers between service encounters; building trust between the firm and its customers; monitoring the service delivery process; properly installing products and training customers in how to use the products they purchase; being available when problems occur; and being willing to expend discretionary effort when needed.

Not all customers may be worth keeping. In general, however, firms focusing their efforts on customer retention programs such as frequency marketing, relationship marketing, aftermarketing, service guarantees, and defection management have found their efforts to be worthwhile and highly profitable.

KEY TERMS

customer retention	defection management
conquest marketing	zero defects model
frequency marketing	zero defections
relationship marketing	price defectors
aftermarketing	product defectors
implicit guarantee	service defectors
specific result guarantee	market defectors
unconditional guarantee	technological defectors
payout	organizational defectors

REVIEW QUESTIONS

1. Why has conquest marketing become an acceptable form of business for many of today's firms?

2. Discuss the problems associated with conquest marketing.

3. Discuss the steps associated with frequency marketing as they relate to frequent-flier programs.

4. How have changes within service distribution channels had an impact on customer retention?

5. Discuss the distinction between zero defects and zero defections.

6. How do service defectors differ from other defector types?

7. Is it always worthwhile to retain a customer?

8. Discuss the characteristics of successful guarantees.

9. What are the trade-offs associated with utilizing implicit guarantees?

NOTES

1. Robert E. Wayland and Paul M. Cole, "Turn Customer Service into Customer Profitability," *Management Review* (July 1994), pp. 22–24.

2. Rahul Jacob, "Why Some Customers Are More Equal than Others," *Fortune*, September 19, 1994, pp. 218, 220.

3. Terry G. Vavra, AFTERMARKETING: *How to Keep Customers for Life through Relationship Marketing* (Homewood, IL: Business One Irwin, 1992), pp. 2–6.

4. Vavra, AFTERMARKETING, p. 1.

5. Ibid., pp. 2–6.

6. Michael W. Lowenstein, "The Voice of the Customer," *Small Business Reports* (December 1993), pp. 57–61.

7. Frederick F. Reichheld and W. Earl Sasser, Jr., "Zero Defections: Quality Comes to Services," *Harvard Business Review* (September–October 1990), pp. 105–111.

8. Barry Farber and Joyce Wycoff, "Customer Service: Evolution and Revolution," *Sales and Marketing Management* (May 1991), pp. 44–51.

9. Reichheld and Sasser, "Zero Defections," p. 107.

10. Adapted from Barton A. Weitz, Stephen B. Castleberry, and John F. Tanner, Jr., *Selling: Building Partnerships* (Homewood IL: Irwin, 1992), pp. 330–340.

11. "Is Customer Retention Worth the Time, Effort and Expense," *Sales and Marketing Management* 143,15 (December 1991), pp. 21–22.

12. Wayland and Cole, "Turn Customer Service," p. 24.

13. Richard Barlow, "Building Customer Loyalty through Frequency Marketing," *The Bankers Magazine* (May/June 1990), pp. 73–76.

14. Jim Ellis, "Frill-Seeking in the Clouds," *Business Week*, September 13, 1993, pp. 104–105.

15. Adam Bryant, "Airlines' Frequent-Flier Miles Not Just for Flying Anymore," *Sunday Star-News*, August 21, 1994, p. 10A.

16. Martin Christopher, Adrian Payne, and David Ballantyne, *Relationship Marketing* (Oxford: Butterworth-Heinemann, 1991).

17. Jacob, "Why Some Customers," p. 222.

18. Ibid., p. 215.

19 Vavra, AFTERMARKETING, p. 1.

20. Jacob, "Why Some Customers," p. 222.

21. Adapted from Christopher W. L. Hart, Leonard A. Schlesinger, and Don Maher, "Guarantees Come to Professional Service Firms," *Sloan Management Review* (Spring 1992), pp. 19–29.

22. Ibid., p. 29.

23. Ibid., p. 28.

24. Ibid., p. 20.

25. "Service Guarantees Yield Surprising Results," *The Cornell H.R.A. Quarterly* (February 1991), pp. 14–15.

26. Hart, Schlesinger, and Maher, "Guarantees Come," p. 20.

27. Reichheld and Sasser, "Zero Defections," p. 110.

28. Ron Zemke, "The Emerging Art of Service Management," *Training* (January 1992), pp. 37–42.

29. Reichheld and Sasser, "Zero Defections," p. 108.

30. "How Five Companies Targeted Their Best Prospects," *Marketing News*, February 18, 1991, p. 22.

31. *The Cellular Telephone Industry: Personal Communication* (Silver Spring, MD: Herschel Shostack Assoc., 1992), p. 122.

32. *The Pager Industry: ProNet Annual Report*, 1989.

33. Reichheld and Sasser, "Zero Defections," p. 108.

34. Lowenstein, "The Voice," p. 57.

35. Patricia Sellers, "Keeping the Buyers," *Fortune* (Autumn/Winter 1993), pp. 56–58.

36. Glenn DeSouza, "Designing a Customer Retention Plan," *The Journal of Business Strategy* (March/April 1992), pp. 24–28.

37. Reichheld and Sasser, "Zero Defections," p. 105.

38. Larry Armstrong, "Beyond May I Help You?," *Business Week/Quality* (1991), pp. 100–103.

39. Sellers, "Keeping the Buyers," p. 58.

40. DeSouza, "Designing," p. 27.

15

PUTTING THE PIECES TOGETHER: CREATING THE SEAMLESS SERVICE FIRM

"*U*sing industrial models to manage service-based corporations makes as little sense as using farm models to run factories.*"

Stanley M. Davis, "Management Models for the Future," *New Management* 1 (Spring 1983)

"*W*hat is needed now is to surround these individuals with the system—a logically and tightly connected seamless set of interrelated parts—that allows people to perform their jobs well.*"

Benjamin Schneider and David E. Bowen, *Winning the Service Game*, (Boston: Harvard Business School Press)

C H A P T E R   O B J E C T I V E S

The purpose of this chapter is to tie together the information presented in this book in a meaningful manner. In order to provide service excellence, the individual components of the firm must act in unison to create a "seamless" organization. The firm will not act as one if the current culture of the organization is based on departmentalization and functionalism. Consequently, creating and supporting a customer-focused organizational culture is critical. Finally, by conducting a service audit, a seamless service culture is fostered as personnel throughout the organization come to appreciate the challenges faced and the contributions made by everyone involved in the firm's final service delivery effort. After reading this chapter, you should be able to

- ▸ Compare and contrast the concept of seamlessness to departmentalization and functionalism.
  - ▸ *Discuss the historical weakness of marketing in service firms.*
- ▸ Explain the basic concepts of the three-tiered model of service firms.
  - ▸ *Explain what is meant by the firm's culture.*
- ▸ Discuss methods that may lead to cultural change.
  - ▸ *Discuss the basic components of a service audit.*

GETTING THE FIRM'S ACT TOGETHER: THE HAVES AND HAVE NOTS

*I*n the preface, you were warned that you may never view your service experiences as customers in the same way again. By now, you should understand the fundamentals of providing good service and be very aware of when poor service is delivered to you personally. In the effort to regain some control or vent frustrations, students often seek out their instructors, who they feel will lend them a sympathetic ear. For good or ill, service instructors often find themselves playing the role of an advice columnist as they listen to one student-generated customer service story after another. Based on the stories told, the two service incidents below are typical of firms that have their act together and those that do not.

ONE OF THE HAVE NOTS

This first incident is about a customer who wanted to drop off his laundry at a local dry cleaner. The firm's advertising promised, "In by 9:00, out by 5:00." The customer entered the dry cleaner at 8:45 A.M. and gave his laundry to an employee, who recorded all the usual information such as name and telephone number. The employee then asked when the customer would like to pick up his laundry. The customer responded that he would like to take advantage of the firm's prompt service offer and get his laundry back that afternoon at 5:00 P.M. The employee then informed the customer that the truck that picks up the day's laundry and delivers it to the firm's main operations site had already arrived and departed. The customer pointed out to the employee the promise of the firm's sign, and the employee responded that she was just an employee and there was nothing she could do for him.

Frustrated, the customer asked to speak to the manager. The employee responded that she was the firm's only representative at that particular site. The customer then asked for the owner's telephone number and for permission to use the laundry's telephone. The employee complied with both requests. Upon reaching the owner, the customer explained his situation. Without any form of apology, the owner responded by saying that he had bigger problems to worry about than what his sign promised and suggested that next time the customer bring his laundry earlier. The owner further suggested that if the customer really wanted his laundry done by 5:00 P.M., "the customer" should drive halfway across town to the firm's main operations and drop off his laundry there. As the customer continued to press the owner to make good on the promise made by the firm's service promise, the owner hung up on the customer.

ONE OF THE HAVES

The second incident concerns a customer who lived in an area that took a direct hit from Hurricane Bertha in July 1996. By coincidence, the customer had left town three days earlier to visit family in the midwest and was not at home when the hurricane ripped through the area. Damage caused by the storm was widespread and consisted primarily of downed trees and branches. Shortly after the storm, the customer was in touch with neighbors who informed him that his house had survived but that the yard was full of debris.

Returning to his home two days later, the customer was surprised to see that his entire yard had been cleaned up by his neighbors and that the debris had been hauled off to a local dump site. The customer was grateful to have such good neighbors. Another surprise was that the customer's State Farm insurance agent had left his card inside the door frame of the house. The agent made a personal trip to the customer's home to see whether the customer and his family required any assistance. In other words, the agent arrived before the customer even attempted to track him down during a period in which the customer believed that getting through to his insurance agent would be next to impossible. Apparently, this type of personalized treatment is part of State Farm's culture—its corporate offices sent an additional 200 agents into the area to assist in assessing and settling claims. In addition, local radio stations aired public service announcements to inform property owners of simple procedures and locations at which to contact insurance personnel.

Although it sounds a bit "corny," when the customer compared the actions of his neighbors with the service he received from his State Farm agent, the company's corporate slogan rang true: "Like a good neighbor, State Farm [was] there!"

**PUTTING THE PIECES
TOGETHER: CREATING
THE SEAMLESS
SERVICE FIRM**

I N T R O D U C T I O N

seamless service

Services that occur without
interruption, confusion, or hassle
to the customer.

Creating a **seamless service** organization means providing services without interruption, confusion, or hassle to the customer.[1] Seamless service firms manage to simultaneously provide reliable, responsive, competent, and empathetic services and have the facilities and resources necessary to get the job done. Seamlessness applies not only to the provision of services but also to service recovery efforts pertaining to core system failures, implicit/explicit customer requests, and employee behavior.

Seamlessness thrives on tightly connected interrelated parts within the service delivery system. Functionalization and departmentalization kills seamlessness. For example, consider the following three memos sent to a young manager of a branch bank on the same day:[2]

> *From the marketing department:*
> We shortly will be launching a new advertising campaign based on the friendliness of our staff. This is in direct response to the increasingly competitive marketplace we face. Please ensure that your staff members deliver the promises we are making.

> *From the operations department:*
> As you are aware, we are facing an increasingly competitive marketplace and, as a result, our profits have come under pressure. It is crucial, therefore, that we minimize waste to keep our costs under control. From today, therefore, no recruitment whatsoever will be allowed.

> *From the personnel department:*
> Our staff members are becoming increasingly militant. This is due, in large part, to the availability of alternative employment with our new competitors. We currently are involved in a particularly delicate set of negotiations and would be grateful if you could minimize any disruptions at the local level.

These instructions from the three different departments obviously conflict with one another. To obey the operations department means no recruitment and, therefore, an increase in the work load of contact personnel. The increased work load will most likely be a hot topic during labor negotiations and could be disastrous for the personnel department. Finally, the increased work load, in all probability, will have a negative effect on staff morale. Given the inseparability of the service, the staff's low morale will be visible to customers and will negatively affect customer satisfaction levels.

If this particular branch bank is marketing oriented, the young manager will attempt to trade off the three sets of instructions, giving added weight to the marketing department's instructions. It should be stressed that, in service firms, it is nearly impossible to be totally marketing-oriented. Customers cannot be given everything they want because of the constraints imposed by the firm's service delivery system. For example, in a restaurant setting, every customer cannot be seated and served immediately upon arrival due to seating and available service (personnel) constraints.

If this branch is operations oriented, added weight will be given to the operations department's set of instructions. The young manager may relay marketing's request to the vice-president of operations and ask for clarification. The operations vice-president, in turn, may fire off an abusive memo to her counterpart in marketing. The memo may ask why marketing was sending memos directly to the branches at all and suggest that in the future, all other requests made by marketing should be cleared by operations.

Firms that continue to cling to functional and departmental mindsets are often besieged by internal conflict as departments compete against one another for resources instead of pulling together to provide exceptional service. Seamlessness is "tooth-to-tail" performance—a term commonly used in the armed forces. "The personnel out front in the trenches need to be backed up with coordinated supplies, information resources, personnel reinforcements, and so on."[3] Similarly, the primary efforts of the service firm should focus on the service delivery process and on the personnel providing customer services.

The conflict that often occurs among marketing, operations, and human resources is not personal.[4] It is a result of their different cultures, which are functions of each department's goals, planning horizons, departmental structure, people-management systems, and the specific individuals in each department. For example, marketing tends to have a longer planning horizon, is less rigidly and hierarchically organized, and tends to reward innovation and creativity compared with its operations counterparts.

In comparison with goods-producing firms, turf wars among departments are more prevalent in service firms due to lack of inventories. Inventories, which provide a buffer between marketing and operations in goods-producing firms, are for the most part nonexistent in service firms. In a service firm, production and consumption often occur simultaneously in a real-time experience.

The Historical Weakness of Marketing in Service Firms[5]

Service firms often find themselves in a three-cornered fight among marketing, operations, and personnel (human resources). (See Figure 15.1.) Somehow, marketing always seems to lose this fight since marketers tend to have less influence in service companies than in goods companies.

At this point, it is necessary to understand the differences among marketing orientation, the marketing function, and the marketing department. **Marketing orientation** means that a firm or organization plans its operations according to

marketing orientation
A firm's view toward planning its operations according to market needs.

PUTTING THE PIECES
TOGETHER: CREATING
THE SEAMLESS
SERVICE FIRM

FIGURE

15.1

THE THREE-CORNERED FIGHT FOR CONTROL

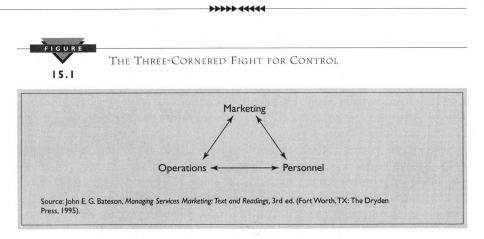

Source: John E. G. Bateson, *Managing Services Marketing: Text and Readings*, 3rd ed. (Fort Worth, TX: The Dryden Press, 1995).

market needs. The objectives of the firm are to satisfy customer needs rather than merely to use production facilities or raw materials.[6] Marketing orientation is clearly an attitude that puts the customer's needs first in any trade-off. Firms do not require a formal marketing department in order to have a marketing orientation.

Marketing functions in a firm include tasks such as the design of the product, pricing, and promotion. Decisions in these areas are made in order for the organization to operate, but they need not necessarily be made by people with marketing titles nor by individuals in a formal **marketing department**—the department that traditionally works on marketing functions in the company.

In a typical goods company, the distinctions among marketing orientation, marketing functions, and marketing department are not necessary. They are, however, necessary in service firms, where a formal marketing department may not necessarily exist. Since the service product is an interactive process, it may be more appropriate to leave the different functional decisions to different departments.

The variety of relationships between marketing and other functions within the organization can be illustrated by the **customization/customer contact matrix** depicted in Figure 15.2. One axis of the matrix relates directly to the degree of contact the firm has with its customers. The higher the level of customer contact, the higher the level of inefficiency because of the uncertainty introduced by customers. This idea is based largely on the concept of inseparability and the participation of consumers in the service delivery process. The second axis relates to the amount of customization of the service available to consumers. Once again, we would expect the "low" state to be preferable for efficiency purposes as it would allow the service delivery system to operate as a production line free from outside influences. A variety of businesses are introduced into the cells to illustrate how the matrix is used.

For example, a travel agency can operate in a number of cells simultaneously. Booking an airline ticket by telephone for a business traveler fits into the low/low cell. But the same travel agency could just as well operate in a different cell if it also maintained a retail operation. From within the retail operation, both high and low customization are possible, depending on whether the customer is a business traveler wanting a ticket or a vacationer planning a multistop European trip.

marketing functions

Tasks such as the design of a product, its pricing, and its promotion.

marketing department

The formal department in an organization that works on the marketing functions of the company.

customization/customer contact matrix

A table that illustrates the variety of relationships between marketing and other functions within the organization.

FIGURE

15.2

THE CUSTOMIZATION/CUSTOMER CONTACT MATRIX

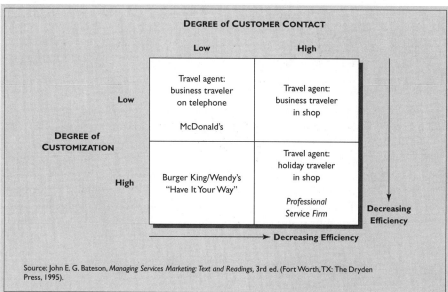

Source: John E. G. Bateson, *Managing Services Marketing: Text and Readings*, 3rd ed. (Fort Worth, TX: The Dryden Press, 1995).

From an operations perspective, the ideal cell is the low/low cell. In this cell, the degree of customization is minimized so that large parts of the organization can be isolated and run like any other manufacturing plant.[7] In addition, the level of customization is also minimized so that the operating system is focused on a limited range of output and its efficiency increased.[8] A move into this cell, however, can have major implications for marketing. Customers may be seeking contact and customization and be willing to pay a premium for them.

A top-quality French restaurant might fit into the high/high cell. Compared with McDonald's, this is a different business with a different formula (but, interestingly, the target segment may be the same person on a very different occasion). The loss of efficiency implied by the high/high cell is compensated for by the price that can be charged.

The importance of the matrix and this discussion is to show how different cells suggest alternative roles and places for the marketing departments of firms operating within them. Two contrasting examples are the provision of legal services by a traditional law firm and by a firm such as Hyatt Legal Services.

Operationally, the traditional firm will fit into the high/high cell in the matrix. The firm's attorneys will be in intensive contact with clients and will customize each service to meet the needs of each individual client. Except for routine cases, there will be little opportunity for economies of scale in this type of legal firm.

PUTTING THE PIECES
TOGETHER: CREATING
THE SEAMLESS
SERVICE FIRM

From a marketing point of view, the service product in the high/high cell often is created in the client's offices, away from the home firm of the attorney. In such situations, it is clear that a central marketing department has little influence over the final product and that most of the marketing needs to be delegated to the field offices, if not to the individual attorneys themselves. The selling function is done by consultants or professionals, so that, too, must be delegated.

The alternative is a firm such as Hyatt Legal Services. This firm represents a clear attempt to move the operating system away from the inefficiency of the high/high cell toward the low/low or, at least, the high contact/low customization cell. By reducing the types of cases handled, operations can be simplified and economies of scale generated. These economies, in turn, can be passed on to the customer through lower fees.

The marketing implications of moving the operation from a high/high cell to a more standardized outcome are relatively straightforward. The service is branded in order to add value for the consumer in a market that traditionally is not heavily branded. The firm depends on systematization and, from an operations point of view, implies centralization. We therefore would expect to find a strong centralized marketing department as well. Clearly, many service firms do not operate in the low/low cell of the matrix, even though they may wish to do so. For many service firms, therefore, the traditional combination of marketing functions in a marketing department breaks down. The result is that there is no strong marketing group to drive a marketing orientation in the organization. The weakness of the marketing function is compounded by the strength of the operations group and the linkages between them.

MOVING BEYOND DEPARTMENTALIZATION AND FUNCTIONALIZATION: THE THREE-TIERED MODEL OF SERVICE FIRMS[9]

three-tiered model
A view of service organizations that reconfigures traditional departmental functions into a customer tier, a boundary tier, and a coordination tier.

Seamless service is based on a **three-tiered model** of the service organization (see Figure 15.3). Traditionally, organizations are sliced by functions such as marketing, human resources, and operations management. In contrast, the three-tiered model consists of a customer tier, a boundary tier, and a coordination tier. Success is based on the effective management and integration of the three tiers.

THE CUSTOMER TIER

customer tier
The tier in the three-tiered model that focuses on customer expectations, needs, and competencies.

As we have discussed throughout the book, attracting and retaining customers is the lifeblood of every service organization. Without customers, the service firm has no reason to exist. The **customer tier** focuses on customer expectations, needs, and competencies. To provide seamless service, management must have a deep understanding of each of these areas from the customer's perspective.

expectations
Consumer expectations pertaining to the service delivery process and final outcome.

Expectations have been discussed throughout this book and are an integral component in developing customer satisfaction evaluations. As firms have realized the importance of customers, experts believe that businesses now have a fairly

▼ **FIGURE** ▼

15.3

THE THREE-TIERED SERVICES MODEL

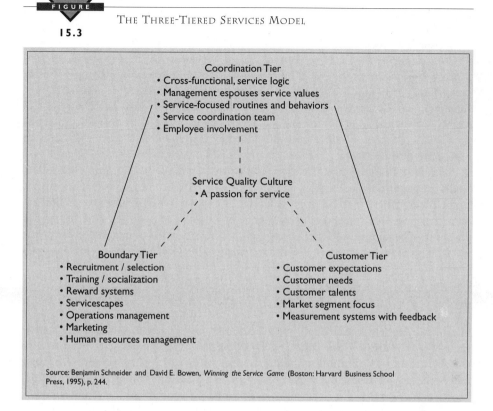

Source: Benjamin Schneider and David E. Bowen, *Winning the Service Game* (Boston: Harvard Business School Press, 1995), p. 244.

good understanding of their customers' expectations but not necessarily of their customers' needs and competencies. At a minimum, service firms must meet customer expectations in order to provide customers what they want, when they want it, and where they want it so that the firms can strategically differentiate themselves from competitors and stay in the service game.

Needs are distinguished from expectations in that customers are generally aware of their expectations but are often unaware of what they need. Chapter Ten provided ample examples of products that met with great success such as minivans, personal computers, and cellular phones, despite early customer research indicating that customers did not feel a need for these products. Service experts believe that firms must deliver three key customer needs in order to deliver service excellence:[10]

1.   Security: The need to feel secure and unthreatened by physical, psychological, or economic harm.
2.   Esteem: The need to feel that one's self-esteem is maintained and enhanced by others.
3.   Justice: The need to feel fairly and justly treated.

needs

Security, esteem and justice; often unrecognized as needs by customers themselves.

PUTTING THE PIECES TOGETHER: CREATING THE SEAMLESS SERVICE FIRM

competencies

The contributions customers bring to the service production process.

Examining and understanding customer needs is the foundation of building a competitive strategy that differentiates the firm from its competitors and of providing service excellence.

Competencies are the contributions customers bring to the service production process. Service firms that excel look beyond their employees as their only human resources. Throughout much of this book, we have discussed the consumer's involvement in the service delivery process. The customer influences the type and length of demand and often is a major determinant in the success or failure of the final outcome. Consequently, appealing to the "best customers" can be a source of competitive advantage.

As an example, Dayton Hudson, the retailer, pursued a strategy that specifically targeted customers who spent more than $1,500 per year in their stores. By involving these customers in designing a program that would attract and retain their business, a special card was developed that entitled the holder to special discounts, free alterations, gift wrapping, free parking, and presale sales days. The information for designing the program was obtained through survey data, which consisted of more than 2,000 detailed responses from targeted clientele.[11]

THE BOUNDARY TIER

boundary tier

The tier in the three-tiered model that concerns itself with the individuals who interact with the customers—the boundary spanners.

While the customer tier deals with customer expectations, needs, and competencies, the **boundary tier** concerns itself with the individuals who interact with the customers—the boundary spanners. The boundary tier is where the customer meets the organization and where the critical incidents or "moments of truth" occur. Service personnel in the boundary tier must be more flexible, communicative, able to deal with stress, and willing to take initiative than their manufacturing counterparts. To the customer, personnel in the boundary tier *are* the organization and occupy a two-way communication role—from the organization to the customer, and from the customer back to the organization.

The key to successfully navigating the boundary tier is to avoid the "human resources trap" that makes the mistake of placing the full burden of "moments of truth" upon boundary-spanning personnel. The firm's nonpersonal services, such as the physical facility, the accuracy and timeliness of billing, and all the support staff who enable the boundary personnel to perform their jobs, must be in place and working together in order for the firm to provide seamless service. Ultimately, boundary personnel are only as good as the service delivery system that supports their efforts.

THE COORDINATION TIER

coordination tier

The tier in the three-tiered model that coordinates activities that help integrate the customer and boundary tiers.

The **coordination tier** is the responsibility of upper management and involves coordinating the activities that help integrate the customer and boundary tiers. Management's most important concerns pertain to (1) defining a target market and developing a strategy for effectively attracting this market; (2) ensuring that the boundary tier has the support necessary to meet the expectations and needs of the customer tier; and (3) ensuring that the expectations and needs of boundary-tier personnel are also being met.

The primary challenge of the coordination tier is to get the various departments within the organization to work with one common goal in mind—serving the customer. Before attempting to integrate the various departments of the firm, it is important to understand that each department is driven by its own **internal logic**—implicit and explicit principles that drive organizational performance.[12] Each department's logic is internally focused on departmental needs and creates seams in the service delivery process. For example, consider the logic behind the following functions: operations management, marketing, and human resources.

internal logic

Implicit and explicit principles of individual departments that drive organizational performance.

Operations logic is driven by the goal of reducing or containing costs through mass production or the use of advanced technologies. Operations and marketing are often in conflict with each other, which creates seams in service delivery. While marketing is concerned with identifying and understanding customer needs and providing goods and services that meet those needs, operations is concerned with how these products and services will be produced and delivered. In essence, marketing is concerned with the management of demand, while operations is concerned with the management of supply. Marketing attempts to focus on meeting demand in the most effective manner in terms of product form, location, price, and promotions, while operations is primarily concerned with meeting demand in the most cost-effective manner. Typical goals of operations management and marketing concerns regarding these goals are displayed in Table 15.1.

operations logic

The reasoning that stresses cost containment/reduction through mass production.

The major challenge for operations in a service setting is the involvement of customers in the production process. Compared with raw materials in a pure manufacturing setting, customers are unpredictable and decrease the efficiency of the delivery system. Operations would like to remove the customer from the production process as much as possible, while marketing promotes the importance of the customer in the production process. Consequently, operations and marketing must establish a point of equilibrium between the variety and depth of products marketing would like to offer and the cost effectiveness of meeting that demand through efficient operations.

While operations management is internally focused, marketing is externally focused on meeting the expectations and needs of consumers. Ideally, the **marketing logic** is to provide customers with options that better enable the service offering to meet individual consumer needs. Although ideal for customers, providing numerous options leads to serious cost inefficiencies in a firm's operations.

marketing logic

The reasoning that stresses providing customers with options that better enable the service offering to meet individual needs.

In addition to often being in conflict with operations, marketing may also find itself in conflict with human resources, creating additional seams in service delivery. For example, marketing would like to staff all personnel positions with individuals who, in addition to being technically competent, possess strong interpersonal skills that enable the organization to better communicate with its customers. Marketing would argue that hiring personnel who happen to be "nice" in

PUTTING THE PIECES
TOGETHER: CREATING
THE SEAMLESS
SERVICE FIRM

TABLE 15.1	OPERATIONS AND MARKETING PERSPECTIVES ON OPERATIONAL ISSUES	
OPERATIONAL ISSUES	**Typical Operations Goals**	**Common Marketing Concerns**
Productivity improvement	Reduce unit cost of production	Strategies may cause decline in service quality
Make-versus-buy decisions	Trade off control against comparative advantage and cost savings	"Make" decisions may result in lower quality and lack of market coverage; "buy" decisions may transfer control to unresponsive suppliers and hurt the firm's image
Facilities location	Reduce costs; provide convenient access for suppliers and employees	Customers may find location unattractive and inaccessible
Standardization	Keep costs low and quality consistent; simplify operations tasks; recruit low-cost employees	Consumers may seek variety, prefer customization to match segmented needs
Batch-versus-unit processing	Seek economies of scale, consistency, efficient use of capacity	Customers may be forced to wait, feel "one of a crowd," be turned off by other customers
Facilities layout and design	Control costs; improve efficiency by ensuring proximity of operationally related tasks; enhance safety and security	Customers may be confused, shunted around unnecessarily, find facility unattractive and inconvenient
Job design	Minimize error, waste, and fraud; make efficient use of technology; simplify tasks for standardization	Operationally oriented employees with narrow roles may be unresponsive to customer needs
Learning curves	Apply experience to reduce time and costs per unit of output	Faster service is not necessarily better service; cost saving may not be passed on as lower prices
Management of capacity	Keep costs down by avoiding wasteful under-utilization of resources	Service may be unavailable when needed; quality may be compromised during high-demand periods
Quality control	Ensure that service execution conforms to predefined standards	Operational definitions of quality may not reflect customer needs, preferences
Management of queues	Optimize use of available capacity by planning for average throughput; maintain customer order, discipline	Customers may be bored and frustrated during wait, see firm as unresponsive

Source: © 1989 by Christopher H. Lovelock. Reprinted with permission from Christopher H. Lovelock. Christopher H. Lovelock, "Managing Interactions Between Operations and Marketing and Their Impact on Customers," in Bowen et al. (eds.) *Service Management Effectiveness* (San Francisco: Jossey Bass, 1990), p. 362.

addition to technically competent is free. In turn, human resources would argue that obtaining and keeping highly trained and personable personnel is much more expensive than hiring people who simply adequately perform their roles in the organization. Furthermore, human resources will point out that certain market segments can be served by personnel who are simply civil with customers and who perform their duties adequately. This point is valid. Does the customer really want a McDonald's worker to engage the customer in a lengthy conversation about the weather, community happenings, and family matters, or would the customer rather have a simply civil employee take the order and deliver the food in a speedy manner? Moreover, the food is more likely to be less expensive when provided by adequate as opposed to superior personnel because of the savings in labor costs.

Human resources logic is to recruit personnel and to develop training that enhances the performance of existing personnel. In the service encounter, operations, marketing, and human resources are inextricably linked. Figure 15.4 depicts the link between operations and human resources. This figure, which compares the degree of customer contact with production efficiency, reveals that no such person as the perfect service employee exists. Characteristics of the "right employee" depend on the characteristics of the particular job in question. Some employees will need to be people oriented, while others will need to be more task oriented to process "things" instead of "people."

The importance of service firm personnel as they interact with customers throughout the service delivery process highlights the link between human resources and marketing. In services, human resources are the only source of quality control. Consequently, the hiring, training, and reward structures developed by human resources will ultimately play a major role in how employees interact with the firm's customers.

Despite the opportunity to make major contributions to the firm's overall service effort, human resources departments are often stuck in their own production orientation and have difficulty getting their own acts together, let alone helping the organization provide superior service. Human resources production-oriented activities include mistakes such as using the same employee evaluation forms for everyone in the firm even though the jobs may be very different, conducting canned employee training programs that never change from year to year, and using generic employee selection procedures for a variety of jobs that actually require different skills. In contrast, service-oriented human resources programs would be co-designed and co-taught with relevant managers, and evaluation forms would be thought of as coaching and evaluating devices rather than as rating forms used solely for compensation decisions. Overall, the service-oriented human resources department would work much more closely with its customers—the employees—and form an ongoing, interactive, long-term relationship in pursuit of supporting those who serve the firm's final consumers.

BUILDING THE SERVICE LOGIC THROUGH CULTURAL CHANGE

The service logic stitches the departmental and functional seams together in order to help the firm provide flawless service. However, before this can happen, the firm's organizational **culture** must be customer focused. The firm's culture reflects the shared values and beliefs that drive the organization—the formally written, the unwritten, and actual occurrences that help employees understand the norms for behavior in the organization. In short, organizational culture establishes the "dos and don'ts" of employee behavior and provides the basis on which various employee behaviors can coalesce.[13]

human resources logic
The reasoning that stresses recruiting personnel and developing training to enhance the performance of existing personnel.

culture
The shared values and beliefs that drive an organization.

PUTTING THE PIECES
TOGETHER: CREATING
THE SEAMLESS
SERVICE FIRM

LINK BETWEEN OPERATIONS AND HUMAN RESOURCES

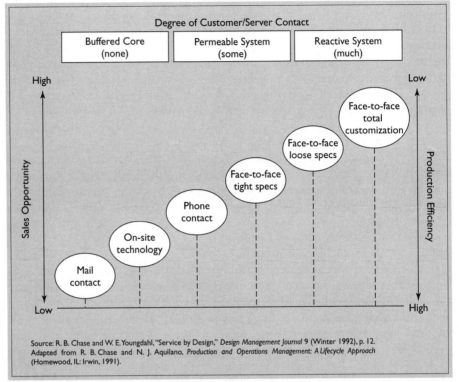

Source: R. B. Chase and W. E. Youngdahl, "Service by Design," *Design Management Journal* 9 (Winter 1992), p. 12. Adapted from R. B. Chase and N. J. Aquilano, *Production and Operations Management: A Lifecycle Approach* (Homewood, IL: Irwin, 1991).

Figure 15.5 presents a simple framework for considering the options available when implementing cultural change in the service organization.[14] The figure suggests that culture is internally linked to and partly an outcome of three organizational components: structure, systems, and people. **Structure** relates to the formal reporting structures normally represented in an organizational chart (such as front-line employees reporting to middle managers, who report to regional managers, who report to national managers, who report to the chief executive officer).

The **systems** component of the framework refers to the people-management systems utilized for control, evaluation, promotion, and recognition. Evaluation and promotion systems include both formal and informal components. For example, management by objectives would be a formal component, while "What do I really have to do around here to get noticed?" would be an informal part of the system. Recognition systems focus on formal and informal rewards as well, ranging from formal rewards such as company trips to informal "pats on the back" such as lunch with the boss.

The other two major components of the culture framework are the people who work in the organization and the firm's current culture. Creating a more

structure

The formal reporting hierarchy normally represented in an organizational chart.

systems

People-management systems of control, evaluation, promotion, and recognition.

FIGURE
15.5

CULTURAL FRAMEWORK

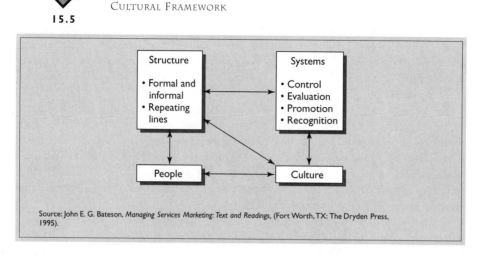

Source: John E. G. Bateson, *Managing Services Marketing: Text and Readings*, (Fort Worth, TX: The Dryden Press, 1995).

customer-focused organization can be accomplished by altering any one of the four components: structure, systems, people, and culture, individually or together.

Changing Culture through Structure

The organization's culture is a function of its structure. Changing culture through structure, however, is a slow process because in many instances, it takes years to successfully implement an organizational change in structure. In the effort to create a more customer-focused organization, two approaches to changing the culture through structure have been tried: (1) utilizing the marketing department as a change agent; and (2) restructuring the firm around the servuction system model.

Marketing Department as Change Agents Marketing departments can be created in order to simply change the current orientation of the firm by creating a customer advocate within the organization. There is a real danger in this approach, however. Once the marketing department has been created, other departments may quickly transfer the complete responsibility for customer satisfaction to the marketing department.[15] Moreover, this transfer is likely to create open warfare among departments in the organization.[16]

Consider again the logic of the operations and the marketing departments. Operations departments, by their very nature, tend to be cost driven; their focus is on evaluating the operation to find costs to save and procedures to simplify. This outlook tends to have a short time horizon. Marketing, by comparison, is looking for product enhancements in order to create a competitive advantage. The creation of such an advantage is not something that firms can expect to achieve in the short run.

The coordination of conflicting departments such as marketing and operations often requires the use of unconventional management techniques. To mesh the

PUTTING THE PIECES
TOGETHER: CREATING
THE SEAMLESS
SERVICE FIRM

interfunctional task force

Problem-solving group in which
individuals with diverse
viewpoints work together and
develop a better understanding
of one another's perspectives.

interfunctional transfers

Moving, via promotion or
transfer, an employee from one
organizational department to
another to foster informal
networks among departments.

logics of the different groups and to allow them to understand one another,
a number of strategies have been suggested by organizational-behavior theory.
Interfunctional task forces are a classic way of forcing individuals with diverse
viewpoints to work together and to develop a better understanding of one
another's perspectives. In the same way, **interfunctional transfers** can create
informal networks of individuals from different departments who understand and
trust one another.

For example, operations managers who are promoted to run a marketing department will face initial problems. Their orientation is toward operations, but
their new roles require a marketing perspective. If such a transfer can be achieved
successfully, the result is usually a general manager who makes rational and clear
trade-offs between operations and marketing. Moreover, it also creates a marketing person who has direct contacts in the operations group and who can overcome
many of the traditional barriers to change.

Once the organization has achieved a strong customer orientation, the marketing department can shrink. For example, in the early 1980s, many professional service firms created marketing departments in this way. The departments focused
on advertising but also on research and customer-satisfaction surveys. The result
was a shift in the culture of the firm and the recognition of the importance of the
customer's needs and expectations.

Restructuring around the Servuction Model A number of service firms have explicitly
or implicitly restructured around the servuction model. For example, one major
airline has all departments that have direct customer contact report to the head of
marketing. Only engineering and the flight crew (pilots) report to the head of operations. Combining all customer-contact departments with the marketing group
has reversed the arguments from, "It will cost too much; it is inefficient," to, "The
customer needs this; how can we make it happen?"

CHANGING CULTURE THROUGH SYSTEMS

The firm's culture is also a function of the systems put into place that control,
evaluate, promote, and recognize the firm's personnel. A number of approaches
have been used to change culture through these systems. Some firms, for example,
have started to give bonuses to managers at all levels based upon the firm's customer satisfaction scores. The firm's overall research effort can be tailored to measure satisfaction down to the branch level, and managers can be rewarded for improved scores. Unfortunately, the problem with this approach is that only part of
the customer's satisfaction is under the control of management. The customer's
expectations can be raised by competitive offerings, and satisfaction scores can
drop as a consequence.

Another approach has been to introduce revenue into branch manager targets.
A major New York bank wanted to change the retail branch manager orientation
from one of considering only costs and security to one of considering customers

first. The bank introduced a revenue-based performance evaluation system. For the first time, managers had to worry about where the customers came from and had to stop thinking of them as "people who made a mess of my branch." Early successes by a few managers produced interesting results. Up to 20 percent of managers left the company, claiming that this was not what they were hired to do. The balance of the managers woke up the bank's sleeping central marketing department to demand help in getting more customers. The long-term result of the change in the system was an increase in customers as well as in bad debt. The managers had discovered that money is an easy product to sell, and the bank had discovered it needed to revamp its credit control function.

Planning systems can also be used to change the orientation of companies. Formal marketing planning can drive organizations through the logic of marketing and can force them to develop an understanding of consumers' needs. Such planning exercises can eventually become "mind-numbing," but for the first two or three cycles, the process can be educational for all personnel involved. This approach is all the more powerful if combined with training and/or direct attacks on culture.

CHANGING CULTURE THROUGH PEOPLE

Outsiders increasingly are being brought into the marketing departments of service firms to try to change the orientation. Such an approach must be supplemented with the development of training programs inside the firm. Operations people need to be trained in marketing, and marketing people need to understand all the areas discussed in this book.

CHANGING CULTURE DIRECTLY

Culture-change programs are becoming increasingly popular. These programs range from broad-scale educational activities to highly empowering personnel in order to re-engineer the firm's entire service delivery process around the customer. Table 15.2 provides a simple way to categorize such activities. Along one axis are the nature of the groups used. Mixed groups are cross-sectional or interdepartmental; family groups can be a department or a naturally occurring group based on process, such as all the individuals involved in loading a particular flight with passengers. The second axis deals with the level of empowerment given to employees. Low levels of empowerment imply that individuals will change their behavior but that the group will have no authority to change the processes and systems of the organization. High-level empowerment implies an ability to change the organization during the event or series of events. The slogans in the cells represent the hypothetical titles of such change programs, which often involve one or more meetings.

The top left cell refers to **"putting the customer first"** programs that take place in mixed groups within the organization. Seated together in sessions, personnel are

**"putting the
customer first"**
The element of the culture
change initiative that teaches
personnel to put the customer
first.

PUTTING THE PIECES
TOGETHER: CREATING
THE SEAMLESS
SERVICE FIRM

TABLE 15.2	CATEGORIZING CULTURE CHANGE INITIATIVES	
	GROUP	
	Mixed	Family
EMPOWERMENT Low	"Putting the Customer First"	"Orientation Change"
High	"Change the Way You Work"	"Change the Way We Work"

Source: John E. G. Bateson, *Managing Services Marketing: Text and Readings*, 3rd ed. (Fort Worth, TX: The Dryden Press, 1995).

"orientation change"

The element of the culture change initiative that teaches "families" of personnel to reinforce one another on the job.

"change the way you work"

The element of the culture change initiative that allows personnel to break the rules in the context of serving their customers.

"change the way we work"

The element of the culture change initiative that teaches personnel to flowchart their activities and to re-engineer the process to better serve their customers.

lectured to and motivated to put the customer first. Through role playing, they are encouraged to recognize the importance of customers and change their behavior accordingly.

These types of programs can be very successful. To be successful, however, the new behavior needs to be reinforced on the job. If management and front-line personnel do not share the same level of enthusiasm and dedication toward the goal of creating a customer-oriented organization, the value of the lessons learned can be wiped out within hours. Without commitment to change, the new behaviors learned will be trivialized by colleagues, the old behaviors will be reinstated quickly, and the value of the program will be a total loss.

The top right cell, **"orientation change,"** overcomes these problems by processing personnel by family groups whose members can reinforce one another on the job. Both cells, however, focus on changing attitudes and individual behaviors. Changing organizational processes and systems are not part of these programs. This potentially produces role conflict as desired individual behaviors are stopped by organizational constraints such as the physical environment or the current operating system.

"Change the way you work," in the lower left cell, draws on the empowerment ideas described in detail in Chapter Ten. It implies active empowerment of the personnel attending the program. Personnel are allowed to break the rules in the context of serving their customers. Because of the mixed group, however, this type of initiative is focused on the individual rather than on process-level empowerment.

The lower right cell, **"change the way we work,"** refers to initiatives that draw on many of the ideas in this book. Groups are in families and can be asked to flowchart their activities. They can then be asked to re-engineer the process to better serve their customers. The level of excitement in such groups is matched only by the anxiety of their bosses. Empowerment at this level really does place the boss in the role of coach and facilitator, and that is exactly what the boss's role should be. In creating a seamless organization, it is not management's job to force or dictate to employees to deliver service excellence. "Management's job is to put together a system that actually makes it possible to deliver quality service."[17]

THE TACTICAL QUESTIONS RELATING TO SEAMLESSNESS: CONDUCTING A SERVICE AUDIT[18]

One helpful approach in creating a seamless organization involves conducting a service audit that addresses a number of questions. The **service audit** directs the firm to think about the forces that drive its current profits and suggests strategies that have been discussed throughout this book that lead to competitive differentiation and long-term profitability. Moreover, the active involvement of front-line and top management personnel in conducting the audit facilitates the change in culture necessary to make the transition from the traditional manufacturing-management approach to an employee- and customer-focused, service-oriented approach.

service audit

A series of questions that force the firm to think about what drives its profits and suggests strategies for competitive differentiation and long-term profitability.

THE SERVICE AUDIT: THE PROFIT AND GROWTH COMPONENT

1. How Does the Firm Define Customer Loyalty? Traditional measures of customer loyalty involve repeat sales, purchase frequency, and increases in amounts purchased. The firm also needs to consider the depth of the relationship. For example, the depth of a customer's banking relationship would be defined by types of transactions and accounts such as savings, checking, certificates of deposit, car loans, home mortgages, savings bond programs, safety deposit box rentals, and so on.

2. Does the Firm Measure Profits from Referrals? Customer loyalty and satisfaction should also be measured in terms of the customers' willingness to refer the firm to friends, family, and colleagues. Given the importance consumers place upon personal sources of information when selecting from among competing services, encouraging referrals or at least creating an atmosphere where customers freely inform others of the firm's services is crucial.

3. What Proportion of the Firm's Development Funds Are Spent on Retaining Customers as Opposed to Attracting New Ones? As discussed in Chapter Fourteen, the benefits of customer retention are clear. Current customers generate referrals, are less expensive to market to, purchase more services more frequently, are knowledgeable about the firm's operating system and, therefore, are more efficient users of the system, and are a great source of information about how the firm can better serve its targeted markets. Unfortunately, under traditional models of management, firms spend the majority of their resources on obtaining new customers while neglecting their existing customers.

4. When Customers Do Not Return, Do We Know Why? Service firms that excel pursue the bad news as well as the good. Traditionally, customer satisfaction assessments are obtained from current customers, who tend to rate the firm toward the more positive end of the scale. Uncovering the reasons customers defect reveals potentially fatal flaws in the firm's service delivery system that other customers have yet to discover and of which the firm may have been unaware. Consequently, contacting customers who have defected provides the firm with the opportunity to make improvements. Moreover, contacting customers who defect makes a positive impression that the firm cares about its customers and may actually lead to recapturing some lost customers.

THE SERVICE AUDIT: THE CUSTOMER SATISFACTION COMPONENT

5. Is Customer Satisfaction Data Collected in a Systematic Manner? In chapters Eleven and Twelve, we discussed a number of methods for assessing customer satisfaction and service quality. The key to successful measurement is consistency so that current assessments can be compared with past benchmarks. Satisfaction measurement should also occur on a regular basis and not only when problems arise. Catching minor problems early through periodic customer satisfaction surveys enables the firm to adjust the service delivery system before major gaps in service occur.

6. What Methods Are Utilized to Obtain Customer Feedback? The service quality information system discussed in Chapter Twelve reveals a number of important methods of obtaining customer feedback on a variety of issues. The active solicitation of customer complaints, after-sale surveys, customer focus-group interviews, mystery shopping, and total market service quality surveys should be used in conjunction with employee surveys. Too often, employees are left out of traditional customer feedback loops even though they are exposed to vast amounts of information about customers' daily interactions with the firm.

7. How Is Customer Satisfaction Data Used? Is the information used at all, or is it stuffed in the bottom drawer of a manager's desk? Customer satisfaction data needs to be shared with employees who provide the service. Front-line employees should feel they are an active part of the firm's overall goals and take pride in improvements in customer satisfaction scores. The data should reveal company strengths that can be used for promotional purposes and weaknesses that can be corrected through training programs or by redesigning the service system itself.

THE SERVICE AUDIT: THE EXTERNAL SERVICE VALUE COMPONENT

8. How Does the Firm Measure Value? One key to providing superior customer service is to define service value from the customer's perspective. Traditional approaches

CHAPTER 15   401

THE TACTICAL
QUESTIONS RELATING
TO SEAMLESSNESS:
CONDUCTING A
SERVICE AUDIT

define value internally and frequently miss what is really important to customers. Remember, buyers' perceptions of value represent a trade-off between the perceived benefits of the service to be purchased and the perceived sacrifice in terms of the total costs to be paid.

9. How Is Information On Customer Perceptions of the Firm's Value Shared within the Company? Keeping customer information in the hands of top management does little to improve the service effort on the front line. By sharing information about customer perceptions with the front line, the employees become sensitized to the behaviors and outcomes that are really important to customers. Improvements made in these specific areas should increase customer satisfaction scores. Similarly, sharing the information with operations, marketing, and human resources personnel should assist each area in understanding the customer's perception of the entire service delivery process.

10. Does the Firm Actively Measure the Gap between Customer Expectations and Perceptions of Services Delivered? Once customer perceptions are obtained, a comparison with customer expectations is vital in assessing customer satisfaction. Customer perceptions alone do not tell the full story. This point was made particularly clear in Chapter Twelve regarding the SERVQUAL scale. Perception scores alone merely reflect whether customers agree with the statement, not whether what they are evaluating is really important to them. Including expectation measures increases the managerial usefulness of the information. Given that making improvements often involves a financial investment, comparing expectations to perceptions assists the firm in allocating resources to the most appropriate areas.

11. Is Service Recovery an Active Strategy Discussed among Management and Employees? Although many firms will spend vast amounts of time and effort to deliver the service right the first time, little discussion centers on appropriate courses of action for employees to take when things do not go according to plan. Consequently, employees are left to fend for themselves while dealing with unhappy customers, and it is apparent that employees often do a poor job in service recovery efforts. Chapter Thirteen stresses the benefits of both service failure and service recovery analysis. Actively tracking failures and recoveries identifies failure points in the system and allows the firm to minimize their occurrence by training employees in service recovery techniques.

THE SERVICE AUDIT: THE EMPLOYEE PRODUCTIVITY COMPONENT

12. How Does the Firm Measure Employee Productivity? If the firm does not measure what it really believes is important, employees will never pay attention to it. In addition, if productivity is measured simply in terms of output and outcomes and not by the behaviors used to achieve these outcomes, the firm may actually be rewarding employees for noncustomer-oriented activities. For example, the employee may be very curt with one customer so that a quick sale can be transacted with another customer who already knows what he or she wants. Service productivity measures such as timeliness, accuracy, and responsiveness need to be developed to reinforce these types of customer-oriented behaviors.

THE SERVICE AUDIT: THE EMPLOYEE LOYALTY COMPONENT

13. Does the Firm Actively Pursue Strategies to Promote Employee Loyalty? Employee loyalty to the organization is often visible to customers and directly influences customer evaluations of the firm. When employees feel more positive about the firm, customers feel more positive about the services the firm delivers. Preaching that employees are the firm's most important asset and then laying off employees in large numbers during periods of downsizing sends a hypocritical message to both employees and customers.

14. Does the Firm Set Employee Retention Goals? Although rarely is 100 percent the correct level, employee retention saves the firm funds in terms of recruiting and training costs. Additionally, customers prefer the continuity of interacting with the same personnel over time so much that the firm's personnel may be its key differential advantage over competitors. When service personnel do leave, their regular customers often seek them out at their new places of employment.

THE SERVICE AUDIT: THE EMPLOYEE SATISFACTION COMPONENT

15. Are Employee Satisfaction Measures Linked to Customer Satisfaction Measures? Employee satisfaction is linked to increases in productivity and external service value. External service value is linked to customer satisfaction and the additional benefit of customer loyalty. The net effects of customer loyalty are increased revenues and profitability for the firm. The outcomes associated with employee satisfaction—external service values, customer satisfaction, customer loyalty, revenue growth, and increased profitability—provide feedback and reinforce the company's internal service quality and employee satisfaction.

16. Are Customer and Organizational Needs Considered When Hiring? Southwest Airlines invites panels of customers to help select flight attendants. Customers are so sold on the idea that some take off time from their own work schedules to be on the selection team. Hiring people with good job skills is important in manufacturing. Hiring people with good job skills *and* good interpersonal skills is vital in services.

17. Are Employee Reward Programs Tied to Customer Satisfaction, Customer Loyalty, and Quality of Employee Performance? Service firms wishing to enhance the customer focus of their employees must implement behavior-based reward systems that

CHAPTER 15 403

THE TACTICAL
QUESTIONS RELATING
TO SEAMLESSNESS:
CONDUCTING A
SERVICE AUDIT

monitor employee activities and evaluate employees on aspects of their job over which they have control. Traditional, outcome-based reward systems often discourage the development of long-term relationships with the firm's customers in pursuit of short-term profitability.

THE SERVICE AUDIT: THE INTERNAL SERVICE QUALITY COMPONENT

18. Are Employees Aware of Internal and External Customers? The ideal service firm should work seamlessly as a team. Each member of the team should understand fully how individual performance affects the performance of other team members as they provide superior service to external customers. Consequently, employees need to understand that the firm's external customers are not the only ones who are depending on their efforts.

19. Do Employees Have the Support Necessary to Do Their Jobs? Does the firm just talk about providing superior service, or does it talk about it and back up it with the support necessary to get the job done right? Over the past few years, Taco Bell has emerged as a firm with some fairly progressive service strategies. Personnel are supported by the latest advances in information technology, self-managing team training, effective food service equipment, and work scheduling that enhances employee performance.

THE SERVICE AUDIT: THE FIRM'S LEADERSHIP COMPONENT

20. Does the Firm's Leadership Help or Hinder the Service Delivery Process? Service personnel frequently find that even though they want to provide good service, their hands are tied by overbearing, conservative, upper-management types. Frequently, upper management is far removed from the front line of the operation and has lost touch with the realities associated with daily service interactions. The leaders of successful firms act as enablers, coaches, and facilitators, and they are participatory managers who listen to employees and encourage creative approaches to solving old problems.

21. Is the Firm's Leadership Creating a Corporate Culture that Helps Employees as They Interact with Customers? Top management sets the tone and provides the resources that support personnel who interact with customers. The links in the service-profit chain discussed in Chapter One reveal that employee satisfaction and customer satisfaction are directly related. Top management's job is, therefore, to create an organization culture in which employees thrive.

THE SERVICE AUDIT: THE MEASUREMENT RELATIONSHIP COMPONENT

22. How Do the Preceding Measures of Service Performance in the Service Audit Relate to the Firm's Overall Profitability? The preceding components of the audit provide strategic measures that aid the provision of superior service. Ideally, the contribution of each measure should be related to the firm's bottom line. Relating these measures to the firm's overall profitability provides a resounding message throughout the company that service and quality pay!

S U M M A R Y

In pursuit of service excellence, the individual departments and functions of the firm must act in unison to create a seamless organization. The firm will not act as one if the current focus of the organization is on departmental and functional needs. The three-tiered model of service firms offers an alternative view of how the organization should focus its efforts by segmenting the operation into a customer tier, a boundary tier, and a coordination tier. The goal is to have those in the coordination tier work in harmony with personnel in the boundary tier so that customers experience seamless service.

Creating and supporting a customer-focused organizational culture is critical when developing a seamless operation. The firm's culture drives employee behavior and directly influences the quality of the firm's service delivery system and subsequent consumer evaluations of the firm's service effort. Firms can change the existing culture of the organization by changing the firm's structure, people-management systems, and/or key personnel, or they can change the culture directly through broad-based educational activities or re-engineering the firm's entire service delivery process.

Finally, by conducting a service audit, a seamless service culture is fostered as organizational personnel throughout the organization come to appreciate the challenges faced and the contributions made by everyone involved in the firm's final service delivery effort. The service audit deals directly with such issues as profit and growth, customer satisfaction, external service value, employee productivity, employee loyalty, employee satisfaction, internal service quality, leadership, and measures that assess the impact of each of these issues on the firm's bottom line.

The service audit also provides a framework for combining the materials that are discussed throughout this book. In closing, we hope that this book has helped develop your understanding of the special challenges involved in the marketing and management of service operations. With challenge comes opportunity, and as you well know, there are plenty of opportunities in the business community to make the service encounter a more productive and pleasant experience for everyone involved—customers and employees alike. The time has come to make a difference . . . and we look forward to writing about the difference you made in future editions of this book.

▶▶▶▶ ◀◀◀◀

KEY TERMS

seamless service

marketing orientation

marketing function

marketing department

customization/customer contact matrix

three-tiered model

customer tier

expectations

needs

competencies

boundary tier

coordination tier

internal logic

operations logic

marketing logic

human resources logic

culture

structure

systems

interfunctional task force

interfunctional transfers

"putting the customer first"

"orientation change"

"change the way you work"

"change the way we work"

service audit

REVIEW QUESTIONS

1. Discuss seamlessness as it relates to "tooth-to-tail" performance.

2. Discuss the fight for control among marketing, operations, and human resources personnel.

3. Define the following terms: marketing orientation, marketing functions, and marketing department. Why is it necessary to distinguish among these terms when discussing service firms? Relate your answer to the customization/customer contact matrix.

4. Discuss each tier of the three-tiered model of service firms separately and then as a combined unit.

5. What is the importance of organizational culture?

6. Explain the relevance of interfunctional task forces and interfunctional transfers as they relate to corporate culture.

7. Discuss the four approaches to directly changing culture as presented in the text.

8. What are the key components of a service audit?

NOTES

1. Benjamin Schneider and David E. Bowen, *Winning the Service Game* (Boston: Harvard Business School Press, 1995), pp. 1–16.

2. This section adapted from John E. G. Bateson, *Managing Services Marketing*, 3rd ed. (Fort Worth, TX: The Dryden Press, 1995), pp. 636–645.

3. Schneider and Bowen, *Winning the Service Game*, p. 199.

4. Bateson, *Managing Services Marketing*, pp. 636–645.

5. Ibid.

6. C. Gronroos, "Designing a Long-Range Marketing Strategy for Services," *Long Range Planning* 13 (April 1980), p. 36.

7. R. B. Chase, "Where Do Customers Fit in a Service Operation?" *Harvard Business Review* 56,6 (November–December 1978), pp. 137–142.

8. W. Skinner, "The Focused Factory," *Harvard Business Review* 52,3 (May–June 1974), pp. 113–121.

9. Schneider and Bowen, *Winning the Service Game*, pp. 1–16.

10. Ibid.

11. Ibid, p. 43.

12. Jane Kingman-Brundage, William R. George, and David E. Bowen, "Service Logic—Achieving Essential Service System Integration," *International Journal of Service Industry Management* (forthcoming).

13. Cynthia Webster, "What Kind of Marketing Culture Exists in Your Service Firm? An Audit," *The Journal of Services Marketing* 6,2 (Spring 1992), pp. 54–67.

14. Bateson, *Managing Services Marketing*, pp. 636–645.

15. Gronroos, "Designing a Long-Range Marketing Strategy," p. 36.

16. C. H. Lovelock, E. Langeard, J. E. G. Bateson, and P. Eiglier, "Some Organizational Problems Facing Marketing in the Service Sector," in J. Donnelly and W. George, eds., *Marketing of Services* (Chicago: American Marketing Association, 1981), pp. 148–153.

17. Schneider and Bowen, *Winning the Service Game*, p. 8.

18. This section was adapted from James L. Heskett, Thomas O. Jones, Gary W. Loveman, W. Earl Sasser, Jr., and Leonard A. Schlesinger, "Putting the Service-Profit Chain to Work," *Harvard Business Review*, (March–April 1994), pp. 165–174.

PART 4

CASES

Emmy's and Maddy's First Service Encounter

August 16, 1995. Our day began at 5:20 A.M. Hurricane Felix was predicted to hit the Carolina coast by the end of the afternoon, and I, like most of the other folks in southeastern North Carolina had spent much of the previous day preparing the house for the upcoming storm. However, my wife and I had one extra concern that the others did not. My wife was six months pregnant with twins, and the prospect of spending lots of time in the car in the attempt to remove ourselves from harm's way was not particularly attractive. We had decided to wait until after my wife's doctor appointment at 9:00 A.M. to make a decision on whether we should leave or stay at home and ride out the storm. We never made it to the doctor appointment.

At 5:20 A.M., I was awakened by the fear in my wife's voice. Her water had broken, and the twins that were due on November 16 had apparently made up their collective minds that they were going to be born 13 weeks early. As first-time parents, we understood that our next move would be to go to the hospital; however, we were unsure as to the best mode of transportation given our particular situation. We had been informed by doctors that multiple-birth pregnancies were high-risk pregnancies and that every precaution should be taken. We quickly called the hospital and asked for advice. The hospital suggested that my wife take a shower, shave her legs, and pack some essentials and that it would be appropriate for us to drive ourselves to the hospital. Too stressed out to take any chances, we passed on the shower advice, quickly threw some things together, and drove to the hospital immediately.

The Emergency Department

Upon our arrival at the hospital, we drove to the emergency entrance, and I quickly exited the car to find a wheelchair. I was immediately confronted by a security guard who had been previously engaged in a casual conversation with another gentleman. I was informed that I could not leave my car in its current position. In response, I informed the security guard that I needed a wheelchair and would move the car after I was able to move my wife inside. The security guard pointed his finger in the direction of the wheelchairs. I grabbed the first wheelchair I could get my hands on and headed back out the sliding doors to assist my wife. At this point, the security guard informed me that I had grabbed a juvenile-sized wheelchair. I headed back inside and grabbed a much larger wheelchair. I returned to the car, assisted my wife into the wheelchair, and headed back inside. The security guard,

Source: K. Douglas Hoffman, "Rude Awakening," *Journal of Health Care Marketing* 16,2 (Summer 1996), pp. 14–20.

while continuing with his other conversation, instructed me to leave my wife with the triage nurse in the emergency department so that I could move my vehicle. I said goodbye to my wife and went to move the vehicle. When I returned, the security guard informed me that they had taken my wife to the maternity ward, located on the third floor.

My wife's encounter with the triage nurse was apparently short and sweet. The triage nurse had called for an orderly to move my wife to the maternity ward. On her way to the third floor, the orderly asked my wife whether she was excited about having the baby. She responded that she was scared to death because she was only six months pregnant. The orderly replied that there was "no way [she was] having a baby that early that [would] survive."

THE MATERNITY WARD

As I exited the elevator on the third floor, I headed for the nurses' station to inquire about my wife's current location. I was greeted by several smiling nurses who escorted me to my wife's room. On my way to the room, I met another nurse who had just exited my wife's room. This nurse pulled me aside and informed me of the orderly's remarks. She continued on to assure me that what he said was not only inappropriate, but more importantly, inaccurate. She also informed me that my wife was very upset and that we needed to work together to help keep her calm. This particular nurse also informed us that she herself had given birth to a premature child, who was approximately the same gestational age as ours, a couple of years earlier.

By this time, it was between 6:00 and 6:30 A.M. The resident on duty entered the room and introduced himself as Dr. Baker. My wife gave me this puzzled and bewildered look. The clinic where my wife is a patient consists of five physicians who rotate their various duty assignments. Dr. Baker is one of the five. However, Dr. Baker was 30 to 40 years older than the resident who had just introduced himself as Dr. Baker. What had happened was that the resident was nervous and had introduced himself as Dr. Baker rather than as Dr. Baker's assistant. Realizing his mistake, he embarrassingly reintroduced himself and informed us that Dr. Baker was the physician on call and that he was being contacted and kept informed of my wife's condition.

The resident left the room and soon reappeared with an ultrasound cart to check the positions of the babies. This time he was accompanied by a person I assumed to be the senior resident on duty. For the next 30 minutes or so, I watched the junior resident attempt to learn how to use the ultrasound equipment. He consistently reported his findings to us in sentences that began with, "I think. . . ." Several times during this period my wife voiced her concern over the babies' conditions, and the location of Dr. Baker. We were reassured by the residents that Dr. Baker was being kept informed and were told that being upset was not going to help the babies' conditions. After about 30 minutes, I informed both residents that despite their advice for us to stay calm, they were not exactly instilling a lot of confidence in either one of us. The senior resident took over the ultrasound exam at this time.

Dr. Baker arrived at the hospital somewhere between 7:00 and 7:30 A.M. He apologized for not being there earlier and mentioned that he was trying to help his wife prepare for the ensuing hurricane. Sometime during this same time period, it was shift-change time for the nurses and also for Dr. Baker. New nurses were now entering the room, and now Dr. Johnson was taking over for Dr. Baker. By approximately 8:00 A.M., Dr. Baker had pulled me aside and informed me that after conferring with Dr. Johnson, they had decided that if my wife's labor subsided, she would remain in the hospital for seven to ten days, flat on her back, before they would deliver the babies. It was explained that with each passing day, the babies would benefit from further development. The lungs were of particular concern.

Upon being admitted to the maternity floor, my wife had immediately been hooked up to an EKG to monitor contractions. Due to the small size of the babies, the contractions were not severe. However, as far as my wife and I could tell, the interval between contractions was definitely getting shorter. Being first-time parents, we were not overly alarmed by this since we figured we were in the hospital and surrounded by health-care providers.

Between 8:00 and 8:30 A.M., two other nurses entered the room with lots of forms for us to complete. Since we were having twins, we needed duplicates of every form. The forms covered the basics: names, addresses, phone numbers, social security numbers, and insurance information. All the same questions that the hospital had sent to us weeks earlier, which we had completed and returned. The nurses asked us the questions, we supplied the information, and they wrote the responses.

By 8:30 A.M., Dr. Baker was informing me that due to one of the babies' breach position, they would deliver the babies by caesarean section. Wondering whether the schedule had been moved up from a week to ten days, I asked when he thought this would be happening. He replied: "In the next hour or so." He then commented that labor had not subsided and that Dr. Johnson would be delivering the babies.

As my wife was being prepared for the operating room, I stood in the hallway outside her room. I noticed another physician limping down the hall with one foot in a cast and a crutch underneath one arm. He stopped outside my wife's room and began to examine her medical charts. He introduced himself as Dr. Arthur (he had broken his foot while attempting to change a tire). Dr. Arthur was the neonatologist, which meant nothing to me at the time. I eventually figured out that my wife had her set of doctors and that my unborn children had their own set of health-care providers. Dr. Arthur asked to speak to my wife and me together. This is when he told us that 90 percent of babies such as ours survive and that 90 percent of those survivors develop normally. He was a calm, pragmatic individual who encouraged us to ask questions. He continued to explain that the babies would spend their next few months in the hospital's Neonatal Intensive Care Unit (NICU) and that if all went well, we could expect to take them home within two weeks of their due date (November 16, 1995).

By 9:00 A.M., all hell had broken loose. My wife had dilated at a quicker pace than had been anticipated . . . the contractions had indeed been occurring at more frequent intervals. Some orderlies and nurses grabbed my wife's bed and quickly rolled her down the hall to the delivery room. I was thrown a pair of scrubs and told to put them on. I was further told that they would come back and get me if they were able. For 10 to 12 very long minutes, I sat on a stool in an empty hospital room by myself, watching The Weather Channel track Hurricane Felix. The volume on the television had been muted, and the only thing I could hear was a woman screaming from labor in the next room. Suddenly, a nurse popped her head in the door and said that a space had been prepared for me in the delivery room.

THE DELIVERY ROOM

As I entered the delivery room, I was overwhelmed by the number of people involved in the process. Myself included, I counted 12 "very busy" people. I was seated next to my wife's head. She had requested to stay awake during the procedure. My wife asked me whether the man assisting Dr. Johnson was the junior resident. Sure enough, I looked up to see the junior resident wearing a surgical gown and mask with a scalpel in his hand. I lied and told her, "No."

Suddenly, we realized that we had not finalized our choices for names. Somehow, what we couldn't decide despite months of discussion, we decided in 30 seconds. Our first baby girl, Emma Lewis (Emmy), was born at 9:15 A.M. Emmy weighed 2 pounds and was 14½ inches long. Our second baby girl, Madeline Stuart (Maddy), was born at 9:16 A.M. and weighed 2 pounds, 2 ounces, and also measured 14½ inches long. Both babies were very active at birth, and their faint cries reassured my wife and I that they had at least made it this far.

Upon being delivered from their mother, the babies were immediately handed to Dr. Arthur and his staff, who had set up examination stations in the delivery room. Each baby had her own team of medical personnel, and I was encouraged by Dr. Arthur, who hopped on one foot across the delivery room, as I watched him examine the girls. The neonatal staff examining the girls "ooohed" and "aaahed," and almost in a competitive manner compared measurements about which baby had better vitals in various areas. Dr. Arthur then suggested that I follow the girls to the Neonatal Intensive Care Unit (NICU) to watch further examinations. He also made sure that my wife got a good look at both babies before they were wheeled out of the delivery room in their respective incubators. My wife and I said our goodbyes, and I was told I could see her again in the recovery room in about 20 to 30 minutes.

THE RECOVERY ROOM

The recovery room and the delivery room are contained within the maternity ward on the third floor of the hospital. The NICU is located on the fourth floor, which is designated as the gynecological floor. The staff on the third floor is geared for moms and babies. The staff on the fourth floor, outside the NICU, is geared for women with gynecological problems.

After receiving the "so far, so good" signals from both my wife's and my babies' doctors, I was permitted to rejoin my wife in the recovery room. It was a basic hospital room with the exception that a nurse was assigned to the room on a full-time basis. One of the hospital volunteers from the maternity floor had taken pictures of each of the babies and taped them to the rails of my wife's hospital bed. The nurses of the third floor maternity ward asked my wife whether she would like a room on the fourth floor so that she could be closer to her babies when she was ready to start walking again. She agreed and spent the next four days in a room on the fourth floor.

Hurricane Felix stayed out to sea and moved up the coastline, missing us completely.

The Fourth Floor

My wife's private room on the fourth floor was small, dingy, and dirty. From an emotional standpoint, the staff on the fourth floor were not prepared to deal with our situation. In fact, one nurse, after discussing the situation with my wife, asked whether we were going to have the babies transported to a major university medical center three hours away.

My wife's quality of care on the fourth floor was sporadic. Some of the nurses were good and some were inattentive—slow to respond to the patient's call button and blaming nurses on other shifts when medications and other scheduled or promised care (e.g., providing the patient with a breast pump) were not provided on a timely basis. Although it might seem trivial to many, the breast pump represented my wife's primary contribution to the care of her babies. It was the only thing she could control. Everything else was out of her hands. My wife was instructed to begin pumping as soon as she felt able, yet due to her location away from the maternity ward, obtaining a breast pump was difficult and became a sore point for my wife.

After receiving a courtesy call by the hospital's patient representative, my wife expressed her concerns. Shortly thereafter, personnel were changed, the quality of care improved, and we were moved to a much larger room on the third afternoon.

The Neonatal Intensive Care Unit

The NICU (pronounced "nick-u") is located in an isolated area of the fourth floor. The primary purpose of the NICU is to provide care for premature babies and for full-term babies requiring special care. The number of babies cared for each day throughout our stay typically averaged 12.

Emmy and Maddy spent approximately seven weeks in the NICU. The staff made every effort to explain the purpose of every piece of machinery and every tube that seemed to cover the babies' bodies. I was repeatedly told that I could and should ask questions at any time and that the staff understood that it was an overwhelming amount of information. Hence, it was understandable and acceptable to ask the same questions day after day. The staff had made signs welcoming each of the babies in bright neon colors and taped them above each of their stations. For ease of access, the girls had not yet been placed in incubators. They laid in what looked like large in/out baskets with raised borders. We celebrated weeks later when they finally had enough tubes removed so that they could be moved into incubators . . . what we called "big-girl beds."

During the first three days, I walked into the NICU to find baby quilts at each of the girls' stations. A local group called Quilters by the Sea had sewn the quilts; apparently they regularly provide the quilts for infants admitted to the NICU. For some reason that I still cannot explain today, the fact that someone outside the hospital who I did not know cared about my girls touched me deeply. The signs the staff had made and the babies' patchwork quilts humanized all the machines and tubes. Somehow, I was no longer looking at two premature infants . . . I was looking at Emmy and Maddy.

Throughout the girls' stay in the NICU, the quality of care delivered was primarily exceptional. The staff not only excelled at the technical aspects of their jobs but also were very good in dealing with parents. Some of the personal touches included numerous pictures of each of the girls for us to take home, homemade birthday cards with pictures from the girls for Mom and Dad on their birthdays, baby stickers on their incubators, and notes of encouragement from staff when a milestone, such as when weighing 3 pounds, was achieved. We arrived one day and found pink bows in the girls' hair. The nurses even signed Emmy's and Maddy's names on the foot cast worn by the baby boy in the next incubator.

Parental involvement in the care of all the infants was encouraged, almost demanded. I had somehow managed to never change a diaper in my life (I was 35 years old). I was threatened, I think jokingly, that the girls would not be allowed to leave the NICU until I demonstrated some form of competency with diaper changes, feedings, and baths. The primarily female staff made me feel at times that my manhood was at stake if I was not able to perform these duties. Personally, I think they all wished they'd had the same chance to train their husbands when they'd had their own babies. I am now an expert in the aforementioned activities.

As for the babies' progress, some days were better than others. We celebrated weight gains and endured a collapsed lung, blood transfusions, respirators, alarms caused by bouts with apnea and bradycardia, and minor operations. Throughout the seven weeks, many of the staff and three neonatologists became our friends. We knew where one another lived, we knew about husbands, wives, boyfriends, and kids. We also heard a lot about the staff's other primary concern . . . scheduling.

THE GROWER ROOM

Sometime after the seventh week, we "graduated" from the NICU and were sent to the Grower Room. The Grower Room acts as a staging area and provides the transition between the NICU and sending the babies home with their parents. Babies who are transferred to the Grower Room no longer require the intensive care provided by the NICU but still require full-time observation. As the name indicates, the Grower Room is for feeding and diaper changing, administering medications, and recording vital statistics—basic activities essential for the growth and development of infants. The Grower Room held a maximum of four infants at any one time.

The Grower Room was located in a converted patient room located in the back corner of the second floor, which is designated as the pediatric floor of the hospital. In general, the Grower Room was staffed by one pediatric nurse and visited by the neonatologists during rounds. As parents who were involved in the care of their babies, being transferred to the Grower Room meant that we had to establish new relationships with another set of health-care providers all over again.

Compared with the "nurturing" culture we had experienced in the NICU, the Grower Room was a big letdown. One of the first nurses we were exposed to informed us that the nurses on the second floor referred to the Grower Room as "The Hole," and that sooner or later they all had to take their turn in "The Hole." We asked the reasons for such a name, and the nurse explained that because the room was stuck back in the corner, the rest of the staff seldom allowed the "grower nurse" to take a break, and because of the constant duties involved, the grower nurse could never leave the room unattended. It was also explained that some of the nurses simply did not feel comfortable caring "for such small little babies." We quickly found that this attitude had manifested itself in a lack of supplies specifically needed for smaller babies, such as premature-sized diapers and sheepskin rugs inside the incubators.

Furthermore, it became quickly apparent that friction existed between the NICU and the Grower Room. The Grower Room was very hesitant to request supplies from the NICU and on several occasions would delay informing NICU that an occupancy existed in the Grower Room. The reason for delay was so that the Grower Room nurse could catch up on other duties and avoid having to undertake the additional duties involved in admitting new patients. The "successful delay" would pass on these activities to the nurse taking the next shift. Apparently, the friction was mutual, since one of the nurses in the NICU commented to us on the way out of the NICU, "Don't let them push you around down there. If you don't think they're doing what they should, you tell them what you want them to do."

When the Grower Room was in need of supplies for our babies and others, I (on more than one occasion) volunteered to ask for supplies from the NICU. Although my foraging attempts were successful, I definitely got the feeling that there was some reluctance on both sides for me to do this. I suspected that the Grower Room nurses did not want to ask for any favors, and the NICU staff felt that it was not their job to keep the Grower Room stocked with supplies. Moreover, I suspect that the NICU and the Grower Room operate from different budgets. Stocking the Grower Room is not one of the objectives of the NICU's budget. However, from my side, my babies needed supplies, and I did not care about either department's budget.

After a few dark days, we established new relationships with the Grower Room personnel and became very involved with the care of our babies. After spending seven weeks in the NICU, we felt more familiar with each baby's personal needs than some of the Grower Room staff were. Recognizing our level of involvement, most of the staff looked forward to our visits since it meant less work for them. By now, we had learned to ask lots of questions, to doublecheck that medications had been provided, and to develop a working relationship with Grower Room personnel. Looking back, it was almost as we and the Grower Room staff trained each other. At the conclusion of our Grower Room experience, my wife and I felt that we had met some good people, but also that the quality of the experience was far lower than what we had grown accustomed to in the NICU.

NESTING

Once the babies had "graduated" from the Grower Room, our last night in the hospital was spent "nesting." Friends of ours joked that this must have involved searching for twigs, grass, and mud. The nesting rooms were located on the second floor of the hospital, in the same general location as the Grower Room. Nesting allows the parents and the babies to spend a night or two together in the hospital before they go home. During the nesting period, parents are solely responsible for all medications, feedings, and general care of the infants. The nesting period allows the parents to ask any last-minute questions and to smooth the transition from, in our case, nine weeks of hospital care to multiple infant care at home.

The nesting room itself was a small patient room that consisted of one single bed and a fold-out lounge chair. By now, the babies had been moved from their incubators to open, plastic bassinets that were wheeled into the room with us. Each baby remained attached to a monitor that measured heart and breathing rates. To say the least, space was limited, but for the first time in nine weeks, the four of us were alone as a family.

Throughout the 22 hours we nested, we were frequently visited by neonatologists, nurses who continued to take the babies' vital signs, the babies' eye doctor, social workers who were assigned to all premature baby cases, hospital insurance personnel, and a wonderful discharge nurse who was in charge of putting everything together so that we could get out the door. Nine weeks to the day after we had entered the hospital, we took our two 4-pound babies home.

QUESTIONS

1. Discuss the relevance of intangibility, inseparability, heterogeneity, and perishability to this case.

2. One of the primary purposes of this case is to illustrate the number of factors that influence patient perceptions regarding the quality of care delivered. Utilizing the

servuction model as a framework, classify the factors or "incidents" that influenced this particular family's health-care experience.

3. Another useful exercise is to interpret the signals sent to the family by the factors that make up the servuction model. By placing yourself "in the shoes" of the parents of Emmy and Maddy, interpret each of the factors that were classified in question 1.

4. Suggest methods for improving the quality of this particular service experience.

EPILOGUE

As of August 1996, Emmy and Maddy both weighed approximately 18 pounds and appeared to be in good overall health. One of the NICU nurses we met at the hospital helps us out in our home on a regular basis, and we have kept in touch with many of the NICU staff as well as with Dr. Arthur. The charges for our hospital stay were more than $250,000. This bill did not include any of the physicians' (e.g., neonatologists, eye doctors, surgeons, or radiologists) charges. Emmy recently returned to the hospital for a cranial ultrasound, which is an outpatient service (the results were negative for brain bleeds, and Emmy is fine). Despite her previous lengthy stay in NICU, we once again had to provide the hospital with all the insurance information one more time. Ironically, the only information the outpatient service had about Emmy was that her "responsible party" was Maddy.

In terms of our overall experience, we are thankful for the lives of our babies and for the health of their mother. We are particularly grateful to the staff of the NICU and to Dr. Arthur.

THE CASE OF
JIM BAKKER AND PTL

Jim Bakker created PTL, a Christian-oriented syndication network, in 1977. Prior to that time, Bakker had spent seven years working for the Christian Broadcast Network (CBN) owned by Pat Robertson. Bakker was not well educated in theology—he had dropped out of North Central Bible College after only three semesters. However, he was a natural on television, where he preached seed-faith and prosperity theology. These theological philosophies had originated with Oral Roberts in the 1940s and by the 1980s were widely embraced by most evangelists.

The seed-faith philosophy taught that if the believers served and gave to God, they would be rewarded by God with an abundance of material needs. Prosperity theology, also known as "health and wealth theology," asserted that God wanted the whole man, including his finances, to be healed. Those practicing prosperity theology recommended that believers pray for a specific outcome or object. Indeed, Bakker recommended that if his supporters prayed for a camper, they should specify the color; otherwise, they were asking God to do their shopping.

Bakker, then, did not preach hard work, saving, and responsible planning. Instead, he subscribed to the belief that the Spirit willed financial miracles as well as the actions of Its followers. Bakker sermonized only on the love of God and ignored the topic of sin. This religious philosophy apparently appealed to a wide cross-section of middle-class Americans, as Bakker's congregation grew rapidly. Only 20 percent of Bakker's supporters came from his own Assemblies of God Pentecostal faith; the remainder came from other Pentecostal denominations, other Protestant denominations, and the Roman Catholic Church. Their contributions and support made PTL one of the three wealthiest and most popular media ministries in the nation. Consequently, by 1984, PTL served 1,300 cable systems of 12 million homes and had accumulated $66 million in revenues and $86 million in assets. PTL also had 900 people on the payroll and enormous operating expenses and debt.

Bakker often prayed, with his television audience, for the financing of specific projects—an evangelical university, a PTL show in Italy or Brazil, or the "Christian Disneyland" labeled Heritage USA. When the money for these projects poured in from viewers, however, Bakker would use the funds for something else because that was the way he had been moved by the Spirit. Because of this style of financial management, PTL debts mounted.

Thus, it was in 1983 that Bakker conceived the idea of selling lifetime partnerships for donations of $1,000 or more. The lifetime partnerships entitled the contributors to three free nights of lodging

Source: This case written by Judy A. Siguaw, Associate Professor of Marketing, Kennesaw State University, and K. Douglas Hoffman, Associate Professor of Marketing, The University of North Carolina at Wilmington.

and recreation at Heritage USA for the remainder of their lives—a package previously valued at $3,000. The funds from the lifetime partnerships were to be designated for completion of construction at Heritage USA. Unfortunately, Bakker sold lifetime partnerships to more donors than he could accommodate at Heritage USA. Further, as the number of lifetime partnerships sold escalated, contributions to the general PTL fund diminished. In order for PTL to continue, funds from the lifetime partnerships had to be diverted for everyday operating expenses. Consequently, construction on the lodging facilities at Heritage USA were never completed.

Bakker's followers were aware of where their contributions were being channelled. The Charlotte *Observer* regularly reported the financial actions of PTL and the Heritage USA construction cost overruns as well as Bakker's purchases, which included three vacation homes, gold-plated bathroom fixtures, an air-conditioned doghouse, and vast amounts of clothing and jewels. Indeed, Bakker would display the headlines on television to demonstrate the hostility of the press. His followers never wavered. They supported and even endorsed Bakker's materialistic lifestyle and promise of financial miracles. After all, Bakker was only acting out what he preached—a religion with standards of excess and tenets of tolerance and freedom from accountability. As a televangelist, he was free to preach what he pleased, and people were free to listen or not. No one coerced monetary contributions from Bakker's supporters—they willingly sent in funds and did not hold Bakker accountable for the disbursement of those funds.

Further, the government was aware of Bakker's actions. Bakker and his PTL operation were extensively investigated in separate incidences by the Federal Communication Commission, the Justice Department, and the Internal Revenue Service beginning in 1979. Even though the agencies had substantial evidence of misconduct involving millions of dollars, no efforts were made to stop Bakker, and none of the agencies moved toward indictment.

Bakker was allowed, indeed, encouraged in his behavior because he personified the culture of the eighties. No government agency or public outcry arose to stop him until after Bakker, fearing reprisal concerning his affair with Jessica Hahn, resigned from PTL. Bakker's actions could hardly be called covert because they had taken place in plain sight, exemplifying the religious philosophy he and his followers had daily espoused.

In 1987, almost a decade after noting apparent misconduct in the operations of PTL, the federal government charged Jim Bakker with 24 counts of fraud and conspiracy, alleging that Bakker had bilked his supporters.

QUESTIONS

1. What service properties inherent in religious groups contribute to consumer vulnerability?

2. Which types of moral philosophies could be argued to be the basis for Bakker's actions?

3. What are the ethical issues involved?

4. What factors, other than moral philosophies, may have influenced the ethical behavior of Jim Bakker?

5. What have been the consequences of Bakker's actions?

6. What strategies would you suggest to help control future abuses by other religious leaders?

REFERENCES

Henry G. Brinton, "Pray TV," *The Washington Monthly* (April 1990), pp. 49–51; Charles Colson, "The Pedestal Complex," *Christianity Today*, February 5, 1990, p. 96; Frances Fitzgerald, "Reflections: Jim and Tammy," *The New Yorker*, April 23, 1990, pp. 45–48; and Kim A. Lawton, "The Remnants of PTL," *Christianity Today*, October 6, 1989, pp. 36–38.

The Case of Ivan Boesky

In the 1980s, the label of "success" was granted only to those people who had the most material possessions. Money was valued, and greed became the norm. This pervasive culture encouraged those who were neurotic or obsessive about money. It was this environment that propelled Ivan Boesky into becoming one of Wall Street's top arbitragers.

A risk arbitrager searches for companies that seem to be likely takeover targets and purchases large blocks of stock at the current market price. A company wishing to acquire another firm typically offers 30 to 40 percent above the market value of the stock. When this event occurs, the arbitrager nets a hefty profit. On the other hand, if the deal does not go through, the arbitrager may suffer major losses. Consequently, arbitragers are constantly seeking information, researching, and listening to the rumor mills. They are not, however, to seek or utilize insider information as a determinant of which stock to purchase. To do so is a violation of federal law.

As one of the major players in a high-stakes game, Boesky attempted to differentiate himself by making bigger, better, and riskier financial deals than others. Boesky became legendary. Obsessed with work, he routinely put in an 18-hour workday and thrived on three hours of sleep. Since information was key to his success, he was never far from a telephone. His office had a 120-line phone console—even his limousine had three telephones. At social events, Boesky talked only business.

Boesky's intense drive and work ethic paid off. He had started his own arbitrage company in 1975 with a $700,000 gift from his father-in-law. Although unusual in the industry, Boesky began actively marketing his services to investors and promoted himself, through the services of a public relations agent, as a researcher gifted at uncovering takeover targets prior to the public announcement. He began hitting big deals in 1977, after only two years in the business, and netted $7 million on the takeover of Babcock and Wilcox. After only a decade as an arbitrager, Boesky had acquired at least $200 million in assets and reportedly had business interests in the Bahamas and France.

Everything came to a screeching halt in 1986, however, when the Securities and Exchange Commission (SEC) charged Boesky with insider trading. In exchange for the names of other inside traders, Boesky plead guilty to only one charge of criminal activity and agreed to pay $100 million in penalties. He also served three years in prison. What remains of his fortune is now subject to lawsuits from those who suffered losses as a result of his insider trading.

Source: This case written by Judy A. Siguaw, Associate Professor of Marketing, Kennesaw State University, and K. Douglas Hoffman, Associate Professor of Marketing, The University of North Carolina at Wilmington.

Ethics experts note that our culture defines ethical behavior. Certainly in the greed era of the eighties, Boesky's behavior fit the definition. The compulsion to best all other arbitragers, though, pushed him beyond the bounds of unethical practice and into illegality.

QUESTIONS

1. What service properties inherent in the brokerage industry contribute to consumer vulnerability?

2. Which types of moral philosophies could be argued to be the basis for Boesky's actions?

3. What are the ethical issues involved?

4. What factors, other than moral philosophies, may have influenced the ethical behavior of Boesky's activities?

5. What strategies would you suggest to help control similar abuses of the financial system?

6. What have been the consequences of Boesky's ethical misconduct? (The titles of the articles used to write this case will give you some pretty good clues.)

REFERENCES

Ann Landi, "When Having Everything Isn't Enough," *Psychology Today*, April 1989, pp. 27–30; Myron Magnet, "The Decline & Fall of Business Ethics," *Fortune*, December 8, 1986, pp. 65–72; "True Greed," *Newsweek*, December 1, 1986, pp. 48–63; Andrew Evan Sewer, "Crook of the Year," *Fortune*, January 5, 1987, pp. 48–50; "We Never Did Trust The Guy," *Time*, November 28, 1988, p. 77; "Tracing Ivan's Deals, Ivan's Money," *U.S. News & World Report*, Feb 2, 1987, p. 47.

The New York City Arboretum

It was a rainy morning in early November 1990, as Mary Saxon, Vice-President of External Affairs for the New York City Arboretum (NYCA), steered her car onto the Bronx River Parkway and made her way to work from her home in Pelham. "How appropriate," she thought, "that the weather is so gloomy. Could this be a preview of the rest of my life?" Yesterday, at the November board meeting, Mary presented the decision to start charging for admission to the Arboretum. However, instead of building cooperation and buy-in for the plan, her presentation had fractioned the employees and board members even more. Mary knew she needed buy-in from all employees to make the switch from free entrance to paying admission a success. She also knew that the Arboretum would need additional funding for initiatives to attract more visitors (and earned revenues) to the Arboretum, and the board's support was integral to raising these additional funds. If her programs failed, the Arboretum would not be able to generate enough revenue to continue operating. If this were to happen, drastic cuts in operating hours, educational programs, and personnel would be undertaken, dramatically changing the scope and mission of the Arboretum.

Had she done the right thing by announcing her decision in yesterday's meeting, or should she have approached the issue differently? She had to come up with a plan for building consensus and support for her program.

She was also concerned about the reaction of the Arboretum's external constituents. In particular, she was concerned about how the community boards in the surrounding neighborhoods would react. The local community had already protested strongly against other decisions the Arboretum had made. And certain Arboretum employees represented another challenge: there was a group, informally represented by the editor of *Arboretum Magazine* (a monthly science and botany magazine published by the NYCA), opposed to the "commercialization" of the Arboretum. Because this group had access to the New York area press, what might have been simply a pesky internal protest had the potential to be aired in public. What would be the best way to manage the Arboretum's communications to its constituents?

Source: This case was prepared by Esther da Silva and Todd Huntley under the supervision of Professor Brian Wansink as a basis for class discussion rather than to illustrate either effective or ineffective handling of an administrative situation. Copyright 1993 by Professor Brian Wansink, Amos Tuck School of Business Administration, Dartmouth College, Hanover NH 03755. All rights reserved. No part of this publication may be reproduced, stored in a retrieval system, or transmitted in any form or by any means without permission.

HISTORY OF THE NEW YORK CITY ARBORETUM

The New York City Arboretum ws founded as a botanical research and public education institution in 1891. Located on a 250-acre tract of land in the Bronx near the New York Zoological Park, it contained educational facilities, display gardens, the largest botanical library in North America, an extensive herbarium (for the cataloguing of dried plant species), a turn-of-the-century conservatory, and scientific research laboratories. The Arboretum also offered 480 educational courses a year, from gardening for children to the art of bonsai, to some 19,500 amateurs and professionals.

Over the years, the Arboretum's mission expanded from botany and horticulture to include environmental education and community gardening programs. James Hastings, who joined the Arboretum as President in 1980, felt that the Arboretum should take a more activist stance. He established the Millbrook, New York-based Institute for Ecosystem Studies, devoted to studying and preventing environmental deterioration. He also founded the Institutes of Economic Botany, which is devoted to conserving the tropical rain forests and to finding new plant sources of food, fuel, and medicine. The Institute of Economic Botany has conducted field studies in South American rain forests in conjunction with the National Cancer Institute, studied use of herbal remedies with a Mayan shaman in Belize, and worked with the Brazilian government to develop new sources of fuel and vitamin C.

FUND RAISING

Although the Arboretum was funded primarily by the City and the State, donations from the private sector became increasingly important, beginning when NYC funding was cut back in the late 1960s and accelerating when the city faced bankruptcy in the 1970s. Arboretum President Hastings proved particularly adept at attracting donations. He augmented the board with CEOs from companies such as Chase Manhattan Bank and General Foods and helped raise $51.7 million during his nine-year tenure.

Closer connections with corporations generated additional fund-raising venues. For example, Chase Manhattan matched every new individual membership ($35) 100 percent.

THE NYCA IN 1989: AN ABUSED TREASURE

Although the Arboretum was intended to function as a living museum of horticultural and natural beauty, its appearance was very much like a park. Consequently, visitors to the Arboretum tended to treat the grounds as they would, say, Central Park in Manhattan. The formal display gardens (such as the Rockefeller

Rose Garden and the Daffodil/Daylily walk) were maintained by experienced gardeners but were often not in pristine condition due to abuse from visitors. Some visitors picked flowers, while others harvested the produce from the Arboretum's vegetable gardens and fruit trees. On weekend days one's first view of the Arboretum's glorious Grand Esplanade was often the sight of families grilling on portable hibachies on the lawn among the towering trees.

The Arboretum grounds also included some natural areas, such as the Forest. Due to the Arboretum's large size and its proximity to troubled neighborhoods, some of these natural areas had become strewn with litter and frequented by drug dealers and users.

Arboretum Visitors

The Arboretum drew visitors from the surrounding neighborhoods as well as from Manhattan and other parts of New York City, Westchester County, Connecticut, and New Jersey. These visitors could be divided into two groups: the neighbors and the non-Bronx visitors. The two groups had different motives for visiting the Arboretum.

People from the neighborhood viewed the Arboretum as their local park and their "back yard" (density of housing was high in this area of the Bronx, so most dwellings did not have yards of their own). These visitors used the Arboretum for walking their dogs, giving their children a large space in which to run, and respite from steaming apartments on hot summer days. For this group of people the Arboretum was an integral part of the neighborhood and an important part of their lives.

Non-Bronx visitors were by nature different because they had to plan a special outing to the Arboretum. As a NYC Arboretum board member noted: "People don't just drop in on the Bronx." These visitors often came with high expectations (raised by frequently placed stories in the NYC media) and admired the manicured display gardens, the Victorian conservatory, the library's collection of botanical illustrations, and the rare orchids on display. This group also came for special events such as the New York Orchid Show and the blooming of Azalea Way. These non-Bronx visitors also composed the majority of those taking classes and attending seminars.

Efforts to Clean Up the Arboretum

With the arrival of Grant Longet as President of the Arboretum in the summer of 1989 came new guidelines and rules for Arboretum visitors. Longet's goal was to make the Arboretum a premier visitor attraction, one that would be revered like the Metropolitan Museum of Art. To that end he began a campaign to clean up the grounds and add visitor amenities. In addition, he brought in talented individuals from industry and other cultural institutions to run the various visitor-oriented departments. Included in Longet's summer 1989 upgrading program were the banning of picnics on the grounds, the elimination of dog walking inside the

Arboretum, the closing of all internal roads to vehicular traffic (in order to make the grounds more pedestrian-friendly), and preliminary plans to add two diesel-powered trams in the spring of 1990 to provide internal transportation for those not wanting to walk.

THE REACTION

These initiatives caused an uproar among the Arboretum's constituencies. Neighborhood groups were incensed by the decision to ban dog walking and picnics and used their local community boards to contact state legislators. There were also organized protests at the main gate (though small, they were still quite visible and therefore potentially damaging), and Kent Lorby, Director of Marketing and Public Relations, estimated that on average five protest letters and 25 phone calls were received per day during the two-week period immediately following the implementation of the policies. Some of these protests dealt with the fact that the policies had been changed abruptly, without consulting the people who would be affected by them. But most protesters were simply irate that the activities had been banned.

There was also dissension from non-Bronx visitors, but their ire tended toward the revoking of driving privileges on Arboretum roadways. Especially disconcerting were the protests from members of the elderly community who claimed that they would be forced to stop visiting the Arboretum if they had to walk through its collections rather than driving. This complaint was easier to mitigate than the others because Longet had already secured funding for trams that would shuttle Arboretum visitors between the entrance and the Old Mill restaurant (on the far side of the property).

Among both Bronx and non-Bronx visitors were Arboretum members. Many members upset by the policy changes were threatening to forgo renewing their memberships, potentially resulting in revenue shortfalls for 1990. In addition, many Arboretum employees were second-guessing Longet's decisions and management style. Already Kate Pierpont, *Arboretum Magazine* editor, had spoken with *New York Times* garden columnist Linda Yang about "Longet's grand scheme to take the Arboretum away from the people."

Despite all the opposition to Longet's policies, there was very little effect on their implementation. Longet did reopen the River Gate (adjacent to the Zoo) as a concession to the community, but all other policy changes remained. As a result, the Arboretum's appearance improved dramatically. No negative articles were published in any of the influential New York publications, and visitation seemed to be on par with that of previous years.[1]

FURTHER ARBORETUM ENHANCEMENTS: 1990

Having weathered the storm in 1989 and with Mary Saxon aboard, Longet launched yet another round of changes to enhance the visitor experience at the

Arboretum. In the spring, as planned, the tram became operational. Because the gift to purchase the tram did not include an endowment to cover operating expenses, a fee of 50 cents was charged for each one-way trip made between the Herbarium and the Old Mill restaurant.

Longet also hired architect Hugh Hardy to design additional recreational structures (an outdoor cafe opposite the Herbarium and a gazebo tram stop) and coordinate a comprehensive Arboretum signage program. Hardy was nationally known for his preservation work[2] and was able to generate publicity for new projects he undertook. In addition, a new Arboretum Shuttle, providing transportation from Manhattan direct to the Arboretum, had been put into operation.[3] Longet had privately raised more than a million dollars for the project, called the Spring 1990 Initiative, and it was completed on time in May 1990. For the first time in the Arboretum's history there were internal transportation and food services available on both sides of the property.

Advertising and Public Relations

The new additions created legitimate "news" for the Arboretum and an aggressive public relations campaign was begun, supplemented by advertising (the initial budget was set at $50,000) for which private donations had been solicited. The Arboretum staff developed a print ad entitled "People Grow Here, Too," which ran in the *New York Times* Weekend section and on billboards inside Metro North Commuter Railroad trains and stations. Since advertising funds were dependent on donations, advertising on a regular basis was nearly impossible. This was in stark contrast with the Bronx Zoo's $1,000,000 advertising budget and assistance from a prominent Madison Avenue advertising agency.

In addition to the above communications, the Arboretum enjoyed a donation from *Town & Country Magazine* in the form of a yearly supplement called *The New York Arboretum Journal*. This was a glossy magazine devoted entirely to the Arboretum. It described projects and improvements underway at the Arboretum and featured key employees and board members, as well as photo collages of attendees at the Arboretum's social events and board meetings. This supplement was distributed free of charge to all *Town & Country* subscribers.

Mary Saxon

Mary Saxon joined the NYC Arboretum in September 1989, as Vice-President of External Relations. She had previously been the Special Events Director at the New York Public Library and was lured to the Arboretum by Longet (with whom she had worked at the library). At the Arboretum, Mary was responsible for all the departments with which outside visitors to the Arboretum came into contact: Marketing, Visitor Services, Volunteers, Membership, Special Events, Public Relations, Tours, and Retailing. Even though she had been there only a short time, Mary had become increasingly frustrated with her position at the Arboretum. She had given up a very prestigious postition to tackle the problems of a neglected public garden in a disadvantaged part of the city. Although she was excited about the prospect of "making a difference," she also wondered whether she had made the right decision to leave the library.

THE DECISION TO CHARGE ADMISSION

Following the direction of Grant Longet, Mary had formulated an admissions plan with the help of Kent Lorby and his marketing staff. After parking their cars, visitors would have to enter the Arboretum grounds through one of three gates. (Access would be limited by an interior fence that ran just inside the Arboretum's perimeter. Due to a mandate from Longet to have the admission plan running in the spring of 1991, construction of the fence had already begun.) Because of the Arboretum's State charter, it was forbidden to require a fee of visitors. But the solicitation of donations was allowed; Mary's plan was to have a visitor host at each pedestrian entrance to the Arboretum asking for specific donations of $3.50 for adults and $2.50 for children. This plan was modeled on the one in use by the Metropolitan Museum of Art and had been presented to and endorsed by Longet.[4]

THE BOARD MEETING: NOVEMBER 1990

One of the most challenging, and frustrating, aspects of Mary's position at the Arboretum was the constant struggle to get agreement about policy changes from the staff and the board member; the brouhaha surrounding the charging of admission was typical. Some constituents refused to acknowledge that there *was* a budget problem, proposing instead increased lobbying of City and State agencies for funding. Others clearly recognized that rising operating costs and decreasing public funding made it imperative that the Arboretum increase its earned revenues in order to avoid a budget deficit.[5]

To assure general acceptance of the decision to charge admission. Mary had prepared a plan for her presentation at the November board meeting. First, she would point out the Arboretum's dire financial position, underlining the need for increased revenues. Then she would bring up the decision to request donations at the Arboretum entrance, pointing to the Metropolitan Museum of Art as an example of successful execution of this strategy. The admission fee discussion would then provide a natural segue to the construction of the fence already underway.

The board meeting was well attended—roughly 20 board members were present, and approximately 10 employees (including Kate Pierpont, some gardeners, and Pat Holmberg, VP: Science) had elected to attend as well.[6] Mary looked at the audience assembled and quickly reviewed the key points of her message. Then she took a deep breath and began her presentation.

Mary Saxon:
As you've heard from Grant and from our Finance VP, Joan Roar, the Arboretum faces difficult times. This year we will surely have a budget deficit.

Next year we anticipate State and City funding to diminish further, and there is no reason to believe that our Development office will be able to generate more private funding. It is therefore imperative that the Arboretum put in place a plan to generate earned revenue.

Mobee Weinstein, Curator of the Fern Collection:
Mary, I'd like to ask a question about the construction that's going on. There are rumors that a fence is being built. If this is true, the horticulture staff is very disturbed. We'd like to hear what's going on.

Mary Saxon:
Yes, Mobee, it is true that a fence is being built, and that is to facilitate the collection of earned revenue. The plan that we have developed—and Kent will present the details of it in just a moment—will allow us to solicit a donation from each and every visitor to the Arboretum.

Grant Longet:
Allow me to interject, Mary. We did a study using last year's visitor figures and compared those to total revenues generated by the Arboretum for the year. What we found was that total revenues from parking, the conservatory, the rock garden, and the Arboretum's rent on the restaurant concessions averaged to only 12 cents per visitor. This is unacceptable.

Board Member 2:
But where is it written that we should be expecting anything from our visitors? This institution was founded for the public, and that is who we should continue to serve. The motion that visitors should be exploited for revenue is absurd.

Board Member 3:
Now, Shelby, that worked very well when the Arboretum was flush with donated funds, but those days are over. The reality is that we are running a business here. Granted, we are not trying to take profits. But we are providing entertainment and education, and the users must contribute toward these operations.

Board Member 4:
Yeah, but at the same time, won't charging a fee drive down the number of visitors? In my experience, as price goes up, demand goes down. How can we be sure that we'll attract enough visitors to realize a gain?

Mary Saxon:
Well, that's part two of our plan. To ensure that we keep attracting visitors to the Arboretum, we'll have to step up our marketing efforts. For example, we could run the "People Grow Here, Too" ad again.

Board Member 4:
Excuse me, Mary. We're looking at what could potentially be a significant downturn in visitation and all you want to do is run that print ad again? I don't know much about marketing for nonprofit, but if all General Foods did was run a print ad every once in a while, we would not be selling much Maxwell House coffee.

Kent Lorby:
Well, we'd supplement the advertising with public relations. Some articles in the *New York Times* Weekend section will generate a lot of interest.

Board Member 4:
That's what the Arboretum always does. I can't imagine that would be enough to overcome the drop in visitation you'll see.

Mary felt a headache coming on, and she was beginning to panic. The meeting was not progressing at all the way she had planned. She had not really given much thought to the marketing communications plan yet and was not prepared to go into much detail.

Grant Longet:
The issue of whether or not the Arboretum needs to raise revenues is not debatable. This institution is at risk. We as a group can either be the stewards of its demise, or we can anticipate the worst and plan to mitigate it. I have asked Mary Saxon and her staff to put together a plan to do just that. Let's take a look at the plan.

Kent Lorby:
I've brought in a map showing the new fence. As you can see, the fence runs from the administration building to the laboratory and has three distinct entrances. At each of these entrances will be a booth with a cash register and a visitor host who will ask each visitor for a suggested donation of $3.50 for adults and $2.50 for children. This host will also distribute a color map of the grounds and will direct the visitor to the gardens of interest on that particular day. There will also be a similar booth and visitor host at the Fordham Gate. The River Gate is rarely used and, therefore, will not be manned.

Mobee Weinstein:
But what about the Arboretum's charter? I thought we couldn't legally charge admission.

Kent Lorby:
That's right. This is a suggested donation.

Kate Pierpont:

I think this is just a way to discriminate against the neighbors who really use the Arboretum. You know most of the community visitors cannot afford to pay that kind of money. And the fence looks disgusting on our beautiful lawn. The Arboretum has already suffered through the addition of those gazebos and that awful cafe. We have too many manmade things in the Arboretum already.

Mary Saxon:

We have to offer such amenities in order to attract more visitors. Restrooms and a cafe are the least that we should offer.

Pat Holmberg:

Why do we want to actively encourage people to visit? This place was perfect when nobody came. It was quiet and peaceful and the people who really appreciated plants had a chance to enjoy them. Now there are people all the time. Science is the backbone of this institution, but some people are trying to turn it into Disneyland. Perhaps we need to consider closing off part of the property and reducing the horticultural headcount.

Rick Muggiero:

I'm not disputing the Arboretum's scientific preeminence, Pat, but the institution has always had a strong horticulture component. Closing down part of the property would be a tragedy. As it is, the horticultural staff is too small to really do the Arboretum's mission as a leading institute of horticulture much justice.

Board Member 1:

I agree that we need to take steps to raise revenue, but $3.50 and $2.50 seems excessive. That would mean that a family of four would pay $12 to get in, $4 to park, $4 to take a round-trip tram ride, and another $12 to go to the conservatory. That's a total of $32.

Grant Longet:

Mary and her staff will work out the pricing details; there will probably be family discounts to bring the net fee down.

Kate Pierpont:

If the Arboretum is in such dire shape, why don't we eliminate some of the tertiary expenditures like the tram and advertising? An institution like the Arboretum should not have to advertise; cutting advertising would save us $50,000.

Board Member 2:

If we are cutting tertiary programs, we'd better look at the Education division. That area is bleeding money.

Grant Longet:
I see that we are out of time. The tram is waiting outside the Administration building to take the board members on a tour of the perennial garden. I move that the meeting be adjourned.

With that, those assembled left the room. Mary heard individual board members discussing the issues as they filed out, but there appeared to be no consensus. Equally ambiguous was the reaction among the employees who had attended the meeting. "I've done nothing here to further our cause," thought Mary. She had expected some opposition, but not the widly divergent views on whether the Arboretum even needed visitors. "Sometimes it feels like we don't even belong to the same organization," she muttered to herself. She wondered whether she had handled this issue correctly and what she could do in the future to get everybody on the same side.

As Mary maneuvered her car into a parking spot at the Arboretum, she reviewed in her mind the key events of the past two years. She was still irritated about yesterday's attack on her marketing efforts. Everyone at the Arboretum had liked the print ad, and although she had no measurements of visitorship, it *seemed* like more people were coming to the Arboretum. She was sure that running the ad again, with public relations backup, would result in a similar increase. She walked back to her office pondering what to do next.

N O T E S

[1] No formal annual visitor count had been undertaken at the Arboretum until Longet implemented one in 1989. Up to that point visitation was reported at "over a million," but was, in fact, suspected to be around 300,000 people per year.

[2] Previous New York City work had included the restaurant kiosks in front of the New York Public Library and the restoration of Bryant Park in midtown Manhattan.

[3] The shuttle made three round trips daily between Manhattan and the Arboretum (with drop-off/pick-up points at The Museum of Natural History and the Metropolitan Museum of Art). The Shuttle used the Henry Hudson Parkway and traversed Riverdale, thereby eliminating visual exposure to blighted areas of the Bronx.

[4] The Met used an elaborate entrance system composed of imposing arches, turnstiles, and signage with specific donation amounts to imply that visitors were expected to donate. Many visitors to the Met believed that the museum *did* charge admission when, in fact, a donation was optional.

[5] Earned revenues were funds gained through parking, which had been charged since the sixties, admission to the Conservatory and the Rock Garden, education department tuition, and group tours.

[6]It was in the Arboretum's charter that all board meetings were open to employees, but only recently had employees taken advantage of this provision.

QUESTIONS

1. Identify the strengths and weaknesses and the opportunities and threats that are faced by the NYC Arboretum.

2. Develop a promotional strategy for attracting guests.

3. Do you believe that the Arboretum should implement the "suggested donation" strategy at all?

4. Recommend a pricing strategy for the Arboretum.

D_EF_{ELICE} & F_{ROST}

Sean Gordon, Director of Development at the law firm of DeFelice & Frost, slammed down the phone and shook his head. He had just spoken with Matt Lennox, a "golden boy" who had recently been hired away from rival law firm Winthrop & Sterling. Matt had called to express his growing frustration:

> You know, Sean, I'm getting a little tired of this. I'm spending so much time on selling that I don't have time to do client work. Mark wants me to join his team working with the State of Tennessee on the Family and Medical Leave Bill, but I can't promise him enough hours to play a major role. And I got a reply today on our bid to the Board of Education. They just can't swallow our hourly rate. They've never been asked to pay more than two hundred dollars an hour before. But what's worse, they told me that some people at Winthrop & Sterling claim I'm infringing the legal code of ethics by even speaking to them. Where am I supposed to focus, on "making rain," on practicing law, or on dealing with Winthrop & Sterling? I need some support here.

Just two months ago, Sean had been basking in the success of hiring Matt as a new senior associate in the Employment and Education Group at DeFelice & Frost. Unfortunately, the initial euphoria had been tainted by Winthrop & Sterling's reaction. Matt's departure from Winthrop & Sterling had been an ugly scene: as soon as he had told the partners of his decision to leave their practice, they had immediately escorted him to the door without time to return to his desk or even say goodbye to his colleagues. Since then, his old firm had begun to malign both Matt's expertise in the Employment and Education area and his new firm (DeFelice & Frost) to clients and the other law firms in Memphis, Tennessee. Winthrop & Sterling claimed that Matt was behaving unethically by attempting to lure clients to D&F. They also implied that, without support from Winthrop & Sterling's other experienced public sector attorneys, his future success was by no means certain. Winthrop & Sterling had even publicly undercut D&F's fee structure on some major assignments. Finally, one of D&F's senior partners had seen Tom McGroary, one of D&F's most able young commercial litigators, leaving the Cotton Exchange building with Edward Winthrop III. Sean wondered: were Winthrop & Sterling trying to poach Tom in retaliation for D&F's hiring Matt Lennox?

THE FIRM

DeFelice & Frost was founded by Charlie DeFelice and Ted Frost in 1983, based primarily on Ted's reputation in construction litigation. Business and construction were booming in Memphis in the

Source: This case was prepared by Brian Wansink, Gillian Blackwell, Fritz Morsches, Carolyn Rhoads, and Ken Carangelo as a basis for class discussion rather than to illustrate either effective or ineffective handling of an administrative situation. Copyright © Brian Wansink.

early 1980s, and the practice grew rapidly. The original five-year business plan called for diversification through aggressive marketing, and D&F soon gained a reputation for its entrepreneurial spirit and extensive client base. Charlie and Ted continued to seek emerging new areas of the law and used lateral hires to develop these areas quickly. For example, in 1987 the partners hired a federal regulator from the Environmental Protection Agency to start an environmental practice.

Charlie's and Ted's priorities were leadership, client management, and client development. They were fond of telling associates, "Lead in law, and in service." They also believed that the practice of law was a business and that the partners should be able to draw upon the expertise of professional management. So, in 1988, they hired an Executive Director with responsibility for administration, accounting, recruiting, marketing and professional development. The next year, D&F broke into the ranks of the top ten law firms in Tennessee. By 1993, D&F employed 58 attorneys, five civil engineers, seven paralegals, and 70 support staff, billing over $15 million in legal fees each year. The firm provided legal services in the following areas:

- ▲ Bankruptcy and creditors' rights
- ▲ Commercial litigation
- ▲ Construction
- ▲ Corporate finance
- ▲ Corporate law
- ▲ Environmental/land use
- ▲ Estate planning and probate
- ▲ General business
- ▲ Health law
- ▲ Intellectual property
- ▲ International trade
- ▲ Labor and employment
- ▲ Real estate, including project financing
- ▲ Surety/Fidelity
- ▲ Tax and employee benefits
- ▲ Venture capital

Their client base was wide and varied and included banking, construction, real estate development, and insurance companies as well as government agencies. D&F's clients ranged in size from Fortune 100 companies to closely held local firms. Although D&F's offices were in Memphis, the firm had represented clients around the United States and gained a reputation as an up-and-coming law firm. Mr. Frost was now interested in building an international practice as well.

From the start, Charlie DeFelice and Ted Frost wanted D&F to be a "different kind of legal practice." Their goal was go be the very antithesis of a "white-shoes" law firm, such as Winthrop & Sterling, by: (1) making D&F a fun place to work, (2) hiring young attorneys with entrepreneurial drive and initiative, and (3) giving them greater autonomy and responsibility than they could expect at other major

firms. For example, D&F associates received more courtroom and client exposure than did associates at comparable firms. Charlie DeFelice also believed in
empowering secretaries to eliminate mid-level administration. As he told *The
Tennessee Law Letter:*

> By increasing people's responsibilities you eliminate waste. They do a better job and
> we avoid mid-level managers.

Charlie and Ted agreed that new hires should not have to work around the
clock for several years to prove their worth. In that same interview, Ted Frost had
said,

> Quality of life is an important theme at DeFelice and Frost. In my Chicago law firm
> days, I spent many a short night on a hard cot in my office, drinking cold coffee until
> three in the morning. You won't see that at D&F.

The partners were also quite open about the firm's performance, regularly
sharing strategic planning and financial information with all levels of the firm,
including the secretarial staff.

THE MARKETING

In the late 1980s, the legal services marketplace had changed radically. The economic slowdown, the decline in merger and acquisition activity, and the slump in
the real estate market reduced the demand for corporate legal services. This effect
was exacerbated by the glut of lawyers who earned their degrees in the 1980s.
Overnight, law firms found themselves submitting bids to win new business,
justifying their hourly fee rates, agreeing to take work on a contingency basis,
and raiding rival firms for clients and partners. As a *Memphis Law Tribune* article
("Law Made to Order," April 1993) stated:

> No longer can the white-shoes firms kick back and wait for the business to roll in. A
> gold-plated name just isn't enough anymore. Firms must scramble for business. Clients
> have become more savvy consumers, which in turn has forced firms to focus on their
> needs and to develop ways to meet those needs efficiently at a fair price.

Charlie DeFelice and Ted Frost knew they had to devote more resources to
developing the firm's client base. To keep the practice viable and growing, they
hired a Marketing Director, a position previously unheard of in law firms. After
doubling D&F's business, the new Director left the firm to found the National
Association of Legal Firm Marketers (NALFM). D&F's innovations did not
stop there, however. In 1991, Charlie and Ted decided to combine marketing and
recruiting into one department, under the premise that there was no point in
marketing the firm's services unless the lawyers were top notch and worked well
together. They hired Sean Gordon as Director of Development, reporting to
the firm's Executive Director. Sean was a Wharton MBA with an impressive marketing background. He had worked for Hallmark Cards, McKinsey & Co., and

a Big Six accounting firm before coming to D&F. Sean was attracted to D&F by the chance to run his own department and to integrate the recruiting and marketing functions. He also sought the quality of life that Memphis could offer.

RECRUITING

Sean was responsible for hiring summer associates, newly minted attorneys, and lateral hires. In all cases, he worked hard to ensure the potential employees were aware of, and would be comfortable in, D&F's unique culture. To ensure that a potential new hire would fit in, he would arrange for him or her to interview with employees from all levels of the organization. Sean looked for lawyers with strong interpersonal skills and a commitment to meeting clients' needs. Several times D&F had decided not to extend full-time offers to very competent summer associates. Although they had performed their tasks with expertise, they had either been too individualistic to fit D&F's team approach or were poor communicators.

MARKETING

Sean was also in charge of marketing for D&F. While the competition divided their lawyers into *"finders, minders, and grinders,"*[1] D&F wanted its lawyers to be as capable of selling to a new client as they were of providing counsel to an existing client.

To develop closer relationships with the firm's clients, Sean focused on two areas. First, he worked hard at developing the lawyers' client relationships and selling abilities. He arranged seminars on practical topics, such as writing and presentation skills, then incorporated these areas into D&F's performance appraisals. The performance appraisals had real meaning, since at D&F salaries were uniquely merit based, not determined by rigid pay bands or a strict billable hours formula.

Second, Sean diligently pursued new clients by increasing awareness of the DeFelice & Frost name. He worked with the lawyers to develop seminars on "hot" legal issues and invited potential clients. Recent seminars included sexual harassment in the workplace and environmental litigation. Sean helped each lawyer become involved with community groups, such as zoning commissions or local business associations, to develop ties with business leaders. The associates participated in these activities for a number of reasons: (1) the partners' example made it a behavioral norm for the organization, (2) billable hour targets were made flexible in order to accommodate such activities, (3) the seminars allowed the associates to develop their own client list, and (4) the extroverted associates that D&F sought to hire generally enjoyed interacting with potential clients in these types of settings.

Sean's group was also responsible for coordinating the firm's involvement in special events, such as The Greater Memphis Open and special musical events at the Orpheum Theater. The group maintained a detailed database of clients and potential clients including such information as the primary client contact, primary and secondary liaisons at D&F, publications received and requested, seminar invitations, business entertainment, and previous holiday gifts.

INTERNAL COMMUNICATION

In keeping with D&F's commitment to a productive, open, and enjoyable work environment, Sean was responsible for internal communications to all staff levels. He and his staff published a weekly newsletter that contained articles on new client assignments, pro bono work being performed by D&F, biographies of firm employees, software user tips, and news on company-sponsored events. Sean's group also coordinated round-table sessions at which one of the two senior partners met with groups of employees to discuss issues affecting the practice. Over a modestly catered lunch, they would discuss topics such as the firm's image, vacation policies, morale, community involvement, billing practices, and new clients.

THE HIRING

Sean drummed his fingers on his mahogany desk as he recalled a conversation with one of D&F's headhunters. Throughout the search process that had culminated with Matt's hiring, the search firm had emphasized D&F's need to seize upon Matt's talents. At the time, Matt had just won the controversial Mud Island Conservation Authority case, and his local reputation and popularity were high. During the final pitch, the headhunter had again pointed out that Matt's expertise in public sector labor law would be in very high demand. He went on to say:

> This guy is on top of the field, he's only twenty-eight, and he's already built a name for himself. He sees a need for a different kind of legal service, but they're not letting him do what he wants where he is now. He's a real entrepreneur and he's ready to move on.

At the other end of the phone, Sean Gordon agreed to set up a meeting the next day so Charlie DeFelice could meet Matt. After Sean hung up, he reexamined Matt's faxed résumé (see Exhibit 1).

Sean called Charlie to give him the good news, then looked out his twenty-sixth story window over the rooftops of downtown Memphis. Charlie was excited about the possibility of hiring Matt Lennox and wanted to meet him as soon as possible. Sean had set up a breakfast meeting with Matt, Charlie, and himself, followed by a series of in-house interviews with other members of the firm. It was difficult to decide where to meet: Memphis was a not a big city, and they all wanted to keep this quiet. Sean had suggested his home in Germantown, just outside the city.

The news about Matthew Lennox was important for several reasons. Sean knew that Mr. DeFelice and Mr. Frost, his firm's founding partners, had wanted to develop the Employment and Education practice at D&F for some time. It would take many years to develop a lawyer internally with the same expertise and contacts as the lawyer from rivals Winthrop & Sterling. Moreover, in the recession of the early 1990s, D&F needed to develop new areas of the practice as traditional corporate legal activity declined.

However, lateral hires in a professional firm were always difficult. There were already five highly qualified lawyers in the Employment and Education practice. How would they feel about a new senior associate being brought into the group? Also, there was the sensitive issue of whether the new lawyer would be able to bring his clients with him. Winthrop & Sterling's client base was based on long-term relationships, many of which dated back decades. Would Matt's clients transfer to D&F, or would they be reluctant to deal with a law firm that had only been around since the early 1980s?

Sean read the résumé more carefully and thought hiring Matt would be a real coup for D&F. The headhunter had only given him 48 hours to make a decision before he began calling other firms, so Sean had to move fast. He hoped Matt would have time to meet everyone on the hectic interview schedule. In general, Sean liked to receive plenty of feedback from a variety of people before recommending a hiring decision. However, he doubted his ability to build full consensus within 48 hours.

Charlie and Matt hit it off well over the breakfast Sean had prepared. When they returned to D&F's offices, Matt made quite a favorable impression. Mark Werner's feedback was positive; his specialty was labor law, and Matt would bring new knowledge about education issues to the firm as a senior associate in the group. Karen Snyder, who had been hired last fall from Washington University's School of Law, was also pleased, telling Sean that she saw this as an opportunity to learn new things from an experienced attorney. Matt also chatted for a few minutes with Elaine Olmstead, Sean's recruiting manager, who was very positive about him. Unfortunately, Sean sensed some problems with Curtis Hopkins. Curtis was senior enough to be made a partner in a few years. When he called to say he could not make his appointment with Matt, Sean sensed a note of hesitation in his voice. Sean guessed he had some natural reservations about a lateral hire being brought in at his level.

Sean was worried that too few people had spoken with Matt to make a decision but knew they had to make the decision soon. Matt had dropped hints that he was speaking to other firms in the area, so D&F was under some time pressure. But Charlie DeFelice had made his decision:

> Sean, I think we should go ahead with Lennox. I've been talking to Mark, he has nothing but good things to say. And I ran into Elaine in the hall. She feels that Matt would be a good fit personality-wise. What do you think?

Sean expressed some reservations about Curtis's reaction but agreed that all the signs seemed to point in one direction. Charlie ended the conversation, saying:

Of course, I'll want you to put your thinking cap on about how we can really leverage Matt and make sure his clients come with him.

After some discussion of the salary package that D&F should offer, Sean signed off with Charlie, and gave Matt a call.

MARKETING MATT

Once Sean made the offer, he waited anxiously for a reply. Matt told him he would get back to him in a day or so. Matt took the time to examine his options, discuss the move with his wife Abbie, and sleep on his decision. The next morning, Matt accepted the offer from D&F.

Sean's enthusiasm about Matt's hiring was infectious. His team began to work hard to integrate Matt into D&F and to ensure that his clients followed him.

- As soon as Matt accepted the position, Sean's group sent out a memo to all employees in Charlie DeFelice's and Ted Frost's names, announcing the new hire and describing his background (see Exhibit 2).
- Sean's recruiting manager arranged a series of round-table discussions with other D&F attorneys. She also wrote an article about Matt for the D&F internal newsletter.
- Sean developed a marketing program for Matt that outlined marketing goals and tactics (see Exhibit 3). DeFelice & Frost sometimes asked lateral hires to propose their own marketing programs before being hired, but Matt's appointment had been so rushed that he had no time to prepare one before he arrived.
- Sean drafted a press release announcing the new hire, sending it to local papers and relevant law journals (see Exhibit 4).
- D&F's marketing manager prepared an announcement on DeFelice & Frost stationery and sent one to each of Matt's clients. Later, he sent the announcements to D&F's other Employment and Education clients.
- Matt personally called all his major clients to inform them of his move, then followed up with a personalized letter. In the letter, he requested permission to transfer the clients' files to D&F (see Exhibit 5).
- Sean urged other D&F attorneys to build awareness of the firm's new area of expertise by describing the addition to their current clients. Also, he integrated material on Matt's typical client assignments into firmwide training materials.
- Matt was asked to submit an article for the June issue of the *Tennessee Employment Update*, the state's monthly newsletter on the subject.

Sean felt good about the steps he had taken to integrate Matt into D&F's practice. However, the nagging problem of Winthrop & Sterling's actions remained.

The Situation

Today, Sean was having second thoughts about the way he handled Matt's hiring back in February. Matt had extensive public-sector experience but had not established himself with private-sector clients. The "rainmaking" that D&F needed was not happening. Furthermore, Memphis was a small town, and its legal community was very tightly knit, almost incestuous. Sean realized that, so far, Matt's move was generating more ill will than new business.

Sean decided to set up a Development Group meeting to help the firm react to Winthrop & Sterling and to improve Matt's position. He scribbled a tentative agenda:

W&S
Defend against poaching
Defamation

Matt
Leverage his skills
Firm support—structural changes?
Things he can do
Things the firm can do
Individual efforts

Sean thought back to what he told Matt just before he presented D&F's offer. At the time, he had been trying to lighten the moment, but his words now seemed painfully inappropriate. "Matt," he had said, "I'd like to make you an offer you can't refuse. . . ."

QUESTIONS

1. Identify the strengths and weaknesses and the opportunities and threats that are faced by DeFelice & Frost.

2. Discuss the overall marketing strategy of DeFelice & Frost.

3. Discuss DeFelice & Frost's hiring practices.

4. What strategy should DeFelice & Frost implement to move forward?

NOTES

[1]Lawyers who, respectively, found the business, took care of and developed accounts, and serviced the accounts.

EXHIBIT   1

Matthew Lennox's Résumé

Matthew J. Lennox
Seven Presley Row
Memphis, TN 38185

ATTORNEY: Attorney, Winthrop & Sterling.

Representing public and private sector employers in many aspects of employee relations and labor and employment law including collective bargaining, discrimination issues, education law, personnel matters, unfair labor practices, grievance and interest arbitrations, organization campaigns and other related matters.

EDUCATION: Georgetown University National Law Center, J.D. 1987
University of Connecticut, B.A. (cum laude) 1983.
Pi Sigma Alpha Honor Society.

EXPERIENCE: Wilk, Carr, Shapiro, Singer and Sporleder, P.C. 1987-1989

Practiced in labor and employment law, representing management in both the public and private sector in many aspects of employee relations, including: contract negotiations, education law and other related matters.

State of Connecticut, Office of Labor Relations 1986-1987

Represented the interests of the State before the State Board of Labor Relations and in contract negotiations and arbitration hearings.

Clerks at Law 1984-1987

Founded and managed Clerks at Law, an organization that offered temporary legal assistance to a large clientele of law firms in Washington.

ACTIVITIES: Treasurer of the Connecticut School Attorneys Council.
Member of the American Bar Association.
Member of the Tennessee and Shelby County Bar Associations.
Member of Tennessee Public Employer Labor Relations Association.
Member of National Organization on Legal Problems in Education.
Responsible for annual review and update of the Municipal Employee Relations Act Manual.

EXHIBIT 2

MEMORANDUM ANNOUNCING MATTHEW LENNOX'S HIRING

DeFelice & Frost

MEMO

To: Everyone at DeFelice & Frost

From: Charlie DeFelice and Ted Frost

Date: March 19, 1993

Re: Matt Lennox

We are pleased to announce that Matthew J. Lennox (Matt) will be joining the firm as an Associate in our Labor and Employment Practice Group.

Since graduating from Georgetown University Law Center in 1987 with a J.D., Matt has practiced as an Associate for Wilk, Carr, Shapiro, Singer and Sporleder, P.C. and, for the past four years, at Winthrop & Sterling, where he represented primarily municipal and board of education clients in aspects of employee relations and labor and employment law.

Matt's experience will complement our Labor and Employment Practice in such areas as collective bargaining, discrimination issues, education law, personnel matters, unfair labor practices, grievance and interest arbitrations, organizational campaigns, and other related matters.

Please join us in welcoming Matt to DeFelice & Frost.

EXHIBIT 3

MARKETING PLAN FOR MATTHEW J. LENNOX

Marketing Plan for Matthew J. Lennox, April–June 1993

1. Background
   - Matt Lennox recently moved his labor practice from Winthrop & Sterling to D&F.
   - Winthrop & Sterling is actively attempting to prevent a number of Matt's clients from moving with him to D&F.
   - A marketing campaign has been developed to assist Matt during his transition to D&F that will enable him to expand and retain his current client base.

2. Marketing Goals
   - Matt Lennox will retain a high percentage of his current public sector clients.
   - Matt will continue to build his labor practice by providing services to current D&F clients and to new clients.

3. Marketing Strategy
   - Build awareness in highly targeted groups, including Tennessee Board of Education, that (1) Matt Lennox has moved his practice to D&F and (2) D&F has the capabilities to serve fully the legal needs of those target groups.

4. Marketing Tactics   Responsibility
   - Formal Announcement
     - Prepare formal announcement   S. Gordon/M. Lennox
     - Send announcement to Matt's mailing list and to current   A. Schaal
       Labor, Employment & Education mailing list
   - Tombstone/Announcement Advertisement
     - Prepare announcement advertisement for selected journals   A. Schaal
   - Press Release
     - Prepare press release for distribution to editors of targeted   S. Gordon
       periodicals (*Tennessee Law Tribune, TABE Journal*, etc.)
   - Client Calls & Letters
     - Call clients, request permission to send information on   M. Lennox
       D&F and to transfer files
     - Finalize statement of qualifications for public sector to mail   S. Gordon
     - Update D&F brochure to include Matt   S. Gordon/A. Schaal
   - Tennessee Employment Update
     - Include "letter from editor" Mark Werner to introduce Matt   M. Werner
     - Write a lead article for June issue on public sector topic   M. Lennox
   - D&F Marketing Database/Mailing List
     - Add Matt's mailing list to main D&F list   A. Schaal
     - Merge Matt's mailing list with Labor, Employment &   A. Schaal
       Education mailing list for newsletter, etc. List Matt as
       primary D&F contact

▶▶▶▶ ◀◀◀◀

E X H I B I T   4

PRESS RELEASE FOR MATTHEW LENNOX

DeFelice & Frost
Law Offices

New Hampshire Square
Memphis, TN 38101
(901) 767-■■■■

FOR IMMEDIATE RELEASE

CONTACT:
Sean T. Gordon
(901) 767-■■■■

MATTHEW J. LENNOX JOINS DEFELICE & FROST

Memphis, Tennessee, April 7, 1993—Charlie E. DeFelice, Managing Partner of DeFelice & Frost, the Memphis, Tennessee, business law firm, announced today that Matthew J. Lennox has joined DeFelice & Frost's Employment and Education Practice Group.

Mr. Lennox is recognized as one of the state's best-known public sector labor lawyers and has many years of experience in representing public and private sector clients with their employee relations and labor and employment matters in such areas as collective bargaining, discrimination, education law, personnel matters, unfair labor practices, grievance and interest arbitrations, organization campaigns, teacher and employee discipline and termination cases, student discipline, school accommodation disputes, unemployment and worker's compensation matters, and wage and hour compliance disputes, among others. He currently serves many municipalities, boards of education, and other public and private sector entities.

Mr. Lennox recently represented a board of education in a binding interest arbitration with its teachers' association. This arbitration resulted in the first salary freeze under the Teacher Negotiations Act, saving the board approximately $400,000 in its salary account.

Mr. Lennox obtained his undergraduate degree from the University of Connecticut and his law degree from the Georgetown University National Law Center. He has practiced as an Associate for Wilk, Carr, Shapiro, Singer and Sporleder, P.C. and, for the past four years, at Winthrop & Sterling. He is an active member of the Connecticut School Attorney's Council and currently serves as its treasurer. Mr. Lennox resides in Memphis with his wife, Abbie.

DeFelice & Frost has grown steadily over the past ten years to become one of the state's leading business law firms. The firm provides comprehensive legal services in the following areas: corporate and securities; intellectual property; international; business succession, tax and estate planning; labor, employment and education; real estate and commercial finance; business litigation; bankruptcy and creditors' rights; construction; surety and fidelity; environmental/land use; and health law.

EXHIBIT   5

MATTHEW LENNOX'S LETTER TO CLIENTS

DeFelice & Frost
Law Offices

New Hampshire Square
Memphis, TN 38101
(901) 767-■■■■

Matthew J. Lennox
Direct Dial 901/767-■■■■

March 22, 1993

Arnold Lansbury
McNairy County Board of Education
336 Lynchburg Road
Hickory Flats, TN 38310

Dear Arnold,

I am pleased to confirm our phone conference regarding my move to the law firm of DeFelice & Frost. I had said that I would be leaving Winthrop & Sterling on April 1, 1993. However, after further discussion with Winthrop & Sterling, we mutually and amicably agreed that I would accelerate my transition and commence work at DeFelice & Frost on March 22, 1993. Although I will be moving to a new firm, my practice will not change; I will continue to represent public and private employers in labor, employment, and education law matters.

Thank you for inviting me to send you information about DeFelice & Frost. The enclosed information should be helpful to the Board of Education as it reviews its legal representation. If you decide to transfer files to DeFelice & Frost, I will be honored to continue our relationship.

I have enclosed a description of DeFelice & Frost, a copy of the *Tennessee Employment Law Letter* (a monthly firm publication), and resumes of the lawyers at DeFelice & Frost who serve as counsel to municipalities. I hope this information is helpful. One point that is difficult to make in a letter relates to the quality of a firm's services. We recognize that the selection of counsel involves intangibles of personality and philosophy. Therefore, my colleagues at DeFelice & Frost and I would be delighted to meet you personally at any time.

A move to DeFelice & Frost will be smooth and positive with no effect on our valued relationship. In accordance with the rules of professional conduct for lawyers, the client is entitled to the possession of all files, can determine what files may be transferred to a new law firm, and holds the prerogative to decide who will represent its interests. Any other issues that may arise as a result of a change in representation will be resolved by the law firms.

Please call me with any questions on my direct line, (901) 767-■■■■.

Very truly yours,

Matthew J. Lennox

Please sign below if you want to transfer files and indicate which files you wish transferred.

_____

Arnold Lansbury

P RITSKER S OFTWARE:
S ALES AND C ONSULTING

"Moklowski, I'm beginning to think you're nothing but an order taker."

These harsh words echoed through Bob Moklowski's mind as he gazed out the window of his Atlanta office. A little over two years ago, he had been promoted to regional sales manager. This was what he had aspired to, but since then, things had not gone well. His sales team had yet to achieve quota, and several important accounts had been lost. Bob knew his boss, Bill Scheffer, was wondering about his competence. Some days he felt like a first-class loser.

Moklowski was beginning to think that Pritsker's pricing policy was impacting his salesmen's ability to generate new accounts. Their traditional separation of consulting services and computer software seemed to be causing considerable anxiety among prospective customers. Bob wanted to find ways to reduce the price of services. But Bill had suggested they bundle both product and services into a fixed-price offering. Their last conversation on this subject ended with Bill saying, "Bob, that's the oldest excuse in the book. Every salesman who can't sell complains about the price being too high. Don't be a whiner, it's not good for your image. My view is that we've got to maintain our margins on both our product and services, But, hey, you're in charge of the region, so I'll leave the decision up to you."

Pritsker Corporation was a small software company with sales of approximately $12 million. The company marketed a line of software products and services mostly to manufacturing companies whose revenues exceeded $100 million. To support the rapid growth in business, the size of the sales force had more than doubled in the past few years. Several salespersons, including Bob Moklowski, had joined the company during this recent growth period.

Accepting the regional manager's position was turning out to be a failed career move for Moklowski. Although he had been a very successful salesman, his performance as a manager was abysmal. During the first year, his five-person sales team sold only 80 percent of their assigned quota, and halfway through his second year they had sold only 25 percent of quota. If a dramatic turnaround didn't occur soon, Bob knew he would be sent back to the ranks. What a disaster that would be. How would he tell his wife? How would he face his obnoxious father-in-law after being demoted? As he pondered his dilemma, he thought of the two presentations he had made at a seminar in Boston last month. His new local salesman, Paul, had been there with him.

TUESDAY JUNE 1

RADCOM

RADCOM, a manufacturer of radar components for the defense industry and the primary supplier of equipment for the Stealth aircraft line, was a fast-track account. Having seen Bob's presentation at the seminar, Rich Beeber, general manager of RADCOM's Radar Products Division, called him in for a sales presentation. The meeting started with Rich offering an explanation of his interest in Pritsker and the issues he thought Pritsker might be able to address. Bob then went on to explain how Pritsker's software system worked and how it could potentially solve Rich's production problem (Exhibit 1).

Following Bob's presentation, a lively discussion ensued. Rich started, "Bob, all this sounds good, but I'm not so sure it will solve my problem. It takes us 25 days to manufacture our product. As I said, we're trying to find a way to bring this down to under 10 days, and I just don't see how your product will fit the bill. Your system sounds like it might work in some shops, but we're completely different."

Trying not to sound completely annoyed at Rich's ignorance, Bob politely responded, "At this point, I won't expect you to agree that our product will solve your cycle-time problem. However, what I'd hope is that you'd give Paul and me the chance to study your operation more closely and to make a more scientific determination of what we can or can't do for your issues. Let's not decide anything until we get all the facts."

"Okay Moklowski," Rich replied, "that sounds like a fair suggestion, but I'm also concerned about the cost of this system. What are we looking at on this?"

Bob was dreading that question, but of course he offered no explanation. "That depends on what we find during our investigation. But a range would be from $150,000 to $250,000, depending on the amount of consulting services required for design and installation."

Bob held his breath, sweat pouring under his arms, hoping for a somewhat positive reaction.

Rich's eyebrows raised a bit. "Well, that sounds a bit high since we can probably do a lot of the work ourselves. In any case, let's arrange for Paul to come back and conduct your investigation."

"Thank you, Lord," Bob muttered as he exhaled in relief. The meeting ended with Paul scheduled to come back later that week.

As they returned to their car, Bob felt that the meeting represented a good start. He liked this feeling of confidence. Although Paul would have to do a substantial amount of work to get ready for the final presentation, Bob felt that was really the only way to convey the benefits of a complex product. Unless RADCOM saw a detailed description of how Pritsker's software would produce tangible savings, their chance of selling the deal were slim to none. Paul had his work cut out for him.

TERADYNE

The second meeting of the day was with an automatic test equipment manufacturer. George Cary, the operations manager at Teradyne's Boston foundry,[1] had also seen Moklowski's seminar presentation and had asked him to make a presentation to his group.

When Bob and Paul arrived at the foundry, they were greeted by Mr. Cary. While walking them to the conference room, George explain why he had called Pritsker. He felt that the divisions his group supplied would soon be demanding delivery on specific days of the week. Although they were 99 percent on-time for weekly delivery, their daily performance was not so impressive.

After listening to Mr. Cary describe his situation, Bob gave the same introductory presentation he had used earlier in the day. George listened intently, and when Bob had finished, he weighed in with several questions:

"That sounds like it might be a lot more than we need here. We've been successful with our current system, right? I see our next step as somehow adding onto it with something just a little more sophisticated. You guys sound like you have a Cadillac, and I think we're looking for a Chevy."

"You'll buy a damned Ferrari if I get my way," Bob thought to himself. He calmly answered this objection, "I understand your concern about complexity. What we've found, though, is that the less complete products offered by our competitors will not do the entire job. They may be able to do 80 percent of it. But you will find that unless the entire system is represented, the software will produce worthless schedules, which your production people will just throw away. Our product's ability to do the whole job will allow you to reach your goal of daily deliveries."

"Well, you have a point there," George agreed, "but I'm still not convinced we need this level of sophistication."

"No, George, an abacus would probably suit you just fine," Bob continued to himself again.

"George, at this point I wouldn't expect you to be certain of our product's value," Moklowski replied. "What I would suggest is that we have Paul come back in and meet with your people so that we can more fully appraise whether our system is right for the foundry. Paul has a strong background in electronics. This will allow him to assess your situation and present to you and your team a clear picture of how the product will benefit Teradyne."

"Okay," said George, "I don't see a reason why we can't do that. Let's have Paul come back in next Tuesday, if that's okay with everyone."

The meeting ended with arrangements for Paul to return the following week. Moklowski was two for two. It was Miller time.

Bob sipped his beer and described what he thought Paul should do with these two accounts over the next few weeks. He explained that Paul should develop a preliminary model based on the information he will have gathered from his meetings. This model, which would not actually be used, would allow Paul to describe the system's functionality in terms familiar to each company. Coupled with this demo would be a standard system demonstration that would take the customer through an operational model to explain how a scheduler would use the software. Finally, Bob explained that a simple benefits analysis should be developed showing how the use of improved scheduling and planning would result in bottom-line savings. This analysis was to use client-provided information on current inventory levels, overtime usage, expediting expenses, etc., to provide a projected savings in cost-of-goods-sold.

As Bob waved goodbye and headed into the terminal, he felt his first sales trip with Paul had been productive. Paul wasn't half the bore he had anticipated. However, there were still a lot of issues to be tackled in this account and others. One was the issue of pricing, a topic Bob had been spending a lot of time thinking about recently. It was a source of great anxiety for him. Pricing was the reason Bob carried two suitcases with him on trips—one for paperwork, and one for blood pressure medicine. He looked forward to his meeting tomorrow with Bill, at which time they planned on discussing the issue at length.

Wednesday, June 2

Pritsker HQ—Atlanta

When Bob arrived at Pritsker's corporate headquarters the next day, he found Bill in a foul mood. Late the previous afternoon, Bill had heard from Moklowski's midwest salesman that an order expected this month would be delayed. Bob was less than pleased, and so was his ulcer. The prospective company's management apparently found Pritsker's final proposal confusing. The region's quota attainment looked to be in jeopardy. Against this backdrop, Bill and Moklowski sat down to hash out a new pricing approach.

Bill was concerned that several accounts in Moklowski's region had opted to purchase the software without Pritsker's consulting services. Although he was grateful for the revenue the sales generated, Bill was worried that these customers would fail to install the system on their own, damaging any follow-on sales potential and margins. He had an idea that he believed would address this issue. Instead of listing software and services as separate line items, he would bundle them together into one big fixed-price offering. To entice prospective customers to purchase such an offering, Bill was prepared to offer extensive pre-sales consulting work to nail down customer benefits and related cost savings. Bill explained to Moklowski, "If management can see the tremendous benefits of this technology in *their* manufacturing operation, they'll be jumping over each other to sign up for our fixed-price offering."

Bob wasn't so sure. He thought the issue was Pritsker's conservative proposal process. Each proposal carried a minimum quotation of 1,000 hours of consulting, estimated using the rate for project manager of $120/hour. Oftentimes, customers would need far fewer than this number of hours, and many of these hours could be handled by lower-paid analysts (see Exhibit 2). In general, Bob found that the analyst with only six month's experience was 85 percent as effective as an experienced person. Based on this, he felt that Paul should be the first to try a lower consulting quotation, especially with the RADCOM account, where price sensitivity was an issue.

As the meeting wore on, it became clear to Moklowski that Bill was steadfast with his new pricing approach. He was in no position to argue, and Bill was as stubborn as a mule. Bob decided the best way out of their impasse was to try each idea in one of Paul's accounts, and let him be the guinea pig. He explained to Bill that Teradyne would be a good test ground for the new approach, but RADCOM would not agree to such an offer. Bill thought about it for a minute, and then agreed to Moklowski's plan.

Having agreed on a pricing strategy, they turned their attention to Bob's regional budget. Bill wasn't sure whether Bob was fielding the right number of people. Keeping a single salesman in the field cost Pritsker almost $150,000 per year. This included not only salary (Exhibit 3) and benefits, but also travel expenses (Miller time), office expenses, and support staff. Currently, there was one pre-sales support person for every 2.5 salesmen. With five salesmen and Bob, the yearly budget was about $900,000. Against this expense, Bob's target was to obtain service and sales revenue of $4.2 million. After discussing various possible reconfigurations, they ended their session deciding to leave things as they were in this area.

FOLLOW-UP VISITS

Throughout June, Paul returned several times to RADCOM and Teradyne to garner information on their current planning and scheduling procedures and their current computer systems. Following his initial data-gathering visits, Paul would return once or twice to review possible approaches, thereby starting the process of educating his prospective customers about Pritsker's product and services. Toward the end of the month, Paul returned to demonstrate the system using a "data only" model combined with one of Pritsker's standard demonstration models. Both companies appeared quite excited about the possibilities, and a final presentation was scheduled with each account at the end of the month.

Besides following up on his two top accounts, Paul had met with 12 other companies throughout the month. Typically, out of 12 such meetings, two companies would have a high enough level of interest to move to the next stage. In addition to these calls, Paul spent a good deal of time on the phone, both qualifying leads received from telemarketing and contacting leads he received from salesmen at other companies. A "slave to the grind," he was working a good 50 hours a week and was just about keeping up. An average day is shown in Exhibit 4.

As the month wound down, Paul turned his full attention to finishing the two proposals for the next day's meetings. During this process, Paul conferred with

Moklowski frequently. Bob suggested the pricing structures which he and Bill had agreed upon earlier. Paul didn't fully agree with this approach but went along, relying on Moklowski's better judgment.

Before finalizing both proposals, Paul called John Marcos, Pritsker's applications manager. John's group would be responsible for doing all post-sales implementation work if Paul's proposals were accepted. John was pleased to hear about the Teradyne proposal, commenting: "We can do just about anything with $160,000 in consulting hours." John was particularly glad that his team would be earning a likely $40,000 premium if the 1,000 hour estimate held up. "Yeah," thought Paul, "I'm bad."

When the subject turned to the RADCOM proposal, John was less sanguine. "Well, I'm concerned about lowering the number of hours and budgeting for more junior staff. Unlike Teradyne, there'll be no firm estimates from the pre-sales study to go on. We may be painting ourselves into a corner on this." Paul's head could be hard deflating.

John went on to remind Paul that several customers who tried cutting corners on consulting hours wound up with unsuccessful implementations. Paul agreed that this was a risk but stressed the cost sensitivity that RADCOM expressed. John relented, but he insisted that his group would approach this strictly on a time-and-materials basis.

By the end of the day, Paul rushed to the nearest FedEx box with both proposals in hand. The pricing seemed to fit each account (Exhibit 5), but Paul wondered how it would be received.

Tuesday, June 30

Final Presentation to RADCOM

The meeting started with Bill making a few introductory remarks about the savings that Pritsker technology had achieved for existing customers. His comments seemed lost on this crowd, so he quickly turned the meeting over to Paul.

Paul proceeded to review the areas of potential cost savings that FACTOR would produce at RADCOM's facility. In addition to achieving their goal of 10-day cycle times, their system would produce a savings of $150,000 in its first full year of operation and $50,000 per year thereafter. The cost of the system was then reviewed, and a suggested implementation schedule introduced. At this time, the floor was opened up for questions. Rich began the discussion, "Most of your proposal makes sense, but I'm not entirely comfortable that your system will deliver the reductions in expenditures you're suggesting. Even if it does, I'm not clear why our staff can't get this thing going. Don't you think our people are smart enough to handle this?"

Bill fielded this one. "What Pritsker can provide with our professional consulting services is a crisp implementation that will allow RADCOM to realize the benefits of this technology in a short time span. Our experience with implementing this product will allow us to steer you clear of any pitfalls that may arise throughout the implementation process."

Following this, Rich answered, "Why can't your people point out these pitfalls before we get started? I was led to believe that installing this thing was fairly straightforward."

The tension mounted, but Bill, a former postal worker, was used to pressure. He smoothly replied, "Sir, the ability to provide successful and timely implementation is Pritsker's forte. The tremendous benefits of this technology will provide a return on your investment within 9 to 12 months. Better still, the cost savings accruing from these benefits can be reinvested in your research, development, and marketing efforts, or flow straight to the bottom line as increased profits."

"From what my production manager told me," Rich whined, "I think this product can solve our problems. I'm not so familiar with the implementation process, but we're usually able to figure things out on our own with help from MIS."

In mild desperation, Moklowski added, "It's possible that RADCOM can install this product on its own. However, our mission is to ensure that the product provides what we say it will. In our experience, a substantial level of involvement up front yields results. Without our input at the various stages of the process, the end product may prove unsatisfactory."

At this point, Rich and his boss excused themselves to discuss the matter in private. When they returned, it was clear that any project initiation would be delayed for the time being.

As they left the building, Moklowksi, Bill, and Paul expressed their disbelief at what had happened. All the previous meetings up until this point had gone well. Rich seemed to understand what the product could do, yet something wasn't quite right. Furious with the situation, Bob remembered Rich being the type of kid he used to pummel in high school for asking too many questions. Bill summed up the team's confusion: "This decision isn't an easy one; $150,000 is a lot of money."

TERADYNE FOLLOW-UP VISIT

On the way to their next meeting, Bob and Paul filled in Bill on the status of the Teradyne account. Paul explained that the previous meeting, where he demonstrated Pritsker's system, generated real enthusiasm. He thought they would be very receptive to Bill's suggestion of a fixed-price offering. Bob concurred with this assessment, adding that the account had proceeded steadily since their first meeting.

Bill began the meeting in earnest by providing the background to Pritsker's new offering.

"We are very excited that we have the opportunity to share our newest offering with Teradyne," he said with a politician's smile. "Our confidence in this new offering reflects the commitment that Pritsker is willing to make to Teradyne, on a pre-sales basis, to crystallize the benefits of deploying this powerful technology within your operations. As Paul and Bob will explain, this offering is replete with benefits."

Following this introduction, Paul went on to explain what was included with Pritsker's fixed-price offering. Essentially, all software and services that were needed to install the product in conformance with a mutually agreed-upon specification were incorporated within the $250,000 offering. Any cost overruns would be absorbed by Pritsker, removing the elements of risk from the implementation. No reaction. They were either lost or in disbelief.

Bob reviewed the extensive pre-sales consulting study that Pritsker would provide in exchange for a good-faith commitment that Teradyne would proceed with the project if the cost savings, as determined by the study, were substantial enough. He explained that, basically, all the evaluative and implementation risk would be borne by Pritsker. Finally, he offered a brief summary of the proposed time frame for the consulting study and then opened the floor to questions.

After a pause of a minute, George Cary laboriously gestured that he was either about to vomit or speak.

"I don't know about the rest of you guys, but this is far more involved than I figured. This just looks totally out of line. It seems that a lot of what you're proposing are services that we don't want. Traditionally, we've done things in-house, right? Our view of consultants has been pretty dim."

Bill replied, "I assure you that our consulting services staff is capable of helping Teradyn achieve the tremendous benefits from this powerful technology. If, after our study is complete, the cost reductions don't exceed our proposal's cost, you can call off the implementation. The risk will be assumd entirely by Pritsker Corporation. All we ask for is a good-faith commitment on your part."

"We just don't have a high opinion of consultants around here," George responded. "We'd have to spend our time at first training your people in how our business works, right? I just don't think we can afford the time to train your people. It seems to me that your other customers have been able to implement this without any input from Pritsker. I talked to the guy in Texas whose name you gave as a reference, and he said that he installed it singlehandedly. This proposal just seems way off base."

"Here we go again," Bob whispered to Paul. "Sir, what you have to understand is that the Texas project was an exception. The individual leading that project had many years of experience working with Pritsker's software systems. He can't be used as an example in this situation."

The conversation continued for a while longer, with no apparent progress. When Bill, Bob, and Paul left for the airport, they had a string of unsuccessful meetings to contend with.

As usual on a weekday afternoon, Boston traffic was at a standstill, allowing plenty of time to ponder the day's events. As his mind wandered (it had a tendency to do that these days), Bob thought about a sales effort earlier in the year at Circuit Center where everything seemd to go perfectly. Lin Alts, Circuit Center's information systems manager, understood how Pritsker's system worked and why it could help his company within 30 minutes of their first meeting. His management science background afforded him an insight into the product that few customers ever developed. Although Lin and his group were clearly capable of doing most of the installation work, the small size of his department made him eager to enlist the help of Pritsker's consultants. While thinking about other satisfied customers, Bob thought that most of them had a lot more in common with Circuit Center than they did with Teradyne and RADCOM. Thank goodness.

WEDNESDAY, JULY 1

PRITSKER HQ—ATLANTA

As Bob went over the events of the past few weeks, he wondered what he should do with his pricing approach. His two experiments in Boston fell flat, and worse yet, he had recently been called by an irate customer whose company was unable to install the product on its own. *He told them so.* Besides addressing these pressing issues, Bob had the nagging feeling that there were other issues he was overlooking. As he sat looking out his office window, he knew that he had better act quickly.

QUESTIONS

1. What do you think might be the *real reasons* (not the stated reasons) why none of the different prospects bought from Bob?

2. As Bob Mokloski, what would you have done differently?

3. What marketing-related suggestions would you make to top management? These might include issues of product design, pricing, service contracts, sales strategies, advertising support, etc.

N O T E S

[1]Actually, PCB boards, not metal ingots, were produced here. The use of the term *foundry* was a holdover from the building's previous owner.

EXHIBIT   1

FINITE PRODUCTION SCHEDULING

Pritsker Corporation developed and marketed production scheduling and planning software—FACTOR—that applied "finite" scheduling techniques. Essentially, the software utilized a detailed model of a firm's manufacturing process and simulated the movement of the firm's production orders through this model. The results of this simulation were then used to modify production schedules and order-release dates.

By modifying production schedules, FACTOR could solve many underlying production problems. For example, inventory was often reduced by as much as 80 percent, resulting in large cycle-time reductions and yield improvements. Another common benefit was a reduction in the use of overtime by smoothing the work flow. Since FACTOR could accurately simulate work flow, it could predict when peaks and valleys would occur and reschedule work to eliminate them.

Finite scheduling had proven to be a great technical advance over older and more generally known technologies, such as Manufacturing Requirements Planning (MRP). Whereas MRP required hard-to-determine data inputs—like average waiting time at a machining center—FACTOR produced accurate predictions of these values. However, the technology was still unfamiliar to most manufacturing executives, and Pritsker's biggest competition was almost always reluctant to change the status quo. In fact, not a single sale had been lost to another software company in the past two years.

EXHIBIT   2

CONSULTING FEE SCHEDULE

Title	Hourly Fee	Avg. Cost/Hour
Sr. Consultant	$120	$50
Consultant	$100	$35
Consultant (new hires)	$100	$30

EXHIBIT   3

SALES PLAN

Compensation for a sales representative consists of both a base salary and commissions as follows:

Base Salary $30,000–$45,000, increases awarded based on performance

Software Commission   0–$200K   2% Paid when order booked
                       $200k–$600K   4%
                       $600k–$1,050K   6%
                       over $1,050K   8%

Services Commission   2 percent paid when booked for fixed-price orders, when billed for time-and-materials orders.

Sales of services count toward software quota attainment. For example, a $200,000 fixed-price services order will move software commission into 4 percent range.

Attaintment bonus: All reps who achieved quota the previous year start at 4 percent.

Typical rep expected to sell $400,000 in services and $650,000 in software.

Regional manager receives a commission override based on regional revenue.

EXHIBIT   4

TYPICAL DAILY SCHEDULE

7:30–8:00	Breakfast meeting with sales rep from another software or hardware company. Exchange leads or discuss accounts.
8:00–8:30	Drive to first meeting.
8:30–9:30	One-hour introductory meeting.
9:30–10:00	Drive to next meeting.
10:00–11:00	One-hour introductory meeting.
11:00–11:45	Use lobby phone to return phone calls and contact home office.
11:45–1:00	Drive to afternoon appointment and stop for lunch.
1:00–3:30	Follow-up meeting, talk with two or three key people.
3:30–4:00	Drive back to office.
4:00–6:00	Return phone calls, prepare letters, contact home office.

One day out of five spent entirely in office qualifying leads by phone, responding to customer problems and preparing sales proposals.

E X H I B I T   5

PROPOSAL PRICING

RADCOM proposal:

Software	$ 65,000
Services	$ 80,000
Training	$ 10,000
Total	$155,000

Services include 300 project manager hours at $120/hr., and 440 analyst hours at $100/hr.

Teradyne proposal:

Software	$ 90,000
—includes all software modules	
Services	$160,000
—includes extensive on-site training	
Total	$250,000

Services includes a two-week pre-sales consulting study. Project sized to use an estimated 1,000 hours of project manager time. All overruns absorbed by Pritsker.

Roscoe Nondestructive Testing

After nine months, Grover Porter, president of Roscoe Nondestructive Testing, Inc. (Roscoe) was beginning to question the success of his new quality improvement program (QIP). Initiated in March 1991, the QIP had produced substantial increases in recent customer satisfaction surveys; however, none of that satisfaction seemed to be fueling a return to growth in either revenue or number of clients. Porter anticipated Roscoe's second down year in a row as the company continued to lose major customers, and he was eager to reestablish the growth that had preceded the last two years of decline.

It was hard to believe that the cyclical downturn in the pulp and paper industry had pushed the boiler inspection business to competing solely on price. Porter still felt that there was room in the industry for a quality service at a fair price, but the ineffectiveness of the QIP had prompted Porter to reconsider adjusting Roscoe's pricing structure.

I. The Nondestructive Testing Industry

Nondestructive testing (NDT) involves the examination of materials to discover microscopic cracks, corrosion, or malformation, using inspection techniques that do not damage the material under scrutiny. Common inspection techniques include the use of x-rays, ultrasonics, and electrical eddy currents.

NDT is used in a wide variety of applications, including the examination of aircraft parts, tanks and vessels of various shapes and sizes, and welds of all kinds. Roscoe primarily uses ultrasonic thickness measuring devices to determine the thickness of metal plating.

NDT technicians are certified by area of expertise (e.g., ultrasonic) and accumulated skill and experience (Levels I–III). Technicians certified in more than one inspection technique are a treasured resource in most firms. They were generally employed by four types of companies:

1. *Mom and pop* labs usually employ less than 25 people and provide a single type of inspection service to a small number of customers. These firms are the low-cost providers

Source: This case was prepared by Brian Wansink and Eric Cannell as a basis for class discussion rather than to illustrate either effective or ineffective handling of an administrative situation.

and are quite willing to bid at cost simply to keep busy. Many are often tied to a single client who wields considerable control over pricing and delivery.

2.   *Nationwide* companies have labs around the country and a high degree of name recognition. These firms also provide inspection services to a large number of different industries; however, individual offices usually serve a narrow segment of the market.

3.   *Specialty* firms target very narrow market segments that require specific needs. These firms make large capital investments in the latest inspection equipment and employ the highest-skilled technicians. Barriers to entry into these specialized markets are high, so specialty firms have traditionally achieved high levels of profitability.

4.   While much larger than the mom and pop labs, *regional* firms lack the name recognition and market strength of the nationwide companies. These firms employ up to 150 technicians and have the resources to tackle the largest inspection jobs. Roscoe is a regional firm, operating primarily in the central southern part of the United States.

All in all, management of NDT firms has been historically uninspired, driven mainly by owner-operators who managed to survive the lean years.

II. History of Roscoe

Roscoe was founded in 1973 by Hans Norregaard in Roscoe, Louisiana. After 30 years as an NDT technician, Norregaard decided to set up shop for himself amidst many of the pulp and paper mills located in western Louisiana. Roscoe focused on the inspection of large boilers, a service designed to monitor the corrosion of the boiler walls. Inspections conducted every two to three years provided mills with sufficient warning to replace weakened, corroded plates in boiler walls before a catastrophic accident occurred.

In 1980, Norregaard sold the company to National Inspection Services (NIS) for $1.75 million. NIS was a subsidiary of Swanson Industries, a large diversified holding company. At that time, NIS brought in Chad Huerlmann (a Harvard MBA) to manage the company. Huerlmann was eager to run a small business and viewed the Roscoe acquisition as a great opportunity.

The company continued well for four years, until the pulp and paper industry bottomed out again. Hampered by misguided directives and burdened by corporate overhead, Roscoe's low-cost position no longer protected it from the growing price pressure facing NDT companies in the pulp and paper industry. Also, Huerlmann failed to establish an effective relationship with the technicians in the company, and many resigned or left the NDT industry altogether. By 1984, Swanson Industries decided to divest of NIS altogether, and Roscoe was once again up for sale.

At that time, Hans Norregaard and a long-time business associate, Grover Porter, decided to get back into the NDT business. Together, they bought back

▶▶▶▶ ◀◀◀◀

Roscoe for about 35 cents on the dollar. They were convinced that by offering an improved inspection service for a fair price, they could rebuild the company's reputation and good fortunes.

After dismissing Huerlmann, Hans and Grover began building a new management team for Roscoe. A new controller, Jane Bottensak, was hired away from MQS Inspection. Ted Witkowski, a staff Professional Engineer (PE) out of Texas A&M, who had previously worked for Exxon, was also taken on. Both men thought Ted would bring some much-needed technical backbone to the company. Also, long-time technician, Ed Brown, was promoted to operations manager. Finally, Roscoe began recruiting technicians from the best vocational tech schools in the country.

In 1987, Hans Norregaard retired, and Grover Porter became president. Roscoe was back on track.

In 1990, Roscoe encountered a downturn in both revenues and customers. Many mills simply decided not to release bids as often as they used to. While Roscoe always lost some contracts to lower bidders, Porter felt the recent slowdown in the pulp and paper industry exacerbated Roscoe's situation by forcing mills to be more cost conscious. Still, Porter felt that there must be room for the services that Roscoe offered:

> Hans and I have put together a great management team over the last three years and our technicians are some of the best in the industry. Roscoe offers an efficient, quality inspection service and we feel that we can price accordingly.

However, the recent loss of established customers caused Grover Porter to question the validity of Roscoe's purported "high-quality" service.

III. Customer Profiles

Although boiler inspections in pulp and paper mills have been standard practice for many years, mills differed widely on the representative who interacted with Roscoe's inspection team. This contact could be almost anyone from the plant manager down to a purchasing agent. The following descriptions illustrate many of the problems that have plagued Roscoe recently.

George McDonald at the Franklin Paper Company was a typical plant manager who reigned over his plant like a king over his castle. As any other plant manager, McDonald was primarily concerned about controlling costs and was hostile to the idea of boiler inspections in general. Since inspections could be conducted only during plant shutdowns, McDonald was unhappy about the lost production time:

> Besides the $85,000 inspection fee, my plant is idle during the two days it takes your team to complete the job. At 750 tons per day, I pay an additional opportunity cost of over $330,000 every day you are in my plant. A boiler will last 20 years without exploding and if it wasn't for corporate HQ, I would never bother with the

inspections. Besides, the only thing that I ever get out of it is an "OK" and a pile of figures that I can't make head nor tail of.

International Paper's plant in Longview, Texas, was one of the few clients that maintained their own NDT department. As with other mills, the department consisted of only one retired NDT technician who interacted with service providers like Roscoe. Bob Kapala typified the kind of NDT person often found in paper mills. He was friendly and eager to help but was actually often more of a hindrance. The last thing a technician wanted was someone looking over his shoulder all the time.

After the inspection was completed, Bob would combine the recent inspection data with a pile of past data and attempt to find trends in corrosion patterns. The fact that different inspection firms provided data in different formats complicated Bob's task.

Jim Bulgrin at the Rockton Paper Mill in Texarkana, Texas, presented a different problem. Bulgrin, a recent graduate of Georgia Tech, had been hired into the mill's engineering services department seven months ago. As one of Roscoe's team supervisors described him, Bulgrin was "as wet behind the ears as a newborn calf." But he was eager to learn and was on top of every detail.

Problems arose when Jim noticed that thickness readings on one section of a boiler were considerably greater than when inspected two years before. After confronting the technicians, who ended up getting very angry, Jim eagerly reported the discrepancy to his boss. It was later discovered that a new plate had been welded onto the boiler in that area, but Roscoe lost the contract with Rockton.

Pulp mill supervisors, like Billy Dunlap at the Lufkin Pulp Mill, were Roscoe's most common contact inside a mill. Dunlap has been cajoling his boiler along for the past 15 years and did not take easily to anyone mistreating his "baby."

Finally, the inevitable contact is the purchasing representative who files the paperwork with accounting. Lucy Boyle in purchasing at Lufkin was never happy about processing paperwork relating to inspection services:

> Corporate headquarters requires us to file additional paperwork for one-time expenses greater than $50,000. With inspection fees well over $75,000, I end up processing over three times more paperwork than normal. My life doesn't return to normal until the mill goes back on-line.

IV. A PRELUDE TO ACTION

In January 1991, while attending the Nondestructive Testing Managers Association meeting in Las Vegas, Grover Porter was still struggling with the question of what defined a quality service. As it turned out, one of the speakers in the New Business Segment of the conference presented a talk on the components of service quality. And in that same month, a number of articles describing quality improvement programs at major aerospace inspection firms ran in both the ASNT and AWS Journals.[1]

At the monthly staff meeting in February, Porter discussed his concerns regarding the level of service provided by Roscoe. "As you all know, we've lost a bunch of accounts in the last few months. I suspect our service quality is not what it should be, and I've been thinking about a quality improvement program. If we don't do something soon, we may be forced to reduce our fees."

Bottensak, the controller, nodded her head in agreement and commented that something had to be done. "Let's go for it! None of us need reminding that 1990 was a bad year, but it looks like this year will be even worse. That's not great for our bonuses!"

Ted Witkowski, the staff PE, and Ed Brown, the operations manager, were extremely skeptical. Ted explained, "Look, we have the best-trained technicians out there with top-of-the-line equipment. They make some mistakes now and then, but when a boiler inspection requires 20,000 readings, that will happen. Besides, the mill has to look at the readings over an entire area and not just a single point. It's not reasonable to inspect every point twice. The mills couldn't afford the cost or the downtime."

After further discussion, Porter suggested that they first conduct a short customer survey to determine whether there were any areas for improvement. No one resisted the idea, so Porter spent the weekend composing the survey, and Bottensak pulled together a mailing list of Roscoe customers from the last five years. On Monday morning, 357 surveys were dropped in the mail.

V. THE SURVEY RESULTS

By the first week of March, Porter had collected 82 responses. With only three responses returned in the last four days, Porter felt his sample was as big as it was going to get and asked Jane Bottensak to aggregate the results into a single report (Exhibit 1). The next morning, Jane walked into Porter's office with a grin:

> Grover, look's like we got something here. I ignored 11 of the responses since they obviously knew nothing about our work. I reckon those surveys didn't even reach the right contact in the mills. Anyway, that left 71 responses. I pulled all the results together to determine the frequency distributions and from what I can see it seems our people skills need work. Even our office staff could use some improvement.

Porter was surprised that the accuracy of inspection data and time to completion rated so highly, considering that business was so tough these last months. But then he recalled that the speaker at the NDTMA Conference last month emphasized the importance of the people aspect in service quality.

Unfortunately, Roscoe did not attract the type of people blessed with an abundance of social grace. The environment around a boiler is not pleasant. There is constant noise, grime, and heat. And if there was a reason to climb inside the boiler, the technician found himself struggling through cramped areas with his equipment and his flashlight. Once out, his clothing and equipment were coated with a black muck that not even Ultra-Tide could remove. Thus, while technicians survived the conditions on-site, they did not necessarily do so quietly.

At the March staff meeting, Porter announced his plans for Roscoe's Quality Improvement Program.

VI. THE QUALITY IMPROVEMENT PROGRAM

The three elements that Porter decided to include in the QIP were initial training, a bonus reward system, and customer surveys at the conclusion of every job. He recognized that the QIP had to be more than a one-shot deal to be successful and felt that the proposed combination of training, surveys, and bonuses would establish the lasting, fundamental changes Roscoe needed.

Training was provided by ABS Consultants of Madison, Wisconsin, who specialized in teaching customer contact skills for industrial service companies. Training consisted of guided roundtable discussions and role playing, through which technicians and office staff explored not only customers' perceptions of Roscoe, but also their perceptions of the customers as well.

ABS also had Ed Brown put together some services guidelines that went beyond the traditional level of service. Brown explained one aspect of the guidelines:

> For example, while on-site, we need to emphasize constant visual inspection of the customer's plant and equipment. If a technician sees some insulation hanging off a section of piping, we expect that person to make a note in his report to the client. It doesn't take much time, and our customers appreciate the extra effort.

Technicians also earned bonus points that were cashed out at the end of the year for $25 per point. Every time a client requested a particular technician to be part of the on-site inspection team, that person received a bonus point. Also, after each job, the client filled out a customer satisfaction survey. At the end of the year, the surveys were ranked, and for each instance that a technician's team was in the top 5 percent, that technician received a bonus point.

Porter also gave a cash bonus to technicians who passed their certification tests and advanced a level. Achieving Level II earned a $150 cash bonus, while reaching Level III earned $500, as this was the most difficult level to achieve. Finally, the customer satisfaction surveys were compiled monthly and the statistics displayed in the shop area.

VII. ANOTHER DISAPPOINTING YEAR

Jane Bottensak wrapped up her part of the December staff meeting:

> Well, as I predicted, 1991 is going to be a disappointing year. Revenues were down again and profits were negligible. However, our performance wasn't as bad as I

expected, so maybe the quality improvement program was more successful than I thought. But, I think we will still need to reevaluate our fee structure for the coming year.

Ted Witkowski agreed that the program was a success and commented that Roscoe had a record number of technicians certified at Levels II and III.

Even Ed Brown conceded that customer satisfaction ratings had improved dramatically over the second half of 1991 (Exhibit 2):

> Most of the experienced technicians are excited about the program. They have been around Roscoe a number of years and have established their families in the area. On the other hand, some of the younger folks have not committed as easily. Part of that is the fact that less-experienced workers get smaller bonuses, on average. But, also, the younger technicians are more mobile and easily move from company to company. Overall, our work force is providing a better service to the customer.

However, regardless of how well the quality improvement program increased customer satisfaction, unless it could support new growth in the company, Grover Porter could only deem the program a failure.

In light of the continued downturn in the pulp and paper industry, Porter felt resigned to restructure the company's pricing policies. And that would mean big changes for Roscoe.

QUESTIONS

1. Evaluate Roscoe's progress with the quality improvement program.

2. Evaluate Roscoe's customer survey.

3. With respect to the QIP and the survey, is Roscoe doing all it can do?

4. Who is Roscoe's customer?

5. What price changes should Roscoe make?

6. Using the Service Quality Gap Model as a point of reference, which gaps appear to be the largest for Roscoe . . . knowledge, specifications, delivery, and/or communications?

N O T E S

[1]Trade journals of the American Society of Nondestructive Testing and the American Welding Society.

EXHIBIT 1

ROSCOE CUSTOMER SATISFACTION SURVEY (MARCH 1991)

Dear Roscoe Customer,

In an effort to provide you with the best inspection service possible, we would like your opinion of Roscoe and the people who work for us. Simply check the appropriate column on the survey and drop it in the mail within the enclosed stamped envelope. Your cooperation is truly appreciated.

Grover Porter
President

Questions	Poor	Below Average	Average	Above Average	Excellent
On-Site Inspection Team					
Accuracy of inspection data	1.3%	5.9%	15.3%	34.7%	42.8%
Time to complete inspection	2.9	4.8	8.4	45.6	38.3
Knowledge of technicians	1.5	11.5	25.6	33.3	28.1
Willingness to make an extra effort	24.6	26.0	23.6	13.5	12.3
Courtesy of technicians	26.1	30.3	18.7	16.2	8.7
Degree of individualized attention	17.6	29.6	38.2	9.9	4.7
Willingness to make an extra effort	13.7	30.1	42.9	8.3	5.0
Conveys trust and confidence	9.2	28.3	34.7	23.8	4.0
Organization of team supervisor	4.2	25.6	37.2	29.9	3.1
Accounting Department					
Accuracy of billing	3.4	8.3	16.1	55.8	16.4
Promptness of billing	9.8	43.9	21.7	16.5	8.1
Courtesy of staff	6.9	24.7	38.6	13.5	16.3
Willingness to help	22.7	25.6	38.1	8.9	4.7
Overall Performance of Roscoe					
Ability to deliver the promised service	2.7	15.6	18.5	39.4	23.8
Variety of services that meet your needs	2.3	13.2	48.8	26.5	9.2
Overall service value for your money	12.7	34.1	43.2	7.8	2.2

Recorded percentages are the frequency distribution of 71 responses compiled by Jane Bottensak, RNDT's controller. An average was taken for respondents who checked adjacent ratings (i.e., poor and below average).

EXHIBIT 2

ROSCOE CUSTOMER SATISFACTION SURVEYS (NOVEMBER 1991)

Questions	Poor	Below Average	Average	Above Average	Excellent
On-Site Inspection Team					
Accuracy of inspection data	1.0%	4.2%	2.1%	24.8%	55.9%
Time to complete inspection	1.4	6.3	7.1	60.0	25.2
Knowledge of technicians	0.9	12.1	20.5	37.4	29.1
Willingness to make an extra effort	11.9	18.2	36.5	27.8	5.6
Courtesy of technicians	9.3	8.9	55.3	16.3	10.2
Degree of individualized attention	2.1	16.7	45.9	30.1	5.2
Willingness to make an extra effort	9.8	17.6	40.3	30.4	1.9
Conveys trust and confidence	3.8	22.7	39.8	30.6	3.1
Organization of team supervisor	0.0	11.9	31.8	44.7	11.6
Accounting Department					
Accuracy of billing	1.5	10.4	19.6	44.2	24.3
Promptness of billing	13.5	33.4	25.6	18.5	9.0
Courtesy of staff	7.9	17.8	33.4	35.1	5.8
Willingness to help	8.6	29.4	30.3	24.6	7.1
Overall Performance of Roscoe					
Ability to deliver the promised service	0.0	13.2	23.1	44.2	19.5
Variety of services that meet your needs	7.4	13.5	56.1	15.3	7.7
Overall service value for your money	10.2	31.2	47.1	11.5	0.0

Compilation of 17 customer satisfaction surveys for inspections completed during November 1991. An average was taken for those respondents who checked adjacent ratings.

Roscoe Nondestructive Testing: Another Quality Improvement Effort

Jim Young was beginning to feel quite concerned. His boss, Grover Porter, would be returning in two days and would be expecting some hard answers about the direction the company's new quality program should take. Since Jim had been with the company for only three months, leading the project to develop the company's new quality program had initially seemed like a great way to get more familiarized with the company's operations.

Many of the managers and technicians at the company were still skeptical of Jim's ability. Grover had hired him for his general business skills and his ability to grow into a leadership position at the company. Jim knew that many of the other managers at Roscoe had objected to his being hired because of his lack of experience in the nondestructive testing (NDT) industry. Jim saw a successful quality project as a big boost to his credibility. Failure of his first big project, on the other hand, would cast real doubt on his abilities.

Jim also knew that a lot more than his reputation was riding on this project. With Roscoe about to acquire another company, a formal quality program was absolutely essential. In less than a month, they would nearly double their workforce, and these new employees had no idea what Roscoe expected in terms of performance or quality. Furthermore, Jim had just learned that a major new contract for the company depended on Jim's ability to design a comprehensive quality program within the week. The company's last attempt, two years ago, to develop a working customer feedback and quality program had been a failure. Jim knew he had to not only develop a new program but be prepared to explain why his program would not fail as well. With less than 48 hours before he presented his recommendations, Jim had only a vague idea of what he should propose.

ROSCOE
NONDESTRUCTIVE
TESTING:
ANOTHER QUALITY
IMPROVEMENT
EFFORT

I. A BIG DIAMOND IN THE ROUGH

ROSCOE AND THE NONDESTRUCTIVE TESTING INDUSTRY

(A detailed description of Roscoe and the Nondestructive Testing Industry is provided in Case 7.)

Nondestructive testing involves the examination of materials to discover microscopic cracks, corrosion, or malformation, using inspection techniques that do not damage the material being tested. Common inspection techniques include the use of x-rays, ultrasonic waves, and electrical eddy currents.

NDT is used in a wide variety of applications, including the examination of aircraft parts, tanks and vessels of various shapes and sizes, and welds of all kinds. Roscoe primarily uses ultrasonic thickness measuring devices to determine the thickness of metal plating on industrial boilers and pipes.

Roscoe has historically been a regional firm, with its largest customer base being the large concentration of pulp and paper mills located in the southeastern United States. The company employs about 140 people and currently has five branch offices. Roscoe competes on the basis of its superior technology in testing equipment and its ability to attract and retain very-high-quality employees.

THE DECISION TO JOIN ROSCOE

Roscoe was not the kind of company that typically attracted a new MBA, but Jim had turned down job offers from a major consulting firm and a Fortune 500 manufacturer to join the company. The work at Roscoe required the kind of long hours he could have expected as a consultant, but about a third of this time was field work under some really horrid conditions. Roscoe also could not pay anywhere near the salary of a consulting firm or a multibillion dollar (sales) company. But Jim wanted to work in a small company where he could have a direct impact on his company's performance and a lot greater control over his career.

Before attending business school, Jim had spent four years in Chicago as a line manager for a large manufacturer of electronic components. He enjoyed the job, but the heavy bureaucracy and the prospects for slow advancement had convinced Jim that he would be much happier at a smaller company. Roscoe was particularly attractive because it offered the opportunity for tremendous advancement as the company grew. Jim knew that Grover also wanted to take the company public as soon as sales revenues reached about $40 million. While this would not occur for several years, it offered the potential for significant financial rewards for the company's management if the public offering was successful.

Jim also felt that he could learn a tremendous amount from Grover. Despite the fact that he had grown a little rough around the edges working with pulp and paper mills for the past decade, Grover was an insightful businessman. Prior to becoming involved in the nondestructive testing industry, he had been quite successful as a group controller with Union Pacific Corp. Jim knew he had a lot to learn about running a business, particularly in the area of finance, where he had little experience outside his business school experience. Grover's intelligence and real strengths in finance and accounting made him an ideal teacher and mentor for Jim.

As is typical in many small companies, there was no one at Roscoe with the business skills to succeed Grover Porter as president of the company. Since suffering a mild heart attack in 1989, Grover had increasingly talked of the need to cut back on his work load, and retirement was probably not more than five years away. The younger technicians at Roscoe joked that Grover had to travel with three suitcases—one for his belongings, one for his heart pills, and one for his cigarettes (three packs a day). Jim knew that he had been hired as the first attempt to bring a potential successor into the company.

Jim was given the title of Special Projects Manager—working directly for Grover. The position was designed to give him an opportunity to learn the NDT business quickly while he helped Grover solve some of the company's pressing problems. As soon as Jim had gained enough experience, he would be given one of the company's divisions (field offices) to manage. Jim thought it would take between six months and one year before he would be ready for a division manager position.

THE NATIONAL EXPANSION EFFORT

Roscoe had been doing quite well, financially, over the past two years (Exhibit 1). Jim's hunch was that this was due almost solely to the improvement in economic conditions after the 1991 recession ended. In any case, strong profitability meant that Roscoe could once again continue to expand the business. The company had actually turned down requests for service from three paper mills during the last shutdown season because of manpower constraints. Grover saw a real opportunity to add technicians and branch offices to meet this growing demand.

Because most small NDT companies lacked any name recognition or "brand equity," they could usually be acquired at the market value of their assets. Grover felt that Roscoe could be worth 4–5 times its assets' value in a public offering because of its name recognition and technological advantages. Thus, new acquisitions could be very lucrative as long as the new divisions were not added too quickly. Furthermore, Grover knew that acquisitions were the only way the company could become large enough to go public in the next five years.

Over the past 18 months, Roscoe had acquired small companies located in Oregon, Maine, and Florida, which became new "divisions" of the company. Each acquired company offered the same type of NDT services as Roscoe, so expansion was primarily geographical, not in breadth of service. In each case, Roscoe purchased only the assets of the company.[1]

Grover saw the national expansion efforts as a way to become the largest supplier of NDT services to the pulp and paper industry. This would give the

ROSCOE
NONDESTRUCTIVE
TESTING:
ANOTHER QUALITY
IMPROVEMENT
EFFORT

company additional name recognition among his primary target customers. Since he always promoted a senior supervisor from Roscoe to run a newly acquired division, expansion also gave Grover the opportunity to reward his most capable employees. By adding the three new divisions, the company had grown from about 80 employees to 132 employees in less than two years.

II. Quality at Roscoe: Searching for Answers

Quality Problems Continue to Grow

Grover was disappointed in the failure of Roscoe's first quality program. With the recent growth of the company, the lack of a formal quality program was really starting to be felt. For Grover, the biggest problem was the increasing difficulty in managing his time. In Jim's estimation, Grover spent about 25 percent of his time dealing with customers who had problems or issues with the quality of service Roscoe provided.

Most of these problems were fairly easy to correct but required a great deal of time on the part of Grover and his division managers. Since Grover was often the only person who consistently dealt with the customers from year to year, he also found himself dealing with issues that could have been handled by a division manager or supervisor. Jim happened to walk into Grover's office after one lengthy and fairly typical phone call.

"You know, Jim, that was the plant manager up at International Paper's containerboard mill in Clarksville. Apparently the report we sent him had some pretty large errors. Now we'll have to drop everything, find whoever supervised the job, figure out how we should correct the report, and have someone drive all the way back up there to deliver it because they need the information ASAP. We'll spend 12 hours doing what should have taken 12 minutes. I think I need to hire a full-time technical writer to try and correct some of these errors before they go out the door. Maybe that will solve these problems."

Three days after the phone call from the Clarksville Plant Manager, Grover had called Jim into his office and asked him to begin working on a quality program for the company.

"I've been thinking about a quality program. When this operation was small, I knew every one of my employees, and we worked great together. Everyone knew what I expected and problems like Clarksville just didn't occur. Now I don't even know the names of half these technicians, and they just don't have the same feel for doing the job right. As we add new employees, the problem gets worse because there are less and less people on every job who really know how it should be done.

"That's why we need a quality program. Something to get people working toward the same goal again, so I don't have to spend all my time dealing with these little problems. I haven't been able to get out of my office to visit prospective customers for almost four weeks, and we will never grow this company if I have to sit here all day patching things up with our current customers.

"Now, I've been thinking that what we really need are some quality teams. If we get these technicians in groups to start thinking about all these issues, they'll begin to realize the problems their sloppy work is causing. They might even come up with some better ways to do some things around here. Hell, I don't even mind paying them to sit around and discuss all the things that seem to be going wrong lately if they can fix only half of them.

"I'll bet that the reason the last quality program didn't work is that we just didn't get the technicians involved enough. Sure, they got a small bonus for doing a great job now and then, but they were never really forced to see all the problems I face every day."

When Jim questioned whether quality teams would be enough to really solve the company's fundamental problems, Grover was quick to reply.

"Of course I don't mean that quality teams can solve every problem just by sitting around over coffee and talking about them. I see quality teams as a way to really get the technicians involved in the problems I face and this company faces. We can have them figure out solutions and work on implementing them if that's what it takes. I'm convinced that our biggest problem is the fact that they just don't realize the problems their inattention to detail in their work causes. Quality teams may not be the entire answer, but I'll bet a month's pay they can be used in one capacity or another to solve 90 percent of my problems.

"What I see happening is that we select about a half-dozen of our best technicians and have them come in someday when things are pretty slow. We can give them a list of our biggest problems, and they can brainstorm about ways to fix things. Hell, in two minutes you and I could come up with our top ten issues right now. Once we get one team working, we can start more so they can get at more and more problems. We can also make the teams responsible for actually putting their ideas to work, and we can give prizes for the most money saved, or something like that. I'll leave you to figure out the details."

Jim walked out of Grover's office unsure of how to proceed. He knew that Grover was right about getting employee involvement. He also felt strongly that quality teams were only a small part of a really effective quality program. Jim had been involved in more than a dozen quality teams with his work prior to business school. He knew it was easy to get employees together to identify solutions initially, but without any focus these teams usually only attack the obvious issues—often only the symptoms of a deeper problem.

Without the proper systems in place to act on their ideas, the teams can quickly become disillusioned and stop functioning. Jim had seen more than one quality team fail in this way. He also knew that it was almost impossible to revive a quality team program once the employees believed it to be a waste of time—so getting it right the first time was critical.

Grover's insistence on quality teams meant that they were going to have to be a part of any quality program that would get his support. Jim figured that he had

ROSCOE
NONDESTRUCTIVE
TESTING:
ANOTHER QUALITY
IMPROVEMENT
EFFORT

better turn his efforts to figuring out what systems needed to be in place to support these teams. Hopefully, he thought, he would be able to delay any quality team formation until he could get these systems up and running. If not, the program was sure to fail.

THE STARTING POINT FOR A NEW QUALITY PROGRAM

To gather information for the quality project, Jim spent at least one or two days per week accompanying inspection teams to their customers' plants and mills. He began to enjoy this opportunity to get out in the field because he felt he was really getting to learn the business quickly. The more information he gathered, however, the more Jim was struck by the difficulty of his task. There were actually tremendous differences between customers.

Of course, the basic tests that Roscoe performed were the same everywhere, but Jim did not believe there was a problem with the technical procedures and equipment used by the technicians to gather data. Roscoe had better technology and people than any of its competitors. The frustrating issues were that each mill or plant had its own safety and operating procedures to learn and follow, and each customer seemed to have a different idea of how the work should be done and how the test results should be prepared.

Jim thought he should start by trying to determine the common problems faced by the inspection teams with the different types of customers Roscoe had. Jim figured the most important type of customer was Roscoe's largest, the pulp and paper mills.

CUSTOMER TYPE I: THE PULP AND PAPER MILL

It was also hard for Jim to imagine a way to develop a quality program that could really be useful in the shutdown environment of a large plant. The environment was nothing short of chaotic, and it seemed that success depended more on the inspection team's ability to remain flexible than anything else. Sean McDevitt was one of Roscoe's most experienced supervisors and was well liked by his fellow employees. Sean was usually very easygoing and cooperative, but when Jim asked him about a quality program, he was quite emphatic.

"I can't believe anybody is stupid enough to think they can come up with a bunch of rules for working in a shutdown. I already have to put up with 40 tons of crap from the [customer's] maintenance supervisor and the last thing I need is more rules from my own company. Look at the team I have today. I got four guys from Orlando, two from Portland, and six guys from the head office. Two of these guys have never been on a shutdown before, so I'll spend half my time just keeping their asses out of trouble.

"Since the job order changed two days ago, I had to get the Portland guys at the last minute, which means I didn't get a chance to safety certify them before they showed up. Now I have to bust my behind just to get them through the gate. Then

I have to have everyone on standby for two or three days waiting for one 12-hour window when we can get in to do the inspection. The mill couldn't give a rat's ass with anything but how fast I get done.

"On top of all that, I have guys who I have to make crawl through the most God-forsaken slime you've ever seen in your life. It'll take you an hour just to scrape the tar off your face. Nobody gets any sleep for about 36 hours. It's hot as hell in the daytime, and then you freeze your ass off being out here all wet and slimy at night. My people are tired , filthy, and generally pissed off when we finally finish the job, but I always manage to get the inspection data we need.

"Fast and accurate, that's my quality program. I don't need to sit around in some circle to figure out why somebody else thinks we're screwed up."

Steve Hericks, a technician who had recently been promoted to supervisor, had this to add:

"The real problem is with these damned mills. They are so busy with the shutdown that they never seem to know which end is up. Sometimes we have to answer to two or three different people who always have their head up their butt and never seem to talk to each other. I've been to some of these mills a dozen times, and every time we go in we have to answer to somebody different who wants us to do the job differently. A quality program would be great, but I really don't see how it will work until the mills figure out what they want us to do from job to job."

Through many conversations with both technicians and mill personnel, Jim knew that Sean and Steve had valid arguments, but the conditions under which Roscoe's teams worked were not likely to change. It would probably be a big boost to both credibility and productivity if inspection teams did not have to be formed differently for every job, but this would be impossible to manage. Each job required a different number of technicians, and one division was simply not large enough to support most of the big jobs alone.

It would also be difficult to get the mills to channel all instructions for the inspection team through one of the customer's employees. The shutdown environment was simply too hectic, and Roscoe had no leverage to demand this of the customer. In general, the success of an inspection team relied heavily on the discretion of the team supervisor. It was not surprising to Jim that the most experienced supervisors rarely let a problem get to the point where Grover had to get involved.

CUSTOMER TYPE II: THE PETROCHEMICAL PLANT

Jim had also spent a lot of time working with the permanent crew at G & C. Since Roscoe won the initial contract at the plant two years ago, the number of technicians working at the plant full-time had grown from six to 12.

The environment at G & C was quite different from that of a mill shutdown because the team was able to work under normal plant conditions. Petrochemical plants do not have to undergo the comprehensive semiannual shutdowns necessary in the pulp and paper industry. Rather, small sections of the plant are shut

ROSCOE
NONDESTRUCTIVE
TESTING:
ANOTHER QUALITY
IMPROVEMENT
EFFORT

down sequentially so that nondestructive testing, as well as other maintenance, can be performed year round.

From what Jim could gather, the oil and chemical industry seemed to be moving toward the sort of long-term contracts Roscoe had with G & C. It was usually cheaper and more efficient to contract for specialty services, such as nondestructive testing, than to perform the work in-house. The success of the G&C operation had made Grover very interested in winning similar contracts with other refineries and petrochemical plants. He had, on more than one occasion, shared his views on the matter with Jim.

"The G & C job has really been a boost for Roscoe. It provides a constant stream of revenue year round, which is very nice from a cash flow standpoint. And, it seems like we really don't have to work very hard to keep them happy. If I could have ten of these contracts, I wouldn't ever have to worry again about answering to every plant manager between Seattle and Orlando, and my finances would be twice as solid. I might even be able to spend more time getting more paper mill customers instead of putting out fires all the time."

Paul Andrews was Roscoe's permanent G & C site supervisor and had been with Roscoe for more than eight years. Jim thought he had more common sense than anyone else he knew at the company. Initially, Jim had hoped to rely heavily on his help to develop the quality program, but Paul just did not believe there was any value in altering the way Roscoe did business.

"I think quality is great, and I wouldn't get the support from G & C that I do if I couldn't produce good results. I just don't know what you think you can improve with more rules and paperwork—which is probably all your quality program will do. I meet with my technicians every day. If I have a problem with anything I talk to the technician involved, and he gets it fixed right away. If it's important, I make the guy work overtime to fix it.

"If Bill [his point of contact and "boss" at G & C] has a problem, he calls me up or it comes up at our weekly meeting. The environment is too fluid to have a lot of meaningless rules about how we operate, and I have yet to see any problem that my team and I couldn't solve ourselves—long before anyone else at Roscoe would even know the problem existed."

Because of the low turnover among Roscoe technicians working at G & C, Paul had developed a team that was very thorough and well respected. No one at G & C had anything but glowing reports about the work he and his team were doing. But Jim thought that much of the success at G & C resulted from Paul's personality and exceptional management skills. If Roscoe expected to win additional contracts in the petrochemical industry, it was important to determine how the G & C performance could be repeated.

Jim also wondered whether there was anything that could be applied from the G & C experience to the company's core pulp and paper mill business. The ability to work with the same team of technicians at the same plant every day made it easy to customize Roscoe's service at G & C. This was probably not possible with the pulp and paper mills. The environment at G & C was also a world apart from that of a shutdown. It was hard to imagine being able to generalize between the two. Jim felt that a separate quality program would probably have to be created for each of the two types of service.

SUSPICIONS ABOUT THE LAST QUALITY PROGRAM

Finally, Jim wondered why the last quality program had failed. Two years after it was begun, there was no evidence the program had even existed. Although he could not be sure, he suspected the program's fate was similar to that of another program developed by Bruce Edwards, an MBA intern the previous summer.

Bruce had developed a very thorough target list to market NDT inspection services to the surface mining industry (strip-mines). Roscoe had developed a specialized technique for x-ray inspection of critical stress points on heavy mining equipment. Bruce had been able to prioritize customers nationwide based on geography, size, and type of equipment. Even the purchasing decision makers were identified for each targeted company.

Unfortunately, after Bruce left, the marketing project was transferred to one of the division managers. The division manager, already overloaded with work, never used the information to actually try and sell the new service line. This was not surprising to Jim since the division managers were rewarded mostly for their division's performance. The new service line would provide only marginal revenues for him, although across the entire company, it would have been significant. By the time Grover discovered that the program was never initiated, the information was already out of date.

To ensure the success of his new quality program, Jim knew he would have to carefully construct incentives for everyone involved in the program. Grover and the division managers would also have to give active support to the program. Given the obvious lack of interest for the last program and Grover's fairly narrow focus on quality teams, Jim really wondered whether a comprehensive program could really succeed.

Jim had some experience of his own with another marketing project at Roscoe. His first project after he arrived had been to initiate a mass mailing campaign to all military procurement offices in the United States. Grover had purchased the Department of Defense list from a marketing agency before Jim had joined the company. The project to send a letter and company brochure to every agency on the list had been assigned to him upon arrival.

As a brand new employee, he had done nothing more than write the form letter and prepare the mailing packets. Still, as Jim stuffed 450 envelopes addressed to places like the Reserve Personnel Center in St. Louis and the Marine Corps Recruiting Depot in San Diego, he wondered what possible business Grover expected to gain from the effort. At one point, Jim asked Grover about the purpose of the marketing campaign.

"Well, I know that some of those places don't need our services. In fact, I don't really know what we'll do for the military. All I know is that there are billions of

ROSCOE
NONDESTRUCTIVE
TESTING:
ANOTHER QUALITY
IMPROVEMENT
EFFORT

dollars spent every year on military contracts, and we must be able to do some of it. By targeting everybody, we're sure to get at least one or two hits. Even if we only get one contract, it will have paid for the $345 I spent to buy the list ten times over."

Jim recalled wondering, at the time, whether Grover had really figured the true cost of such an unfocused effort. If the same time and energy had been spent marketing Roscoe's services to a more select group of customers, it certainly might have been more productive. Still, $345 was not much money, and the project had only taken him a couple of days from start to finish.

What Jim was sure of now, however, was that if the same lack of focus applied to the last quality program, it is no wonder it failed. Jim knew that he would have to be very selective in making his own quality recommendations. Too broad a plan would be just as likely to fail as one that was too narrow.

III. A Sense of Urgency

A Large Acquisition Presents Trouble

Jim had been working on the quality project for over a month, gathering information in between working on several other projects. Until now, there had been no real sense of urgency.

Roscoe was about to acquire Louisiana Testing Services (LTS), another medium-sized nondestructive testing company headquartered in Baton Rouge. The acquisition would add about 85 employees and four branch offices to Roscoe. The deal had been stalled for several months, but now it looked almost certain that it would be finalized within a few weeks. After the acquisition, Roscoe would be the largest NDT company in the Southeast. LTS had a base of customers similar to Roscoe—mostly pulp and paper mills and a few oil and gas refineries. But LTS did not have the same technological advantages or the same high-quality employees as Roscoe. The company competed largely on the basis of low price and average service. Historically, the company had provided service almost exclusively to the oil and gas industry until that industry began to have serious profitability problems in the early 1980s. Only in the last three or four years did LTS begin to shift its emphasis to the pulp and paper industry. Its technicians did not, therefore, have the same depth of experience in these mills as Roscoe's.

LTS was being offered for sale because its owner/president wanted to devote his energies to a new financial services firm he had recently begun. The asking price of the company was quite attractive, and Grover saw the opportunity to really dominate the southeastern United States with the addition of four more branch offices in the region. But the LTS deal would be much different from any of Roscoe's prior acquisitions. Roscoe's three previous acquisitions had been much smaller single-office companies. None of them had a substantial administrative staff, and the transition to becoming a Roscoe division was accomplished with relative ease. LTS was five times larger than any of the previous acquisitions and had a substantial administrative infrastructure that would need to be consolidated after the acquisition (Exhibit 2). Furthermore, one of LTS's branch offices was located near Roscoe's main office and would also need to be consolidated for efficiency. The biggest problem, though, was the absorption of approximately 70 technicians. With the smaller acquisitions, Grover had been able to select a loyal and talented employee to run each new division. This ensured that each newly acquired company soon learned, as Grover would say, "to do business the Roscoe way." LTS was too big for Grover to replace all the key managers, so there was no way to micro-manage the transition the way the other acquisitions had been handled. Furthermore, the president of LTS had been disinterested in his NDT business for quite a while, and the company was in real need of leadership.

The LTS technicians would begin performing work under the Roscoe name as soon as the deal was finalized. It was critical that they quickly learn to use Roscoe's advanced technology and provide the same high quality of service. Without a formal system to control quality, Grover knew that it would take only a short time to destroy the reputation that he had built over the years. Unfortunately, Grover had been so busy with the financial side of the deal that he had not been able to give proper attention to the other critical organizational issues. With the deal suddenly only weeks away, he realized that Jim's program was critical to the success of the acquisition. Jim was given a deadline to present an outline of his program to Grover and the division managers at their quarterly meeting in two weeks.

PRELIMINARY IDEAS FOR THE QUALITY PROGRAM

Since the absorption of LTS would entail some organizational changes at Roscoe, it was an ideal time to make any additional changes to support the new quality program. One preliminary idea Jim had was to create a company quality control department to help ensure that the new quality program did not simply fade away like the last program. Of course, this would be costly, and Jim thought there might be other changes that could less expensively support his quality goals.

One of the issues that intrigued Jim was the idea of using salesmen. LTS employed a small sales force consisting of one vice-president of sales and four salesmen. Each salesman was assigned to one of four geographical regions and was responsible for all customers within that region. Roscoe did not employ any type of a sales force, and Grover was not inclined to change this: "I figure we'll keep those salesmen for a couple of months, but unless they are worth their weight in gold, I'm going to can them all. We already have more work than we can handle at peak season, and I'm sure the other division managers and I can do just as good a job during the off-season as any salesmen. Besides, for the same cost I can hire a few top-notched technicians who will generate more revenue for the company."

ROSCOE
NONDESTRUCTIVE
TESTING:
ANOTHER QUALITY
IMPROVEMENT
EFFORT

Jim did not think Grover had fully considered the value of having a technical sales force (all the salesmen were former ASNT level III Technicians—the highest rating given). But if he wanted to propose any kind of a sales force at Roscoe as part of his quality program, he knew he would have to justify his plan very soon. His chances to effect this change would be gone if he waited until Grover finalized his postacquisition organizational structure in the next two or three weeks.

The idea of developing a system of accountability for quality among supervisors and division managers was also something Jim felt was essential. The trouble was that Jim still did not know how to define quality and what metric to use for this accountability. Anything substantial enough to really provide the right incentives would probably have to involve quite a lot of bonus money—and that would mean the program would have to be well thought out. What Jim really wanted to do was get the supervisors and managers together to get some more input on this issue, but there simply wasn't time.

Of course, Jim would have to incorporate quality teams into his recommendations, but he wondered how he could focus them on helping to solve the fundamental quality problems at Roscoe. If the teams were set up to focus only on certain issues, they may be prevented from looking at the big picture to find these fundamental problems. If the teams were not forced to be focused, they would probably not dig deep enough into any one issue to really develop their recommendations into something useful. Jim wondered whether he could use Grover's idea of rewarding the teams for their solutions to manage this problem.

THE TEXAS STANDARD CHEMICAL COMPANY CONTRACT

"When it rains, it pours," thought Jim. He had just gotten off the phone with Grover, who was visiting the division office in Orlando, Florida. Grover had found out that Roscoe had been selected as a finalist in the bid for a major contract, and he was FAXing Jim the company's quality requirements. Grover would be making a presentation to the bid selection committee in less than one week, and the final award of the contract seemed to hinge on Jim's quality program.

Texas Standard had a petrochemical plant even larger than G & C's. They had decided to eliminate the plant's internal NDT department and contract for the services on a long-term basis. The contract to provide all NDT services at the plant would run for a minimum of five years and would employ at least 20 NDT technicians full time. One month ago, Grover had heard of the bid through a friend and had immediately submitted a proposal to Texas Standard.

Winning the contract could mean almost $1 million in revenues per year. Roscoe had been selected as one of three finalists for the job, and the selection process was getting increasingly rigorous. Only the first cut from among 23 initial bidders was made on price. The final cut was being made on quality and safety.

Texas Standard provided Roscoe with a list of the criteria they would use to select from among the three finalists. In five days a Texas Standard selection team would visit Roscoe. They expected a presentation on the company's quality and safety programs at that time. Since Roscoe had an excellent safety program, it was apparent that winning the contract would depend on quality.

The Texas Standard Contractor Quality Requirements were extensive (Exhibit 3). As Jim reviewed the list, he thought that these were all things Roscoe should be doing anyway. Most of the quality requirements were derived from the ISO 9000 standards,[2] which were rapidly becoming a requirement for competition throughout the world. Even if Roscoe did not win this contract, he was quite sure that similar quality issues would play a major role in any future contracts of this type.

Jim thought it was amazing that two senior managers from G & C thought so much of Roscoe that they had agreed to travel to the Roscoe headquarters and meet privately with the Texas Standard evaluation team during the visit. For competitive reasons, G & C would not allow the Texas Standard personnel into their plant to actually see Roscoe's operations there. They were, however, eager to describe the operation and provide a strong personal recommendation for Roscoe.

Still, the Texas Standard people seemed to be quite sophisticated and would not easily be swayed by one recommendation. It was likely that Roscoe could win the contract based on their technology and safety records if they had at least begun to implement a strong quality program. If Jim could present a solid outline to Grover in two days, there was a chance there would be enough time to pull together a presentation for Texas Standard. But as he pondered his list of preliminary ideas for the quality program, Jim knew he could not look just to the Texas Standard contract. If his proposal was to get the support it needed to succeed it would have to apply to all of the company and all of its customers. With the LTS acquisition around the corner and the mounting quality problems throughout Roscoe, Jim knew he had to make the right recommendations this first time around.

QUESTIONS

1. What are the relevent issues pertaining to the development of a Quality Improvement Program (QIP) for Roscoe?

2. Develop your own proposal for QIP.

NOTES

[1]In an asset purchase, only the company's assets are purchased. The acquired company's corporate status is dissolved so that no liability carries forward to the acquiring company.

[2]ISO 9000 stands for International Standards Organization series 9000. It is a standard developed for the European Community that has rapidly become the worldwide standard for quality, particularly for companies wishing to compete in Europe.

E X H I B I T   1

ROSCOE'S INCOME STATEMENT (ALL NUMBERS IN THOUSANDS)

Year	1989	1990	1991	1992
Revenues				
Sales Revenue (1)	1856	2491	4198	7983
Other Revenue	142	159	233	285
Total Revenue	1998	2650	4431	8268
Expenses				
Administrative	499	742	1550	2397
Sales (2)	59	53	66	207
Labor	639	954	1728	2563
R & D (3)	69	74	93	380
Other	438	485	572	1779
Operating Income	294	342	422	942
Interest	16	19	23	52
Taxes	94	109	135	302
Net Income	184	214	264	589

Notes to Income Statement:

1. With 147 technicians, the company had $54,306 in sales revenue per billable employee.
2. Sales Expense is staff's/manager's travel expenses for sales calls and customer recruitment and the expense of setting up an exhibit at several annual trade fairs.
3. A separate Applied Research Division was established in 1992.

Expenses as a Percent of Sales Revenues

Year	1989	1990	1991	1992
Administrative	25.0%	28.0%	35.0%	29.0%
Sales	3.0%	2.0%	1.5%	2.5%
Labor	32.0%	36.0%	39.0%	31.0%
R & D	3.5%	2.8%	2.1%	4.6%
Other	21.9%	18.3%	12.9%	21.5%

EXHIBIT   2

ROSCOE AND LOUISIANA SERVICES ORGANIZATION CHARTS

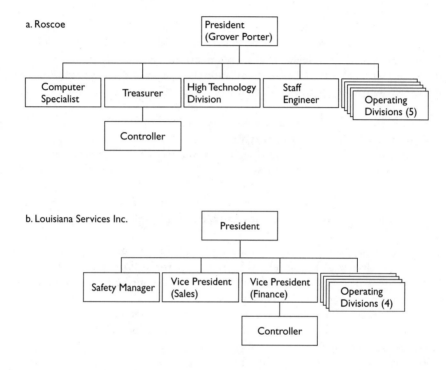

a. Roscoe

b. Louisiana Services Inc.

▶▶▶▶ ◀◀◀◀

E X H I B I T   3

TEXAS STANDARD CHEMICAL CONTRACTOR REQUIREMENTS

General: Each contractor to the Texas Standard Chemical Plant will define and document its policy and objectives for, and commitment to, quality. The contractor shall ensure that this policy is understood, implemented, and maintained at all levels in the organization.

Responsibility: The responsibility, authority, and interrelation of all personnel who manage, perform, and verify work affecting quality shall be defined, particularly for personnel who are responsible to:

1. Initiate action to prevent the occurrence of any quality problems
2. Identify and record any product quality problems
3. Initiate, recommend, or provide solutions through designated channels
4. Verify the implementation of solutions

Definition: The contractor will, with the appropriate Texas Standard department, clearly identify and communicate the quality goals, objectives, and standards applicable to the work being performed for Texas Standard.

Training: The contractor will establish and maintain procedures for identifying the training needs of all personnel performing activities affecting quality. The contractor will provide for the training of all personnel based on the identification of these training needs. The contractor will keep detailed records of all quality-related training provided to its personnel.

Management Representative: The contractor will appoint a management representative who, irrespective of other responsibilities, shall have defined authority and responsibility for ensuring that the requirements of Texas Standard are implemented and maintained.

Management Review: The quality system adopted to satisfy the Texas Standard requirements shall be jointly reviewed a minimum of twice per year to ensure continuing suitability and effectiveness of all quality procedures, policies, and requirements.

Quality Requirements: All Texas Standard contractors will establish and maintain a documented quality system as a means of ensuring that all work conforms to specified requirements. This system will entail, as a minimum, the following:

1. The preparation of quality plans and a quality manual in accordance with the specified requirements.
2. The identification and acquisition of any controls, processes, inspection equipment, fixtures, total production resources, and skills that may be needed to achieve the required quality.
3. The updating, as necessary, of quality control, inspection, and testing techniques, including the development of new instrumentation.
4. The identification and clarification of standards of acceptability for all features and requirements, including those with a subjective element.

5. The establishment, to the greatest extent possible, of written standards and requirements for all workmanship performed for Texas Standard.
6. The identification and preparation of quality records.

Documentation: Each contractor will establish and maintain procedures to control all documents and data that relate to the requirements of Texas Standard. These documents will be reviewed and approved for adequacy by Texas Standard Management prior to issue. Documentation will ensure that:

1. The pertinent issues of appropriate documents are available at all locations where operations essential to the effective functioning of the quality system are performed.
2. Obsolete documents are promptly removed from all points of issue or use.

Subcontractors: Each contractor will be held strictly responsible for ensuring that all subcontractors meet the requirements of this quality standard.

Inspection, Measuring, and Testing Equipment: Each contractor will control, calibrate, and maintain inspection, measuring, and test equipment, whether owned by the contractor or on loan, to demonstrate the conformance of the equipment to specified requirements. Equipment will be used in a manner which ensures that measurement uncertainty is known and is consistent with the required measurement capability. The contractor will:

1. Identify the measurements to be made and the accuracy required and select the appropriate inspection, measuring, and test equipment.
2. Identify, calibrate, and adjust all inspection, measuring, and test equipment and devices that can affect product quality at prescribed intervals, or prior to use, against certified equipment having a known valid relationship to nationally recognized standards—where no standards exist, the basis used for calibration shall be documented.
3. Establish, document, and maintain calibration procedures, including details of equipment type, identification number, location, frequency of checks, check method, acceptance criteria, and the action to be taken when results are unsatisfactory.
4. Maintain calibration records for inspection, measuring, and test equipment.
5. Ensure that the handling, preservation, and storage of inspection, measuring, and test equipment is such that the accuracy and fitness for use is maintained.
6. Records shall identify the inspection authority responsible for the inspection and calibration of all inspection, measuring, and test equipment.

Corrective Action: Each contractor will establish, document, and maintain procedures for:

1. Investigating the cause of all quality issues or problems and the corrective action needed to prevent recurrence.
2. Analyzing all processes, work operations, concessions, quality records, service reports, and complaints to detect and eliminate potential causes of nonconformance.
3. Initiating preventive actions to deal with problems to a level corresponding to the risks encountered.

4.   Applying controls to ensure that corrective actions are taken and that they are effective.
5.   Implementing and recording changes in procedures resulting from corrective action.

Quality Audits: Each contractor shall carry out a comprehensive system of planned and documented internal quality audits to verify whether quality activities comply with the planned arrangements and to determine the effectiveness of the quality system. These audits will be:

1.   Scheduled on the basis of status and importance of the activity, but never less than every three months.
2.   Carried out in accordance with documented procedures.

Verification of Quality: Each contractor will identify in-house verification requirements, provide adequate resources, and assign trained personnel for verification activities for all aspects of the quality program. Verification activities shall include inspection, test, and monitoring of all aspects of each service or product provided and reviews and audits of the quality system. Verification will be carried out by personnel independent of those having direct responsibility for the work being performed.

9

O'Keefe Associates

I've watched this firm grow just like I've watched my own children, and perhaps with as much love and care. This makes the decision I face even more difficult. But like most painful decisions, it is inevitable.

The partner meeting of O'Keefe Associates[1], a preeminent management consulting firm, had gotten underway and Kevin O'Keefe, the founding father of the firm, had just announced that he would be removing himself from all decision-making positions. He would be passing control of the firm to its vice-presidents, the new partners of the firm.

Recent events had made this departure inevitable, and it had been expected for some time. Despite this, Aviva Katz felt a lump form in her throat, and she quickly reached for the glass of Dom Perignon in front of her. In her haste, she knocked it clean across the shining mahogany into the lap of Henning Amelung who, even as he felt the wetness permeate his clothes, directed his gaze calmly at her, kind of waiting for an apology. She had half a mind to not offer one but decided to leave personal battles for another day, for today belonged to Kevin O'Keefe, the patriarch who had started the firm 18 years ago. She gestured an apology to the unruffled Henning and her mind started to churn. Kevin's departure meant that the vice-presidents had to quickly regroup and decide the immediate fate of the firm. The consulting industry had been declining for the past two years, and O'Keefe Associates had born the brunt of the downturn due to their connection with a recent, well-publicized lawsuit. The right moves now could stem client erosion, reverse reputation damage, and set the firm on the course to rejuvenation; the wrong moves would mean a slow demise.

Brief History of O'Keefe

Kevin O'Keefe had stepped into the management consulting world with the start-up Boston Consulting Group (BCG). Industry watchers and insiders attributed his meteoric rise within BCG to an undying commitment to deliver to his clients' bottom line. He succeeded in consistently doing so by coming up with unorthodox ideas and ensuring that his recommendations were implementable. In 1971 he left BCG with three of his colleagues to form O'Keefe Associates. In an interview at a later date, he gave the following reason for his move: "Paul [another O'Keefe founding father] and I were bringing in about half the revenue for the firm. We operated independently and, over time, drifted away from everyone at BCG. Finally, my entrepreneurial urge got the better of me and I decided to start O'Keefe Associates."

Kevin had built a strong reputation for himself. His clients openly commended him. He earned the respect of colleagues and competitors after creating the highly effective O'Keefe Model for strategy formulation, which was first published in the *Harvard Business Review* and won the award for the year's

Source: Copyright © 1996 by Professor Brian Wansink.

best article. When he moved out on his own, his clients decided to continue retaining him. At the same time, three of his colleagues—Paul Vivek, John Hartmann, and Ted Chesner—decided to join him. They decided to split up the ownership of the firm based on the projected revenues each could bring. Consequently, Kevin held 37 percent ownership, Paul 33 percent, and John and Michael, 15 percent each.

O'Keefe Associates focused on high-level corporate and business-unit strategy consulting and shied away from industry specialization. Charging the highest billing rates in the industry, they introduced the concept of relationship consulting[2] and focused on a single client in each industry. In return, they asked that their clients not engage any other consulting firm. This one-to-one relationship set the firm apart in the industry and gave CEOs the assurance that their company's secrets and strengths would not be exposed to potential and existing competitors.

Each of the partners had the potential to be a powerful rainmaker at most firms in the industry; together they formed a powerhouse. They leveraged Kevin's reputation and warm personality very effectively with clients as well as with potential recruits at the top three business schools in the United States. As a start-up that promised to reach stellar heights, O'Keefe Associates attracted the topmost talent at schools. As a consulting firm that brought a unique proposition to the table, they attracted Fortune 500 clients from all industries. The result was the perfect high-growth formula, and by 1980, a mere nine years after its birth, O'Keefe Associates had registered itself on the radar of the bigger, more established consulting firms.

As it grew, O'Keefe Associates won friends as well as enemies. While about 80 percent of clients had nothing but praise for them, others felt they had been poorly served. In response to a question asking for their opinion of the firm, respondents had this to say:

> O'Keefe has the brightest talent in the industry. Moreover, their people are not snobs like most consultants are. They mix well with our employees, come up with truly innovative out-of-the-box ideas, and work at convincing all levels of our hierarchy. They know how to address bottom-line concerns and they know how to produce bottom-line results. If I were stranded on a remote desert island, the one thing I'd want with me is an O'Keefe consultant.
>
> —CEO of a Fortune 500 chemicals company

> O'Keefe may be good intellectually, but they have been inconsistent in dealing with us. Some of the advice they gave us set the company back 10 years. Once when I needed support to defend one of their recommendations to my CEO, they just did an about-face on me, like they had never made the recommendation! They leave me with the feeling that they would do anything to save their own necks!
>
> —SBU Manager of a Fortune 500 manufacturer

One of the probable reasons for this variation in quality of service was the growth rate: O'Keefe could not grow its people into experienced consultants fast enough to serve the needs of the entire client base. As a result, some clients suffered. Business media, which thrives on reporting the out-of-the-ordinary, picked up on stories disgruntled clients had to tell. The ensuing bad press hurt O'Keefe's image and, by many accounts, they managed to survive only because clients found it impossible to change consultants due to contractual obligations and costs involved in getting new consultants up to speed. Over the next two years or so, the founding partners worked hard at avoiding similar embarrassment by building good relations with the media, convincing clients with success stories to speak out, and implementing rigorous recruiting and training procedures. Their efforts at improving quality and cleaning up the image of the firm worked, and they were able to continue commanding the highest billing rates in the industry.

O'KEEFE'S ORGANIZATION

O'Keefe Associates was organized like most other partnerships. After inception, part of the firm's ownership was given to employees via the Employee Stock Ownership Plan (ESOP), primarily as an incentive for them to help the firm grow. The four founding fathers continued to hold most of the equity in the firm, and vice-presidents held the rest (about 10 percent). The 27 vice-presidents, all officers of the firm, reported to the partners and managed the activities of 68 managers while having complete responsibility for relationships with two to seven clients (depending on the size of the clients). Managers were responsible for one to three cases that were staffed by senior associates, associates, and research associates (RAs). Senior associates helped in conducting the case while assuming responsibility for case modules.[3] Associates managed case modules. RAs helped case teams analyze data and came up with helpful insights. They were high-performing undergraduates, while associates were the top graduates of the three most highly rated business schools in the country. A typical case team was made up of one vice-president, one manager, two senior associates, four associates, and two RAs. Turnover among associates and RAs was high, with about 50 percent of recruits staying on till the three-year mark, at which they made senior associate. Senior associates made manager within about two years. Managers who showed an aptitude for managing client relationships were promoted to vice-president after about three years. Base compensation at all levels was high (an associate started at $70,000 a year plus a $30,000 sign-up bonus) and above industry norms. Top performers earned annual bonuses of up to about 50 percent of the base salary.

THE MANAGEMENT CONSULTING INDUSTRY

Although the management consulting industry can be entered easily by engaging any one client, it is one of the toughest service industries to survive in. The following characteristics explain why.

Consultants face the toughest business problems. Consulting firms have high billing rates, and each engagement costs the client a lot of money and other resources.

Consequently, businesses tend to call in consultants if they offer innovative solutions (e.g., CSC Index's reengineering, BCG's Matrix) or if the management is perplexed about a certain problem. Problems that perplex upper management are tough to solve, since the upper management of large businesses is made up of very bright people.

Convincing management about recommendations is an arduous task. As mentioned earlier, senior management is made up of bright people who have known their business and industry well for many years. As a result, all recommendations have to be thoroughly supported, and all levels of the client's hierarchy have to buy in to them.

In many cases, it is difficult to measure results. The nature of the problems is such that it is difficult to discern the impact of a recommended solution. The result of adopting a recommended strategy may not be visible for years. Observed outcomes could be the result of factors other than the recommendation. Even when the result can be distinctly identified, it is impossible to tell whether a better recommendation could have been made. This also leads to difficulty in discerning the quality of advice.

Good employees are hard to come by. Employees are the largest constituent of the costs incurred by a consulting firm and are the factor that allows a firm to distinguish itself. Consequently, the recruiting process is rigorous and expensive (see Exhibit 1). Also, since many firms end up competing for the same people, recruitment yields[4] are lower than in other industries.

It is difficult to retain employees. After expending a great number of resources on recruiting, consulting firms face the challenge of retaining employees. This is primarily because consultants lead high-pressure lives plagued with immovable deadlines and consequently long hours. Many recruits burn out quickly, while others leave due to lifestyle issues.

Consultants are always viewed as expendable. If profits come under severe pressure, businesses will first dispense with consultants. This can lead to consulting firms' facing costs without getting revenues; this pressures them to cut costs by laying off employees. This action not only results in the loss of superior resources but also creates a poor reputation for future recruiting efforts.

It is important to be differentiated, clearly positioned, and well reputed. Only distinguishable firms are consistently able to attract talented employees as well as clients; others succumb to vagaries of the economy or to competition.

The management consulting industry can be divided into five categories.[5] These categories are the following:

1. *Pure strategy advisors:* These are small firms that provide high-cost advice to corporate and business-unit management (O'Keefe belongs in this category). The competiton is strong, though gentlemanly. These firms compete for the topmost talent and compensate their employees extremely well. Their costs are consequently the highest among all segments. Examples of this category are The Boston Consulting Group, LEK Partnership, and Bain & Company.

2. *Traditional management consultants:* These firms consult in all areas and are somewhat diversified in that sense. They offer strategy consulting services as well as advice in functional areas. These are large in size, and competition between them is keen but polite. Examples are Booz Allen & Hamilton, McKinsey & Co., and Arthur D. Little.

3. *Accounting firms (Big 6):* These firms are recent entrants looking for new sources of revenue. They have well-established client relationships due to their accounting services and are now trying to leverage these relationships. Traditionally, these firms dealt in functional areas such as accounting and information services. Through acquisitions of specialist strategy boutiques and in-house expansion, they are now encroaching on the territory of management consultants. Competition among these firms is high, and costs are relatively low. Examples are Andersen Consulting, Coopers & Lybrand, and Deloitte Touche.

4. *Human resource firms:* These are mid-sized firms designing compensation packages for clients. Their costs are low since they do not recruit at top business schools. Competition in this category is intense. Examples are Sibson & Co., and Johnson & Higgins.

5. *Specialized firms:* These firms advise clients in specialized areas (e.g., financial services). Their costs are at a level between those of accounting firms and traditional firms. This category includes sole practitioners (college professors, retired executives, etc.). Competition in this category is fierce. Examples are Oliver Wyman & Co., and Marketing Corporation of America (MCA).

The management consulting industry enjoyed spectacular success and grew at the rate of about 20 percent annually through the last decade.[6] This boom had attracted many new entrants. A downturn in the U.S. economy started the current decline two years ago. Financially strapped clients started terminating engagements prematurely, and recent entrants started falling like ninepins. New engagements were being given to the lower-priced accounting firms.[7] Faced with global competition and technological changes, clients looked for help from specialists, and the demand for the services of generalists crashed. The industry began to consolidate, with outside buyers recognizing an opportunity to buy several firms and merge them. Summarily, the industry was experiencing change like it had never experienced before, and the foreseeable future did not seem to promise any stability.

CUSTOMERS

O'Keefe's clients were CEOs or divisional heads of Fortune 500 companies seeking advice on strategy formulation or implementation. They engaged O'Keefe because they looked for top-quality advice and an exclusive relationship. Client business units typically had revenues greater than $100 million since smaller operators could not afford O'Keefe's billing rates.

Customers for the management consulting industry cut across all industries and come in all shapes and sizes. Some require ongoing advice, while others call in consultants on an "as needed" basis. Matters on which they need advice range from corporate strategy to operational improvement. Some clients have substantial in-house capability to implement recommendations, while others need ongoing support and help during implementation. Without variation, all customers pay top dollar and demand top performance.

Recent Occurrences at O'Keefe Associates

The last two years had brought rough times to O'Keefe Associates. The decline in the consulting market resulting from the economy-wide decline had forced clients to cut engagements and stretch receivables to the maximum. This placed tremendous financial pressure on O'Keefe, but the company was able to handle it reasonably well by finding new clients. However, as the market decline commenced, an employee at the Canadian office was named as a co-defendant in a lawsuit brought by client shareholders against client management for undervaluing a recent divestiture.

The lawsuit was fairly complicated. In it, the shareholders claimed that some senior managers were part owners of the closely held acquiring firm. By undervaluing the divestiture, management had cheated shareholders for personal gain. The O'Keefe consultant claimed he was innocent and had no knowledge of any wrongdoing. His name was finally dissociated from the lawsuit, but only after he had agreed to testify against client management. The scandal had been well publicized by the popular and business press, and O'Keefe's reputation had been badly damaged. Moreover, the Canadian client had engaged 40 O'Keefe consultants, who were suddenly left without a case to work on. The loss in revenue and poor market conditions had forced O'Keefe to lay off 65 employees.

The story did not end there. The firm was also in deep financial trouble. During the growth years (O'Keefe revenues grew at about 40 percent annually), the firm's financial needs had been met through internally generated cash and limited bank borrowing. Seeing the steady, low-debt-burden growth of the firm, the founding partners had decided to cash in on their success by selling their holdings to the ESOP. To compensate them, the ESOP had to borrow heavily from various banks, and this placed a heavy debt burden on the firm. In the current downturn, it became impossible for the firm to meet its debt commitments: it was brought to the verge of declaring bankruptcy. Rumor also had it that Kevin O'Keefe had conducted negotiations to sell the firm to an outside buyer but that they had been unable to see eye to eye.

Facing the combined onslaught of reduced business and financial distress, O'Keefe had no choice but to cut costs further. A second round of layoffs was followed by a third. The crisis that ensued had finally forced Kevin O'Keefe to step down as managing director. It had also been decided that the firm would restructure its debt after the founding fathers agreed to revalue the firm and return some of the money they had taken from the ESOP. Consequently, the debt burden would become somewhat more manageable. Challenges that still faced the vice-presidents were

The Canadian lawsuit and financial trouble had severely hurt the firm's reputation among current and potential clients. Consequently, there was a danger of losing more clients without gaining any.

The skeletal staff remaining was barely able to service the needs of clients. Experienced consultants had been retained, but associates and RAs (who had been laid off) were sorely needed. However, the layoffs had hurt O'Keefe's reputation on college campuses, and potential recruits were largely ignoring the firm.

Remaining consultants were insecure in their positions, and morale was low. There was a danger that many more would leave very soon if nothing were done to address their concerns. Those leaving first would probably be the best since they would be in high demand.

The departing leadership had left a void, and the firm needed to establish direction quickly.

O'Keefe Now

Following Kevin's departure, the first order of business for the new partners was to elect a new leader for the firm. The partner meeting for this election had been scheduled already, and the two vice-presidents that were expected to be nominated for managing director were Aviva Katz and Henning Amelung. The following profiles characterize these two well.

Aviva Katz

Aviva was one of the earliest employees of O'Keefe Associates. Prior to attending Harvard Business School, she was a nurse with the U.S. Army. She had dazzled professors and fellow students at Harvard with her intellectual prowess and sharp wit. During her summer job at O'Keefe, she was convinced that she wanted to come back and share in and contribute to the success of the firm. Once there, she had quickly won the confidence of the founding fathers and had built a strong client base in the consumer products area. Through the late seventies and early eighties, Aviva was the top revenue earner for the firm. More recently, she had cut back on work hours to spend more time with her family. Aviva was well respected and fondly liked by most colleagues. For many, she was the ideal choice for managing director.

Henning Amelung

The descendant of a wealthy German family, Henning Amelung had graduated from the Amos Tuck School and joined the firm in 1981. Within the first two years he had distinguished himself and won accolades for creative solutions that helped in turning around some steel industry clients. Seeing his penchant for finance, Kevin O'Keefe had allowed him to start a venture capital subsidiary, which turned out to be a super success. While Henning drew respect from colleagues and clients, he had a reputation for being a ruthless driver of case teams. One RA had this to say about his experience working with Henning:

> Its almost as though you are a piece of machinery. Your feelings do not exist, you are tireless, and you respond without questioning. That's how he treats you. I was told when I joined that vacation is considered sacred by all at O'Keefe and by and large I have found that to be true. But Henning considers nothing sacred except the directions he gives you. If I'm assigned to another case with him, I'm quitting!

Henning ws an extremely hard worker and expected others to follow suit. His entrepreneurial success, "nose for the money," and drive made him a strong candidate for managing director.

AVIVA'S PLATFORM

Aviva was acutely aware that in making their choice for managing director, partners would consider the nominee's views about the future strategy of the firm. Consequently, she was confident she would win since she felt her stick-to-historical-strengths perspective was more popular. Salient aspects of this viewpoint were:

Maintain the one-client-per-industry offering. This had helped in setting the firm apart from the rest of the industry and had helped their initial growth. No other firm had built this capability, and it promised O'Keefe a competitive advantage.

Remain general management consultants. The firm had built a reputation for being generalists and had the talent pool to support that position. Specialization in functional or industry areas mean (a) building expertise in them, probaby by hiring experienced people,[8] and (b) dealing with functional management instead of top management that O'Keefe had customarily dealt with.

Maintain a wide geographical presence. During its high-growth years, O'Keefe had expanded nationwide and internationally by establishing offices in 16 cities. This had been done to (a) be closer to clients to create a stronger partnership with them and (b) reduce travel requirements for employees. Many partners felt that both issues were extremely important and that O'Keefe should not change this position in any way.

While Aviva espoused these views, she had heard from colleagues that Henning's view was markedly different and was based on the premise that the firm's situation would not improve without radical change. He felt that O'Keefe's strategy had been appropriate for entry and initial growth but that now it had to adapt to the times and the competitive environment. Hearsay had it that his views were

O'Keefe should accept more than one client per industry. In the past, they had turned away business to honor their one-client-per-industry policy, and there was no telling how much revenue had been foregone. Some partners felt that in the current situation, they could not afford to be picky and turn away more business.

O'Keefe should be general management consultants with specialized strengths in some areas. Specialization was important as the market demand was heading in that direction. But there were very few general management firms left in the marketplace, and while there was a temporary lull in demand, many industry watchers expected it to bounce back. Keeping the general management strength would mean carrying some employees and partners without adequate business to keep them busy. Building specialization would mean training senior staff and hiring experienced people.

Operations should be consolidated geographically; service coverage should be maintained. Since prestigious firms buy or rent prestigious office space, O'Keefe's lease and mortgage payments were astronomical. Although most internal services were centralized in Washington, D.C., some office staff and services were required to support each location. The current level of business in most offices did not justify maintaining them.

Aviva realized that Henning's perspective was not altogether without merit; however, she was confident that the majority of partners wanted the firm to continue doing what it knew best. She was sure that the discussion about respective platforms prior to the vote would position her well. There was, however, the possibility of the group's digressing to the issue of the firm's reputation. In the recent past, Aviva had been very vocal about her stand on this issue and had discovered, much to her surprise, that the majority opposed her views. While she had tried to tone down her stand on the issue, a complete about-face would not have reflected well on her. Besides, she did feel very strongly about her beliefs. She advocated that

- O'Keefe must rebuild its reputation through high-quality advice and renewed commitment to client bottom lines—much the way it had done in the past. The resulting favorable word-of-mouth will ensure reestablishment of O'Keefe's reputation.
- To regain high visibility in a positive light, O'Keefe's partners and employees should publish their work in business periodicals and journals, form alliances with prominent universities, and encourage employees to become involved in community services.

▲ Under no circumstances should O'Keefe increase starting salaries to become more attractive on campuses. This would be self-defeating since potential recruits would see this as a sign of weakening reputation.[9] Besides, this would necessitate revising salaries for all employees, resulting in higher cost when the firm least needed them.

She was sure that Henning saw the merit in her position on the reputation issue. Her sources had informed her, though, that he had opportunistically aligned himself with the perceived majority, which favored

▲ Undertaking a concerted advertising effort via advertisements indicating that O'Keefe was still a strong player. Placed in eminent business periodicals, these would emphasize O'Keefe's past successes and current strengths by quoting clients. They would assert that O'Keefe's had always focused on bottom-line results. Such a strategy had recently been executed by Andersen Consulting with significant success.

▲ Actively promoting positive word-of-mouth. This could be done by targeting champion CEO(s) and offering O'Keefe's services with a guarantee or at concessional terms. Champions would be high-profile enterpreneurs or executives who are quoted in the media often and are respected for their opinions.

▲ Offering new recruits higher starting salaries and bonuses. Money was a strong motivator, and there would be a salary level beyond which recruits would have a very hard time declining offers. O'Keefe's weakened reputation was no secret; not raising salaries was not going to fool anyone.

Aviva was critical of these views, especially the aggressive promotion of word-of-mouth. Arranging for a *quid pro quo* with senior level executives was unthinkable. Even if one were arranged, how could O'Keefe offer guarantees? In case of success stories, how could they be sure that O'Keefe would get desired exposure? She just did not think these ideas were implementable, and even if they were, she felt they would not go down well with clients.

The partners' meeting was still about an hour away, and Aviva decided to go get some coffee. When she returned she found Michael Silfen, a rising star and currently a manager, waiting for her. Aviva was Michael's mentor[10] and had also worked with him in the past. They shared a strong, positive relationship.

Hi, Michael! What can I do for you?

Hi, Aviva, Something's come up and I need your advice, that is if you have the time.

I have a few minutes. What's up?

Well, it's like this. A headhunter cold-called me about two weeks age. We struck up a conversation, and to cut a long story short, I have received a very, very attractive offer from a competitor. I'm torn between memories of the good times and the sheer frustration of being here now. Any ideas about what I should do?

Aviva heaved a quiet sigh. This was going to be a long evening, and the battle had already begun.

QUESTIONS

1. Identify the strengths and weaknesses and the opportunities and threats that are faced by O'Keefe Associates.

2. Who will be voted managing director?

3. What should the firm's strategy be going forward?

4. How should the firm handle its reputation problem?

5. What should Aviva say to Michael Silfen? If you were in his shoes, would you take the competitor's job offer?

N O T E S

[1] O'Keefe and O'Keefe Associates have been used synonymously.

[2] Relationship consulting means that the client and the consulting firm maintain an ongoing relationship as opposed to having a relationship for the term of an engagement only.

[3] Managers usually divided a case assignment into related tasks known as case modules.

[4] Recruitment yield is defined as the ratio between the number of recruits accepting the firm's offer to the total number of offers given out by the firm. At 66 percent, O'Keefe's ratio was one of the highest in the industry.

[5] Shankar Suryanarayanan, "Trends and Outlook for US Consulting," *Journal of Management Consulting* 5, 4(1989), pp. 4–5.

[6] Ibid.

[7] Ibid.

[8] This would be a marked departure for O'Keefe. Prestigious firms traditionally hired fresh MBAs and groomed them to fit the firm's culture. Although there had been instances of competitors' relaxing this rule, many within O'Keefe were quite opposed to doing so.

[9] While high salaries were important to recruits, many surveys had shown that firm reputation and prestige were the topmost considerations.

[10] O'Keefe had a mentoring system in which new associates were assigned to mentors, usually vice-presidents. These mentors advised mentees on matters regarding performance, social adjustment, and career planning.

EXHIBIT 1

THE CONSULTING RECRUITING PROCESS

Consulting firms have a rigorous recruitment process. This process is also costly since employees have to be pulled off cases to visit campuses to conduct interviews and select candidates. Candidates selected on campus then visit the office of the hiring firm and are interviewed by more employees. The following is an excerpt from a guide to interviewing with consulting firms.

Most consulting firms conduct case interviews. The primary purpose of these interviews is to get an idea of how well you break a problem down and then logically try to solve it. Due to the nature of the interview they also get to see how you think on your feet and how well you keep your composure. At times, they also get to see how quickly you bounce back after making mistakes.

In addition to problem-solving ability, interviewers make judgments about your ability to work in teams and lead at client sites. Usually, the last question the interviewer has to answer on the evaluation form is, "Would you like this person to be on your team tomorrow?"

Consulting firms recruit through a multiround process. Some firms have three rounds, while others have only two. In the first round, you interview with one person, and in subsequent rounds you have back-to-back interviews with two to three people. Each of these interviews ranges from 30 to 45 minutes.

In addition to other factors, doing well at case interviews requires skill. Like all other skills, this one can be learned by practice.

ANATOMY OF A CASE INTERVIEW

An interview typically begins with 2–10 minutes of résumé-based discussion. During this, the usual set of questions (why consulting, etc.) are asked. Following this, the interviewer presents a business case and asks you general/specific questions. Your analysis will probably be guided in the direction your interviewer wants you to go, so do not ignore comments or instructions. With each additional insight, the interviewer will probe deeper and push you to the next issue. While there is *no right answer* to any case, you will generally be expected to take a stand (state a hypothesis) at the end of the case. You should base this stand on what your analysis reveals, any assumptions you want to make, and any input the interviewer gives you. The following are examples of case questions:

- An overseas construction firm wants to establish its presence in a growing regional U.S. market. What advice would you give it?

▲ A major airline is considering acquiring an existing route from Tokyo to New York. How can it determine whether the route is a good idea?

▲ An Israeli travel agent has been extremely successful. His primary source of revenue is customers who fly to and from the United States. He manages to fill up over two planeloads on a daily basis. Given his success, he is considering buying an aircraft and plying the U.S.–Tel Aviv route himself. What advice would you give him?

▲ How would you compare the airline industry with the baby food industry? In which would you invest your own money?

Index